W9-DGU-570

VIRGIL

Aeneid

Translated with Notes by
FREDERICK AHL

With an Introduction by
ELAINE FANTHAM

OXFORD
UNIVERSITY PRESS

OXFORD

UNIVERSITY PRESS

Great Clarendon Street, Oxford ox2 6DP

Oxford University Press is a department of the University of Oxford.
It furthers the University's objective of excellence in research, scholarship,
and education by publishing worldwide in

Oxford New York

Auckland Cape Town Dar es Salaam Hong Kong Karachi
Kuala Lumpur Madrid Melbourne Mexico City Nairobi
New Delhi Shanghai Taipei Toronto

With offices in

Argentina Austria Brazil Chile Czech Republic France Greece
Guatemala Hungary Italy Japan Poland Portugal Singapore
South Korea Switzerland Thailand Turkey Ukraine Vietnam

Oxford is a registered trade mark of Oxford University Press
in the UK and in certain other countries

British Library Cataloguing-in-Publication Data

Data available

Library of Congress Cataloging in Publication Data

Virgil.
[Aeneis. English]
The Aeneid / Virgil ; translated with notes by Frederick Ahl ; with an introduction
by Elaine Fantham.
Includes bibliographical references and index.
1. Epic poetry, Latin—Translations into English. 2. Aeneas (Legendary character)—Poetry.
3. Legends—Rome—Poetry. I. Ahl, Frederick, 1941– II. Title.
PA6807.A5A38 2007   873´.01—dc22   2007014605

Typeset by Cepha Imaging Private Ltd., Bangalore, India
Printed in Great Britain
on acid-free paper by
Clays Ltd, St Ives plc.

ISBN 978-0-19-283206-1

For Elaine and Nicola

ACKNOWLEDGEMENTS

MANY people helped me in many ways to bring this work to completion, but none more than Elaine Fantham and Nicola Minott-Ahl, to whom I dedicate this volume. Dealing with an absent-minded recluse cannot have been easy. Judith Luna really belongs in the dedication too; her wisdom and clear judgement saved me from many errors. Elizabeth Stratford has also helped me catch many slips and infelicities.

I am deeply grateful to John and Marie Corbin of the University of Kent, who so often shared their home with me, and to Martin Winkler of George Mason University, a dear friend over many years, who maintained unflagging support. Thanks also to some other Ahls: Kate, Sid, and Mary, for their tolerance and encouragement. Then there are those who introduced me to Virgil's epic: T. A. Williams, Malcolm Wilcock, and J. P. Sullivan; Archie Ammons, who gave me the courage to write poetry; Virgil Espino of the Texas Military Institute, who helped me grasp how much I needed to learn. Many colleagues (some now deceased) at various institutions have, over many years, taken time to discuss and dispute ideas (often hotly) with me: R. D. Armstrong, Rhiannon Ash, R. G. Basto, Martin Bernal, Max Brecher, Jonathan Culler, Michael Davies, Martha Davis, John Fitch, G. Karl Galinsky, John Garthwaite, G. K. Gresseth, Brent Hannah, Robert Helbling, Roald Hoffmann, Gail Holst-Warhaft, Thomas Hubbard, Pat Johnson, Jane Wilson Joyce, Ian Kidd, Douglas Little, Don Maguire, Martha Malamud, Gordon Messing, Katrina Neff, S. Georgia Nugent, Peter Kuniholm, Dolores O'Higgins, Kerrill O'Neill, Bill Owens, Douglass Parker, Michael Paschalis, Sue Payne, Arthur Pomeroy, Pietro Pucci, Michael Putnam, Andrew Ramage, Nancy Ramage, Jay Reed, Hanna Roisman, Joseph Roisman, Jeffrey Rusten, Janice Siegel, Victoria Surliuga, Christiana Sogno, Michael Stokes, Lynette Thompson, Tobias Torgerson, Giannis Tsiogas, Michael Vickers, Raina Weaver, Winthrop Wetherbee, and Frederick Williams. I am especially grateful to Mike Black of Hobart and William Smith Colleges who made it possible to record excerpts of the translation for the Oxford University Press website. A word of thanks also to my colleagues at College Year in Athens and the Athens Centre, especially Steve Diamant, Rosemary Donnelly, Kimon Giokarinis, John Raisch, Rhea Scourta, and Sally Tong; and to friends now gone: Alan Ansen, Carol Buckley, Dan Booth, Robert Farrell, Lucianne Katzenberger, David Keller, and David Wyatt. Last, but not least, I thank Clayton and Lucia Minott, for whom this translation has a special importance, and Jordan and Olivia Cruger who, I hope, will some day read it.

Folkestone, Kent
January 2007

CONTENTS

INTRODUCTION

The Aeneas Tradition

WHEN the poet Propertius heard the anticipatory excitement about Virgil's forthcoming *Aeneid*, he hailed the news: 'something is coming to birth greater even than the *Iliad*' (2.34.66). What sort of poem would Romans expect when they heard that Virgil was composing an epic about Aeneas? (*Aeneid*, like the title *Odyssey*, announces itself as a poem about a hero—the man whom Virgil himself introduces in his first line 'Arms and the man I sing . . .')

Unless they were educated, Romans would have had little reason to know the name of Aeneas. Certainly they might have handled the silver denarii of 47 or 46 BC on which Caesar displayed Venus Genetrix (founder of the Julian clan) on the obverse with Aeneas on the reverse, carrying his father Anchises and the sacred image of Pallas Athena (known as the 'Palladium') from Troy; again, primitive terracottas of Aeneas carrying his father have been found in Etruria, as near to Rome as Veii. But it would be from literature, not religious cult, that they would know of this hero. Fragments of Rome's first historical poet, Naevius, speak of Aeneas and his father leaving Troy with heads covered, and someone asks Aeneas to tell the story of his escape.[1] And Ennius' more celebrated *Annales* speak more than once of Anchises' ancestry and prophetic wisdom: although Aeneas is not named, Ennius has made him father of Ilia, and grandfather of Rome's legendary founder, Romulus. Later poets like Accius and Lucretius would call the Romans 'Children of Aeneas'. But if they knew of Aeneas it would be as an ancestor of the Julian clan or a Homeric founder of their city.

Educated Romans would have met Aeneas far earlier in life and more directly when they learned to read the *Iliad* with their elementary teacher, the *grammaticus*.[2] It is from the Greek text of Homer that they would have formed their ideas of Aeneas as a prince and a warrior. Because Homer's Aeneas is so different from Virgil's, an outline of his

---

[1] Naevius, *Punic War*, lines 2–10 and 19–20, in *Remains of Old Latin*, vol. ii, ed. E. H. Warmington (Cambridge, Mass., 1936).

[2] This man would be expected to teach both reading (of Greek and Latin) and the interpretation of the poetic texts from which his pupils learned to read. Hence the discipline called *grammatice* covers both language and literature.

role in Homer's battles provides a point of departure and shows just what Virgil chose to leave behind and what to develop. While Roman readers would have been embarrassed by any impression of weakness or vulnerability in their ancestral hero, Virgil could stress that the gods favoured Aeneas and destined him to become the founder of a mighty dynasty: he could replace mere prowess in battle with the long-term endurance and commitment of a national leader, and honour qualities that would implicitly honour Aeneas' descendant Octavian, Rome's powerful ruler and Virgil's patron, soon to be the first citizen and commander-in-chief (*princeps* and *imperator*) Augustus.

Aeneas is prominent in two widely separated books of the *Iliad*, book 5 and book 20, both exceptional in the extent to which the gods participate in the combat: some gods support the Trojans, others the Greeks. When the Greek Diomedes enters battle in book 5 Athena (who is Pallas or Minerva in Virgil) breathes into him strength three times greater than his own. Aeneas urges the Trojan archer Pandarus to help him attack this unknown warrior. Fighting from Aeneas' chariot, Pandarus challenges Diomedes and casts a spear at him, but Diomedes' counterthrust is more deadly and he kills Pandarus effortlessly. When Aeneas dismounts to defend his friend's body he is seriously wounded by a rock cast by Diomedes and falls to the ground. Only the instant intervention of his mother Aphrodite (Virgil's Venus) saves him from death. Diomedes takes possession of Aeneas' horses, then chases Aphrodite and wounds her arm. Aphrodite drops her son, who is snatched up and covered in a dark cloud by Apollo. Even under Apollo's charge Aeneas is not out of range; three times Diomedes leaps at Aeneas in rage, and three times Apollo repels him, but the fourth time Apollo rebukes him for trying to fight with a god. He raises Aeneas up to his sanctuary in Troy's citadel where Aeneas is healed and made more splendid by Apollo's divine mother, Leto (Virgil's Latona), and sister Artemis (Virgil's Diana). As a distraction Apollo creates a phantom Aeneas (a device which Virgil will adapt in Juno's attempt to rescue Turnus in *Aeneid* 10), which becomes the target of the fighting for Trojans and Greeks alike. Aeneas makes one more appearance in this battle, when the Greek commander-in-chief Agamemnon kills one of his companions. Aeneas retaliates by killing two Greeks. When Agamemnon's brother Menelaus is about to fight Aeneas and is joined by another warrior, Aeneas feels he cannot confront both men together.

Homer's Aeneas is a warrior praised by the poet for his ancestry, but marked more by discretion than heroic courage. In book 20, Aeneas is

measured against the greatest Greek warrior, Achilles. Again, the gods
are involved. Apollo, in disguise, prompts Aeneas to challenge Achilles
and suggests that Aeneas' divine mother is a reason for him to expect
victory, since Achilles' mother is only a minor goddess. When Aeneas
and Achilles approach each other, Aeneas offers the first challenge, but
Achilles speaks first. He jeers at Aeneas for daring to meet him. Is he
prompted by ambition to take over Priam's kingdom? Achilles reminds
Aeneas that he had put Aeneas to flight once before, when Aeneas was
herding on Mount Ida, and had only been rescued by Zeus (Virgil's
Jupiter) and the other gods (20.178–98). When Achilles pierces Aeneas'
shield with a spear and draws his sword to finish him off, Aeneas
is saved by divine decision. Although Poseidon (Virgil's Neptune) is
fighting against Troy, he urges the other gods to rescue Aeneas, for a
mixture of moral and prudential reasons; Aeneas has a moral claim
because he is without guilt and always makes the gods welcome offerings.
And the gods must save him in their own interest, so as to avoid Zeus's
anger if Achilles should kill him. Poseidon swoops down and casts a
mist before Achilles' eyes, uproots the spear from Aeneas' shield, and
lifts Aeneas above the battle, then scolds him for challenging a superior
fighter. (Homeric warriors are rated and handicapped like sporting
champions.) Apollo now tells Aeneas he should not have challenged
Achilles, but once Achilles has been killed he will be able to fight in the
front ranks, for no other Greek will be able to kill him.

The outcome of the encounter between Aeneas and Achilles is in
some ways less important than what we are told of Aeneas' genealogy.
Before they join combat, Aeneas says he is the son of Anchises and
Aphrodite and traces his descent from Zeus through Dardanus and
Erichthonius. Erichthonius was father of Tros, who had three sons,
Ilus, Assaracus, and Ganymede. The eldest son, Ilus, was father of King
Laomedon, and grandfather of King Priam, the ruler of Troy during the
Trojan War. Assaracus, as father of Capys, was grandfather of Anchises.
Later, as Achilles is about to kill Aeneas, Poseidon observes that he must
be saved, 'because he is fated to escape, so that Dardanus' race shall
not die out. For Zeus loves Dardanus above all his children by mortal
women, but he has come to hate the descent of Priam and the mighty
Aeneas will now become king of the Trojans, as will the sons of his
sons who shall be born hereafter.' Aeneas, then, is to be the restorer of
the dynasty. And it is that dynasty that later Greek and Roman tradition moves to Italy. Significantly, Aeneas' first adversary, Diomedes, is
also moved to Italy.

As Roman boys read or heard their *Iliad* they would receive the mixed message of Aeneas as a warrior less skilled than brave, who was saved from defeat at the hands of better fighters because the gods either loved him or recognized his destiny; defeated, he was nonetheless spared the imputation of cowardice by the same divine concern which also gave him merit as a future leader, the man destined to revive Troy. Perhaps they understood Aeneas' career as encouragement to go on fighting even in defeat, as Rome had fought on despite the victories of Hannibal in the Second Punic War. But when they read Poseidon's argument they surely thought that Aeneas had the power of the gods behind him because he was to be the founder of Rome—or the Latin city from which Rome was settled.

From the lost cycle of epics composed by Homer's successors, only Arctinus' *Sack of Troy* mentions Aeneas, and that incidentally, when his followers retire from Troy after the serpents have killed Laocoön and his sons and the Trojans decide to bring the treacherous horse inside their city.[3] The Greek world knew many variants on the tale of Aeneas before and after the city's fall: it was commonly said that when Paris had abducted Helen from her husband Menelaus and brought her to Troy, Aeneas and Antenor, the future founder of Padua mentioned as Aeneas' peer by both Virgil and Livy, had recommended returning Helen to the Greeks, and some versions even saw them as collaborators, even traitors, who had been allowed by the Greeks to leave Troy laden with treasure. Other versions had celebrated Aeneas as founder of various communities in the Troad, and across the Aegean, as also in Sicily. There were so many self-interested local traditions that when Virgil came to make this Trojan prince the hero of his poem he had numerous, often conflicting, myths to adapt to shape his hero's westward journey and ultimate reception in Latium.

Of Rome, Virgil, and his Times

Two generations before Virgil's birth Rome was becoming a sophisticated metropolis, commanding an empire which her senatorial government was no longer equipped to rule. The influx of wealth from conquered Asia Minor had swollen the discrepancy between the riches of the elite and the endangered farmsteads of the peasants who made

[3] See Proclus' summary in the Loeb volume, *Hesiod and the Homeric Poems* (Cambridge, Mass., 1914).

up Rome's citizen army. In Virgil's youth the older generation (we may take Cicero as representative) saw the beginning of the threat to traditional government with the Gracchus brothers, idealists from the heart of Rome's aristocracy. First, Tiberius Gracchus tried to use the office of tribune to legislate redistribution of public land; ten years later his brother Gaius extended his proposals to embrace social legislation including colonies. Each time a combination of property owners and politicians who saw them as aiming at tyrannical power used violence to bring down each brother, massacring or prosecuting their supporters. When Rome was fighting off a Gallic invasion of north Italy the shortage of yeoman soldiers led Marius to open the ranks to propertiless men who would henceforth depend on their commander for their livelihood. Backed by their armies, Marius and his younger rival Cornelius Sulla would each ruthlessly turn his forces against their own city and its civilian inhabitants. The generation of Virgil's father did not forget Sulla's proscriptions, which outlawed first political antagonists, then anyone whose property was coveted by kin or neighbours. In the eyes of the governing class Sulla was an ambiguous figure: he had restored senatorial control (without remedying the economic plight of the underprivileged) but there was no one who did not recall the loss of friends or family among his victims.

About the time of Virgil's birth in 70 BC, it seemed that the two most successful generals, Crassus and Pompey, were prepared to accept the restored control of the Senate, at least until Pompey was offered legitimate commands, first against the rampant piracy infecting all the Mediterranean, then to carry through the war against Mithridates. In his absence, a corrupt aristocrat, Sergius Catilina, twice rejected in elections for the consulship, began to prepare for a coup at Rome and uprisings both in Etruria and southern Gaul against the elected consul Cicero. While Cicero may have exaggerated the danger to excuse the Senate's unconstitutional decision to execute Catilina's elite allies, Virgil himself makes a villain of Catilina when he places him among the great sinners of Hades (*Aeneid* 8.668–70) and sets in judgement over him Cato, the fiercest of Rome's conservatives. What Sallust and Cicero tell us, but Virgil has no reason to mention, is that Caesar may have sympathized with the Catilinarians (he certainly spoke against their execution), and Cato was the most passionate and principled opponent of Caesar, dying by his own hand at Utica when Caesar's victory was assured.

After his decisive defeat of Pompey and the Republicans at Pharsalus (in Thessaly) Caesar forgave many distinguished senators like Cicero and Varro, and actively promoted younger ex-Republicans like Brutus and Cassius. When Caesar assumed the unlimited role of dictator for life, shortly before he planned to lead his expedition against Parthia in March 44, it was these men who killed him at the foot of Pompey's statue in the Senate room of Pompey's theatre. This was the state of Rome when Virgil was 25.

How, then, did Virgil come to contemplate writing an epic on the Trojan hero? This was not anything that could have been anticipated by those who knew the young Virgil or read his early poetry. According to the chief sources for his early life, the biographies attributed to Suetonius and Donatus,[4] after his childhood as son of a prosperous farmer near Mantua, Virgil had been sent first to Milan, then to Rome for his education: we should bear in mind that the poems of Catullus and Lucretius would have begun to circulate about the time he came of age. We know that he was delicate, and continued his studies at Naples, where the Epicurean poet and critic Philodemus was teaching, as were Roman critics Siro and Valerius Cato. If there was money (and his health did not fit him for a military career or an active public life), he could have stayed on in Naples when Julius Caesar made himself master of Italy in 49 and even after Caesar's assassination. As a self-governing city, Naples would have been a safe place for neutrality.

In fact, Caesar's assassination only led to political confusion. Mark Antony as consul was the chief source of authority at Rome when Caesar's great-nephew Octavian acted to obtain public confirmation of his adoption as Caesar's heir, and came south to Campania to rouse the support of the legions his great-uncle had planned to lead against the Parthians. The following year, 43, with the support of Caesar's veterans, Octavian was first endorsed by the Senate with praetorian status as its champion against Mark Antony, then forced the Senate to recognize him as consul, turning around from his victory at Mutina to join with Antony and demand their recognition (with Lepidus) as triumvirs with power to reorganize the state. Brutus and Cassius had been amassing legions and finances in Syria and Asia Minor, but in 42 the new triumvirs met and defeated them in two battles spread over three weeks at Philippi in Macedonia.

In Italy, Octavian's legates Pollio and Varus were sent to take over lands for veteran colonies from cities such as Cremona. Virgil's first

---

[4] Both lives are printed in the Oxford Classical Text of the *Vitae virgilianae*; Suetonius' life, from his lost collection of Lives of the Poets, is translated in the second Loeb volume of Suetonius.

poetry book, the *Eclogues*, on which he spent three years, includes poems dedicated to and praising Pollio and Varus (*Eclogues* 3, 4, and 8), and two poems (6 and 10) honouring his friend the elegist Gallus.[5] We seem to see the reflection of the land displacements of the late 40s in the laments of Virgil's shepherds in two other poems. Both the reinstatement of the slave-shepherd Tityrus by the young leader at Rome in *Eclogue* 1, and the failure of the singer Menalcas to recover the expropriated land for his friends in *Eclogue* 9 must be evocations rather than literal reports of what happened in Virgil's neighbourhood, but the divine young leader who restored Tityrus' pastures is surely Octavian, and it is most likely that Virgil paid him this honour because of favour he extended to Virgil directly or through his subordinates.

The defeat of Brutus and Cassius did not end Octavian's difficulties in maintaining relations with Mark Antony or opposing Pompey's son Sextus Pompeius, who now controlled Sicily and the seaways for the supply of grain for the million people of the metropolis. With the aid of his great friend Agrippa, Octavian would finally defeat Sextus Pompey in the naval battle off Naulochus (off northern Sicily) in 36, but relations with Antony had not yet come to a crisis. It was about this time that Virgil began his *Georgics*.

The opening of this poem in four books proudly invokes Octavian as Caesar, destined to become a god, urging him to help the poet bring comfort to the farmers, and the internal proem of book 3 speaks of setting Caesar in his own temple in the midst of Virgil's poetic celebrations and incorporates references (3.26–33) to present and future imperial victories. Is this an undertaking to compose a poetic celebration of Caesar himself? The last lines of the poem, as Virgil signs off (4.559–66), contrast the heroic Caesar flashing thunder by the Euphrates and bestowing justice on the nations, with the poet's own inglorious leisure in peaceful Parthenope; it seems, then, that he has kept his home at Naples.

Locating Caesar in the far East dates the closing lines of *Georgics* to 31–30 BC, after Octavian's great naval victory at Actium over Antony and Cleopatra, and we should place the conception of the *Aeneid* no later than this time. This would also fit the biographers' claim that when the poet died in 19 BC, he had devoted eleven years to the poem's twelve books.

---

[5] Gallus was also a successful soldier, and would become Octavian's first Prefect of Egypt after the deaths of Antony and Cleopatra in 30. He was later disgraced for boasting of his military feats, and committed suicide.

What kind of pressure did Virgil feel to honour the victorious Caesar—soon to be renamed Augustus—with an epic? It had become a Roman tradition that poets composed epics around the victorious campaigns of generals; even Cicero, for example, had set to writing an epic on Caesar's invasion of Britain. Dealing with contemporary warfare, such assignments left little room for inspiration, however. The fourth-century critic Servius[6] says Virgil's object was to praise Augustus through his ancestry. It might be better to say that by choosing to construct a narrative of questing and struggle around the Roman ancestor who was known from Homer, but not known in too much detail, the poet gave himself the scope to construct an idealized founder and leader whose sufferings and moral decisions would be both a model to Augustus and to some extent a model of Augustus, suggesting to the Roman public an interpretation of their young leader's achievements. Something of the same shift in emphasis can be seen in Caesar Octavian's own choice of title, since *Augustus* combined a quasi-religious reverence with an altogether new kind of authority—the more powerful because it was not constitutionally defined.

Yet although the immediate popularity of the *Aeneid* (it was used in schools a few years after its release was authorized by Augustus) was certainly fostered by the model it offered to the sons of the elite as future leaders, the epic would not have absorbed and kept the interest of even disillusioned generations like our own if it had not been rich with both moral and aesthetic complexity, with depth of implications and beauty of expression. Nor would it have much claim on our hearts and minds if its theme were limited to the destiny of Rome and its once and future leader. Certainly our age can no longer, as Roman boys and British nineteenth-century schoolboys did, read Virgil with confidence that Fate—or God—is on our side, because we use our power justly and benevolently. But the poem shows a concern for all humanity and its struggles to combine virtue and happiness.[7] As for the 'man of destiny', the charmed conduit of history, the chief undercurrent of Virgil's narrative seems to be the cost of success, not just the cost of national

---

[6] On Servius and his commentary on the *Aeneid*, see Don Fowler, 'The Virgil Commentary of Servius', in C. R. Martindale, *The Cambridge Companion to Virgil* (Cambridge, 1997), 72–9.

[7] Two critics half a century apart, Richard Heinze (*Virgil's Epic Technique* (1915), trans. H. and D. Harvey and F. Robertson (Berkeley, 1993)) and Brookes Otis (*Virgil: A Study in Civilized Poetry* (Oxford, 1964)), offer the best introduction to the psychological dimensions of Virgil's narrative.

victory in casualties, the lives of officers and men, but the personal self-denial and hardship required of any leader, whether pioneering a new community or simply maintaining morale in an existing one.

The Aeneid

Before turning to analysis of Virgil's epic something should be said about the first Roman epics, and the rival claims of Aeneas and Romulus in Rome's ostensibly double-foundation legend, which came from early ignorance of chronology and from the competing claims of Latin cities to have given Rome its founder. Naevius, the first poet of Roman history, made his focus the first war against Carthage, in which he is believed to have fought. To readers familiar with the *Aeneid*, a single fragment of Naevius' retrospective narrative of Aeneas' adventures suggests he too may have brought Aeneas to Carthage and had him converse with Dido, its queen, but it does not name the person who 'with charm and learning asks how Aeneas had left the city of Troy'.[8] Scholars who are not prepared to speculate that this was Aeneas' Carthaginian hostess make the speaker Latinus or an unidentified host.

The chief obstacle to introducing Dido into Naevius' tale of Aeneas would be chronology, if Hellenistic Greek chronology had not been unknown to both Naevius and his close successor Ennius. The third-century chronographer Eratosthenes calculated the place of events in history in relation to the Trojan War, reckoning that Troy fell early in the twelfth century BC, but dated the foundations of both Rome and Carthage four centuries later: Carthage to 814 BC and Rome either at the same time or two generations after. By the time Virgil was a young man, however, his older contemporaries Atticus and Varro had stabilized the foundation date of Rome to 753 BC (the date still used by historians). So how could Aeneas share in the foundation of Rome? For Ennius, he was father of Ilia (and presumably ruler of Lavinium), grandfather of her sons Romulus and Remus. Once Romans realized the chronological gap between the Homeric age of Troy and Rome's foundation, they needed king-lists to fill it, and so the tradition arose, fostered by the Julii and other families from Alba, that there were fourteen generations of Alban kings between Aeneas' son and Numitor, the father of Romulus.

---

[8] Naevius 19–20 (ed. Warmington). The subject is not named, nor is the gender specified, but the adverbs *blande* and *docte* may encourage thinking that a woman, and a well-informed woman like Dido, whose temple shows knowledge of the Trojan War, is the speaker.

Hence Virgil needed to give due importance to both Lavinium and Alba in his prologue (*Aeneid* 1.2 and 1.7); hence Jupiter allows three hundred and thirty-three years in all from Aeneas' foundation of Lavinium to the birth of Romulus (1.265–74). Even so the numbers fall short!

In teaching the *Aeneid* in both Latin and English, I have found that the complexity of the epic causes students and other readers to pass over many details both of narrative continuity and of characterization. For this reason I have tried to combine three functions in the book-by-book summary that follows. Besides stressing where and how Virgil has shaped his narrative to recall the world and actions of Homer's epics[9] I have aimed to provide a summary of events that traces the interweaving threads of divine and human action; at the same time I have tried to bring out consistently aspects of the behaviour of Aeneas and others which seem to ask to be judged by different standards from our own. Scholars have long debated the apparent conflict between Virgil's public and his private voice.[10] Perhaps the humane poet recognized the necessity for public figures to take actions that go against their private principles and personal choice.

If the proem of **Book 1** opens by setting its theme in the *longue durée* of human history, 'the man . . . of Troy, who . . . suffered profoundly in war to establish a city, | Settle his gods into Latium, making this land of the Latins | Future home to the Elders of Alba and Rome's mighty ramparts' (1.1 and 5–7), it swiftly moves beyond the human Aeneas to the divine instigator of his sufferings, the anger of savage Juno.[11] Virgil is setting both hero and goddess against a huge canvas of history: Juno is not, like Poseidon in the *Odyssey*, angry with Aeneas over any act he has committed—as Odysseus blinded Poseidon's son Polyphemus—but has gathered her resentment against his race over past generations and many generations to come. Juno is angry because of what will happen after almost a thousand years: she loves Carthage above all

---

[9] Such intertextual allusion may work with Homer's text as a model (of language, of imagery, etc.) or as generic norm for types of scene and action. See G. B. Conte, *The Rhetoric of Imitation: Genre and Poetic Memory in Virgil and Other Latin Poets* (Ithaca, NY, and London, 1986).

[10] The pioneering study is A. Parry, 'The Two Voices of Virgil's Aeneid', in S. Commager, *Virgil: A Collection of Critical Essays* (Englewood Cliffs, NJ, 1966), 107–23; see also R. A. O. M. Lyne, *Further Voices in Virgil's Aeneid* (Oxford, 1974).

[11] On the role played by Juno, Venus, and other gods see D. C. Feeney, *Gods in Epic* (Oxford, 1991), 129–87: his chapters on earlier epic add further understanding of the gods in the *Aeneid*.

cities, and has learned it will be overthrown by the descendants of this man. And she is angry because she hates the descendants of Dardanus, child of Jupiter's mistress Electra, and Ganymede, his boy-favourite, and of Paris, who preferred Venus/Aphrodite's beauty to her own.

When the action begins it is already seven years after the fall of Troy: tossed over land and sea Aeneas is beginning the relatively short voyage from western Sicily to Latium, when Juno provokes a violent storm that blows his fleet off course. Just as we first meet Odysseus in the despair of shipwreck when Poseidon sends the storm against him, so as its full force strikes the ship Aeneas wishes in his heart he was dead (and recalls to Virgil's readers his Homeric defeat and escape): 'O Tydeus' son, Diomedes | Bravest Danaän of all, why could *I* not have fallen on Ilium's | Plains, spilled forth my soul under *your* right hand?' (1.96–8). The divinely roused storm will be divinely calmed, and Virgil shows here and throughout the book how gods skew the human narrative. Aeneas is saved when Neptune observes the havoc Aeolus king of the winds has created to oblige Juno, and puts an end to it, restoring the ships, just as the authority of a wise citizen quells an incipient riot. Cast up on land Aeneas forces an expression of hope on his features, giving his men reassurance he does not himself feel.

> Crewmates, by now we are hardly strangers to evil and hardship.
> We've suffered worse. God will grant us an end to these sufferings also. . . .
>   Take heart once again and dispel your fears and depression.
> Maybe the day'll come when even this will be joy to remember.
>
> (1.198–9, 202–3)

As the castaways share a makeshift feast from the deer which Aeneas has shot, Virgil moves to the divine level, and with Jupiter's words of reassurance to Venus (1.257–96) introduces the first of three great panoramas that reach across Roman history to Augustus and the present age (the others come from Anchises' survey of the parade of heroes in Book 6 and from the shield designed by Vulcan for Aeneas in Book 8). Aeneas will win through and reign three years in Latium, then his son Ascanius will rule thirty years, transferring his city from Lavinium to Alba, then will come three hundred years of Alban kings before Romulus will found the city and Juno relent.[12] Agamemnon's city of Mycenae will be subdued, and Aeneas' descendant, Trojan Caesar, will create an

[12] See D. C. Feeney, 'The Reconciliation of Juno', in S. J. Harrison, *Oxford Readings in Virgil's Aeneid* (Oxford, 1990).

empire limited only by the ocean and the stars. His era will bring justice and end all warfare, imprisoning savage fury within the gates of war. Is this Caesar, who is also called Iulius (the Julian), meant for the man we call Julius Caesar? More likely Virgil is evoking not the Julius who died with wars still to fight, but Caesar Augustus, the 'son' who took his name.

Narrative on the human level is blended with further divine intervention as Mercury flies down to win over the hearts of Dido and her Carthaginians, for fear that, 'not knowing what's fated' (1.299) she should drive off Aeneas and his men. In fact, Aeneas will openly declare to Dido his mission to Italy (2.780–4, 3.163–71, etc.), but she blinds herself to his fate, and Venus intervenes so as to aggravate her self-deception. To accost her own son, the goddess disguises herself as a young virgin out hunting. It is Venus who provides our introduction to the tragic prehistory of Dido, widowed of a beloved husband, Sychaeus, and leader of a bold new colony grudgingly tolerated by the aboriginal Africans. And Venus' speech should alert the readers to Dido's susceptibility, stressing the details of her loving anxiety when her wicked brother conceals the killing of her husband (1.351–2). But it is his mother's disguise that troubles Aeneas. Reticent as he is,[13] he gives a good account of himself and his mission to seek a homeland in Italy aided by his divine mother, but the goddess does not reveal her divine person before she has left him. We share his indignation that she will not let him clasp her hand, but why does he accuse her of *so often* deceiving him with disguises? She has not done so before, and when Aeneas as narrator of the fall of Troy in Book 2 describes his mother's previous appearance to him she holds nothing back in revealing herself, and the divine agency behind the city's downfall.

From now on the human narrative which brings Aeneas to Carthage and its queen is infused with divine meddling. Venus conceals Aeneas and Achates in a mist while they observe and envy the newly founded city, until Dido herself appears and receives Ilioneus and other Trojans kindly. Through Aeneas' eyes the readers see the story of Troy retold on the walls of Juno's temple, chiefly in terms of Greek triumph, but with Aeneas himself depicted fighting in a kind of visual Homeric cycle.[14] The warrior who greets the queen is already celebrated, and

[13] Aeneas is characterized throughout the epic as speaking only what is necessary: see ibid.

[14] On this and other *ekphrases* (descriptions of visual narrative art works), see A. Barchiesi, '*Ekphrasis*', in Martindale, *Cambridge Companion*.

the affinities between these two colonists with their personal bereavements are great enough to have generated love without Venus' gratuitous intervention, as she substitutes the contagious Cupid for Aeneas' little son, and infects the hospitable queen with the affliction that will destroy her.

I have surveyed the first book at some length so as to convey the different levels of narrative.[15] Aeneas begins shipwrecked and despairing like Odysseus in *Odyssey* 5, and is kindly received just like Odysseus in Phaeacia (*Odyssey* 6–8). But as with Odysseus' inset reminiscences in *Odyssey* 9–12, the next books do not move forward in time but go back to the crisis that drove Aeneas from Troy (Book 2) and the years of wandering that he has endured since (Book 3). In **Book 2** the hero who is so sparing of personal response elsewhere in Virgil's narrative tells his own version of the fall of Troy, and one which seems to show the mature man as aware of his past youthful blunders. It may be helpful to read the book of Troy as in part an apology for Troy's defeat, in part for his own flight. Repeatedly, Aeneas stresses Greek deceit, over the horse (2.13–20) and the lying tale of Sinon (2.65–6: 'Mark how Danaäns set traps. From this one criminal instance | You'll learn them all', and more fully 2.195–8), but Sinon's tale seems to be confirmed by the monstrous serpents[16] which strangle Laocoön and his sons. Aeneas' people, whom neither Diomedes nor Achilles could overcome, were betrayed by deceit. But when he is warned by Hector's ghost (2.289–95) Aeneas is too loyal and proud to take flight and squanders time in a useless guerrilla action. It is after this failure that Aeneas leaves his narrative to swear to his ancestral shades that: 'Had *my* death been fated | *My* deeds done would have earned it' (2.433–4). This is not just the self-questioning of the survivor; it is necessary to obliterate any echoes of hostile tradition.

After Aeneas has described the brutal end of Troy's king as the palace is sacked, he reaches the turning point with Venus' epiphany. This may have been the stimulus for a passage which many scholars reject as post-Virgilian (in part because it is preserved only in Servius' commentary), the so-called 'Helen episode', where Aeneas sees Helen lurking in sanctuary and longs to kill her as cause of Troy's ruin.

---

[15] On Virgilian variations of 'order duration and frequency' see Don Fowler, in Martindale, *Cambridge Companion*, 259–70.

[16] On the interweaving of serpents and flame in the narrative and imagery of Book 2, see B. W. Knox, 'The Serpent and the Flame: The Imagery of the Second Book of the *Aeneid*', in Commager, *Virgil*.

Certainly Venus opens her rebuke to her son by insisting that Helen is not to blame, but the gods themselves. In order to convince her son it is his duty to flee, she now strips the mist of human ignorance from his eyes to show him the forces of the gods (Neptune, Juno, Athena, Jupiter himself) in battle array physically destroying the city. Lucretius had praised Epicurus for lifting the mist from men's eyes to show them the true serenity of the gods, and their freedom from intervention in human affairs. Venus affirms the opposite, stressing with a rare word, *inclementia*, the ruthless nature of the gods.

The vision is unforgettable:

> . . . in her place, there appeared the appalling faces and mighty
> Forces divine that detested Troy.
> That's when my eyes really saw all Ilium slowly subsiding
> Into the fires. . .

$$(2.622-5)$$

But when Aeneas obeys her command to escape (2.619) and seeks out his family, a new obstacle arises as Anchises, who also tells his son to flee (2.638–40), refuses to go with them. It takes a divine portent—the harmless flame crowning young Iulus—to change his mind and release them. In one last episode, as he carries Anchises and leads little Iulus, his wife Creusa is lost. (In Naevius' epic she had left Troy safely, but she needed to die for Aeneas to be free for his destined wife Lavinia and his undestined lover Dido.) Creusa is the source of Aeneas' last authorization to escape: she has been taken up to heaven by Cybele, the Mother Goddess, but he will finally reach Hesperia and the river Tiber where royal power and a royal wife await him. Grieving, he joins his followers as they retreat to Mount Ida and prepare a fleet.

Virgil continues Aeneas' narrative in **Book 3** without returning to the banquet-scene. The adventures which he describes (the blood of murdered Polydorus in Thrace, the plague in Crete, the nauseating Harpies on the Strophades islands, and Odysseus' hazards, Scylla, Charybdis, and the cannibal Cyclops) are beset with horrors on land and sea. But Aeneas gives more prominence to the divinely prompted messages of encouragement for the future and the warning against cherishing the past. While the vision of his household gods urges him on to leave Crete for Italy and Corythus' city, the true homeland of Dardanus (3.161–71), the Harpy Celaeno threatens them with a hunger that will drive them to eat their tables before they can settle in Italy (3.253–7). Sailing on to Epirus, they are welcomed to Buthrotum

by lost kin, Helenus and Andromache, who have created a replica of
Troy, but Andromache lives only in the past, and the prophetic Helenus
contrasts their retirement from life's struggles with Aeneas' onward
voyage; Italy may be near, but its nearer (eastern and southern) shores
are full of Greek settlements: Aeneas and his men must travel further,
even visiting the lakes of the underworld (3.386), before they come to
the region of Italy, where the portent of a white sow with thirty young
will mark their destination. And when they approach Sicily, they must
follow its east and south coast, to avoid Scylla and Charybdis. Religious
instructions constitute an important element in Helenus' long speech
of guidance (parallel to that of Circe in *Odyssey* 12): to cover the head
in sacrifice (3.403–9) and give reverence to Juno (3.435–40).[17] The last
part of Helenus' advice foreshadows Book 6, warning Aeneas to demand
the personal guidance of the Cumaean Sibyl instead of the unreliable
lots cast by fluttering leaves.

For the remainder of this book Aeneas sails in the wake of Odysseus'
adventures, steering away from Scylla and Charybdis along the east
coast of Sicily, past the volcano of Mount Etna, and rescues Odysseus'
marooned comrade Achaemenides, escaping before the Cyclops can
sink their ship. Aeneas ends his narrative (we must not forget that he
is telling his experiences to Dido) with a rapid cruise westwards past
the Sicilian Greek cities, breaking off with an outcry of grief at the
death of his father Anchises, a loss none of his prophetic interlocutors
had foretold.

Book 3, where Aeneas portrays himself as a questing colonist, skil-
fully selects legends and landscapes to convey the length and variety of
Aeneas' travels. It also provides the best illustrations of what James
O'Hara has called the optimistic prophecy—for true as they are, the
prophecies are always partial, and mislead by omission.[18]

In the defence of his love poetry addressed to Augustus, Ovid would
insist that even Virgil took his arms and the man into a Carthaginian
bed, and that no part of the *Aeneid* was more famous than this unlaw-
ful love affair.[19] In Roman Africa four hundred years later, according
to his *Confessions*, the young Augustine wept over Dido, and it is
Virgil's achievement to have created a noble heroine and worthy
queen, destroyed by the gods like the hero of a Euripidean tragedy.

---

[17] On the constantly recurring details of ritual in the epic (quite distinct from the role
of the gods in the action), see C. Bailey, *Religion in Virgil* (Oxford, 1935).

[18] J. J. O'Hara, *Death and the Optimistic Prophecy* (Ann Arbor, 1990).

[19] Ovid, *Tristia* 2.533–6.

The queen whom Virgil compares at her first appearance (1.496–503) to the goddess Diana, superior in beauty to her dancing maidens, bringing silent joy to her mother's heart, is the peer of the prince whom the poet compares at greater length to Apollo as master of the dance in 4.141–50. In his introduction to **Book 4**, the commentator Servius claims that it is entirely derived from the third book of the *Argonautica*, in which Apollonius presents Medea in love: and there is no doubt that Virgil has adapted much of his portrayal of Dido's fever-ish passion from Apollonius, but Dido is closer in situation to Jason's other love, the widowed queen Hypsipyle of Lemnos, with whom Jason stays some months on his way to his destined quest for the fleece. Emotionally, it is harder to see her resemblance to any of the three women whom Odysseus meets: the innocent and hospitable Nausicaa (although Virgil has adapted the Diana-simile to Dido from Homer's introduction of Nausicaa), the charming immortal Calypso—whom Odysseus leaves only after seven years, and at Hermes' command—and the dangerous but seductive Circe, with whom he stays twelve months. But the divine manipulation of Venus and her enemy Juno, who agree for conflicting reasons to unite Dido with Aeneas, put her more in the position of Euripides' Phaedra, used by Aphrodite as a mere instrument of her desire to punish Hippolytus: as Phaedra struggles to suppress her love of her stepson, so Dido strug-gles to resist her growing love for Aeneas and to keep faith with her dead husband.

Beyond the mythical heroines of Greek poetry there are three further elements to colour Roman response to this Carthaginian queen. First of all, Romans and Italians too would remember three wars with Carthage, and above all the supposed treachery of the nation embodied in its great leader Hannibal. (This is why Dido will invoke the future general as her avenger in 4.625–9.) More recently, Augustus' rival Antony had betrayed his country and his wife, Augustus' virtuous sister Octavia, with another African queen, Cleopatra, who would take her own life with proud courage after her lover had left her (by suicide in defeat). But Virgil's Dido has nothing of the debauchery attributed to Cleopatra by other Augustan poets, and no allusions suggest that Virgil wanted to diminish his queen by any association with the Egyptian seductress. It is less significant that in portraying Dido's sister Anna Virgil changed a version attributed to Varro in which it was Anna, not Dido, who loved Aeneas: but here too he has enhanced Dido's innocence, by showing how Anna (unmentioned in Book 1) has applied her unscrupulous pragmatism to persuade Dido to abandon her vow of chaste fidelity to Sychaeus, as Phaedra's nurse or Medea's sister Chalciope in Apollonius had weakened the heroine's virtuous resolve.

From the opening of Book 4, Virgil creates a number of unforgettable images to convey Dido's affliction.[20] Starting with the wound piercing deep into her heart like that of a doe shot by a hunter unaware, Virgil will show the queen raving through her city like a bacchante at the news of Aeneas' plan to leave her, and later as plagued by nightmares and portents, like the madmen Pentheus or Orestes pursued across the stage by Furies. And the moment of consummation, when queen and prince shelter from the storm, is described in contradictory terms: there is a marriage (modelled on Medea's clandestine marriage to Jason) with Juno as matron of honour, and a chorus of nymphs, but then the poet changes his wording: it is Dido who *calls* this a marriage, using the name to disguise her offence. Of Aeneas' emotions we hear nothing, until Mercury descends with Jupiter's summons to move on. He even instructs his men to prepare their departure without a word and disguise it—words with which Dido opens her denunciation: 'Was it your hope to *disguise* . . . such a monstrous | Wrong, to get out, *with no word said* . . .' (4.305–6). His short and formal attempt at explanation is perhaps a mark of self-discipline: the mission is absolute and any attempt at tenderness would simply increase their pain. When Anna entreats him on Dido's behalf he is deaf as the fates block all pleas, like an oak tree buffeted by the winds but held firm by its deep roots. This powerful simile contrasts with the felling of the ash tree which is Virgil's simile for the final collapse of Troy (2.636–41)—and its length and detail is a kind of compensation for the restraint of Aeneas' last speech to Dido. The hero feels emotions deeply (note the rare form *persentit*, 4.448) in his great heart, but his intention is fixed, and the tears that fall have no effect.

Rather than relive Dido's sufferings, we must note that she stands for the future of her city. When Dido stabs herself upon her funeral pyre Rumour, the same destructive spirit that precipitated the lovers' separation, now raves through the city as if all Carthage (like Troy) was falling to enemy occupation and being consumed by flames. The greatest wrong done by Dido's love for Aeneas was arguably to her own people. But Dido's 'famous city' did not fall. Virgil's Rome knew

---

[20] The best study of both this imagery and other key images in the *Aeneid* is still V. Pöschl, *Virgil's Poetic Art*, trans. G. Seligson (Ann Arbor, 1962).

that it had grown to be a mighty rival of Rome; that Rome came near to defeat under her curse:[21]

> No love must ever exist between our two peoples, no treaties.
> Rise from my bones, my avenger—and there *will be* an avenger!—
> So you can hound these Dardan settlers with hot fire and cold steel,
> Now, or some day in the future . . .

$$(4.624-7)$$

And Juno, at last, takes pity on the woman she has helped to ruin.

Such is the intensity of this book that the poet needed to draw a deep breath. As **Book 5** opens the Trojans at sea note the grim omen of flames in the city, but Aeneas is resolved, even confident, of his journey and a few lines bring him back to the land of Eryx, which his fleet had left as the epic began, and where his father had died in his narrative to Dido at the end of Book 3. Trojan Acestes greets them with gladness at their safe return (well he might!), and Aeneas devotes the next day to ceremonies for the dead Anchises. As part of the honour due to his father he decrees games on the ninth day—a boat race, a foot race, competitions in javelin throwing and archery, and a boxing contest. As at the funeral of Patroclus in *Iliad* 23, games not only honour the dead, they create a space for co-operative and collective activity before the business of life resumes. In the Greek world the sacred games were a time of truce when citizens of every community could participate in peace, and an occasion for glory without the death risk of warfare.

Virgil's games echo some of the events of Achilles' games for Patroclus, and to some extent the more modest Phaeacian games of *Odyssey* 8, but corresponding events display both material differences and differences of characterization. The race between four ships and their captains in the coastal waters corresponds to Homer's far longer chariot race in *Iliad* 23, with the same humorous account of interaction between participants and spectators, but a sharper moral message; thus Gyas, who throws his steersman overboard, comes in last, whereas Cloanthus, falling behind, prays to the gods and urges his men to a heroic victory; they win because the gods, prompted by his promises of sacrifices, push him ahead.

---

[21] Professor Pelling has made the nice point that Dido's curse (like Celaeno's near-curse) is a 'pessimistic prophecy', literally true, but suggesting to the reader a far more desperate future than will actually result.

The foot race is used to introduce Nisus and Euryalus, the doomed lovers and heroes of Book 9. When Nisus in the lead slips in a pool of sacrificial blood he uses his own fall to trip the man running second so that his friend Euryalus can win—as he does. But Aeneas is a generous master of ceremonies and finds prizes for those who should have won as well as those who cheated. The boxing contest, too, is presented as the comeuppance of the boastful Dares and a well-earned victory for the aged champion Entellus, originally too modest to enter the ring. The Homeric contest of javelin-throwing is forgotten; instead, when the champions compete to shoot the dove tied to a ship's mast Mnestheus shoots and cuts the rope, and Eurytion hits the flying dove in mid-air. There is now no target left for Acestes, but he shoots into the sky and receives a positive omen as his arrow trails fire like a comet.

The book is becoming more serious. After the competitive games comes a display evoking the past glories of Troy and future of Augustan Rome, as young Ascanius leads one of the three cavalry troops deploying in the ancestral Game of Troy. And at this moment of pride Juno brings disaster, inciting the women, sitting neglected on the seashore, to set fire to the ships in hope of ending their voyages. (It was she who tried to wreck the fleet in Book 1; and the fleet will be endangered again in Book 9.) The crisis stimulates young Ascanius' leadership as he rides up and shames them, while Aeneas' impassioned prayer to Jupiter brings on a downpour which extinguishes the fire. Inspired by a vision of Anchises, he founds a settlement (called Troy) for the women and the weary, and makes Acestes its ruler; now only the fighting men will continue to Italy. (This will leave them free to marry Latin wives and found the new composite Latin–Trojan nation once peace has been achieved.) Virgil transfers the narrative to the divine level as Venus persuades Neptune to take only one life as the price for Aeneas' safe journey to his destination: that life will be the conscientious helmsman Palinurus, who is drugged into a treacherous sleep and hurled into the sea. Virgil's sympathy for the victim is ironically reinforced when Aeneas takes over the helm but mistakenly assumes his helmsman was in some way to blame. Denied burial and so admission to the underworld, Palinurus will at least report the truth to Aeneas in the sixth book, and receive the cold comfort of giving his name to a Campanian landmark.

The first six books are often called Virgil's *Odyssey*, although only the framework of Odysseus' travels and his personal narrative provide correspondences with Books 1 and 3–5. However, with Aeneas' *katabasis* (journey beneath the earth) in **Book 6** Virgil combines much closer correspondences to Odysseus' report of his visit to the dead at the ends of the earth with entirely new elements both before and within the journey to the underworld. Landing at Cumae, Aeneas realizes that he is a latecomer among heroes travelling to the west, just as he is among heroes descending to the underworld. Just as he was greeted at Carthage by the sight of the temple reliefs depicting the Trojan War, so he is confronted at Cumae with the reliefs carved on the doors of Apollo's temple by Daedalus, telling his own history. Like Aeneas, Daedalus had felt pity for a queen's great love (Pasiphaë, treated with unexpected sympathy); unlike Aeneas, Daedalus had lost his beloved son Icarus on his flight (in both senses) from Crete when the boy's wings melted and he drowned in the sea. While Virgil reports Daedalus' emotional distress as he repeatedly tried and failed to depict the death of Icarus, he passes over Aeneas' reaction, as the Sibyl summons him to her oracular cave. When she feels the onset of the god and urges Aeneas to make his request, he first promises to honour her with a great temple if she will only grant the Trojans settlement in Italy. It is not hers to grant, and her reply outlines the grim battles that await him on land—worse than he has suffered by sea: the Trojans will reach Lavinium but

> ... another Achilles is now born for Latium. He's also
> Son of a goddess. There's also the Teucrians' incubus, Juno,
> She'll haunt you every day, everywhere. Which of all Italy's peoples,
> Which cities *won't* you approach for assistance, a destitute suppliant?
> Once more the cause of such evil's a wife, who'll be hostess to Teucrians,
> Once more a foreign bridal affair.
> Don't give way to these evils, but move the more boldly against them ...
>
> (6.89–95)

This is the outline of what is to come in the six Iliadic books of Aeneas' struggle to settle in Italy, a message which only becomes clear as Virgil's narrative moves in Book 7 from initial welcome to the tumultuous resistance stirred up by Juno. But Aeneas has a more immediate demand—to see his beloved father—and he cites the precedents. Did not Orpheus enter the underworld, and Pollux, and Theseus, and Hercules? Hercules had been ordered to bring back Cerberus as one of his labours; Theseus had freely gone down to rescue his beloved Pirithoüs, as the half-divine Pollux had gone to rescue his twin Castor. And the descent of Orpheus had become part of the credo of the Orphic cult.

(Virgil was the first to change the outcome of Orpheus' descent to redeem Eurydice, imposing on Orpheus a failure caused by his own excessive love and impatience, in the miniature *katabasis* of *Georgics* 4.467–93.) The Sibyl now imposes two more delays before Aeneas can embark on his journey: Aeneas will need to equip himself with a magic golden bough (6.136–48) to give to Persephone, and he must oversee the burial of one of his men who has met sudden death (6.149–55). Both these tasks are described at length as Virgil deliberately defers the crossing into the other world. When Aeneas finds the precious bough it is because his mother's doves have led him to the tree where it grows. The Sibyl had told him it would come away in his hand, but now it resists his eager grasp. What does this imply? Next we follow Aeneas through the funeral rituals on the shore, before he can return to the Sibyl's cave and perform the sacrifices to Hecate and the spirits of the dead. Still another step is needed. Only after the Sibyl has dismissed the uninitiated does the poet speak in his own voice, marking his intrusion on the world of the dead by asking pardon for speaking of all that is hidden in darkness below, which he has (only) heard about.

Odysseus had seen the crowd of gibbering ghosts rush to drink the blood in his sacrificial trench. Aeneas instead sees a crowd of the unburied swarming towards Charon's boat, desperate to cross the Styx, and among them Palinurus, who begs Aeneas for burial and receives small comfort when the Sibyl guarantees that the local peoples will do expiation to his bones. Palinurus is the counterpart of Odysseus' foolish young companion Elpenor, left unburied after an accidental death. Odysseus actually pushes away his own mother's ghost until he has learned his future fate from the seer Tiresias; first the future, then the present, as his mother describes the state of his household, including his father's self-imposed poverty. Aeneas will learn his own fate and the glorious future of his descendants from his father at the climax of his journey, but both heroes experience the frustrated embrace of a beloved but insubstantial parent. Once across the Styx the early phases of Aeneas' experiences follow the Odyssean outline: but Homer's parade of noble women becomes in Virgil the fields of mourning for those who took their own lives; there he meets Dido, who scorns his apologies and would-be consolation as the angry Ajax had spurned Odysseus' attempts to conciliate him. Odysseus meets his old commander Agamemnon among the warriors and learns of his brutal murder by his treacherous wife and his cousin Aegisthus. Aeneas, tracing his life backwards to the fall of Troy, meets the almost unrecognizably mutilated Deiphobus, Helen's last Trojan husband, who tells him of his wife's unspeakable treachery. Virgil offers no counterpart to the encounter with Achilles, who told Odysseus that he would rather be an indentured serf on earth than king below it. Homer has no Elysian fields, but both poets include a description of the judge (Minos, *Odyssey* 11.568–71; Rhadamanthus, *Aeneid* 6.566–9) and the great sinners punished in Tartarus (Virgil has added nameless offenders to the traditional sinners, and portrays Theseus as confined there for all eternity), before Aeneas is able to deposit the golden bough at Persephone's gate.

Only now does Virgil leave Homer behind, as Aeneas enters the Elysian fields where heroic athletes and warriors enjoy a different sunlight and practise their old activities, along with priests and prophets, poets and musicians. Here he seeks and finds Anchises, who shows his son the souls gathered for rebirth and offers a pantheistic eschatology, in which human souls must be pure, or purified by centuries of exposure to the elements, before they can come to Elysium and be reborn free of all memory (6.724–51). But there are also the special souls of Aeneas' own descendants, 'what *your* fateful destiny offers' (6.759). The last and longest instalment of this journey of discovery is the parade of the Trojan descendants of Ascanius/Iulus and the Italians who will be born to Silvius, Aeneas' posthumous son by Lavinia (6.763). For Roman readers (especially for Augustus), this is their hour of glory, including tribute to Romulus, to Augustus (6.789–807), offset by the evocation of the civil war between Pompey and his son-in-law, Aeneas' descendant Julius Caesar (6.826–35).[22] In this past projected as future, the poet can speak as though the quarrel might still be averted, as Anchises urges Caesar in vain to hold back.

Two other moments in this long speech call for attention. Anchises' famous concession of the fine arts to other nations, in favour of Roman excellence in the arts of war and government: 'Mercy for those cast down and relentless war upon proud men' (6.853), was to have been his last message, and it has often been cited in criticism of Aeneas' last exercise of the victor's right to kill. But in 23 BC, before Virgil recited this book (with Books 2 and 4) to Augustus, young Marcellus, the emperor's nephew, designated as his future heir by marriage to Augustus' only child, died of a fever, and the poet felt obliged to add

---

[22] On the role of this and other 'Augustan' passages, see D. Quint, *Epic and Empire: Politics and Generic Form from Virgil to Milton* (Princeton, 1990).

a speech of tribute and of mourning. It is said that as Virgil read the passage Octavia, Marcellus' mother, fainted away.

After Anchises has sent his living son and the prophetess back to the upper world, Aeneas never speaks of his experience in the world of the dead to anyone. Yet he has clearly gained a new confidence and is much less hesitant in confronting the unknown. When **Book 7** begins Virgil carries the Trojans from Cumae past the last landmark to recall Aeneas' former life—the tomb where his nurse Caieta is buried—and past the last Odyssean echo, Circe's island, on to the shores of Latium. So readers share with Aeneas this last lap to his destination, before Virgil's carefully delayed second proem[23] proclaims the greater themes to come, of Latium's society, its kings, and its warfare.

In the first third of the book every sight and sound seems to contribute to hope of a peaceful new settlement. Not only is King Latinus without an heir; a series of omens mark his daughter Lavinia for an unforeseen destiny, and the oracle of Latinus' father confirms that she must marry a newcomer from abroad. From now on Aeneas' progress will be marked by omens of divine blessing, and his grateful acts of piety. The almost comical omen of Ascanius' allusion to eating their crusts at the picnic leads to libations and prayers, before the Trojans set out their camp and send envoys to King Latinus, who receives them with lavish gifts, the promise of a treaty and land settlement, and an offer of marriage.

But this cannot last: Juno breaks into the action with a speech of hatred for Aeneas and his men even more vehement than her words and actions at the beginning of Book 1: she is now determined to invoke the powers of hell. The hideous Fury Allecto is her instrument, and an instrument willing and eager to exceed her mission. In three episodes, Allecto exploits the passion and hot temper, first of Latinus' queen Amata who had wanted to see her nephew Turnus as son-in-law; once infected with Allecto's symbolic serpent, Amata goes from reasoned protest to her husband to a Bacchic frenzy as she snatches up her daughter and rouses a revolt among the matrons. Next, Allecto visits the sleeping Turnus disguised as a priestess, and urges him to fight for his rights; when he objects, she fires him with a torch that sends him calling his men to arms. Her third assault uses a more innocent

---

[23] On this delayed proem, which is also a 'proem in the middle', see Fraenkel in Harrison, *Oxford Readings*, and G. B. Conte, 'Proems in the Middle', *Yale Classical Studies*, 29 (1992), 147–59.

vehicle, as Ascanius while hunting wounds a much-loved and petted young stag which crawls dying to its Latin mistress. The countrymen are enraged and Allecto sounds the horn for open fighting between the unarmed peasants and the hunters.

At the supernatural level, Juno has to call off her vicious underling; at court, King Latinus is besieged by angry husbands, warriors, and peasants demanding war. Here Virgil introduces as his climax a powerful ritual known from Rome itself: to begin a war the consul had to open the gates of Janus' temple, so now Latinus tries to resist the pressure, like a rock battered by the angry seas. Indeed, the rock does stand firm, but correspondence between the simile and its tenor breaks down: Latinus feebly gives way and withdraws from his office into private obscurity, while Juno herself seizes a crowbar and forces open the gates. Now nothing can stop the momentum as the cities of Latium urgently forge new weapons, until the narrative reaches the march past of the Latin forces, Homeric in the vivid evocation of their homelands and their picturesque armour, headed by the tyrant Mezentius (who will be prominent in Books 8 and 10), with other contingents led by expatriate Greek warriors and by sons of Theseus (Hippolytus) and Hercules (Aventinus). The parade appears to end with Turnus himself, marked by the fire-breathing Chimaera on his helmet, but it is not quite over; last comes the warrior maiden Camilla, whose exploits will fill the second half of Book 11.

With **Book 8** the action divides, as Aeneas is prompted by a night vision of the Tiber god to seek the alliance of Evander and the Arcadian settlers at Pallanteum. For two days and nights he will be separated from his son and the officers guarding the Trojan camp. His pious prayer of thanks for the river-god's encouragement is answered by a further portent; the white sow of Alba with her thirty sucklings, which he sacrifices to Juno. After a marvellous and mysterious description of the journey upstream, Aeneas reaches Pallanteum, the site of the city which his descendants will one day found, and is welcomed by Evander's young son Pallas. This is a devout and harmonious community, occupied in celebrating the festival of their saviour Hercules. Hercules will be presented by Evander (and Virgil) as a model for Aeneas, and, more subtly, as a model or type of Rome's current saviour Augustus. Indeed the heart of this book (8.175–369, 455–584) is filled as much with the memory of the hero as with the present welcome to Aeneas and the foreshadowing of the future world capital.

Let me briefly digress to set this memory in context. Hercules himself belongs to the generation before the Greek expedition to Troy: he had saved Troy from the sea-monster and then taken the ungrateful city by storm when Priam was still a child. At this time, as Evander tells Aeneas, Anchises was a young man, and visited Arcadia, where Evander was an impressionable boy. But when Evander fled Arcadia to settle in Latium, Hercules would be Evander's guest on his return from his exploits taking the cattle of Geryon in Spain. Before Virgil completed the *Aeneid* Livy too had introduced Evander into Rome's prehistory, with Hercules as his guest. Both writers explain the foundation of Rome's first cult, the Great Altar of Hercules, by the hero's exploit in killing the robber Cacus who had stolen some of his (that is, Geryon's!) cattle. Where Virgil has innovated is in bringing Aeneas to the site of Rome and making the now aged Evander his host. There are bonds of kinship as well as Evander's past hero-worship of Anchises, and the bond is intensified when Evander entrusts Pallas, his only son, to learn warfare under Aeneas.

When Evander gives a full epic account of Hercules' defeat of Cacus it is ostensibly to justify the religious celebration which will end with a pious hymn to the hero (8.297–306), but this heroic combat serves the larger purpose not only of foreshadowing Aeneas' own forthcoming struggle but also of prefiguring Octavian–Augustus' continent-wide struggle against Mark Antony. Virgil has given this duel cosmic dimensions by turning the brigand Cacus (*Kakos*, or 'badman') into a supernatural son of Vulcan, a cave-dwelling monster belching fire and smoke, like Polyphemus in Book 3, or his counterpart Typhoeus, last of the giants to be overthrown by the enlightened power of Jupiter: the combat between Hercules and Cacus has become a gigantomachy.[24] But while there is no doubt of Cacus' evil powers, and the hugeness of the struggle reflected by the shock of sky, land, and river, and the hellish nature of his cave (8.239–46), Virgil presents Hercules, not as a strong but dispassionate executioner, but as repeatedly driven by fury ('Rueful pain at his loss and the bilious blackness of anger | Now set Hercules blazing', 8.219–20); a few lines later Hercules

> was arriving in utter
> Fury, his face moving this way and that to check each point of access,
> Gnashing his teeth. And he circled the whole of the Aventine three times,
> Boiling with anger.
>
> (8.228–31)

---

[24] The combat between Hercules and Cacus is discussed by P. R. Hardie, *Virgil's Aeneid: Cosmos and Imperium* (Oxford, 1986), 110–18, with other allusions to gigantomachy which exalt the narrative to a cosmic level.

The hero's violence as he gets to grips with Cacus (8.260–1) is as furious and explosive as that of his enemy. And this is Aeneas' model! Are we to condemn them both, or to understand that violent evil has to be overcome by a greater violence?

Through the ritual details of the original foundation of Hercules' altar, and the present commemorative wreath, libation, and hymn, Virgil returns to the calm and cheerful evocation of the pastoral community and its Roman setting. On the first evening Evander accompanies Aeneas from the altar and Capena gate into what will be Rome's sacred centre, the Capitoline Hill,

Golden now; in the past just bristling forested thickets.
Even then, grim awe of the place terrified superstitious
Peasants. When no more than boulders and woods, it could strike them with terror.
'This grove,' he said, 'this hill with the leaf-covered summit, is some god's
Dwelling, though *which* god we don't know. Arcadians believe they have sighted
Jupiter up there in person . . .'

(8.348–53)

As Aeneas goes to rest where Hercules once slept, Virgil changes the scene to Olympus, and a note of comedy, as Venus sets herself to seduce her husband into forging divine armour for the mortal Anchises' son. And the humour surely persists when Vulcan dutifully rises before dawn to visit his forge, and is compared to a woman who rises early so as to support her children by her diligent weaving and keep her husband's bed chaste. The supernatural armour is quickly ready: when Evander makes a morning call on his guest and advises him to seek the alliance of the Etruscans at Agylla (Caere), whose tyrant has taken refuge with Turnus, Venus sends a celestial portent of arms glittering and rattling in the sky. Aeneas declares that his mother had promised this sign, and even the arms forged by Vulcan; he knows he is called by the gods and can only pity Latinus' people and his enemy Turnus for the slaughter they will suffer.

His departure for Caere with Pallas and his cavalry seems full of hope, but is fraught with Evander's prayers for his son and the reader's forebodings. A quickening of pace soon brings them to the grove of Silvanus near Caere, near the Etruscan camp. Venus seeks Aeneas when he is alone by the stream, and now openly embraces him, leaving the arms beneath an oak (the tree Romans used for the military crown for saving a fellow citizen and depicted on Augustus' coinage). The rest of the book is taken over by Rome's history depicted through an *ekphrasis* of the scenes on Aeneas' shield. Homer had devoted much of *Iliad* 18 to the description of the scenes on the shield made by Hephaestus/ Vulcan for Achilles, but these were scenes representing all of Greek life—the cities and countryside at peace and at war, harvest, and ritual dance. What Aeneas sees are episodes from his future city; the cave where Romulus and Remus are suckled (the cave of Mars in 8.630, but the Lupercal of Lycaean Pan in 8.343–4), the rape of the Sabines, which ensured the next generation and alliance with Tatius. The vignette of Manlius and the geese defending the Capitol (8.652–3) stands out because we have heard its name earlier (8.347); now the barbarian Gauls are driven back, and women and priests share in the religious rites of communal rejoicing.

But more than half of Virgil's vivid description is occupied by the central scenes of very recent history: Augustus' naval victory at Actium and triumphal entry into Rome. In the first scene, surrounded by enamelled and silver waves, the seas are crowded with the fleets of the Roman leader, 'Caesar Augustus, on this side, is leading Italians to combat, | Backed by the senate and people, the household spirits and great gods', illuminated by the twin flames of his crest (here, as in Anchises' review of history (6.792), he is honoured by both names). Augustus and his loyal Agrippa advance to oppose the barbarian forces of Antony and his abominable Egyptian wife:

> In its midst, the queen cheers on her troops with the sistrum, her nation's
> Symbol. As yet she has not looked back at the twin snakes behind her.
> Every conceivable monstrous god, even barking Anubis,
> Points weapons at counterbalancing figures of Neptune and Venus . . .
>
> (8.696–9)

Above the human scene, all the gods are enumerated, Rome's Olympian supporters, against the monstrous animal divinities of Egypt, but also hovering overhead are the evil gods of war itself (8.700–3) before the crucial moment of Apollo's bowshot puts the enemy—even Cleopatra herself—with 'Pallor of death yet to come on her face' to flight. But the city, too, is crowded with rejoicing at Augustus' entrance in triple triumph, paying his vow before the city's three hundred shrines, and followed by an unending parade of conquered peoples from all points of the empire. One is tempted to compare it to the grand finale of a theatrical show. But when Virgil renounced the idea of an epic that would celebrate Augustus' military achievements he knew that he would have to find a spectacular form of indirect celebration.

As for Aeneas, he marvels, but shoulders his new equipment and his nation's future without understanding its meaning.

We know from the ancient Lives of Virgil that he first composed a draft outline of his whole poetic narrative, then painstakingly worked on small sections, accomplishing only a few lines each day: he said that he refined their details as a mother bear licks her cubs into shape. So he must have designed the apparent alternation of tension between dramatic books like the fall of Troy, or the tragedy of Dido, and the more even progress of Aeneas' travels (Book 3), or the games of Book 5. We have seen that Book 7 broke the pattern, building a crescendo of tension, but in **Book 9** events at the Trojan camp are muted by Aeneas' absence. Prompted by Juno, Turnus decides to fire the Trojan ships, but the poet interrupts to reassure his readers that the ships will not burn; a god will fend off the flames. Virgil adopts the tone and pace of a storyteller to explain how Cybele obtained from Jupiter the favour that these ships built from her sacred wood would not burn, but be transformed into sea-goddesses. As Turnus brandishes his torch a divine voice orders the ships to break free, and they re-emerge from the sea as nymphs. Despite his pretence of confidence he must call off the attack, and the Latins return to spend the night in feasting.

Book 9 belongs to the young. In a fully developed episode, the young lovers Nisus and Euryalus volunteer to break through the camp and carry news of the siege to Aeneas, but they are distracted by their successful slaughter and greed for spoil. Lingering, they are surprised by a Latin relief force, which captures young Euryalus; when Nisus exposes himself to spare his beloved both are killed and their severed heads set outside the camp, impaled on spikes. Ascanius had promised to look after Euryalus' mother if they were killed, as he would his own (the lost Creusa). She is the only woman to come this far with the army, and now rumour alarms her into a tirade of grief. With a pointed irony, Virgil shows how military authority hustles her out of sight to protect morale. But he is quick to replace the bitter taste of this affair with Ascanius' own success in dispatching Numanus, in retaliation for his boasts of Italian hardihood and insults to the supposedly effete Trojans from the decadent East. The ethnic stereotypes would be familiar to every Roman, whose belief in the moral and military superiority of native Italians would be only partly shaken by the young boy's lucky shot. Here too discipline takes over. The disguised Apollo congratulates the boy but sends him off the field (9.649–62). His destiny is to survive.

The last phase of this book sees the new initiative of Turnus, who pursues a miscalculated Trojan sortie back into their own camp, where he fights a series of death-dealing duels (as Alexander the Great had notoriously battled unaided in an Indian fortress). When the Trojans rally and focus on him alone (Jupiter has forbidden Juno to give him aid) he leaps over the battlements into the Tiber. The river washes him free of bloodshed and bears him safely back to his comrades.

We cannot truly admire a hero unless his opponents, too, are heroic. Turnus may be prompted by pride and ambition, but he is defending his own people against outsiders, and the river's benevolence is a testimony to his courage and leadership. The fierce fighting in **Book 10**, when Aeneas returns with the Etruscan forces and relieves the besieged camp, will bring out vicious aspects of both Turnus and Aeneas, revealed in their very different treatment of the two doomed young fighters Pallas and Lausus. But the book opens on a higher plane as Jupiter summons a council of the gods to impose neutrality (on Juno and Venus, who denounces Juno for interfering, and provokes a passionate and mocking reply).[25] At ground level the book maintains the lower tension of Book 9, with a holding action on land, and Aeneas' night voyage, accompanied by a catalogue of the ships from Etruscan cities. Continuity with Book 9 is provided by his nocturnal encounter with the nymphs that had been his ships; they give him the news of the siege which Nisus and Euryalus failed to deliver. An opening clash on the seashore between Turnus' force and the Etruscans is inconclusive, despite Aeneas' many victims, then Pallas on the further side rallies his Latin horsemen, and kills a series of warriors, last of them the Latin commander Halaesus.

The rest of this book will alternate the slaughter of almost anonymous warriors with a chain of causality that implicates the veteran warriors in the fate of the young fighters new to battle. Thus when Pallas confronts Halaesus, he prays to Tiber for victory and is granted this success. The other young hero, Lausus, whom Virgil presents as Pallas' counterpart, is also slaying his quota of warriors, but Virgil warns in advance that they are fated not to meet, since they must die at the hands of greater warriors: fortune will not grant either young man a safe return.

It is to support Lausus that Turnus now demands to fight young Pallas, but Virgil does not sentimentalize the unequal odds. Both fighters

---

[25] On this, Virgil's only council of the gods, see Feeney, *Gods in Epic*, 144–5.

taunt each other with Homeric cruelty; Turnus wishes that Evander could see his son slaughtered. Pallas prays to his father's guest Hercules that Turnus, wounded and dying, may see him strip away his armour. Olympus itself is absorbed into the outcome as Hercules weeps, and Jupiter reminds him that he had to let his own son Sarpedon die; the only comfort he offers is that Turnus, too, will soon die. And Virgil stresses the act that will decide Turnus' fate. As he answers Pallas' spear cast with a fatal blow and offers the return of the boy's body to his father he catches sight of Pallas' sword-belt with its image of the Danaids' collective crime,[26] and takes it to wear as spoils.

The death of Pallas changes the course and focus of the battle. Fighting far away, Aeneas hears the terrible news and reacts as Achilles did on the death of his beloved Patroclus, by running amok and showing no mercy, not even after he has taken eight captives for a human sacrifice to the shades of Pallas (10.517–20). Because Juno succeeds in luring Turnus away from the fighting (to his bitter shame, as he is swept away on shipboard) the conflict is now dominated by the Etruscan Mezentius (from 10.689), who holds all the lesser warriors at bay like a wild boar, as he advances to challenge Aeneas. The man is a blasphemer, who sees his right arm as his only god, and boasts that he will adorn his son with the trophies captured from Aeneas. It is a kind of warped justice that when Aeneas succeeds in wounding Mezentius his virtuous son is driven to step into the combat so that his father can withdraw. Assailed with a hail of spears by Lausus and his men Aeneas begs him not to incur his death out of loyalty but is almost obliged (by the warrior code) to give the fatal sword-wound. We should pause here to note Aeneas' surge of 'Ferocious wrath' (10.813): Lausus has done nothing to warrant indignation. I would suggest that Virgil gives Aeneas this uncharacteristic violence of spirit because it is both physically necessary and a kind of moral extenuation of the boy's killing.

At the news of Lausus' death his crippled father can only mount his horse and charge Aeneas; with nothing to lose, he fights on desperately until Aeneas brings the warhorse crashing down on his rider.

[26] In the Greek legend the fifty Danaids (daughters of Danaus) were forced by their father to murder their new husbands on their bridal night; a dreadful violation of trust. These husbands were also their cousins, the fifty sons of Aegyptus, but while this encouraged Greek drama to treat the women leniently, receiving them into Athens by the decision of their king and people, it is not clear how Romans read the legend. What we do know is that Augustus had statues of the Danaids and their father with drawn sword set up in the porticoes of the Palatine temple of Apollo, which Virgil would have seen when it was inaugurated in 28 BC. Scholars disagree in their interpretation.

Now Mezentius asks only to be buried with his son, and welcomes Aeneas' fatal stab as a *coup de grâce*. The book anticipates the end of the poem by ending in a death without further closure.

The grim first half of **Book 11** is the inevitable aftermath of the battle. Aeneas erects a trophy of Mezentius' arms, as a mark of (partial) victory, then orders the burial of the Trojan casualties and utters a speech over Pallas' corpse that is as much self-reproach as eulogy (11.42–58) before sending the bier to Evander with a vast procession of attendants, enemy spoils, and captives. His last words combine the recognition that he is fated to experience more losses with an intense farewell. But the completion of this narrative thread by Evander's heartbroken reception of his dead son (11.139–81) is postponed as Latin envoys come requesting permission to bury their dead, led by Drances, whose response to Aeneas' generosity is discredited by his feud with Turnus. The sad monotony of redoubled funeral pyres and ritual mourning, first performed by Trojans, then repeated on the Latin side, barely conveys the twelve days of truce in which public emotions are torn between rejection of the war and support for Turnus. The action and narrative mode changes when Venulus returns from his embassy, reporting that Diomedes himself favours Aeneas, convinced by his recent experiences and memories of Aeneas as a powerful opponent, equal to Hector but superior to him in piety (11.282–92, rewriting *Iliad* 20): he urges them not to fight but to ally themselves with Aeneas. As connoisseurs of political rhetoric, Romans would relish the ensuing debate called by Latinus, in which Drances' denunciation of Turnus, provoking Turnus' passionate reply, echoes the mutual abuse of Venus and Juno in the divine council. Taking up the challenge, Turnus now vows to face Aeneas alone: 'I, Turnus, vow both to you and my father by marriage, Latinus, | My life's blood' (11.440–1).

When the debate is broken up by news of Aeneas' mobilization the focus shifts, not only from Aeneas but from Turnus, who returns eagerly to combat, but drops out of the narrative as he plans to ambush Aeneas and his main force in a woodland pass: he delegates to Camilla the task of opposing the Etruscan cavalry (11.515–16, 523–31).

The narrative of Camilla's heroic deeds and death is shaped by the story of her past life which Diana tells her nymph Opis (rather as Venus tells Aeneas Dido's past history). The warrior maid with garlanded spear who brings up the rear in the Italian march past (7.803–17) was dedicated to Diana by her father when he had to flee his city, and she has been reared in the forest; but now that she is fated to die, it is Opis' task to ensure vengeance on her killer. Even in this minor battle the gods interfere; when the Etruscans are failing Jupiter sends Tarchon to rally them. Virgil is more even handed. While he shows Camilla fighting fairly against the dishonest Aunus, he makes her betray herself by her greed for the luxurious spoils of a Trojan priest, which blinds her to the bowshot of Arruns. But if Apollo grants Arruns his prayer to kill Camilla (and her death is deeply pathetic), Diana's agent hunts down Arruns, leaving him to die unburied.

With the death of Camilla, Book 11 ends in a rout as the cavalry flees to the city, many trapped outside the gates. In keeping with Camilla's heroism, even the Latin mothers hurl makeshift missiles from the walls, longing to die for their city. At the news of Camilla's death Turnus calls off his ambush, letting Aeneas through, and both forces make for the city. Only nightfall makes battle impossible until the next day.

Book 12 begins with Turnus, twice characterized with animal similes that convey his violent spirit, as wounded lion (12.4–9) and as battling bull (12.101–6). This first scene, which sees him resolved to fight, despite the pleas of Latinus and Amata and the silent distress of Lavinia, will be answered by the crisis within the city when Aeneas is prompted by Venus to besiege it, and Turnus' death is falsely reported, leading to Amata's suicide and Latinus' despair (12.593–614). Aeneas, too, is 'no less a savage . . . self-lashed in his anger' (12.107–8). But at first the narrative presents both armies and their leaders preparing for the religious offerings that will sanctify a truce. It is Juno's intervention that sends the disguised Juturna to provoke a violation of the truce in order to save her brother. (This breach and the wounding of Aeneas are modelled on the truce before the duel of Menelaus and Paris that is violated by Pandarus' wounding of Menelaus in *Iliad* 3.) When Aeneas is driven from the irregular battle by his wound Turnus leaps into his chariot and wreaks havoc,[27] until Venus intervenes by bringing the herb dittany to heal Aeneas. As he returns to the fight, Turnus and the Italians see him with terror, but Juturna again intervenes, disguising herself as Turnus' charioteer and driving him away from the part of the battle where Aeneas is fighting. For some fifty lines the poet treats the two champions as equals, reporting their slaughter in parallel as both rush over the battlefield like fires or rivers in spate, their

---

[27] He is actually compared to Mars (12.331–6), but this is the bloodthirsty Ares of *Aeneid* 8.700–3, rather than the strong father of Romulus.

anger seething and their invincible hearts bursting. This deliberate matching of champions is an innovation in epic, and seems to suggest that they share a story which must end with their reduction to a single figure.

It is now that Venus prompts Aeneas to attack the city, which will go up in flames as Turnus is driven ever further from the fighting. How can the reader not pity this warrior, victimized by deities who are postponing his death at the cost of his honour? Only when Turnus has been twice warned of the threat to the city is he finally overwhelmed with turbulent emotions of shame and love and courage: he casts off his sister and rushes on foot to the city, clamouring for the hostilities to be suspended so that he can fight his duel.

We have reached the last phase, but there will be more obstacles before the final combat. Every detail of diction and imagery enhances the superhuman stature of Aeneas, thundering in his weapons, towering like Athos or Eryx, as the champions from different worlds converge like bulls (again) fighting for dominance of the herd, and a mighty crash fills the heavens. But Jupiter is in control, weighing the two men's fates to determine which one will meet death. The shattered blade of Turnus (who mistakenly took his charioteer's sword) sends him running for his life, until Aeneas' spear sticks fast in the stump of Faunus' sacred wild olive, which the Trojans themselves had mutilated. Juturna restores Turnus' sword to him, and Venus pulls out and restores Aeneas' spear. There will be two more episodes before the battle can be completed. First, Jupiter accosts his sister-wife Juno demanding that she put an end to her actions, in return for his guarantees (here each element is ideologically important to the self-image of Roman Italy): that Troy will stay dead and the Latins keep their language name and way of life; the Trojans will contribute only their physical paternity (as future fathers of children by Latin wives) and Jupiter will make all the Italians Latins with a single tongue, creating a glorious race whose piety will celebrate Juno beyond all other nations.

But when Juno agrees and withdraws Jupiter resorts to infernal agents. He summons two *Dirae* (dreadful Furies), which we hear regularly attend his throne, and which he uses to spread plague and terrify cities. One he now sends to drive off Juturna; this creature becomes a bird that shrills, hovering in Turnus' face and beating his shield. Turnus is terrified and Juturna, recognizing that it is acting at Jupiter's command, laments her brother's doom and sinks beneath her stream. (The other Fury is not used.)

Now Turnus answers Aeneas' mockery: he knows that Jupiter (and the gods) are his enemies. He tries to hurl a huge boulder, but he fails, and the Fury prevents every valiant attempt. When Aeneas hurls his spear with the force of a siege weapon it pierces Turnus' thigh and he falls helpless. No scene in the entire epic has provoked more dispute than what follows. The poet calls Turnus humbled and suppliant, and his last words surrender his bride; he admits his defeat, asking only that he or his corpse be returned to his father. Aeneas himself hesitates until he catches sight of the baldric stripped from Pallas. 'As his eyes drink in these mementoes of savage | Pain, these so bitter spoils, Aeneas grows fearsome in anger, | Burning with fire of the Furies.' Aeneas claims that it is Pallas who gives the death-blow. Does anger at Pallas' pathetic death, or shame at failing to protect him, justify him in over-riding Anchises' precept of sparing the humbled? Here most recent scholars, especially in North America, believe that Virgil withholds his approval from Aeneas' act, and that the emphasis on his anger marks the poet's disavowal of Aeneas' action. There is another way of reading the act, however: remembering Hercules' anger with Cacus, and Aeneas' own rage at the innocent and honourable Lausus, I would suggest that Aeneas' anger can be seen as psychologically necessary, if he is to kill his humbled opponent, and that it is even more necessary, politically, for Turnus to die. We might also recall Virgil's advice to his beekeeper in the *Georgics* on how to deal with rival leaders for the swarm: for the sake of the swarm the inferior rival must be killed. Although we each read this last act of the epic in terms of our own and our nation's experience, we can agree that Virgil is not directing us towards an official verdict. He leaves his reader to appreciate both Aeneas' hesitation and his final blow.

When Virgil died in 19 BC he had already devoted eleven years to the *Aeneid* but according to his biographers he had wanted to spend another three years on refining his text. There are some local traces of changes needed, notably in inconsistent references to earlier narrative details[28] and in half-lines, where the poet had not yet fused passages he had worked on separately. It is difficult to believe that he was so

---

[28] The standard example is the statement in 7.123–7 that Anchises had foretold the omen of 'eating their tables'. The prophecy was actually made by the harpy Celaeno in 3.253–7. But we might also ask whether a revision would have put the second Fury to use at the end of the epic: why did not Virgil send one Fury against Turnus and the other directly against Juturna?

dissatisfied with the state of the poem that he ordered his friends Tucca and Varius to burn it, but if he did, and his will was overruled by Augustus, as the biographers tell us, we must be thankful. Within a decade Virgil's poem was being explicated by the teacher and critic Caecilius Epirota, and even his greatest poetic successor, Ovid, built constant allusions into his epic *Metamorphoses*: the *Aeneid* became *the* model for Seneca's moral allegorizing, for the poetic eloquence of the new orators like Marcus Aper and for Quintilian's rhetorical instructions on pathos, and on figured speech. More dramatically, in the grim later years of Nero's principate, as the end of Augustus' dynasty approached eighty years after Virgil's death, the *Aeneid* became an anti-model for young Lucan's passionate narrative of how the great Roman *respublica* (which Augustus claimed to have restored) was destroyed by the civil war of the first of the Caesars: Caesar's ageing opponent Pompey becomes a failed counterpart of Aeneas, leaving the shores of Italy for an irreversible defeat at Pharsalus. In Lucan's epic *Civil War* (also known as *Pharsalia*), Caesar's victory brought slavery and ruin. Italy is again depopulated, and its fields clamour for the hands of farmers, while uninhabited towns are reduced to a miserable shadow of past greatness (*Pharsalia* 1.24–32, cf. 7.391–407). It seems that Rome and Italy have returned to the devastation of the *Georgics* years. But the resonance of Virgil's poetry through pagan and Christian antiquity, and the afterlife of his great epic in the European Middle Ages and Renaissance, is a theme too great for these pages.

TRANSLATOR'S NOTE

TRANSLATING the *Aeneid* is a humbling experience. Even a very careful version will inevitably fall far short of the original, one of the world's greatest works of literary art, and will also be very different from it. Few contemporary languages are so alike that poetry can be moved from one to another without significant loss, no matter how minutely the details are transposed. And we are more distant in time and culture from Virgil's Rome than Virgil was from mythic Troy. English, one of Europe's youngest languages, is so saturated with the Christian thought into which it was born that it is a poor vehicle for the pre-Christian philosophies of the *Aeneid*, itself long assimilated into Christian tradition (as the *Iliad* and *Odyssey* never were). To translate it accurately, therefore, one must in some ways defamiliarize it, and thereby run the risk of outraging one's readers. Further, the best translations suffice only for a generation or so. None will ever satisfy all who consult it. Many potential readers, justifiably, want a version that is itself a work of literature: they must be able to sense through it that the original really is as good as its admirers claim. There are also many student readers, who are the hardest to satisfy without compromising Virgil, the translator, and other readers.

What makes such an apparently hopeless labour worthwhile for me is an irrational love of the poem which drives me to want to convince others about its magnificence. That is why I, like many before me, have spent years trying to produce an exciting, readable, and performable translation that is intelligible to listeners as well as readers, one that might catch and hold the attention of even the reader in a hurry, despite the fact that it refuses to simplify the text. I wanted it to be a version that the literary-minded could appreciate, but which would not play fast and loose with the original to win approval. On the contrary, I tried to stay close enough to the original for a struggling Latin student, if necessary, to be able to use it as a crib.

Finding an appropriate level of diction has been hard. The idiom, I feel, has to be more or less contemporary, as direct and Anglo-Saxon as possible, using the normal vocabulary and the contracted forms of non-scholarly literature, unless special emphasis is required. I have avoided archaisms, unless I thought them indispensable to a particular context, or when there really is no acceptable modern word to describe a piece of armour or the equipment of an ancient ship. Occasionally I have heightened the intensity of what might otherwise be an inert metaphor in English by choosing a word more dramatic than the Latin original, or have borrowed a word more familiar in New Zealand than in New York ('hogget', to describe a sheep too old to be lamb, to young to be mutton). Otherwise I have avoided regional usages: I did not want to make it too American for the English, Australian, and Indian eye or too English for the North American eye.

I could not, however, render the *Aeneid* as prose, because I don't know how to refashion poetry into prose without losing the essence of what makes the original poetic. An epic poem must sing. Even the best prose versions of Greek and Roman epics have about them a false aura of history or the novel. The *Aeneid* is neither. It would not compare favourably with real novels and histories unless vastly expanded and made explicit where it is allusive. But verse involves assumptions about the pronunciation of English. It cannot be neutral to the ear as it can sometimes be neutral to the eye. Words sound differently in 'standard' North American and 'standard' British usage, in so far as any standard exists. I opted to observe the word–stress and vowel quantities heard (until recently) on the BBC World Service and still, by and large, listed as preferred or variant usages in American dictionaries. But my own ear is not perfect in this regard, since I have lived most of my life in the United States.

Athough my idiom is informal, often colloquial, I have used a version of Virgil's ancient hexameter, a swift-moving line varying between twelve and seventeen syllables, divided among six feet, each of which carries its principal stress on the *first* syllable.[1] I move freely between present and past tenses, as Virgil does, but not always in the same places. The first syllable of each line is always stressed. Here is an example of what I mean, with the stressed syllables accented (3.583–7):

> Dúring that níght we endúred, under fórestland cóver, appálling
> Hórrors. And, fúrther, we júst couldn't sée what was caúsing the noíses.
> Nó star's gléam, no lúminous váult with its bríght constellátions
> Óffered us líght. There were óvercast skíes, fog-shróuded, entómbing
> Móon in a dúngeon of clóud; it was níght without tíme, utter dárkness.

---

[1] Because the metre I use has fairly strict rules about the number and length of syllables in a line, I have taken advantage of both conventions for expressing the English possessive of words ending in 's': 'Venus' child' (treating 'Venus' as two syllables) and 'Venus's child' (treating 'Venus's' as three syllables).

There are the same number of lines in this translation as in the original and the reader who wants to check it against Virgil's Latin or a commentary can do so readily.

The *Aeneid*, like much ancient (and some medieval) verse in European languages, uses not only regular metre but also carefully crafted resonances of sound. By this I do not mean rhyme (which Virgil hardly ever uses), but elaborate patterns of wordplay, including anagrams, which have not been a distinguishing feature of English poetry since Chaucer's day. When Latin wordplay is regenerated in English some readers are upset, believing that wordplay is better avoided in 'serious' literature. Since the days of Dr Johnson we have been taught to associate puns almost exclusively with levity. Scholars often deplore the propensity for puns they note in Chaucer, Shakespeare, Donne, and Herbert. Modern English translations of Chaucer, in fact, routinely suppress almost all his wordplay. I have followed the opposite course with Virgil. Wherever he uses two or more Latin words of similar sound or structure in close proximity, I have tried either to reproduce the effect in English or to express it in some other way.

Anagrams are more of a problem, since they usually cannot be 'heard' in English: 'thread' and 'hatred', for example, are anagrams only by conventions of spelling. In Latin, anagrams are audible. Latin letters have fairly predictable values regardless of placement within a word. Young Romans were trained to recite their letters (and syllables) as we recite numbers: backwards as well as forwards, and in various other groupings. To approximate the effect of Virgil's anagrams I therefore had to depart at least a little from the 'dictionary' meaning of the text, and thereby invite accusations of mistranslation.

One does not have to understand Latin to *see* the problem. Here are the only two words in one of Virgil's incomplete lines, *Aeneid* 7.702: *pulsa palus*. The poet is describing the ripples in the surface of a lake (*palus*) caused by the sound of the cries of swans striking (*pulsa*) its surface. The impact of the sound destabilizes and rearranges the elements of the word *palus* itself, not just of the lake the word indicates. The closest I could get was 'pools' and 'loops'. Whenever syllables have to be inverted, I make their *sound*, not their spelling, the basis of my equivalent wordplays.

I realized as I translated the catalogue of troops in Book 7 that Virgil had, throughout, leavened what I once thought flat and uninteresting lines with an often ebullient wit. We have no business making poetry dull because we disapprove of wordplay. To shear away Virgil's luxuriance is not to separate the painting from a (superfluous) gilded frame, but to lacerate the canvas. Like Shakespeare and the Greek tragedians, Virgil grasped that humour and earnestness are not mutually exclusive in art, any more than they are in life. We should read the *Aeneid*, not in solemn homage, but for enjoyment.

I have transposed Virgil's puns, anagrams, and other figured usages into comparable but generally less intrusive figures in English without leaving the 'dictionary' sense too far behind. I rarely trespass farther than making *nemus* 'a wooded area' or 'a (wooded) hollow' rather than 'a wood'. I avoid English words that generate multiple resonances when the Latin does not, unless it is simply impossible to avoid them, as in the case of the visual doublet of the name Dares and the verb 'dares' in Book 5. But I could not find a way to bring out most of Virgil's persistent cross-language wordplay between Latin and Greek. So one entire section of the Virgilian verbal orchestra is missing. This translation will, nonetheless, read quite differently, in several places, from many others since it retains elements that are usually jettisoned.

Translators, like all readers, try to formulate a mental profile of their authors. But Virgil is exceptionally elusive. His persona, though it saturates his work, is the engine powering the art-form rather than the artistic focus of attention. Virgil assumes so many different masks that I could not privilege any as representative of the poet's inner feelings— even his own persona as narrator. Here I differ from many predecessors. The *Aeneid* is often so translated as to accommodate either the widely accepted assumption that it is Virgil's *intent* to glorify Rome and its emperor, or the increasingly popular counterassumption: that his *intent* is to mount a covert attack on Rome and the Caesars. The translator has no business imposing any such intentionalist framework. The epic should be allowed to speak, in so far as a translation can achieve this goal, for itself. English, with its vastly larger vocabulary than Latin in most areas, allows one to generate distinctions Roman writers had no means of expressing, and to justify changes in the original by using the dictionary shrewdly. Translators routinely render the adjective *superbus* differently, for example, depending on whether they (as translators) approve or disapprove of the person or place it is applied to, thereby conveying the false impression that this is what Virgil is doing. Although the 'doorposts' of a monster's cave and of a god's temple are described by the same adjective, *superbus*, those of the cave often appear in English as 'arrogant' or 'haughty', those of the temple as 'proud'. I follow Virgil and use 'proud' in both cases, since pride can be virtue or vice in English.

Some Latin words I have felt obliged to translate by the same English equivalents at all times because I wanted the reader to be able to track them down, since scholarly literature pays them particular attention. The main instances are: the adjectives *felix*, *infelix*, and *pius* (along with its corresponding noun *pietas*). I always render *felix* with 'fulfilled' or with the noun 'fulfilment', and *infelix* with 'unfulfilled', or a formula indicating the failure of 'fulfilment', to capture what I take to be the word's essential idea: the ability (or lack of ability) to bear fruit. *Pius* and *pietas* are more problematic, since their English equivalents 'pious' and 'piety' are now redolent with hypocrisy. I settled on 'righteous' and 'righteousness', though they too have acquired negative shading. Latin *fama* is also difficult. Our derivative, 'fame', is almost always positive, whereas *fama* usually (but not invariably) indicates a bad report of someone's behaviour. If one is *famosus* one is 'notorious', not 'famous'. I translate *fama* as 'rumour' throughout, but often add an extra word to round out the meaning when 'rumour' alone isn't enough.

Virgil rarely presents us with a consistently binary opposition between right and wrong, truth and falsehood, reality and illusion. His is more the world of paradox, of multiple and apparently conflicting simultaneous realities which often flare in unexpected ways as different planes of meaning intersect. Wherever I sensed the text leading me in different directions at the same time, I have left the reader the ambiguity or contradiction Virgil left me. What he says, and what he has his characters say—even Jupiter, king of the gods—varies from one context to another, depending on whom the speaker is addressing and under what circumstances. I did not want to smooth out these differences. Virgil's characters, like their counterparts in real life, do not always tell everyone the same thing. Jupiter himself often resembles an administrator who promises someone the world in private, but backs down in front of a contentious assembly. Further, Virgil does not always tell us, as novelists often do, when a speaker is lying. We have to note this for ourselves. Indeed, he sometimes teases us into thinking a character is lying when there is nothing untrue in what he says.

Not only does Virgil's epic sing, it sings in a variety of registers. His style constantly shifts mood, pace, and tone. He is a complete master of rhetorical nuance. In Book 7, for example, we encounter the complex and sensuous language describing the land of the enchantress Circe which, in turn, yields to a passage outlining the myth-history of Latium and echoes the prose of the Roman historian Livy. The speeches in the *Aeneid* have distinctive styles, ranging from the studiedly ambiguous narratives of Aeneas and Latinus' devious attempts at diplomacy to the pompous arrogance of Ilioneus and the witty sarcasm of Juno. And his characters change and evolve. These features I have attempted to distinguish by corresponding modifications of style, as one would in a drama. Virgil meticulously marks his speakers' voices off from his own narrative voice. He also startles us with some of the most complex psychological analysis found in any ancient writer, Greek or Roman; and, for the bloodthirsty, he offers what are arguably among the most thrilling (I would argue the *most* thrilling) descriptions of battle in all ancient epic.

No translation, of course, can (or should) provide within the text all that readers two thousand years later need to appreciate the *Aeneid*. For if it strays too far into the territory of the commentator it ceases to be a translation. Virgil assumes of his reader a familiarity with Roman and Greek language, myth, history, and culture which we do not necessarily possess. While some minor adjustments can, I think, be made within a translation to accommodate things known to an ancient reader but unknown to many modern readers, one must not clarify what would also have puzzled an ancient, or a character within the epic, as it puzzles us. When Virgil's Anchises talks to Aeneas of a Roman father-in-law and son-in-law who will clash in war, he mentions no names. Aeneas has no more idea than the novice reader who it is that Anchises is talking about. The *Aeneid* is, in this sense, an interactive text, relying on us to adduce our own observations and knowledge to complete the meaning. Sometimes we can't. Sometimes no one can. In Book 4, for instance, we are suddenly informed that the queen of Carthage, Dido, has a sister who appears to have become a close confidante of Aeneas even as Dido is floundering, ever more helplessly, in her love for him. The poet tells us there is another door in the room, as it were, but he never opens it for us. We are often confronted in the *Aeneid* with a kind of reversed dramatic irony: his characters do things and know things to which the poet alludes, but which he otherwise passes over in resolute silence.

For this kind of information one must resort to notes. New vistas open if the reader spends even a little time among them to see where Virgil found Anna, or how he builds his text from an assortment of different traditions, and deploys his mythic narrative against a backdrop of events closer to, even within, his own lifetime. Neither the Introduction nor the notes, of course, are intended as a substitute for a full commentary. The notes, except those on Book 6, are intended merely to draw attention to, and clarify, issues and problems raised in the text, or to explain choices I have made when preferring one

manuscript reading to another. I have tried to avoid dictating to readers how they must read the *Aeneid*; but I do try to ask some new questions of the text. I have indulged myself a little more in the case of
Book 6 because it raises so many complex issues that I felt the reader
unfamiliar with the historical and literary backdrop needed more support without having to put the book down and look elsewhere.

Virgil's refractions of poetic predecessors and of contemporaries are
extensive and have prompted critical volumes written by scholars far
more learned than I. No less extensive is his use of the multiple and
varied mythic, historical, and cultural data that subtend his epic. However
much Virgil conveys the impression that he is simply recounting the
traditional 'Tale of Aeneas', there is reason to believe that he created
most of the story and its extraordinarily vivid cast of mythic and
fictional characters (almost all new to full epic characterization) all by
himself out of scattered fragments. There is really nothing to rival this
achievement in Greek and Latin poetry.

Latin editions of the *Aeneid* are based on a textual tradition that
survived for 1,500 years in handwritten copies. There are a number of
places where the surviving manuscripts disagree with one another, and
leave editors in disagreement. I have offered alternative translations in
some places where these differences are important. I have, with the
exception of a couple of lines universally rejected, translated the entire
received text, including the often omitted prefatory lines. In a handful
of places, an unimportant short line has been conflated with the next
in the translation; this is reflected in the marginal line numbers.
The edition I have followed throughout is Hirtzel's Oxford Classical
Text, though I have adjusted it in places to take account of more
modern editions of the *Aeneid* as a whole, editions of individual books,
and a number of important articles.

SELECT BIBLIOGRAPHY

Note: only works written in English and wholly or partially intelligible to readers who do not know Latin or Greek are included.

Historical/Mythic Background on Troy, Sicily, and Italy

Ahl, F., *Reading the* Aeneid: *A Commentary for the Reader in Translation* (Oxford, forthcoming).

Bonfante, L., *Etruscan Art* (Berkeley and London, 1990).

Bremmer, J., and Horsfall, N., *Roman Myth and Mythography* (London, 1987).

Erskine, A., *Troy between Greece and Rome: Local Tradition and Imperial Power* (Oxford, 2001).

Galinsky, G. K., *Aeneas, Sicily, and Rome* (Princeton, 1969).

Gowing, A., *The Triumviral Narratives of Appian and Cassius Dio* (Ann Arbor, 1991).

de Grummond, N. (ed.), *A Guide to Etruscan Mirrors* (Tallahassee, Fla., 1982).

Horsfall, N., *A Companion to the Study of Virgil* (Leiden and New York, 1995).

MacNamara, E., *The Etruscans* (London, 1990).

Malkin, I., *The Returns of Odysseus* (Berkeley, 1998).

Martindale, C. R., *The Cambridge Companion to Virgil* (Cambridge, 1997).

Ogilvie, R. M. (ed.), *A Commentary on Livy, Books 1–5* (Oxford, 1970).

Salmon, E. T., *Samnium and the Samnites* (Cambridge, 1967).

Wilson, R. J. A., *Sicily under the Roman Empire: The Archaeology of a Roman Province 36 BC to AD 535* (Warminster, 1990).

Virgil's Language and Use of Earlier Latin Poets

Ahl, F., *Metaformations: Soundplay and Wordplay in Ovid and other Classical Poets* (Ithaca, NY, and London, 1985).

Goldberg, S. M., 'Saturnian Epic: Livius and Naevius', in Boyle, *Roman Epic: Livius and Naevius* (1993), 19–36.

O'Hara, J. J., *Death and the Optimistic Prophecy* (Ann Arbor, 1990).

Paschalis, M., *Virgil's Aeneid: Semantic Relations and Proper Names* (Oxford, 1997).

Wigodsky, M., *Vergil and Early Latin Poetry* (Wiesbaden, 1972).

Virgil's Religion, Philosophy, and Rhetoric

Ahl, F., 'Homer, Vergil, and Complex Narrative Structures in Latin Epic: An Essay', *Illinois Classical Studies*, 14 (1989), 1–31.

—— 'The Rider and the Horse: Politics and Power in Roman Poetry from Horace to Statius', *Aufstieg und Niedergang der römischen Welt*, 2.32.1 (1984), 40–110.

Bailey, C., *Religion in Virgil* (Oxford, 1935).

Conte, G. B., *The Rhetoric of Imitation: Genre and Poetic Memory in Virgil and Other Latin Poets* (Ithaca, NY, and London, 1986).

Feeney, D. C., *Gods in Epic* (Oxford, 1991).

Hardie, P. R., *Virgil's Aeneid: Cosmos and Imperium* (Oxford, 1986).

Lyne, R. A. O. M., *Further Voices in Virgil's Aeneid* (Oxford, 1974).

Parke, H. W., *Sibyls and Sibylline Prophecy in Classical Antiquity*, ed. B. C. McGing (London, 1988).

Various Interpretations of the Aeneid

Boyle, A. J., *The Chaonian Dove: Studies in the Eclogues, Georgics, and Aeneid of Virgil* (Leiden, 1986).

—— *Roman Epic* (London and New York, 1993).

Clausen, W. J. (1965), 'An Interpretation of the Aeneid', in S. Commager, *Virgil: A Collection of Critical Essays* (Englewood Cliffs, NJ, 1966), 75–88.

Commager, S., *Virgil: A Collection of Critical Essays* (Englewood Cliffs, NJ, 1966).

Gillis, D., *Eros and Death in the Aeneid* (Rome, 1983).

Harrison, S. J., *Oxford Readings in Virgil's Aeneid* (Oxford, 1990).

Heinze, R., *Virgil's Epic Technique* (1915), trans. H. and D. Harvey, F. Robertson (Berkeley, 1997).

Jenkyns, R., *Virgil's Experience: Nature and History. Times, Names, and Places* (Oxford, 1998).

Otis, B., *Virgil: A Study in Civilized Poetry* (Oxford, 1962).

Pöschl, V., *Virgil's Poetic Art*, trans. G. Seligson (Ann Arbor, 1962).

Putnam, M. C. J., *The Poetry of the Aeneid: Four Studies* (Harvard, 1988).

Virgilian Influence on Later Writers

Comparetti, D., *Vergil in the Middle Ages* (1872), trans. E. F. M. Benecke, with a new introduction by Jan M. Ziolkowski (Princeton, 1997).

Quint, D., *Epic and Empire: Politics and Generic Form from Virgil to Milton* (Princeton, 1993).

Thomas, R. F., *Virgil and Augustan Reception* (Cambridge, 2001).

Studies of Particular Aspects of the Aeneid

Barchiesi, A., '*Ekphrasis*', in C. R. Martindale, *The Cambridge Companion to Virgil* (Cambridge, 1997).

Conte, G. B., 'Proems in the Middle', *Yale Classical Studies*, 29 (1992), 147–59.

Feeney, D. C., 'The Taciturnity of Aeneas', in S. J. Harrison, *Oxford Readings in Virgil's Aeneid* (Oxford, 1990), 167–90.

—— 'The Reconciliations of Juno', in S. J. Harrison, *Oxford Readings in Virgil's Aeneid* (Oxford, 1990), 339–62.

Fowler, D., 'The Virgil Commentary of Servius', in C. R. Martindale, *The Cambridge Companion to Virgil* (Cambridge, 1997), 72–9.

—— 'Story Telling', in C. R. Martindale, *The Cambridge Companion to Virgil* (Cambridge, 1997), 259–70.

Galinsky, G. K., 'The Anger of Aeneas', *American Journal of Philology*, 109 (1988), 321–48.

Gill, C., 'Reactive and Objective Attitudes: Anger in Virgil's *Aeneid* and Hellenistic Philosophy', in S. Braund and G. W. Most (eds.), *Ancient Anger: Perspectives from Homer to Galen*, Yale Classical Studies, 32 (New Haven, 2003), 208–28.

Knox, B. W., 'The Serpent and the Flame: The Imagery of the Second Book of the *Aeneid*', in S. Commager, *Virgil: A Collection of Critical Essays* (Englewood Cliffs, NJ, 1966), 124–42.

Parry, A., 'The Two Voices of Virgil's *Aeneid*', in S. Commager, *Virgil*, 107–23.

Zetzel, J., '*Romane Memento*: Justice and Judgment in *Aeneid* 6', *TAPA* 119 (1989), 263–84.

Further Reading in Oxford World's Classics

Homer, *The Iliad*, trans. Robert Fitzgerald, ed. G. S. Kirk.

—— *The Odyssey*, trans. Walter Shewring, ed. G. S. Kirk.

Lucretius, *On the Nature of the Universe*, trans. Ronald Melville, ed. Don Fowler and Peta Fowler.

Milton, John, *Paradise Lost*, ed. Stephen Orgel and Jonathan Goldberg.

A CHRONOLOGY OF VIRGIL

All dates are BC.

70 Crassus and Pompey consuls; Virgil born 15 October at Andes near Mantua.

55 Crassus and Pompey consuls for second time. Virgil comes of age; goes away to study at Milan and Rome.

49 Civil war breaks out; Caesar occupies Italy, has himself elected dictator at Rome. Pompey and Republican forces evacuate to Epirus, followed by Caesar. (It is likely that Virgil withdrew to the neutral safety of Naples now if not earlier, to avoid fighting and to study philosophy. We do not know when he returned to live in Rome.)

48 Caesar defeats Pompey and Republicans at Pharsalus; Pompey assassinated by Egyptian king. Caesar in Egypt until 47.

44 15 March: assassination of Caesar. Octavian declared his heir, supported by the Senate against Mark Antony.

43 'Second' triumvirate of Octavian, Antony, and Lepidus.

42 Octavian and Antony defeat Brutus and Cassius at Philippi.

41 Octavian besieges and sacks Perusia, held by supporters of Antony, and begins confiscation of land from northern cities to settle his veterans.

40 Virgil's 4th Eclogue honours Pollio's consulship. (The book of *Eclogues* took three years to write but was complete before 35. During these years Virgil was befriended by Maecenas, and given a house on the Esquiline: he probably spent more time at Rome from now on.)

36 Octavian defeats Sextus Pompey at Naulochus.

35 *Georgics* begun this year; the work takes Virgil seven years.

31 Octavian defeats Mark Antony and Cleopatra at Actium.

30 1 August: Octavian occupies Alexandria.

29 *Georgics* completed: read by Virgil to the returning Octavian. Virgil must have begun the *Aeneid* now if not earlier: it is reported to have taken him eleven years.

27 Octavian returns formal control of Republic to the Senate and is given the title 'Augustus'. (During this decade the critic Caecilius Epirota began to give young men formal instruction in Virgil's poetry along with the work of the New Poets of Catullus' circle.)

23 Virgil reads *Aeneid* 2, 4, and 6 to Augustus and his sister Octavia after the death of her son Marcellus.

19 Virgil travels to Greece, falls ill while returning with Augustus, and dies at
    Brindisi. (The *Aeneid*, which he had wanted to destroy as unfinished, was
    published at an unknown date by order of Augustus, possibly edited by his
    friends Varius and Tucca.)

AENEAS' TRAVELS

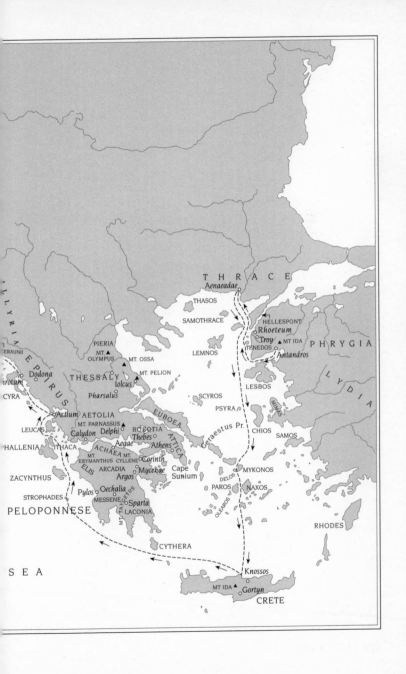

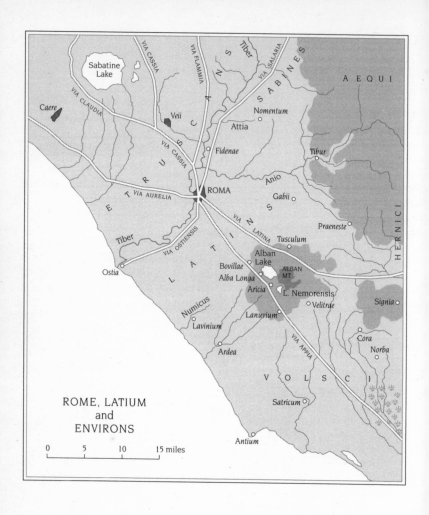

ROME, LATIUM
and
ENVIRONS

0   5   10   15 miles

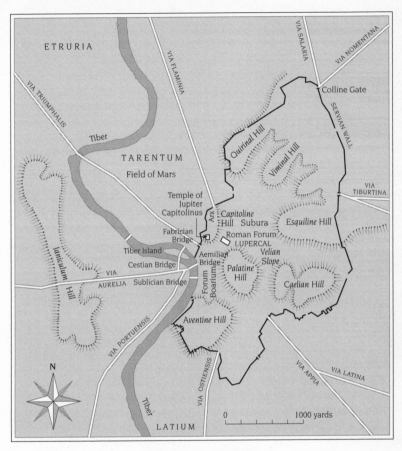

THE HILLS OF ROME

AENEID

BOOK ONE

I'm the same man* who once coaxed music from slenderest reed pipes,
Then, upon leaving the forests, I worked in the neighbouring ploughlands,
Making them yield their resources to even the greediest settler:
Farmers all loved this work. Now I turn to the horrors of battle,

ARMS and the man I sing of Troy,* who first from its seashores,
Italy-bound, fate's refugee, arrived at Lavinia's
Coastlands. How he was battered about over land, over high deep
Seas by the powers above! Savage Juno's anger remembered
Him, and he suffered profoundly in war to establish a city,   5
Settle his gods into Latium, making this land of the Latins
Future home to the Elders of Alba and Rome's mighty ramparts.
Muse, let the memories spill through me. What divine will was
      wounded,
What deep hurt made the queen of the gods thrust a famously
      righteous
Man into so many spirals of chance to face so many labours?   10
Anger so great: can it really reside in the spirits of heaven?

Once, an old city existed, and Tyrian settlers controlled it:
Carthage,* a distant menace to Italy, facing the Tiber's
Estuary, rich in resources, ferocious in practice of warfare.
Juno reportedly cherished this one land more than all others,   15
Even than Samos. In Carthage she kept both her chariot and
      weapons.
This was her candidate city to rule as the king of all nations
If fate allowed. For this role she was grooming it even in those days.
But there was being produced, she'd heard, from the bloodline of
      Trojans,
Offspring that would one day overturn her Tyrian fortress,   20
People who'd rule far and wide like kings, full of pride in their
      war skills,
Sure to arrive and cut Libya's thread spun on Destiny's spindles.
    Fearing this, haunted by memories, too, of a war from the deep
      past,
One she had fought at Troy for her well-loved Argives, Saturnian

Juno had never let fall from her mind these causes of anger,   25
Savaging pains. For they stuck, stored fast in her mind's deep
     awareness.
One was the Judgement of Paris* that bypassed, insulted her beauty.
Hate for Troy evilled her eye. Add Ganymede,* raped and exalted.
Burning with these thoughts too, she battered all over the high
     seas
Remnants of Troy that the Greeks and their never-gentle Achilles   30
Missed. She relentlessly kept them at bay, far distant from Latium.
Many the years, fate-driven, they strayed over sea after salt sea.
Planting the Roman nation's roots was a task of immense scale.

Scarcely had Sicily faded from view. They were setting their canvas,
Spirits high, on the deep. Bronze prows ploughed brine into foam
     spray.
                                                        35
Juno, who kept her wound eternally fresh in her bosom,
Said to herself: 'Am I beaten, my plans all dead? Is preventing
Teucer's descendant from landing as Italy's king beyond *my* power?
Granted, the Fates are opposed. But if so, how was Pallas
     empowered,
Just for the insane crime of a single man, son of Oileus,   40
Ajax, to burn an entire Greek navy and drown all its sailors?
Out of the clouds she herself hurled Jupiter's lightning; she
     scattered
Vessels, her storm winds churned calm seas. And, so much for Ajax,
Lungs thunderbolted, he vomited fire: she dispatched a tornado,
Whirled him away as he died and impaled him upon a sharp
     reef rock.   45
I, meanwhile, who rank as the queen of gods, Jupiter's sister,
Jupiter's wife, have been waging war with this one single nation
All these years. Will anyone now still pray for my favour,
Offering humbly, on bended knee, his gifts at my altars?'
    Inwardly spinning such thoughts, heart blazing with anger, the
     goddess   50
Comes to Aeolia, storm-cloud land, ever raging with tempests.
Aeolus rules here as king and restrains with imperial power,
Deep in a cavern's vastness, the struggling winds and the howling
Hurricanes, bridling their rage with a prison's chains and portcullis.
Hating restraint, they seethe all round their bolted escape
     routes,
                                                        55

Making the mountain roar. Here Aeolus, holding a sceptre,
Sits on a high peak, soothes winds' fury, tempers their anger.
If he did not, they would tear straight out and swirl away with them
Oceans, land, vast sky, swept off like dust upon breezes.
Fearing precisely this, the Almighty Father confined them   60
Deep within caves, then superimposed high mountainous masses,
Gave them a ruler who'd understand, from a well-defined contract,
How to restrain and, upon his command, give rein to their
     movements.
  Juno came humbly begging his help, and addressed him as
     follows:
'Aeolus, I come to you since the father of gods and men's ruler   65
Granted you power both to quieten waves and to raise them with
     windstorms.
Sailing the Tuscan Sea is a people unfriendly towards me,
Ferrying Ilium and already conquered gods of its households
Over to Italy. Make your winds hurricanes! Shatter their navy!
Sink them, or split their forces and litter the waves with their
     bodies!   70
I, by the way, have fourteen nymphs with simply outstanding
Bodies. The one with the prettiest figure is Deiopea.
I'll designate her as yours, join you both in a durable marriage.
Thus she can spend all time with you, in return for your service
Rendered, and make you the father, as well, of some beautiful
     children.'   75
  Aeolus answered: 'My ruler, your task is but this: to discover
What you desire to achieve. My duty's obedience to orders.
You ensure Jupiter's backing for my control of this kingdom,
Such as it is. And *you* assign seats at the banquets of heaven.
You make decisions on who has control over storm clouds and
     tempests.'   80
  This said, he pointed his spearhead down, then pierced through
     the hollow
Flank of the mountain. The winds, like legions marshalled for
     battle,
Stream through the portal supplied, blast out across earth in
     tornadoes,
East wind and south wind together, and storm-packed African
     tempests
Sweep upon seas, churn waters up from the bottommost seabeds,   85

Curling immense and destructive wave-crests over the coastlands.
Then follow roars: men's shouts; rasped screeches of hawsers
    protesting.
Billowing up in a trice, clouds tear away heaven and daylight,
Blinding Teucrians' eyes; dark night settles ghastly on ocean.
Sky roars thunder above, air flashes and flashes with lightning.   90
All signs menace the men with immediate death and destruction.

Now, in a flash, shivers send all Aeneas' limbs into spasm.
Groaning aloud, he extends both palms, reaches upwards to heaven
Uttering these cries: 'Greater by three, even four times, the
    blessing
Chance gave those with the fortune to die beneath Troy's mighty
    ramparts   95
Under their fathers' gaze! O Tydeus' son, Diomedes,
Bravest Danaän of all,* why could *I* not have fallen on Ilium's
Plains, spilled forth my soul under *your* right hand? That's where
    savage
Hector was killed by Achilles' spear, where the mighty Sarpedon
Died, where the Simoïs snatched up and rolled in the swirl of its
    waters   100
So many warriors' shields, men's helmets, and valiant bodies!'
    While he is bellowing this, fierce, screaming gusts of the north wind
Batter his sail head-on, thrust waves star-high to the heavens.
Oars split, the bow yaws sharply, the ship veers broadside to sea's
    swell
Just as the surge curves up, in a mountain of water, a huge Alp.   105
Some hang high on the crest, others see, as the trough opens vastly,
Land disclosed between waves where tempests rage upon dry sand.
Southerlies toss onto lurking reefs three ships they have snatched up,
Reefs the Italians call Altars, exposed in the sea when it's choppy
Like some monstrous spine hidden under the surface. The east
    wind   110
Blasts three more into shallows and sandbanks (a sad sight to witness),
Slithers them onto the shoals, then walls them in among sand dunes.
    Right before his own eyes, one vessel carrying Lycians,
Trusty Orontes too, is battered by huge breakers cresting
Over her aft deck. The helmsman, wrenched from his oar, is sent
    spinning   115
Headlong. Three times round that same surge spirals the vessel,

Spinning it down through its suctioning throat, and devours it
    completely.
Up bobs a swimmer afloat, here and there, in this drain of destruction,
Arms of the men, planks, paintings, and treasure from Troy fleck
    the waters.
Now Ilioneus' well-built galley, now valiant Achates',   120
Abas' vessel, the ship that is carrying agèd Aletes
Storm lashed, start to go down; in their hulls' seams, dowelling and
    tendons
Snap, locked joints split apart, springing murderous leaks shipping
    water.

Meanwhile, Neptune perceived that an unleashed tempest was
    raging,
Sensed that the sea was a thunderously massive upheaval of salt
    brine   125
Churned from its still, calm depths; and he found it deeply
    disturbing.
So, looking up, he lifted his tranquil head to the surface.
Scattered on ocean's expanse he observed Aeneas's navy,
Trojans beleaguered by high-running seas and the heavens'
    implosion.
Juno's plots and her anger in no way eluded her brother.   130
Summoning east wind and zephyr to him he addressed them as
    follows:
'Could you have so much trust in your family connections, you mere
    winds,
That, without my consent, you dare make earth and the heavens
Chaos again and create so monstrous a mass of confusion?
You, that I . . . Wait! First business must be to bring calm to the
    waters.   135
Then you will pay for your crimes. *Your* lashing won't be just
    verbal.
Get on your way and be quick. And relay these words to your ruler:
Ocean's High Command and the savage Trident of Office
Weren't allotted to *him* but to *me*. His province is large rocks,
Homes, east wind, for your kind. That's the right court for
    Aeolus' bluster,   140
Playing at king. But the winds must be kept in their cells
    with the doors locked!'

This said, more quickly in fact than he spoke, he levels the
    swelling
Seas, rounds up, then disperses the clouds, re-establishes sunshine.
Cymothoë (Triton helps her) does hard work levering vessels
Up from the jagged reefs. The god prises them free with his trident, 145
Opens the quicksands' vastness, levels the seas back to flatness
Skimming the wave-tops on feather-light wheels in his
    swift-running chariot.
Much the same happens* within a great nation, where lawlessness
    often
Bursts into riots, where people become mobs savage with passion,
Firebrands, stones start flying through air (fury furnishes weapons) 150
Then, if they happen to glimpse a man worth their respect for his
    righteous
Conduct, they're silenced. They prick up their ears and await his
    instructions.
He, with his words, brings passions to heel, lulls panting to calmness.
    So all the crash of the sea died down, as soon as the Father
Looked at the surface, cleared up the skies, and with only a guiding 155
Flick to his horses, established his course, and flew on under
    free rein.
    Tired out, Aeneas' men put all their strength into gaining
Landfall as close as they can, setting course for the Libyan coastline.
Deep in an inlet there's somewhere to beach, where the flanks of an
    island
Jutting across force breakers to crash and to channel their fury 160
Into its various coves. It's a natural port,* and around it
Vast cliffs shield both sides, dual rock-masses surge towards heaven.
Sheltered beneath these menacing peaks are silent, expansive
Stretches of safe, calm water, around which a backdrop of shuddering
Woods loom down from above, dark forests bristling shadows. 165
Under the seaward face, there's a cave where rocks dangle in long
    tusks.
Fresh running water within and ledges of still-living limestone
Fashion a dwelling for Nymphs. No cables are needed for mooring
Vessels, no grappling anchors to grasp onto land with a firm bite.
Here, with a squadron of seven ships left from his navy, Aeneas 170
Puts ashore. Trojans, ecstatic with joy at regaining the dry land,
Leap from the ships and establish themselves on the sand-covered
    coastline,

Stretch out brine-encrusted limbs full-length on the beaches.
First action came from Achates, who struck out a spark from a
     flintstone,
Caught it in leaves, made a flame which he nurtured with kindling
     of dry wood,   175
Fanned it to blazing life by waving the smouldering tinder.
Next, though exhausted by what had occurred, they salvaged their
     wheat stores—
Ceres,* swollen with brine—found equipment for processing cereals,
Started to dry out the grains over fire and to grind them with
     millstones.

Meanwhile, Aeneas is climbing a cliff to survey the horizon   180
Far and wide out to sea for a glimpse of the Phrygian biremes,
Seeking a sign that, say, Antheus or Capys has weathered the tempest.
Maybe he might even see Caïcus' arms on his tall ships.
Though not a vessel's in sight, he detects, down below, by the
     seashore,
Three buck deer straying freely; behind them, straggling through
     valleys,   185
Whole herds follow in single file cropping grass as they amble.
Halting, he stands very still. And his hands grab the bow and the
     arrows,
Weapons that faithful Achates is carrying strapped to his shoulders.
First shots lay low the leaders, their tall heads crested with antlers
Branching like trees; then his shafts create havoc by routing the
     common   190
Herd and dispersing disordered ranks into leaf-sheltered woodlands.
He doesn't stop his victorious onslaught till seven enormous
Carcasses lie on the ground: one for each of the ships in his squadron.
Then, heading back to the harbour, he shares them among all his
     crewmen.
Next, he distributes the wine jars, the ones that the generous hero, 195
Noble Acestes, loaded as gifts when they sailed from Trinacrian
Sicily. Last, he adds soothing words, lulling hearts full of sorrow:
'Crewmates, by now we are hardly strangers to evil and hardship.
We've suffered worse. God will grant us an end to these sufferings also.
You've been close to the rabid rage and the deep-bellied thunder   200
Roaring from Scylla's cliffs, you've experienced boulders the Cyclops
Hurled. Take heart once again and dispel your fears and depression.

Maybe the day'll come when even this will be joy to remember.
Through all these varied events, these many critical junctures,
We're reaching out towards Latium, where fate reaches out to us,
    offering   205
Homes where we'll settle in peace, where Troy has the right to
    reburgeon.
Just hold firm, conserving your strength for the good days to follow.'
Such were the words that he voiced. He, sick as he was with his
    worries,
Masked his expression with hope, kept gloom in his heart, deeply
    buried.
    Clothes hitched up, they tackle the spoils, make ready for
    feasting,   210
Ripping the hides from the ribs, pulling out and exposing the raw
    flesh.
Some hack meat into chunks and impale them, pulsing, on skewers;
Others set cauldrons of bronze on the beaches and stoke up the fires.
Then they revitalize vigour with vittles and, spilling all over
Meadowlands, fill up on vintage Bacchus and succulent wild game.   215
    After they've feasted their hunger away and removed all the tables,
Comrades lost are the grief-stricken quest of their long conversations;
Wondering, poised between hope and fear, whether they should
    believe them
Still living or now dead and unable to hear voices calling,
Most of all, righteous Aeneas, who now mourns fiery Orontes   220
Lost, now Amycus, lost—though he keeps it all silent within him—
Lycus' fate too, and Gyas the steadfast and steadfast Cloanthus.

Now that the crisis was past, lord Jupiter, high in the bright air,
Looked down below on the sail-billowed sea and the motionless
    dry land,
Looked on its shores and its far-flung peoples, and paused upon
    heaven's   225
Summit. He focused the light of his glance* on the Libyan kingdoms.
And, as he tossed round, deep in his heart, such anxious reflections,
Venus, her shining eyes full of tears and grimmer than usual,
Spoke to him: 'Lord who controls the affairs both of gods and of
    mortals,
Ruling, eternal in power, bringing terror with flashes of lightning, 230
What could *my* son Aeneas have done to offend you so greatly,

What could the Trojans have done, that they should, after deaths in
    their thousands,
Find that, to keep them from Italy now, the whole world has been
    sealed off?
From them Roman commanders were sure, some day in the future's
Rolling years, to arise. There'd be born, from restored blood of
    Teucer,   235
Men who would hold all lands, all seas, under their jurisdiction.
That was your promise.
               So whose is the mind* that has changed you, dear father?
This vow was my consolation as Troy slid down to destruction:
Destined success counterpoising destined doom in the balance.
Now it's the same old fortune pursuing men driven by countless   240
Random disasters. What end will you set to their troubles, great ruler?
Antenor slipped through the midst of Achaeans, successfully, safely
Thrusting on up through the lap of Illyria's coves and Liburnia's
Deepest recesses and mounting his way to the source of Timavus.
Down comes the flow as the peak moans mightily, out through its
    nine mouths   245
Bursting, a sea with the roar of an ocean, all over the ploughlands.
This man has made it. He's founded his city, his home for the
    Teucrians,
Padua, given his people a name, he has put up his Trojan
Weapons. Now peacefully settled, he basks in tranquillity's calmness.
  'We, your own children, to whom you accord full access to
    heaven,   250
Have, a disgrace beyond words, and through one individual's anger,
Lost our ships, been betrayed, held far from Italy's coastline.
This is your way of rewarding the righteous, restoring our power?'
  Smiling at her, the begetter of life for mankind and immortals,
Showing the face that he uses to clear skies, pacify tempests,   255
Offers his daughter some kisses and speaks to her much in this
    manner:
'Spare these personal fears, Cytherea!* Your own and your children's
Fate that I've stated stays unchanged. You *will* see Lavinium's
City and promised walls, and you *will* raise great-souled Aeneas
Up to the stars of the skies. No one's mind has changed my
    opinion.   260
Since this anxiety constantly gnaws you, I'll make my
    pronouncements.

I will unwind rather more of my scroll of the fates and their secrets.
He'll wage widespread war throughout Italy, crushing ferocious
Peoples; he'll give men civilized ways and fortified ramparts,
Till the third summer has seen him reigning as ruler in Latium,   265
Till he's camped three times in the winter and conquered Rutulians.
Youthful Ascanius, who'll now be known by a new name, "Iulus",—
"Ilus" it was while the Ilian state still ruled in the Troad—
He will go on to complete full thirty cycles of rolling
Months in command. Then he'll transfer the centre of power from
     Lavinium   270
And, with a huge show of force, make Alba Longa his fortress.
Over the next three centuries, then, this will be the command post
Ruled by the people of Hector, until such time as a royal
Priestess named Ilia, pregnant by Mars, gives birth to her twin boys.*
Romulus, happy to wear the tan hide from the she-wolf who
     nursed him,   275
Then will inherit the line. And, in Mars' honour, he'll found a
     city,
Giving its people a name he derives from his own name: the Romans.
I am imposing no bounds on his realm, no temporal limits.
Empire that has no end* is my gift. Even Juno, whose harshness
Now is exhausting the sea and the earth and the heavens with
     terror,   280
Will, one day, change plans for the better, and, with me, she'll
     nurture
Romans, that people in togas, the masters of all in existence.
That's my decree. And an age will come, as festivals glide by,
When Assaracus' house sets Phthia in slavery's shackles,
Famous Mycenae, too. It will conquer and master the Argives.   285
There will be born of this splendid lineage a Caesar, a Trojan.
He'll make Ocean the bounds of his power, and the stars of his glory,
He will be Julius—a name that derives from the mighty Iulus.
One day, anxiety gone, you'll take him up to the heavens
Loaded with spoils from the East. He too will be called on in prayer. 290
Then all wars will cease. These Ages of Harshness will soften.
Vesta and white-haired Trust, Quirinus, along with his brother
Remus, will make laws together. The merciless, reinforced iron
Portals of War* will be closed. Unrighteous Madness within them,
Sitting on weapons of murder, his hands bound back by a hundred   295
Bronze-locked chains, face bathed in blood, will rage in contortions.'

This said, he sends Maia's son from on high to the newly built
  stronghold,
Carthage, so he can ensure that the land and the city keep open
Welcome for Teucer's men, so that Dido,* not knowing what's fated,
Doesn't just keep them clear of her boundaries. Mercury, flying   300
Over expanses of air, wings serving as oars, arrives quickly
Down on the Libyan coast, does as ordered. Phoenicians abandon,
As god wills, all fierceness of heart; and, above all, their ruler
Takes on a calmness of soul and a kind disposition to Teucrians.

Righteous Aeneas, whose thoughts spanned night in countless
  gyrations,   305
Took a decision, at dawn's first comforting light, to go outside,
Scout out the new terrain, figure out what shores they'd been
  blown to
And who controlled them, humans or beasts (he'd seen no cultivation).
Once he had answered these questions, he'd bring back news to his
  comrades.
So, camouflaging the fleet under cliff-tops eroded and hollow   310
Covered above with a woodland canopy—trees and their bristling
Damp shade circled the ships—he set off, having only Achates'
Company, clasping a matched pair of spears tipped stoutly in iron.
  Deep in the forest, his mother approached him, assuming a virgin's
Face and attire, bearing arms, like an unmarried virgin from
  Sparta   315
Or like Harpalyce (*that* girl from Thrace can tire out a racehorse
And, in a sprint, run faster than Hebrus, a swift-flowing torrent!).
She, as if hunting for venison, slung, in their style from her shoulders,
Strung for quick action, a bow, and she'd let her hair blow in the
  breezes,
Gathered her flowing dress up in a knot, thus exposing a bare
  knee.   320
'Hey!' she spoke first. 'You lads! If you've seen, perhaps, one of my
  sisters
Wandering here, tell me where! She'd be wearing a quiver about her,
Over the hide of a dappled lynx. She could also be hunting,
Hot in pursuit of a foaming boar, and raising a loud cry.'
So Venus spoke; Venus' son then responded to her in this manner: 325
'I haven't heard, and I'm sure I've not seen, any one of your
  sisters—

What shall I call you, O virgin? For neither your face nor expression
Seems merely human and, further, your voice doesn't sound like a
    mortal's.
Surely you *must* be a god. Phoebus' sister? Related to some Nymph?
Bring us fulfilment, whoever you are, please lighten our struggle!   330
Please inform us, at least, where under the sun we are stranded,
Where in the world are these shores? We know neither the place
    nor the people;
We are just wandering lost, driven here by the winds and the wild
    seas;
Many a victim will fall by our hands to show thanks at your altars.'
    Venus said: 'I don't think I deserve any honours of that sort.   335
Wearing the quiver is normal style for us Tyrian virgins,
As are the calf-high costume boots laced tight, and in purple.
Tyrians live here. Phoenician settlements: Agenor's city,
That's what you see, but on Libyan soil among war-toughened
    peoples.
Dido's the ruler in charge. She came here to escape from her
    brother,   340
Sailing from Tyre. It's a long tale of wrong and injustice,
    a long tale:
Twists, turns, full of deceit. But I'll summarize most of the main
    points.
    Dido had married Sychaeus, the richest of all the Phoenician
Landowners. She, poor girl, loved him deeply. For she was a virgin
Child-bride, betrothed the first time that her father had checked
    wedding omens.   345
Ruling Tyre, in those days, was Pygmalion.* He was her brother,
And quite a monster of crime, far surpassing all possible rivals.
Conflict arose among in-laws. Pygmalion, secure in his sister's
Love for them both, lusting blindly for gold, killed Sychaeus in
    cold blood
Secretly, catching him quite off guard and in front of an altar.   350
Evil, unrighteous man, he concealed what he'd done for a long time,
Toyed with the lovesick bride, raised false hopes, crafted illusions.
But in her dreams, the true form of her unburied husband
    approached her,
Raising before her a face that was wasted with terrible pallor,
Baring the truth of the brutal crime at the altar, the daggered   355
Breast, and disclosing each unseen crime concealed in the palace.

Then the dream urges her on to craft speedy escape from her homeland,
And, as resources for travel, reveals where there's long-buried treasure,
Massive ingots, silver and gold. No one knew they existed.
Dido, moved by all this, made her plans, sought allies in exile.　　360
All those who felt cruel hate for the tyrant, all people who feared him
Keenly, assembled; then, pirating ships which, by chance, were already
Outfitted, loaded the gold. So greedy Pygmalion's riches
Take to the open seaways—a bold coup, led by a woman.

　'Putting in here, at this very place where you now see enormous　365
Ramparts, the rising castle of Carthage's new town, they purchased
Land, just as much as one could mark off with the hide of a single
Ox. And they called it Byrsa, "The Hide",* to recall the transaction.
What about you? Who are you? What part of the world have you
　　come from?
Where are you travelling to?' In response to her various enquiries,　370
He gave a sigh, reached into his heart, gave a genuine answer:
'Goddess, were I to retrace the whole tale from its very beginning,
If you had free time to hear our chronicles, all of our troubles,
Venus, the Evening Star,* would end daylight and close up Olympus.

　'Ancient Troy was our home, though I wonder if Troy's name
　　has ever　　375
Passed through the ears of you gods. We've been blown over various
　　seaways;
Now, some self-willed tempest has beached us on Libya's coastline.
I am Aeneas the Righteous. I carry with me on my vessel
Household gods that I saved from the foe. My fame reaches heaven.
Seeking a homeland in Italy, I, mighty Jupiter's offspring,　380
Had, when I launched upon Phrygian seas, two squadrons of ten
　　ships.
My goddess mother showed me my course. Fate commanded. I
　　followed.
Just seven ships have survived, all damaged by high seas and east
　　winds.
Nobody knows me, I've nothing, I'm wandering Libyan deserts.
Europe and Asia reject me.'
　　　　　　　　　　　　　But Venus would suffer no further　385
Lists of complaints. So she spoke, interrupting his pain and his
　　sorrow:
'You, I believe, whoever you are, are not hated by heaven.
You're still alive, still breathe; and you've come to a Tyrian city.

Keep going, make your way out of this spot, get yourself to the ruler's
Palace. I've news. Your companions have made it, your fleet is
    recovered,   390
Saved when the eager winds from the north veered off, if my
    parents
Didn't misteach me my augury, didn't just fill me with nonsense.
Look, and you'll see twelve swans* in a row moving joyfully
    forward.
Jupiter's bird had been rousting them down out of clear, open
    heavens,
Swooping upon them from skies far above. Now they seem to be
    either   395
Landing in one long line or looking at others who've landed.
See: these birds, now safe, flap whistling wings. They are playful,
Now that they've circled the sky in a flock and have sung out their
    swans' song.
Knowingly then, I can say that your vessels and vassals have either
Made it to port or are nearing its mouth, flying under full canvas.   400
Just keep going, direct your step wherever the path leads.'
    This said, she turned on her heels. And her neck gleamed brightly
    as roses;
Down from her head, her ambrosial hair breathed heavenly perfumes
Gods breathe forth, and her dress streamed down to the top of her
    ankles,
Making it clear, as she walked, that she was a real goddess. Aeneas   405
Now recognized his mother. He spoke to her thus as she vanished:
'You're cruel too! Oh how often you toy with me, crafting illusions!
Why? I'm your son! Why can't *we* ever link *our* right hands together,
Why are we never allowed to hear genuine questions and answers?'
Such were the charges he made while directing his steps to the city.   410
    Venus with her divine power, fenced them, as they walked,
    with a rampart,
Fashioned from opaque air, pouring cloud in a deep misty mantle
Round them, so no one could see them and no one could touch
    them or even
Cause them delay, or interrogate them as to why they were coming.
She, then, soars through the air off to Paphos, delighted to visit   415
Her own home with its temple and hundred altars all breathing
Perfume of fresh-cut blossoms and hot with the incense of Sheba.*

Meanwhile, they've hurried the length of the route pointed out
　　by the pathway
And are ascending a hill whose menacing heights offer full views
Over the city and look both across at, and down on, its castle.   420
Awed by the massive construction, where once there were rickety
　　hovels,
Awed by the gates, by the noise, the paved roadways, Aeneas just
　　marvels.
Fired-up Tyrians work at their tasks; some extend the defence walls,
Strengthen the castle and, with bare hands, lever masonry uphill.
Some decide housing-sites, mark boundary lines with a furrow.   425
Magistrates, legal codes, and a sacred senate are chosen.
Others excavate ports, still others are laying foundations,
Deep in the ground, for a theatre. Some chisel out from the cliff-sides
Tall columns, massive in size: decor for a stage in the future.*
　　Work keeps bees just as busy as this in the sunshine of early   430
Summer across meadows covered with flowers when they lead out
　　the now grown
New generation from hives, as they store up the streams of their honey,
Stretching the combs' wax cells to the full with the sweetness of
　　nectar,
Or when unloading the incoming swarm, or when, massed like an army,
Driving those useless creatures, the drones, from the bounds
　　of their compound.   435
Work seethes; thyme's sweet savour enhances the fragrance of honey.
'Oh, how blessed are people whose ramparts are already rising!'
So Aeneas observes, looking up at the roofs of the city,
Fenced, as he walks, by a fortress of cloud (it's a marvellous story)
Moving along in their midst unseen,* yet mingling with people.   440
　　Centrally placed in the city a park, most delightfully shaded,
Marked where Phoenicians, battered by waves and by violent
　　storm winds,
Landed and dug up the sign pointed out as an omen by ruling
Juno: the head of a spirited horse, foretelling the nation's
Future: distinction in war and in steady traffic of commerce.   445
Dido of Sidon was here constructing a temple to Juno,
Grand in its scale, in its votive gifts, in its goddess's presence;
Tall banked steps made approach to a threshhold of bronze and
　　its framing

Bronze-bound beams, and the doors rasped open on hinges of
    wrought brass.
Here, in this park, something new first touched him now, and it gentled
Fears; now Aeneas dared, for the first time, dream of survival,   451
Dared to put greater trust in events, despite his reversals.
For, while awaiting the ruler below the huge temple, he took in
All its details, marvelling at how that city had prospered,
Noting the artists' skill, the combined success of their labours.   455
Awestruck, he saw the whole series of battles at Troy represented,
Wars that were already famed world-wide in rumour and story:
Atreus' sons, Priam too, and Achilles, savage to both sides.
'Is there a place,' he said, stopped in his tracks, tears flowing, 'Achates,
Is there a land in the world not steeped in our troubles and sorrow?   460
Look! Priam's here. Even here great deeds win due recognition,
Human events stir tears; what dies has the power to move minds.
Cast off fear! These rumours, this fame,* will bring you some safety!'
This said, he feasted his soul on the ghostly figures before him,
Groaning a great deal, bedewing his face with a river of weeping,   465
Constantly seeing the fighters circling Troy in their battles:
Greeks here, routed and hotly pursued by the young Trojan soldiers,
Phrygians there, pressed hard from his chariot by crested Achilles.
Not far away, he can see (and recall) the white canvas of Rhesus'
Tents* through his tears, men betrayed in their first night's sleep
    near the city,   470
Hideously butchered by Tydeus' blood-drenched son, Diomedes.
He seized Rhesus' fiery steeds, drove them off to the Greek camp
So they could not first crop Troy's grass and drink of the Xanthus.
    Elsewhere, a young boy, unfulfilled, no match for Achilles,
Troilus, throws down his shield as he flees, borne away by his
    horses,   475
Rolls backwards out of his chariot, unseated, but still he is clinging,
Clutching the reins while his neck and his hair drag over the hard
    ground,
While the fine tip of his spear points downwards and writes in the
    dry dust.
Grim-faced women of Troy, meanwhile, hair streaming, unribboned,
Walk to the temple of Pallas—the goddess was hardly impartial—   480
Suppliants, beating their breasts and bringing a robe as an offering.
Head turned away, eyes fixed on the ground, though, the goddess
    ignores them.

Here, selling Hector's lifeless cadaver for gold, was Achilles—
After he'd dragged that corpse three times round Ilium's ramparts.
Huge sighs welled from the depths of Aeneas's heart as he noted   485
His friend's plundered armour and chariot, his actual cadaver;
Priam too, whose unarmed hands stretched, pleading for pity.
And he detected himself, mixed in with Achaean commanders,*
Eastern contingents too: black Memnon's own special armour.
Here, leading thousands of Amazon troops, shields curved in a
          crescent,   490
Penthesilea appears, all ablaze in her full battle fury.
Bracing her naked breast with a halter of gold, a fierce warrior
Virgin, a woman who dares to engage with the men in their battles.

While these marvellous works hold Dardan Aeneas' attention,
While he stands stock-still, eyes fixed, gaze totally focused,   495
Dido the queen is approaching the shrine, supreme in her beauty,
Flanked by a numerous escort of youths. She appears like Diana
Leading her dancers out on the banks of the Spartan Eurotas,
Or along ridges of Cynthus in Delos, with thousands of mountain
Nymphs in a cluster about her, on this side and that side, yet
          towering   500
High above all of the rest as she strides, quiver strapped to her
          shoulder.
Joy even tempts the impassive heart of her mother Latona!
Such then was Dido and as such she bore herself: confident, cheerful,
Right through their midst, intent on her tasks, on the kingdom that
          must rise.
Then, at the entrance to Juno's shrine, and under the temple's   505
Shielding roof, fenced tightly by spears, she sat, elevated
High on a throne, issued laws, defined rights for her men, and she
          justly
Portioned out various tasks, or assigned them by lot, for completion.
Now, of a sudden, Aeneas observes, in a large crowd approaching,
Antheus, with him Sergestus, along with the steadfast Cloanthus,   510
And other Teucrians scattered by pitch-black gales on the high seas,
Driven far up upon different and distant points on the coastline.
Stunned stock-still, Aeneas himself, and likewise Achates,
Felt shock, ecstasy, fear, all at once. They are greedy to grasp hands,
Hot with desire, yet deeply disturbed by the whole situation's   515
Unknown nature. Maintaining disguise, clad in cavernous, veiling

Cloud, they are watching for clues: what has happened to these men?
Where is their fleet beached, why are they here? Delegations from
    each ship
Now are approaching the temple and shouting, yes, pleading for
    mercy.
  Once they have entered, and gained their request for a personal
    hearing,   520
Captain elect Ilioneus begins quite coolly and calmly:
'Ruler and queen, to whom Jupiter granted the right to establish
This new city, the right to rein in with the firm hand of justice
Spirited peoples, we beg you, we suffering Trojans who've wandered
Every sea: keep fire, that unspeakable doom, from our vessels.   525
Spare us; we're righteous folk. Take a closer look at our quandary.
We did not come to annihilate* Libya's temples and peoples,
Nor to conduct pillage, rape, or to carry off spoils to the beaches.
Violence, pride such as this isn't found in the souls of the conquered!
There is a place that the Greeks call Hesperia. It is an ancient   530
Country, mighty in arms and strong in its richness of ploughland,
Tilled by men once called Oenotrians. But, Rumour says, their
    successors
Named both the people and land after Italus. He was their leader.
That was our course, as planned.
Wintry Orion, however, arose with a sudden upsurge of high seas,   535
Drove us on unseen shoals, scattered us, with the force of relentless
South winds, deep among waves that crashed over us, deep into
    hopeless
Mazes of reefs. We few that you see swam ashore to your beaches.
What kind of humans are these? What barbarous sort of a country
Tolerates conduct like this? Our welcome? They keep us from
    landing,   540
Start up a war and forbid us to take a step over their borders!
Even if you despise humankind and have no fear of mortal
Arms, be assured gods remember what's holy and what is unholy.
No man was ever more just than our ruler: his name was Aeneas.
No man was ever more righteous, more valiant in arms and in
    combat.   545
If fate still keeps this man safe, if he's still breathing vital
Air from the skies and has not yet succumbed to the brute world
    of shadows,
Mutual fear has no place. You could well, with impunity, battle

Him as to who was more generous.

                              In Sicily too there are cities,
Ploughlands, and someone of Trojan bloodline, the famous Acestes.   550
Please let us haul our storm-ravaged navy ashore on your beaches,
Cut down wood from your forests to craft new planking and oarage;
So, if we *can* go to Italy, comrades and ruler recovered,
We'll be elated to go off to Italy, heading for Latium.
But, if our saviour is lost, if the Libyan seas have your body,   555
Best of the Teucrians, father, if hopes for Iulus are useless,
Still we can head back to Sicily's seas—that's where we've just
     sailed from.
There we have homes that are ready for us; and a ruler: Acestes.'
So Ilioneus spoke; Dardanians shouted with one voice
Total assent.   560
    Dido relaxed her expression at this point and briefly responded:
'Unknot the fear in your hearts, shut the door on anxieties, Teucrians.
Brutal realities, newness to power, compel me to order
Such measures, force me to post such guards the full length of our
     borders.
Who couldn't know of Aeneas's people, of Troy and its city,   565
Heroes, heroic deeds, and the blazing fires of a huge war?
We Carthaginians are not quite *that* insensate and heartless,
Nor does the Sun yoke his team *that* far from our Tyrian city!
Whether you choose great Hesperian shores and Saturnian
     ploughlands
Or prefer Eryx's realm, and to have, as your ruler, Acestes,   570
I'll send you safely away, and I'll help, with support and resources.
Or, you can stay here with me upon equal terms in this kingdom,
Should you so wish. For the city I'm founding is yours. Beach your
     vessels.
Trojan and Tyrian: both shall be one and the same in my judgements.
I wish this same south wind had driven your ruler Aeneas   575
Here, so he'd be with us now! For my part, I'll dispatch an elite
     corps
Off down the shores with instructions to search the whole Libyan
     coastline.
Maybe he's been washed ashore and is lost in our cities or forests.'
    Spirits raised by the words she had uttered, the valiant Achates,
Father Aeneas as well, had been burning to burst through the
     veiling   580

Cloud for some time. Then Achates spoke first, saying this to
    Aeneas:
'*Now* what kind of decision suggests itself, son of the goddess?
All is secure, as you see: our comrades and fleet are recovered.
One's missing, true; but we saw him ourselves overwhelmed on the
    high seas.
Otherwise everything matches your mother's report quite precisely.'   585
    Scarcely have these words come from his mouth when the cloud
        veil around them
Suddenly splits wide apart and evaporates into the bright air,
Leaving Aeneas fully in view in the daylight and gleaming
Bright as a god in his face and his shoulders. For Venus the Mother,
Sees her son's hair will have lustre, sheds youth's bright radiance
    upon him,   590
Livening the glance of his eyes with joyfulness and with distinction,
Much as a sculptor's hands* add sheen to an ivory, or as
Deep yellow gold gives a highlight to silver or marble from Paros.
Speaking these words to the queen, he startles them all with his
    sudden
Visible presence: 'You're looking for me. I am right here before you,   595
Trojan Aeneas, snatched from the storms upon Libyan waters.
You, you alone, have shown pity for Troy's inexpressible anguish,
Pitied us remnants missed by the Greeks, who've absorbed each
    disaster
Land and sea can inflict, who are utterly destitute. Yet you
Give us a share in your city and home. We have not the resources,   600
Dido, to pay back in full what we owe you, nor have other fragments
Left of our Dardan race scattered anywhere else on the wide earth.
If there exist any powers watching over the righteous, if somewhere
Justice rules, if there's somewhere a mind that's aware of what's proper,
Oh, may the gods repay you in kind! What age of contentment   605
Bore you? What marvellous parents produced so noble a daughter?
While rivers flow to the seas, while shadows sweep across mountain
Vales each day, while stars are grazed on the pastures of heaven,
You, your name and your glory, the praise you've earned, will for ever
Live and endure, whatever land calls me.' This said, he extended   610
One hand to dear Ilioneus, his right, and his left to Serestus,
Then greeted others: both Gyas the steadfast and steadfast Cloanthus.
    Stunned by her first sight of the man, by his massive misfortunes,
Dido of Sidon shaped her response: 'Son born to a goddess,

What force of chance has been dogging your heels throughout all
    of these dangers?   615
What kind of violence haunted your way to this menacing coastline?
You, then, are famous Aeneas, the child blessed Venus once bore to
Dardanus' offspring, Anchises, near Simoïs' waters in Phrygia?
I myself can recall when Teucer* came over to Sidon.
He'd been expelled from his homeland and was, with assistance
    from Belus,   620
Looking for some new realm. Now Belus, my father, was looting
Cyprus of treasures at that time; he'd conquered it, made it his
    fiefdom.
Ever since that day the city of Troy, what misfortunes befell it,
Your name, the kings of Pelasgian Greeks, have been part of my
    knowledge.
Teucer, your foe, used to speak very well of his foemen, the
    Teucrians,   625
Claiming that he was himself born of ancient Teucrian lineage.
So then, young men, come on in, move into our homes. Make them
    your homes.
Fortune has battered me too, with some similar twists, through so
    many
Trials, yet finally willed that I settle down here in this country.
I am no stranger to hardship. I'm learning to help those who suffer.'   630

So her words ran; action followed at once. She conducted Aeneas
Into her halls, ordered sacrifice offered in all the gods' temples,
Sent, simultaneously, down to his friends (who were still on the
    seashore)
Twenty bulls and a hundred hogs, hides bristling and massive,
Also a hundred well-fed lambs along with their mothers,   635
Gifts for the day's celebrations.
Inside, the palace is given the feel of extravagant, regal
Luxury. Places are set in the central hall for a banquet:
Fabrics produced by long, skilled toil and the proud purple
    mollusc;*
Massive silver plates on the tables, a service with golden   640
Inlay, narrating ancestral deeds in an endless procession
Through many heroes back to the ancient birth of their people.
    Love would not let Aeneas's mind stop nursing a father's
Thoughts. So Achates was sent, at a run, to the ships to bring instant

News to Ascanius, then bring the boy with him back to the city.   645
All care a parent can feel he lavished on his dear Ascanius.
Further, he ordered that presents be brought, pieces snatched from
    the Trojan
Ruins: a mantle stiffened with figured designs and with gold thread;
Also a veil, trim borders embroidered with saffron acanthus,
Finery Argive Helen had brought* from Mycenae when sailing   650
Over to Pergamum, fully intent on an unapproved wedding.
Wonderful handwork it was and a present from Leda, her mother;
Also a sceptre that, in past times, Ilione, the eldest
Daughter of Priam, had carried, along with her pearl-studded necklace,
Even her two-tiered golden crown with its setting of gemstones.   655
Charged with these orders, Achates sped off to the ships at their
    moorings.

Venus, Cythera's goddess, however, was spinning some new tricks,
New plots deep in her heart. Her intent was that Cupid, her own
    child,*
Switch his appearance and face, then come in to replace sweet
    Ascanius,
Madden the queen, kindle fire with the gifts, set her bone-marrow
    blazing.   660
Moods at the palace, she feared, could shift; double-talk was a Tyrian
Art-form. Juno was ruthless—that burned in her mind, and at
    night-time
Anxious cares coursed back. So she said this to Love, wingèd Amor:
'Son, you're my strength, you alone are the principal source of my
    power.
Thunderbolts mighty Jupiter launched at Typhoeus don't worry   665
You. So it's you that I run to and kneel to, whose grace I'm
    beseeching.
You're well aware that Aeneas, your brother,* is now being harried,
Tossed all over the world by the bitter hatred of Juno.
You've felt my rue and my pain, often sharing that ruefulness
    with me.
Now a Phoenician, Dido, controls him, and she, with her smooth
    talk,   670
Makes him delay. I'm afraid of the ends to which Juno might channel
This hospitality. *She* won't stop at this pivotal moment.
My plan is then: Strike first; take the queen by a ruse, with encircling

Fences of fire so she won't change course through divine
    interference,
Bind her to me, then, with bonds of a mighty love for Aeneas.   675
Now, as to how you can manage this task. Just pursue my suggestion.
My chief concern is the royal prince. He's at this time preparing,
At his dear father's behest, to come into the city of Carthage
Carrying gifts that survived both the burning of Troy and the voyage.
I, then, will drug him to sleep and I'll tuck him away in my
    sacred   680
Shrine in Cythera's heights or within my Idalian temple
So he has no way to learn, or to hinder, the ruse I'm devising.
Your job is making the ruse work on Dido by feigning his features,*
Just for one night, no more. You're a boy. A boy's facial
    expressions
Are, thus, familiar to you. So, when Bacchic juices are flowing   685
During the banquet, when Dido takes *you* in her lap, oh so blissful,
Hugs you and cuddles you, plants on your forehead a few tender
    kisses,
You can rouse unseen fire, deceive her with venomous love-draughts.'
Amor obeys his dear mother's instructions and now sheds his
    feathered
Wings, takes Iulus's manner and mien and enjoys what he's doing.   690
Venus, for her part, drips sleep's calming dew on Ascanius'
Limbs, and then carries him up, nestled close to her breast, to her
    gardens
High on Idalia, where marjoram softly enfolds him in gently
Shaded embrace as it soothes him with fragrant breath from its
    flowers.
    Cupid, obeying his parent's words, strode on, bringing regal   695
Gifts for the Tyrians, thrilled that Achates was there to escort him.
When he arrives, Dido's already taken her place in the centre,
Seating herself on a gilded divan, amid sumptuous draperies.
Father Aeneas and Troy's young men are joining the gathering,
Shown to their couches. And now they're reclining on coverings
    of purple.   700
Slaves pour water over their hands, serve baskets of Ceres'
Breads, and supply serviettes whose nap has been razored to
    smoothness.
Fifty storehouse maids inside lay dishes in long lines
Side by side, and keep light in the fires at the shrines of Penates.

Then there's a hundred more, and a hundred boys of the same age,   705
Loading the tables with fine foods, setting out goblets for drinking.
Tyrians have also been crowding through doors set ringing with
     laughter;
They too are guided to pre-assigned places on needleworked couches.
All are impressed by Aeneas's presents, impressed by Iulus—
Or, rather, by the god's dazzling face and his staged
     conversation—   710
And Helen's mantle and veil embroidered with saffron acanthus.
She above all, the descendant of Phoenix,* cannot sate her senses,
Unfulfilled* and vowed as an offering for future destruction,
Burns as she stares, roused equally both by the gifts and the
     young boy.
After embracing Aeneas and hugging his neck, satisfying   715
All the quite genuine love of a father who wasn't his father,
Amor made for the queen. And she, with her eyes and her whole
     heart
Clung to him, took him, at times, in her lap, poor Dido, not knowing
How great a god set snares for her there to suffuse her with torment.
Amor, recalling his Acidalian* mother, now slowly   720
Starts to erase Sychaeus and tries to surprise, with a living
Passion, a heart where the fire has died and where love is a memory.

Banqueting now takes a break; for the first time, tables are cleared off;
Huge bowls placed for the mixing of wine are encircled with
     garlands.
Chatter crescendoes within; cascading voices roll on through   725
Huge halls; fixtures suspended from ceilings, fretted and gilded,
Gleam as the lamps light; torches ablaze rescue daytime from
     darkness.
Dido calls for a chalice of gold encrusted with jewels,
Weighty traditional vessel of Belus and Belus' successors,
Fills it with unmixed wine. Now the halls fall suddenly silent.   730
'Jupiter, people maintain *you* wrote hospitality's handbook.
Make the day happy for Tyrians and those who set out from the
     Troad,
Make it a day that our children will always remember! So grant it!
Bacchus, you give us our joy, so be with us; and you, goodly Juno!
Tyrians, celebrate our close bonding with your full approval!'   735

So she spoke; and she poured on the table a flowing libation,
Then, the libation made, first touched her lips to the chalice,
Passed it on then with a challenge to Bitias, who, without pausing,
Drained the still bubbling cup—took a bath in its gold as he
     did so!
While other lords follow suit, a student of Atlas, the maestro,   740
Livens the air with his gilded harp. For the long-haired Iopas
Sings of the unpredictable moon, of the sun and its labours,
Origins human and animal, causes of fire and of moisture,
Stars (Lesser, Greater Bear, rainy Hyades, also Arcturus),
Why in the winter the sun so hurries to dive in the Ocean,   745
What slows winter's lingering nights, what blocks and delays them.
Tyrians encore, applaud. Thus cued, Troy's men show approval.
Talking of this and of that to extend night's span ever further
Dido, unfulfilled, drank deeply of love's heady vintage.
Question on question about Priam; many, as well, about Hector;   750
What was the armour the son of Aurora would wear into battle?
Could he describe Diomedes' steeds?* How great was Achilles?
'Come, better yet, tell us, guest, of the trap that was sprung, from
     its earliest
Planning,' she said, 'by Danaäns; of your own family misfortunes;
And of your drifting at sea. This summer's already the seventh   755
Season that's portaged you on all lands, and on waves as you drifted.'

BOOK TWO

S ILENCE came over them all; eyes focused upon him intently.
Father Aeneas arose on his deep-pillowed couch and began thus:*

'Words can't express, my queen, what you bid me relive, all the rueful
Pain: telling how the Danaäns destroyed Troy's wealth and its power
Makes for a dirge of lament. Heartbreaking events. And I saw them,   5
I was a major part of them all. What Myrmidon soldier,
Or what Dolopian, what man who served under callous Ulysses
Could find words, yet hold back tears? And, besides, night is shedding
Dew from the sky, and stars as they fade persuade us to slumber.
    'Still, if you're so much enamoured with learning how ruin
        befell me,   10
Also with hearing, though briefly, of Troy's last afflictions, its
        death-throes,
Though my soul, still shocked by the memory, recoils from the
        anguish,*
Let me begin.
                    'The Danaän command, now shattered by warfare,
Beaten aside by the fates, seeing years slither on into more years,
Crafted a horse, thanks to Pallas' divine skill, high as a mountain,   15
Built on a framework of ribbing with interlocked sections of pitch pine.
"Vowed to ensure our return!" was the lie passed onwards by
        rumour.
Inside its flanks, unseeing, unseen, they secretly sealed up
Bodies of men they'd selected—for lots had been drawn. And they
        loaded
Deep in its vast hollow spaces, its womb, quite an army of soldiers.   20
    'From Troy's shores you can make out an island called Tenedos,
        famous,
While Priam's empire endured, for its wealth of resources, now merely
Coasts with a bay that affords unreliable mooring for vessels.
That's where the other Greeks sailed. And they hid on its desolate
        coastline.
We, though, concluded they'd now shipped out on the winds for
        Mycenae.   25
So all Teucria too cast off long moorings to anguish.

Gates were flung open. What pleasure it was to go into the Greek camp,
See the deserted sites and the beaches abandoned and empty!
Here's where Dolopians tautened their tents; there, savage Achilles.
Here's where the fleets once lay; over there occurred most of the
    fighting.   30
Some just gawked at the ruinous gift from the virgin Minerva,
Marvelled at its sheer mass. Thymoetes was first to encourage
Bringing the horse inside our walls to a place in the castle:
Treachery maybe; perhaps Troy's fate already in motion.
Capys, however, and others whose minds proved sounder in
    judgement,   35
Thought it a ruse the Danaäns had planned, a suspicious donation,
Argued for pushing it into the sea, lighting bonfires beneath it,
Or drilling into, and probing, its womb's hollow caves of concealment.
Popular sentiment wavered and split into two opposed factions.

    'Enter Laocoön first—and a large crowd of followers with him—   40
Running, ahead of the rest, from the citadel, blazing with passion,
Shouting while still far off: "Poor citizens, what utter madness
Seizes you? Do you believe the foe's gone, or that gifts from Danaän
Donors don't involve ruses? Is that what we know of Ulysses?
Either this structure of wood is concealing Achaeans inside it,   45
Or it's an engine of war they've designed to destroy our defences,
Spy on our homes, make aerial assault on our city, or some less
Evident trap. Sons of Teucer, whatever this horse is, be careful.
I am afraid of Danaäns, not least when they offer donations."
This said, he launched at its flank, with enormous force, a huge
    javelin   50
Into the wild beast's paunch, at a curve in the joints of its structure,
And hit his mark. For it stuck there and quivered. The cavernous
    hollows
Rang with the sound of the wounded womb and emitted a deep moan.
Had not god-given fates, divine minds (and our own) been against us,
That would have driven our swords to turn Argive lair into
    bloodbath,   55
Troy would endure to this today; you'd still stand, fortress of Priam.

    'Meanwhile, observe, some Dardanian shepherds are dragging a
    young man,
Hands tied behind him, straight to the king, with a great deal of
    shouting.

They didn't know him. The youth had approached them himself to
    surrender
Willingly, and with a purpose: to open up Troy to Achaeans.   60
Trusting his own courage, he was prepared for both possible outcomes:
Either he'd pull off his treacherous ruse or he'd die, that was certain.
Eager to view him, the young men of Troy surged up, spilled
    around him,
Each one vying to outdo the others in taunting the captive.
Mark how Danaäns set traps. From this one criminal instance   65
You'll learn them all.*
Well, as he stood before everyone's gaze, roughed up and defenceless,
As he surveyed with his eyes all the Phrygian forces around him,
"Oh," he said, "what land on earth, what oceans can ever accept me?
More to the point, what hope of survival remains in my grim plight?   70
I've no possible place with Danaäns; Dardanians also
Hate me, as one of the foe. They demand retribution and bloodshed."
Attitudes changed as he groaned, thus suppressing all urge to
    attack him.
Rather, we begged him declare where he came from and tell us his
    bloodline,
Say what he wanted, explain why he'd trust us and risk being captured.
   'Finally, setting his terrors aside, he addressed us as follows: 76
"Truth, sir, whatever the cost," he began, "I'll admit to you frankly,
All of it. I won't deny I'm an Argive by birth. That's the first truth.
See, none* of Fortune's twists that have bent Sinon low as a beggar
Will also craftily bend him so low as a fraud and a liar.   80
Possibly you've heard the name of a man that they call Palamedes,
Belus' descendant.* His glory, once rumour, is now a tradition.
Well, the Pelasgians tried him on trumped-up charges of treason—
Since he was always opposing the war. Though he never was guilty,
They planted evidence, put him to death. Now they're sorry they
    killed him.   85
He was, by blood, close kin of my own; so my penniless father
Sent me here to the wars in his company during those first years.
While his status as king stayed safe—and in our kingly counsels
Weight was accorded his words—I enjoyed some importance and
    standing.
When he departed the shores of this life, thanks to guileful Ulysses'   90
Envious eye—and I'm not saying things that you don't know already—
I was crushed too; and I trudged through life in the dark grip of anguish,

Fiercely resenting the fall of my friend, who was guiltless, as I was.
Mindlessly, I didn't keep my mouth closed: I vowed I'd avenge him,
If chance arose, if we won, if I ever got home to my native   95
Argos. In speaking these words, I set vicious hatred in motion.
This was when I commenced my own slide to disaster. Ulysses
Kept me, from now on, in terror with endless new accusations,
Spread ambiguous talk in the ranks, plotted, hunted for allies.
Nor did he rest till the day when, with Calchas'* priestly
     assistance . . .   100
Why am I wasting time unscrolling a tale of no interest?
Why delay now? You have heard quite enough, if you catalogue
     all Greeks
Under one heading: I'm Greek. So get on with it, carry out sentence.
That's what Ulysses would want. The Atreidae would amply
     reward you."
This left us burning to delve even deeper and find out the reasons.   105
We didn't know the full scope of Pelasgian criminal cunning.
   'Feigning fear, he resumed, and, with crafted sincerity, added:
"Often Danaäns yearned to quit Troy and effect a withdrawal,
Get themselves out of a lengthy war that had left them exhausted.
How I wish they had gone! Often violent storms on the seaways   110
Cut off escape. When they sailed, southwesterlies beached them in terror.
That day was special. The horse built with planking of interlocked
     maple*
Stood complete. But the whole vast sky was rumbling with storm
     clouds.
Baffled, we sent Eurypylus* off to find answers at Phoebus'
Oracle. But his report from the shrine was completely
     horrendous: 115
'Blood was your means of placating the winds—for you slaughtered
     a virgin
When you were first on your way, you Danaäns, to Ilium's coastline.
Blood is the price, if you want to go home, and the sacrifice human:*
Argive, again.' When the sound of his voice reached their ears, every
     soldier's
Heart stopped, stunned. Through their bones' very marrow ran
     shivers of icy   120
Fear as to whom fate readied to strike, who was sought by Apollo.
Major uproar ensued when Ulysses dragged the seer Calchas
Into our midst at this moment, demanding that he explain clearly

What the gods willed. Many now were predicting that this cruel
    schemer's
Target of crime would be me, but stayed quiet and watched what
    developed.   125
Calchas withdrew into silence for ten days, wouldn't surrender
Anyone by any word he might say and condemn him to slaughter.
Forced, only just, to agree, by the Ithacan's loud protestations,
He, at last, burst into speech; marked me to be killed on the altar.
Everyone shouted approval. All energy feeding each person's   130
Fears for himself was refocused on one poor wretch, to destroy him.
   '"Now that indescribable day was approaching. The detailed
Rites for my death were in hand: salted meal, ribboned bands for
    my temples.
Well, I admit it, I broke my restraints, I escaped my appointed
Death. I hid all night unseen in the sedge of a mud-filled   135
Swamp. I was waiting for them to set sail, if by some chance they
    did sail.
There's no hope that I'll ever again see *my* former homeland,
My dear sons or my father—and oh, how much I have missed him!
There's a good chance that the Greeks will penalize *them* because
    I fled,
Make *them* pay, poor things, full price for *my* sin with *their* lives. 140
So, by the powers above, such forces as know what the truth is,
By any trust, any pledge, that remains unbroken by mortals
Anywhere now, I implore you! Oh, pity my terrible sufferings,
Pity a soul who's enduring a lot undeserved and unworthy!"
   'Tears won him life, which we granted. We freely gave him
    our pity.   145
Priam himself took the lead, giving orders to strike off his shackles
And the connecting chains, then addressed him in tones full of
    friendship:
"Henceforth, whoever you are, forget you have lost Greece for ever.
You will be ours. Now tell me the truth as I ask you this question:
Why did they build this enormous hulk of a horse? Who designed it? 150
What's the idea? Some rite of religion? Some engine of warfare?"
This said, he, well-schooled in ruse and Pelasgian cunning,
Raised up his hands, all chains now shed, palms high to the heavens.
"O eternal fires, whose will lies beyond violation,
O unholy altars and steel-edged blades I've evaded,   155
O ribbons, sacred to god, that I wore as a victim, bear witness!

Justice absolves me of oaths, which Greeks hold solemn and sacred,
Justice demands that I hate these men, that I bring all their secrets
Out in the open. I'm bound by none of the laws of my homeland.
All I ask—if you're saved—is that *you* honour *your* vows and
    pledges,   160
Troy, if I tell you the truth and I pay back your kindness with
    interest.

  ' "Every Danaän hope and assurance in war, once it started,
Always relied upon Pallas's help. This fact was the reason
Tydeus' unrighteous son* and that expert in outrage, Ulysses,
Came for and stole that fatal talisman, Pallas's image,   165
Out of its holy shrine, and butchered the citadel's sentries.
They stole the sacred Palladium away, desecrating her ribboned
Temples, divinity's vital and virginal symbols, with bloodstained
Hands. After this, the Danaäns' hopes turned to water beneath them,
Seeping away. Strength snapped. The goddess's mind remained
    hostile.   170
There was no doubting the signs the Tritonian gave: they were
    monstrous.
Hardly was her image placed in the camp when its eyes began bulging,
Flared wide, leaping with flames. Salt sweat oozed over its body.
Three times the goddess herself, like a flash (it's a marvel to mention),
Leaped from the ground as she brandished her shield and her
    spear—and they quivered.   175
  ' "Out of the templed sky* it flashed upon Calchas that they must
Make an attempt to sail home, since Argive steel couldn't uproot
Pergamum till they'd retaken the omens at Argos, and brought back
Numinous powers they had plundered away in the holds of their vessels.
That's why they've now gone heading off home on the winds for
    Mycenae.   180
Arms and the gods are prepared—reinforcements as well. Then
    they'll recross
Seaways and catch you off guard. So Calchas interprets the omens.
  ' "Warned to make up for profaning the image and power of Pallas,
Greeks, to atone for their ugly injustice, created this creature.
Calchas required that a statue be built of enormous proportions,   185
Stretched up high as the sky in a structure of interlocked planking:
That meant it couldn't be brought past the gates, dragged into the city,
Shielding its folk through traditional bonding of gods with their
    dwellings.

Yet, if some Trojan hand violated this gift to Minerva,
Wholesale disaster would fall upon Phrygians, upon Priam's
    empire—   190
Heaven forbid! May the gods turn back this curse upon Calchas!—
Were it, said Calchas, to enter your city, if *your* hands should drag it,
Asia would triumph and march on the fortifications of Pelops:
Such would be fate's doom in store for our people's descendants."
   'So spoke Sinon, an artist in perjury, setting his ambush.   195
And we believed him. He fooled us with well-staged weeping and ruses,
Conquering men neither Tydeus' son nor Larissa's Achilles,
Not even war's ten years and its thousand vessels could vanquish.

'Then, something greater was cast in our hapless way, something
    far more
Frightful. It startled and muddled our minds. We could not have
    foreseen it.   200
Neptune's priest, Laocoön, chosen by lot for this honour,
Stood sacrificing a victim, a monstrous bull, at the altars.
Look! Across tranquil depths, out of Tenedos, writhing and coiling,
Big orbs swishing a course, twin serpents—I shudder, recalling—
Slither the sea's face, stretch for the shore in their parallel lunges.   205
Now, amid surf, chests standing erect, crests mane-like, in aspect
Blood-red, up they surge on the swell, bodies skimming the water,
Spiralling measureless tails in whiplash whirls of propulsion.
Foaming brine crashes noise. In a trice they have reached the
    enclosure.
Flickering, viperous tongues lick mouths spitting sibilant hisses,   211
Eyes blaze, reddened with fire and with blood in a sanguine suffusion.   210
Anguished and pale at the sight, we scatter; they form into columns,
Seeking Laocoön. First, each serpent entwines his two children's
Tiny bodies in coils of embrace and, poor little fellows,
Feasts upon limbs that its jaws just crunch and ingest at a single   215
Gulp. When he seizes his weapons and runs up to help them, the
    serpents
Pluck him away and constrict him in monstrous spirals; already
Two coils squeeze the man's waist; and their scaly backs, interlacing,
Noose two more round his throat. Their necks, their heads, tower
    above him.
Struggling to push them away with his hands, and to rip their
    garrotting   220

Knots from his throat, he's awash in their poisonous blood-blackened
    venom.
Constant, appalling screams he shrills and shrills to the starry
Sky, like the bellowing pain of the bull who's escaped from his altar
Maimed, and who's shaken the badly aimed axe from his neck where
    it struck him.
Meanwhile the dragon pair slithers up to the high temple
    summit,   225
Fleeing for refuge within the ferocious Tritonian's fortress,
Finding protection beneath the goddess's feet and her shield's orb.
  'New terror sneaks into every heart, each already pulsing
Wild in its fear; and Laocoön, men begin saying, has simply
Paid for his crime, as he surely deserved, since he had, with his
    blade-point,   230
Pierced holy wood, stabbed the horse in the back with a murderous
    spear-cast.
Soon there's a general demand that this symbol be brought to the
    temple
And that the goddess's grace be implored.
We start to breach our own walls, we open our city's defences.
Everyone joins in the work: setting rollers under the creature's   235
Feet, to facilitate sliding, and hawsers of hemp, to get traction,
Over the neck. Thus war's fatal engine, pregnant with soldiers,
Scales our walls. Young boys all round her and unmarried
    maidens
Hymn her with songs, take delight in the touch and the tug of her
    hang ropes.
She follows, meek in her menace, and glides to the heart of our city. 240
Ilium, fatherland, home of my gods, so famous in warfare,
City of Dardanus' sons! Four times she gets stuck and she falters
Not at our gate but upon the gate's slabstone. And four times the
    weapons
Clang in her womb. We press on, though, blind in our madness,
    oblivious,
Placing this monstrous fulfilment of doom in our citadel's sanctum.   245
Even now Cassandra discloses our doom, but, as always,
God's divine orders ensure that we Teucrians fail to believe her.
We, poor fools, decorated our deities' shrines in the city,
Wreathed them with boughs for a feast on the day Troy died, as the
    gods willed.

'Hours and the sky roll on. Night falls, spreading out from remotest
Ocean, enshrouding, in dankness and dark, both earth and the
    heavens—   251
Myrmidon treachery, too. Draped over the ramparts, the Teucrians
Slump into silence, limbs hugged tight by the sleep of exhaustion.
Argive infantry, now like marines in a naval formation,
Put out from Tenedos, tacitly, lovingly, lanterned by moonlight, 255
Heading for beaches they know. On a signal of fire from the flagship,
Sinon, protected by fate and iniquitous gods, slips the pinewood
Bolts from their slots, as a burglar does, and releases Danaäns
Locked in the equine womb. Once opened, the horse starts restoring
Soldiers to fresh air. They spring from the hardwood caverns
    delighted: 260
Captain Thersander and Sthenelus too, and ruthless Ulysses,
Shimmying down a suspended rope; there was Acamas, Thoas,
Peleus' grandson too, Neoptolemus; first was Machaon,*
Then Menelaus and then this ruse's designer: Epeus.
In they march, on a city embalmed in a wine-sodden slumber.   265
Sentries are slaughtered, and every gate unbolted and opened.
Now they can let in the troops, join ranks with their allies in purpose.

'This was the time when sleep's first wave sweeps over our mortal
Frailty, and gods' most agreeable gift slithers into our beings.
There in my dreams, right in front of my eyes, I seemed to see
    Hector   270
Nearby, deeply depressed, flooding tears in a copious torrent,
Blackened with gore-clotted dust, as he was that day when the chariot
Dragged him by straps threading gashes slashed in his still swelling
    insteps.
Oh, how he looked! How changed, alas, from the Hector I'd once seen
Clad in Achilles' arms sloughed off in defeat by Patroclus,   275
Or when he torched the Danaän ships with his Phrygian firebrands!
Filth now covered his beard and his clumped hair, matted and
    blood-caked;
Now he wore only the numerous wounds he'd received round his
    homeland's
Walls. I saw myself, through my tears, make the first move,
    addressing
Hector, in tones of despair, and expressing these thoughts to the hero: 280
"O Dardania's light, most reliable hope of the Teucrians,

What has delayed you so long? Oh, Hector, what land have you
　　come from?
How we've been waiting for you! And to see you like this! We're
　　exhausted—
Many you know are now dead, we've endured every kind of affliction,
Human and civic. What act of dishonour has savaged your features　285
Once so calm and sublime? Or why else am I seeing you wounded?"*
Wasting no time, not a word of response, on my vacuous questions,
He just groaned a deep groan from the innermost depths of his being:
"Oh," he said, "flee now, child of the goddess, get out of this firestorm.
Foemen have taken the walls. Troy has fallen, from peak into chasm.　290
Priam and homeland are finished. If Pergamum could be defended
My right hand would already have done the defending in *my* time.
Troy is entrusting to you its icons, its guardian spirits.
Take them as fate's fellow travellers, find great walls to protect them,
Walls you will build when your sea-borne wanderings reach their
　　conclusion."　　　　　　　　　　　　　　　　　　　　　　295
This said, he thrust in my hands the ribbons and image of potent
Vesta and brought her eternal flame from her innermost sanctum.
　　'Anguish in all of its forms, meanwhile, echoes all through the
　　city,
Louder and louder, its chaos of screams. Though my father
　　Anchises'
House was so well tucked away, a retreat overarched by its tall trees,　300
Sounds start to sharpen, the ghastly rasping of weapons advances.
Shaking off sleep, I climb to the highest point of the rooftop,
Stand there, listening for sounds, my ears pricked up and attentive.
Think of a wildfire's sweep through wheatfields, powered by the
　　roaring
Southerlies. Think of a flash flood exploding through banks of a
　　mountain　　　　　　　　　　　　　　　　　　　　　　　　305
Cataract, flattening fields, ripe crops, all the hard work of oxen,
Ripping whole forests away. Add a shepherd high on a rock ridge
Far above, hearing he doesn't know what kind of sound in his stupor.
　　'Then truth dawns on the eye. We begin to see how the Danaäns
Trapped us. Deiphobus' opulent home has imploded, erupting　310
Vulcan's flames to the sky and his neighbour Ucalegon's mansion
Blazes. The straits of Sigeum are now a vast mirror of fire.
Clamour of warriors rises and blends with the clangour of trumpets;
Mindlessly, I seize arms, without thinking too clearly what purpose

Arms should serve. Grab a fistful of comrades and rush to the
    fortress,   315
Fight! That's the fire in my soul. Wrath and fury have jettisoned reason.
Taking its place is a slogan: that death, under arms, has its beauty.
   'Up comes Panthus,* who's just now eluded Achaean
    bombardments,
Panthus, Othrys's son, who was priest of the fortress and Phoebus,
Running with arms full of relics and vanquished gods, dragging
    one small   320
Grandson, and scurrying up to my house, mind lost in his panic.
"Where's the real heart of the fight? What point should we take as
    our stronghold,
Panthus?" I'd hardly spoken these words when he said with a
    deep groan:
"Doomsday has come, inescapable hour of Dardania's destruction.
Trojans we were. But no more. No more Ilium, no more
    stupendous   325
Glory for Teucer's sons. Savage Jupiter's moved it to Argos,
All of it. Now, in our blazing city Danaäns are masters.
Standing tall in the centre of town, that horse is disgorging
Armoured hordes. Sinon, gleeful in victory, mocks us and scatters
Fire. Of the thousands who ever arrived from the mighty Mycenae,   330
Some keep watch at our great double gates, others cordon off narrow
Alleyways, spears levelled, ready for action. A battle formation
Solid with steel is unsheathed, blades honed to a glittering sharpness,
Poised for the kill. Even those on our front lines, the guards at the
    gateways,
Mount hardly any resistance; they're fighting a foe that they
    can't see."   335
   'Stung by the words of Othrys's son and by promptings from
    heaven,
Off I'm whirled into flames, into combat wherever Erinys,
War's grim demon, and uproar and sky-pulsing clamour direct me.
Rhipeus joins me and Epytus too, a remarkable fighter,
Allies emerging in moonlight, then Dymas and Hypanis also,   340
Gather around at my side, and, with them, the youthful Coroebus,*
Mygdon's son, who was, so it chanced, at Troy during those days.
Mad, burning love for Cassandra had forced him to come there, as
    would-be
Son-in-law, bringing his aid and support to the Phrygians and Priam.

He went unfulfilled, not heeding advice that his pledged bride　　345
Uttered in clairvoyant frenzy.

　'I, when I saw these warriors united and burning for battle,
Offered these words: "Young men, you bravest of hearts in a
　　hopeless
Cause, if your clear desire is to follow a leader who boldly
Challenges death, this is it. You *see* how our fortunes are faring:　　350
All of the gods, on whose strength this empire stood, have forsaken
Altars and shrines. They're all gone. You are running to save an
　　already
Burned city. So, let's die, let's rush to the thick of the fighting.
There's just one way to live with defeat: Don't hope to outlive it!"

　'Youthful courage is thus augmented by rage. We are henceforth　　355
Predators roving the mist-veiled dark, wolves driven by raging
Bellies and blindly forced from our lairs, where cubs we've abandoned
Wait dry-jawed. We stride through the volleys of arrows, through
　　foemen,
On to a death beyond doubt in a resolute march to the city's
Centre as dark night circles her caverns of shadow about us.　　360
Who could translate into words that night's disaster and killings?
Who could shed tears that express those oceans of pain that
　　engulfed us?
That day an old city died after so many years of dominion.
Everywhere bodies were strewn in her streets, in her houses,
　　her sacred
Shrines dedicated to gods, bodies numberless, motionless, lifeless.　　365
Teucrians weren't alone in their shedding of blood in atonement.
Even in conquered hearts, now and then, courage found resurrection.
Swords struck conquering Danaäns as well. Everywhere there was
　　cruel
Anguish, everywhere terror—and death in its manifold guises.

'Our first Danaän, Androgeos, heading a large squad of soldiers,　　370
Thought, for he didn't know better, that we were an allied
　　contingent.
So, he came up and addressed us with friendly, spontaneous banter:
"Hurry up, lads! You're late! What's holding you back? Are you idle
Slackers? The others have torched all Pergamum, and they're enjoying
Plunder and rape. Have you only just now come ashore from the
　　tall ships?"　　375

Then he divined in a flash—for our less than convincing responses
Roused his suspicions—that we, those he'd just fallen in with, were
    foemen.
Dumbstruck, suppressing his stride and his voice, he began to edge
    backwards,
Just as one suddenly backs off in terror, while sweating through rugged
Bush, if one's foot presses down on an unnoticed viper that rears up   380
Angrily, puffing its dark-hooded neck. So Androgeos faltered,
Trembling at what he'd just seen, and began to retreat in the same way.
We rushed in and engulfed them in one massed onslaught of weapons.
Trapped as they were by their shock, in an unfamiliar location,
We simply killed them at will. Thus Fortune smiled on our first
    deed.   385
   'Arrogant in our success, and emboldened at this point, Coroebus
Said: "Let us follow, my comrades, the route towards safety that
    Fortune's
First stroke points to, a way where she shows herself ready to help us:
Let's switch shields with them, let's put on this Danaän equipment.
Ruses or bravery, who cares which when you're dealing with
    foemen?   390
They'll be our armourers!" This said, he donned Androgeos' helmet,
Crested with plumes, then he strapped on his shield, quite superbly
    emblazoned,
Fitted an Argive sword at his hip, readjusting the buckle.
Rhipeus did just the same, so did Dymas and all of the young men,
Joyfully, each one arming himself* with the fresh fruit of plunder.   395
   'Marching, but under this borrowed protection, we mixed with
    Danaäns.*
In the indifferent blindness of night, we provoked and engaged in
Battles galore, sent Danaäns galore to the dark pit of Orcus.
Some scatter back to the ships, racing off for the shorelines they
    can trust.
One group, shameless in fear, climbs back once more up the
    ladders   400
Into the monstrous horse, nestles deep in the womb they remember.

   'No one may justly trust in the gods when the gods won't be trusted.
Here, alas, was Cassandra, the virgin daughter of Priam,
Dragged by her unribboned hair from Minerva's temple and
    sanctum,

Vainly extending the blazing light of her eyes toward heaven,   405
Only her eyes; for chains locked her delicate palms in their bondage.
This sight taxed to its limits the frenzied mind of Coroebus
Who, determined to die, now hurled himself at her captors.
All of us followed in tight formation and charged at the column.
   'Now's the first time we are crushed by our own side's volleys
     of missiles   410
Launched from the shrine's high roof. It's the start of a pitiful
     slaughter
Caused by the misjudged look of our arms, by our helmets with
     Greek crests.
Then the Danaäns attack, drawn in from all sides by the angry
Crying and groans as the virgin's abducted: the hotheaded Ajax,
Atreus' pair of sons too, and the whole Dolopian army.   415
Much as colliding fronts in a storm will produce a tornado:
Westerlies crash into south winds and easterlies, loving to joyride
Horses of sunrise. Woodlands are howling and Nereus, frothing
     with fury,
Whips up the sea from its bottommost depths with the swish of his
     trident.
Even the troops that we once, in disguise, under cover of night-time,   420
Chased through the shadows, dispersed in their panic all over the city,
Now reappear. They are first to detect that our shields and our
     weapons
Lie about who we are, and to note that our language is different.
Sheer numbers now overwhelm us in seconds. Our first loss,
     Coroebus,
Falls to Peneleus' hand at the altar of armoured Minerva.   425
Rhipeus is next. He was Troy's most just individual of all time,
Ultimate champion of fairness. He dies—for the gods took a
     different
View of him. Dymas and Hypanis perished, the victims of friendly
Volleys and, Panthus, your utterly righteous life and Apollo's
Ribbons of priesthood gave *you* no protection when *you* began
     stumbling.   430
Ashes of Ilium, flames that destroyed my people for ever,
Witness my oath: as you fell, I had no wish to live by avoiding
Any Danaän devices or weapons. Had *my* death been fated,
My deeds done would have earned it.
                    'But we were just torn from the action,

Instantly called, by the uproar and shouts, to the palace of Priam,   435
Iphitus, Pelias, and I. Just three; and old age was impeding
Iphitus. Pelias, too, had been slowed by a wound from Ulysses.*
  'Here we saw raging a battle so large that it was as if conflict
Couldn't occur elsewhere, as if no other people were dying
All through the city: a total war with Danaäns assaulting   440
Rooftops, attacking beleaguered portals in tortoise formation:*
Ladders clamp against walls, men fight on the rungs for a footing
Straight below gateposts. Left hands thrust out shields against
    arrows,
Ward off spear-casts, right hands grasp at the parapet's crenels.
Dardans respond, tear turrets apart, strip down entire rooftops.   445
These, as they stare death full in the face and can see it's their last
    stand,
These are the weapons deployed in defence as they hunt for projectiles,
Toppling gilded rafters, the height and the glory of ancient
Heritage, down on the foe. Others form into close ranks, blockading
Lower approaches and guarding them, swords drawn, ready for
    action.   450
  'Courage arose in us now to run up to the king's palace, bringing
Vital relief to its veteran defence, new verve to the vanquished.

  'Hidden from sight was a doorway, the access point to connecting
Tunnels within Priam's palace: a postern ignored by attackers.
Through it Andromache, unfulfilled even while the realm lasted,   455
Frequently walked to her in-laws' suite with her son, unescorted,
Dragging* Astyanax up to his grandfather's rooms for a visit.
Entering here, I climbed to the top of the roof's highest apex
From which the Teucrians pelted a hand-launched, useless
    bombardment.
Over the roof, itself high to the heavens, a tower had been raised up,   460
Standing above a precipitous drop. One would go there to look out
All over Troy, at Danaän ships and Achaean encampments.
Prising with steel all around, where the upper structural courses
Showed signs of slippage, we tore it away from its seating support
    beams,
Then pushed hard. First it slid, then it suddenly crumpled,   465
Burst, with a roar, into showers of debris that spread over Danaän
Forces. But others moved up. There was no intermission in volleys
Either of rocks or of all other kinds of projectile.

'Right at the palace's gate and directly in front of the courtyard
Pyrrhus dances* in glittering bronze, ecstatic in swordplay,   470
Much like a viper emerging to light from his frigidly frost-clad
Den below ground, all swollen from feeding on poisonous grasses.
Now, though, he's sloughed the old skin, he's reborn to youth's
     colourful brilliance,
Coiling his slippery back, he lifts breast and head high to the sunlight,
Darts forked tongue from his mouth, flashes brightly in flickering
     menace.   475
     'With him, huge Periphas stands, and his squire, who'd once
     driven Achilles'
Horses, Automedon. They, joined by all the young fighters from
     Scyros,
Launch an attack on the palace, pitch firebrands onto the rooftops.
Pyrrhus, up front, double axe in his hand, tries breaching the massive
Gateway and tearing the bronze-clad doors from their hinges and
     mountings.   480
Cutting a cross-beam loose, he smashes the solid oak inward,
Opening up a great window* revealing a wide panorama:
Views of the palace within are disclosed, long stretches of courtyard;
Views of the innermost chambers of Priam and kings of the old days.
Now they see bodyguards standing at arms right there at the
     entrance.   485
     'Screaming chaos reigns in the heart of the palace. The hollow
Hallways howl with the keening of women's laments and the
     rhythmic
Beating of breasts: vast sound drums glistening stars in its uproar.
Terrified mothers roam aimlessly through huge chambers, embracing,
Clinging to, fixing their kisses upon their defenders: the doorposts.   490
     'Pyrrhus, true heir to his father's violence, persists. Neither locked
     bolts
Nor armed guards can withstand him. He's using a ram now, and
     batters
Furiously. Doors yield, ripped from their mounts, crashing down to
     inertia.
Force surges forward. Danaäns burst in through the entrance and
     slaughter
Front-line defenders, then fill the whole breadth of the courtyard
     with soldiers,   495
Wilder than foaming floodwaters bursting escape through the levees,

Sweeping all structures set in their way with their violent torrents,
Racing in rage through the ploughlands, dragging both cattle and
    cowsheds
Over the plains in a single mass. I saw with my own eyes
Pyrrhus, frenzied with killing, and Atreus' twins at the entrance.   500
Hecuba, her hundred daughters, I saw them, and, sprawled on an altar,
Priam, his own blood polluting the holy fires he had kindled.
Fifty bedrooms he had, grand hopes for a new generation,
Doorways gilt with barbarian gold, decorated with plunder,
All lying desolate. Where fires fail, the Danaäns take over.   505

'Maybe you'd like to hear Priam's fate* recounted in detail.
Once he had seen Troy's capture and fall and the breach of his palace
Gates and the enemy right in the heart of his own private quarters,
He, though long out of practice and elderly, pulled on his armour,
Vainly—his shoulders were palsied with age—buckled on his now
    useless   510
Sword and set off on his own to meet death where the foe gathered
    densely.
Centrally placed in the palace, completely exposed to the heavens,
Stood a huge altar, adjacent to which was a very old laurel,
Leaning across it, enfolding the household gods in its shadow.
Hecuba, also her daughters, were crowded in vain at this altar   515
Where, like doves, they had swooped to escape the dark tempest
    approaching,
And were now sitting, embracing the various deities' statues.
When she saw Priam himself rigged out in the arms of his young days,*
"My dear pitiful husband," she said, "what ghastly decision
Prompted your arming yourself like this? And where are you
    rushing?   520
This kind of help, and defenders like you, are not what the crisis
Needs. My own Hector, were he with us now, wouldn't make any
    difference.
Come here instead, lord. For either this altar will give you protection
Or you will die with the rest!" When she'd said this she drew him
    towards her,
Seating this ancient man in a holy sanctuary's refuge.   525
   'Look, one of Priam's sons, named Polites, has just escaped
    Pyrrhus'
Murderous hand. He has fled through the spears, past the foeman

Down through long colonnades and is crossing the now empty
    courtyard
Wounded. But hot on his heels, and intent on inflicting the
    death-blow
Pyrrhus pursues, and he's now within arm's reach, he's thrusting
    his javelin.   530
Lurching in front of the faces and eyes of his parents, Polites
Finally crumples and spews out life in a fountain of dark blood.
Priam, at this point, though already trapped in a circle of killing,
Can't hold back. For he doesn't suppress all his wrath, he proclaims it.
"*You* will pay dear for this crime," he declares, "you will *pay* for
    this outrage.   535
If any power in heaven feels righteous concern in such matters,
May gods show you the thanks you deserve, pay you back in the
    proper
Coinage for staging my son's death here, and for making me watch it,
You have disfigured a father's face with the blood of his son's death.
You are no child of Achilles, you liar. He never mistreated   540
Priam, his foe, like this! He blushed for shame, he respected
Rights that are granted a suppliant, he showed good faith by returning
Hector's blood-drained corpse* for interment, and me to my kingdom."
Once he'd spoken, the elderly man made a feeble strike with a
    powerless
Spear. And it fell, with a clang, on the bronze shield, instantly halted, 545
Then dangled limply down from the top of its central embossment.
Pyrrhus replied: "You'll report this, then, to my father Achilles,
Fully, in person. Remember to tell him the tale of my grisly
Actions. Describe Neoptolemus just as he is: a degenerate bastard.
Now: die."
        'While he was speaking, he pounced on the quivering Priam,
Dragged the king, slipping in pools of his own son's blood, to the
    altar,   551
Grabbed his hair, yanked back his head with his left, with his right
    drew his gleaming
Sword which he then buried up to the hilt in the flank of the old king.
So ended Priam's role, as prescribed by the fates. His allotted
Exit made him a spectator at Troy's Fires,* Pergamum's Ruin,   555
This man once in command of so many countries and peoples,
Ruler of Asia! He's now a huge trunk lying dead on the seashore,
Head torn away from his shoulders, a thing without name, a cadaver.

'Then, for the first time, brutal horror beset me on all sides.
Rooted me down stock-still. Stealing into my mind came my
          cherished   560
Father's face as I watched that king, just his age, being butchered,
Gasping his life out. Then in stole the thought of Creusa, deserted,
Thoughts of my home being plundered, the fate of my little Iulus.
Glancing around, I assess what forces I have to support me.
All have deserted, exhausted. They've either just hurled their own
          weakened   565
Bodies down to the ground or consigned them to death in the fires.

   'I was the last one alive* when I saw her on guard there at Vesta's
Shrine,* keeping silent and well out of sight, in its innermost sanctum:
Helen, Tyndareus' daughter.* The flames, as I wandered at random,
Passing my eyes over everything, shed the light needed to see her.   570
She, common demon of war for both Troy and her homeland,
          foreseeing
Teucrian wrath because Pergamum fell, then Danaän reprisals,
Then the rough ire of the husband she'd left, had now hidden in terror,
Crouched by the fires of the altar, unseen by their eyes full of hatred.
Flames were now rife in my soul, ire rose up within me, demanding   575
Vengeance for my dying homeland and summary, criminal justice.
"Must she see Sparta again unharmed—and her uncle's* Mycenae—
Riding in glory, a queen who has just given birth to a triumph?
Is she to see married life, her ancestral home and her children,
Served by a court full of women from Troy and of Phrygian
          pageboys,   580
Though Priam died by the sword, though Troy is but one massive
          bonfire,
Though our Dardanian shore has sweated out blood beyond measure?
No! While you don't win a glorious name if you punish a woman,
Here is a victory earning its own special kind of approval.
I will be praised for destroying the blight of a curse, for exacting   585
Punishment earned, and my soul will be glad it has duly
          accomplished
Vengeance we burned for*—and sated the thirsting ash of my nation."
Such were my rioting thoughts as my mind's rage swept me
          towards her.

   'Then, so presenting herself to my eyes that I had to observe her,
Clearer than ever before, and illumining night with her brilliant   590

Radiance, my gracious mother shone forth in that nature and stature
Usually visible solely to gods. She, proclaiming her godhood
Thus, took my right hand in hers and restrained me. Her rosy lips
      added:
"Son, what monstrous pain spurs such uncontrollable anger?
Why do you rage? Where's your care for me, and your family,
      vanished?   595
Why not look first where you've stranded Anchises? He's old and
      he's tired,
And he's your father. See whether Creusa, your wife, is still living,
What of Ascanius, your boy? Greek forces are everywhere, wandering
Round them, encircling them all, and if I didn't love and protect them,
Flames would be snatching them now, foe's swords would be
      draining their lifeblood.   600
Blame doesn't lie with the evil-eyed face of Tyndareus' destested
Spartan bitch, or with Paris. It's gods' inclemency,* gods' will,
Ruining all this wealth, dashing Troy from its heights into rubble.
Look, I will tear back the whole of the veil now shrouding your vision,
Clouding death-doomed eyes into dullness with blurring and
      misty,   605
Darkness. But you mustn't now be afraid of your parent's instructions.
And don't refuse to obey these commands whose force is apparent.
   ' "Here, where you see massive bastions wrecked, blocks torn from
      supporting
Blocks, where smoke intermingled with dust sweeps upwards in billows,
Neptune is shaking foundations and toppling walls with his mighty   610
Trident. He's prising the whole city up and away from its bedrock.
Juno, most brutal of all, is the first in control of the Scaean
Gates over here, with a sword at her side, in a frenzy, and calling
Allied troops from the fleet.
There, look, Tritonian Pallas, who's taken the citadel's summit,   615
Sits in a cloud flashing lightning, ferocious with aegis and gorgon.*
Jupiter boosts courage, heightens success for Danaäns, in person,
And himself rallies the gods into war on Dardanian forces.
Son, get out quickly, escape. Put an end to this effort you're making.
I'll be on hand the whole time and I'll get you home safe to your
      father's."   620
This said, she merged herself back among ghostly shadows of
      night-time.
And, in her place, there appeared the appalling faces and mighty

Forces divine that detested Troy.
That's when my eyes really saw all Ilium slowly subsiding
Into the fires, saw Neptune's Troy prised up from its deep-set   625
Roots, like an ancient ash on a mountain's peak when the farmers
Cut her and hack her with steel, with relentless blows of their axes,
Vying to fell her for sport. She's been threatening to crash, she's
    been yawing,
Tresses of foliage shivered, her head in incessant convulsion,
Slowly succumbing to gashes and rips before rumbling her final   630
Death crackle, torn from her ridge, sprawled prone in destructive
    destruction.

'On my descent, I set out between foeman and flame with the goddess
Guiding me.* Weapons withdraw from my path, flames back off
    before me.
Yet, when I actually made it through to the gate of my family's
Home and ancestral estate, my father, the first one I looked for,   635
First one I wanted to carry away to the heights of the mountain,
Flatly refused to extend his own life, now Troy was cut from it,
And face the rigours of exile. "It's you," he said, "you with the solid
Strength of physique and as yet of an age when you're fit and
    full-blooded,
You who must make your escape!   640
Me? Had the gods in their heavens willed *me* to extend my own
    lifespan,
They'd have preserved me my homeland. I've already seen Troy
Fall once.* That's much more than enough; I've lived through its
    capture.
Think of me now as a corpse laid out, say farewell and get going!
I'll figure out how to die. Some foeman will show me his mercy,   645
He'll have his thoughts on the spoils. Dispensing with burial's easy.
Gods' evil eye has been on me. For years I've been helpless and useless,
Just killing time since that moment the father of gods and men's ruler
Blasted me down* with his lightning and scarred me with burns
    from its fire."
Voicing such memories, he stood fast, immovably stubborn.   650
We—that's Creusa, my wife, and Ascanius, in fact, the whole
    household—
Argue, with torrents of tears, that he shouldn't, as head of the family,
Wilfully wreck it along with himself, and increase our oppressive

Fate. He refuses and sticks to his plan, sits tight in the same spot.
    'Total despair gets me back under arms. I now want, I now choose
        death.   655
What other course did fortune allow? What choice was I granted?
"Father, did you think or hope I could run off and leave you
        abandoned?
Did such a monstrously unjust thought find voice in my father's
Mouth? If the gods want to leave not a trace of a once mighty city,
And, if it's settled, resolved, to add both you and yours to the
        doomed Troy's   660
Ruin, your doorway to death's wide open. For Pyrrhus is coming,
Fresh from the bloody disposal of Priam, beheading the ruler's
Son right in front of his father; the father on top of an altar.
Mother divine, did you snatch me away through the fighting and
        fires
Just so I'd see the foe here in the innermost rooms of my own
        home,   665
Watch as Ascanius dies, see my father, along with Creusa,
Slaughtered like beasts, each one all awash in the blood of another?
Arms, men, stand to your arms! Life's last day summons the
        vanquished!
Throw me upon the Danaäns again, let me go back and restart
Combat. Never shall all of us die this day without vengeance."   670
    'Buckling a sword on again,* I was sliding my arm into shield-
        straps,
Making them taut, and preparing to leave my house for a second
Time. But my wife blocks the door, won't budge, grabs hold of my
        ankles,
Keeps pushing little Iulus directly in front of his father.
"If you're just leaving to die, rush us off to face everything with
        you.   675
Taking up arms* means to lay down a wager on winning. You know
        this!
Yet you abandon your little Iulus, your father, and me too—
Once called your partner in marriage— to who knows what. Guard
        your home first!"
    'Such were her cries. She was filling the house with her echoing
        sorrows
When there arose a most sudden, remarkably wonderful portent.   680
During the conflict of looks, words, arms between desperate parents,

Look, a slim halo of light seems to shine from the crown of Iulus'
Head. And it's shedding a glow that can touch without burning: a
      gentle
Flame licking over his tresses and grazing the down on his temples.
Scared by the sight into spasms of fear, we flail the ignited   685
Hair and extinguish the sacred flames with our fountains of water.
Father Anchises, however, eyes raised to the stars in elation,
Stretched out his palms, reached out with his voice to the heights of
      the heavens:
"Mightiest Jupiter, if your resolve ever bends when petitioned,
Look at us, that's all I ask. If our righteousness shows we
      deserve it,   690
Then, Father, show us an augural sign* that this was a true omen."
      'Hardly were these words said by our family elder, when thunder
Suddenly crackled away to our left and a star shot from heaven,
Trailing a flare most intensely bright as it dashed through the
      darkness.
Over our rooftops it sped in its fall. And we watched as its
      brilliance   695
Then disappeared in the mountain forests of Ida, defining
Where we must go. And the pathway its long trajectory furrowed
Glowed light; all of the area round us was smoky with sulphur.
That's when my father admitted defeat. For he raised himself
      upwards,
Made his address to the gods, offered prayers to their sacrosanct
      comet.   700
"No more delay for us now. I am here. Where you lead, there I
      follow!
Gods of my homeland, look after this house, and look after my
      grandson.
This is your augural sign. Troy now has its being in your will.
Yes, son, I yield. I no longer refuse to leave here as your comrade."
That's all he said.
                  'Now we heard, spreading all through the city, much clearer
Sounds of the fire. Hot winds roll billowing flames ever closer.   706
"Come, my dear father, let's leave! Set the weight of your limbs upon
      my neck.
I'll support *you* on my shoulders. This labour won't burden me
      greatly.
Come what may in the fall of events, we'll share every danger.

Safety for one will be safety for both. Let the little Iulus   710
Walk alongside, and my wife follow on* in our tracks at a distance.
Slaves, you must pay full attention now as I'm giving instructions.
Just as you're leaving the city, you'll find there's a mound and an
    ancient
Temple of Ceres* Abandoned, and, near it, a very old cypress,
Nursed over many long years by our fathers' attentive devotion.   715
This will be our one point of assembly from every direction.
You, father, take in your arms our ancestral gods and the relics.
I cannot, for I have come from a huge battle and recent bloodshed:
That would be sacrilege—till I am cleansed in a live source of
    running
Water."   720
  'This said, I stoop and slip over my neck and broad shoulders a
    tawny
Lion's skin for a cloak; then I raise up my burden. Iulus,
Still the small boy, takes my right hand and holds it with intertwined
    fingers,
And, since his stride's not as long, lags behind, trailing after his
    father.
Further back comes my wife. On we go through the darkest of
    places.   725
I, who, just moments ago, didn't flinch at a volley of javelins
Or at contingents of Greeks falling out from their march to attack us,
Cowered whenever a breeze blew now, so tense that the slightest
Sound made me twitch out of equal fear for my comrade and burden.
Now I was nearing the gates. In my mind, I could see myself past
    them,   730
Totally clear, when persistent sounds seemed to steal on our hearing
Suddenly, as of the tramping of feet. Looking out through the
    darkness,
Father exclaimed: "Hurry, son! Son they're getting so very much
    closer!
Shields glowing bright and the flash of their bronze: I can actually
    see them!"
This is when some malign power exploited my panic and
    plundered   735
What confused part of my mind I still had. While I took to the side
    streets,
Ran well beyond the network of roads that were known and familiar,

Lord, was it pitiful fate that made off with my wife? Did Creusa
Pause for a rest or stray from the path or slump in exhaustion?
There's no way to be sure. She was never restored to my eyesight.*   740
I didn't know she was gone. For I didn't look back, didn't even
Think back about her until we'd arrived at the mound and the sacred
Precinct of Ceres the Ancient. When all those assembled were counted
She was the only one lost, fooling comrades, her son, and her husband.
What human being, what god did I not accuse in my madness?   745
Or what crueller sight* did I see in the sack of the city?

'Handing Ascanius, Teucrian gods, and my father Anchises
Over to comrades, I leave them concealed in the bowl of a valley,
Put on my glittering armour, head back on my own to the city.
It's my resolve to retrace each step that we took, each occurrence,   750
All through Troy, to expose my person, again, to the dangers.
First, I go back to the walls and the dark passage under the gateway
Through which we'd left, looking out for, and carefully tracking
     the footprints,
Back through the darkness of night, with my only lantern my eyesight.
Horror beleaguered my mind; even silence itself brought me
     terror.   755
First I head back to my home, just in case, by some chance, some
     remote chance,
She'd returned there. The Danaäns had stormed in, controlled the
     whole building.
Up it goes! Fire is consuming my house, bellowed high by the
     updraughts,
Up to the roof. Flames roar to the sky in a mad dance of triumph.
  'I press on. I revisit the fortress and palace of Priam.*   760
Now, in the emptied cloisters of Juno's Shrine for the Helpless,
Chosen guards stand watch: they are Phoenix and ruthless Ulysses,
Keeping their thefts clear of thieves. At this central point, all the
     treasures
Stripped from the burned-out temples of Troy are collected: the holy
Tables, the solid gold chalices too, all the prisoners' clothing   765
Dumped in a heap. Children, and, set in long, ranked terror, their
     mothers,
Stand in a circle.
This didn't stop me from daring to hurl my cries through the ghostly
Darkness and filling the streets with my shouts of "Creusa! Creusa!"
Calling her vainly, again and again with the loud voice of anguish.   770

Then my eyes saw, while I dashed in an endless search through the
    city's
Buildings, a vision, my fear's worst fulfilment: the ghost of Creusa,*
Looming before me: her image was as I remembered, but grander.
Stunned, hair standing erect, voice choked in my throat, I stood
    stock-still.
Uttering words to allay my concerns,* she addressed me in this way: 775
"Why, sweet husband and partner, are you indulging your frantic
Grief so intensely? For these events haven't evolved without heaven's
Guidance. You can't take Creusa from here as companion. That isn't
God's will. The ruler of lofty Olympus expressly forbids it.
Long years of exile await; you must plough vast stretches of salt sea.   780
Then you will reach the Hesperian land, where the Lydian Tiber
Flows a straight course without waves amid farmlands fruitful and
    peopled.
Born for you there is a blessèd state, royal power and a royal
Partner in marriage. So staunch all tears for beloved Creusa.
I'll never see the proud lands of the Myrmidons or the Dolopians,   785
I won't go as a slave to the housewives of Greece. I'm of Dardan
Blood, and by marriage, a daughter of Venus divine.
Mighty Cybele, Mother of Gods, keeps me here on her home shores.
Now farewell. Maintain your love for the son that we both made."
When she'd said this, though I wept and so wanted to utter so
    many   790
Words, she deserted me, fading away on the winds without substance.
Three times I tried to encircle her neck with my arms as I stood there,
Three times, alas, all in vain. For the image eluded my grasping
Hands, like a slight puff of air, as a dream flutters off from a dreamer.

'So it all ends, and the night's used up. I go back to my
    comrades.   795
And, when I get there, I'm awed to discover there's been an impressive
Influx of newcomers,* mothers and fighters, the cream of our young folk
Massed for a journey to exile—a host of the sad and dejected
Gathered from everywhere, ready in heart and equipment to travel
Over the seas to whatever terrain I might want them to settle.   800
   'Venus, star of the morning,* was rising above Ida's topmost
Ridges restoring the daylight; Danaän blockades were controlling
Every approach to the gates. There was no hope of help whatsoever.
Shouldering father I made for the mountains. I'd lost, and I knew it.'

BOOK THREE

' AFTER the powers on high had approved* the destruction of Priam's
Innocent people and Asia's empire, Ilium's proud heights
Fell. All Neptune's Troy lay razed to the ground: ashes smoking.
Forced to pursue, by what we divined of the gods' will, our different,
Far-off places of exile, deserted lands, we constructed,   5
Under Antandros and under the ridges of Phrygian Ida,
Ships,* though we'd no idea where fate would take us or where we'd
Settle. We muster our men. By the early days of the summer,
Father Anchises is issuing orders to sail at the fates' call.
Tears in my eyes, I am leaving the shores of my homeland behind me,   10
Leaving the harbours and fields where Troy once stood. I'm an exile,
Borne on the deep with my comrades, my son, and our household's
      great gods.

'Far off lies Mars' special domain, vast arable flatlands
Ploughed by the Thracians and ruled, long ago, by savage Lycurgus.
Thrace, though, had long shared friendship with Troy, shared cult
      and religious   15
Ties—while Fortune held. Carried there, I established my first town,
Down on its curving shores, though the fates seemed to curse my arrival,
Called it Aeneadae*—simply a name we derived from my own name.
I began making my offerings now to my mother, Dione's
Child,* and to such other gods as might bless the work started. To
      honour   20
Jupiter, king of the gods, I was ready to slaughter a handsome
Bull on the shore. Nearby, as it chanced, stood a mound topped
      with dogwood
Clumps and some dense-packed thickets of bristling myrtle.
This I climbed. And I tried to uproot green wood from its groundsoil,
Eager to cover my altars with living and leaf-covered branches.   25
Just as I snapped the first shrub from its roots to extract it, I noticed
Something that made *me* bristle with fear, and which makes an
      astounding
Story; for dark blood started to ooze, dripping downwards in large
      drops,

Staining the soil with its putrid gore. A shudder of ice-cold
Horror shivered my limbs. And my blood froze, clotted in terror.   30
Still, I persisted, and tried once again to extract a reluctant
Shaft from another bush, seeking the latent cause of the problem.
Dark blood flowed from the bark of this second tree, in the same way.
Thoughts crowded into my mind. I began saying prayers to the rural
Nymphs and their father, Mars, under whose heavy heel lie the
     Thracian   35
Fields, so they'd make what I'd witnessed a lighter, more favourable
     omen.

  'After I'd tackled a third group of shafts, and with even more effort,
Wrestling, down on my knees, with the sand that resisted my
     struggles—
Now—should I speak or be silent?—a moan that would drive you
     to heartbreak
Rose to my ears from the depths of the mound; a voice drifted on
     breezes.   40
"Why do you mutilate me? I have suffered, Aeneas, I'm buried!
Spare me, and spare your own righteous hands from a crime. I'm a
     Trojan,
Not some bizarre plant's shoot dripping ghastly blood; and you
     know me.
Flee from this brutal land, get away from this greed-haunted
     seashore.
I'm Polydorus;* and spiked into me was a seeding of iron   45
Weapons which sprouted and yielded a harvest of sharp-pointed
     spear-shafts."*
Fear then assumed a more complex face. Mind crushed by the portent,
Stunned, hair standing on end, voice caught in my throat, I stood
     stock-still.

  'Priam, as ever, unfulfilled, had, earlier, sent off
This Polydorus, loaded with gold, to be raised by the Thracian   50
King. It was secretly done. Priam's confidence in the Dardanian
Army was lost now; the city, he saw, was completely encircled.
But, once Teucrian power was destroyed, deserted by Fortune,
This king of Thrace chose the conquering side and he joined
     Agamemnon,
Thus breaching all moral laws. He hacked Polydorus to pieces,   55
Seized all the gold. Cursèd hunger for gold, is there no crime you
     won't drive

Mortal hearts to attempt?

        'When my bone-chilling fear fled, I brought back
News of these heaven-sent horrors to delegates picked by the people,
And, above all, to my father. I asked for a judgement and ruling.
All were of like mind: abandon this criminal land and escape its   60
Fouled hospitality; we must sail with our fleet on the south winds.
Therefore we give Polydorus a funeral. Over his earthen
Mound an immense layer of topsoil is piled. His remains now have
    altars,
Sombrely ribboned in black, wreathed dark with funereal cypress;
Women of Troy form a circle, hair ritually loose and unribboned.   65
Next we bring bowls full of warm, frothing milk, bear chalices holding
Blood from the sacrificed beasts, and we settle the soul of the dead man
Deep in his tomb while our voices blare Last Call at the graveside.
Then, just as soon as the main can be trusted, and winds give us
    lake-smooth
Waters, and rustling softness of south winds summons us seaward,   70
Sailors begin to haul ships to the surf, fanning over the beaches.
Out of the harbour we sail, and the cities and land are receding.

'In mid-sea there's a land held sacred, an island that's dearly
Loved by the Nereids' mother and Neptune who rules the Aegean:
Delos. It once drifted freely from this coast to that—till Apollo,
    the archer,   75
Righteously tethered his birthplace to Mykonos and to the craggy
Gyaros, granting it power to be still, and to laugh at the breezes.
That's where I sailed.

        'The safe harbour of Delos gave tired crews its calmest
Welcome.* When we disembarked, we paid homage to Phoebus's city.
Anius* met us, the king, and not only the king but Apollo's   80
Priest, with the god's holy laurels and ribbons encircling his temples.
Seeing Anchises, he knew him at once as a friend from the old days.
Handshakes and greetings exchanged, we stepped into the buildings
    before us.
There I paid homage at Phoebus' ancient temple of hewn stone.
"Give us a home of our own, god of Thymbra, give walls to the
    weary,   85
Give us a future, a city that lasts. Preserve, for a new Troy,
Pergamum's remnants missed by the Greeks and ungentle Achilles.
Who do we follow? Or where do you tell us to go or to settle?

Give us a sign to interpret, slip into our minds and inspire us!"
  'Hardly had I said this, when everything seemed to start
    shaking   90
Suddenly, even the god's own gateway and laurels; the mountain
Seemed to revolve and the tripod to roar as its shrine was hurled open.
We threw ourselves to the ground, and our ears were assailed by a
    huge voice:
"Dardanus' rugged sons:* the first land that nurtured your parents'
Roots will, on your return, take you back to her welcoming
    bosom.   95
Go, then, in careful search of your ancient, original mother!
That's where Aeneas's house will establish a worldwide dominion,
Kept by the sons of its sons and by those who'll be born of their
    offspring."
Phoebus had spoken and happiness surged, though the sound of
    contention
Mingled. They all wished to know what city was meant and precisely   100
What land Phoebus was calling their wandering souls to return to.
  'Father's mind turned over the memories of old men in old times.
"Listen," he said, "you commanders, and learn what it is you can
    hope for.
Crete, great Jupiter's isle, lies out in the midst of the high seas.
There Mount Ida is found. It's the cradle of our people's
    being—   105
Welcoming, well-peopled land, with a hundred considerable cities.
That's where Teucer,* our father, had come from, if I now remember
Rightly what I once heard, when he first went ashore at Rhoeteum.
Wanting the place as his realm. No Ilium existed in those days,
No Castle Pergamum. People just lived deep down in the valleys. 110
Crete gave us our Great Mother* who lives in and blesses Cybelus,
Gave us the Corybants' cymbals, the sacred woodlands of Ida,
Cybele's sacraments hallowed by silence, her chariot's submissive
Lions in yoked pairs. So: where gods' bidding leads, let us follow!
Come, let's charm the good winds, let's sail for the kingdoms of
    Knossos!   115
Crossing a distance so short will be easy, if Jupiter's with us.
Dawn on the third day will see our vessels anchored on Cretan
Shores." When he'd said this, he slaughtered appropriate beasts at
    the altars:
Honouring Neptune, a bull; and a bull for you, lovely Apollo,

Black is the sheep for the storm winds; white for the favouring
    zephyrs.   120

'Rumour is flying that Idomeneus,* the king, is in exile,
Cast from his father's throne, and that all Crete's shores are deserted:
That means no foe in the palace, and houses, abandoned, but standing.
Leaving Ortygian Delos' port, we ourselves begin flying
Over the seas, past the wildly Bacchic mountains of Naxos,   125
Verdant Donysa, Olearos, snow-white Paros—the sea-strewn
Cyclades—threading our way through waterways crowded with
    islands.
Shouts from the sailors arise as they vie in their various contests:
Crewmen, all urging us onwards to Crete, to the land of our fathers.
Tailwinds rise, and they chase us along on the course we've been
    plotting.   130
Soon we glide in on the ancient shores of a folk called Curetes.
  'Now I'm impatient. I'm building the walls of the city I've
    prayed for,
Naming the place, to my people's delight, Pergamea, and urging
All to feel love for their homes—and add height to the citadel's
    structures.
  'Sands underneath beached vessels were almost dry now, the
    young folk   135
Busied with weddings, new lands for the plough. I myself was allotting
Homes, I was drafting laws. Then, suddenly, out of some sickened
Part of the heavens, a plague fell upon us. It rotted our bodies,
Piteously blighted our trees and our crops. What a year of destruction!
People let go of the sweet breath of life or they dragged ailing bodies   140
Painfully. Sirius' heat withered growth on our farms in the summer.
Grasslands parched and the ailing crops refused us their nurture.
"Back to the Delian oracle, trace back your sea-routes to Phoebus!"
That's what my father was urging. "And pray that he grant us
    forgiveness,
Ask him what end he can bring to this state of exhaustion, what
    helpful   145
Sources he bids us approach in our toils, what land we should sail to."

'Night reigned; sleep was controlling earth and its living and conscious
Creatures.* And my sleeping mind saw, standing in front of my
    own closed

Eyes, holy statues of gods and the household spirits of Phrygia—
Effigies I'd brought with me from Troy, refugees from the blazing   150
City. They stood forth, clear in the generous light which the full moon
Poured through the slats of the shutters. And then they appeared to
        address me,
Uttering words to allay my concerns,* and expressing them this way:
"All that Apollo intends to declare when you reach his Ortygian
Delos, he sings for you here. See, he's sent us directly to *your* home!   155
We, when the Dardan city was burned, followed you and your forces,
We measured great sea's swelling expanse under you, and with your
        fleet,
And it is we who will raise your descendants high to the heavens;
We'll give your city imperial power. You must furnish that mighty
Future with mighty defences. Don't give up your flight and its
        long toil!   160
Move, as you must, from this place! It's not *this* land the Delian
        suggested;
Crete's not the place where Apollo's instructions advised you to settle.
But such a place does exist. It's an ancient land called Hesperia,
'Twilight Land',* by the Greeks, strong in armies, rich in its
        cropfields.
Once the Oenotrians tilled it. Now rumour reports that successors   165
Renamed it 'Italy' after the family name of their leader.
That's where it's right that we settle: where Dardanus came from,
        and also
Father Iasius. They are the ultimate source of our bloodlines.
Come on, get up! And report what we've said to your elderly father
Joyfully. It's beyond doubt! Let him seek out Corythus, seek out   170
Lands in Ausonia. Jupiter's dictates ban you from Dicte."*
    'Struck by such visions and voices of gods as by thunder, I leaped up.
These were no phantoms of sleep, but known identities, witnessed
Closely. I seemed to be seeing their veiled hair, actual faces.
Icy sweat was beginning to seep from all over my body.   175
Out of my bed in a flash, I stretched hands high toward heaven,
Palms facing up, voice raised. Then I poured out the purest libations
Over the fires. When content that I'd done all the ritual honours,
I told the news to Anchises, expounding the details in order.
Grasping that there were two lines in our ancestry, twin sets of
        parents,   180
Seeing that he'd been misled by a new error mixing up old sites,

"Son," he recalled, "you who've anguished so much about Ilium's
    future,
Only Cassandra kept singing to me about this sort of outcome.
Now, as I think back, she claimed this land was our family's due
    realm,
Often she'd talk of Hesperia, often of Italy's kingdoms.   185
Who'd believe Teucrians, though, would arrive on Hesperia's beaches,
Who, at the time, could be stirred, anyway, by Cassandra's predictions?
Let's go along with what Phoebus advises. It's better. Let's follow."
That's what he said. We all cheered in our joy and obeyed his
    instructions.

'So, we deserted this settlement too—leaving only a small group— 190
Sails set, speeding across vast seas in our hollows of timber.
After our vessels gained open seas, as we sighted no further
Land, saw sea on all sides, up above saw only the heavens,
Rain clouds, black as the deep, formed over our heads, bringing
    with them
Night-time and winter gales, seas shuddering, stippled with
    darkness.   195
Instantly winds roll water to waves; sea's immensity surges
Huge. We are scattered and tossed in its spinning and suctioning
    vastness.
Black storms smother the day, night's dankness rips away heaven,
Fire flashes out from exploding clouds, forks thunderously doubled.
Shaken off course we are wandering, lost in the blindness of water. 200
And Palinurus himself says he cannot distinguish in heaven
Day from night, or remember the course in the midst of the high seas.
Three full cycles of unseen sun we wander in sultry
Darkness over the deep, the same number of nights without starlight.
  'Then, on the fourth day, at last, land seems to emerge for the
    first time,   205
Opening distant vistas of mountains and billowing smoke plumes.
Down goes the canvas, we rush to the oars; in an instant the sailors'
Muscles are churning foam as strokes sweep wide on the blue deep.
  'Strophades is what the Greeks call the islands whose coastlands
    receive me
First, as I'm saved from the waves, Strophades in the spreading
    Ionian   210
Sea. There the Demon Celaeno, along with the rest of the Harpies,*

Dwells, now that Phineus' door has been closed to their hunger,
Forcing the creatures, in fear, to give up their old banqueting tables.
No grimmer monster than these, worse plague, or divine show of
    anger
Ever protruded its fiendish head from Stygian waters: 215
Harpies can fly; they have faces like girls', and discharge from their
    bellies
Foulest filth. They have hands like claws, they have cheeks ever pallid,
Hungering mouths.
  'Once we've arrived and have entered the port, what a vista
    before us!
Herds of contented cattle that graze at will in the meadows,   220
Goats flocking, cropping the grass—no herdsman to watch or
    control them.
In we rush.* And we butcher them all, and invite the gods' presence,
Specially Jupiter, so they too may share in our plunder.
Next, on the curving beach we set couches and dine there superbly.
  'Then, in a sudden and spine chilling swoop from the mountains,
    the Harpies   225
Pounce in a flash and wreak havoc with thunderous clangour of
    wingbeats,
Tearing our banquet to pieces, their unclean contact befouling
Everything. Hellish screeching resounds in the midst of a vile stench.
So, in a deep recess, under cliffs hollowed out by erosion,
Covered above with a woodland canopy—trees and their bristling   230
Shadows encircle it—we set our tables again and rekindle
Altar fires. And again, from their unseen lairs, from a different
Quarter, the screeching mob, talons poised, flies over the plunder,
Fouling the feast with their mouths. So I order my crews to grab
    weapons,
War, I declare, must now be waged with this nation of fiends.   235
Acting precisely as ordered, they hide their swords, which they scatter
Variously over the grass, bury shields where they can't be detected.
So, when the foe swoops, blaring its screech through the curve of
    the seashore,
High in his sentinel post, Misenus, with hollow brass trumpet,
Sounds the alarm. Then my comrades attack in a new form of battle,   240
Try to dismember with steel these foul, disgustatory seabirds.*
They, unscarred by wounds to their backs or blows to their plumage,
Swiftly soar to the stars, while leaving behind them their carrion

Half-eaten, torn from the tables now spoiled with the marks of
    their foulness.
    'One of them perches on top of a very high cliff: she's Celaeno,   245
Prophet of failed fulfilment for us. She breaks forth with these words:
"Sons of Laomedon,* are you prepared to wage war on the Harpies,
War for our bulls, which you butchered, and over our cows, which
    you slaughtered,
And to expel us, who've done you no harm, from the land of our
    fathers?
Carry on into your minds* my words, then. Grasp them securely.   250
These are predictions the Father Almighty gave Phoebus Apollo,
Phoebus told me. Now I pass them to you, I, direst of Demons.*
Italy's where you're steering your course. You'll summon up fair winds,
You'll be allowed to reach Italy's coast, to sail into her harbours.
But you will never surround your allotted city with ramparts   255
Till dire famine* avenging the wrong done to us by this slaughter
Drives you to gnaw with your jaws at your tables and then to devour
    them."
This said, she rose on her wings and flew back to the sheltering forest.
    'Blood froze rigid as ice in my comrades' veins at this sudden,
Frightening vision. Their spirits fell. Their demand was no longer
Peace won by warfare, but peace won by offerings, prayers, and
    petitions,   261
Whether these beings were gods or disgusting birds of ill-omen.
Palms stretched upwards in prayer, on the shore, my father, Anchises,
Calls upon heaven's great powers and offers them ritual honours:
"Gods, keep us safe from these threats! O gods, please avert such
    disaster!   265
Grant to the righteous salvation and peace." Then he orders the
    moorings
Slipped and the yard ropes loosed, all sail unfurled for departure.
Southerlies belly the canvas, we flee, wake foaming behind us.

'Setting a course now mapped by a helmsman and guided by breezes.
On the horizon we soon catch glimpses of wooded Zacynthus,   270
Samë, Dulichium, Neritus too, raised high on its steep cliffs,
Far to our leeward, we hold craggy Ithaca, realm of Laërtes.
Roundly cursing this land which had suckled the savage Ulysses.
Leucas's cloudy peaks* soon appear, and its shrine of Apollo,
Shores that a sailor would normally dread; but we, now exhausted,   275

Set a direct course towards it, put in at its miniature city.
Anchor is cast from the prow; ship's sterns stand beached on the
   seashore.
Since we've at last achieved landfall, unplanned, yet beyond all our
   wildest
Hopes, we now wash ourselves clean, and, in Jupiter's honour, set
   altars
Blazing with gifts, hold Ilian games upon Actium's beaches.   280
Naked and slippery with oil, my crews do traditional Trojan
Wrestling, delighted we've safely eluded the grip of so many
Argive cities, effected escape through the midst of our foemen.

   'Meanwhile, the sun has completed one more long year in its orbit;
Icy winter churns seas wild with the blasts of the north wind.   285
Out on the gateposts, I nail up a shield made of bronze, hammered
   concave,
Carried by great Abas once, and inscribe my gift with a poem:
"Arms from Danaän victors,* these, and vowed by Aeneas."
Then I give orders to leave our haven and get to the benches.
Crews compete, strike sea with their oars, sweep over the surface.   290
Quickly we tuck out of sight* Phaeacia's mist-covered towers,
Skirt past the Epirote shoreline and enter Chaonian harbours,
Drawing in close to the lofty heights of a city: Buthrotum.

   'Here, our ears are assailed by a true but incredible rumour:
Helenus, Priam's son,* now possesses the wife and the sceptre   295
Once held by Pyrrhus, of Aeacus' blood. He's a king and he's ruling
Greek cities. Once more Andromache marries a man from her
   homeland!
Stunned, I could feel my heart overcome by astonished and burning
Passion to talk to the man, learn the cause of events so momentous.
Leaving the shore and my navy, I made my way up from the
   harbour,   300
Just as Andromache chanced to be standing in front of the city.
There in a grove by the streams of a make-believe Simoïs, she held
Rites of remembrance, with food for the dead, sad gifts, and libations,
Calling on Hector's empty tomb that she'd hallowed with green turf,
And upon altars, twinned, like the cause of her tears: son and
   husband.   305
   'When she observed me approaching and saw, in a panic, our Trojan
Arms all round, she reacted in terror as if to a monstrous

Phantasm, stiffening in mid-glance. Warmth fled her bones and she
    fainted.
Finally, after a long time had passed, she could speak,* but just
    barely.
"You! Is it really your face I see, really telling me you're here?   310
Son of the goddess, are you still alive? Or, if sweet light has left me,
Where's Hector?" Speech now yielded to streaming tears as her
    loud cries
Flooded the whole place. And while she was out of control, I could
    scarcely
Slip a few words in. Confused, I began with a phrase here, a phrase
    there:
"I am alive. Yes it's me, though I lead a life stretched to my limits.   315
Don't doubt it. What you are seeing is real.
Oh, what befell to uplift you,* when left cast down by your great
    spouse?
Hector's Andromache, say what worthy—well, adequate—Fortune
Visits you? Do you maintain your spousal relations* with Pyrrhus?"
  'Head bowed, eyes downcast, voice down to a murmur, she
    answered: 320
"How much more fulfilled than the rest of us women was Priam's
Single daughter left virgin,* and ordered to die on a foe's grave
Under the high walls of Troy. She was never the prize in a raffle,
Shamed as a captive to feel the touch of her winner and master's
Bedding. But we, when they'd burned up our homeland, were split
    up and shipped off   325
Far away over the seas. I bore the conceit of Achilles'
Offshoot, arrogant youth, bore the pains of birth as his slave-girl.
He, then, went chasing Hermione, Leda's grandchild, a decent
Lacedaemonian wedding!—signed over the rights to his housemaid,
Me, to a house-slave, Helenus, but—now enter Orestes,*   330
Blazing with passionate love for the girl (who's the wife he's been
    robbed of).
Maddened by ghosts of his crimes he catches his rival when off guard,
Butchering him at his father's shrine. Neoptolemus now dead,
Deeds assign Helenus part of his realm, and he names it for Trojan
Chaon—hence the 'Chaonian Plains' and the region,
    'Chaonia'—   335
And, on the heights, he sets Pergamum too, and an Ilian fortress.
But what winds, what forces of fate, set *you* on a course here?

Did some god drive you here to the shores you did not know were ours?
What of your son? Did Ascanius survive, is he living and thriving?
He's the one Troy left you . . .   340
Does he still grieve now for his lost mother,* and does his father's
Fame, does Aeneas inspire him to old-fashioned courage, a real man's
Greatness of soul, does the thought that his uncle was Hector
     inspire him?"
Words like these, intermingled with tears, she continued to pour forth,
Raising a lengthy and hopeless lament, as the hero, as Priam's   345
Son, made his way from the walls, with a sizeable group of retainers.
   Helenus knows us as kinsmen and ushers us into his city
Joyfully, though each word has to sob through the flood* of his
     weeping.
On getting closer I know it: a miniature Troy, simulating
Mighty Pergamum, even a bone-dry creek that is now named   350
Xanthus. And I'm at the Scaean Gate, and embracing its threshold.
Teucrians too find similar joy in this city of kinsmen,
Ample courtyards enabled the king to admit their whole number.
Out in the centre, they started to offer libations to Bacchus,
Sacred feasts, set on service of gold, great chalices held high.   355

'Day followed day in procession, another, another. The breezes
Cried for our sails, and persistent southerlies bellied the canvas.
Statements and questions like these on my lips, I go up to the prophet:
"Helenus, born within Troy, translator of gods, you decipher
Phoebus' will, his oracular tripods, his laurel of Claros,   360
Movements of stars, birds' language and ominous patterns of
     flying.
Speak to me. Every traditional source has been kind and informed me
Where I should go; all the powers above, in their signs, recommended
Sailing for Italy, testing out lands far off in the distance.
Only the Harpy Celaeno proclaims new omens, abhorrent   365
Even to name, invokes curses of vengeance upon us: disgusting
Famine. So what are the first of the hazards I should be avoiding?
What course must I pursue to ensure we survive all these troubles?"
   'Helenus' first response was the ritual slaughter of heifers,
Prior to begging the gods to grant peace. Then he stripped off the
     ribbons   370
Binding his sacred hair, and, since such intense divine pressures
Paralysed me, took my hand, led me into your temple, Apollo.

There, as a priest with divine inspiration, he sang these predictions:
"Son of the goddess: that you're being guided and watched by
     some major
Powers as you travel the deep is quite obviously true. For God's
     ruler   375
Thus divides fate into lots, creates change. That's how order
     progresses.
Of these numerous signs, I'll translate you a few into verbal
Form: so you'll find safer passage, while guest of the seas, so you
     can then
Reach an Ausonian port. But the Fates prevent Helenus knowing
All the remainder; and speaking them's banned by Saturnian Juno.   380
     '"In the beginning, this Italy you think close and whose harbours,
Ignorant man,* you're preparing to wade to as if they were next door,
Lies aloof, long lands away on a long, impassable passage.
Ere you arrive, your oar must be slowed by Trinacrian waters,
Leagues of Ausonian seaways must also be crossed by your vessels,   385
Lakes of the underworld too, and Circe's island, Aeaea.
Only then may you find safe land to assemble your city.
Signs there will be. I will tell you them. Store them deep in your
     memory.
     '"When, under pressure, you come to the streams of a well-hidden river,
Under the bankside's oak-shrub brush you'll find an immense
     sow   390
Lying sprawled on the soil, on her side—an albino, with thirty
Newborn piglets, albino themselves, at her teats in a cluster.*
This is the seat for your future state and your refuge from troubles.
Don't live in terror about this impending gnawing of tables.
Fates will discover a way;* when you call him, Apollo will be there.   395
But, stay clear of the shores and the lands around Italy's closest
Coasts, those washed by the swell from our own Ionian waters.
All the communities there have been settled by Greeks who are wicked.
Locrians, Ajax's people from Naryx built walls there, and that's where
Idomeneus from Lyctos encamped, with his troops, on Salento's   400
Broad plains. Terraced Petelia, too. It is tiny but famous;
Now Philoctetes' abode, since he fled from his home, Meliboea.
Then, once your fleet has completed its mission and halted its motion,
While setting altars down by the shore, making good all your solemn
Vows, you must cover your hair with a veiling mantle of purple*   405
So that no evil-eyed enemy face can intrude on your hallowed

Flames lit to honour the gods, thereby disrupting the omens.
You, both your crew and yourself, make this a religious tradition!
May your descendants maintain this rite with unceasing devotion!
  ' "Then, when you set sail again, when the wind moves you on to
          Sicilian   410
Shores, where Pelorus' tongue-slim promontory narrows to nothing,
Run, though it makes for a lengthy loop, for the land to the larboard,
Larboard seas. Steer clear of the shores and the waters to starboard.
These two regions once formed a single, contiguous landmass,
Then, it is said, they rifted apart in a vast, devastating   415
Earthquake. Remote antiquity's hugeness of time can accomplish
Changes like this. In a violent flood, sea gushed through the chasm,
Severed Hesperian flank from Sicilian, washed with its narrow
Rip-tides between ploughed fields, between cities now sundered by
          coastlines.
Scylla keeps watch on the starboard side; on the larboard, Charybdis 420
Suctions vast waves down an abyss spun deep by her whirling
Spirals of tides three times each day; then, reversing her motion,
Vomits them up to the skies, strikes stars with a whiplash of water.
Scylla, confined to a cavern's concealing protection of darkness,
Constantly darts out her mouth, drags ships onto reefs of
          destruction.   425
First glance shows one a human face and a girl with a pretty
Torso, as far as the groin. But below that, a sea-serpent's monstrous
Body with wolfish bellies that merge into dolphin-like tail flukes.
Take time! Better to double Trinacria's Cape of Pachynus,
Though it's a long and circuitous course, than to get just a single   430
Glimpse of deformed Scylla lurking within her cavernous vastness
And hear the reef's ringing echoes as dark hounds bark amid breakers.
  ' "If, in addition, this seer, your Helenus, has any foresight,
If one can trust him at all and his soul is replete with Apollo's
Truths, I'll predict one thing to you, son of the goddess, just one
          thing;   435
Over and over again I'll repeat this advice and this warning:
Juno's great force *must be the first* you respect in your prayers,
Sing to her heartfelt vows, win over this powerful mistress,
Juno, with gifts, on your knees. That way, in the end, you will triumph,
Leave the Trinacrian land, and be sent on to Italy's borders.   440
  ' "When you've arrived there and made your approach to the city
          of Cumae,

Lakes dedicated to gods and Avernus's echoing forests,
Then you'll observe a mad seer* who sings, from the depths of a cavern,
Fate's decrees, using leaves to record all names and all details.
Each word this virgin writes upon leaves as her song of the future,   445
She then arranges in sequence and stores in her cave, behind
    locked doors.
These all stay unmoved, and in place, never fall out of order.
But, just the slightest draught, as the door rotates on its hinges,
Blows them away. For its opening scatters the featherlike foliage.
All through her hollow cave leaves flutter, but she never bothers,   450
After this happens, to catch, to replace, or assemble the verses.
People go off without answers, detesting the shrine of the Sibyl.
Don't count the cost of delay very high when you visit. No matter
How crews grumble, how strongly your voyage demands that you set sail
Now, or what favouring winds now blow and would belly your
    canvas,   455
Don't fail to go to the seer. Ask, *beg* her, to open her own throat,
Sing you her oracles willingly, orally, now, and in person.
She'll tell you all about Italy's peoples, and wars that are coming,
What methods you should employ to avoid or endure every problem.
And, if you show her respect, she will grant you success in your
    journeys.   460
That's it. No further warnings to you from my voice are permitted.
Forward! And with your deeds, raise Troy's great name to the heavens!"
    'Such were his friendly words. And the seer orders gifts to be carried
Onto my ships: items heavy with gold and with sawn elephantine
Ivory,* loading the keels with a huge store of silver and cauldrons   465
Brought from Dodona.* Among these is Neoptolemus' armour,
Namely a corslet of interlocked loops interwoven with tripled
Gold, and a helmet beautifully coned, topped off with a handsome
Horsehair crest. And my father, too, receives personal presents.
Also he adds horses, adds a few pilots,   470
Strengthens our benches with rowers, supplies new equipment for
    crewmen.

    'Meanwhile, Anchises was issuing orders to get the fleet's rigging
Ready for sail so there'd be no delay should a favouring wind rise.
Phoebus' spokesman approached him with great deferential politeness:
"You were thought worthy, Anchises, of proud honour, marriage
    to Venus,   475

You're the gods' special concern, twice rescued from Pergamum's ruin,
Look, there it is, your Ausonian land! Hoist canvas and take it!
Yet—*you really must* glide past the near coast on the high seas:
Phoebus Apollo shows *you* the distant Ausonian *west* coast.
Forward!" he cries. "Your righteous son brings hopes to fulfilment!   480
Why am I talking so much and delaying the south winds? They're
       rising!"

     'Saddened by this last parting, Andromache too offered presents:
Garments embroidered with figures of gold threaded into the fabric,
And, for Ascanius, a Phrygian cloak* (he wasn't forgotten!).
Weighing him down with her textile gifts, she spoke much as
       follows: 485
"Take these too. May my hands' work serve you as memorials,
Witnessing, dear boy, the lasting love of Andromache, Hector's
Wife. Take these. They're the final gifts that your kinsmen can give you,
You, sole image surviving to me of Astyanax, my son.
You have his eyes, hands, face, his expressions, precisely his
       movements.   490
He would be your age now: a youth on the threshold of manhood."

     'I told them as I went on my way with tears flowing freely:
"Live fulfilled lives, you whose struggles with fortune are over
Now. We're *still* being challenged by one fate after another.
You're celebrating the birth of your stillness; no more ploughing
       salt seas   495
Nor any quest for Ausonian fields that are always receding
Farther away. You see Xanthus's image, a Troy that your own hands
Built under auspices which, I hope, prove better, a Troy that
Might prove less of a hindrance to Greeks.* Should it be that I ever
Enter the Tiber and enter the ploughlands bordering the Tiber,   500
See the walls granted my people, some distant day in the future,
We'll bring our two states together, uniting our neighbouring nations,
Linking Hesperia to Epirus. This same Dardanus founded
Both of our bloodlines, each bore identical hardships. In each mind
Troy shall be one and the same. Here's a task for our grandsons to
       settle!"   505

     'Northward we press on the sea, with Ceraunia's ridges to starboard,
Gaining the point from which Italy's reached by the shortest of
       crossings.*
Sun sets, dense dark mountains now merge deep into shadows.

There we lie in the welcome dry land's lap, near the water,
Clasping the oars we're allotted, and randomly sprawled on the dry
    sand, 510
Tending our bodies, as sleep pours balm over limbs now exhausted.
Night, driven on by the Hours, wasn't yet approaching its mid-point
When Palinurus, always alert, leaped up from his bedroll,
Checked all the winds, gauged movements of air with his sensitive
    hearing,
Marked the progression of stars* in the silence of heaven: Arcturus, 515
Hyades, promising rain, he observes, the Triones, the twin Bears,
Also Orion with weapons of gold. When his survey's completed—
All observations concur that the sky is serene—he then signals
Clearly from up on the aft-deck; and we break camp for departure.
Sails unfurled are our wings as we start our attempt at a crossing. 520
  'Dawn is now duly blushing to red and the stars have been routed
When we see dim, vague hills in the distance and, low in its profile,
Italy. "Italy!" shouted Achates who first hailed the sighting,
"Italy!" sang out the crew in a joyful and clamorous greeting.
Father Anchises then circled a mixing bowl with a garland, 525
Filled it with unmixed wine* and, standing high on the aft-deck,
Voiced his appeal to the gods.
"Gods who have power over sea, over earth, over sky and its tempests,
Grant us a crossing eased by a wind, breathe favourably on us!"
Breezes pick up, as we've hoped. There's a port, getting closer and
    closer; 530
High on Minerva's Castle, a temple appears. So the sailors
Shorten their sail, swing about all prows on a tack for the coastline.
Pounding seas from the east have curved this port in a bow-shape.
Spits jutting outwards foam with the spattering spray of the salt sea,
Hiding the actual harbour, formed by the downward extending 535
Spurs of a turreted ridge which create two embankments. The temple
Backs far away from the shore. Here I saw the first omen, four horses
White as the snow, freely ranging the flat plains, cropping the
    grasses.
Father Anchises observed: "Host land, you are bringing us warfare.
Horses are bridled for war and it's war that these animals threaten. 540
These same four-footed creatures, though, may be trained for the
    chariot*
Some day and, yoked, may produce that concord born of the harness.
Peace can be hoped for."

     'We then offered prayers to a sacred, divine power:
Pallas the Armoured, who greeted us first when we landed
   triumphant.
Then, just as Helenus had so emphatically ordered, we duly   546
Veiled our heads, as we stood before altars, in Phrygian mantles,   545
And honoured Juno the Argive by burning the specified offerings.
Once we'd completed our rites in due order, we instantly started
Hauling the rig on the masts and the yards of our sails round to
   windward,
Leaving behind us the port, Greek towns, and the land we
   mistrusted.   550

'Next into view comes the bay of Tarentum which, rightly or
   wrongly,
Rumour had Hercules visit. Lacinium's temple of Juno
Rises to face it, then Caulon's heights, Scylla's headland, the sailor's
Graveyard.* Far off, up from the swell, Trinacrian Etna
Looms into view. We hear monstrously roaring seas thunder over   555
Outcrops of rock, voices screaming on coasts, fragmented by distance,
Shoals leaping high in a riotous dance, sand swirling in sea's surge.
Father Anchises observes: "This must be the famous Charybdis.
These are the crags and the jagged reefs named in Helenus' warning.
Comrades, get us away! Be a team! Put your backs into rowing."   560
   'Crews do no less than they're ordered. The first to respond,
   Palinurus,
Torques ropes, forces the rasping prow hard over to larboard;
Each crew veers to a larboard tack, under oar-power and canvas.
Up to the heavens we're raised on the spiralling waves, the next
   moment
Down we sink to the depths of the dead as the waters are sucked
   back.   565
Three times cliffs amid hollows of rock roar thunderous echoes;
Three times we see foam wash clear, see stars dripping water.
Meanwhile the wind and the daylight abandon us, leave us
   exhausted.
Not knowing where we are, we've beached on the shores of the
   Cyclops.
   'Huge and calm as the harbour itself is, for no breezes enter,   570
Nearby Etna thunders horrific cascades of destruction.
Sometimes she shoots dark clouds up high, enshrouding the heavens,

Billows out eddying pitch-black smoke, ash blazing and white hot,
Catapults fiery globes, great flames which lick at the gleaming
Stars. And she'll sometimes hurl forth crags, she will tear out and
      vomit   575
Her own mountainous guts, she'll boil into air, from her deepest
Pits, rocks liquefied, rounded, with painful groans, into lava.
    'Rumour contends that beneath her mass, Enceladus' body*
Lies trapped, charred by a thunderbolt. Over him, hugeness on
      hugeness,
Etna was placed, and she bellows out flame where her furnaces
      rupture.   580
Each time he tires and turns on his side, Trinacria's whole mass
Shudders and roars, and envelops the sky in a mantle of dark smoke.
    'During that night we endured, under forestland cover, appalling
Horrors. And, further, we just couldn't see what was causing the
      noises.
No star's gleam, no luminous vault with its bright constellations   585
Offered us light. There were overcast skies, fog-shrouded, entombing
Moon in a dungeon of cloud; it was night without time, utter darkness.

'Now it's the next day. Dawn, as the first gleam of sun at its rising,
Sweeps away dankness of shadowy dark from the vault of the heavens.
Suddenly, out of the forest, a figure appears, unlike any   590
We've ever seen, starved gaunt, quite pitiably squalid—an unknown
Man coming down to the shore, hands outstretched, begging for mercy.
We just stare. Though his filth is disgusting, his beard in an untrimmed
Tangle, what passes for clothes sewn together with thorns, he's in
      all else
Greek, once sent against Troy in his father's inherited armour.   595
    'He, when he noticed our Trojan attire, when he glimpsed, at a
      distance,
Armour from Troy, stopped short in his tracks. What he saw, for an
      instant,
Froze him in terror. He soon made a dash for the shore, though,
      imploring,
Tears in his eyes: "May the stars, may the powers above bear me witness,
May this light we absorb from the sky now support my petition: 600
Teucrians, take me away, take me where in the world it may please you.
That's all I ask. Yes, I know I'm a man from the fleet of Danaäns,
And I admit that I came to attack Troy's temples and households.

If damage done by my crime is too great, then punish my actions,
Scatter me, limb by limb on the waves, plunge me into the vast sea.   605
If I'm to die, I will happily die at the hands of a human."
This said, he clung to my knees as he swayed on his own: a determined
Suppliant. He wouldn't budge. "Who are you?" we urge him to tell us.
"Tell us about your family, explain what caused your misfortunes."
Father Anchises himself took his hand* with but slight hesitation,   610
Giving the youth courage, building it, through this significant gesture.

'He, when at last he's recovered from fright, tells us this as his story:
"I am from Ithaca; I served Ulysses who found no fulfilment;
I'm Achaemenides. Since Adamastus, my father, had nothing—
Oh, staying poor would have been good fortune for me!—I set off
      for   615
Troy. But it's here my companions marooned me. While nervously
      slipping
Out past the gate of our brutal confinement, they didn't remember
Me in the Cyclops' monstrous cave.
                                   ' "Inside, it's enormous,
Dark. It's a filthy home for a banquet of blood. He's gigantic,
High as the stars (gods, keep earth free of such pestilent creatures!).   620
Looking at him isn't easy; conversing is out of the question.
Victuals, for him, are his victims' vital sinews and dark blood.
I myself have watched as he scooped two members of our group
Up in his massive hand, then reclined in the heart of the cavern,
Cracked them on rock, spraying fluids and filth that left entrances   625
Swimming. I've watched as he gnawed through limbs still awash
      with and pulsing
Gore, I've seen warm, living tendons responding to teeth with a
      shudder.
Not that they died unavenged. This was not let pass by Ulysses.
Ithaca's son, in this crisis, did not lose his veteran cunning.
   ' "Once Polyphemus was gorged with his feast, and the wine had
      embalmed him,   630
Once he had lain down his drooping neck, his immensity sprawling
All through the cave, as he vomited up, in his sleep, half-digested
Chunks, gore-clots all blended with blood-thick, previously unmixed
Wine, we prayed to the great divine powers, drew lots, and, in one wave,
Poured in a circle around him and bored, with a sharply honed
      weapon,   635

Clear through his huge, sole, luminous eye set deep in his fierce brow,
Large as an Argive shield or the solar lantern of Phoebus.
Thus, with delight, we at last avenged the shades of our comrades.
  '"But get away, poor fools, get away, break the ropes from their
      shoreside
Moorings!   640
This Polyphemus who milks woolly flocks and who uses a hollow
Cave to enclose them is not unique in his size or his nature.
There are a hundred more indescribable Cyclopes, whole clans,
Living along this curving coast, roaming high in the mountains.
Now, for the third time, the moon's bright horns are rounding to
      full light.   645
That's how long I've been eking out life in the woods, through
      deserted
Wild beast ranges and lairs, keeping watch, from a cliff, on the
      monstrous
Cyclopes, trembling at thumps of their footfalls, sounds of their voices.
Branches yield me an unfulfilling diet of berries,
Stony cornelian cherries; I graze upon grass I've uprooted.   650
This, though I've constantly watched all seas, is the first fleet I've
      spotted
Putting ashore. I had sworn I would yield to whatever that first group
Turned out to be, just content to escape these unspeakable people.
I'd rather *you* take my life—and by *any* death whatsoever."
  'Almost before he has finished, we see Polyphemus: a
      shepherd   655
Moving around among flocks on the top of a mountain, and vastly
Huge. He is making his way to the shores that he knows—an enormous,
Monster so ugly and fearsome, his sole eye ravaged and sightless,
Crutching his hand and supporting his feet on a pine stripped of
      branches.
Wool-bearing sheep give him company—they are the one
      consolation,   660
Sole pleasure left for his pain.
Once he's arrived at the sea and detected the touch of the high waves,
Groaning, and grinding his teeth, he rinses the blood that still oozes
Out of his gouged-out eyesight. He's wading far into the sea now
But waves still don't reach all the way to his towering ribcage.   665
We, in a panicky rush to escape far away from the region,
Take our deserving suppliant aboard, slash hawsers in silence,

Churn seas up, flat out at our oars, in a race for survival.
  'Sensing the movements, he twisted his steps toward the sound
    of our voices.
When opportunity fails to empower his hand, when his own powers   670
Waver, unseasoned for chasing us over the deeper Ionian
Waters, he raises a scream beyond measure which shivers not only
Ocean, but every wave. The terrain that is Italy trembles,
Terrorized down to its core, Mount Etna roars from its crater.
Roused from the forest, the Cyclops tribe rushes down from the
    mountain   675
Heights, races into the harbour and fills up all of the shoreline.
Oh, what a frightening assembly this was, these brothers from Etna,
Standing alert, heads high as the heavens, each eye full of futile
Menace frustrated! We watch them intently. They stand there like
    oak trees,
Tall tops towering up into air, like coniferous cypress,   680
High forests sacred to Jupiter, groves that belong to Diana.
Fear's sharp spurs drive us madly away in whatever direction
Sheets shaken loose let us run, and where following winds tauten
    canvas,
Flouting Helenus' plea that I not hold a course that meant favouring
Either Charybdis or Scylla,* routes more or less equally deadly.   685

'Then we must double back on our course. So we haul round our
    canvas.
Look now! A northerly breeze picks up from Pelorus's narrow
Headland, I'm swept past Pantagia's estuary, known for its living
Rock caves, on past Megara's gulf, past low-lying Thapsus.
These Achaemenides shows us, for he is retracing the coastline   690
He's travelled once before with Ulysses who found no fulfilment.
  'Reaching across a Sicilian bay and facing Plemyrium's
Surf-washed shores is an isle men of old called Ortygia. Rumour
Tells that a river in Elis, the Alpheus, brings here by secret
Passages under the sea to this harbour in Sicily, fresh streams   695
Spurting assault on the sea through the mouth of your spring,
    Arethusa.
Passing from here—our respects to the local and powerful spirits
Paid—I then sail past the fertile marshland loam of Helorus.
Next, when we've skirted Pachynus' high cliff peaks and projecting
Reefs, Camerina appears in the distance, though fate never grants us   700

Closer approach, then the plains called Geloan, or "laughing",
    then Gela,
Named for its mighty river that roars with the thunder of laughter.
Acragas, high on the cliffs, comes next, now displaying its massive
Walls from afar—once famed for its breeding of thoroughbred horses.
Rising winds let me leave your palms well behind us, Selinus.*   705
Off Lilybaeum, I thread among sharp reefs lurking in shallows.
Drepanum's harbour* receives me next. But it's no joyous haven.
  'Here, alas, not in those high sea's storms that so often beset me,
I lost him who'd brought me to life, Anchises. He lightened
Every disaster and care. You left me, my wonderful father,   710
Here, to exhaustion. Alas, you were saved from such perils for nothing.
This was a grief neither Helenus, seer as he was, in his many
Forecasts of horror, predicted to me, nor did fearsome Celaeno.
This was my hardest test, the decisive turn on a long road.
Then a god drove me clear off the course,* to your people and
    your shores.'   715

Father Aeneas, a single voice in a hall full of listeners,
Thus retold gods' story of Fate* and explained all his movements.
Now he fell silent at last. His end was accomplished. He rested.

BOOK FOUR

Now though, the queen, long since pierced through by her
terrible anguish,
Nurtures the wound with her veins. Passion's blind fire feeds on the
harvest.
Images course through her mind: of his courage, his family
distinction.
Each word he's spoken is fixed in her heart, each facial expression.
Anguish grants no peaceful repose, no respite for tired limbs.   5

Next day's Dawn had dismissed sky's dew-dank dark, and was shining
Earth with Apollo's lantern, when Dido, her sanity fading,
Came to what was her soul's other self, in a manner: her sister:
'Anna my sister,* what sleepless dreams suspend me in terror!
Who is this newcomer guest who has set up his quarters in our home? 10
Oh, what a grand look he has, how brave in his heart and in battle!
Gods generated his line; I believe this, not simply on blind faith.
Base-born, degenerate souls are exposed by their fear. What a
beating
Destiny gave him! What wearying wars sang out in his story!
Were it not rooted, immovably fixed in my mind, that I'd never   15
So much as wish to ally myself with another in marriage,
After my first great love deceived me and failed me by dying,
Were I not weary of weddings, my thoughts about marriage so altered,
I, perhaps, could rest easily with this—one point of censure.
Anna, I have to confess: ever since my poor husband Sychaeus   20
Died and my brother stained our household's shrines with his
slaughter,
This is the one man who's suppled my senses and pummelled my
fainting
Mind's resolution. These embers of long-lost fires, I recall them.
I'd rather see Earth yawning her bottommost chasms before me,
Feel the Omnipotent Father's fire thrust me to the shadows—   25
Erebus' pale, dank shadows, and Night's sea of darkness—than ever
Violate you, my own honour, or loosen the vows that I make you:
He, who first coupled me to himself, robbed me of my love life.
So, let him keep it and guard it in death's unlovely confinement.'*

This said, tears welled up in her eyes and dampened her bosom. 30
 Anna responds: 'You are dearer than life's very light to your sister.
Will you then squander your youth in your solitude, harvesting
  sorrow,
Not knowing joys Venus offers: delights that she yields, and those
  sweet sons?*
Dead souls, urns full of ash set aside, do you think they'll be troubled?
Suitors' pleas, in the past, failed to move you, sick in your grieving: 35
Tyrians earlier, Libyans now. You rejected Iarbas
Scornfully, and other princes that Africa, goldfield for triumphs,*
Nurtures. Will you still fight off love even when it's appealing?
Aren't you concerned about peoples who share these lands you
  have settled?
We are surrounded: Gaetulian cities, invincible warriors. 40
Who can control the Numidians, tame wild tidelands of Syrtis?
South lies a region of desert and thirst and of savage Barcaean
Nomads. I hardly need talk about Tyre's impending invasion,
Threats from your brother.
I think the gods gave us excellent omens when Ilian vessels 45
Sailed this way on the winds to our land. We have Juno's approval.*
Joined in a marriage with him, what a city you'll see, what a kingdom
Rising in front of your eyes! In alliance with Teucrian forces,
Punic Carthage will soar to the summit of glorious achievement.
Ask the gods' pardon, that's all you must do, make the right kind of
  offerings. 50
Play lavish hostess, and reef in his hawsers with reasons for staying:
Winter and rainy Orion, of course, whip seas to a fury,
Ships need refitting; the overcast skies prevent safe navigation.'
 Stirring an already smouldering soul to love's rashness of passion,
Anna fed hope to a hesitant mind, severed chastity's moorings. 55
Off to the shrines they went first, these two, and from altar to altar
Searched out omens of peace; they selected and ritually slaughtered
Hoggets for Ceres the lawgiver, Phoebus, and father Lyaeus,
And, above all, for the power that controls all marriages: Juno.
Loveliest Dido herself, in her own right hand, holds the goblet, 60
Pouring the contents between the two horns of a gleaming white heifer.
 Sometimes she paces, before heaven's eyes, to the rich smoke of
  altars,
Starting the day with her offerings, staring intently as cattle's
Cavernous chests are cut open, consulting their still living entrails.

This is the insight of seers? Pure ignorance! What use are votive   65
Offerings or shrines when you're mad? It is *she* whose soft tissue
     the fire eats,
Hers is the chest still alive with a wound that won't offer responses.*
Dido, unfulfilled, burns on and, in raving obsession,
Randomly wanders the town, like a deer pierced through by an arrow
Hit long range, when off guard, in the Cretan woods, by a shepherd   70
Armed for the hunt. He has left his steel-tipped shaft in her body,
Not knowing he's hit his mark. In her flight, she ranges all Dicte's*
Meadows and woods. Barbed deep in her haunch is the reed that
     will kill her.
Now Dido's leading Aeneas all over the heart of her fortress,
Showing him Sidon's resources, explaining her plans for the city,   75
Starting to tell him her thoughts, stopping short, halfway through
     a sentence.
Now, day drooping to dusk, she's the same. She repeats the same
     banquet:
Crazily pleading to hear once more what the Trojans have suffered,
Once more hanging in awe on his lips as he tells her the story.
   Later, when others are gone, when the already dim moon, in its
     turn,   80
Snuffs out its light, and the stars as they fade persuade slumber, she
     lingers
Ghostlike in grief on the couch he's abandoned, the sole presence
     haunting
Emptied halls. He's not here, but she hears him; not there but she
     sees him.
Charmed he's his father's image, she'll take in her lap young Ascanius,
Hoping that she can delude Love's* inexpressible passion.   85
Bastions started no longer rise, youths' military training
Halts. The port's harbour defences aren't readied for war. As
     construction
Ceases, the growth of the daunting and massive walls is disrupted:
Cranes that reach high to the skies are left dangling in idle suspension.

Jupiter's darling wife, Saturn's daughter, upon diagnosing   90
What kind of plague gripped Dido, and knowing that fear of the
     damage
Rumour might cause wouldn't stifle her madness, said these words
     to Venus:

'Marvellously regal glory you've won, war's spoils in abundance,
You and this young boy of yours—this memorable might of divine
     power!
Thanks to a ruse, two gods tally up one woman defeated.   95
Your false tricks don't hide your genuine fear of my city,
I knew how much you distrusted the mansions of powerful Carthage!
Where will you stop, how far will you go in your wild competition?
Why not, instead, work together, for endless peace and a marriage
Sealing it? See, you've attained what you spent your whole intellect
     planning: 100
Dido is burning with passion, love's madness has seeped to her
     marrow.
Under matched auspices, then, let us rule their combined populations
Jointly. I grant that she'll serve as the bride of a Phrygian husband,
And, as her dowry, deliver the Tyrians into your keeping.'
     Venus, who grasped that her words were staged to disguise her
     intention—   105
Namely, transferral to Libyan shores of Italian kingship—
Counter-attacked in this way: 'One would have to be mad not to
     honour
Terms such as these, to prefer fighting you in a war—that's assuming
Fortune favours and follows the plan your proposals envisage.
Yet I'm not clear about fate, not sure whether Jupiter wishes   110
One city shared by the Tyrians and those who have sailed from
     the Troad.
Does he approve such a mixture of peoples, such union by treaties?
You, as his conjugal partner, have rights to implore him,* to fathom
What's on his mind. I'll follow, you lead!' Royal Juno responded:
'That will be my special chore. Now let me explain very briefly   115
How we will manage the task that we face. So please pay attention.
Dido, poor woman, lays down with Aeneas the plans for a wild game
Hunt in the forests tomorrow when Titan pulls back the wide world's
Covers and radiantly blazes the day's first blushes of sunrise.
While their wings flurry their flanks,* while they're setting up snares
     around clearings,   120
I'll set a blackening storm-cloud on *them*, rain mingled with hailstones
Pouring to earth from above, and I'll rumble the whole sky with
     thunder.
All their companions will scatter; they'll vanish, disguised by the
     darkness.

Dido and Troy's chief will come down together inside the same
    cavern.
I'll be there too. And, if I am sure *you'll* co-operate freely,   125
I'll designate her as his, join them both in a durable marriage.*
This is the day they'll be wed.' Cytherea voiced no opposition,
Nodded assent, then laughed. She had seen through these obvious
    ruses.

Golden Aurora, surging aloft, left the damp bed of Ocean.
Out from the gates, as sun's rays rose, rode a youthful select corps,   130
Then came a torrent of fine nets, snares, broad iron-tipped hunting
Javelins, troops of Massylian horse, and scent-catching dog power.
Still in her boudoir, the queen takes time; the elite Punic nobles
Crowd at her doorway and wait. And her steed stands waiting, but
    wildly
Champing its froth-covered bit, quite resplendent in gold and in
    purple.   135
Finally, she makes her entrance, attended by hosts of retainers,
Draped in Sidonian fabric with needlework fringes, her shoulders
Armed with a quiver of gold, hair clasped by a golden tiara,
Cloaked in a bright purple mantle secured by a brooch-pin of pure
    gold.
Clusters of Phrygian friends come along; the delighted Iulus,   140
Too. But most lovely of all, outshining the others, Aeneas
Joins with the host as an ally and merges his troops with their columns.
  He's like Apollo, deserting his wintertime home by the Lycian
Streams of the Xanthus to visit his mother's homeland of Delos,
Where he's the sponsor of ritual dance. Round his altars there
    mingle   145
Cretans, tattooed Agathyrsians, Dryopes, all celebrating.
He strides the ridges of Cynthus above, and to pin his loose tresses,
Twines supple branches to fashion a garland, secures them with
    gold loops.
High on his back, arrows rattle. Aeneas is no less impressive,
Riding among, yet surpassing the others and regal in splendour.   150
  Once they have reached high mountain terrain past the end of the
    footpaths,
Look, wild she-goats, dislodged from the ledges of rock at the
    summit,
Leap down the ridges; and there, racing out from a different direction,

Deer run a course down the mountains and then fan out into columns
Pounding up dust as they bound in their flight across open expanses. 155
Down in the heart of the valley, the youthful Ascanius passes
This group and that, at a gallop. He's thrilled by his horse's quick
     spirit,
Prays that among these helpless herds of unchallenging livestock,
He'll find a wild boar leaving the heights, or a tawny-backed lion.
     Meanwhile the massive rumbling of thunder begins to roil turmoil 160
All through the heavens. Then follows a cloudburst of rain mixed
     with hailstones.
Tyrian troopers and Troy's young warriors mingle at random,
Venus's Dardan grandson too, all hunt in fear for such scattered
Shelter as fields offer. Now it is rivers that rush down the mountains!
Dido and Troy's chief come down together inside the same cavern. 165
Earth gives the sign that the rites have begun, as does Juno, the nuptial
Sponsor. The torches are lightning, the shrewd sky's brilliance* is
     witness,
Hymns for the wedding are howling moans of the nymphs upon high
     peaks.

That first day* caused death, that first day began the disasters.
Dido no longer worries about how it looks or what rumour 170
Says, and no longer thinks of enjoying a secret liaison.
Now she is calling it marriage; she's veiling her sin with a title.

Out in a flash through Libya's cities Rumour is blazing.
No other evil is swifter than she. Rumour's being is fuelled
By her mobility, gaining additional strength as she travels. 175
Not very fearsome at first, she's soon puffs large on the breezes,
Striding the ground, but thrusting her head up high into cloud-caps.
Earth was her mother, they say, bearing this last child in her angry
Spite at the gods. Thus Coeus, Enceladus too, got a sister
Fast on her feet, and provided with wings of astonishing power, 180
Huge and horrendous, a monster whose body conceals beneath feathers
Just the same number of spying eyes (a remarkable feature),
Just the same number of tongues, and of mouths, and of ears pricked
     to eavesdrop.
Flying at night between heaven and earth, she screeches through
     darkness,
Nor does she grant any sweetness of sleep to her eyes ever searching. 185

Seated by day, she does sentinel duty aloft on a rooftop,
Or, up in some tall tower, ripples terror through powerful cities,
Clinging to fiction and falsehood as often as telling the plain truth.
Now, she is flooding the people with many crosscurrents of gossip,
Singing of things done, things not done, without any distinction: 190
That some man named Aeneas has come; that his bloodline is Trojan.
That lovely Dido is deeming it proper to join herself with him;
That they are passing long winter hours in the high life together;
Cupid's slaves in a shameless love, their kingdoms forgotten.
Such is the gossip the foul goddess* scatters at random on men's
    tongues.   195
  Quickly, she twisted her devious course to the ruler Iarbas,
Kindled his spirit with words, added more words, fuelling his anger.
Born of a raped Garamantian wood-nymph and fathered by
    Ammon,*
This man erected a hundred enormous temples, a hundred
Altars in Jupiter's honour, all over his far-reaching kingdom,   200
There dedicating eternal flames, gods' vigilant sentries,
Floors rich with animal blood, doors blooming with garlands of all
    kinds.
Rumour dissolves his aroused love in sourness and razes his reason.
He, it's said, falls to his knees, amidst gods at their altars,* a
    changed man.
Desperate, hands stretched upward to Jupiter, pleading intently: 205
'Mightiest Jupiter, you to whom Moors make our first dedications
When, as we feast on our tapestried couches, we honour the
    winepress:
Father, do *you* see *this*? Or are *we* quite needlessly trembling
Each time you spin off a thunderbolt? Is it just unseeing, cloud-borne
Fire that frightens our souls, compounded by meaningless rumbles?   210
Here is a woman who wandered within our borders, and founded,
Cash down, a very small city. We gave her a few coastal ploughlands,
Leased on a contract. And then she rejected our offer of marriage,
Took in Aeneas, and made him her master and lord of her kingdom.
Helped by his eunuch entourage,* this latter-day Paris,   215
Chin kept in place by Maeonian bows, and his hair by conditioning
Perfumes, controls what he's raped. We, meanwhile, consecrate
    offerings
Made in your temples, and place our faith in what's just idle Rumour.'*
  He, with his prayer so phrased, and tenacious presence at altars,

Caught the Almighty's ears; Jove's eyes blazed round to the royal   220
Walls and to lovers blind to their need of more favourable rumours.
Speaking to Mercury, then, he dispatched him with some such
     instructions:
'Get under way, wake the zephyrs, my son, let your wings glide you
     downwards!
Speak to the Dardan leader, who's now lodged in Tyrian Carthage,
Wasting time with no thought or respect for the cities that fate's
     words   225
Grant him. Deliver my dictates now through the swift-flowing breezes:
That's not the kind of behaviour that loveliest Venus, his mother,
Promised us. God knows,* it wasn't for *this* that she saved him from
     Greek spears
Twice. Wasn't he once supposed to make *Italy* pregnant with empires,
Seething with wars, to rule *her*, sire *there* a new breed out of noble   230
Teucer's blood, and to force the entire world under his law's yoke?
If, then, the glory of such great deeds doesn't fire up his spirit,
Being indifferent himself to the plaudits earned by this hard work,
Can he, a father, with envious eye, begrudge Rome to Ascanius?*
What does he hope he can build* by delay in this enemy nation,   235
Sparing no thought for Ausonian sons and Lavinian ploughlands?
Tell him to sail. That's final. Let this serve him notice of our will.'
   So he spoke. And the other prepared to obey these parental
Orders.* He first straps boots to his feet. They are ankle-high, golden,
And, having wings, take him upwards in flight over seas, over
     dry land,   240
Swift as a rising current of air. Next he picks up his special
Wand, which he uses to call up the pale, wan spirits from Orcus,*
Or to dispatch others down below earth, into Tartarus' grimness.
With it, he gives or takes sleep, makes eyes remain open on deathbeds,
And, with its help, he can navigate winds, weather turbulent
     cloudbanks.   245
Now, as he swoops, he discerns both the summit and steep flanks
     of rugged
Atlas, who levers aloft, on his peak, all the weight of the heavens,
Atlas, whose pine-covered head* is eternally banded with storm
     clouds,
Battered by wind and by rain. Round his shoulders is strewn a mantle
Thickened with snowfall; and down from the chin of this elderly
     being   250

Cataracts plunge, and his beard-bristle freezes to icicled stiffness.
Here Mount Cyllene's god, powered in on his glistening paired wings,
First touched down. From there, powered out by the weight of his
    body,
Seaward he dived like a tern, who's been circling shorelines and cliff
    pools
Teeming with fish, skimming wave-tops. In turn, one knowingly
    pictures   255
How Cyllene's child now descended from his own maternal
Grandfather, feathered his flight between heaven and earth to the sandy
Coastland of Libya, cleaving his winding way through the breezes.
  Then the god, just as his winged feet land in the outskirts* of
    Carthage,
Glimpses Aeneas constructing defences, refurbishing houses,*   260
Wearing a sword with a star-speckled inlay of yellow-green jasper,
Shoulders ablaze with a trailing mantle of Tyrian purple,
Wealthy Dido's tribute of honour, the work of her own hands,
Threaded with highlights of fine-spun gold worked into the
    cross-weave.*
Instantly on the attack: '*You*, laying foundations for mighty   265
Carthage!' he said. 'Obsessed with your wife, you're now building
    a lovely
City for her. You've forgotten your own obligations and kingdom!
Heaven's own king, who spins both the sky and the earth with his
    power,
Sends me to you himself, directly from gleaming Olympus,
Tells me himself to convey these instructions through swift-moving
    breezes: 270
What do you hope you can build, you deserter,* in Libya's deserts?
If, in fact, glory from such great deeds doesn't fire up your spirit,
Being indifferent yourself to the plaudits earned by this hard work,
Think of the growing Ascanius, the dreams for Iulus to cherish.
He is your heir. Thus Rome's fine earth and Italy's kingship   275
Stand as his due.' The Cyllenian addressed him in just such a manner,
Yet, before all had been said, much less answered, he fled mortal
    vision,
Vanished away* in the thinness of air, far distant from eyesight.
  Not that Aeneas could have replied. For the sight left him
    speechless,
Senses lost, hair bristling in shock, voice frozen in locked jaws.   280

Still, though, he burns to get out, to escape from the lands that
    delight him,
Stunned by the mighty force of the gods' commandment and warning,
Wondering what he should do, how he'd dare to get round the besotted
Ruler* with some explanation, or find ways of broaching the subject.
This way and that, he channelled his swift mind, testing his options,   285
Every alternative he could conceive. He approached from all angles.
This, as his thoughts vacillated, appeared the most forceful decision:
So he calls Mnestheus, Sergestus as well, and the valiant Serestus;
Then, he instructs them to refit the ships, muster crews on the
    seashore,
Ready their weapons. *No word must get out*. The entire
    re-equipment   290
Must be disguised. In the meantime, since excellent Dido knew
    nothing,
And wouldn't dream that their great love affair* was in fact being
    shattered,
He would himself test out some approaches, and find the most tactful
Times for a talk, and how best he could frame it. Reaction was instant.
Each obeyed orders and followed instructions. They all were
    delighted.*   295

Still though, the queen detected his ruse. Who *could* fool a lover?*
Scared because things seemed safe, she discovered his plans for
    departure
First. Rumour, ever unrighteous, informed on him, telling the furious
Ruler the navy was being refitted and readied for sailing.
Mind now out of control, all ablaze, she screams through the
    city,   300
Bacchic in fury, resembling a Thyiad* frenzied by brandished
Thyrsus and loud Bacchic cries when Thebes' biennial orgies
Madden her soul, when Cithaeron's voice howls shrill in the night-time.
Finally, *she* broached the subject, addressing Aeneas as follows:
'Was it your hope to *disguise*, you perfidious* cheat, such a
    monstrous   305
Wrong, to get out, *with no word said*, from this land that I govern?
You are not bound by our union of love, by the hand you once
    gave me,
Nor does Dido, doomed to a cruel death,* now detain you.
Why so much work on your fleet? Constellations tell us it's winter,

Yet you are rushing to put out to sea, cruel man, while the north
    winds   310
Rule. Why is this? Were you not in pursuit of some other man's
    ploughlands,
Unknown homes, and if ancient Troy were still in existence,
Would Troy, then, be the goal for your fleet on the water's
    expanses?
Could you be running from me? Let me urge you, with tears, by
    your right hand
(Thanks to my pitiful conduct that's all I have left now to swear by),   315
Urge you by love we have shared, by the steps we have taken to
    marriage:
If I have ever earned your thanks for services rendered,
Or given you any pleasure, I beg you, if prayer still has meaning,
Pity this falling house, shrug off your present intention.
Libyan tribesmen, nomad sheikhs all loathe me. The Tyrians   320
Hate me on your account; and on your account I have ruined
My sole claim to a stellar distinction: my chastity's good name,
Once honoured, even by Rumour. I'm dying, and yet you desert me,
Houseguest—the lone name left for the man I called "partner in
    marriage".*
What should I wait for? My brother Pygmalion's attack on my city?   325
Or till I'm captured and wed by Gaetulia's monarch, Iarbas?
If I'd at least, before you ran off, conceived from our closeness
Some child fathered by you, if there just were a baby Aeneas*
Playing inside my halls, whose face might in some way recall you,
I would not feel so wholly trapped yet wholly deserted.'   330
    That's what she said. He, conscious, however, of Jupiter's warning,
Never once blinked, and he struggled to keep his anxiety stifled
Deep in his heart. Yet he briefly replied: 'That I owe you, my ruler,*
All you could list in your speech I would never deny. You have
    earned it.
Memory will never elicit regret for my missing Elissa*   335
While I remember myself, while my spirit rules in this body!
Now, a few words in defence.* This escape: slipping out like a bandit,
That was *not* what I hoped. Don't *twist* my words. And I never
Formally wed you nor did I endorse any contract as "husband".
If fate's orders allowed me to live out the life of my choosing,   340
Putting my anguish to rest as I myself would have wanted,
Troy is the city where I'd be now, looking after my own folk's

Relics and remnants; the great house of Priam would still stand in
     spirit,
My own hands would have rebuilt Pergamum's shrines for the
     vanquished.
But, great Italy now is the land that Apollo of Grynia   345
And Lycian oracles tell me to seize, it is Italy's great land.
This is my love and my homeland. If you, since you are a Phoenician,
Focus your gaze on the towers of Carthage, your Libyan city,
Why does the vision of Teucrians settling the land of Ausonia
Evil your eye? We too have the right to seek overseas kingdoms.   350
Each time night cloaks earth with opaque, dank shadows of spectral
Darkness, and fire-born stars rise upwards, my father, Anchises'
Angry face* in my dreams chastises me, stalks me with terror,
As does my son, Ascanius. The damage I've done his dear person!
Cheating him out of his destined Hesperian kingdom and croplands!   355
Jupiter now has dispatched his divine intercessor, who bears me
Personal orders, I swear by them both, through the swift-blowing
     breezes.
I myself, in clear day's light, saw Mercury enter
These very walls, and my own ears heard each word he was saying.
Stop enraging me, and yourself, with all this complaining.   360
Going to Italy's not my choice.'*
     Such was his tally of words. For a while, she just watched him
          obliquely,
Eyes flashing this way and that as he spoke, scrutinizing at random
His whole being with silent looks. Then her anger exploded:
'No goddess gave you birth, no Dardanus authored your bloodline!   365
Caucasus, jagged with flint, fathered *you*—in Hyrcania! Savage
Tigresses stuck their teats in your mouth, you perfidious liar!
Why disguise what I feel, hold back, knowing worse is to follow?
When I wept, did he groan, did he soften his glance or surrender,
Conquered by torrents of tears? Did he pity the woman who
     loved him?   370
Which thought shall I express first? It's clear neither mightiest Juno
Nor Saturn's son, the great Father, looks fairly at this situation.
Nowhere can one treat trust as secure. I found you in dire need,
Shipwrecked; and, fool that I was, I gave you a share in my kingdom,
Brought back the fleet you'd lost, at the same time saving your
     comrades.   375
Oh, I am burning with fury! Now: enter Apollo the Augur;

Lycian oracles next; then, in person, Jupiter sending
Gods' intercessor down, bringing hideous commands through the
    breezes.
Maybe this *is* a dilemma for powers above, anguish to trouble
Their deep inertia.
                'I won't try to keep you, or craft a rebuttal.   380
Go with the winds! Pursue Italy! Chase across seas for your kingdoms!
My hope, if righteous forces prevail, is that, out on some mid-sea
Reefs, you'll drink retribution in deep draughts, often invoking
Dido's name. When I'm absent, I'll chase you with dark fire!
    When cold death
Snaps away body from soul, evil man, my dank ghost will haunt you.   385
My destination is yours. There'll be no impunity. You'll pay.
Tireless Rumour will come to my buried remains. I will hear her.'

Breaking away before all had been said, she escaped from the outside
Breezes. She felt quite sick, as she turned and then fled from his
    vision.
He was left trapped: hesitating through fear to say much, and yet
    so much   390
Wanting to speak. Dido's failing limbs were supported by handmaids
Back to her marbled chamber and there set to rest on her mattress.
Righteous Aeneas, much as he wished he could soften her angry
Pain by consoling her grief and find words to rechannel her anguish,
Much as he groaned and felt shaken at heart by the great force of
    love's power,*   395
Nonetheless followed the gods' commands, and returned to his navy.
   That's when the Teucrians fell to their work, started hauling the
    tall ships
Down to the far-stretched beaches, where hulls were retarred and
    refloated.
Eager to launch, crews brought in, as timber for oarage and planking,
Leaf-covered branches and unhewn trunks.   400
Into and out of the city you'd see them, everywhere, streaming.
Ants getting ready for winter* do this: they attack an enormous
Mountain of grain and they carry it off to provision their anthill.
Spanning fields, their black formation snakes across grassland,
Hauling spoils: one long slim track. Some lever and trundle   405
Monstrous kernels, shoulders strained; some enforce the formation,
Bullying idlers along, their entire path seething with labour.

Dido, what did you feel when you noted and watched this
    commotion?
Oh, what groans you expressed, looking out from the citadel's summit:
Seeing the shore set aboil, and the whole expanse of the water   410
Stretching before your eyes churn choppy and noisy in uproar!
Ruthless Love! Hearts break, humans die. How far must you force us?
Dido is forced once again into tears, once again attempts pleading,
Bending her pride to its knees before love. For she wants to leave
    nothing
Unexplored to ensure that her long-doomed death isn't
    pointless.   415
'Anna, you see how the shore now seethes as they hurry departure.
In they come, this way and that; furled canvas keens for the breezes,
Sailors are happy, festooning the vessels with garlands of flowers.
Sister, if I've had the personal strength to foresee this intense pain,
I'll have the strength to endure it. But Anna, I'm miserable,
    help me!   420
Do me this last honour. You're the sole person his perfidy visits,
Trusts with his innermost secrets.* This makes you the sole person
    expert
As to the when and the how of making him tactful approaches.
Go, my sister, and speak to our proud-hearted foe as a suppliant.
I wasn't with the Danaäns in Aulis when they vowed to wrench
    Troy   425
Up by its roots, and Pergamum wasn't attacked by my navy;
I didn't dig up the ashes and ghost of his father Anchises.
Why, then, does he refuse to admit my words to his harsh ears?
Why the great haste? Let him grant his poor lover this final concession:
Simply to wait for an easy escape and for winds in his favour.   430
It's not our long-gone marriage, which he has betrayed, that I'm
    begging,
Nor that he live without lovely Latium or give up his kingdom.
Time's what I ask, nothing tangible: space for my frenzy to calm down,
So, now I'm beaten, misfortune can train me to cope with my anguish.
This is the final extension I beg (please pity your sister);   435
If he approves, I'll repay him, with interest, when my time expires.'*
   Such her insistent plea; and such lamentations her sister,
Saddest of all, has to act, re-enact. To laments, he proves passive,
Motionless; and to their voices, the words that he hears, unresponsive.
Fate blocks, god obstructs what he, as a man, would hear calmly.   440

So, in the Alps, wild gales from the north gust this way and that way,
Vying among themselves to uproot some vigorous oak tree,
Massive with centuries' growth: there's a roar, and the uppermost foliage
Flies off and carpets the ground as the trunk shudders. Yet the old
    oak tree
Sticks to the crags;* and as high as its crest reaches up towards
    heaven's   445
Brightness, its roots stretch down just as low into Tartarus' darkness.
Such was the pounding of voices, this way and that way, the hero
Underwent ceaselessly; he, in his great heart, felt all the anguish.
But, in his mind, he remained unmoved; tears flood, but are wasted.

Dido, denied fulfilment as doom closes in, bringing terror,   450
Now begs for death. It is wearying torture to look at the arched skies.
And what resolved her to work for this goal and escape from the
    day's light
Was that while setting her gifts upon altars smoky with incense,
She saw an omen grim to describe: for the sanctified water
Blackened, the wine poured out transformed into sickening
    blood-clots.   455
No one was told of *this* prodigy. No, not her very own sister.
Further, there was in the palace a marble temple that honoured
Dido's previous husband, which she maintained with astounding
Care, decorated with snow-white fleeces and festival garlands.
From it, she thought she could hear both the voice and the words
    of her husband   460
Calling, when night held earth in the anxious grip of its darkness.
High on a rooftop, a lone screech owl keened death in repeated
Dirges, and wailed shrill cries drawn out into pulses of sobbing.
Many predictions of old-time seers with their hideous warnings
Deepened her terror. Aeneas, a ravenous beast in her fevered   465
Nightmares, hunted her down. Yet she seemed ever wandering lonely
Endless paths, left all by herself without any companion,
Looking, alone, for her Tyrian people in desolate landscapes.*
She was like Pentheus, stripped of his mind, seeing armies of Furies,
Seeing the sole sun* double, and Thebes in a duplicate presence;   470
Like Agamemnon's child, driven mad in a drama: Orestes,
Fleeing his mother who's armoured with flames and with dark
    hissing serpents,
While, at the door of the palace, avenging Furies sit waiting.*

She, then, in total surrender to pain, became pregnant with
    madness.
Passing sentence of death, she determines the time and the
    method   475
In her own counsels. Yet she, when addressing her sorrowful sister,
Masks all trace of her plans and presents a facade of serene hope.
'*I've* found a way, dear soulmate (so say "Well done!" to your sister).
I'll either get him back, or get rid of the love that he causes.
Close by Ocean's edge, near to sunset, lies the remotest   480
Outpost of Ethiopian rule. It's where Atlas the mighty
Spins sky's sphere, all studded with burning stars, on his shoulders.
Someone has just let me know of a priestess from there, a Massylian,
Once warden of the Hesperides' shrine, in charge there of feeding
Food to the dragon, and guarding the tree with the magical
    branches.   485
Using a mixture of honey and sleep-bringing opium poppy,*
She, with the right spells, claims she can liberate minds when she
    chooses,
But that, in others, her power can induce intractable anguish.
Hers is the power to stop rivers, reverse heaven's stars in rotation.
She makes dead spirits stalk dark night; you'll see the earth
    rumbling   490
Under your feet; you'll see ash trees striding down from the
    mountains.
Dearest, I swear by the gods and by you, by your sweet life, my
    soulmate,
I didn't want to invite and embrace such practice of magic.
  'Build me, in secret, an open-air pyre in our innermost courtyard.
Then place upon it the arms of the man, which that unrighteous
    villain   495
Fixed on our bedroom walls, other gear he cast off, and the bridal
Bed where I came to my grief. The idea is to kill, says the priestess,
All of the odious memories that impious man left to haunt me.'
After these words, she fell silent; her cheeks were invaded by pallor.
  Anna, for her part, didn't believe that her soulmate was
    shrouding   500
Her death with these novel cults. Anna's mind can't conceive such
    obsessive
Madness, and fears nothing worse than occurred at the death of
    Sychaeus.

She, then, acts as instructed.

Now, though, the queen, once her pyre is complete in the innermost
    sanctum,
Stacked sky-high in the open with logs cut from ilex and pitch-pine,
Strews the location with wreaths, festoons it with funeral garlands. 506
Over it, she sets a bed with the gear he has left, his abandoned
Sword, and his person, in effigy*—knowing full well what will
    happen.
Altars are built all round. Then a priestess, hair flowing freely,
Thunders by name three hundred gods plus Erebus, Chaos,   510
Hecate's trinity, all three faces of virgin Diana.
Water, symbolic of death and Avernus,* is used for lustration,
Fresh young herbs are obtained, lactating with juice of black venom,
Sickled with curved bronze blades and gathered at night in the
    moonlight.
Also sought is the love-charm torn, at birth, from a colt's head,   515
Taken before its mother can snatch it.
She, hands righteously cleansed, offers sacred grain at the altars,
Wearing her clothes, and one of her sandals, loose and unknotted.
Death-doomed, she calls upon gods and the fate-telling stars to
    bear witness,
Prays to a power that is just (if there is one), a power that
    remembers,   520
Whose jurisdiction embraces all lovers with one-sided contracts.

Night reigned: all through the world tired bodies were harvesting
    tranquil
Slumber. The woods and the savage seas lay calmed into stillness,
Stars at this hour were midway along their rolling procession.
Each flock in each field is quiet, and all of the bright-painted birdlife, 525
Species at large on the liquid lakes or the rough rural thickets,
Nestle themselves into sleep beneath night-time's blanket of silence.
Fears are now gentled and hearts now lost to the memory of struggles.
Not so the unfulfilled of soul, the descendant of Phoenix:*
Never was she set drifting in sleep; she never did welcome   530
Night with her eyes or her heart. Her anguish redoubles and her love,
Rising again, flares wild as she tosses on flood tides of anger.
Then this notion took hold in her heart and she span thoughts
    around it:

'What am I doing? Come on! Shall I check out my previous suitors?
How they'd laugh! Should I beg on my knees just to marry a nomad   535
When I've so often disdained them all as possible suitors?
    'Or, shall I follow the Ilian fleet—and Teucrian orders?
That's what's left, is it? They will agree since I aided them earlier,
They will be grateful for past good treatment. But *will* they
    remember?
Who'll let me come, who'll take me aboard their proud sailing
    vessels?   540
Hate for me speaks in their eyes. Don't you know, mad fool, don't
    you sense it?
Perjury's quite a tradition among Laomedon's people!

'What? Be a runaway woman alone among jubilant sailors?
Well then, suppose I'm protected by all my Tyrians, full force?

'These are the same troops it took all my efforts to root out of
    Sidon,   545
Must I again force them onto the seas and command them to hoist sail?

'Just go and die! You deserve to. Go parry your pain with a steel blade!

'*You*, sister, *you* gave in to my tears, *you* burdened my raving
Soul with its first load of evil. You served me up to my foeman!
Out of the question, you said, that I should, with no scandal,
    but no mate,   550
Eke out a bestial life that avoided the hint of such anguish.
I then broke every promise I made to Sychaeus's ashes.'
Such was the voice of her grief breaking forth from her heart's
    desolation.

High on his aft-deck, Aeneas, his business duly accomplished,
Sure he could now set sail, was reaping a harvest of slumber.   555
Then, some shape of a god* represented itself to his dreaming
Mind, coming back, the same look in his eye, again seeming to warn him.
Every detail suggested Mercury: yes, the complexion,
Sound of the voice, blond hair, and the limbs so young and attractive:
'Son of the goddess, how *can* you take charge, in this crisis, by
    sleeping?   560
Don't you detect, then, the dangers that have you completely encircled?

Don't your ears tell you, you madman, that zephyrs, that fair winds,
    are blowing?
She's got some ruse in her heart, she has some atrocity brewing;
She's set on dying, she's rousing the changeable tides of her anger.
Why aren't you getting out fast while a fast getaway's still an option?   565
Soon you'll see timber churn up waves, massed menacing firebrands
Burst into flame, beaches leap with the fires of a blazing inferno,
If, that is, dawn's light catches you still hanging round in this country!
Hang the delays!* What you face is a complex and changeable constant:
Woman.' When he'd said this, he mingled himself with the dark
    night.   570

    Terrified now by this sudden upsurge of phantoms, Aeneas
Snatches his body from sleep, then awakens and haggles his
    crewmen:
'Wake up and get up, my lads, settle down to your oars on the benches,
Set all sail! Make it quick! Yet again a god sent down from heaven
Urgently drives us to speed our departure and cut through the
    looping   575
Hawsers. Whoever you are, holy god, we follow you gladly
And, yet again, we obey your command with a feeling of triumph!
Stay by our side, we implore, treat us kindly, provide us auspicious
Stars in the sky.' So he spoke. And he pulled out his blade like a
    sudden
Lightning flash* from its sheath and with bared steel sheared
    through the moorings.   580
All feel the same fire instantly, grab their equipment and make haste.
Coasts are already astern, sea's surface concealed by the navy.
Straining backs and arms churn foam, oars sweep the blue waters.

Dawn was by now beginning to stipple the earth with new brightness,
Leaving Tithonus' saffron bed. From her watchtower, the ruler   585
Watched as the early light whitened and noticed the fleet under full sail*
Standing seaward, well under way, and observed that the empty
Coastline displayed not a single oarsman strolling the harbours.
    Three times, four times she pounds on her beautiful breast, and
    rips golden
Hair from her head by the roots. 'Oh Jupiter! Shall this intruder   590
Go on his way,' she exclaims, 'mocking me and the power of my
    kingdom?
Get a force fitted, pursue them with all of our city's resources,

Others must haul out our vessels from storage docks. Go to it, right
    now!
Hurry, bring fire, issue weapons, have rowers press hard upon oarlocks!
  'What am I saying? Where *am* I? What madness is warping my
    reason? 595
Unfulfilled Dido, your unrighteous acts come to haunt you!*
When action *was* the appropriate course,* you were giving him
    your power.
  'Witness the word and the honour of one, who, they say, carries
    with him,
Gods of ancestral shrines, who once took on his shoulders his agèd
Father! Could *I* not have taken him off, torn his body to pieces, 600
Scattered it over the sea, or murdered his comrades, and even
Served up Ascanius himself as a treat for his banqueting father?*
If war'd ensued, though, the outcome was not, and could not have
    been,* certain.
Whom did I fear? I was going to die. I'd have torched his encampment,
Filled up his holds with my fires, and once I'd extinguished the
    father, 605
Child, and the whole of his race, I'd have thrown myself onto the
    bonfire.
  'Sun: your cleansing flames survey all earthly endeavours!
Juno: you sense, and are my intercessor in, all of my anguish!
Hecate: your name is howled by night throughout cities, at crossroads!
Demons of vengeance, gods of the dying, forgotten Elissa!* 610
Take it all in, focus your divine will, as you should, on my sufferings.
Hear what I pray. If it *must* be that this indescribable person
Makes it to port, that he floats back to dry land, and if this is really
Jupiter's last word on fate and he *must* reach the goal of his journey,
Let him be hammered in war* by the armies of valiant people, 615
Forced from his borders, torn far away from Iulus' embraces.
Let him beg help, let him watch as his men are disgracefully
    slaughtered!
When he surrenders himself to an unjust peace and its strict terms,
Grant him no joy in his realm or the light he so loves. Let him
    lie dead,
Well before his due day, halfway up a beach and unburied. 620
This is my prayer; these final words I express with my life-blood:
Tyrians, drive with relentless hate against *his* stock and every
Future brood, and dispatch them as ritual gifts to my ashes.*

No love must ever exist between our two peoples, no treaties.
Rise from my bones, my avenger—and there *will be* an
    avenger!—   625
So you can hound these Dardan settlers with hot fire and cold steel,
Now, or some day in the future, whenever that strength coalesces.
Menace of coast against coast and of waters hurled against waters,
Arms against arms, I invoke. Let them fight, they themselves and
    their grandsons!'
  This said, she started to let her thoughts wander in every
    direction,   630
Seeking to douse, just as soon as she could douse, the light she
    detested.
Then she spoke briefly to Barce,* who'd once served as nurse to
    Sychaeus—
Her nurse was back in the old homeland where her ashes were buried.
'Please bring Anna to me, nurse dear to me, get me my sister.
Tell her to hurry and sprinkle her body with fresh-flowing
    water,   635
And to bring with her the cattle and placatory gifts designated.
Please have her come. You yourself should righteously ribbon your
    temples.
This is for Stygian Jupiter's rites:* I intend to complete them.
All the first steps I have duly prepared. I will now end my anguish
And set flames to the pyre of that cursed Dardanian creature.'   640
Done. The nurse used any speed old feet still had to assist her.

Dido, fearful yet crazed at the ghastly extent of her planning,
Frantically glances about her with bloodshot gaze, and impending
Death now discolours her quivering cheeks with its pallor and blotches.
Bursting through doors to the innermost courtyard in frenzy, she
    clambers   645
Up to the top of the pyre, then unsheathes the Dardanian swordblade.
This was the special gift she'd requested, but not for this purpose.
Here, catching sight of the Ilian clothing and bed so familiar,
She, for an instant, delayed deadly purpose in tears and reflection,
Fell, ghostlike, on the bed where she uttered a few final phrases: 650
'Spoils that were so sweet once, while fate and its god gave permission,
Take to yourselves this soul. Cut me loose from all of this anguish.
Fortune assigned me a course. I have run it. My life is accomplished,
And now the image of me that will pass beneath earth has its greatness.

I've laid the ground for a famous city; I've seen my own walls rise,   655
I have avenged my husband and punished my brother, my foeman.
So fulfilled, fulfilled to excess if only Dardanian
Vessels had never, oh never, touched in on the shores of my country.'
This said, she pressed her face to the covers: 'We'll die without
      vengeance,
But let us die! This is it, this the path that I choose to the dead
      world.   660
This is the fire that, far out to sea, the cruel Dardanian's
Eyes must absorb. He must carry with him these omens of our death.'*
   Such were her words; and while she was speaking, attendants
      observed her
Slumped on the sword, saw the blade foam streaming blood from
      her body,
Saw that her hands were drenched. And their cry soared high
      through the courtyard's   665
Open roof. Rumour now raged wild through a city left bludgeoned.
Homes are a chaos of noises: laments, groans, keening of women.
Skies far above re-echo the breast-drumming, grief-stricken sobbing,
Rather as if, after enemy forces had breached the defences,
Carthage or ancient Tyre faced final collapse,* and the raging   670
Flames rolled in over rooftops of mortal men and immortals.
   Hearing the uproar in terror, her soul now lost to her body,*
Panicked, her sister tore through the crowds, nails clawing her features,
Fists beating breasts, and she called her by name as she lay there,
      expiring:
'This was your scheme, dear soulmate? Your fraud had *me* as its
      target?   675
That's what this pyre meant for me? That's what altars and fires were
      preparing?
What, now you've left me, should I protest first? Have you not spurned
      your sister's
Friendship in dying like this? If you'd called me to share in the same
      death,
Then the same pain from the sword, the same hour would have killed
      us together.
My hands built this pyre, my voice called out to our fathers'   680
Gods. Did you cruelly arrange that I'd not be attending your deathbed?
You've killed me and yourself, the Sidonian people and senate,
Sister, your city as well. Give me water to cleanse all these gashes;

If any breath should stray from her mouth in its final expression,
Let me absorb it in mine.' Before ending, she'd mounted the
    towering   685
Steps, nestled snug in her lap her now half-animate soulmate,
Groaned as she blotted the blood's dark flow with the clothes she was
    wearing.
Dido attempted to lift heavy eyes once again, but her body
Failed her. The wounding sword, jammed deep, rasped hard on her
    ribcage.
Three times she rose up and she propped herself up on her forearm,   690
Three times she slumped back on the couch as her eyes, in their
    wandering,
Searched for the light high up in the sky; then she moaned when
    they found it.
  Juno Almighty pitied her difficult death with its painful
Anguish long drawn out, and dispatched to her, down from Olympus,
Iris, to unmoor her struggling soul from the limbs' web of bondage.   695
Dido was dying a death that was neither deserved nor predestined,
But premature: a poor woman, swept up by the quick fire of madness.
So, as Prosperpina hadn't yet taken the locks of her golden
Tresses, and thereby consigned her being to Stygian Orcus,
Iris, rosy with dew, skimmed down through the sky upon crocus   700
Wings. And her wake, as she passed by the sun, traced colours in
    thousands.
Standing by Dido's head, she spoke: 'I take, as instructed,
Locks consecrated to Dis. I untether your self from your body.'
Then, as her right hand severed the hair, all warmth escaped Dido;
And as it did, life fluttered away from her into the breezes.   705

BOOK FIVE

Meanwhile,* Aeneas was holding a steady course with his navy,
Confident, even while cutting through waves growing dark
    from the north wind's
Gusts, and while gazing back at the city ablaze with Elissa
Burning, unfulfilled. What ignited this huge conflagration
Lurked unexplained. But great love's pain, edged sharp by betrayal,   5
That is proverbial; as is what a woman can do in her fury.
Teucrians, then, in their hearts, made a grim assessment of omens.

Now, as their vessels gained boundless seas, as they sighted no further
Land, saw sea this way, that way saw only the heavens,
Rain clouds, black as the deep, formed over their heads, bringing
    with them   10
Night-time and winter gales, waves shuddering, dappled with darkness.*
High on the stern, Palinurus, the helmsman, reacted:
'Odd how this storm-belt has blocked out the sunlight from every
    direction—
Ah! father Neptune, what are you about?' When he'd said this, he
    ordered
Tackling rendered secure, oars manned, plied swiftly and stoutly.   15
Then, when he'd shifted his canvas aslant to the wind, he continued:
'Great as your soul is, Aeneas, I'd not hope for Italy given
These skies, even if Jupiter swore me a personal promise.
Winds have veered, blowing wild, broadside from the west where the
    sky's dark,
Rising fast. The air's humid and densely compressed into fog banks.   20
Can't even ride out *these* crosswinds, much less try to fight them.
So, since we're left to the mercy of Fortune, it's wiser to follow,
Steering our course where she calls. Now I think we're not far
    from your brother
Eryx's coasts.* You can trust them, and trust a Sicilian harbour.
All's well if I can recall and re-plot stellar readings from last time.'   25
Righteous Aeneas said: 'I have myself been observing, for some hours,
How the winds force this upon us, how vainly you've battled for
    headway.
Alter your course. I doubt I could find any land more delightful,

Or any place that I'd rather put in with my sea-weary vessels.
This land has treated my Dardan comrade, Acestes, so kindly,　　30
And, in its bosom, embraces the bones of my father Anchises.'
This said, they head for the port; as they sail on, favouring zephyrs
Belly their canvas taut; so the fleet speeds swift on the sea's swell.
Finally, gratefully, pulling ashore on familiar beaches.

　　Far away, high on a mountain crest, Acestes,* astonished,　　35
Saw the approaching fleet was an ally's and ran down to meet it,
Shaggily bristling with spears and the pelt of a Libyan sow-bear.
Son of a Trojan mother he was; Crimisus, the river,
Fathered his life. Since he'd never forgotten his ancient, parental
Ties, he was happy to see and receive them with all of the treasures　　40
Farms can provide; and, with this friendly bounty, he soothes their
　　exhaustion.

When, the next morning, the stars had been routed by sunrise and
　　brilliant
Daylight, Aeneas assembled his crews from along the whole seashore.
Then, from the top of an earthen mound, he made this announcement:
'Dardanus' sons, great men who are born of the gods' noble
　　bloodline,　　45
Months have been passing. Their cycle's complete. They add up to
　　exactly
One year since we interred my divine father's bones and his relics.
Well, it will soon be the day, if I've not made a slip,* which I'll always
Cherish—you gods have so willed—as a bitter, but honoured
　　memorial.　　50
If I were spending this day as an exile in Libyan quicksands,
Or in the Argive gulf, as a prisoner held in Mycenae,
Still I would, each year, mark his passing with rituals, solemn
Prayer and processions, with suitable offerings placed on his altars.
Now, under no constraints—for the harbour we've entered is
　　friendly—　　55
We—and I don't think this happened without heaven's will and
　　gods' blessing—
Stand where my father's ashes and bones are actually buried.
Come then, let's all celebrate what makes this a happy memorial.
Ask him for winds. Let us pray that he'll want to make this day a yearly
Festival held at a shrine of his own when my city is founded.*　　60
Two head of cattle per ship, that's the gift that the noble Acestes,

True son of Troy, offers you. There's a feast! So invite your ancestral
Patron gods and the gods that Acestes, your host, honours deeply.
Further, if on the ninth day from today Aurora gives mortals
Daylight's blessing, revealing our world once again with her bright
    rays,   65
I'll set up games for the Teucrians. First, for the warships, a boat race;*
Then, for the runners: a foot race; and then, for the strong and
    aggressive,
Contests to see who's best with the spear or the light-shafted arrow.
And, for the crueller expert in leather and lead, there'll be boxing.
All of you, come. If you win, there'll be palms to show merit
    rewarded.   70
Now, show respect with your silence! Set garlands of leaves on your
    temples!'
This said, he circled his temples with myrtle, his own mother's
    sacred
Tree, as did Helymus;* so did Acestes, whom years had now ripened,
So did Ascanius, the boy, whose example the other youths followed.
From the assembly Aeneas set off for the tomb. Many thousands   75
Went with him, forming a large entourage of which he was the centre.
There, in a ritual libation, he emptied two beakers of pure, strong
Bacchus, two beakers of fresh-drawn milk, two of sacrificed beasts'
    blood,
Over the earth, scattered colourful flowers, and spoke words such as
    follow:
'Greetings to you, blessèd father, and greetings again, my dear
    parent's   80
Ashes, your ghostly remains and your spirit. I saved you for nothing.
Fate didn't let me reach Italy's coast and the farmlands we're
    promised,
Or find Ausonian Tiber*—whatever that is—in your lifetime.'
This said, there oozed from the deep-set shafts of the tomb an
    enormous
Serpent whose slithering length issued forth in the coils of its seven   85
Loops. And it rippled this sevenfold spiral, encircled the grave
    mound,
Slid between altars caressingly, calmly. Its back, stippled dark blue,
Flashed with the blaze of its gold-flecked scales like the shafts of a
    thousand
Hues of refracted sunlight fired by a rainbow at black clouds.

Then, as Aeneas, stunned by the sight, stood rooted, the serpent   90
Snaked like a long line of troops round his father's bowls,* among burnished
Goblets, and sampled the feast, ate offerings set on the altars,
Then slithered harmlessly back to within the mound's inner recesses.
  Keener still to press on with the rites for his father, Aeneas
Can't decide whether he's seen some local god* or Anchises'   95
Ghostly familiar. As ritual prescribes, he now slaughters two hoggets,
Two pigs, two black bullocks. And then there's the wine for libations,
Emptied from bowls as Aeneas invokes both the soul and the ghostly
Presence of great Anchises, released from the Acheron's waters.
Crewmen are glad to bring offerings too: each as much as his own means   100
Lets him bestow. So the altars are heaped, and the bullocks are slaughtered.
Some arrange bronze pans neatly in rows and, dispersed through the meadows,
Set live charcoal under the spits, grilling red meat and innards.

Now it's the long-expected day and the steeds of Phaëthon*
Usher that ninth Dawn in; and she's clear and she's bright to perfection.   105
Rumour gets round, and the link with Acestes' name—they all knew him—
Draws in the neighbouring peoples. The beaches are crowded and festive.
Some come to see Aeneas's folk, some to enter the contests.
First, a display of the prizes is placed in the midst of the oval
Field: votive tripods, garlands of green leaves, and, for the victors,   110
Palms; then there's armour, and garments expensively dyed with the purple
Mollusc, and silver, pounds upon pounds, plus gold by the ingot.
Trumpet-calls rasp loud from a mound in the centre: they're starting.
  Four ships picked from the fleet as a whole are to open the contest,
Well matched, heavily oared. There's the *Pristis*,* speedy and keenly   115
Crewed by its oarsmen. It's captained by Mnestheus—soon to be known as
Mnestheus of Italy. And from his name comes Memmius' bloodline.

Gyas commands the *Chimaera*,* a monster of monstrous proportions,
Big as a city and powered by Dardan youths in a threefold
Layer of tiers, whose triple-banked oars strike water together.   120
Riding a large vessel, *Centaur*, we find Sergestus,* the founder
Claimed by the Sergian clan, while Cloanthus captains the dark-blue
Scylla—and he is your Roman family's founder, Cluentius.*
  Far offshore is a reef directly facing the foaming
Beaches; and every so often, when seas swell high, when the wintry   125
Northerlies bury the stars, it's pounded and swept under water.
During a calm, when the seas lie still, it protrudes through the
       surface;
Cormorants land on its level expanses to bask in the sunlight.
Father Aeneas sets here a green marker of holm-oak in full leaf
So that the sailors will know where to turn in the long race, and
       double   130
Back for the final leg. There's a drawing of lots to determine
Who starts where, and commanders themselves are aboard on the
       aft-decks,
Clearly discerned from afar in their glistening gold-leaf and purple.
Other young people, the crew, have their foreheads shaded with
       real leaves
Shorn from a poplar. Their gleam is of oil poured thick over naked   135
Muscle. They sit, arms tensed, at the oars, packed close on the
       benches,
Tense in themselves as they wait for the start. Throbbing nerves
       and the stiffened
Lust for the promise of praise drain blood out of hearts that are
       pounding.
Then, when the clear-pitched trumpet sounds, each ship, in an instant,
Surges away from the start. And the oarsmen's shouts assault
       heaven.   140
Arms pulled back against chests as they strike set salt water foaming;
Parallel furrows are cloven in seas, whose surface is wholly
Chasmed and churned by the oars and the three-pronged beaks of
       the galleys.
Two-horse chariots don't burst forth so swiftly at races
When they're released from the gates to the course in a torrent of
       motion,   145
Nor do the charioteers whip rippling reins with such vigour
Over their free running pairs or bend to such angles to lash them.

Then the applause: fierce roaring of men, wild cheering of factions,
Livens the woodlands with noise, the enclosed bays roll back the echo,
Hilltops drummed by the uproar bounce back sound to the
    beaches.   150
  Gyas slips into the lead, amid all the confusion and shouting,
Right from the first strokes. Giving him chase is Cloanthus, with better
Oarsmen and oarblades but slowed by the weight of his pine-timbered
    vessel.
Pristis and *Centaur* are just the same distance behind the two leaders,
Locked in a race of their own, each trying to slip past the other.   155
Sometimes it's *Pristis* pulling ahead, sometimes it's the massive
Centaur, and sometimes, bow beside bow, both race like a yoked team,
Long keels dredging their furrows all over the saltness of water.
As they are nearing the rock—within reach of the turning-point
    marker,
Gyas, the leader, the first-half winner, in fact, at mid-water,   160
Shouts these words at his vessel's helmsman and pilot, Menoetes:
'Why are you pulling me so far to starboard? Direct your course
    this way!
Run in close to the shore, let the oars grate reefs on the larboard!'
Fearing the unseen shoals, Menoetes, ignoring the order,
Sheers the bow round towards open sea with a wrench on the
    steering.   165
'Why are you pulling about?' Gyas yells. 'To the rock shore, Menoetes!'
Trying to get him to turn. Then he looks back—and there is
    Cloanthus,
Sailing, right in his wake, on the closer course by the shoreline,
Heading between Gyas' ship and the rumbling roar of the breakers,
Letting his larboard oars scrape shoals. Sneaking past on the inside,   170
Suddenly he's in the lead, makes the turn, and he's back in safe
    waters.
Humiliation and anger blaze from the bones of young Gyas,
Tears of frustration dampen his cheeks. Forgetting decorum,
Dignity, safety of crew, he pummels the timid Menoetes,
Tosses him head first into the sea* from the top of the aft-deck.   175
He takes total command himself as pilot and helmsman,
Cheers his men on, tugs the steering around for a course to the
    shoreline.
Well, it takes time for the sodden Menoetes to rise from the seabed.
Since he is quite an old man, he is lucky to make it. He clambers,

Waterlogged, streaming with brine, on top of the reef, and then
    slumps down   180
Onto a dry rock. They laugh as he falls, and they laugh at him
    swimming,
And, as he spews salt floods from his lungs, the Teucrians still laugh.*
  Hope and delight are sparked in the straggling Sergestus and
    Mnestheus
By these events. Each thinks he can pass the now floundering Gyas.
Nearing the reef, Sergestus seizes the lead. But it's only   185
Part of his ship that's in front. So his lead doesn't come to a
    whole length.
Pristis, his rival, with armoured prow, still threatens at mid-ship.
Mnestheus moves to the waist of his vessel, right there with his
    crewmen,
Yelling encouragement: 'Stand to your oars, now, allies of Hector,
Stand! You're the men I chose in Troy's last hours as my comrades.   190
Now is the time to deploy that strength and the courage you've
    shown me
There, in the Libyan Gulf, on the Syrtis sandbanks, and there too
In the Ionian Sea and in Malea's dangerous currents.
I, Mnestheus, don't aim to come first or strive to be victor.
Yet . . . oh! Neptune, I pray, let whoever you've picked be the
    winner . . .   195
What a disgrace to be last, though! Citizens, make this your triumph:
Stave off the really unspeakable!' They, with all strength they can
    muster,
Bend to the oars. Vast strokes send a shudder through all the ship's
    bronze-plate,
Sea slips under the keel, breath panted in gasps shivers muscles,
Quivers already dry mouths, sweat wells up rivers and gushes.   200
Yet what brought them the honour they craved was an accident, really.
Mind-obsessed, Sergestus was spurting around on the inner
Course, prow aimed at the reef, but *he* ran aground as he entered
Shoals of uneven depth, stuck fast on the rocky protrusions,
Hopes now unfulfilled, with a jarring shock. Then the struggling   205
Oars split on sharp shell crusts, and the beached prow dangles in
    mid-air.
Sailors leap to their feet, shout loudly, and try to back water,
Pulling out iron-tipped boathooks, sharp-pointed ship-poles, and
    scooping

Cracked oars out of the swirling surf.
                                    Mnestheus is delighted.
Made more determined by such a successful turn of his fortunes,   210
He, with an orderly, fast strike rate, and a prayer to the wind gods,
Heads for the homeward stretch, speeds along over seas that are
     reefless.
Think: if you suddenly frighten a dove* from her home, from her cosy
Nest in a secret bubble of pumice deep in a cavern,
Out above farmlands, in terror she flies, wings frantically, loudly   215
Thrashing. Yet, after a while, she'll be gliding aloft in the calm air,
Hardly touching her frictionless road, not moving her swift wings.
That's how Mnestheus sails, as the *Pristis* sails, on the final
Stretches of sea. For her own sheer impetus keeps her in motion.
First it's Sergestus she leaves in her wake, high and dry on a
     reef-top,   220
Struggling madly in shallowest shallows, and shouting out hopeless
Cries for assistance and learning the art of broken-oar racing.
Gyas is next: the *Chimaera* herself, in her monstrous proportions,
Now overhauled. For, deprived of her helmsman, she's lost to the
     contest.
Now there is only Cloanthus left, and they're nearing the finish.   225
Each ounce of strength he can summon goes into the chase, and the
     cheering
Doubles at this, for the crowds on the shore all support the pursuer,
They're on his side. And the skies overhead re-echo the uproar.
One ship's crew, thinking victory theirs, honour won, cannot cope with
Thoughts of conceding it now. And, for glory, they'd eagerly
     trade life.   230
Feeding the others: success. They can win, for it seems that they
     can win.
Now prow to prow, there's a chance that the challengers would become
     winners,
Had not Cloanthus extended both palms in appeals to the salt sea,
Had he not poured out prayers, begged divine help, vowed to pay
     tribute:
'Gods with command of the seas, on whose very surface I'm racing,   235
Gladly I make you a promise that I will present at your altars,
Here on this shore, a white bull, and its entrails I'll cast on your salty
Waters. I'll also pour libations of wine in your honour.'
Far down under the waves, the whole chorus of Nereids heard him,

Phorcus's dancers too and Panopea, the virgin.   240
Father Portunus himself drove him swiftly ahead with his massive
Hand. So the ship flew faster than southerly gales to its landfall,
Faster in flight than an arrow,* and plunged itself deep in its haven.
     Summoning all, in traditional fashion, the son of Anchises
Calls on a herald to make it official: the winner's Cloanthus,   245
Wreathes the man's temples with green laurel leaves, then grants
     to each vessel
Rights to select and remove from the herd three bullocks, and also
Wine from the stores—plus one full talent* in ingots of silver.
Each individual captain, besides, gets additional prizes.
First place garners an exquisite cloak embroidered with gold thread   250
Round whose hem runs a double meander of deep Meliboean
Purple. The weaving depicts the young prince, Ganymede, upon leafy
Ida. He's hotly pursuing—and tiring—some fast-moving buckdeer,
Javelin in hand, and he seems to be panting. From Ida, an eagle,
Bearer of Jupiter's arms, swoops down, has him fast in its talons,   255
Sweeps him away. Here men, very old, stretch hands towards heaven,
Hopelessly. They are his guards. Here dogs bark wildly at breezes.
     Second place earns, for its courage and skill, a fine corslet of
     chain mail:
Intricate interlocked loops interwoven with gold, triple-threaded.
This piece Aeneas, in person, had ripped from Demoleos,*
     vanquished   260
Close to the Simoïs' ravenous streams, beneath Ilium's towers.
Now it's a permanent gift that gives style, and protection, in battle.
Phegeus and Sagaris, Mnestheus' slaves, had a problem just hoisting
All its layers on their shoulders. Demoleos once—what a contrast!—
Wore it routinely while sprinting to catch up with straggling
     Trojans.   265
     Third place earns, as a gift, two matching cauldrons of cast bronze,
Goblets of silver as well, each embossed with exquisite relief-work.
     All of them now had their gifts and were off on their way with a
     swagger,
Proud of the riches they'd won, foreheads ribboned with tassels of
     purple,
Just as Sergestus was putting ashore in disgrace. How they jeered
     him!*   270
Prising the ship, though, off murderous reefs required seamanship,
     pure skill.

Oars had been lost—one entire bank was crippled. They'd only just
    made it.
Think of a snake that, like many, is caught, as he glides on a raised
    road's
Flagstones,* by, say, a wheel's bronze rim, cutting in at an angle,
Or who's been mangled and left half-dead by a traveller's hurled
    stone.   275
Struggling vainly to ripple escape through the length of his body,
Part of him fiery-eyed, fierce, head reared, still hisses defiance;
Part, paralysed by the wound, holds back as he wreathes into
    squirming
Knots, writhes back on himself, coils tangled about his own body.
That was the state of the ship's banked oars as she forced herself
    forward.   280
Still, she got canvas aloft—made port under full rig of canvas!
Gifts are bestowed on Sergestus, as promised before. For Aeneas,
Happy he's salvaged the vessel, preserved—and come home
    with—his crew safe,
Gives him a servant whose home was once Crete. Quite adept at
    Minerva's
Arts, this slave, Pholoë,* is a nursing mother with twin sons.   285

Now that this contest was over, Aeneas moved on to a level,
Grass-covered meadow completely enclosed by a circle of woodlands,
Contoured by hillside slopes. In this amphitheatrical valley's
Heart was a circular track. Here the hero, escorted by thousands,
Entered and sat on a podium raised in the heart of the gathering.   290
Here, by announcing and showing the prizes, he quickens the sprinter's
Spirit in those who just love to compete in a race. They come
    thronging,*
Trojans, Sicanians, this way and that way, from every direction.
Nisus, Euryalus with him, are first.
Perfect physique, and the live sap of youth, make Euryalus famous;   295
Nisus is known for his love of the boy, so respectful and righteous.
Next comes Diores, a towering king among Priam's once flocking
Sons. Neck and neck follow Salius and Patron: one Acarnanian,
One of Arcadian blood, from a clan that had roots in Tegea.
Helymus, Panopes too, come next. Both youths are Sicilian,   300
Men of the forest, companions at arms of the aging Acestes.
Lots more besides, all rumour of whom has been shrouded and buried.

Here's what Aeneas announced from the midst of the crowd at this
    juncture:
'Grasp what I'm saying with gladness of heart! Pay lively attention!
None of this group will depart without getting my personal
    present.   305
Two Cretan arrows apiece I will give, steel tipped, highly burnished;
Also an axe with an inlay of silver—identical trophies
Honouring all. They are theirs to take home. Those who place in the
    top three
Get further prizes. Their heads will wear garlands of sallow-leafed
    olive.
First place wins you a stallion equipped with a full set of
    trappings;   310
Second, an Amazon quiver that's loaded with Thracian arrows,
Mounted upon a retaining harness finished with broad gold
Plate, and attached by a clasp with a smooth, polished gemstone.
Third place will have to go home content with this helmet from Argos.'
    This said, they go to their marks; like a storm cloud, the moment
    the signal—   315
Oh, how they eat up the distance!—is heard,* they are off from the
    start-line,
Billowing out, and they signal the end in their starting momentum.
First individual to break from the crowd, with a long lead, is Nisus,
Flashing off fleeter than wind or the wings of a thunderbolt striking.
Following him, although following him at a very long distance,   320
Salius comes in pursuit. After him, there's a gap, and then running
Third is Euryalus.
Chasing Euryalus, Helymus; right behind him there comes flying,
Look! there he is, brushing heel against heel, pressing shoulder to
    shoulder,
Right at his back. It's Diores. Were more space and time still
    remaining,   325
He would ease round him and pass to the front, or at least run him even.
Now they're approaching the final stretch, they're exhausted, but nearly
There at the finish. Then Nisus slips in a thin pool of liquid
Blood, hopes unfulfilled. They'd been slaughtering bulls here, it
    happened:
Blood spilled over the ground, left the green grass utterly sodden.   330
That's where the youth, thinking victory his, celebrating his triumph,
Lost footing just as his feet hit the patch, couldn't get back his balance,

Fell face first in that unclean sludge*—in that blood consecrated.
Still, he did not fail to think of Euryalus and of his passion.
For as he rose from the slime, he positioned himself so that Salius*   335
Tripped, spinning head over heels to the blood-clotted sand, where
    he lay sprawled.
Flashing to victory now is Euryalus, thanks to his lover's
Sacrifice. First place is his, and he flies amid cheering and clapping.
Helymus follows and now, for the third palm frond, comes Diores.
    This is when Salius fills the whole gathering in the enormous   340
Hollow with ringing complaints made straight in the faces of front-row
Elders, demanding return of his prize, so dishonestly stolen.
Sentiment favours Euryalus, though; his tears so become him.
Virtue is much more appealing when found in a beautiful body.
Strongly supporting his cause, at the top of his lungs, is Diores.   345
He has sneaked in for a palm, and has thus qualified for the last prize
All to no end, if they're then to restore prime honours to Salius.
Father Aeneas now speaks: 'Your rewards have been set, and they'll
    stay fixed,
Boys. You can keep them. There's been no change in the order of
    palm fronds.
Still, you'll permit me to pity the fall of an innocent comrade.'   350
This said, he offers to Salius the monstrous hide of a Libyan
Lion—a quite enormous weight with its mane and its gilt claws.
Nisus reacts: 'If the losers', he says, 'get such wonderful prizes,
If those who fall win your pity, what worthy gift will you offer
Nisus? I've earned top honours on merit, and I would possess them   355
Right now if Fortune had not turned vicious on me, as on Salius.'
He, as he spoke, made sure they observed both his face and his body
Filthy with wet slime; this brought a laugh from the excellent father.
Bidding them bring him a shield, fine work by the skilled Didymaon,
Stolen by Greeks* from the entrance of Neptune's shrine. He
    presented   360
This to the youth who stood out from the flock: an outstanding
    donation.

After the races are over and all of the prizes awarded,
'Now is the time', he declares, 'when all men with a stout heart and
    courage
Ought to come forth, arms raised, and their own palms wreathed—
    but in leather!'*

Then he proposes a double award for the boxing: the victor   365
Wins a young bull, gold plate on its horns, all covered with garlands;
Then there's a sword and a very fine helmet to solace the vanquished.*
Instantly, Dares sticks up his face and his muscular, virile
Vastness, and raises himself to a rumbling roar from the menfolk.
This was the lone soul who'd often solicit a contest with Paris;   370
He was the one, who, right on the tomb of Hector the Mighty,
Battered Bebrycian Butes,* from Amycus' blood, so he boasted,
Massive in stature, a champion. But Dares gave him a thrashing,
Left him sprawled on the tan-coloured sand and slowly expiring.
Such, then, was Dares, his head raised high for the start of the
    contest,   375
Flexing the breadth of his shoulders and stretching one arm, then
    the other,
Out as he pummelled and slashed at the air with a series of punches.
  Someone is needed to fight him. In all the great army assembled,
Nobody dares* to get near him or put on the gloves for a contest.
So, then, supposing they've all given up on the palm, he astutely   380
Stands at Aeneas's feet, and with no hesitation whatever,
Sets his left hand on the horn of the bull and declares, in this manner:
'Son of the goddess, if nobody dares put his trust in his knuckles,
When does the standstill stop? How long are you planning to keep me
Waiting? Command them to bring out the gifts!' With unanimous
    uproar,   385
All Dardanians command that this man get the prize that was
    promised.
  This prompts Acestes to turn to Entellus* who sits at his elbow
There on the green grass, soft as a couch, and reproach him in
    earnest:
'Does it mean nothing, Entellus, that you were the bravest of heroes
Once? Are you *so* passive now that you'll let someone else,
    uncontested,   390
Haul off a wonderful prize? Where's our god and your much-vaunted
    trainer,
Eryx, in this? Has it *all* gone to waste? Where's your great reputation,
All over Sicily, gone, and those trophies that hung from your rafters?'
He, in response, says: 'Fear hasn't pummelled my love of the glory,
Or my pride, into quitting. My blood runs cold because old age   395
Slows me, because my whole body is stiff as an icicle, strengthless.
If, though, I had what I once *did* have, and what this cheap imposter

Trusts in and brags about, youth, if I had that now, I'd have
     stepped up,
Not for the lure of the prize, I should add, or to get me that handsome
Bullock. I don't waste a thought on the purse.' Then, as soon as
     he's spoken,   400
Out he throws, into the ring, a pair of gigantically weighty
Gloves routinely worn by Eryx the Fierce when his fists went
Out into combat, bound up as far as the forearms with tough hide.
Everyone freezes on seeing these gloves, made of seven gigantic
Oxhides rigid with iron and lead* sewn in between layers.   405
Dares especially, stupefied, pulls himself back to a distance.
Generous-hearted Aeneas, Anchises' son, checks the massive
Weight and voluminous bindings, and turns them first this way
     then that way.
Then the old man makes a heartfelt statement much along these lines:
'What would reactions have been if you'd seen those gloves and
     equipment   410
Hercules wore when he boxed, and the grim match fought on this very
Beach? Now, these were the gloves once worn by your own brother Eryx.
Look, you can still see the stains from the blood and the brains that
     were spattered.
These he was wearing the day he faced Hercules. These were my usual
Gear when more vigorous blood gave me strength, before *my* greatest
     rival,   415
Old age, with time on his side, spattered both of my temples* with
     whiteness.
But if the Trojan Dares baulks at confronting these weapons,
And if Aeneas the Righteous approves—and our sponsor, Acestes—
Let's fight on equal terms. So for you I'll renounce Eryx' gauntlets,
Don't be afraid! And remove your Trojan gloves for the contest.'   420
This said, he strips from his shoulders the double-thick cloak he is
     wearing
Baring his huge and muscular limbs, huge forearms and huge bones,
Standing, a giant, there in the heart of the coastal arena.
Father Aeneas, Anchises' son, then brings out some matching
Gloves, and arms both men's palms with equal, uniform bindings.   425
Both, in a flash, are up on their feet, bolt upright, on tiptoe,
All terror banished as arms stretch up to the breezes of heaven.
Keeping their heads high, well drawn back, to evade any punches,
Sparring and taunting, fist against fist, they tangle in combat.

One has superior footwork, exploiting his youthful advantage;   430
Muscle and mass are the other man's strength, but his knees are
     unsteady,
Prone to give way, and his vast limbs are shivered with asthmatic
     gasping.
Both men exchange many punches that miss; but a good many thunder
Down with a thud upon cavernous ribs; vast chests echo loudly.
Flickering fists dance frantic and wild, around ears, around temples,   435
Punishing uppercuts crackle and crunch into jaws. But Entellus
Stands in the same tense pose, immovable, solidly planted,
Dodging the blows by alertness of eye, by a twist of his torso.
Dares, like someone attacking a towering city with siegeworks,
Someone with troops under arms who's surrounding a mountaintop
     fortress,   440
Tests this approach, that approach, and explores every inch of the layout
Cannily, varies his tactics in mounting assaults—and gets nowhere.
Then there's an upward surge by Entellus. His right is extended,
Raised for a hammer blow, but—his opponent, who's quick, sees
     the arc crest,
Sees the fist coming, slips swiftly aside with a swerve of his body.   445
Energy whaling at winds whips the feet out from under Entellus;
Massive the man is, and massive his fall to the earth as his vastness
Crashes as, every so often, on tall Erymanthus or Ida,
Pines that are hollow inside get uprooted and just topple over.
Up on their feet now, the Teucrians cheer, young Sicilians are
     gasping.   450
Uproar soars to the skies. First man on the scene is Acestes,
Sorry for his old friend and contemporary, running to raise him.
But, neither slowed by his fall nor grounded in terror, the hero's
Back in the fight. He is sharper, for anger has kindled his violence;
Shame and awareness of manhood forge this force into pure
     strength.   455
Over the flatness, ardent as fire, he hammers at Dares'
Frantic withdrawal: a right, then a left: a two-fisted, relentless
Pounding without intermission. As hail from a storm when it rattles
Rooftop tiles, so punch after punch, right, left, from the hero's
Hands pelt down thick and fast, send Dares reeling and spinning.   460
   Father Aeneas won't let this anger intensify further,
Or let Entellus' embittered rage turn him into a monster.
Therefore he calls the fight over, pulls Dares, exhausted, to safety,

Trying to calm him with words. So he offers the following comments:
'What utter madness has taken your mind, now you find your
    ambitions   465
Unfulfilled? Don't you sense your opponent's strength or the changing
Favour of heaven? Give way to the god!' And his voice stops the
    contest.
Trusted friends lead Dares off to the ships. He is dragging
Failing legs, and his head flip-flops. From his mouth he is spitting
Gore in clots and, mixed with the blood, there's a sprinkling of
    smashed teeth.   470
When the result is announced, his friends take the sword and the helmet
On his behalf, but abandon the palm (and the bull) to Entellus.
Heart full of triumph, the champion speaks (and the bull makes him
    swagger):
'Son of the goddess,' he says, 'other Teucrians too, now discover
Both what muscular power I had when my body was younger   475
And what a death was in store, had you not interceded, for Dares.'
This said, he takes a position directly confronting the bullock,
Just now won as his prize, and conveniently standing beside him.
Up goes his gloved fist, back, till he's found the right balance, then
    smashes
Down, in between the two horns, crushing ruptured brain against
    skull-bone.   480
Felled, and though quivering still, sprawled dead on the earth, lies
    the great ox.*
Over its body he offers this heartfelt, brief dedication:
'Eryx, I'm now fulfilling my vow by slaying a victim
Nobler than Dares. With this win I lay down my gloves and my boxing.'

Archery's swift-flying arrows are next, with Aeneas inviting   485
All comers wishing to hazard a test of their skills. There are prizes.
Numerous hands are recruited to hoist up the mast on Serestus'
Ship. To the masthead he ties, by a cord with a slipknot, a fluttering
Dove as a target at which they can shoot their iron-tipped arrows.*
Once the contestants are gathered and lots are tossed into a
    helmet,   490
Hyrtacus' son, named Hippocoön, gets the first shot, for his token
Tumbles out first, amid partisan cheers; and right after him, Mnestheus,
Follows, who's just put ashore from his boat race victory:* Mnestheus,
Hair now bound in a victor's fresh green garland of olive.

Third is Eurytion—your brother, Pandarus, you who, at one time,   495
Earned great attention by breaking, on orders, a solemn agreement:*
Firing the first arrow into the thick of the massing Achaeans.
Last is Acestes, whose lot settled deep in the crown of the helmet,
Yet who's had courage to try out his hand at a young man's
      endeavours.
Strong arms then arch bows into crescents. And each individual   500
Fans out before him the shafts he's selected and drawn from his quiver.
Now comes the twang of a bowstring: the first arrow cracks through
      the fluttering
Winds like a whip as it shoots through the sky from Hippocoön's
      fingers,
Flies to its target, encounters the mast's solid timber, and sticks fast.
As the mast shivers, the dove is dislodged, wings beating in
      frenzied   505
Terror. The whole place erupts in a thunder of cheering and clapping.
Mnestheus, who's next, stands, bowstring taut, in intense
      concentration,
Gauging the arc of his shot with his eyes and the line of his arrow.
Still the poor man cannot quite hit his target, the bird, with its iron
Point; but he severs the cordage of hemp and the slipknot that
      tethers   510
One of her feet to the masthead and dangles her high like a pennant.
Off she now speeds into lowering skies on the wings of the south wind.
   Seizing the moment, Eurytion, long since ready with bowstring
Taut, sets eye on the dove, bright white on a backdrop of black cloud,
Flapping and clapping her wings in joy at escape through the
      empty   515
Skies. So he prays to his brother, and fires off a shot, and he strikes her.
Lifeless, she drops to the earth, soul lost in the billowing stardust,
And, as she falls, transfixed, she restores spent arrow to archer.
Only Acestes is left. Though the victor's palm is already
Won, the old man takes aim at the billowing breezes, displaying   520
Technical art arched tense* for a canticle hummed by a bowstring.
That's when an omen confronted their eyes: inescapable, sudden
Symbol of what lay ahead—as events of significance later
Showed, and as prophets of doom, later on sang loudly, but too late.*
For, as it winged swift flight through the shifting cloud banks, the
      arrow   525
Burst into flame, blazed fire in its path, then tapered and vanished

Tracelessly into the winds, as stars, once fixed in the heavens,
Break loose, shoot across skies some nights, hair streaming behind
    them.
Minds stunned, motions stilled, both Teucrian men and Sicilians
Prayed to the gods. Then Aeneas, who could have said no—the
    decision,   530
Rested with him—ruled the omen was real, and spoke thus, while
    embracing
Joyful Acestes, and showering gifts in abundance upon him:
'Father, accept them. It's clearly the will of the king of Olympus—
Witness these favourable signs—that you merit extraordinary honours.
Your gift will be this piece once owned by the long-lived Anchises,   535
This bowl, with figured reliefs, that Thracian Cisseus* presented
Long ago now, to my father Anchises: a splendid donation,
Meant to stir thoughts of the donor: in symbol, a child of their
    love-pledge.'
This said, he circled Acestes' temples with green laurel garlands,
Hailing him now as the victor supreme for the whole of the contest.   540
What a good sport Eurytion was! He alone brought the dove down
Out of the sky. Yet his eye shot the man who displaced him no
    malice.
Next, in the order of prizes, was he who had severed the cordage,
Last, was the one who had pierced the mast with his swift-flying arrow.

Father Aeneas had, even before these games were concluded,   545
Summoned Epytides, youthful Iulus' guard and companion,
Over, and whispered these words in an ear that he knew could be
    trusted.
'Go, have Ascanius make his appearance in armour, and lead out
Troops in his grandfather's honour, provided he's got the boys'
    squadron
With him, and ready, and marshalled to execute horseback
    manoeuvres.   550
Tell him!' He now orders all those people who've flooded the circle's
Lengthy expanse to withdraw and to leave the flat areas open.
On ride the boys in formation in front of the eyes of their parents,
Horses under control, all aglitter. Admiring approval
Roars as they pass in review before Troy's and Sicily's massed youth. 555
Each has his hair bound in uniform style with a neatly trimmed
    garland,

Each bears two matched lances of cornel-wood, heads tipped with iron.
Some wear bright quivers strapped to their backs, but they all wear
     a pliant
Circlet of spiralled gold as a torc where the chest meets the neckline.
Three troops of cavalry, each with a captain, ride at an easy   560
Canter. And two squads of six boys apiece follow each of the captains,
Parting the column in two flashing lines under uniform orders.
Leading one youthful and cocky platoon is a junior Priam,
Bringing new life to his grandfather's name, your fine son, Polites,*
Soon to make Italy greater. The courser he rides is a Thracian   565
Piebald, gleamingly dappled, displaying the white of its forehead
Showily high and displaying fore-pasterns of white as it prances.
Atys comes next (claimed by Latins of Atius' clan* as their founder),
Atys, so little, but loved, the way boys love boys, by Iulus.
Last, but in beauty supreme, rides Iulus, his mount a Sidonian*   570
Splendid Dido (so lovely herself) had bestowed: a donation
Meant to stir thoughts of the donor: a pledge of her love and affection.
Other boys ride on Sicilian horses that aging Acestes
Lends for their use.
     Dardans, while cheering the nervous lads, enjoy scanning their
     faces,   575
Finding their parents, as they once were, writ large in their features.
After they've happily ridden the ritual lap past the gathered
Crowds and their parents' gaze, Epytides, off on the sidelines,
Snaps out the order to start, gives a crack of his whip. And they're ready.
Galloping off right and left, the three companies break from their
     columns,   580
Split into squadrons of six. Orders bark, and they wheel about, charging
Back once again, lances levelled, as if they were meeting in combat.
Other manoeuvres and counter-manoeuvres ensue as the two groups
Face off across the arena: they intertwine circles with circles,
Conjure up representations of armed men fighting a battle,   585
Now they're exposing their backs in retreat, now they're levelling
     lances,
On the attack, and now peace has been made, and they ride round
     together.
     There was a labyrinth* once, it's reported, in Crete, land of
     mountains,
Crossed by a road threading blindly amid blank walls, and dividing
Into a thousand routes as a ruse to deprive you of guiding   590

Signposts and hope of return as you strayed in a maze beyond
    mind's grasp.
Such are the textures of tracks intertwining that sons of the Teucrians
Weave in their patterns of rout and attack in their games as they
    gallop,
Much like dolphins at play in Carpathian or Libyan seaways,
Cutting their way up and down through the waves.   595
This was the style of the horse-shows and contests revived by Ascanius
When he first started a circuit of walls to surround Alba Longa,
Teaching the Latins of years gone by all the details of staging,
Just as he'd staged them himself as a boy with the other young Trojans.
Albans instructed their boys, then mightiest Rome, when its turn
    came,   600
Later maintained these games as an honoured ancestral tradition.
Boys who take part are called 'Troy'; their formation is known as
    'The Trojan'.

With this performance, the games for the Sainted Father concluded.
Fortune, though, started to change—thus reviving belief in her power.
While men conducted their rites at the grave with their various
    contests,   605
Juno, the daughter of Saturn sent Iris down* from the heavens,
Blowing a breeze that would waft her directly to Ilium's navy.
Honour unsatisfied, pained by old wounds, she'd set big plans in
    motion.
   Iris speeds on her way, down a path in the skies through a rainbow's
Thousand hues, not perceived as a girl. She observes, on arrival,   610
How big the gathering is; then, while she's surveying the coastline,
Notes that the harbour's deserted: the fleet has been left unprotected.
But, far off, on a lonely beach, in seclusion, the Trojan
Wives are lamenting the loss of Anchises. They all, while lamenting,
Stare at the deep sea's surge: 'We're exhausted, yet so many
    seaways,   615
So much water is still to be crossed!' Many voices sing one song.
Tired of enduring the high seas' hardships, they pray for a city.
   Not unskilled in the criminal arts, Iris thrusts herself, therefore,
Into their midst, sheds clothes and appearance that prove her a
    goddess,
Re-forms as Beroë,* Tmarian Doryclus' wife of advanced
    years—   620

Status, a good name, and children: all these she'd have had in her
    heyday—
As such she took stage centre among the Dardanian mothers.
'Pity us all,' she began, 'whom the hands of Achaeans did *not* drag
Off to a wartime death near our homeland's walls. O my people
Unfulfilled, for what terrible doom has Fortune preserved you?   625
Summers have passed, almost seven by now, since Troy was
    demolished.
We, though, are still mapping all lands, seas, cruel reefs, constellations
Far beyond count, we're shipped over the vast deep, rolled by the
    heaving
Waves, chasing Italy—which, in turn, tries hard to escape us.
Here we have brotherly Eryx's land; and a host in Acestes.   630
Who says we *can't* put up walls and give *citizens* something: a city?
Homeland and household gods! What a waste! You were saved from
    the foeman,
But will there never be walls to make Troy's name real? Will I never
See Hector's rivers, the Xanthus and Simoïs, redefined somewhere?
Come then—why don't you?—and join me in burning these
    miserable galleys!   635
I've had a vision, in dreams, of Cassandra, who's prophecy's poet,
Giving me torches of fire: "Look here for your Troy," she instructed,
"Here's where your home *should* be! Now's the time to take action,
    not dither!
Portents are *so* strong! Look! Four altars are blazing for Neptune
Right where we stand! So the god provides fire and the courage to
    use it!"'   640
   She, as she spoke, made the first move: she snatched up a
    menacing firebrand,
Raised it up high in her hand, whirled flames into fury and hurled it
Far. Now the minds of the women of Troy had been roused to
    attention.
Hearts, though, were stunned with amazement. The eldest in years
    and importance,
Pyrgo, once royal nurse to the numerous children of Priam,   645
Spoke: 'It's not Beroë, Doryclus' Rhoetian wife, that you're hearing,
Ladies! Notice her beauty, like that of a god, note her blazing
Eyes, all her energy, notice the sound of her voice, her expression,
Look at the grace in her movements! But Beroë's ill. I've just left her
Sickbed to come here myself. She was so upset when I saw her,   650

Angry that she was the only one who would miss the memorial
Service, that she couldn't pay her respects, as she should, to
     Anchises.'
That's what she said.
Well, as the ladies, at first, were in two minds (yet casting an evil
Eye on the ships), hearts torn between pitiful love for this real,   655
Tangible land, and the call of the powerful realms that fate promised,
Iris rose on symmetrical wings and sped off through the heavens,
Etching a rainbow prodigiously large beneath mantles of storm clouds.
Shocked by the ominous signs, energized by their fury, the women
Burst into one great scream, seize burning logs from the sacred   660
Hearths. Some plunder the altars of wreaths, leafy branches, and
     torches:
Kindling to hurl. Fires rage along oars, along benches, through painted
Pinewood hulls: all Vulcan's power unstoppably unleashed.

News that the ships are ablaze is announced to the crowds at
     Anchises'
Tomb and the theatre's tiers by Eumelus. A glance at the ashes   665
Billowing black in a menacing cloud just behind them confirms it.
First to respond is Ascanius, as piqued now as he'd been delighted
Earlier, leading the cavalry show. And he gallops his stallion
Into the rioting camp. Though his trainers try hard, they can't
     stop him.
'What is this new form of madness?' he asks. 'What's your goal or
     your purpose,   670
Citizens, pitiful creatures? For shame! We're not foemen! You're
     torching
Your own hopes, not an Argive attack-force. It's me, your Ascanius,
Look!' And he tore off and flung at their feet the toy helmet he'd
     sported
During the games, when they'd staged mock versions of combat and
     warfare.
Enter Aeneas in haste, and, approaching the scene at the same time,   675
Teucrian troops, full force. Fear scatters the women all over
Various parts of the beach as they scurry to hide under hollow
Rocks or in woods. They regret what they've done, recognize their
     own people,
Wish they could vanish. They've changed. Juno's hold on their
     hearts has been broken.

Fire, however, and flame were not thereby inspired to diminish   680
Their invincible force. Underneath the damp oak, the pitch caulking
Bubbles with life, spews forth thick smoke. Slow, smouldering
      embers
Eat through the hulls like a cancerous blight spreading all through
      the body.
Heroes' muscles and constant streams of water are useless.
   Righteous Aeneas now rips off the cloak draped over his
      shoulder,   685
Raises his arms to the heavens and calls on the gods for assistance.
'Mightiest Jupiter, if you don't heartily hate all the Trojans
Down to the very last man, if your old-time righteousness values
Human sorrows and toil, let the navy escape from this firestorm!
Now, father, rescue from death the slim relics of Teucrian
      statehood!   690
Or, if it's what I deserve, take the alternate course: let your own hand
Blast me to death with a lightning bolt that expresses your anger.'
Hardly are these words out of his mouth when an unprecedented
Storm* explodes in a fury of dark and torrential downpours.
Thunder rocks hilltops and plains, rain streams black as night from
      the heavens'   695
Whole expanse, lashing drops plumped huge by the southerlies'
      moisture.
Vessels fill up and brim over; half-burned oak planks become sodden.
So, in the end, all embers are doused, all hulls can be salvaged—
Well, except four that are lost. They've survived fire's feverous
      onslaught.
   Father Aeneas, however, is stunned by this bitter misfortune.   700
Stress and anxiety press him; he turns problems this way and that way,
Changing perspectives. Should he forget fate, settle here in Sicilian
Farmlands? Perhaps he should try, though, for Italy's coastline.
Nautes, an elder, broke in at this point. Pallas, god of Tritonis,
Made him her one student, bringing him fame for his deep skill and
      learning.   705
What does divine anger, when it is strong, portend for the future?
What does fate's sequence of causes demand? She gave him the answers.
He touched Aeneas's lonely thoughts with words bringing comfort:
'Child of a goddess, let's follow where fate drags* us, onwards or
      backwards.
Each turn of fortune we meet, we survive, and defeat, by endurance.   710

Help does exist. You have Dardan Acestes, a man of divine birth.
So, take him in on your plans as a partner. He's certainly willing.
Give him the crews from the vessels you've lost and, besides them,
    the people
Sick and tired both of grand adventure *and* your achievements,
Those well on in their years, those mothers weary of high seas;   715
Elements weakening your ranks, those frightened when danger
    confronts them,
Weed them away. Give the weary their chance to have walls in this
    country.
If you permit it, they'll give this city the name of Acesta.'
While such words from his agèd friend spark fire in Aeneas.
Still, in his heart, anxieties tear resolution to pieces.   720

Now, as the surging horses of Night grip heaven in darkness
Down from the skies* above slips an apparition resembling
Father Anchises. And from it a voice wells instantly upward:
'Son, you were dearer than life to me even when life lingered in me.
Oh, what you've suffered, my son, through Ilium's fate and its
    downfall.   725
Jupiter's orders have brought me to you. It was he who extinguished
Fire on the ships. He's at last taken pity, up high in the heavens.
Agèd Nautes has given advice. It is excellent. Heed it!
Pick out the best of the young men for Italy, hearts that are stoutest.
Take them. The people that you must defeat there in Latium are
    hard men,   730
Raised to be tough. But before all this, make your way to the buried
Palace of Dis, to the world of the Dead, through the depths of Avernus.
There your encounter's with me. No, I'm not where they keep the
    unrighteous,
Tartarus, held among ghosts that are grim. I reside with the righteous
Gathered in pleasant surroundings: Elysium. There the chaste
    Sibyl,   735
After a great deal of black sheep's blood has been shed, will escort you.
Then you will learn your whole family line and the cities they're
    granted.
Goodbye now! Damp Night is rounding her course at its midpoint,
Sunrise comes cruelly upon me with panting horses and hot breath.'
This said, he now disappears like a puff of smoke on the
    breezes.   740

'Where are you rushing so soon?' says Aeneas. 'What's all of this
      haste for?
Who are you running away from?* Who's keeping you from my
      embraces?'
He, as his thoughts become words, stirs ashes, awakens the fire,
Prays on his knees both to Pergamum's god and the altars of ashen
Vesta, and offers the ritual grain and full measure of incense.   745
Straight from devotions, he sends for his crews and, above all,
      Acestes;
Sets forth Jupiter's mandates,* then his dear father's instructions,
Then what his *own* decree rules. As debate means delay, it's omitted.
Nor does Acestes refuse to obey. They transfer all the married
Mothers to his city's citizen rolls and they offload   750
People so wishing: those spirits that don't feel lost without glory.
They replace benches for rowers themselves; and where the fire's
      damaged
Planking, they fit it anew and they craft new oarage and rigging.
Small though their numbers be, their courage is blazing for battle.
Meanwhile Aeneas is marking the site for a city with furrows;   755
Home sites he portions by lot. One zone's called Troy, as he orders,
Ilium is yet another. His realm is a joy to Acestes,
Trojan himself. He declares an assembly, he summons a senate,
Drafts it a code. Work starts on a shrine for Idalian Venus,
Close to the stars, upon Eryx's peak. And the tomb of Anchises   760
Gets both a priest of its own and a broad tract of sanctified woodland.

Nine days now: the whole people has feasted, the altars received due
Sacrifice. Seas have been lulled by gentle breezes to flatness:
Southerlies mostly, whose breath once more is a summons to set sail.
Rising along the curved crescent of shore, a crescendo of weeping   765
Swells as embraces delay by a day and a night their departure.
Now the same mothers, the same men who saw, only recently, brutal
Harshness etched in the face of the deep, and who hated to hear sea
Mentioned, were ready to go, and endure all the struggles of exile.
These good Aeneas attempts to console with words stressing
      friendship.   770
Tears in his eyes, he commends them to their own kinsman, Acestes.
First he commands three calves to be slaughtered in honour of Eryx,
Next, to the storm winds, a lamb; then he calls out the order to
      cast off.

Standing remote on the prow, head crowned with a trimmed olive's
      foliage,
Sacral bowl in his hands, he scatters the entrails on salt sea,   775
Pours out the liquid wine on the surging waters beneath him.
Winds, picking up well astern, chase after them on their departure;
Rival crews strike sea with their oars' sweep, feathering its surface.

Venus, in anxious distress, meanwhile, has been speaking to Neptune,
Pouring upon him her heartfelt complaints in the following
      manner: 780
'Juno's implacable heart and her wrath which defies saturation*
Force me, Neptune, to sink to the humblest levels of prayer.
No long passage of time, no act of righteousness softens
Her. Neither Fate nor Jupiter's orders can break her. She never
Rests. Though she's eaten the city right out of the Phrygian
      heartland,   785
Dragged Troy's last remains through every conceivable torment.
Still her unsated hate goes on. She hunts the dead body's
Ashes and bones. Only she knows the causes that prompt such a
      passion.
You are my witness yourself to that recent mess which she stirred up
Out of the blue, in the Libyan Sea, making "earth and the heavens   790
Chaos again." In her hopeless straits, she used Aeolus' tempests.
All this she dared in your very own realms.
Look at her now! She's made Trojan mothers her criminal weapons,
Vilely burned up their ships, and because their navy's been ruined,
Forces them now to abandon their crews in a country that's
      unknown!   795
Grant, I implore, that whatever survives may sail upon your seas
Safely, and come to the Laurentine Tiber—if my plea's is in order,
If city walls there are granted by Destiny's thread-spinning Sisters.'*
Here's the response Saturn's son, deep ocean's master, delivered:
'Queen of Cythera, it's totally right you should trust what is my
      realm,   800
Since it's the source of your birth. And I've earned that trust. I have
      often
Choked back the madness and monstrous rage of the sky and the salt
      seas.
Nor have I failed you on land—Simoïs will bear witness and Xanthus—
All to protect your Aeneas. At Troy once, Achilles was pinning

Terrified Trojans back to their walls as he went on a rampage,   805
Dealing out thousands of deaths. Yes, overfilled rivers were groaning:
Xanthus could not rediscover his course and roll out to the salt sea.
That's when Aeneas, no match in support from the gods or in
       sheer strength,
Challenged that brave son of Peleus. I snatched him away* in a hollow
Cloud, though my own dear goal was the utter destruction of
       Troy's walls,   810
Walls that I'd built for those liars with my own hands. So don't worry.
I'm in the same frame of mind at this moment as well. There's been
       no change.
He'll arrive safely for you, as you pray, at the port of Avernus.*
One man alone will be lost. You will search for him* out on the
       sea's swell:
One single life shall be offered to save many.'   815
   Now he has soothed and delighted her heart with these words,
       father Neptune
Yokes up his horses in harness of gold and attaches their foam-flecked
Bits as a curb, for they're fierce. Yet his hands give them totally
       free rein.
Lightly he skims sea's surface* aboard his chariot of dark blue.
Waves subside and the heaving sea-swell settles to stillness   820
Under his axle's roar; clouds vanish in vastness of sunlight.
Comrades of varied appearance* escort him: the whales in their
       hugeness,
Glaucus, with elderly dancers, and Ino's beloved Palaemon,
Darting Tritons, the shoaling armies of Phorcus in full force,
Thetis and Melite there on his left, Panopea the virgin,   825
Spio, Nesaeë, and Thalia—and there was Cymodoce too.
   This was the moment the lure of delight took a turn at beguiling
Father Aeneas's tenseness of mind. All masts to be hoisted,
Swift as you can, was his order, all canvas set on the yardarms.
Acting as one, each crew sets sheets, and with canny precision,   830
Drops sails larboard and starboard; as one, they tighten or slacken
Tension on each yard's horn for the tack. And the fleet has its sailwinds.
Captain-in-chief of the close line of ships, Palinurus, is sailing
Out in the lead. Others hold to his course, in accordance with orders.

Damp Night now has almost attained her mid-point in heaven.   835
Gratefully, sailors, relaxing their limbs, sprawl over unyielding

Benches and under the oars for a rest. Then, out from the high sky's
Stars, soft Sleep* slithers down and he nudges apart the tenacious
Darkness of air, pushing on through the dankness of shadows,
Making for you, Palinurus, for you, in your innocence, bringing　840
Nightmarish horrors. Alighting upon the raised aft-deck, adopting
Phorbas' features,* the god streams words in a soothing profusion.
'Iasus's son, Palinurus: the fair seas are moving your navy
All by themselves. Fair winds now blow. It's a good time for resting.
Lay down your head, steal weary eyes from their labour of vigil.　845
I'll offer you a replacement—myself—for a while. I will spell you.'*
Now barely able to open his eyes, Palinurus responded:
'You're telling *me* not to monitor salt sea's mood when there's no swell,
When it appears to be calm? You want *me* to trust ominous stillness?
Why should I now be entrusting Aeneas to treacherous breezes　850
And to the skies? I've so often been tricked by delusory calmness!'
Over and over he echoed these words. He held on, he stuck firmly,
Never lost grip on the steering, kept eyes fixed fast on the sky's stars.
　Look! the god's shaking a bough, saturated with droplets of
　　Lethe's
Sleep-drugged Stygian power, over each of his temples,
　　unmooring,　855
Though he resists it, the sight from his eyes which are already swimming.
Hardly had this unexpected repose loosened limbs and relaxed him
When the god stooped, picked him up, hurled him overboard into
　　the ship's wake
Headlong—and with him went part of the stern and the steering
　　equipment.
Time and again he cried out to his comrades for help. It was futile.　860
Sleep soared up on his wings, flitting off to the delicate breezes.
　Yet the fleet sped on her course, nonetheless, upon fair seas, in safety,
Free of ungrounded fears; Father Neptune had made her a promise.
Sailing along, she was already nearing the cliffs of the Sirens,*
Once very hard to evade, bleached white with the bones of so many,　865
Now distant ceaselessly surf-hammered rock-cliffs raucously booming.
This was the moment the father perceived that his vessel was drifting,
Helmsman lost. So he steered it himself through the waves, in the
　　darkness,
Groaning a lot, mind stunned by the doom that had taken his comrade.
'You, Palinurus, placed too much trust in the sky and the ocean's　870
Calm. You'll lie naked and dead on the sands of an unknown seashore.'

BOOK SIX

S o HE declares as he weeps. Then he lets the fleet run under full sail,
Finally putting ashore at Euboea's colony, Cumae.*
Prows veer round to face seaward; then anchors secure all the vessels
Fast to the land with the bite of their teeth. Curved sterns add a
    patterned
Fringe* to the seashore. A handful of youths, blazing eager,   5
Flashes ashore onto Twilight's Land.* Some strike for the dormant
Seeds of a flame in a flint vein; others tear off into forests,
Wildlife's dense-roofed homes, find streams,* point out their
    locations.
Righteous Aeneas, though, heads for the citadel's heights where Apollo
Rules, and towards a huge cave, the secluded haunt of the Sibyl.*   10
She sends a shiver through distant hearts. For the seer of Delos
Breathes into her the great force of his mind, disclosing the future.
They're in the grove now, the gilded shrine of the Goddess at
    Crossroads.*

   Daedalus,* so rumour has it, when fleeing from Minos's kingdom,
Dared put his faith in the heavens, and birdlike, on ominous swift
    wings,*   15
Sailed an unusual course not by but towards the cold Bear Stars.*
Since he first gently alit on the hill-tops of Chalcis, when landing
Back on the earth, it was here, and to you, Phoebus, he dedicated
Wings that had served him as oars* and a temple of massive
    proportions.
   Shown on the doors is Androgeos' murder; then Cecrops's
    children*   20
Ordered—and how grim it was—to pay out as a penalty, each year,
Seven live bodies of sons.* Over there stands the urn, with the lots
    drawn.*
Opposite, balancing these, raised up from the sea: Cretan Knossos.
Here's cruel love for a bull, here's Pasiphaë under him, mated
Guilefully; here is her hybrid child, showing traits of both parents: 25
Named Minotaur, monumental reminder of Venus perverted.
Here is the beast's house, an intricate puzzle,* defying solution.
   Daedalus pitied a ruler* in her great love. He untangled
Ruses and structural mazes and ruled them a route upon unseen

Tracks with a guiding thread. You, Icarus, too would have
　figured　　　　　　　　　　　　　　　　　　　　　　30
Large in this masterly work, if his rueful pain had permitted.
Twice he attempted to shape what befell you, in golden relief-work;
Twice, what fell were your father's hands.*
　　　　　　　　　　　　They'd have scanned every detail
Had not Achates, sent in advance, now arrived, bringing with him
Glaucus' daughter, Deiphobe,* priest to the Goddess at Crossroads　35
And to Apollo. She said to the king: 'Your casual sightseeing* isn't
What this occasion demands. You'd do rather better to slaughter
Seven young bulls from a virgin herd, a like number of young ewes
Chosen as rite prescribes.' Once she's spoken this way to Aeneas,
No time's lost. Men ready the offerings demanded. The priestess　40
Summons the Teucrians into the depths of her towering temple.

Mined* from a Euboean cliff's broad flank is a cavern of vast size.
Into it lead a full hundred broad-shanked shafts, a full hundred
Mouths; out spills the same tally of voices: the Sibyl's responses.
So, when they came to an entrance, the virgin exclaimed: 'Now's
　the moment:　　　　　　　　　　　　　　　　　　　45
Ask for the statements of god. See the god, look, the god's here!'
　While speaking,
Facing the doors, she abruptly transformed: her expression, her colour
Totally altered. Her hair sprang loose, gasped struggles to draw breath
Shuddered her chest. Heart, lungs puffed huge in her bestial madness.
Looming much larger in size, no longer sounding just human,　50
Bellowed by god's spirit, nearer now: 'Have you stopped your
　devotions,
Trojan Aeneas?' she cried. 'Have you stopped praying? Think about
　this then!
Not till you pray will the dumbstruck mouths of the great dwelling
　open.'
This said, she lapsed into silence, and ice shivered toughness in
　Trojan
Bones. But the king found voice for his prayers, which he poured
　from his heart's depths:　　　　　　　　　　　　　　55
'Phoebus, you've always shown pity for Troy and her burdens of
　suffering.
You once directed a Dardan arrow from Paris's bowstring
Into the flesh of Achilles, and you were my guide as I travelled

Far into so many seas that enclose massive lands with their waters:
Even to Syrtis' gulf where the distant Numidian people's   60
Land juts forth. Now Italy's coastlands, ever receding,
Lie in our grasp. Let our Trojan luck pursue us no further!
Gods, who thought Ilium's existence and Dardan national glory
Stood in your way, all goddesses too! It is right that you now cease
Harming Pergamum's nation. And you too, holiest priestess,   65
You know the future beforehand. Permit Teucer's sons and the vagrant
Gods and uprooted spirits of Troy to resettle in Latium.
What I request is merely the kingdom my destiny owes me.
Then I'll build Phoebus and Hecate, Goddess at Crossroads, a solid
Marble temple,* I'll institute festivals sacred to Phoebus.   70
Sibyl, a great shrine awaits you too in the heart of our kingdom.
Here I will store your responses* and statements of fate's inner secrets
Voiced to my people. I'll also ordain select men as its keepers.
One thing I ask: don't encode your predictions in leaves, blessèd lady,
Sing them yourself, I entreat. For I fear they'll fly off and be
          scattered,   75
Mocked by the plundering winds.' This said, he fell silent. The prophet,
Monstrous still, isn't broken in yet to the bridle of Phoebus.
Rather, as if Bacchus ruled her, she rages around in the cavern,
Hoping to buck the huge god from her breast. But he wearies her
          froth-flecked
Mouth even more, as he tames her heart's wildness, and shapes her
          with pressure.*   80
   Now all hundred mouths of the shrine fling open their portals,
Willingly bearing the seer's oracular words through the breezes:
'You who've at last passed on, with success, beyond perils of salt sea—
Though greater dangers await you on land—the Dardanians will enter
Into the realms of Lavinium.* Dismiss your concerns on this issue!   85
But: they will also wish they had never arrived. I see warfare,
Hideous warfare, the Tiber frothing with torrents of bloodshed.
Simoïs, Xanthus, the Dorian camp:* there'll be features to match them,
Even another Achilles* is now born for Latium. He's also
Son of a goddess. There's also the Teucrians' incubus, Juno,   90
She'll haunt you every day, everywhere. Which of all Italy's peoples,
Which cities *won't* you approach for assistance, a destitute suppliant?
Once more the cause of such evil's a wife, who'll be hostess to
          Teucrians,
Once more a foreign bridal affair.

Don't give way to these evils, but move the more boldly against
    them,   95
Turn any way* that your fortune permits. The first pathway to safety,
One you anticipate least, will emerge from a Greek city's* portals.'
Fearsome, ambiguous words such as these are the Sibyl of Cumae's
Song from her sanctum. She rolls up the truth in obscurity's riddles,*
Rumbling the cavern with echoes. Apollo shakes hard on the
    bridle's   100
Reins as she raves, and he's raking her breast with his spurs to
    control her.

   Then, when her frenzy has ceased and her foaming mouth fallen
    silent,
'Maiden,' Aeneas, the hero, begins, 'no struggle you mention
Comes unexpected by me, or as news.* I have pondered these issues
Well in advance of your words, I've gone over them all in my own
    mind.   105
One thing I ask. Since the gate to the king of the underworld regions
Is, they say, here, and since here is the place where the Acheron*
    surges
Up to a dark lake, grant me the chance for a glimpse of my dearest
Father's face. Could you teach me the route,* could you open the sacred
Gates? For I snatched him away through the flames, through a
    thousand pursuing   110
Javelins, safe on my shoulders, from out of the midst of our foemen.
He was my journey's companion, he sailed every seaway beside me,
Constantly bore every menace the deep and the heavens inflicted.
He wasn't strong—yet his vigour surpassed what is normal in old age.
He himself urged me, implored me to find you, to seek your
    assistance   115
Here and to come to your shrine. Holy woman, I beg you to pity
Father and son. It is all in your power. Hecate, with good reason
Put full command of the woodland groves of Avernus in *your* hands!

   'Orpheus found, in the resonant strings of his Thracian lyre,
Power to conjure his dead wife's ghost back into existence;   120
Pollux bought back his brother by sharing his death and so often
Treading, retreading this path—one could also add Theseus and
    mighty
Hercules.* Why not me? I too claim descent from Almighty
Jupiter.' While he was praying his prayers and was gripping the altar
Tightly, the seer interrupted: 'O Trojan child of Anchises,   125

Born from the blood of the gods, going down to Avernus* is easy.
All nights, all days too, dark Dis's* portals lie open.
But to recall those steps, to escape to the fresh air above you,
There lies the challenge, the labour! A few have succeeded, those
    people
Fair-minded Jupiter loved or whom blazing manliness wafted   130
High to the heavens, men born of the gods.
                                        'The whole centre is forest.
Deep-channelled Cocytus'* serpentine waters encircle it darkly.
Yet, if there's love so strong in your mind, so mighty a passion
Twice to float over the Stygian lakes, twice gaze upon deep black
Tartarus,* if it's your pleasure to wanton in labours of madness,   135
Grasp what you must do first. On a dense dark tree lurks a hidden
Bough, and its leaves and its pliable, willowy stem are all golden,
Sacred, they say, to the underworld's Juno.* It's masked by the
    forest,
Dank shadows lock it inside hollow coombs of protective concealment.
No one's permitted descent beneath earth's deep mantle without
    first   140
Harvesting this gold-tressed live growth from the tree where it's
    nurtured.
This is the gift you must steal, fair Proserpina rules, as her tribute.
When the first bough's wrenched off, it's replaced, without fail, by
    another
Growing identically golden; its branch leafs just the same metal.
So, track it down, but with eyes looking up. When you've found it in
    due course   145
Harvest it, but, with your hand. It will come away, easy and willing,
Only if fate calls *you*. If not, you'll be powerless to wrench it
No matter what force you use, or to hack it away with a steel blade.
One more thing. I'm afraid you don't know, but a friend of yours*
    now lies
Lost to you, dead, and defiling the fleet with his lifeless cadaver,   150
Now, while you're hunting for oracles, hanging around at our
    entrance.
Find him first, bring him back to a tomb of his own and inter him.
Round up some black cattle. Use them in your first rites of
    appeasement.
After this you'll see the groves of the Styx, the terrain through whose
    defiles

Life cannot pass.' She had spoken. Her mouth was now muted
    and silent.   155

Downcast, Aeneas departs from the cave, eyes lowered, expression
Sombre as he moves along, as his mind turns over and over
What, in his blindness, he's failed to observe. His faithful Achates
Keeps pace, step by step, at his side. He too was in mourning.
Many ideas they scatter like seed in exchanges of chatter:*   160
Who was the dead friend the priestess meant, what body was needing
Burial? Then, while approaching Misenum, they saw, on the dry
    beach,
Cut off by death without honour, a corpse that, in fact, was Misenus,*
Offspring of Aeolus. None could surpass him in raising men's spirits
High with the bugle's brass. He set Mars all ablaze with its blaring.   165
Hector the Great's companion in war, he'd served with distinction,
Fighting in Hector's entourage with his lance and his bugle.
He, when Achilles, in triumph, had stripped away Hector's existence,
Joined up with Dardan Aeneas's friends, this bravest of heroes,
Following what was a cause and a destiny no whit the lesser.   170
Then, as it chanced, one day, as he echoed the seas with his conch-call,
Losing his senses, he challenged the gods to a contest in bugling.
Triton, his rival, at once took him up—if the story's worth credit—
Only to plunge the man down into rock-strewn sea-spray, and
    drown him.
  Everyone now gathered round him with cries of intense
    lamentation,   175
Notably righteous Aeneas. They hastened, unslowed by the flowing
Tears, to do just what the Sibyl had ordered. They vied in constructing,
Tree upon tree, sky high, a cremation fire for his last rites.
Into an ancient forest* they go, tall lairs for the wild beasts.
Spruces crash to the ground and the ilex and trunks of the
    rowan   180
Ring under axe-strokes; fracturing oak splits, sundered by wedges;
Down from the mountains they trundle enormous flowering ashes.
  Up amid all of the work is Aeneas himself, as a foreman
Urging his crews on, equipped with a lumberjack's tools like the others.
As he surveys* the extent of the woodlands, his gloomy depression   185
Makes him turn over these thoughts, which, it chances, he voices
    as prayers:
'What a huge forest! If only that golden bough would just reach out

All by itself, right in front of us now! Why not? For the priestess
Was, alas, all too truthful a prophet in your case, Misenus!'
Just as he says this, in front of his eyes, twin doves,* by convenient   190
Chance, manage somehow to swoop from the skies and to land on
       the green-turfed
Soil. The divinely born hero supreme recognizes his mother's
Own special birds and expresses delight in a prayer that he offers:
'Oh! Be my guides, if there *is* any pathway, and set a direct course
Through the cold air to the groves where that rich bough darkens
       the fertile   195
Earth. O divine mother, don't you fail me in this time of crisis!'
Once he has spoken these fateful words, he stops in his traces,
Noting such ominous signs as the birds make, and where they're
       proceeding.
Since they keep stopping to scavenge, the birds fly ahead in their
       passage
Only as far as the eyes of their trackers can follow their
       progress.   200
Nearing the venue assigned, they've arrived at Avernus's reeking
Jaws. They ascend in a flash, and then glide on the currents of breezes
Down to a perch on the hybrid tree, where he's hoped they would
       settle,
Just where the glittering contrast of gold gleams coldly through
       branches,
Growing as mistletoe grows. For it's not a real shoot of its host tree. 205
Mistletoe loves bearing green leaves fresh in the frosts of the solstice,
Looping the woods' smooth trunks with its berries, yellow as crocus:
That's how the leafing gold met his eye on the dark of the ilex,
That's how its thin foil crackled insistently under the light wind.
Instantly grabbing the bough from its seat, though it struggles,*
       Aeneas,   210
Greedily snaps it and takes it home to his seer, the Sibyl.

Meanwhile, back on the shore, the laments for Misenus continue.
Teucrians give last rites to his unappreciative ashes.
First, they've constructed a massive pyre, rich in resinous pitch-pine,
Split oak too, whose sides they've been weaving with garlands of
       dark leaves.   215
Cypresses, symbols of death, they arrange in an upright position

Fronting it; and, on top, they set out all his glittering armour.
Some set water to boil—bronze cauldrons with wavelets of liquid
Seething on flames—and they wash and anoint the now ice-cold
   cadaver.
Groans echo round. They lay out on a couch limbs duly lamented,   220
Casting upon them his oh so familiar vestment: his mantle
Crimson as fire. Other men—it's a grim, sad service to render—
Shoulder the massive bier and they, as their parents before them,
Turn away faces while kindling the pyre with their torches. The
   heaped gifts
Burn: there is incense and food, olive oil that they've poured into
   large bowls.   225
After the embers collapse and the searing flames have subsided,
Men lave ashes with wine: the remains are still glowing and thirsty.
Bones are collected; and these Corynaeus seals in a bronze urn.
This same man thrice circles his comrades with pure, holy water,
And, with the bough of a fruit-bearing olive, he sprinkles a
   light dew,   230
Ritually cleansing the men, then pronounces the last benediction.
Righteous Aeneas constructs him a tomb in a huge mound, enclosing
Arms for the man, and his bugle and oar, at the foot of a towering
Mountain that up to this day bears a name in his honour: Misenus.
Such is the name it retains for eternity, all through the ages.   235
This done, he's quickly completed the rites that the Sibyl has
   ordered.

Shaped by an outcrop of rock was a high cavern,* opening a monstrous,
Gaping mouth, guarded well by a black lake and woodland's
   tenacious
Shadows. Above it no creature that flies could, without severe peril,
Pass upon fluttering wings, so appalling the breath that came
   spewing   240
Out of its blackened jaws to the vaulted dome of the heavens.
That's why the Greeks named Avernus *Aornos*, 'The Place that is
   Birdless':*
Here's where the priestess prepares four black-skinned* bullocks for
   slaughter,
Trickles their foreheads with wine, crops tips of the tough bristle
   growing
Midway between the two horntips, and sets them as ritual first fruits

Over the sacred fires. She next prays aloud, while invoking   246
Hecate, goddess with power both in Erebus and in the bright sky.
  Others press ritual knives to the throats, catch the warm blood in
      vessels
Held underneath. And Aeneas, to show his respect for the Furies'*
Mother and powerful sister, now kills with his own sword a
      dark-fleeced   250
She-lamb. For you then, Proserpina, he kills an unmated heifer.
Next he establishes altars, at night, for the Stygian ruler,
Places unsundered bulls on the flames, and drenches the blazing
Innards with fresh-pressed oil.
                              Look now: as the sun at its rising
Starts to emerge from beneath its solar threshhold, the solid   255
Earth bellows under men's feet. Forests yoking the hilltops together
Start into motion and hounds seem to loom up, howling through
      shadows,
Hailing the deity's advent.* 'Away, clear away, those who must stand
Outside the shrine!' Thus the god's seer cries. 'Clear out of the
      whole grove!
You, set forth on your path, pull your blade from its sheath* now,
      Aeneas!   260
Now you need resolute courage and stout-hearted firmness of spirit.'
Thus, in her frenzy she spoke, plunging into the cave which had opened.
Matching his leader's steps as she strode, he followed her, fearless.

Gods, under whose command are the breeze-like souls, and you silent
Ghost-shadows, Chaos* and Phlegethon, speechless spaces,
      extending   265
Deep into night, say it's right to give voice to the things I have heard of,
Grant your assent to disclose what's submerged in the earth's pit of
      darkness.

Moving, blocked from sight under night's isolation, through shadows,
Through Dis's empty homes they strode, through realms that are
      nothing,
As one would travel through moonlight's shimmering vagueness,
      beneath light's   270
Treasonous dimness, in forests when Jupiter buries the sky's vaults
Deep beneath ghost shadows, when black night robs substance of
      colour.

Facing the entrance hall, just past the gate, in the gullet of Orcus,*
Sorrows* have set up their quarters, and Heartaches crying for
    vengeance.
Here pale Diseases reside, grim Senility, Terror, and Hunger   275
Powering evil and crime, and Poverty, vile and degrading:
Shapes terrifying the eyes that behold. Then there's Death and
    Hard Labour.
Next lurks listless Sleep, Death's blood-relation, and nearby
Evil Pleasures of Mind and, across, in the opposite threshhold,
War, who is bearer of Death, steeled bedrooms of Family
    Vengeance,   280
Mad Civil Strife, viper hair interlaced by her gore-clotted ribbons.
Centrally set: a dark elm with extending branches, its forearms,
Centuries old, peopled strangely. It's here that what men deem elusive
Dreams wreathe nests, it is said, clinging tightly beneath all its
    foliage.
Many additional monsters lurk here, bestial hybrids: 285
Centaurs have stables adjoining the gates, as do Scyllas—part human,
Part beast—Briareus, too, with his hundred arms, and the Hydra
Hissing out terror; Chimaera, whose weapons are flames; then the
    Gorgons,
Harpies, and Cerberus' shape with its three-bodied shadow.* Aeneas,
Trembling, fear welling up at the sight of them, grabs for his steel
    sword's   290
Edge as a line of defence as they surge at him. He would be lunging,
Uselessly slashing the menacing shadows apart with his steel blade,
Did not his scholarly escort explain that they're bodiless, flimsy,
No more than flickers of life in the hollow illusion of shaped form.*

Here's where the pathway to Acheron, Tartarus' river, commences.   295
Here, in a riot of mud and a suctioning vortex, a whirlpool
Seethes before vomiting up into Cocytus all of its thick silt.*
Charon,* repulsive in frightening filth, is the ferryman, plying
Passage across these turbulent waters. A matted and wolf-grey
Beard clings thick to his chin and his eyes glare flame in their
    bright gaze.   300
Dirt-soiled clothes hang dangling down from a knot at his shoulders.
He works alone. He's propelling his skiff with a pole, trimming
    canvas
Sails as he ferries the bodies across in his iron-girt vessel,

Elderly now—but there's fresh green sap in his elderly godhood.
Pouring his way, all the seething crowd spills down to the stream's
　　　banks: 305
Mothers and full-grown men and the bodies of great-hearted heroes
Finished with life, young boys, young girls who have never been married,
Youths in their prime set on funeral pyres while their parents are
　　　watching:*
Countless as leaves,*during autumn's first frost, falling in forests,
Countless, as clustered birds escaping the turbulent deep sea,   310
Flocking towards dry land when the freezing cold of the season
Routs them across great seas, propels them to lands that are
　　　sun-warmed.
Each soul that stands there begs to be first to accomplish the crossing,
Stretches out hands in a yearning love for the shore on the far side.
Now the grim sailor lets some come aboard, now decides upon
　　　others,   315
Others he just drives off and keeps far away from the bankside.
Moved and amazed by the crowds and the uproar, Aeneas says:
　　　'Tell me,
Maiden, what does it mean, this gathering down at the waters?
What are the spirits attempting to get? What determines selection?
Why is it some go away, others sweep dark waters with oar
　　　strokes?'   320
Brief in her answer, the long-lived priestess responded in this way:
'Child of Anchises, beyond any doubt you're an offshoot of gods' stock,
You're seeing Cocytus' still, deep pools and the Stygian marshes
By whose power gods dread to make oaths. For they dread not to
　　　keep them.
All this mob you observe is the helpless folk, the unburied.   325
Charon's the ferryman; those who have tombs are conveyed on the
　　　waters.
Statutes forbid transportation of souls beyond these banks of horror,
Over these torrents of groans, till their bones receive proper interment.
Lost, they must pass a full century wandering, haunting this shoreline,
Then, at long last, they may pass, and revisit the waters they've
　　　yearned for.'   330
　　Stopped in his tracks, Anchises' son stands motionless, thinking
Deeply, and pitying deep in his soul the injustice they suffer.
Here, in this group, he observes Leucaspis* along with Orontes,
Admiral, once, of the Lycian fleet, sad souls lacking death's dues.

Southerly gales had submerged and engulfed both the men and
    their vessel   335
While they were sailing from Troy over wind-swept seaways together.
Look, Palinurus the helmsman is guiding his footsteps among them.
He, while observing the stars on the recent voyage from Carthage,*
Fell from the aft-deck and spilled overboard in the water at
    mid-course.
  Scarcely aware who this sad being was, so intense was the
    shrouding   340
Darkness, Aeneas spoke first: 'Which one of the gods,* Palinurus,
Tore you from us in mid-voyage and plunged you beneath the sea's
    surface?
Tell me, come on. Though Apollo has never before proved deceitful,
He, in this one response, had my mind completely deluded.
You'd be unharmed on the seas, so his oracles always insisted,   345
You'd reach Ausonian land. Well, so much for the worth of that
    promise!'
  'Son of Anchises, commander,' he answered, 'the cauldron of
    Phoebus*
Didn't deceive you; no god plunged *me** underneath the sea's
    surface.
Violent but random force ripped our steering away. I, as captain,
Charged with both plotting and holding our course, clung fast
    to the tiller   350
Which, as I hurtled down, I dragged with me, and, by the rough seas,
I felt no fear for myself, I swear, near as strong as my terror
That, stripped of steerage, its helmsman ejected, our vessel might
    founder,
Sunk in the swelling surge that seethed so wildly around us.
Three tempestuous nights I spent in the water, as violent   355
Southerlies drove me across vast seas; On the fourth day, I just glimpsed
Italy's coastline ahead as I rose up high on a wave-crest.
Slowly but surely I swam towards land, I was grasping at safety,
Hooking my hands round the crags of the cliff-top. And I would
    have made it
Had cruel people, ignorant men, not attacked me with cold
    steel,   360
Thinking I was fair game, weighed down as I was by my wet clothes;
Now I belong to the waves; winds roll me about on the seashore.
So, by the wonderful daylight and breezes of heaven, I pray you,

And by your father, by dreams that you cherish for growing Iulus,
Save me from this vile doom! You're a man who is never
        defeated.   365
Throw earth upon me! You can! Go about, head for Velia's harbour!*
Or—since you're not, I believe, now preparing to cross such a mighty
Torrent and sail on the waters of Styx without some god's
        approval—
Give a poor fellow your hand, take me *with* you over the waters
If there's a way you can find, if the goddess who bore you
        reveals one,   370
So I can rest, at least now that I'm dead, in a place that is tranquil.'
Such were his prayers and such was the prophet's immediate
        reaction:
'What brings this terrible urge that sweeps over you now, Palinurus?
You, an unburied soul, plan to gaze upon Stygian waters,
Pitiless Furies' streams? You'll cross to those banks uninvited?   375
Cease to hope fate, once spoken by gods, can be altered by prayer!
Grasp and remember these words to console you in bitter misfortune.
Those living near—driven far, driven wide, by celestial omens,
City to city—will offer your bones last ritual appeasement;
Build you a mound. And they'll send to that mound solemn,
        annual tributes.   380
Through the remainder of time that site will be named Palinurus.'
All of his sorrows are driven away. From his heart, sad and aching,
Pain is, for just a brief moment, expelled; he delights in the
        land's name.

Then they continued the journey begun and moved close to the river.
When, from his boat on the water, the sailor observed them
        approaching   385
Down through the silent grove and directing their steps to the bankside,
He, with a verbal assault, challenged them before they could
        address him:
'Tell me, come on, whoever you are, who now march on our river
Armed to the teeth—Halt!—Why are you here? Speak where you
        are standing!
This is a land for the shades, and for sleep, and for night that brings
        numbness.   390
It's an offence to convey *live* bodies on Stygian vessels.
I wasn't happy at all to take Hercules, when he came this way,

Onto the lake, or, for that matter, Theseus, Pirithoüs either,
Though they were born of the gods and invincibly powerful heroes.
Hercules came into Tartarus planning to chain up its watchdog,   395
Actually dragged the beast trembling with fear from the king's
    throne. The others
Came with intent to abduct Dis' mistress out of his bedroom.'
  Briefly the seer of the god who himself had defied death,*
    responded:
'No such treachery here! So stop getting angry! These weapons.
Don't threaten force. Your great big doorman can bark on for
    ever   400
Inside his cave, let him terrify ghosts that have no blood to drain out,
And let Proserpina stay unabused in her own uncle's household.
Trojan Aeneas, renowned for his righteousness—and martial valour—
Goes to the deepest shadows of Erebus seeking his father.
But, if no icon of righteousness on such a scale can impress you,   405
Still, you'd acknowledge this bough'—disclosing the bough that lay
    hidden
Under her robe. Wrath gone, his surging emotions subsided.
No more was said. As he gazes, in awe, at the marvellous offering,
Destiny's fateful branch, seen now after long years of waiting,
Charon reverses his dark vessel's course and approaches the
    bankside,   410
Hurls out other souls already seated across the boat's long thwarts,
Frees up the gangways and, as he does, takes massive Aeneas
Into his reed-woven hull. But when *his* weight is added, the
    twine-sewn
Skiff gives a groan, shipping gallons of water through gaps in its fabric.
Still, it gets seer and hero across, and deposits them safely,   415
Over the waters, in shifting mud, amid grey river grasses.

Cerberus, monstrous, massively stretching out in a cavern
Facing them, sets this whole realm booming with three-throated
    barking.
Seeing his snake-spiked collar erect now, the seer distracts him,
Tossing him sleep-bringing drug-drenched cakes with a coating of
    honey.   420
Opening three throats wide, that dog, quite rabid with hunger,
Snaps up the treats he is tossed; then, his monstrous shoulders
    relaxing,

Slumps to the ground, sprawled massively over the whole of the
     cave floor.
Now that its guardian's entombed, Aeneas leaps for the entrance,
Swiftly escaping the banks of the river that knows no re-crossing.   425
   Instantly voices are heard: massed wailing, the weeping of
     children:*
Souls never able to speak, just over the boundary's threshhold,
Stolen by death's dark day, ripped away from the breasts of their
     mothers,
Plunged in the grave's bitter sourness without any share of the
     sweetness
Life brings; next are those sentenced to death upon false
     accusations.   430
Placement here's not assigned without lot or a process of judgement.
Minos presides* in a court, shakes lots in an urn, summons silent
Crowds for a hearing, investigates lives and the charges against them.
Innocent folk who despaired are their neighbours: people whose own
     hands
Birthed their own deaths in disgust at the world's light, cast away
     living   435
Souls. How they'd *long** to get back now beneath sky's limitless, open
Brightness, and suffer in poverty, tolerate gruelling labours!
Heaven forbids it; and that grim lake's unlovable waters
Bind them; the spiralling Styx loops ninefold moats of constriction.*

Not far from here, their attention is drawn to what men call the
     Grieving   440
Meadows that sprawl their tremendous expanses in every direction.
Here reside people that hardhearted Love, with his cruel corrosion,
Wholly consumed. Tracks, traceless and secret, conceal them, and
     myrtle
Forests enclose them. For, even in death, anxiety's heartaches
Fail to desert them. Aeneas discerns here Phaedra and Procris,   445
And Eriphyle displaying the wounds that her pitiless son dealt.
There is Evadne, Pasiphaë too; at their side Laodamia
Walks. And there's Caeneus,* a man for a while, now, again, she's a
     woman:
Fate has reversed its account; she's returned to her former appearance.
   Wandering the vast forest, lost, among women of Greece,* was
     Phoenician   450

Dido, fresh from her wound. Troy's hero, as soon as he neared her,
Knew who she was, in the dark of her heartache, there among
    shadows,
Dimly, the way one sees, or imagines one *has* seen, the wandering
Moon on the first of the month rise up through a veil of enshrouding
Clouds. As he let tears fall, he addressed her with love in its
    sweetness: 455
'Dido unfulfilled, then it really was true, news that reached me,
News that your life had been quenched, that you'd ended it all with a
    sword point?
Have I, alas, been the cause of your death? Oh, I swear by the heavens'
Powers above, by the stars, by whatever one trusts in the earth's
    depths:
It was no choice of my will, good queen, to withdraw from your
    country.*   460
Rather, commands of the gods, which now compel me to pass
    through
Ghost-shadows, regions vile with decay, night's oceans of darkness,
Drove me with power supreme. And I couldn't believe* I was bringing
Grief so intense, so painful to you, when I made my departure.
Don't walk away, don't draw yourself back from my eyes as
    I watch you.   465
Who are you running from?* Fate gives me this last chance to address
    you.'
That's how Aeneas attempted to quiet a soul that was blazing,
Glaring in anger: with words such as these. And he set his eyes
    weeping.
She turned her back on him, stared at the ground, eyes fixed, her
    expression
No more moved by these efforts at conversation than hard flint   470
Slabs, or the marble face on the crags of Marpessus in Paros.*
She, in the end, made the break herself, full of hate, and took refuge
Deep in the ghost-shadowed grove where her earlier husband,
    Sychaeus,
Matches her cares with his own and whose love equals hers very fairly.
    Stunned by her unfair doom, and despite her reaction, Aeneas,   475
Follows her far with his tears; he feels pity for her as she leaves him.

Travelling onwards as planned needed effort, but soon they were
    reaching

Distant secluded fields, where the heroes of battle assemble.
Tydeus encounters him here and, famed for his prowess in combat,
Parthenopaeus, along with the ghost of the pallid Adrastus.*   480
Here too were Dardanus' sons, those fallen in battle and deeply
Wept to the heavens. Aeneas, on seeing them all in formation,
Gave out a groan: there was Glaucus, and Medon, Thersilochus* also,
Three sons of Antenor, Ceres' votary too, Polyboetes,
And, still holding fast to his weapons and chariot, Idaeus.*   485
Round him to left and to right these spirits crowd in a circle.
It's not enough just to glance at him once; for they love to delay him,
Stroll at his side as he walks, and discover his reasons for coming.

    But, when Danaän commanders, and infantry lines Agamemnon*
Led, see the man and his arms flash lightning-bright through the
    shadows,   490
They all tremble in fear. Some turn tail, as in the old days
When they ran off to their ships. Others, trying to raise a thin war-cry,
Find that the shouts don't emerge from their mouths, though they
    open them widely.
Here he sees Priam's son,* every part of whose body is mangled:
This is Deiphobus, all of whose face is completely disfigured,   495
Face, yes, and both of his hands: ears ripped from dehumanized
    temples,
Nose lopped off as a common criminal's mark of dishonour.
Just, only just, recognizing the man as he cowered and covered
Punishment's terrible scars, he exclaims in a voice still familiar:
'Master of weapons,* Deiphobus, prince of the bloodline of noble   500
Teucer! What judge in his ruling imposed such a barbarous sentence?
Who had the licence to do this to you? I heard rumours, that final
Night: people said you'd collapsed on a mountain of intertwined
    corpses,
Worn out by killing Pelasgians during an orgy of slaughter.
I myself built an empty tomb for you, down at Rhoeteum's
Harbour, and cried out the Call for the Dead three times in a loud
    voice.   505
Guarding the spot are your name and your arms.* But I couldn't
    distinguish
You, my dear friend, and set you, as I left, in the earth of our homeland.'
Priam's son answered: 'My friend, for your part, you have
    overlooked nothing,
You've done the rites due Deiphobus, and to his ghost, at the
    graveside.   510

My own fate and the deadly crime of that bitch of a Spartan
Sank me in all of these evils: she left me these scars as mementoes.
  'That last night: how we squandered its hours in our false
    celebrations,
You well know. One is forced to recall it too hideously clearly.
Up from the plain came the fateful horse, leaping over our towering   515
Pergamum, pregnant with infantry, heavily armed, in its belly.
She staged what seemed like a chorus, and led, in a circle around it,*
Phrygian women who screamed in a wild celebration of Bacchus.
She, in their midst, was brandishing fires that would ruin a nation,
Calling Danaäns forth from the citadel's crest. I, exhausted,   520
Heavy with sleep and with cares, lay trapped in the bed of our marriage,
Unfulfilled and accursed, as a sweet, deep slumber like tranquil
Death pressed down on my stillness. My wife, royal pick of the
    whole flock,
Strips, meanwhile, all arms* from the house, even eases my trusty
Sword out from under my head, opens doors, calls in
    Menelaus,   525
Hoping, I'm sure, this would make a grand gift for her lover and
    stamp out
Rumours based on her past that had made her a byword for evil.
Why draw it out? They burst into my bedroom along with Ulysses,
Aeolus' spawn,* always ready to prompt an atrocity. Oh gods!
Pay the Greeks back in kind, if my prayer for justice is
    righteous.   530
  'Now it is your turn. Explain what occurred that has brought you
Here while you're still alive? Were you lost, washed in by the wayward
Seas or did gods so advise? Or were *you* so wearied by Fortune's
Blows as to seek out the land of unrest, grim homes without sunlight?'
While they exchanged conversation, Dawn* had already
    completed   535
Half of her arching course through the skies in her roseate chariot.
Chances were good they'd consume all allotted time on such matters.
But his companion, the Sibyl, advised him of this, and said briefly:
'Night is upon us, Aeneas. We're squandering hours in weeping.
Here is the place where the road subdivides into two distinct
    pathways: 540
This one, the right, leads up past the fortress of Great Dis: it's
    our route
Straight to Elysium* now. But the left marches those who are evil
Off to their torments, to Tartarus, dungeon for all the unrighteous.'

'Don't get so angry and harsh, great priestess,' Deiphobus
　　counters.
'I'll go away, I'll be there for the count, I'll surrender to darkness.　545
March on, glory of Troy, march on! May *your* fate be kinder!'
That's all he said, and he turned on his heels while his voice was
　　still speaking.

Suddenly, under a cliff to his left, as he glances, Aeneas
Sees an extensive fortress, encircled by triple defence walls.
Round them Phlegethon roars. Grim Tartarus' river of lava　550
Blazes with white-hot flame, spits rocks out hissing and clashing.
Blocking the entrance, a huge gate stands set in uprights of solid
Adamant, such as defy any force that a human or even
Heaven could bring to attack and uproot them, encased in a soaring
Turret of iron. Tisiphone,* swathed in a blood-dripping mantle,　555
Sleeplessly, day and night, stands permanent guard at the entrance.
Screams can be heard from within, and the crackle of merciless
　　floggings;
Followed by rasping of iron and chains as they're cranked under torsion.
Halted and frozen with terror, Aeneas absorbs all the bedlam.
'Maiden, can you put a face on the crimes or describe me what
　　torments　560
Punish them? What is provoking the torrent of screams that I'm
　　hearing?'*
So then, the prophet began: 'Famous chief of the Teucrian nation,
Innocent people may never set foot on that criminal threshold.
Hecate, though, when she put me in charge of the groves of Avernus,
Taught me herself how the gods punish wrongs, took me through*
　　the whole system.　565
　　'This is hell's toughest regime: Rhadamanthus, its warden from
　　Knossos,
Punishes, hears accusations of treachery, forces confession
When someone smugly delights in illusory flight from detection
While still alive, and defers his atonement till death, when it's too late.
Vengeance is swift on the guilty: Tisiphone, armed with her lashes,　570
Leaps up to whip them herself, thrusts her left hand, teeming with
　　angry
Snakes, at their faces, then calls in her armies of merciless sisters.
That's when the hinges scream and the hideously rasping, accursèd
Gates yawn wide. You can see what manner of jailer is posted

Here at the entrance, what kind of a face watches over the
     threshold.   575
Inside is stationed an even more pitiless monster, with fifty
Raven and gaping throats. It's the Hydra. Then Tartarus proper
Opens a chasm extending on down twice as far* into darkness
As the eye's view of Olympus extends up high into brightness.
Here's where the ancient offspring of Earth, great warrior
     Titans,*   580
Toppled by lightning bolts, now squirm on the floor of her bedrock.
Here I have seen Aloeus's twins.* Their bodies are monstrous.
They, bare-handed, attacked and attempted to tear down the vast sky's
Vault, to cast Jupiter down from his realms up above in the heavens.
I've seen Salmoneus* too as he suffers in cruel retribution: 585
He used to ride in a four-horse chariot, parading in triumph,
Brandishing torches of fire, among peoples of Greece, through Olympia
Right in the heartland of Elis. He mimicked the really Olympian
Jupiter's thunder and fire and demanded men grant him official
Status as god. How insane! To use bronze and the clatter of
     hard-hoofed   590
Horses to simulate storms and their unreproducible lightning.
But the omnipotent father, within thick and genuine storm clouds,
Torqued up a thunderbolt—no simple torches in his case, no smoky
Pinewood brands—and he blasted him down with a monster tornado.

'Tityos,* stepchild of Earth who is mother of all, with his body   595
Stretched over nine full acres, was there to be seen. And a monstrous
Vulture was trimming his liver that can't die, snipping with curving
Beak as it probed through his guts that regenerate tissue and
     raw pain,
Plucking out food for its feast, tucked under his tall ribs and nesting:
Flesh reborn is not granted a respite for even an instant.   600

'Need I remind you of Lapiths: Pirithoüs, Ixion* also?
Over them looms a black boulder of flint that will fall any moment,
Seems to be falling now. Gold gleams in the frames elevating
Couches for feasts; and in front of their eyes are set banquets of regal
Splendour. But right at their elbows reclines that direst of
     Demons*   605
Blocking their ghostly hands from touching the food on the tables,
Rearing up, raising her fiery torch while her mouth bellows thunder.

'Here are the men who, during their lives, earned hate from their
     brothers,

Lashed out at parents and beat them, or tricked and defrauded
    dependants,
Men who acquired great wealth then roosted alone on their
    nest-eggs,   610
Setting no portion aside for their families (this group is largest!).
Then those killed for adultery, those who fought wars for unrighteous
Causes, and those unafraid to betray oaths sworn to their masters.
They're locked up, pending punishment. Please don't ask me* to
    teach you
Details of punishment, forms it assumes, individual cases.   615
Some move large rocks, some stretched taut, lashed tight onto
    wheel spokes,
Hang. There is one who just sits; he'll continue to sit there for ever
Unfulfilled: Theseus. Then Phlegyas,* misery's symbol,
Cries out his warning, his booming voice bears witness among ghosts:
"Learn what justice means! Be warned! Don't underrate gods'
    power!"   620
  '*He* sold his country* for gold, set upon it a powerful tyrant:
He fixed laws in bronze, for a price; for a price he unfixed them.
This one invaded his daughter's room for incestuous marriage.
All of them dared some atrocious wrong and accomplished that daring.
Had I a hundred tongues and a hundred mouths* and an iron   625
Voice, I would still fall short of the power I would need to encompass
Every species of crime or name all of the judgements inflicted.'
  Phoebus's long-lived priestess, her overview finished, adds these
    words:
'Now reap the fruits of your journey. You started an offering;
    complete it!
But we must hurry. I see walls wrought upon Cyclopes' anvils,   630
Also the gates whose arches we're facing. That's where our
    instructions
Tell us we must now deposit these gifts.' As soon as she's spoken,
Both race, side by side, down the path's last stretches of darkness,
Hurtling along as they're closing the gap and approaching the gateway.
Gaining the entrance, Aeneas besprinkles his body with
    fresh-drawn   635
Water, then fixes the bough on the castle entrance before him.

Once this rite was performed and the goddess's offering completed,
Down they went to the zone of joy, the green of idyllic

Fortune's groves: the Estates of the Blest. A more generously lustrous
Brightness of sky dresses meadows here with a colourful
    brilliance.   640
They know a sun shining only for them* and the stars are their own
    stars.
Some keep their bodies in shape on the open-air lawns of gymnasiums,
Hold competitions in sport, even wrestle each other on blond sand.
Some beat feet to the rhythms of dance, recite poetry, music.
And there is also a Thracian priest in his long, flowing
    vestments,   645
Bridging the seven distinctive notes of his lyre, which he's plucking
Now with his fingers, now with a shuttling ivory plectrum.
Here resides Teucer's family of old, such a handsome assemblage,
Great-hearted heroes they are, who were born in an age that was
    better:
Ilus, Assaracus, Dardanus* too, Troy's father and founder.   650
Arms, in the distance, and chariots of men catch his gaze: hollow,
    empty.
Spears stand fixed, points down in the earth, while untethered horses
Wander at random and graze all over the plain. For the pleasure
Men, when alive, took in chariots and arms, and in raising their
    well-groomed
Horses, remains, and it follows them under the earth when they're
    buried.   655
Look, he sees others spread out to the left and the right in a meadow,
Feasting, and singing a paean of joy as they dance through the fragrant
Clusters of laurels in groves from whose springs the Eridanus* surges
Up to the surface and rolls in its ample flow through the forest.
Here there are clusters of men who were wounded defending their
    country,   660
Priests who kept chastity's vows intact through the course of their
    lifetimes,
Poets and seers who were righteous and spoke words worthy of
    Phoebus,
All who enriched human life with the arts and the skills they discovered,
All whose noble deeds earned life in the memory of others.
Every forehead is ringed with a ribbon as white as the pure
    snow.   665
  As they encircled Aeneas, the Sibyl addressed them, with special
Thought for Musaeus, the focal point of the largest escorting

Throng, and regarded with awe as he stood head and shoulders
    above them:
'Souls who have found your fulfilment, and you, supreme poet and
    prophet,
Tell me what district* is housing Anchises and at what location?   670
He's why we've come here and crossed the large span of the Erebus
    river.'
In just a few words, the hero supplied his response to her question:
'Nobody here has a home you can point to. Our dwellings are dark
    groves,
River-banks serve as our bedding and meadows freshened by brooklets.
That's where we live. Still, if this is your wish, and the choice that
    your heart prompts,   675
Climb up this ridge over here. I will plot you a path you can manage.'
This said, he strode out in front and he showed them, from up on
    the summit,
Well-tended grasslands below. So they left the high hill and descended.
Father Anchises, deep in a hollow valley of greenness,
Was, as it chanced, making careful review of the souls in
    confinement   680
Who, in time, would ascend to the light. He was holding a census.*
Counting up all his descendants, the grandsons he doted on, weighing
Fates and fortunes of men, strength of character, power of body.
But, when he noticed Aeneas approach, reaching out across meadows,
He too opened his arms, reached both hands eagerly forward.   685
Tears were now flooding his cheeks, words poured from his mouth
    in a torrent:
'Have you at last really come? Did righteous love for your father
Conquer the rough road here as I thought it would! Son, can I really
Gaze at your face, hear the voice that I know, and be able to answer?
This thought I nurtured live in my mind, I was sure it would
    happen,   690
While I was counting the days. And my anxious hopes didn't fool me!
I have you now! I've heard of the lands, the extent of the seaways
You, dear son, have traversed. What a beating you've taken from
    danger!
Oh, how I worried that Libya's powers might harm you in some way!'
He, in reply, said: 'Father, your sad image, rising before me   695
Time and again compelled me to push to this boundary's threshold.
Anchors are down in Etruscan waters.* We've made it! So, father,

Give me your hand! Give it, don't pull away as I hug and
    embrace you!'
Waves of tears washed over his cheeks as he spoke in frustration:
Three attempts made to encircle his father's neck with his
    outstretched   700
Arms yielded three utter failures. The image eluded his grasping
Hands like the puff of a breeze, as a dream flits away from a dreamer.

Through this,* Aeneas observes in a nearby vale, a secluded
Grove with its green-leafed canopy rustling over the woodlands,
And river Lethe* too, flowing on past dwellings of calmness.   705
Peoples and nations, too many to count, seethe all around, swarming
Much as, on summer's serene, warm days, honey bees* in the meadows
Settle on so many species of flowers, pour over the lilies'
Whiteness. The countryside's live with the hum of their buzzing.
Shocked by this sudden sight, unaware of its meaning, Aeneas   710
Asks for some answers: what river might this be which flows over
    yonder,
Who are the people who've crowded the banks* in a giant formation.
Father Anchises replies: 'They're souls that are due second bodies:
So fate rules, and they're drinking now from the waters of Lethe,
Draughts that will free them of care and ensure long years of
    oblivion.   715
  'These are the souls, my family's line I've been wanting for ages
Just to parade in your presence, to set in your mind, name and
    number,
So you can, now you've found Italy, share my delight more
    profoundly.'
'Father, must I then suppose some souls of ineffable lightness
Soar, once again, to the sky just for reincarnation* in clumsy   720
Bodies? What terrible passion for daylight possesses the poor things?'
'Son, I will not hold *you* in suspense,' Anchises commences.
'*I'll* tell you now.' He proceeds to reveal every detail in order:
  'First, you must grasp that the heaven and earth and the sea's
    liquid flatness,
Also the gleaming sphere of the moon, constellations, the huge sun   725
Feed on internal Energy.* Mind, which suffuses these cosmic
Limbs, pervades the vast body and keeps the mass vital. This
    mixture
Generates life within humans and beasts, flying creatures, and also

Monsters Ocean spawns below marbled plains on its surface.
Fire endows them with force, and the source of the seeds for
    that fire   730
Is, though it's slowed and restricted by noxious bodies, the heavens.
Earth-made flesh, limbs slouching to death, dull much of its vital
Force, causing people to fear and desire, suffer pain, and feel pleasure,
Fail to see open skies in their prisons of darkness and blindness.
Even when life has departed, along with their last glimpse of
    daylight,   735
Not all traces of evil are gone from these pitiful creatures,
Not all bodily maladies leave. Of necessity, many
Harden and grow, become deeply ingrained in mysterious manners.
Therefore the souls are both punished and cleansed, and they pay off
    the hanging
Balance of crimes in the past. Some are stretched, hung up to the
    empty   740
Breezes, while others are cleansed of their ingrained crime by
    immersion
Deep in a giant whirlpool, or burned from within by a fire.
Each of us suffers his ghostly pain.* When it's over, we're sent out,
All through Elysium's breadth. Just a few of us stay in the Blessèd
Fields. When the circle of time is complete, some day in the
    future,   745
Purged of the last trace of crime ingrained, they are left with ethereal
Power of perception, the fire of its clear breath, pure and untainted.
  'God summons all these souls, when they've rolled time's wheel
    for a thousand
Years,* to convene in a mass at the Lethe, Oblivion's waters,
So, with their memories wholly erased, they can walk beneath
    heaven's   750
Dome yet again and begin to desire to go back into bodies.'

Finished, Anchises propelled both Aeneas and, with him, the Sibyl
Into the midst of the seething and noisy assemblage, and clambered
High on a mound from whose top he could plainly distinguish the faces
Passing in long lines before him and note their identities clearly. 755
  'Come now: I'll set out in words the whole sequence of glory that
    follows*
Dardan sons in the future: illustrious spirits, descendants,
Souls that remain to be born of Italian peoples and go forth

Bearing our name. And I'll teach you what *your* fateful destiny offers.
  '*That* man, you see him, the youth who now leans on an as yet
     unblooded   760
Spear, is allotted the next place in line: he's the first who'll be rising
Up to the bright sky's breezes. His blood will be partly Italian:
Silvius—"Woodsman", an Alban name. He's your posthumous
    offspring,*
Child of advanced old age.* So your wife, Lavinia, will rear him,
Too late for you, in the woods, to be king and the father of more
    kings.   765
Our descendants, through him, will long be the masters of Alba.*
  'Procas* is next, over there, he's the glory of Troy and its people,
Then Capys, Numitor too, and the man who'll give *your* name
    revival:
Silvius Aeneas,* as righteous in life as he's valiant in warfare,
He'll be king among kings, if he ever becomes king of Alba.   770
Fine young men! Take a look! What a great show of strength they
    can proffer,
Shading their brows with the Citizens' Oak for their rescue of others.
  'These men will found Nomentum for you, Gabii and Fidenae.
These men will place Collatia's fortress high on the hilltops,
Also Pometia and Castrum Inui, Bola and Cora.*   775
They will exist in the future as names; now they're lands, but they're
    nameless.
  'Next, Mars' son will join the parade as his grandfather's comrade:
Romulus* born of a mother, herself of Assaracus' bloodline:
Ilia. See how this man has twin crests crowning his helmet,
And how the father himself now marks him with *his* stamp of
    godhood?   780
  'Here's the man* under whose auspices famous Rome will encompass
Earth's full extent with her power; and in courage will rival Olympus!
One city's circuit of walls will embrace seven citadel summits,
Well fulfilled in her offspring of men, as is mighty Cybele,*
Who, in her turreted crown, rides a chariot drawn through the
    Phrygian   785
Cities, the radiant mother of gods who embraces a hundred
Grandchildren: all live in heaven, each claiming the sky as a birthright.
  'Marshal your eyes' twin gaze this way now! Look at this people,
Look at your Romans! For Caesar is here,* all Iulus' descendants,
Marching towards their places beneath sky's arching expanses.   790

Here's the man you've heard promised to you so often, he's here now:
Caesar Augustus, born of a god, who will one day establish
All through the farmlands of Latium once, long ago, ruled by Saturn,
Ages of Gold. He'll extend Roman power beyond far Garamantes,
East beyond India too, to a land that lies under no mapped stars,   795
Outside the paths of the year and the sun, where sky-bearing Atlas
Spins on his shoulders the blaze of the star-studded orb of the heavens.
Caspian kingdoms* already await his arrival, and shudder,
As does Maeotia's land, at the gods' oracular warnings.
Nile's seven mouths to the sea now riot in turmoil of terror.   800
Not even Hercules crossed so much of the earth in his travels,
What if he shot down a bronze-hoofed doe, if he tamed Erymanthus'
Forested woodlands, what if he terrified Lerna with arrows?
Conqueror Bacchus' journey was shorter when guiding his chariot's
Tigress team from the summit of Nysa with reins made of ivy.   805
So, do we still hesitate to extend our strength by our manhood?
Are we afraid of establishing roots in Ausonia's land now?

   'Who's the man far over there, decorated with branches of olive,
Carrying ritual symbols? I know, by the hair and the untrimmed
Beard, he's the Roman king* who'll establish the city as leading   810
Framer of laws, and be sent to imperial power from a pauper's
Land, tiny Cures.

                            'And next after him in the line we see Tullus:*
This man will shatter his homeland's inertia and stir up its idle
Men to take arms, rouse armies who've grown unaccustomed to
        triumphs.
Following closely behind him, comes Ancus.* He's overly boastful,   815
Finds too much joy, even now, in the breezes of popular favour.
   'Won't you observe these Tarquin kings,* and that proud spirit
        bringing
Vengeance, restoring our *fasces*, our emblems of government, Brutus?
He'll be the first to take consular power and the merciless axes;
He, their own father, will pass on his sons, when they stir
        revolution,   820
Sentence of death, for the sake of beautiful freedom. This action
Costs him his own fulfilment—however posterity takes it.
Other loves yield before love of one's homeland and passion for glory.
   'Look at the Decii there, and the Drusi, and, far off, Torquatus,
Merciless axeman, and also Camillus* who brings back our
        standards!   825

'Those, though, the souls that you see all ablaze in identical armour,*
Hearts so harmonious now—and as long as the darkness constrains
    them—
Oh, what a massive war, what battles they'll kindle between them,
What great slaughter, if they should arrive in the light of the living!
Father-in-law swoops down from the Alps and from Monaco's
    fortress;   830
Son-in-law lines up opposing troops from the lands of the sunrise.
No, my boys, no! Don't accustom your spirits to wars of such huge
    scope,
Don't use your strength and your vigour to disembowel your
    country!
You be the first to show pity, you, who are sprung from Olympus!
Throw down the sword in your hand, son of my blood! . . .   835
    'That man will drive to the Capitol's heights in his chariot,
        triumphant
Victor of Corinth,* distinguished for all the Achaeans he's
    slaughtered.
That man* destroys Agamemnon's city, Mycenae, and Argos
And the descendant of Aeacus, scion of warrior Achilles:
He'll avenge his Troy's blood and the looted shrine of Minerva.   840
    'Who'd leave you unnamed, Great Cato,* or you, Cossus?*
        Who'd leave
Gracchus's stock* from the count—war's twin bolts of lightning, either:
Scipiadae,* spelling African doom? Or Fabricius,* the peasant
General? Serranus* the ploughman serrating and sowing the furrows?
    'Fabii,* where do you rush me? I'm tired. You're Fabius the
        Greatest: 845
You alone slow action down to restore our republic.
    'Others* will hammer out bronzes that breathe in more lifelike
        and gentler
Ways, I suspect, create truer expressions of life out of marble,
Make better speeches, or plot, with the sweep of their compass, the
    heaven's
Movements, predict the ascent of the sky's constellations. Well,
    let them!   850
You, who are Roman, recall how to govern mankind with your power.
These will be your special "Arts": the enforcement of peace as a
    habit,
Mercy* for those cast down and relentless war upon proud men.'

So spoke his father Anchises, then adds—for they're watching in
　　wonder:
'Look! How Marcellus* is striding, aglow in his Spoils of
　　Distinction!　　　　　　　　　　　　　　　　　　　　　855
He, as conqueror, towers so high above all other heroes.
He'll stabilize Rome's state in a turbulent crisis, he'll ride down
Punic foes, kill a Gallic chief in a duel, thus becoming
Third to present these captured spoils* to our father, Quirinus.'
　　Now came Aeneas's turn. For he saw, with Marcellus, a
　　young man　　　　　　　　　　　　　　　　　　　　　860
Who, in his beauty and armour's flash, stood out from the flocking
Crowds. Yet his forehead displayed little joy; his expression* was
　　downcast,
As were his eyes. 'Who's the man who is walking that way in the hero's
Company, father? His son? Or his nephew, some noble descendant?*
Oh, what an uproar his comrades are making! And what an
　　impressive　　　　　　　　　　　　　　　　　　　　　865
Figure he cuts! Yet the night flutters menacing shadows about him,
Darkens his head.' Eyes brimming with tears, his father Anchises
Broke in: 'Son, don't ask of your land's great national sorrow.
Fate grants earth a mere glimpse of his face; it won't let
　　him continue
Living. For Roman growth seemed to you too great in potential,　870
Powers above, had such gifts as these been our lasting possession.
Oh, how the Campus Martius will flood his great city with heroes'
Massed lamentations!* And oh, what a funeral, Lord of the Tiber,
You'll see while flowing your way past the newly built mound at the
　　gravesite!
No boy of Ilian blood will hereafter lift elders of Latium　　875
Higher in hope, nor will Romulus' land any time in the future
Swell with such boastful pride over anyone else she has nurtured.
Oh, for his righteousness, oh, for his old-fashioned honour, his
　　right hand
Never defeated* in war! No man would have lived if he'd challenged
Him to a fight, as an infantryman marching forth at his foeman,　880
Or as a knight putting spurs to the flanks of a foam-frothing stallion!
Boy to be pitied, alas, if you break harsh destiny's barrier,
You'll be Marcellus. Fill hands full of lilies to shower upon him.
I'll scatter crimson flowers. Let me thus, at least, solace our kinsman's
Soul with an offering* of gifts and a hollow oblation.'

They wander   885
Randomly on in this way through the whole of the region's expansive
Prairies of mist while subjecting them all to the light of enquiry.
After he's guided his son around, detail by detail, and kindled
Love for the glory to come as a flame in his spirit, Anchises
Then puts the hero in mind of the wars he must fight in the
     future,   890
Tells him about the Laurentian peoples, Latinus's city,
Also what way to elude or confront each labour encountered.

Sleep opens twin double portals.* The first, made of horns, grants
     an easy
Exit, it's said, for real ghosts. On the second, one sees a rich lustre,
Crafted with dentils of elephant tusk in fantastic perfection.   895
Dead souls, though, send deceptive dreams up above to the heavens.
Here's where Anchises, his last words said to his son and the Sibyl,
Bids them farewell, sends them off on their way through the ivory
     portal.*
Cutting on back to the fleet now, Aeneas revisits his comrades,
Then sets out for Caieta's port,* running close to the seashore.   900
Anchors are tossed from the prows; aft decks stand beached on the
     seashore.*

BOOK SEVEN

Y<small>OU</small> too gave to our coasts, Caieta, nurse of Aeneas,
Undying fame when you died, thanks to rumour. For here in the
mighty
Twilight Land, your name still marks your bones, you ennoble
This site even today—if that's in itself any glory.

Righteous in ritual detail, Aeneas completes the interment, 5
Building a rising mound; then, after tranquillity settles
Over the deep, hoists sail for the voyage and slips from the harbour.
Soft winds breathe through the night, and a dazzling moon doesn't
hinder
Sailing. The silvered sea glitters bright with her shimmering
radiance.
Circe's Aeaean land is the next shore they pass without stopping. 10
There she, child of the Sun,* enchants inaccessible forests,
Ringing their depths with eternal song, and, proud in her palace,
Kindles the fragrant cedar, illumining night while her weaving
Coaxes her shuttle to sing as it runs the slim threads of her loom's
warp.

Groans full of anger are overheard from this region, as lions 15
Chafe at their chains in the deep night hours and roar as the ropes rasp.
Coarse-haired boars and penned-in bears bristle savage in fury,
Shapes as of massive wolves howl loudly. They're Circe's creations.
She, savage goddess, has drugged them with herbs out of human
appearance
Fashioned them into these brute beast hides and facial expressions. 20
Fearing that righteous Trojans too faced monstrous abuses
If they were forced into port or approached these terrible coastlands,
Neptune bellied their sails with favouring winds, and accorded
Chance to escape. He conveyed them beyond these turbulent waters.

Sea was already beaming with blushes; Aurora was glowing 25
High in the heavens, in saffron attire and in roseate chariot,
When the winds dropped; every puff of the breezes was suddenly
stillness.
Oar blades struggled in slow, dense brine, flat, heavily marbled.
Here, though, Aeneas observes, as he looks from the deep, a great
forest
Through which the Tiber's idyllic flow bursts out into open 30

Sea in a series of spiralling swirls, scrawled densely with yellow
Sand. All around and above it, the varied birds of the river's
Channels and banks are enchanting the skies with the charm of their
　　singing,
Flying from place to place in the forest. Aeneas then orders
Crews to adjust their courses and face prows in for a landing.　　35
This done, he joyfully enters the shaded course of the river.

Come now, Erato!* Who were the kings? What happened at which time?
What kind of state was the Latium of old when that immigrant army
First drove its vessels to land on the shores of Ausonia? All this
I will explain, I'll recall what led to the start of the fighting.　　40
You, goddess, prompt your seer.* I'll speak about hideous warfare,
I'll speak of battles, of kings who were driven to death by their courage,
What part Etruscans played, how Hesperia's whole land was bullied
Into the fight. As the worldview birthing within me is greater.
My labour's greater too.
　　　　　　　　　King Latinus had governed the tranquil　　45
Farmlands and cities through years of prolonged peace. Now he was
　　ageing.
He was born Faunus's* child by a Laurentine nymph named Marica,
So we are told. Now the father of Faunus was Picus, and he claimed
You, Saturn, fathered him and were ultimate source of his bloodline.
By gods' fate, though, Latinus had neither legitimate son nor　　50
Any male stock. One rose; but was rooted out early in manhood.
Only a daughter sustained his home and position of power.
She was now ripe for a husband, now fully of age to be married.
Many a man from great Latium, indeed, from all over Ausonia,
Sued for her hand. And the loveliest suitor among them was
　　Turnus.　　55
He'd strong ancestry backing his claim; and the queen of the Latins*
Pushed to have him join the house as her son-in-law with quite amazing
Love. But divine portents, raising a number of fears, were a hindrance.
Right in the midst of their palace's high inner courts stood a laurel,*
Nursed over many long years with respect. For its leaves were
　　thought sacred.　　60
Father Latinus was said to have found it himself and declared it
Sacred to Phoebus, when first he commenced constructing his city,
And, it's said, he named his settlers 'Laurentines', in the tree's honour.
　Here came a portent: bees in a dense swarm* swept through the
　　liquid

Air with a shrill and intense buzz, besetting the crest of the laurel,   65
Then, interlocking their feet, they became, in a flash, just a single
Blanketing mass hanging over, and down from, the leaf-covered
        branches.
Instantly, out speaks a seer: 'We discern here a man and an army
Coming to us from abroad, from *that* same quarter to *this* same
Quarter, and gaining control of the topmost heights of the city.'   70
Virgin Lavinia,* standing alongside her father and kindling
Fires on the altars with burning torches held in her chaste hands,
Seemed,* a bad sign from the gods, to catch the fire up in her trailing
Tresses. Her headdress appeared to be wholly consumed by the
        crackling
Flames. Royal hair was set blazing, her crown, with its jewelled
        insignia,   75
Blazing. Enshrouded with smoke, silhouetted in dull glare of orange,
She, so it seemed, spread Vulcan's fire through the whole palace
        complex.
This was declared to be both a grim omen and marvellous vision:
Seers sang that she would shine in her fate and be famous in rumour.
But, for the people, a mighty war was the portent's prediction.   80
    Troubled by prodigies, then, this king approached Faunus his father's
Oracle, destiny's voice. So he went for advice to his forest
Under Albunea's heights.* It's the greatest of groves. Here the sacred
Fountain roars amid shadows, with fierce exhalations of sulphur.
Peoples of Italy, all of Oenotria, come here for answers   85
When there's a crisis. The priestess* brings offerings here and the
        night-time's
Silence sees her on slaughtered sheep's skins scattered in layers,
Waiting for dreams, seeking sleep. And she does see numerous
        ghostly
Images dancing before her in marvellous ways; she hears voices,
So many different kinds, joins deities in conversation,   90
And talks to Acheron down in the bottommost depths of Avernus.
Here, then, is where Latinus too now came, as a father,
Seeking responses. A hundred wool-bearing hoggets he slaughtered
Ritually, propped himself up on their backs, lying down on their
        fleeces.
Suddenly, out of the depths of the grove, a voice called to him,
        saying: 95
'Don't seek to marry your daughter within any Latin alliance,

Son of my blood, don't trust in an easy and ready-made wedding!
Sons-in-law will arrive from a foreign world* and, with their blood,
Raise our name to the stars! The descendants of their stock will
    one day
See all lands the Sun sees, in his cyclical course between either   100
Ocean, rolling beneath their feet and subjected to their rule.'
On these responses and warnings that issued from Faunus, his father,
Night remained silent. Latinus himself, though, did not seal his
    own lips.
Rumour had started flitting the news all round the Ausonian
Cities before Laomedon's youth* ran ashore with their hawsers,   105
Mooring their fleet to the rising slope of a grassy embankment.

Captains of units, Aeneas himself, and lovely Iulus
Settled beneath some tall trees' shade, relaxing their bodies.
And getting ready to eat. So, as Jupiter's own voice suggested,
Over the grass, as a base for their food, they set sections of flat
    bread,   110
And they arranged, on this Cereal base, country produce and berries.
When, so it chanced, they had eaten all else, acute shortage of rations
Drove them to turn their teeth upon Ceres' wafer-thin trenchers,
And, with their hands and audacious jaws, break into the fateful,
Outer circle of bread, even take squared sections of
    starch-wheat.   115
'Hey, we are eating our tables as well!' said the lovely Iulus.
That's all it was: just a joke. But his words, when heard, were the
    first sign
Marking the end of their toils; for his father, the moment he'd spoken,
Pounced on, corralled these words,* and, stunned by this show of
    divine will,
Instantly cried: 'Hail, land owed me by the fates as a debt due,   120
Hail to you too, Troy's guardian gods, who have kept your
    commitments!
This is my home and my homeland. It tallies with secrets my father*
Left me, that talked about fate. I recall now the words of Anchises:
"Son, when you're brought to an unknown coast, and when hunger
    compels you,
After you've eaten the scraps of your meal, to start eating your
    tables,   125
Then, though you're weary, remember to hope for a home, to position

Your first houses *there*, with your *own* hand. And shield them with
    ramparts."
This was the hunger referred to, our very last trial that awaited,
Bringing a definite end to our exile.*
Let's then go out at the joyous sun's first brightness tomorrow,   130
Check what the land's like, what people controls it, and find where
    that nation's
City is built. Let's fan from the harbour in different directions!
Now make libations on patens to Jupiter; and, in your prayers,
Call on Anchises, my father. Set wine once again on the tables.'
    After he's spoken these words, he garlands his temples with
        leafing   135
Sprigs. Then, addressing the area's local spirit,* invoking
Earth as the first among gods, then the Nymphs, and the rivers not
    yet known,
Night and the night-rising stars, he now offers his prayers. In his
    order,
Jupiter, Ida's lord, comes next, then the Phrygian Mother,
Both of his parents then: one in heaven, one in Erebus' darkness.*   140
    Now three times from the heights of the sky the Omnipotent Father
Thundered aloud and he thrust into view from the heavens a storm
    cloud
Whirled by his hand into blazes of gold, into daggers of sunlight.
Instantly rumour spreads through the rank and file of the Trojans:
Claiming the day has arrived for the city they're owed to be
    founded.   145
Racing each other to start a real feast, overjoyed by the mighty
Omen, they set out bowls for the wine, which they circle with garlands.
    Just as the next day's fresh-risen dawn is surveying the landscape
By the first glow of her lantern, they fan out, to note down this people's
Frontiers, city, and coasts. Their report is that these are
    Numicus'   150
Spring-fed marshes, this river the Tiber, that here live the valiant
Latins. Anchises' son bids a hundred men, gifted in language,*
Picked from among all ranks, now approach the august royal palace,
Each one screening his face with a branch cut from Pallas's olive.
They're to bring gifts to the ruler, to ask of him peace for the
    Teucrians.   155
There's no delay; they make haste, as instructed, proceeding with
    rapid

Strides.

He himself ploughs a shallow trench that will outline his city's
Bounds,* starts work on the site, and encloses their first coastal
    dwellings,
Just like an army encampment, with crenellate walls and a rampart.

Now the young men had completed their march. They could make
    out the Latins' 160
Turrets and tall-roofed buildings; and the wall was there, looming
    before them.
Outside the city, the boys and the youths in the first flower of manhood
Practise their horsemanship, raise up dust as they master their chariots,
Dart arched bows' taut strings,* muscle whip-lashing spin into javelins,
Challenge each other to race or to box.

Then a messenger, mounted,
Sent to report to the agèd king in advance and in person, 166
Says that some large foreign men have arrived, wearing most unfamiliar
Clothing. Latinus gives orders to summon them inside the palace,
Then takes his royal seat at the heart of his ancestors' throne-room.

Towering over the city, its huge roof raised by a hundred 170
Columns,* august and sublime, stood the palace of Laurentine Picus,
Eerie with bristling forests and old superstitious traditions.
Here kings were given their sceptres and took up the *fasces** of office,
Since this conferred a good omen. It was, too, their senate and
    temple,
Site for their holy-day banquets. And here, when the ram had been
    slaughtered, 175
Elders would sit side by side at communal tables for dining.
Further, it housed, in the entrance, the old cedar statues of bygone
Ancestors, neatly in order: they've Italus, father Sabinus,*
Founder of vineyards (maintaining his curved sickle here on his image),
Elderly Saturn as well, and the double-faced image of Janus.* 180
Next to them stood other regional kings of original settlers,
Then those wounded while fighting the nation's battles in wartime.
Add to these numerous weapons attached to the sacrosanct doorposts,
Captured chariots suspended, the curving edges of axe-blades,
Helmet plumage and monstrous bolts from the gateways of
    cities, 185
And spears and shields and rams* ripped from the timber of warships.

Shown seated, holding Quirinus's staff, enrobed in a small, striped
Toga,* and bearing the sacral shield in his left hand, was Picus,
Tamer of horses, himself. Obsessed by her passion to wed him,
Circe attacked with her golden wand and administered poisons,   190
Turning him into a bird, then striping his plumage with colours.*
  Such was the temple of gods to whose halls Latinus now
      summoned
Teucrians to see him. He'd taken his seat on the seat of his fathers.
And, once they'd entered, he spoke the first words and addressed
      them sedately:
'Tell me, Dardanians—yes, we are not unaware of your lineage   195
And city. Yes, you were heard to be plotting this course on the high
      seas.
What are you after? What purpose, what need, has transported your
      vessels
Here to Ausonia's shore over so many darkening seaways?
Did you lose bearings and course? Were you driven to land by bad
      weather?
Sailors experience many such dangers when out on the high seas.   200
That's why you've entered the river, is it? Why you've settled at
      moorings?
Don't avoid being our guests,* don't fail to observe that the Latins,
Saturn's people, are *just*—not through fear of the law and of prison,
But of their own free will. For they follow the old god's example.
And I recall, though with years the tradition has darkened to
      rumour,   205
Tales that Auruncan* old-timers told: that Dardanus grew up
Here, but he then thrust on into Phrygia's cities near Ida,
Samothrace* too—which was known back then as Thracian Samos.
There, this man who'd set out from Corythus' home* in Etruria,
Passed on, and sits on a throne in the golden palace of starry   210
Heaven,* and adds to the number of gods that we honour with altars.'
  That's what he said. What he said was developed thus by Ilioneus:*
'King, prime lord of Faunus's stock, in *this* case there were no
Storms forcing men at the mercy of waves to put in at your people's
Land, and no misread stars on our way, no coastlines mistaken.   215
Pre-set plans and free-willed souls brought *us* to this city,
All of us. We'd been expelled from our kingdom, which once was
      the greatest
Seen by the sun as he comes from the farthest Olympian heavens.

In our beginnings was Jove;* young Dardans delight in their Jovian
Grandfather.* Our king himself is of Jove's own consummate
    bloodline.   220
Trojan Aeneas has sent us here to the doors of your palace.
  'How huge a hurricane rolled out of savage Mycenae all over
Ida's plains, what forces of destiny drove into conflict
Europe and Asia, two distinct spheres: there's a tale that the whole
    world's
Heard, even someone in some remote land where the breakers of
    Ocean's   225
Far side crash, or who lives in a southern zone, beyond sunlight's
Central and hottest of sky's five zones, in complete isolation.
  'Out of that primal flood, men borne over so many vast seas
Ask, for our fathers' gods, just a tiny home, just a harmless
Haven, and water and air, which are nobody's private possessions.   230
We won't disgrace your realm; your fame won't diminish to rumour,
Never will thanks for a great deed done grow dim in our conscience,
Nor will Ausonians come to regret taking Troy to their bosoms.
This I swear by Aeneas's destiny and by his right hand,
Mighty, as men know who've tested his word—or his weapons in
    battle.   235
Don't take us lightly because we have made the first move, and
    extended
Branches and words of entreaty. We're numerous peoples' and nations'
Allies of choice for themselves. They have willingly sought our alliance.
God-declared destiny, though, led *us* to come looking for *your* lands
By its commands. Here Dardanus started; he's calling us back
    here.   240
Powerful orders Apollo once gave drive us on to the Tuscan
Tiber and sacred spring-fed pools of the river Numicus.*
He, besides, offers you these small gifts from our previous fortune—
Relics salvaged from Troy as it burned. Once, with this golden vessel,
Father Anchises would pour his libations to gods at their altars.   245
This was regalia Priam would wear* when he made his judicial
Rulings at public assemblies: his sceptre and sacred tiara,
Vestments, the handwork of women of Troy.'
So Ilioneus speaks. But Latinus displays no reaction:
Unmoved, face lowered, focus fixed on the ground—though his
    flashing   250
Eyes show a mind that's at work. Neither tapestried purple nor Priam's

Sceptre impel the king forward as strongly as thoughts of his daughter's
Wedding and who she should marry are holding him back.*
    He's unscrolling
Old Faunus' prophecy deep in his heart as it flashes before him.
This is the man who, fates foretold, would set out from a foreign   255
Land and be summoned as son-in-law into his realm under
    well-matched
Augural signs, and whose future descendants would show an
    outstanding
Manliness, manage to seize and control the whole world with their
    power.
    He at last answered with joy: 'May the gods bless what we are starting
And what they augur themselves. Man of Troy, what you wish will
    be granted,   260
Nor do I spurn your gifts. You won't lose, while Latinus is ruling,
Access to nurture from this rich soil or to Troy's great endowments.*
Still, though, Aeneas *should*, if his passion for us is so mighty,
If he's so keen to be hugged as guest, to be hailed as an ally,
Come here in person and not fear faces expressing their friendship.   265
Part of my peace terms will be simply touching the hand of the tyrant.*
    'You'll now convey my commands to your king, my counterproposal:
I have a daughter that my own father's shrine, in predictions,
Will not permit me to wed to a man of our nation. And many
Omens from heaven agree. Our sons-in-law will, sing the prophets,   270
Come from a foreign shore. That is Latium's lot. And they'll carry
Our name in blood that runs high to the stars. I think this man's
    the person
Fate demands; and, if my mind reads omens correctly, he's *my* choice.'
    This said, the father now makes a selection from out of his whole
    herd
(Three hundred well-groomed horses were kept in his sizeable
    stables),   275
Ordering, right on the spot, that for each of the Teucrian envoys,
One by one, a fine racer be brought, with a horsecloth of purple,
Needleworked blanket, medallion of gold hung on pectoral harness,
Bridle covered with gold, teeth chomping the yellow of pure gold.
And, for the absent Aeneas, he orders a chariot* and matched
    pair,   280
Seed of the blazing sky; they breathe fire out of their nostrils.
Born of the bloodline Circe stole from her father, they're cross-breeds
Sired on a mother she guilefully mated with Daedalan cunning.*

Such were Latinus's presents and words. So the sons of Aeneas
Ride back high on their horses, reporting that peace terms are
      settled.   285

Look though! For while coming back from the city of Inachus, Argos,
While holding course in the skies, still airborne, Jupiter's savage
Wife has observed both the Dardan fleet and the joyful Aeneas
From far astern, high above the Sicilian headland, Pachynus.
Now she can see them building homes, putting trust in the dry
      land,   290
Sees they've deserted their ships. Raw pain strikes deep with its arrows.
Then she starts shaking her head; her emotions well over with these
      words:
'Damn these creatures* that evil my eye, damn the Phrygians' future,
Blocking the future as I had it planned! Could they die on Sigeum's
Plains, stayed captured when captured? Of course not! When Troy
      was a bonfire   295
Didn't she burn up her menfolk? Oh no! They discovered a pathway,
Right through the thick of the front and the fires. I believe my divine
      powers
Have, at last, wilted and died. Or I'm past saturation with hatred,
Dead to myself.
            'They were tossed from their home. As they fled, I pursued them
Boldly, remorselessly, over the waves. Where they sailed,
      I obstructed.   300
All sea's and heaven's resources were spent in opposing the Teucrians.
What use was Syrtis or Scylla to me, what use was Charybdis'
Vastness? They have what they wished, they've established
      themselves in the Tiber's
Channel, untroubled by seas or by me.
                              'Yet Mars could demolish
All of the monstrous Lapiths.* The father of gods handed
      ancient   305
Calydon* over to suffer the rage of the angry Diana.
What was the Lapiths' big crime? What had Calydon done to deserve
      this?
I, Jupiter's mighty wife, though, I, who couldn't leave any
Challenge untried or direction unprobed, am denied my fulfilment.
I'm being crushed by Aeneas. And if my own authority isn't   310
Great enough, I shouldn't baulk at appeals to more adequate sources.
If I can't influence powers above, I'll move Acheron's waters.

Granted, I won't be allowed to repel him from Latium's kingdoms,
And it's immovably fixed in the fates that he'll marry Lavinia.
Yet . . . there is room to prolong and delay these momentous
    proceedings,   315
Room to depopulate both kings' ranks by tearing their roots out.
Son-in-law, father-in-law, let them consummate union at this price
Paid by their peoples. Young bride, you'll receive both Rutulian*
    and Trojan
Dowries of blood. And Bellona* awaits you as matron of honour.
Hecuba wasn't alone when her womb birthed torches of marriage,   320
Pregnant by funeral fire. For the same's true of this second Paris,
Venus' son; again marriage brings death to a Troy resurrected.'
    This declared, she headed down into earth as a figure of terror,
And, from the grip of the shadows below, from the home of the
    Demons,
Summons Allecto,* the bringer of grief, whose delight is in dismal   325
War and in anger, betrayal, and damaging criminal charges.
Pluto, her own father, loathes her, her sisters in Tartarus loathe her;
She, even there, is a monster, transforming herself into countless
Faces and vicious expressions, and darkly erupting with serpents.
    Juno spoke these words as a spur to her instincts, observing: 330
'Do me this task as a favour, young Virgin, daughter of Night-time:
Skilled work. Ensure that my honour, my fame in this place, will not
    vanish,
Shattered by rumour. Prevent, too, Aeneas's people from using
Marriage to get round Latinus and take over Italy's borders.
You can get brothers, harmonious souls, to don armour for battle,   335
Overturn households with hate, you can introduce floggings and
    death-fires
Into men's homes. You have names by the thousand, a thousand
    artistic
Methods of hurting the world. So shake down the fruits of your bosom,
Scatter the sheaves of this peace, sow grievances leading to warfare.
Make youths want, demand, reach for their weapons in one single
    instant!'   340

Thus cued, Allecto set off, bathed foully in venom of Gorgons,
First towards Latium, towards the high halls of the Laurentine tyrant.
Once there, she settled herself at the silent door to Amata's
Quarters. The ardently partisan queen had been boiling with anger,

Racked by anxieties she, as a woman, felt over the Teucrians'   345
Presence and Turnus's marriage. The goddess plucked one of the
    serpents
Lodged in her sea-dark hair, then directed its course, introduced it
Into Amata's breast, where the heart meets the lungs, first to madden
Her and, by this display, cause chaos throughout her whole household.
Slipping between her gown and her smooth bosom, rippling,
    but never   350
Touching, it fills her with viperous breath, injects fury unnoticed.
  Now the huge snake is the golden torc on her neck, now her bonnet
Trailing with ribbons. It twines through her hair, slithers free on
    her body.
  While the first flow of the transfused poison's assault on her senses
Seeps, while it's threading her bones with its fire, while her spirit
    has not yet   355
Felt the effects of the flame in the whole of her heart and her reason,
She has that gentler tone in her speech you'd expect of a mother:
Tears upon tears for her daughter, distress at her Phrygian marriage:
'Exiles, Teucrians, are given Lavinia to take as their wedded
Wife? Don't *you* feel sorry for *her* or yourself—you're her father!—
    and sorry   360
Too for her mother? He'll scoop up our girl on the first breath of
    north wind,
Leave me and head for his high sea's lair, this perfidious pirate!
Isn't this just how that Phrygian sheep-boy* poked into Sparta,
Carrying Leda's Helen away to the cities of Troy's land?
What about your solemn word? And your old-time love for your
    family?   365
Didn't you pledge her to Turnus, our own blood, with many a
    handshake?
Granted: it's settled that what's sought for Latins is some kind of
    foreign
Son-in-law. Granted: you're pressured by orders from Faunus, your
    parent.
"Foreign", I think, includes every land that is separately settled,
Free of our sceptre's control. I think *that's* what the gods are
    declaring.   370
Further, if you traced Turnus' roots, in his ancestry* you'd find
Inachus and, yes, Acrisius too, bluest blood in Mycenae.'
  Nothing was gained by these arguments used as she tested Latinus.

He, she could see, stood opposed. And the viperous venom of fury
Now seeps deep in her entrails, courses the whole of her being.   375
All fulfilment denied, driven wild by the monsters within her,
She's now a force of fury herself unleashed through the city's
Vastness, whirling about like a whip-lashed top such as children,
Rapt in their play, will propel in a great circle all round empty
Courtyards. When lashed into motion, it travels in segments of
          curving   380
Arcs; and the uncomprehending young throng stands in a stupor
Over it, gazing in awe at the fast-spinning figure of boxwood
Energized by their blows.
                    And Amata's propelled in no slower
Course through the centres of cities, amid some ferocious peoples.
She even runs out into the woodlands, pretending that Bacchus'   385
Spirit possesses her, rising to higher offence, raising madness
Higher, concealing her child in the shelter of leaf-covered mountains,
Robbing the Teucrians, she hoped, of their bride, and delaying the
          wedding.
'Evohé, Bacchus!' she cried. 'Only you're good enough for this virgin!'
Such was her shout. 'It's for you that she takes up the gentling
          thyrsus,*   390
Dances the ritual dance, and she lets her hair grow in your honour.'
Rumour takes wing, the same ardour takes hold among mothers in
          general,
Kindled by fury at just the same instant. It drives them to seek out
New homes. They've run away, necks bared, hair free to the breezes.
Others have strapped on hides, bear spear-shafts coiling with
          tendrilled   395
Vines and make heaven above pulsate with the wail of their wolf-howls.
She herself stands in their midst and she seethes as she brandishes
          burning
Pitch-pine and keens her nuptial hymn for her daughter and
          Turnus,
Whirling the bloodied edge of her glance. Then she suddenly, wildly
Screams aloud: 'Ho, mothers hear me, wherever you are, Latin
          mothers!   400
If any goodwill remains, among righteous souls, for Amata
Unfulfilled, if a mother's rights are an issue that gnaws you,
Tear ribbons out of your hair, join me in the ritual revels!'
     That was the queen, as Allecto lashed her into the forests,

Where only wild beasts live, all beset by the promptings of Bacchus.   405

Once it was clear she'd sufficiently honed the first onslaught of
    madness,
Shattered Latinus' political scheme—and the whole of his
    household—
Off flew the grim goddess, instantly soaring on dark-feathered pinions
Straight to the walls of the daring Rutulian's homeland, a city
Danaë founded with Acrisionian settlers* when south winds   410
Drove her ashore—that's the common opinion. Our fathers once
    called it
Ardea,* long, long ago. Though its great name, Ardea, still lives,
Fortune has left nothing else. Here now, in his towering palace,
Turnus was midway through reaping the dark night's harvest of
    slumber.
    Shedding her menacing face and her Fury's body, Allecto   415
Made herself over to stage and express an old woman's appearance,
Ploughed wrinkles into a forehead deformed, and then added some
    bone-white
Hair, capped with ribbons, which she intertwined with the branch
    of an olive.
She became Calybe,* Juno's old maidservant, priest at her temple,
And she presented herself to the young man's eyes with these
    comments: 420
'Turnus, will you let all of your labour's sweat run for nothing,
And let the sceptre that's yours be signed over to immigrant Dardans?
He's going back, this king, on the marriage he promised you, dowries
You shed blood to acquire. The required crown prince must be
    foreign.
Off you go, then, and be mocked as you hazard your life to face
    dangers   425
Unthanked! Flatten Etruscan lines, shield the peace of the Latins!
This is what Saturn's almighty daughter, in person, commanded
Me to tell you to your face while you lay in night's stillness,
    unconscious.
Come on, be glad to arm up for a fight, get your lads into armour,
Ready to march through the gate. Burn out these Phrygian
    captains   430
Squatting on our lovely river and burn up their brightly daubed navy!
Spirits of heaven with huge raw force so bid. If Latinus

Doesn't declare that he'll give you your marriage and do what you
    tell him,
Let the king finally learn, first hand, what it's like to fight Turnus.'
   It was the young man who mocked at the seer when he offered
    responses   435
Uttered by his own mouth. 'The report that a navy has entered
Tiber's waters has not, as you fancy, eluded my hearing.
Don't fashion me your large-scale terrors. For Juno, my guiding
Queen still remembers me.
Mother, decades in this spot,* old age tired out from conceiving   440
Truthfulness racks you with meaningless worries, deluding its seer,
Making up these false figures of fright, amid kings and their armies.
Your worry should be maintaining the statues of gods and their temples.
Men decide war and peace, because men must decide a war's battles.'
   These words kindled Allecto to fury. She flared up in anger.   445
Seizures suddenly shuddered the young man's limbs and a rigid
Stare, as he spoke, locked both of his eyes. Raw Strife,* with her
    countless
Serpents, hissed; and her monstrous face thrust through. Then she
    drove him
Back with the whirling force of her blazing glare, though he struggled,
Trying to say more. Up from her tresses she made twin constrictors
Rise, crackled whips, and, foaming with rage, added: 'So: I'm "decayed"
    then: 451
Now see how old age deludes "this pot" "tired out from conceiving
Truthfulness, with its false figures of fright amid kings and their
    armies."
See what I've brought. I have come from the realm of the Sisters of
    Terror,
I decide wars, and death, with my own hand.'   455
   This said, she pointed a flaming brand at the youth and implanted
Smoke-darkened light in his heart, the torches of death* and of
    marriage.
Frightful and massive shock bursts in on his sleep, and erupting
Sweat from his whole body drenches him through to his bones and
    his tendons.
Mindlessly screaming for arms, he hunts arms in his chamber and
    palace.   460
Love of the sword linked with criminal madness for war brutalizes:
Top it with anger and it's like the roaring of firewood kindled
Under the ribs of a bubbling cauldron of copper. The surface

Dances with joy as it heats. Underneath it, the upsurge of water
Seethes and it steams and it spurts spray high with exuberant
    splashing.   465
Water's not water, but vapour that flits and that blurs into breezes.
Therefore he ordered his warrior captains to march on Latinus:
He was the king who had ruined the peace. They must ready their
    weapons
And, to keep Italy safe, expel their foe from its borders.
Turnus could come in and handle, he said, both Latins and
    Teucrians.   470
When he had made this announcement, and called on the gods to
    bear witness,
All the Rutulians vied in their exhortations to battle.
Some men were moved by his youth and his strikingly uncommon
    beauty,
Some by his kingly ancestry, some by his prowess in battle.

Meanwhile, as Turnus inspired the Rutulians with courage and
    daring,   475
On sped Allecto, on Stygian wings to her Teucrian targets.
Trying a fresh ploy, she scouted a place where the lovely Iulus
Eagerly hunted and trapped wild game by the banks of the river.
Here, this girl from the Cocytus* laid down a new track which
    promptly
Drove the dogs wild as the oh so familiar scent reached their
    nostrils,   480
Set them off hot in pursuit of a stag. That's how the real suffering
Started: events that stirred passion for war in the hearts of the
    peasants.
He was a handsome buck, well horned with a huge rack of antlers;*
Tyrrhus's boys had been feeding him since he'd been torn from his
    mother's
Dugs. So had Tyrrhus, their father, the man set in charge of the
    royal   485
Herds and entrusted with guarding the open parklands in general.
Silvia, their sister, would lovingly drape his antlers with supple
Circles of garlands. For he had been tamed, he was trained to
    obedience.
She used to comb this beast of the wild and to bathe him in clear
    springs.
He let them touch him, he usually lay by his masters at table.   490

And, though he strayed through the sylvan* parks, he could find his
     way homeward,
No matter how late at night, to the long familiar doorway.
This was the stag that the frantic hounds of Iulus, out hunting,
Started, as he strayed far from his home. As it chanced, he was drifting
Downstream, escaping the heat of the bankside grass in the water.   495
It was Ascanius, fired by his love of distinguished approval,
Who himself levelled a shaft in the curve of his horn-bow of antlers.
His hand strayed,* but not from the path god wanted. The arrow,
Torqued with a loud twang, passed through the stomach and groin of
     its victim.
Wounded, the quadruped fled to within its familiar dwelling,   500
Entered the stables bellowing, streaming with blood, made the whole
     house
Ring with his plaintive cries, like a human begging for mercy.
First it's the sister, flailing her arms with her cupped hands, it's
     Silvia
Calling for help, shouting loudly to rouse tough peasants to action.
And—who'd have thought it?—they come, for the raucous voice of
     the Fury   505
Lurks in the speechless sylvan expanse. One's armed with a fire-hard
Branch; one carries the weight of a knotted club. Out of each man's
Rummagings, anger makes weapons. And Tyrrhus takes charge of
     the forces.
He, as it chanced, had been quartering chocked oak cracked by his
     wedge-blocks,
So, he just grabbed up his axe as he panted in huge exhalations.   510
   Up in her look-out, the brute goddess seized a fine chance to do
     damage,
She headed up to the tall stable's roof, and from there on the summit,
Sounded the shepherd's alarm, as her voice deep as Tartarus bellowed
Out through the curving horn. In an instant the whole wooded hollow
Trembled, the forests beyond rang loud with the blare, and
     Diana's   515
Faraway Lake of the Crossroads and sulphurous Nar with his whitish
Waters could both hear it, as could the springs flowing into Velinus.
Mothers now clasped sons up close to their bosoms in terror.
   Off men speed for the source of the sound, where the grimly demonic
Bugle has signalled. These farmers who've never been tamed grab
     for weapons   520

Everywhere. But, at the same time, the Trojan warriors also
Open their camp gates, unleashing a flood tide of help for Ascanius.
Battle-lines form. It's no longer a rivals' brawl among peasants
Fought with a flurry of hardwood clubs or fire-toughened fence-poles.
These men are fighting with double-edged steel, to the death; the
    black harvest   525
Bristling the broad fields is unsheathed swords.* Now the sun-dazzled
    bronzework
Flashes and tosses the sunlight's bolts back up to the sky's clouds.
Motion grows, as a wave grows white when the wind begins rising.
Little by little, the sea swells up and pushes its rollers
Higher, and finally reaches the skies from the floor of the ocean.   530
  Here's a youth caught in front line of battle, brought down by a
    screeching
Arrow. He's Almo. Till then he'd been eldest of Tyrrhus's children.
Under his throat the shaft stuck, and it choked off his moist vocal
    passage,
And the thin airflow that gave him his life, with the surge of his own
    blood.
Many more men fell as corpses around him. The ageing Galaesus   535
Died as he stepped in their midst as a peacemaker. He was the
    most just
Man of all time in Ausonia's lands, and, at one point, the richest:
Five flocks of bleaters he had, and five herds of cattle to shelter,
And so much land that he needed a hundred ploughs for the tilling.

While this action occurred on the plains, Mars favouring neither*   540
Faction, the goddess, her promise completed—she'd made the
    war bloody
And had accomplished deaths in the first battle—now left Hesperia's
Twilight Land to itself, travelled upwards through breezes of heaven,
And, with a conqueror's pride in her voice, spoke this way to Juno:
'See! There you have it! Your setting is grim war and discord's the
    jewel!   545
Tell them to couple in friendship now and to sign up for treaties!
Since, then, I have indeed spattered Teucrians with blood of
    Ausonia,
I will add this as a bonus, if *you'll* assure *me* that it's your will:
I'll draw the neighbouring cities right into the conflict with rumours,
I'll set their souls on fire with love for the lunatic War God,   550

I'll get them in from all round to assist. I'll seed farmlands with
    armour . . .'

Juno broke in and opposed: 'We have terrors and fraud in abundance.

Causes for war are established. There's hand-to-hand conflict with
    weapons.

Weapons that chance first proffered are now steeped freshly in
    bloodshed.

Let the prime pick of Venus's stock, let the real king, Latinus,   555

Celebrate *this* as their coupling, and *this* as the bride's consummation!

   'But having *you* freely licensed to wander through air's upper
    brightness,

Would not be what the Great Father would wish,* Lord of highest
    Olympus.

Get out! *I'll* take charge myself if the chance for some further

Action occurs.' That's the tone that the daughter of Saturn
    adopted.   560

All that Allecto could do was to raise wings hissing with serpents,

Leave heaven's heights, and set off for her home by the Cocytus'
    waters.

There is a place beneath mountainous summits at Italy's centre,

Rumours of which are lodged in the memories of many a nation,

Famous Ampsanctus Valley.* The edge of the forest
    encroaching,   565

On both sides, sheds a dense, leaf-canopied darkness. A crashing

Torrent thunders with boulders torqued in a swirl at the centre.

There people point out the sight of a spine-chilling cavern where brutal

Dis breathes out, where a whirlpool enlarged by the Acheron's upward

Thrust yawns open its toxic jaws. It was through these the
    Fury,   570

Shocking the eyesight, plunged, thus lightening earth and the heavens.

Meanwhile, the daughter of Saturn, for all that she's said, sets a final

Hand of control on the war. The entire contingent of shepherds

Rushes from battle to city returning those killed in the slaughter:

Almo, the young boy, and also the head of the butchered Galaesus,   575

Begging the gods and imploring Latinus to come and be witness.

Turnus is there. Amid death-fires and charges of slaughter,
    he doubles

Panic. The Teucrians, he says, have been asked to take over the
    kingdom;

Mating with Phrygian stock is required; he himself has been kicked out.
Husbands whose mind-blown wives are dancing for Bacchus in
    backwood   580
Wilds as a chorus (Amata's name, after all, carries some weight)
Gather from everywhere, merge in a group, chant endlessly:
    'Mars! Mars!'
Some perverse force makes them want—just saying the word should
    be outlawed—
War. They don't care that it goes against omens and fate set by
    heaven.
Jostling each other they crowd all around King Latinus's
    palace.   585
    He's like a crag as it stands unmoved against battering high seas,
He's like a crag* in the high seas, as breakers crash down upon it,
Self-maintained by its own sheer mass while, relentlessly, rollers
Bark all around, and around it the rocks and the reefs rumble endless
Protests. The kelp that is washed up its flanks slips away in the
    backwash.   590
    When, though, he's granted no power in himself to surmount
    their collective
Blind intent, and events follow savage Juno's directions,
Father Latinus calls on the gods and the hollow winds to bear witness:
'We're being shattered by fate,' he declared, 'swept off by a tempest!
Poor fools, you'll pay the price for all this with your own
    sacrilegious   595
Blood. You too, Turnus; you're now accursed, and the sentence
    awaiting
You some day will be grim. You'll be praying to gods when it's
    too late.
This is my birthday of death. I'm inside death's haven completely,
Yet I die robbed of fulfilment.' His words stopped. Fenced in
    his palace,
He now withdrew from all public affairs, dropped the reins of
    his kingdom.   600

Men had a custom in Latium's Hesperian days, which the later
Alban cities adopted and hallowed. It now is the practice in mighty
Rome's great empire, when men rouse Mars for a new set of battles:
Say, for example, they're planning to bring war's tears to the Getae,*
Or to Hyrcanians or Arabs, or reach towards India's people,   605

March in pursuit of the Dawn and request standards back from the
    Parthians.*
  War has twin matched portals* (the name they are known by is
    'War Gates')
Sacred in cult and in frightening symbols of Mars the Relentless.
Sealed by a hundred barrier bolts made of bronze and eternal
Hardness of iron. And Janus is never off guard at the entrance.   610
When there's a clear call to arms, in a ruling passed by the senate,
These are the shrieking doors that the consul uncouples in person,
Wearing Quirinus' toga, cinched in what's known as the Gabine
Style, and himself shouts 'to arms'; then the rest of the warriors
    follow.
Bronze horns blare their concerted blasts in raucous approval.   615
But when Latinus was told to declare war within this tradition
Now, on Aeneas' sons, and uncouple the grim double portals,
He wouldn't touch them; the father, instead, turned his back and
    avoided
Serving repugnant goals, and he buried himself in the shadows
Well out of sight. Then the queen of the gods, slipping down from
    the heavens,   620
Pushed the reluctant gates with her own hand. Turning the hinges,
Saturn's daughter ruptured the War Gates' iron-bound casings.
  Motionless until now, and untroubled, Ausonia is blazing:
Some are preparing to march across plains; some are mad for a gallop
High up in billows of dust upon horses. They all need their
    weapons.   625
People are cleaning the grease off shields and off javelins: smoothing,
Shining them brightly and honing the blades of their axes on
    whetstones.
Marching with colours and hearing the call of the trumpet excites them.
Five great cities, in all, set up anvils and forge new equipment:
There's Amitina,* a powerful place, the proud city of Tibur,   630
Ardea, Crustumerium too, tall-towered Antemnae.
Some craft the rounded protection of helmets, or weave willow
    withies
Into supports for a shield. Others pound bronze flat to form
    breastplates,
Or stretch silver's softness out to make greaves fitting smoothly.
Here's where they've shifted respect for the sickle and share, where
    they've transferred   635

All love for ploughing. They reforge their fathers' swords in the
     furnace.
Bugles are calling. The token symbolic of war* is now issued.
Here someone grabs for his helmet and rushes from home.
     Here another
Struggles to yoke nervous horses. He buckles his shield and his corslet,
Mail, triple-threaded with gold, and he straps on his sword, ever
     trusty.   640

Goddesses,* open up Helicon now, set your music in motion,
Naming the kings who were roused for the war and the armies that
     followed
Each as they filled up the plains. Name the men with whom our
     blessed Italian
Land blossomed bright even then, and the weapons, which scorched
     her with fire.
Goddesses, you can remember it all and recite it from memory.   645
We, though, feel hardly the slenderest breath of a rumour from
     those days.
  First to enlist in the war is a tough man from Tuscan dominions,
God-despising Mezentius,* who arms and now leads out his forces.
Riding beside him is Lausus, his son. There was no other person
Lovelier than he, if we don't count the body of Laurentine
     Turnus.   650
Lausus, a tamer of horses and deadly slayer of wild beasts,
Leads out a thousand troops from their city, Agylla,* who've
     followed
All in vain. He deserved more cheer than he got from his service
Under his father, deserved that his father should not be Mezentius.
Next after them, lovely Hercules' lovely son, Aventinus*   655
Shows off his chariot, marked by a palm, and his champion horses,
Over the meadows. His shield bears a marker proclaiming his father:
Snakes, a full hundred, and Hydra herself, surrounded by serpents.
He was the son born in secret to Rhea, a priestess, who brought him
Out across daylight's shores on the Aventine Hill in the
     woodlands.   660
Womanhood blended with god when, following Geryon's extinction,
Tiryns' triumphant Greek reached Italy's Laurentine ploughlands,
Bathing his Spanish bulls in the Tuscan waters of Tiber.
Spears and brutish pikes are their arms as they march off to battle,

And, in the thick of the fight, smooth blades and the Samnian
    rapier.*   665
He knots a huge lion's hide as a mantle around him, its uncombed
Fearsomely bristling mane and its white teeth cowling his features.
That's how he made his approach, now on foot, to the palace of
    monarchs,
Shoulders swathed with the rough-cut wildness of Hercules' outfit.
  Twin brothers now sweep out from the city of Tibur whose
    people's   670
Name, in this case, is derived from another brother, Tiburtus.*
These youths, Catillus and Coras the Fierce, trace roots back to Argos.
They gallop round in the hailstorm of spears out ahead of the front
    lines
Like two centaurs birthed from the clouds,* pelting down from a
    mountain's
Peak, spilling out from the snowcap of Othrys or Homole, rushing   675
Swift as a torrent. The hugeness of forest concedes them a passage;
Underbrush, thunderously crackling, yields to the sweep of their
    onrush.
  Nor was Praeneste's founder,* Caeculus, lost to the muster.
Every age has believed him a foundling left by a fireside,
Vulcan's child, and a king among flocking livestock of peasant   680
Farmers. A legion of peasants accompanies him from all over:
Men who live up in Praeneste's heights and in Gabii's farmlands
(Juno's domain), along ice-cold Anio, Hernican rocklands'
Dew-trickled rills; those men that you feed on your riches, Anagnia,
Those, Amasenus, to whom you are father. Not all of these
    peoples   685
Rattled with chariots, shields, real arms. The majority volleys
Bullets of dark lead slingshot; and some wave a couple of pointed
Wooden shafts in their hands, and they wear, to give heads some
    protection,
Yellowish wolfskin caps. They observe a tradition of keeping
Soles of the left foot bare and a raw leather shoe on the
    right foot.   690
  Neptune's offspring, Messapus,* the tamer of horses, whom neither
Fire nor sword have the power to destroy no matter who wields them,
Suddenly tugs out his sword and gives marching orders to peoples
Long settled back into peace, who have unlearned war and its
    practice.

These are the men of Fescennium, forces of Aequi Falisci,   695
Men who inhabit Soracte's heights and the farms of Flavina,
Ciminus' lake in the mountains, and also the shrines of Capena.
They'd strut in time to the beat of the line as they sang of their leader,
Rather like snow-white swans flying back, in formation, from feeding
In and out of the yielding clouds, piping sonorous music   700
Down long necks, resonating below in the Asian river, and pulsing
Loops in its pools.*
No one would find the potential for brass-hard battle-lines lurking
Here in this column; you'd think it a breeze-borne cloudbank of raucous
Birds on the wing pressing hard for the coast from the swirl of the
    high seas.   705
    Look! Here's Clausus,* from old-time Sabine blood, who's collected
Quite a colossal column; he's quite a columnar colossus
All by himself. Thanks to him the whole Claudian family *and* tribe
Spreads over Latium now, after Rome's partly ceded to Sabines.
Old-time Quirites turn out beside Amiternum's well-peopled   710
Squad, gathered hands from Eretum and olive-producing Mutuscae,
Men from Nomentum's town, rustic Roseans from the Velinus,
Craggy Tetrica's cliff-dwellers, mountain men from Severus,
Men from Casperia, Foruli, men from the river Himella,
Drinkers of Tiber's and Fabaris' waters, men sent by icy   715
Nursia, Orta's knights and the Latinienses of old days,
Folk cut apart by the streams of the Allia,* cursed as that name is.
Countless as rolling waves on the marbled Libyan sea-swell
When fierce Orion is setting in wintry and turbulent waters,
Dense as ears of grain as they roast in the new season's sunshine   720
Over the plains by the Hermus or Lycia's goldening farmlands,
Shields clatter, terrified earth's ground down by the trample of
    footbeats.
    Next, Agamemnon's lad,* foe of anything Trojan, is yoking
Horses to chariot for Turnus. Halaesus is plucking a thousand
Wild-living peoples who rake over Massicus' soil,* bringing
    Bacchus   725
Perfect fulfilment; and men sent down from the hills by Auruncan
Fathers and those Sidicinum's nearby plains are dispatching,
Men leaving Cales, an odd resident from Volturnus's shallow
Flow matched up for the march beside one of Saticula's tough men.
Then there's a handful of Oscans. Their weapons are *aclydes*, short,
    smooth   730

Spears it's their practice to torque with a length of fine strapping;
　　and leather
Shields give their left arms protection; up close they use swords
　　shaped like sickles.
　　Oebalus, you won't escape a citation in our writs of epic*
Either. Report indicates that an elderly person named Telon
Fathered this man on Sebethis, a nymph, while ruling Capreae,　　735
Where Teleboeans live; said son, not constrained by his father's
Holdings, commenced even then to force under his broad
　　jurisdiction
People known as Sarrastes, the plains that are watered by Sarnus,
Rufrae's and Batulus' denizens, owners of farms at Celemnae,
And such as one may observe from Abella, the city of orchards.*　　740
They hurl boomerangs, Oscan style*—that's their regular practice—
And, as protection for heads, wear bark that they strip from the
　　cork-tree.
Bronze plate glints on their light shields, bronze glitters light* on
　　their sword-blades.
　　You too were sent into battle, in this case by mountainous Nersae,
Ufens, glorious in folklore and rumour, fulfilled as a fighter.　　745
Your people, Aequiculi, whose soil can't be equalled* in hardness,
Take rough life to extremes with their constant hunting in
　　backwoods.
They work the land with their weapons, delighting in harvests of
　　always
Fresh fruits of pillage, and living on what they can garner by plunder.
　　Even a priest from Marruvium came, trimly kempt with an olive　　750
Garland over his helmet, symbolic of fruitful fulfilment.
Ordered to war by his ruler, Archippus, the utterly fearless
Umbro's* more usual species of contact was serpents: aquatic
Venomous snakes. He could charm them to sleep with a touch or by
　　singing,
Calm down their anger, alleviate bites with his curative powers.　　755
Yet he had no power to heal himself from the strike of a Dardan
Spear; his hypnotic songs, and his herbs culled high on the Marsi's
Hillsides were no help at all when applied to his wounds in the battle.
Anguish for you choked the woods of Angitia, glassy Fucinus
Rippled lament, lakes wept you with tears.　　760
　　Virbius, loveliest shoot of Hippolytus' stem,* went to war too,
Sent by Aricia, his mother, who'd raised this youth for distinction

Deep in Egeria's grove, on the moistened soil of the lakeside
Close to Diana's blood-rich altar, which still needs appeasement.
Rumour persists that Hippolytus, after his stepmother shrewdly   765
Killed him and he'd paid in blood the full penalty set by his father's
Curse, sundered limb from limb by his horses, returned beneath
     heaven's
Stars. He again breathed the breath of the skies up above, resurrected,
Thanks to Asclepius' curative herbs and the love of Diana.
Outraged that anyone doomed to death should rise from infernal   770
Darkness to brightness of light, the Omnipotent Father then blasted
Phoebus's own son,* inventor of medical skills so perfected,
Down to the Stygian waters himself with a bolt of his lightning.
Still, though, the Goddess at Crossroads buried Hippolytus far off,
Hiding him in her remote shrine, the nymph Egeria's woodlands,   775
So he could live life alone and unknown within Italy's forests,
Renamed Virbius: saving his life by erasing its meaning.*
That's why horn-footed stallions are exorcised from both the
     Crossroads
Temple and sacred grove: for they spilled both the youth and his
     chariot
Over and out on the beach when the sighting of sea-monsters
     spooked them.   780
This doesn't stop his son* exercising his fiery stallions
Over the sea-flat plains and racing his chariot to battle.
     Turnus, outstanding in build and in height, a full head above others,
Heads in and out among leaders, in person, and brandishes weapons.
Under the three tall plumes of his helmet he bears the
     Chimaera,*   785
Blasting Etna's fires from her jaws. The more fiercely she's roaring,
Bestially wild with her menacing flames, the more rawly the battle's
Gushing of blood spouts brutally high. Decorating his smooth shield,
Horns elevated, is Io,* chased clearly in gold and already
Covered all over with bristling hide and already a bovine,   790
Arguing family claims. Guarding girl and her girlhood is Argus.
Her father, Inachus, from an incised urn, streams out his river.
     Following Turnus, a storm cloud of infantry marches, its columns
Armoured with shields, packed dense over all of the flatlands: the
     Argive
Warriors, Auruncan contingents, Rutulians, Sicanians of old
     stock,   795

Troops of Sacrani as well and Labici with shields brightly painted,
Men, river Tiber, who till in your vales or beside the Numicus'
Sacred banks,* men who toil the Rutulian hilltops and Circe's
Ridge with their ploughshares, the farmlands that Jupiter Anxur
Rules with his presence, Feronia thrilled by the green of her
          precinct,   800
And where Satura's marsh lies death-dark, and bone-chilling Ufens*
Hunts for a course through the valley's depths to its tomb in the
          salt sea.

    One further leader arrives: from the Volscian people,* Camilla,
Leading a cavalry column.* Her squads bloom bright in their
          bronze-plate.
She is a woman of war who has never accustomed her female   805
Hands to Minerva's spindle and baskets. She's hardened for battle's
Hardness, this virgin, her swift feet could outrun the winds in a
          foot race,
She could fly over the top of the highest stalks in a grainfield,
Leaving the tender ears of the crop unharmed by her crossing.
She could pass over the breadth of the sea, over waves, over
          sea-swell   810
High up, speeding through air, never touching her feet to the surface.
All the young people pour out of the fields, out of homes, in amazement,
As do their mothers, in crowds, just to watch from afar as she passes.
Oh, how they gape, how they're stunned that a kingly splendour of
          purple
Mantles such delicate shoulders, that gold clasps thread through her
          well-groomed   815
Tresses, that she's bearing weapons herself, both a Lycian quiver
And, though it's capped with a spearhead, a shepherd's staff made
          of myrtle.*

BOOK EIGHT

Turnus has hoisted the signal for war on the Laurentine castle;
Trumpets have shrilled out an ear-splitting blare, and he's
    goaded his fiery
Horses to frenzy, his spear drums loud on his shield. In an instant
Passions explode, fierce youth turns brute, all Latium conspires in
Jittery fury. The leading commanders, Messapus and Ufens,   5
God-despising Mezentius too, are enforcing conscription
Everywhere, plundering farms all round of their planters and reapers.
Venulus* heads a legation dispatched to the great Diomedes'
City, requesting his aid, bringing news that a fleet-load of Teucrians   10
Led by Aeneas has landed and settled in Latium, importing
Already vanquished cults. They're to say that this Dardan is claiming
Fate has appointed him king, and that numerous peoples have
    joined him,
And that Aeneas's name is on more and more lips throughout Latium.
What he might build on this basis, what outcome he'd want from
    the battle   15
If Fortune favours, they'll say, Diomedes would find more apparent
Than either Turnus, their king or their king* Latinus imagines.
    Such is the tally of Latium's ills. Once Laomedon's kinsman*
Drinks in this vision, the hero is swept on a swell of emotions,
Scurrying thoughts into this or that channel of choice and decision,   20
Surging in random directions, examining every perspective,
Just as the shimmering light from a watery surface in bronze-lipped
Cauldrons—itself but reflected sun, or the radiant, mirrored
Face of the moon—ripples all round a room, leaps up through the
    yielding
Air where it flickers on fretted beams panelled high on the ceiling.   25

Night reigned;* all across earth, sleep dulled living creatures' exhausted
Consciousness, ruled all the various species of birds and of livestock.
Under the cold sky's vault, on the river-bank, father Aeneas,
Though sick at heart and confused by the outbreak of war and its
    grimness,
Lay down, permitting the rest he'd deferred to diffuse through
    his body.   30

Then Tiberinus, the region's god, seemed to rise up before him
Out of idyllic waters edged by a border of leafy
Poplars, in person, quite elderly, shrouded in greyish, translucent
Flaxen attire, hair veiled by a shadowy mantle of sedge-grass.
Then the god seemed to allay his concerns* and address him in
          this way: 35
'Seed of divine stock, you, who bring Troy's city home to us once
          more
Out of the foeman's grasp and keep Pergamum's fortress eternal,
You, long awaited by Laurentine soil and the ploughlands of Latium!
Here is your destined home, and the destined gods of your household.
Don't turn away. Don't be scared by the threats of a war. All the
          swollen   40
Anger of gods has abated.
Now, here's proof, so you won't think sleep's just crafting a fiction:
Under my bankside's oak-shrub brush you'll find an immense sow
Lying sprawled on the soil, on her side—an albino, with thirty
Newborn piglets, albino themselves, at her teats in a cluster.   45
[This is the seat for your future state and your refuge from troubles.]*
This means Ascanius will, after thirty seasons have rolled by,
Found an illustrious city known, in their honour, as Alba.
What I foretell is not subject to change. How to solve the immediate
Problem—winning this war—I will briefly explain. Listen closely!   50
People descended from Pallas* have come to these shores. These
          Arcadians
Followed the flag of Evander, their king, on this venture. They've
          chosen
Where they will settle and, up in the hills, they've established a city
Which, in great-grandfather Pallas' honour, they've named Pallanteum.
They now sustain a relentless war against all of the Latin   55
Peoples. So make them your allies in battle, establish a treaty.
I will myself guide you there on a straight course marked by my
          stream's banks.
You, though, must conquer my flow with your oars, since the
          journey is upstream.
Child of the goddess, arise and, as soon as the first stars are setting,
Offer to Juno your formal prayers, and, with humble devotions,   60
Conquer her anger and menace. You pay me my own debt of honour
Simply by winning. For I am the force that you see in its full flow
Rasping at banksides, slicing its way through the rich soil of farmland,

I am the sea-dark Tiber, a river most pleasing to heaven.
Here's where my mighty domain emerges, crowned with high cities.'   65
This said, the stream sank down to the bottommost bed of his lake-calm
Depths.
          Now night and its dreams ebb away from Aeneas. He rises,
Faces the dawning glow of a sky that is streaming with sun's rays,
Ritually cups in his palms fresh waters drawn from the racing
River, then raises his hands as he pours these words to the heavens: 70
'Nymphs, you Laurentine nymphs, you fountains that rivers
          descend from,
You, father Tiber too, with the sacred flow of your waters,
All of you, carry Aeneas, protect him, for once, from all dangers.
River who pities our troubles, whatever the lakes where your sources
Spring, and whatever the soil *you* pass through, emerging in beauty,   75
You I will honour for ever with gifts and for ever with feast-days,
Horned river, ruler of waters not western but Hesperidean.*
Stand by us now, though, I beg you. Confirm your support more
          directly.'
Those were his words. And he picks from the fleet two identical
          biremes,
Fits them with oars, assigns crews with appropriate arms and
          equipment.   80
   Suddenly, there she is! And the prodigy shocks and bewilders
Eyes brought to bear on a sow* as she lies, stretched out on the green
          bank
Gleamingly white through the woods with a brood the same colour,
          albino.
Instantly, righteous Aeneas, in your honour, mightiest Juno,
Ritually slaughters* both her and her brood, sets them all on an altar.   85

Tiber, throughout the duration of night, had eased off his swelling
Surge and, reversing his flow, so slowed waves silenced to stillness
That, smooth-faced as a pond or a surfless lake, he was soothing
Rough waters' rush to an unruffled flatness so oars wouldn't
          struggle.
Thus they set off at a pace further quickened by cheering behind
          them.   90
Fine-oiled fir keels slip through the shallows, amazing the waters;*
Woods are amazed, unused to the far-flashing glint of the dazzling
Shields of the men and of painted vessels afloat on their river.

Wearying all of the night and a day at the oars, they press onward,
Rounding the long river bends beneath shadows cast by the varied   95
Trees, cutting clearance through woods mirrored green in the
     motionless surface.
  Fiery Sun had arrived at the peak of his orbit of heaven
When, in the distance, they saw a town's fortress and walls, and
     some scattered
Buildings—a place Rome's dominant power raises high as the
     heavens
Now, but in those days no more than Evander's impoverished
     holdings.*   100
Quickly adjusting their course, they began their approach to the city.
  That very day the Arcadian king, as it chanced, was observing
Yearly rites for Amphitryon's son* and the gods in a sacred
Grove just in front of the city. And Pallas, his son, was there with him,
So, too, were all of the leading youths and the penniless senate,*   105
Offering smouldering incense. Warm blood steamed on the altars.
But, when they saw tall ships glide up through the shadowy forest,
Silent men plying oars, this sight, unexpected and sudden,
Struck them with terror. They all rose at once and abandoned
     their tables.
Pallas, however, was bold. He forbade them to break off the rituals.   110
Snatching a spear, he himself flew down to confront the intruders.
Hailing them, high on a mound, at a distance: 'What motives, young
     warriors,
Drive you', he asked, 'to try routes never travelled? Where is it
     you're heading?
What people are you? Where's home? Are you coming in peace or
     attacking?'
Father Aeneas then answered him thus from the top of his
     aft-deck,   115
Stretching an olive branch out, as a symbol that peace was his mission.
'Men born in Troy, weapons hostile to Latins. *That's* what you're
     seeing.
We sought asylum.* They drove us away. Pride prompted
     aggression.
Now it's Evander we seek. Bring him this news, men,* tell him chosen
Dardan leaders have come to request his alliance in warfare.'   120
Stunned by so famous a name, Pallas stood stock-still for a moment.
Then he resumed: 'Well, whoever you are, come ashore, talk to father

Face to face, enter our home as the guest of our gods and their
　　household.'
Taking his guest's right hand in his own hand, he clasped it and held it,
Then they walked forward into the grove and away from the river.　125
　　Once there, Aeneas addresses the king in the language of
　　　friendship:
'Best of all Greek-born men, it is Fortune's will that I'm bearing
Branches of ribboned olive to you, that I come as your suppliant.
I didn't fear you, although you're Arcadian, a king of Danaäns,
Though you have also ancestral links with the twin sons of Atreus.　130
My courage brought me, and so did the gods' sacred oracles, so did
Kinship ties of our fathers and your world-wide reputation.
All this linked me to you. Fate drove me, but I followed gladly.
Dardanus,* first true father and founder of Ilium's city,
Born, so Greeks maintain, of Electra, the daughter of Atlas,　135
Came to the Teucrians. Atlas the Mighty, who carries the heavens'
Spheres on his shoulders, had fathered Electra. Your family's father,
Mercury, then, was conceived on the ice-cold peaks of Cyllene,
Gushed into life by the fair nymph Maia. Now, if we're to credit
What we have heard, Maia's father was Atlas. And he is the selfsame　140
Atlas who props all sky's constellations high on his shoulders.
Both of our family trees are thus branches of one single lifeline.
Trusting in this, I did not employ envoys or make some initial
Crafty approach to you. No. I have risked my own personal safety,
My own head; and I've come, upon bended knee, to your doorway.　145
　　'Daunus's clan, the same people that hunts you down in a brutal
War, hunts me. They believe that, if they can expel us, then nothing
Stands in the way of their sending the whole of Hesperia entirely
Under their yoke and controlling her seas, both the Upper and Lower.*
Take up our pledge, then give us your own. In war we have valiant　150
Hearts—and our courage and troops have been tested and witnessed
　　in action.'
　　So spoke Aeneas. Evander had long been observing the speaker,
Noting his face and his eyes, and assessing the whole of his person.
Briefly, he said in response: 'How happy I am to receive you,
Bravest of Teucrians.* I know who you are. How well I remember　155
Words your great father Anchises said, and his voice, his expressions!
He, I recall, went to visit his sister Hesione's kingdom,*
Salamis: Priam, I mean, Laomedon's son. On his way there he also
Visited us where we lived, in Arcadia's ice-covered regions.

Manhood was then just beginning to clothe my cheeks with its
    fresh down.   160
Awed, I gazed at the Teucrian leaders, gazed at the great man,
Son of Laomedon. But, walking taller than all, was Anchises.
My mind blazed with a young man's love to come up and establish
Contact with him, shake the hero's hand with my own.
    I approached him;
How I was thrilled, as I led him on through Pheneus' defences.   165
He, when he left, gave me gifts: a fine quiver and Lycian arrows,
Also a military cloak made of golden brocade and a golden
Matched pair of bits for my horses which Pallas, my son, now possesses.
Therefore: my right hand now joins yours in the pact you're requesting.
And, when tomorrow's light first brings back a glow to the
    landscape,   170
I'll send you happily off, reinforced, and I'll help with resources.
Meanwhile—you've come here as friends, after all, and deferring
    our yearly
Festival would be a slight to the gods—be so good as to join in,
Celebrate with us, get used, right away, to the feasts of your allies.'
    This said, he orders the dishes and goblets, removed in the panic,   175
Set back in place. He himself shows the men where to sit in the
    meadows,
Honours Aeneas, his privileged guest, with a cushion and fine-maned
Lionskin, then he invites him to sit on a throne made of maple.
Chosen youths, and the priest who has slaughtered the bulls at the altar,
Rush to distribute the grilled flesh, load up baskets with bounty   180
Ceres provides when toiled into bread, pour Bacchus in goblets.
Warriors of Troy and Aeneas are now all feeding together
Off an entire ox carcass and ritually sacrificed entrails.
    Hunger removed, and the frenzy for feeding stuffed to its limits,
'These sacred rites,* said Evander, the king, 'this traditional, yearly   185
Banquet and altar established to honour a powerful spirit
Aren't imposed by an ignorant cult unaware of the old gods,
Guest from Troy. No, we offer these novel and well-deserved tributes,
Thankful that we've been saved from a brutal nexus of dangers.
First, take a look at this cliff, overhung by its uppermost
    rock-ledge;   190
Note where its mass is extensively shattered and where an abandoned
Cave-dwelling* stands, though the overhang's fall wrought enormous
    destruction.
This was at one time a cave stretching far back under the hillside,

Hiding within it, where rays of the sun couldn't enter, the fearsome
Visage of subhuman Cacus.* The groundsoil was warmed into
    humus   195
Constantly freshened with slaughter; and nailed with pride at the entrance
Hung human heads, each face decomposing grimly to greyness.
Vulcan had fathered this monster. So *his* were the fires that the
    beast's face
Vomited dark from its mouth as it set its immense mass in motion.

  'Finally, time brought even to us the relief that we prayed for: 200
Help, in the form of a god: the Avenger Supreme came among us,
Proud of his spoils and of killing all three of Geryon's bodies,*
Hercules passed through town on his travels, a conqueror, herding
Massive bulls. And the cattle took over the valley and river.
Wild passion rustled in Cacus's mind, for it couldn't bear leaving   205
Any activity, crime or ruse, undared, unattempted.
Four prime bulls he cut out from the grazing herd, and as many
Gorgeously fine-bodied heifers. And then, so they wouldn't leave any
Tell-tale hoofprints marking their forward direction, he dragged them
Into his cave by their tails,* thereby reversing the track marks   210
Tracing their path. So the thief kept them hidden in stone-covered
    darkness,
Leaving a searcher no obvious clue that might lead to the cavern.

  'Meanwhile, Amphitryon's son got the cattle, now sated with grazing,
Back on the move and was starting to ready the herd for departure.
Cows began mooing as they headed out, and the whole of the
    valley   215
Filled with their grumbles, the hills were left rumbling and booming
    with echoes.
One of the oxen imprisoned by Cacus found voice and responded,
Mooing inside vast, resonant chambers, betraying its captor.
Rueful pain at his loss and the bilious blackness of anger
Now set Hercules blazing. He seized up his weapon, his knotted,   220
Weighty club, heading up at a run for the mists of the hilltop.
That was the first time we all saw Cacus actually frightened,
Panic alive in his eyes. He took off, and he fled to his cavern
Faster than wind from the east. And his feet found wings in his terror.

  'Just as he'd shut himself in and had broken the chains he had
    crafted,   225
Thanks to his father's art, out of steel, and had dropped a suspended
Huge slab, blocking the entrance, augmenting the strength of the
    uprights,

Hercules, stone-built Tiryns's child,* was arriving in utter
Fury, his face moving this way and that to check each point of access,
Gnashing his teeth. And he circled the whole of the Aventine*
    three times,   230
Boiling with anger. He made three efforts to break through the
    rock-firm
Entrance, in vain. Three times he collapsed in the valley, exhausted.
  'Rising high, to an onlooker's eye, up over the cavern's
Spine, all surrounding rock sheared away, stood a jagged, serrated
Quartz crag—the perfect home for accursed carrion vultures.   235
Since it was tilting away from its ridge to the left, towards the river,
Hercules pushed from the right, full force, shook it loose, and then
    ripped it
Free from its roots in the clifftop and suddenly toppled it over.
Bright sky's vastness thundered response to the impact, the river's
Banks leaped apart, Tiberinus himself flowed backwards in terror.   240
Down went the roof over Cacus's grotto, disclosing his monstrous
Palace. Its ghost-ridden cavern's abysses of darkness lay open,
Just as if some great force had made earth's depths yawn in a chasm,
Breaking the locks upon hell, unbarring the kingdoms of pallor
Loathed by the eyes of the gods, as if one could see down into
    death's dark   245
Pit, while the shades shuddered, scared by intrusive brightness and
    vision.
  'Hercules, thus, had him caught by the light of a quite unexpected
Dawn. Cacus, trapped in his rock hollow, now roared differently
    somehow.
Everything served as a weapon as Hercules pressed him with volleys
Hurled from above: tree branches, boulders as massive as
    millstones.   250
Cacus had thus no further chance to go running from danger,
So, and it is a remarkable tale, he vomited massive
Billows of smoke from his jaws and enveloped his home in a blinding
Fiery darkness that robbed one of sight. In his cave he created
Night with his eddying smoke-clouds, a choking and flame-flickered
    darkness.   255
Hercules' rage couldn't take this. He hurled himself down with a
    great leap
Over the edge, through the fire, to where smoke billowed forth the
    most densely,

Where the immense cave boiled up vaporous fogbanks of blackness.
Here he ensnared Cacus, trapped in the dark and still vomiting useless
Flames. He encircled his neck in an unrelenting constriction   260
Forcing his eyes from their sockets and choking the blood from
     his gullet.
Down in a flash came the doors, torn off, thus exposing his darkened
Home, and the oxen, whose theft he'd denied,* dragged out in the open,
Stand on display. Cacus' hideous carcass is hauled by its ankles
Outside the cave. People stare at his terrible eyes, at this half-beast's   265
Facial expressions and thick-bristled chest, at his jaws' now extinguished
Flames. And they can't glut their hearts to the full with the pleasures
     of gazing.'
Since then* this deed has been marked by a feast; and each new generation
Joyfully keeps the day holy. Potitius started the practice
(And the Pinarian House became wardens of Hercules' honours).   270
He built this altar surrounded by trees we'll for ever describe as
Greatest of Altars. And it will indeed be for ever our greatest.*
'Come then, my warrior friends, and in tribute to marvellous valour,
Garland your heads, lift your goblets and hold them with right hand
     extended,
Call on the god that our peoples share, offer wine in your gladness!'   275
   Hercules' shadowy wreath, intertwining the hair with its dangling
Silvery-backed green poplar leaves now veiled him. A sacred
Beaker of wood filled the palm of his hand. They all quickly and gladly
Poured their libations of wine on the table and prayed for the gods'
     grace.

Meanwhile the Evening star was approaching, as heaven's
     Olympian   280
Brightness sank. Priests draped in their ritual pelts, with Potitius*
Leading, began to process, and to bring in the torches of fire.
Feasting began once again; and this second phase of the banquet
Brought pleasant gifts, piled altars high with its food-loaded platters.
Then came the Salii, temples bound with the boughs of the poplar,   285
Chanting their hymns as they danced round the kindled fires on the
     altars.
One of their troupes was of men in their prime and the other of elders,
Singing the glory of Hercules' deeds: how he crushed his first monsters,
Bare-handed, strangling his stepmother Juno's pair of constrictors;
How the same hero dismantled two cities, outstandingly warlike,   290

Troy and Oechalia; how he endured and completed a thousand
Difficult labours,* when, under Eurystheus' rule, through the unjust
Juno's notion of fate: 'You, hero unconquered, have slaughtered
Centaurs born of a cloud, with your hand, Hylaeus and Pholus,
Crete's giant bull, and the huge lion laired in the hills of Nemea,   295
You made the lake-still Styx and Orcus's guardian* shiver
Over his half-gnawed bones as he lay in his blood-spattered cavern.
Fear has no face that deters you, not even gigantic Typhoeus
Standing in armour before you. The viperous Hydra of Lerna
Circling you with any army of heads didn't find you resourceless.   300
Hail to you, true son of Jupiter, brilliance added to godhood!
Come to us, favour your festival now with your prowess at dancing!'
    Such were the deeds celebrated in song. They performed, as finale,
'Cacus' Cave', representing the monster himself, spewing fire.
All the grove joined in the chorus, the drummed hills danced to the
        rhythm.   305

Once they'd completed the rites for the gods, they all went off together,
Back to the city. The king, who was hobbled by age, progressed slowly,
And, as he kept both his son and Aeneas close, as companions,
Lessened the strain of the walk with discussion of various topics.
    Letting his eyes roam freely, Aeneas surveyed his surroundings,   310
Taken by places he saw. In delight, he asked what this or that was,
Listened to men of the old days recalled in the monuments round him.
Then King Evander, the Roman citadel's founder,* expounded:
'These woods belonged to indigenous Fauns* and to Nymphs in the
        olden
Days, and to people birthed from the trunks of the trees and from
        oaken   315
Hardwood, devoid of all manners or culture, who hadn't a notion
How to yoke oxen, store grain, or to manage the produce they'd
        garnered.
Branches and primitive hunting supplied them with food for survival.
Saturn was first to arrive from outside, from the heights of Olympus,
Stripped of his power, as a fugitive fleeing from Jupiter's
        weapons.   320
He got this untamed species, dispersed through the highlands, together
Gave them a law code and honoured this land where he'd lately lain
        hidden
Unmutilated, made Latium its name* as his ultimate preference.

Under this ruler occurred what tradition describes as the Golden
Centuries, such was the peace and the calm of his rule over
    peoples.   325
These gave way over time to a rather debased and discoloured
Age that was rabid for war and when love became greed* for
    possessions.
Then the Ausonians came, and Sicanian peoples.* Too often
Saturn's homeland surrendered its name* and identity. That's when
Kings came, notably Thybris, a brute of gigantic proportions,   330
And we Italians* would later rename, in his honour, the river
Tiber. Thus ancient Albula* lost her correct name for ever.
Here is the place unavoidable Fate and omnipotent Fortune
Set me when I was expelled from my homeland and sought the remotest
Reaches of ocean, the place where the nymph Carmentis,* my
    mother,   335
Drove me with terrible warnings whose ultimate source was Apollo.'
   Just as he spoke, he had reached, and was showing Aeneas, the altar
And what the Romans commemorate now as the Gate of Carmentis.
Since old times they've honoured that nymph Carmentis, prophetic
Mouthpiece of fate. Her voice first sang of Aeneas' descendants'   340
Greatness to come and the noble distinction of Pallanteum.
Passing the great park Romulus* shrewdly used for his outlaws'
Refuge, he notes the chill flow in the Lupercal* grotto, the Wolf Cave
Honouring Pan, in Arcadian style, as Lycaeus, the Wolf God.
Further, he points out the grove with its shrine called the
    Argiletum,*   345
Calls it to witness the truth in the death of his guest, the late Argus.
   Up to Tarpeia's rock* and the Capitol Hill he escorts him,
Golden now; in the past just bristling forested thickets.
Even then, grim awe of the place terrified superstitious
Peasants. When no more than boulders and woods, it could strike
    them with terror.   350
'This grove,' he said, 'this hill with the leaf-covered summit, is
    some god's
Dwelling, though *which* god we don't know. Arcadians believe they
    have sighted
Jupiter up there in person and shaking his aegis, which often
Darkens the sky, in his hand, as he rouses the storm clouds to action.
Those two additional towns you can see where the walls have been
    shattered,   355

Those are what's left of the previous folk and recall their existence.
This one had Janus as father and founder, the other had Saturn.
This, when it stood, bore the name of Janiculum,* that of Saturnia.'
    Verbal exchanges like this ran on as they entered Evander's
City, a pauper's realm. They saw cattle grazing at random,   360
Mooing around what's now Rome's forum and spotless Carinae.*
When they arrived at his house, he said: 'This is the threshold victorious
Hercules crossed, and this palace was ample enough to contain him.
Dare to be worthy of this god, my guest, and think nothing of riches:
Pattern your being on his. Don't be harsh on my poverty.
        Enter.'   365
This said, he ushered Aeneas, a man of considerable stature,
Under the roof of his far from august house, and laid him a blanket
Bolstered with mattressing leaves and the hide of a Libyan sow-bear.*
    Night swooped down and enveloped the earth with her feathers
        of darkness.

Venus, being a mother, was heartsick with not at all groundless   370
Terror at threats from the Laurentines, wracked by their stubborn
        disorder.
So, she had words with her husband in Vulcan's bedroom of wrought
        gold,
Breathily stirring a passion divine with her words. She began thus:
'While those Argolid kings waged war that left Pergamum wasteland,
As it deserved, and assaulted a citadel doomed to a foeman's   375
Fires, I requested no help for their misery, asked for no armour
Wrought by your skill and resources. For I, most dearly belovèd
Husband, did not want *you* to put in all your labour for nothing,
Even though I myself owed much to the children of Priam,
And had shed many a tear for the hard labour borne by Aeneas.   380
Now, and at Jupiter's orders, he stands on Rutulian coastlands.*
I come to you on my knees, in the same kind of crisis, requesting
Arms from a power I revere, for a son, as Motherhood's goddess.*
Nereus' child and Tithonus's wife* softened you just by weeping.
Look at those peoples coming together! See how many
        strongholds   385
Seal their gates tight, whetting blades to bring me and my loved ones
        to ruin.'
    This said, he still hesitated.* The goddess's hands began moving,
Fondling him this way and that in her pliant embrace. In an instant,

He felt the same old flame flare up, the familiar hotness
Surged through his bones' very marrow and raced through his
    loosened   390
Joints, just as sometimes a dazzling fracture of fire spurts brightness
Clear through a cloud when it bursts from a brilliant explosion of
    thunder.*
She, well aware of her beauty, could feel her ruse work and was happy.
Chained* by his undying love and its passion, the father responded:
'Why hunt for precedents up in the skies? Since when have
    you, goddess,   395
Lost faith in *your* power with me? Had you felt any similar worry
Even then, there was no law to stop us from arming the Teucrians!
Neither the Father Almighty nor fate was denying a further
Ten years for Troy* to survive or for Priam's continued existence!
Now, too, if you're preparing to fight, and your mind's set
    in this way,   400
I will extend my art to its fullest potential to lighten
Your cares: whatever one *can* forge from steel or from molten electrum,
Pushing the limits of bellows and fire, I'll forge. But your begging
Shows it's your own power you doubt. Stop it now!' When he'd said
    this he gave her
Just the embraces she wanted and, melting away in his wife's lap,   405
Sought there the pleasing calm of relief throughout all his members.

Night had already passed the mid-point of her circuit. Relaxing
Sleep's first phase banished drowsiness. Now it's the hour of the
    woman,
Forced to put up with a lifetime of spinning and all of Minerva's
Trivial skills. So she stirs ashes, rouses the comatose fires,   410
Adds night hours to the workday, busies her slave-girls with extra
Wool to be spun by the light of the fire to ensure that her husband's
Bed remains chaste and that she can bring up small children correctly.
Just like her, and at no idler hour, the Igniter of Fire
Rises from comfort in bed to attend to his tasks* in the workshop.   415
   Up close to Sicily's flank and to Lipara, in the Aeolian
Islands, there rises a towering, smoke-spewing insular rock mass,
Deep beneath which lies a cavern and chambers connecting to Etna,
Gnawed out for foundries by Cyclopes, echoing audible thunder:
Mighty blows upon anvils, the groans and the screams of
    compacted   420

Ingots of Chalyban iron and furnaces' fire-bellowed gasping.
Down here is Vulcan's home, and Volcania's the name of the island,
Here the Igniter of Fire now descended from high in the heavens.
Cyclopes tempered the steel in the vast cave; Brontes was crafting
Thunder, and Steropes lightning; Pyracmon pounded the anvil,   425
Stripped bare. Hammered to shape by their hands was a thunderbolt,
     such as
Jupiter hurls at the earth from all over the sky in abundance.
Part of the work was completed and part needed finishing touches.
Three spring-coiled rain belts were in place, three of water-compacted
Cloud, three bright with the scarlet of fire and with swift-winging
     south wind.   430
Now they compounded, and melded in metalwork, frightening flashes,
Rumbles and terror, and vengeful wrath that can target and track you.
Elsewhere, a group was creating for Mars a new chariot equipped with
Swiftly rotating wheels to whirl cities and men into battle.
Some raced to finish a blood-chilling aegis, the armour for
     angered   435
Pallas, with viperous scales done in gold, showing intertwined serpents
And, on the goddess's bosom, the Gorgon herself with her glaring
Eyes still in motion, alive in a head on a neck wholly severed.
'Stop all your work,' he said. 'Clear away all those tasks you have started,
Cyclopes, creatures of Etna, give this your immediate attention.   440
Arms must be made for a keen-edged man. So summon your full force
Now, we need quick hands, now we need all of your consummate
     skill NOW!
Don't put it off with delays!' And he says nothing more; they all swiftly
Fall to their work and apportion the tasks in an even division.
Bronze and a mineful of gold begin flowing in rivulets, lethal   445
Hard steel liquefies deep in the vast vatted furnaces. They then
Hammer out one huge shield to repel every weapon the Latins
Hurl, and, to form it, they fuse seven round layers tightly together,
Circle to circle. While some draw the breezes in with the bellows'
Suction, expel them as wind gusts, yet others are plunging the
     screeching   450
Bronze into pools, and the cave floor groans beneath tonnage of anvils.
Raised arms' huge force, this first, then that, beat out a rhythm,
Hands grip the ingot with tongs, flip it over and pound it to flatness.

Now, as the father from Lemnos* speeds round Aeolian coastlands,

Gentle daylight is stirring Evander to step from his humble   455
Shelter, along with the morning birds singing under his gables.
Rising, the elderly man dons a tunic to cover his body,
Slips his feet into Tuscan sandals and ties up the laces,
Straps a Tegean sword to his hip by a belt from his shoulder,
Then knots the skin of a panther about him. It hangs from his
    left side.   460
Further, a couple of guardians posted up high at the entrance
Dash out in front as he walks. These dogs are their master's retainers.*
Straight to Aeneas's hut went the hero, and entered the private
Room of his guest. He remembered their talk and the favours he'd
    promised.
Morning had brought forth Aeneas as well. He was up and in
    motion.   465
Pallas came out to his father; Achates escorted Aeneas.
After the meeting and handshakes, they sat in the heart of the building
Making the most of this overdue chance for a real conversation.
'Greatest of Teucrian leaders,' the king began, 'while you are living,
I won't ever admit Troy's kingdom and power have been
    conquered.   471
We have but slender resources to help in a war for a famous
Cause, hemmed in, as we are, by the Tuscan Tiber on this flank,
Pressed by Rutulian forces who're ringing our walls on the other.
Still, I'm prepared to ally to your cause very populous nations,   475
Armies richly equipped by their realms. It's relief unexpected
Chance offers up. Though you came of your own will, it's what the
    fates wanted.
  'Not far from here are a people who live in a city, Agylla,
Founded on age-old rock in the Tuscan hills by a famous
Warrior people who came, long ago,* from their Lydian
    homeland.   480
Over the years it succeeded and thrived. Then a king named
    Mezentius
Crushed it with powerful pride maintained by a ruthless militia.
Why recall slaughter that words can't describe, or a tyrant's
    subhuman
Actions? May gods bring it back on his head and the heads of
    his children!
He, I'd point out, made a habit of tying dead bodies to live men,   485
Hands bound together with hands, even faces lashed against faces,

His special version of torture. It killed people ever so slowly,
Strapped in a grisly embrace as they oozed with decay and corruption.
Finally, citizens tired of his passion for horrors beyond words,
Took up arms, set siege to the tyrant himself and his palace,   490
Slaughtered his henchmen, bombarded his rooftop with torches of fire.
During the carnage, he slipped out across the Rutulian border,
Made his escape and, as guest, was protected by Turnus's forces.
All Etruria rose in a righteous fury, demanding,
On pain of instant war, that they hand back the king to be
     punished.   495
     'You I will add to these thousands, Aeneas, to serve as their leader.
All down the coast there's commotion, you see. A whole war fleet's
     assembled.
Though they're demanding invasion, an ancient diviner restrains
     them,
Singing of fate: "You, the pick of Maeonia's young, you, the flowering
Blossom, the manhood, of men in the old days! Legitimate outrage   500
Drives you. But though this Mezentius deserves all wrath he has
     kindled,
Gods' law forbids you to harness a nation so great to Italian
Leadership.* Pray for some foreign commanders." That's when the
     Etruscan
Army collapsed on the field where it drilled, in its terror at gods' words.
Tarchon himself sent me delegates, bearing the sceptre and
     kingdom's   505
Crown. He entrusts the regalia to me so I'll join his alliance
And take control of Etruria's kingdoms myself. But my old age
Slows me with ice-stiff limbs, worn out by decades, and bedevils
Me as a leader. My strength is too far beyond prime for heroics.
I'd be suggesting my son. But his mother is Sabine. His mixed
     blood   510
Means he's just partly expatriate. You, to whom fate has been kinder
Both in your age and your origins, you, whom divine powers summon,
Step forth, bravest of Teucrian, and of Italian, leaders.
Pallas, my hope and my solace, I'll also assign to your service.
So, let this young man learn, as apprentice, with you as his
     master,   515
How to endure what a soldier must bear, the grim burden of warfare,
And let him witness your deeds, from his first years grow to admire you.
I'll give him horsemen, two hundred Arcadians, selecting the toughest

Youths, the same number that Pallas will pass on to you in his own
    name.'

  Scarcely had he said this when—no,* for Aeneas, Anchises' 520
Son and the faithful Achates were keeping their heads lowered, thinking
Numerous problems through. They'd have stayed so, had not Cytherea
Given a sign from the cloudless blue. For a flicker of lightning
Shivered from out of the startled skies, crashed down amid thunder.
Suddenly everything seemed to implode, and a trumpet's
    Etruscan 525
Blare seemed to low, like a bellowing ox, up high through the heavens.
As they look up, there's the ratatat rattle of crackling thunder.
And, between clouds in a tranquil region of sky, they see armour
Blazing the dry air scarlet, and pealing out booms as it clashes.
Others' minds went numb. The heroic Trojan, however, 530
Knows both the sound and the items his parent, the goddess, has
    promised.
Then he explains: 'Don't look any further, good host, to discover
What kind of outcome these omens portend: I am called by Olympus.
This is the sign my Creator Divine once predicted she'd send me
Should war arise, and she promised she'd bring through the air,
    to assist me, 535
Weapons that Vulcan would make.
Pitiful Laurentine men, how huge is the slaughter impending!
Oh, what a penalty, Turnus, you'll pay me! And how many men's
    shields,
Helmets and valiant corpses will you, Father Tiber, be rolling
Under your waters! So let them demand battle, let them break
    treaties!' 540
  When he had spoken, he rose from his tall chair and, as his first
    action,
Stirred up flames from the altar's embers in Hercules' honour,
Joyfully prayed to the god of the house and the far from pretentious
Spirits he'd known just a day. Then Evander, along with the Trojans,
Side by side, slaughtered hoggets, selected as ritual demanded. 545
This done, Aeneas returned to the ships to revisit his comrades
Out of whose ranks he selected to come and assist him in warfare
Only the brave, the most manly. The rest float away on the tranquil
Waters, lazily drift downstream with the river's assistance,
Charged with informing Ascanius about these events—and his
    father. 550

Horses are given to Teucrians now as they head for Etruscan
Lands. A fine mount is reserved for Aeneas. Its back is entirely
Masked with a lion's tawny hide, claws glittered with gold-plate.
Rumour takes wing among ordinary folk in this minuscule city:
'Cavalry's galloping off to the king of Etruria's palace.'   555
Mothers, in fear, double prayers as the gulf between terror and danger
Narrows. As Mars closes in, war's spectre looms ever larger.
Pallas is ready to leave, but Evander still hugs him. His father
Weeps inconsolable tears as he clings to his son and keeps talking:
'Oh for my bygone years, could Jupiter only restore them,   560
Make me the man that I was when I once, at the siege of Praeneste,*
Flattened the foe's front line, piled shields up in triumph and burned
          them,
Sending King Erulus down into Tartarus' pit with my own hand.
     'When he was born—and the tale makes me shudder—his
          mother, Feronia,
Granted him three lives, three distinct changes of armour to fight in,   565
Three death-blows were thus needed to kill him. That day, though,
          my right hand,
Robbed him of all three lives, stripped all of his three suits of armour.
Son, if I were what I was, I would never be torn from your loving
Arms. For Mezentius wouldn't have trampled on that kind of
          neighbour's
Head to begin with. He'd never have dealt out so much and such
          brutal   570
Death with his sword, left our city a void without citizens, widowed.
Powers in heaven, and you, who are ruler supreme over all gods,
Jupiter, pity, I beg you, this king from Arcadia, *your* land.
Listen to prayers from a father. If your divine will preserves Pallas
Safely for me, if he's spared by the fates, if I'm going to see him   575
While I'm alive, if I'm going to meet him again, I'm requesting
Life and I'll put up with labour and hardship, no matter how awful.
If, though, you threaten us, Fortune, with random, unspeakable ruin,
Let me die now, let me now snap the grip of a cruel existence
While my anxieties waver, while hope for the future can flicker,   580
While, my dear boy, I still hold you, my sole and my last source of
          pleasure,
Here in my arms. May no dire news strike at my heart through my
          hearing.'
These words a father shed over his son as they parted for ever.

Then he collapsed; slaves raised him and carried him into the building.

Gates had been opened, the cavalry troop had now passed to the
     outside.   585
Riding up at the front were Aeneas and faithful Achates,
Followed by Troy's other chiefs. Pallas, though, was himself at the
     column's
Centre, so easy to see in his cloak and his colourful armour,
Bright as the star that brings daylight, cleansed by the sparkle of
     Ocean's
Waves, and belovèd of Venus beyond other heavenly star-fires,   590
Raising its sacred face in the sky and dissolving the darkness.
Still, on the walls mothers stand, fear live in their eyes which are
     tracking
Dust as it forms into cloud and the squadrons whose bronze fittings
     glisten.
Though they are clad in full armour they ride across thickets of
     scrubland,
Taking the shortest of routes. There's a shout. They get into
     formation.   595
Galloping, clattering quadruped hoofs quiver prairie to powder.

Huge woods crowd in close to the ice-cold river of Caere,
Widely revered in traditional cults, and encompassed by curving
Hillsides which buttress the grove with a dark black edging of fir trees.
Rumour says ancient Pelasgians, first to possess what were later   600
Latin domains, dedicated these lands to the cult of Silvanus,*
God of the ploughlands and cattle. They honoured him there with a
     feast-day.
Not far away, in a fortress protected by nature's defences,
Tarchon's Etruscan forces were camped. From the heights of the hilltop
All of his legion was there to be seen, deployed on the broad
     plains.   605
That's where Aeneas, the father, and youths he'd selected for
     warfare
Now entered. And they were weary. They rested their mounts and
     their bodies.
   Venus, gleaming white amid dark clouds up in the bright sky
Now arrived, bringing the gifts. And she saw her son from a distance
Sheltered within a secluded vale near the chill river's waters.   610

These were the words that she spoke as she brought herself into his
  presence:
'See, they're completed, these offerings crafted with skill by my
  husband
Just as I promised. My son, show no further reluctance to challenge
Either proud Laurentines or even Turnus, fearsome in battle.'
This said, Cythera's goddess approached so her son could
  embrace her,   615
Set the arms under an oak tree's radiate branches* before him.
He, in delight at the gifts and the singular honour accorded,
Just couldn't sate his eyes as he scanned each item in detail,
Awed as he held in his hands, or put over his arms, or rotated
First the grim helmet, the shock of its plumes, eructations of fire;   620
Next, the sword, agent of death; then the rigid and bronze-stiffened
  corslet,
Blood-coloured, massive, resembling a sea-grey cloud that the sun's rays
Kindle and blazon with fire and which shimmers and glows in the
  distance;
Next, greaves fashioned in purest refinement of gold and electrum;
Then the spear; lastly the shield's indescribable texture and
  context.   625
 There the Igniter of Fire, who was neither unversed in the seers'
Prophecies nor uninformed about future events, had expounded
Italy's history, the triumphs of Roman achievement: Ascanius'
Future line of descendants, and battles they fought, set in order.*
Mars' green Lupercal cave he had wrought, and the Tale of the
  She-Wolf.   630
There she reclined with the litter she raised; and the twin boys she
  nurtured*
Dangled and played at her dugs and were fearlessly drawing their
  mother's
Milk, and the wolf stretched back her smooth neck toward them,
  caressing
Each in his turn and, with licks from her tongue, groomed both of
  their bodies.
Not far away he'd set Rome and the lawless Rape of the Sabine   635
Women, abducted from seats at the sacred games in the Circus,
Showing the sudden resurgence of war between Romulus' nation
And the austere folk of Cures whose king was the elderly Tatius.
Then these same two kings, their mutual conflict abandoned,

Stood, still armed,* before Jupiter's altar, goblets uplifted,   640
Joining in treaties* over a sow struck down and disjointed.
Not far away from this scene, swift four-horse chariots had sundered
Mettius,* limb from limb. You should stand by your word, man of Alba!
Tullus was there, strewing this disembowelled liar's intestines
All through the woods; and the brambles were damp with the dew
     of the bloodshed.   645
Lars Porsenna* was there, telling Romans to bring back the exiled
Tarquin, and pressing his claim with a large-scale siege of the city.
Sons of Aeneas rushed down on his swords in defence of their freedom.
Lars, you could see, looked like someone enraged, like a man full of
     menace,
All because Cocles was daringly smashing the bridge, and
     Cloelia*   650
Breaking the chains in her prison, escaping, and swimming the river.
High on Tarpeia's citadel rock* was its sentinel, Manlius,
Standing in front of the temple and guarding the Capitol's summit.
And, as in Romulus' day, fresh thatch made the palace look rustic.
Here was a gander in silver relief flapping out from a gilded   655
Portico, rousing men up with no paltry alarm: that the Gallic*
Host was now perched at the gates. Safe in shadows, abetted by
     moonless
Night, Gauls spread among thickets were gaining control of the
     stronghold.
Gold is employed for their unscissored hair* and each garment is
     golden,
Tartan gleams on each cape, on each milk-white neck there's a
     twisting   660
Necklace of gold, each man carries two bright spears of the Alpine
Type in his hand, and their full-length shields give their bodies
     protection.
     Hammered in high relief were the dancing Salii, naked
Lupercal priests with their bonnets of wool, and the shields* that had
     fallen
Out of the sky. Chaste mothers, in well-cushioned coaches,
     escorted   665
Relics in city parades. At a distance from these, he's appended
Tartarus' homes of the dead and the deep-down entrance to Pluto's
Realm and the crimes punished there. He shows you, Catiline,* and
     you're dangling

Over a chasm and facing, in terror, the jaws of the Furies.

Righteous souls set apart have their personal law-giver, Cato.*   670

Running the width of the shield, and dividing the scenes, ran a golden

Picture of rough dark seas, waves' foam set in highlights of whiteness.

Edged all around by a circle of sparkling dolphins in silver,

Whipping the surface with tails, cutting neatly through surges of
      sea-swell.

   Centrally placed, fleets depicted in bronze, the whole conflict at
      Actium*   675

Opened to view. You could see, as decks cleared for battle, all Leucas

Seething with action and churning with waves flashing white against
      gold-plate.

Caesar Augustus, on this side, is leading Italians to combat,

Backed by the senate and people, the household spirits and great gods,

Stationed high on the aft-deck, his joyful temples erupting   680

Twin flame-plumes. His paternal star* is the badge on his helmet.

Elsewhere, and towering high, in command of the fleet, is Agrippa

Favoured by winds and divine support. On his temples is blazing

War's proud medal, the Naval Crown* with its pattern of ships' rams.

   Antony, backed by a foreigner's wealth, international forces,   685

Faces them, fresh from the Red Sea and Gulf and the conquest of
      eastern

Peoples. He brings with him Egypt, the Middle East's strength, and
      remotest

Bactria. Following him (what a crime!) is his wife, who's Egyptian.*

   Vessels all rush out together, the whole sea's surface is foaming,

Thrashed by the tug of the oars and the three-pronged rams on the
      ships' prows.   690

Out into open waters they race. You would think the Cycladic

Islands uprooted* and swimming the seas, or high mountains colliding,

Such was the mass in which men gave battle in turreted warships.

Torches of blazing pitch, hand-launched, scatter, as do the flying

Steel-tipped shafts. And on Neptune's fields it's the slaughter that
      blossoms   695

Red.

      In its midst, the queen cheers on her troops with the sistrum,
      her nation's

Symbol. As yet she has not looked back at the twin snakes* behind her.

Every conceivable monstrous god, even barking Anubis,*

Points weapons at counterbalancing figures of Neptune and Venus,

Points at Minerva. And, figured in steel at the heart of the
    fighting,   700
Mars runs wild, grim Demons observe from the heavens, and Discord
Gleefully rushes about with her garment in tatters; Bellona,
Blood-spattered bullwhip in hand, follows closely. Above them, Apollo,
Actium's god, has been noting all this and is stretching his bowstrings.
Every Egyptian is terrified, Indians, each of the Arabs,   705
All of the Shebans are scared. They begin to turn tail, they're defecting.
Even the queen seems to call for the winds and the canvas, to slacken
Yard-ropes and lower the sail. The Igniter of Fire had depicted
Pallor of death yet to come on her face even now, in this carnage,
Even as winds from Italian coasts steal her over the waters.   710

    Facing her, he'd represented the Nile as a giant, in mourning,
Opening wide each fold in his mantle to welcome the vanquished
Into his sea-blue lap with its undular layers of concealment.

    Now, Caesar:* he was conveyed within Roman walls in a three-fold
Triumph. To Italy's gods he made vows that would bind him
    for ever: 715
Three hundred large-scale shrines to be built throughout all of the city.
Streets were a riot of joy, of performance, applause, and approval.
All temples rang with the singing of mothers, all temples had altars,
Altars had thresholds strewn with the young bulls slaughtered for
    Caesar.*
He's seated right before dazzling Phoebus's snowy white sanctum,   720
Thanking his peoples for gifts now attached with pride at its portals.*
    Vanquished nations approach in a long line, varied in language
As in their clothing and weapons. The Gentler of Iron had carved out
Nomad peoples and Africans too, quite distinct in their loose robes,
Leleges, Carians here, and Gelonians shouldering quivers.   725
Now, as it flowed, the Euphrates was moving more gently; Morini,
Farthest away of all peoples, were checked, and the Rhine, with its
    two prongs,
Untamed Scythians as well, and Araxes resentful of bridges.

Such is the tale* upon Vulcan's shield, on the gift of his parent.
Ignorant as to its substance, yet awed by the artwork, Aeneas   730
Shoulders with joy fame's rumours and fate's vows for his descendants.

BOOK NINE

WHILE these actions occurred* in the depths of a different region,
Juno, the daughter of Saturn, sent Iris down from the heavens
Straight towards Turnus the Bold. He was seated, it chanced, in a
    sacred
Hollow containing the shrine of his ancestors' father, Pilumnus.*
This is how Thaumas' child, with her lips red as roses, addressed
    him: 5
'Turnus, observe that the scrolling of time has, without any prompting,
Offered what no god would *dare* promise you, if you asked it. Aeneas,
Leaving his city, his allies, his navy abandoned, has set out,
Hot in pursuit of the sceptre and Palatine realm of Evander.*
Not just that—he's struck deeper: to Corythus' outermost Tuscan   10
Cities, recruiting the Lydian peasants and giving them weapons.
Why dither? Now is the time to be calling for chariot and horses!
Smash any force that delays you and capture their camp! You'll wreak
    havoc.'
This said, she rose on symmetrical wings and sped off through the
    heavens,
Etching a rainbow prodigiously large beneath mantles of storm
    clouds.   15
Turnus now knew who she was, so he stretched both his palms to the
    starry
Heights, and dispatched words hot in pursuit as she fled from his vision:
'Iris, glory of skies, who has driven you earthwards through veiling
Clouds just for me? What's causing this change in the air, all this
    sudden
Brilliance? I'm seeing the sky split apart at its vault, constellations   20
Moving in space. So, whoever you are who now call me to battle,
I'll follow this great an omen!' That said, he strode up to the river,
Drew fresh draughts from its gurgling flow at the surface and uttered
Numerous prayers to the gods, heaped promises high to the heavens.

Now, across stretches of open plains, the whole army's advancing,   25
Rich in its horses and rich in embroidered apparel and gold trim.
Leading the front-line troops is Messapus, commanding the
    rearguard

Tyrrhus' sons, and, in charge of the centre, their general, Turnus
[Passing along under arms, head and shoulders above all the others].*
Forward they sweep like the Ganges,* majestic in silence,
    its seven   30
Tributaries feeding its flood, like the Nile ebbing back, its enriching
Flow withdrawn from the flatlands, returned to its regular channel.
Teucrians notice a sudden explosion of dust, darkly billowed
Into a cloud, and see menacing shadows arise over meadows.
Warning comes first from Caïcus,* who's high on the facing
    embankment: 35
'Citizens, some cloud, dark as a smoky fire, is approaching.
Hurry to arms, issue weapons, and man all the battlements quickly!
Enemy sighted! On guard!' Voices merge in an uproar as Teucrians
Pour through the gates for protection, and mass, full force, on the
    ramparts.

   When he departed, Aeneas, an expert on tactics, had ordered   40
Just this response, if Fortune took any such turn in his absence.
No, they must not offer battle or hazard a chance in the open,
Simply protect both the camp and the walls on their solid
    embankment.
So, although anger and shame urge a counter-attack, they continue,
Nonetheless, following orders, they keep the gates sealed shut and
    bolted,   45
Wait, under arms, for the foe in the cavernous safety of turrets.

   Turnus breaks from the slow moving column with twenty selected
Cavalrymen at his flanks, speeds off, and arrives at the city
Sooner than one would have thought. He is riding a Thracian piebald
Dappled with white, and he's masked by a red-plumed helmet of
    pure gold.   50
'Who's going to join me in being the first at the enemy, soldiers?
Look!' Then he spins off a well-torqued javelin high towards heaven,
Marking the start of the fight. Then he prances in pride on the
    meadow.
Up goes a bloodcurdling roar as his squad joins in on the war-cry,
Adding its own yells. The Teucrians' lack of response is a puzzle: 55
Why don't they come out and fight, on the level, take arms against
    foemen's
Arms and be men, and not hide in a camp? In a mad gallop this way
Round the walls, that way, he hunts a way in, where no way's in
    existence,

Just like the midnight wolf in his personal siege of a dense-packed
Sheep-pen, snarling at gaps in the fencing, wind-whipped and
    rain-lashed.   60
Ruthless and rough in his rage, long starving and tortured by
    pent-up
Cravings of hunger, by parched jaws thirsty for blood, he is madly
Howling at lambs lying just beyond reach. They are tucked beneath
    mothers,
Safe and secure, their incessant bleating's their only reaction.
So, as he checks out the walls and the fort, the Rutulian's anger   65
Flares. Frustration's pain burns fire deep into his tough bones.
What should his strategy be to get in, or to shake out the Teucrians
Huddled inside the stockade, and to pour them all over the sea-flat
Surface? The fleet!* It lay sidled away out of view at the stronghold's
Side with a circling defence of both river-fed moats and
    embankments.   70
This he breaks through. Then he calls on his cheering companions
    for fire,
Fervidly seizing a handful of blazing torches of pitch-pine.
Turnus' example inspires the rest, who now work with a passion.
All the young men are equipping themselves with such ominous
    firebrands,
Stripping the wood out of hearths. Smoky torches emit a
    pitch-darkened   75
Brilliance and Vulcan erupts to the stars fire mingled with ashes.

Muses, which god kept this brute act of arson from harming the
    Teucrians?
Who stopped the great blaze destroying the ships? For belief in the
    story
Died long ago,* though it lives on in rumour, as folklore. You tell it!
Once, upon that first time when Aeneas was building a navy   80
High upon Phrygian Ida, preparing to head for the high seas,
Popular tales say Cybele, the Great Berecyntian Mother,
Spoke thus to Jupiter: 'Give me, my son, one wish, which I ask you,
Now that you've tamed Mount Olympus,* to give to your dearly
    loved mother.
Centrally placed on the peaks, giving shady relief with its maple   86
Beams and its black pitch-pine, was a park where the people brought
    offerings,   87

Woodlands of pine that had given me year after year of enjoyment.   85
These I was happy to give to the Dardan youth when he really
Needed a fleet. Now I'm troubled, I'm choking, I'm strangled with
     terror.
Loosen the grip of my fears, let her prayers win this much for your
     mother: 90
Power to keep my trees from destruction when battered by any
Voyage, tornado, or gale. Let them profit from birth on my mountains.'
He whose energy drives heaven's stars, her son, then responded:
'Mother, what call are you issuing fate? What's your goal for these
     objects?
Should vessels crafted by death-doomed hands have the right to be
     deathless?*   95
How can Aeneas complete a predicted journey whose dangers
Can't be predicted? What god is permitted the power to compute
     that?
No, when their useful life's at an end and they're berthed in Ausonian
Havens, those that survive sea's surge, and convey the Dardanian
Leader as far as the Laurentine land, I will strip of their
     death-doomed   100
Beauty and form and I'll bid them be goddesses there on the great sea's
Surface, and cut through the ocean's foaming brine with their bosoms,
As do the fair Galatea and Doto, the daughter of Nereus.'
These words gave his assent. Then he swore a great oath by his
     brother's
Molten, pitch-scorched banks of the Styx,* by its dark-eddied
     torrents.   105
That one nod of his head shivered all of Olympus with tremors.
   This was the promised day, the day fate fully paid out the vessels'
Time due. Turnus' assault warned the Mother to ward off the
     firebrands
Launched at their sacred timbers. The first sign that she was reacting
Came when a strange new light dazzled eyes and a huge cloud was
     noticed   110
Scudding the sky from the eastern dawn and, with it, ecstatic
Corybant* dancers from Ida. Then down through the air fell a
     frightening
Voice overwhelming the ranks of the Trojans and ranks of Rutulians:
'Teucrians, don't arm up for a desperate defence of my vessels!
Turnus will sooner be granted the right to set fire to the oceans   115

Than to destroy my sacred pines.* You are free of your moorings,
Go! You are gods of the sea! Go on as your mother instructs you.'
Instantly each vessel severs the ties of its riverside moorings
And, beak first, like a dolphin, dives down deep under water,
Straight to the river-bed. Then they emerge (an astonishing
        portent),   120
[Matching the number of bronze figured prows once beached on the
        seashore]*
Shaped into so many female forms swimming out to the high seas.
   Shock froze Rutulian hearts, and Messapus, whose horses were
      rearing,
Joined in their terror himself. Tiberinus, who's normally raucous,
Slowed to a trickle and pulled back his muddying foot from the
        salt sea.   125
Turnus, however, felt no lessened trust in his confident boldness.
Seizing the chance to raise spirits with words, he now issued this
      challenge:*
'*These* portents menace the Trojans, not us. They've been stripped of
      their usual
Refuge by Jupiter. *He* didn't need to wait round for Rutulian
Weapons and flames. So the Teucrians, you see, cannot now use
        the seaways.   130
Hence, they've no hope of escape. They've been robbed of the land,
      their one other
Way to get out. We control it. For Italy's peoples, so many
Thousands, are now under arms. Those divine, fatalistic responses
Phrygians scatter at random don't terrify me in the slightest.
Venus and fate have their due. Trojan feet made contact with
        ploughlands   135
Here in our fertile Ausonia. But I have my destiny also,
Countering theirs: the destruction of their whole criminal nation.
They, on the eve of our wedding, abducted my wife. Menelaus
Isn't alone in his pain and Mycenae isn't the only
City allowed to take arms. "Dying once is enough," says the
        proverb;   140
One prior rape would have been crime enough, if they hadn't so deeply
Loathed the whole female sex. Their trust in the rampart between us,
Trenches that may slow us down, the thin line between life and
        destruction,
Give reassurance. But didn't they see Troy's fortifications

Crafted by Neptune's hand sink down as the fires devoured
    them?   145
You, our elite! Which of you is prepared to dismantle this rampart,
Join my attack, plunge into this castle of quivering cowards?
I don't have arms made by Vulcan,* I don't have, I don't need, a
    thousand
Ships to beat Teucrians. Let all the Etruscans enrol as their allies!
This time they needn't be scared of the dark or of amateur
    burglars   150
Stealing the statue of Pallas and butchering citadel sentries,*   151
Or fear we'll hide in a horse's paunch unseen. We're resolved that
Our fires start during daylight, at outside walls, in the open.
I'll guarantee they won't say that it's like their defeat by Danaäns
And by Pelasgian forces that Hector held off more than nine
    years!   155
Well, since the day's better part is now over, spend what's still remaining
Looking to bodily needs. Be content. A great deal's been accomplished
Nicely. And hope, gentlemen, that a battle is now in the making.'

Meanwhile, Messapus is charged with maintaining the siege of the
    gateways,
Picketing sentries, and keeping the fortress encircled with bonfires.   160
Fourteen Rutulians,* picked as the duty-officers, stand watch
Over the enemy walls, each commanding a force of a hundred
Troops wearing purple plumes, with the glitter of gold on their armour.
Off to their various postings they go. Guards change. Then they're
    sprawling*
Over the grass in the pleasures of wine, and upending the bronze
    cups.   165
Fires burn bright all round and the sentry passes his sleepless
Night playing dice.
All this the Trojans observe from the top of their rampart. They're
    keeping
High points guarded, and anxiously, nervously, checking the gateways,
Anchoring gangways, linking the barbicans, brandishing weapons.   170
Mnestheus* keeps up the pressure, along with the fearsome Serestus;
Father Aeneas appointed them as—should a crisis demand it —
Generals in charge of the forces; in matters of state, full commanders.
There's a whole legion now lining the wall. They've apportioned
    the danger,

Each stands guard in rotation, each watches what he is
    assigned to. 175
  Nisus* mounted guard at the gate, one of Hyrtacus' children,
Quick with a spear and light arrows, an expert in handling weapons.
Ida, that heaven for hunters, sent him as Aeneas's comrade.
Close by, his own special comrade, Euryalus, stood. In Aeneas'
Group, in the whole Trojan army, this boy had no rival in beauty. 180
Face still unshaven, he just now was showing the first signs of
    manhood.
They were as one in their love. They charged as a pair into battle.
So now too they guarded the gate on the watch they were sharing.
'Is it, Euryalus, gods who implant these obsessions,' said Nisus,
'Deep in our minds? Or do each individual's passions
    become god? 185
My mind's been nagging me now for a while to try battle, or something
Major. It isn't the least bit content with this tranquil inertia.
See how complacent Rutulians are about how things are going?
Just an occasional glimmer of fire. They're asleep. They are dead drunk,*
Flat on their faces. The silence is total out there. Now think over 190
Why I'm debating myself, what's emerging as my resolution.
Everyone, senate and people, demands that Aeneas be summoned
Back, and that men should be sent to report this demand to Aeneas.
If they will promise to give what I'm asking for you (since the good name
Brought by the deed is sufficient for me) then I think that I might
    just 195
Find there's a path, under that mound* there, up to walled Pallanteum.'
Stunned by his great love of glory, Euryalus, rooted and dumbstruck
Still managed this in response to his friend who was blazing with passion:
'So, you're avoiding *me*, cutting *me* from your greatest adventure,
Nisus? Am I just to send you alone to face dangers so daunting? 200
That's not the way that my father, Opheltes,* toughened in battle,
Shaped me from my raw birth between Troy's dying labours and
    Argive
Terror, nor how I conducted myself at your side when I followed
Great-souled Aeneas and every extreme of his destiny's anguish.
Here lives a soul, lives a soul unconcerned with life's light. It would
    reckon 205
Honour, the kind that you reach for, a bargain, though bought with
    its life's blood.'
Nisus said: 'No such fear had occurred to me. That would be sinful.

That's not the way I'd be if great Jupiter or any power,
Looking at all this with unbiased eyes brought me, in my triumph,
Back home to you. But if some force (in crises like this you see
    many)   210
If some force, be it chance, be it god, were to drag me to ruin,
I'd want *you* to survive. Your youth gives your life more importance.
I need a person who'd snatch up my body from battle or pay out
Ransom, then bury me, *that's* what I need. Or if Fortune, as often,
Doesn't allow this, he'd build me a cenotaph and, in my
    absence,   215
Give me my rites. Don't make me the cause of your poor mother's
    desperate
Grief. She alone among so many mothers still follows her own son;
She didn't give all her love to the city of noble Acestes.'
'Don't waste time', said the other, 'in stringing together such useless
Arguments. My mind still hasn't changed; it maintains its
    position.   220
Let's hurry up!' As he speaks he is waking the guards, who relieve them,
Taking their turn on watch. He abandons his post, and as Nisus'
Comrade, walks at his side. They're beginning their quest for their ruler.

All through the earth other conscious creatures* were yielding their
    anxious
Tensions to sleep. Their hearts had forgotten the weight of their
    burdens.   225
Top-ranking Teucrian officers, though, the select of the army,
Gathered in conference now on affairs of the utmost importance:
What should they do? Who should go out and pass on the news to
    Aeneas?
Propped upon long spears, there they stood, shields held in a tight grip,
Right in the heart of the camp, in its open parade ground.
    Then Nisus   230
Urgently begged (and Euryalus too) for immediate admission:
Major concerns, worth the price of delay, they contended. Iulus
Made the first move, let the nervous pair in, and told Nisus to
    speak out.
Hyrtacus' son began thus: 'Listen, sons of Aeneas,* with open
Minds. Don't assess our report by our age. The Rutulians are
    quiet,   235
Drifting away in a wine-sodden sleep. We ourselves have detected

Where we can set up an ambush: unmonitored space where the
    footpath
Leading towards the gate nearest the sea makes a fork. Here the
    watchfires'
Circle is broken, a black smoke plume rises high to the starry
Skies. If you grant us permission to use this good fortune for
    finding   240
Just where Aeneas is, and for going to walled Pallanteum,
You'll see us back very soon with the spoils from an orgy of slaughter.
We won't get lost on the way. We've sighted the city's outlying
Regions from deep within well-shaded valleys when out on our frequent
Forays to hunt, and we know very well the whole length of the
    river.'   245
    That's when the solemn Aletes,* a well-seasoned mind, added
    these words:
'Gods of my homeland, your will has been Troy's clear guidance at
    all times.
You're not poised, after all, for the utter destruction of Teucrians
When you've instilled such courage in our young men, such determined
Hearts!' As he spoke he was gripping the two men's hands and their
    shoulders,   250
Weeping profusely, his face, his expressions, awash with emotion.
'What would I reckon might square your account, what honours
    befitting
Such a heroic deed, fine men, what actual prizes?
Noblest, and first, will be those that the gods and your own moral
    standards
Give you. And righteous Aeneas will pay the rest promptly.
    Ascanius—   255
He has a long life before him—will never forget what he owes you.'
'No,' interjected Ascanius, 'I won't. I've just one hope for safety:
Getting my father back. So, Nisus, I beg by my household's
Great gods as well as Assaracus' spirit, and ashen-haired Vesta's
Shrine, and I set in your laps my whole fortune and trust in the
    future: 260
Summon my father back. Bring him back here, where I can see him.
There'll be no sadness and grief once he's back with us, safely recovered.
I'll give two goblets of exquisite silver, embossed with relief-work,
Plunder my father obtained in the capture and sack of Arisbe,
Matching tripods as well, plus gold: two talents of bullion,*   265

Also an antique chalice, a gift from Sidonian Dido.
If, though, he happens to win in the war, capture Italy, gaining
Absolute royal power and the right to apportion the booty,
I will remove from the lottery something you've seen: it's the stallion
Turnus was riding, his armour,* a vision of gold. These are
    all now   270
Yours, Nisus, prizes for you: horse, shield, and his plumage of crimson.
Further, my father will give you a dozen top-quality female
Bodies, all mothers, and male prisoners too, each complete with his
    armour.
Plus any good flat land King Latinus himself now possesses.
  'You, though, a boy one should worship, a person my young age
    is trailing   275
Rather more closely, I take you with all my heart, I embrace you
Into my future, each turn of events, as my personal comrade.
No quest for glory in all my engagements will happen without you,
Whether it's war that I'm waging, or peace, you'll be my most
    important
Friend and adviser in actions and words.' Then Euryalus
    answered   280
This way: 'The day'll never dawn that will catch me behaving in any
Different way in such bold undertakings, so long as my fortune's
Now fair breeze doesn't veer into headwinds. But more than all
    gifts,* one
Favour I ask. I've a mother, descendant of Priam's most ancient
House. The poor soul wasn't kept back on Ilian soil. She left
    with me.   285
Nor is she in King Acestes' city. She's here. And I'm leaving
Her now. She neither knows of this danger (whatever its nature)
Nor got a farewell from me (this I swear by the night and your
    right hand)
I simply could not bear all the tears of a parent's deep sorrow.
I, then implore you, console her. She's helpless, forsaken.
    Support her,   290
Grant me this hope in *you* to take with me, and I'll face whatever
Chance throws my way the more bravely!' Old sons of Dardanus,*
    minds stunned,
All wept, but none wept more than lovely Iulus, his being
Touched by the image it conjured of righteous love for a father.*
Then he declares: 295

'Take as assured everything your great enterprise shows that you merit.
This woman now will be my mother too, with just one detail missing:
Her name isn't Creusa. That she gave you birth does ensure her
No little thanks. Whatsoever the outcome may be of this action,
I now swear by this head which my father used always to
　　swear by:　　　　　　　　　　　　　　　　　　　　　　　300
All that I promise to you if you come back,* your mission successful,
These same things will remain as my pledge to your mother and family.'
So he speaks, and in tears, while he strips from his shoulders the harness
Holding his gold-chased sword that Lycaon of Knossos* had crafted,
Exquisite work, which was handily sheathed in an ivory casing.　　305
Mnestheus gives Nisus the spoils of a hunt. It's the frighteningly shaggy
Skin of a lion. And trusty Aletes exchanges his helmet.
　　Once they are armed they are off. A whole cluster of leaders escorts
　　　　them,
Wishing them well, both the young and the old, as they move to the
　　　　gateway.
Lovely Iulus came too. He affected a spirit transcending　　　　310
Childhood's years, a man's anxious demeanour, persisted in giving
Numerous instructions to take to his father, each one of which breezes
Picked up and wafted away to the clouds as a meaningless present.*
　　Now they're outside, they are over the trenches, they're heading
　　　　through ghostly
Night to a camp that's determined to kill them but where they will
　　　　slaughter　　　　　　　　　　　　　　　　　　　　315
Many before that occurs. They see, randomly strewn upon meadows,
Sleep-flattened, wine-sodden bodies, and chariots down at the water's
Edge, poles high, men tangled in wheels and in harness, their
　　　　weapons
Lying as dead as their wine-jugs. And Hyrtacus' son said the first
　　　　words:
'Now show your right hand's boldness, Euryalus. This scene
　　　　invites it.　　　　　　　　　　　　　　　　　　　　320
Here's where we'll hack out a path. Your task is to keep a broad lookout,
Guard against any potential attack they might launch from behind us.
I'll lay all this waste, and I'll cut a wide swath you can follow.'
This said, he smothers his voice; and with hand upon sword he
　　　　approaches
Rhamnes* the Proud who, it chanced, was laid out on a mountain
　　　　of carpets,　　　　　　　　　　　　　　　　　　　325

Bellowing whole-lunged sleep. This king was another king's augur,
Turnus' favourite, in fact. But his augural powers simply couldn't
Drive *this* pestilence off. Nisus then kills a trio of slave-boys,
Close by, stupidly dead to the world, not at, but among arms,
Then Remus'* armourer, then the man's charioteer, who was
        taken   330
Right by his horses, whose long drooped necks Nisus slashed with a
        sword-stroke,
Then it's their master whose head he lops off, whom he leaves a
        truncated
Torso pulsing blood; dark gore streams warmth through the sodden
Earth, soils bedding with dampness. It's Lamyrus now, now it's
        Lamus.*
Youthful Serranus* too, what a handsome face! He had
        gambled   335
Most of the night-time away and was now out cold, all his limbs limp,
Smashed by an excess of god. Luck's fulfilment was his if he'd only
Kept the odds even with night and had gambled on until daybreak.
Nisus, a lion unfed amid fullness, gone mad in a sheepfold
(Hunger's a ruthless persuader), now gnaws, rips, tears at the
        tender   340
Lambs numbed dumb by their fear; growls rumble through jaws
        dripping slaughter.
Nor is Euryalus slower to kill. He's in full battle fury,
Pure fire sweeping the numberless, nameless rankers before him:
Fadus, Herbesus,* and Rhoetus, and Abaris, dazed and bewildered.
Rhoetus was fully awake; he saw all that occurred but was
        hiding,   345
Watching in fear from behind a huge bowl where the wine had been
        blended.
But he arose as the enemy neared and Euryalus plunged his
Blade hilt-deep in his chest, then withdrew. Death came in
        abundance.
Spewing the crimson of life, he returns to the bowl a new mixture:
Wine and his blood as he dies.
                                        The assassin persists in his fury.   350
Now he goes after Messapus's cavalry, there where the outer
Watchfires are faint. He can see who they are, since their horses
        are grazing
Properly tethered. But Nisus has these few words for his comrade,

Knowing this orgy of slaughter, this passion, is stealing his reason:
'Let's call it off,' he declares. 'Dawn's approaching and she will
      betray us.   355
We've drunk deep* in our vengeance. A path through the foe is
      created.'
Many a fine piece of pure silver warrior art they abandon:
Weaponry, winebowls too, not to mention the beautiful carpets.
Rhamnes' medallions Euryalus does take, and also the harness
Studded with gold-wrought amulets, sent as a gift by the
      wealthy   360
Caedicus once to secure, while away, good relations with Tibur's
Ruler Remulus.* He, on his death passed them on to his grandson.
And, in the war when he died, the Rutulians won them in battle.
   These he strapped on,* though they'd do him no good, to his
      valiant shoulders,
Adding the well-fitted helmet and elegant plumes of Messapus.   365
Off they go, out of the camp, and set forth on the pathway to safety.
   Meanwhile a cavalry unit dispatched in advance of the army's
Main body (still held back on the plains, though in battle formation),
Rode from Latinus's city, reporting to Turnus, as monarch:
Three hundred men, all first-line troops. Their commander was
      Volcens.*   370
They were already approaching the camp, set to pass its defensive
Wall, when they saw the youths veering off to the left in the distance.
Then in the night shadows' low luminescence, Euryalus' helmet
Met and reflected a moonbeam,* betraying its thoughtless possessor.
Only a glimpse, but not wasted. And 'Halt!' came the shout from the
      column.   375
'Why are you travelling?' Volcens asked. 'You are soldiers. Who *are* you?
Where are you going to?' They made no answer at all to his questions.
Rather, they quickened their rush to the woods, hoping night would
      protect them.
This way, that way, the cavalry fanned to block off the familiar
Side-tracks and set up a cordon of guards around all points
      of exit.   380
Bristling underbrush, dark holly oak spread over the forest
Floor: every gap wattled thickly with tangles of brier and bramble,
Trails just sporadic ribbons of light along overgrown track-marks.
Struggles with grappling shadowy branches and cumbersome plunder
Slow down Euryalus' feet. Fear muddles his sense of direction.   385

Nisus gets clear; he'd eluded the foe with improvident prudence,
Passed what were later called Alban Resorts (so named after Alba),
Then just a high market-station for King Latinus's livestock.
Stopping, he noticed his friend wasn't with him, looked back. It was
    useless.*
'Where did I leave you, Euryalus, robbed of your glory's
    fulfilment?   390
How can I get to you?' Thinking his way back all through the twisting
Maze of the woodlands, and, at the same time, hunting for footprints,
Tracking them backwards, he wanders the thickets, unhelpfully silent.
Horses! He hears them, he's hearing the search party's bustle
    and signals,
And, in a matter of moments, as shouts start to pound on his
    eardrums,   395
Actually sees his Euryalus, ambushed by forest and darkness,
Roughed up in sudden and massive attack by the whole of the squadron,
Captured and now carried off, still attempting a futile resistance.
   Nisus, what is he to do? What force could he use for a daring
Rescue, what weapons? Perhaps he should hurl himself out upon
    their swords,   400
Choosing to die a quick, beautiful death in a flurry of slashes?
Swiftly deciding, he drew back his arm to put spin on a javelin,
Then, looking up at the Moon overhead, offered this as his prayer:
'You, goddess, you, please be with us now and assist in our effort,
Glory of stars and Latona's daughter, the Guardian of
    Woodlands.   405
Let me, if ever my father, Hyrtacus, brought to your altars
Offerings on my behalf, and if *I've* added trophies from *my* hunts,
Hung in your dome or attached outside to its sacrosanct gables,
Rout this cluster of men, and guide my spears through the breezes.'
This said, he whirls off the iron-tipped shaft, puts his whole body's
    full force   410
Into it. On flies the javelin, lashing a path among night-time's
Shades till it plunges in Sulmo,* who's just turned round, so it
    strikes him
Full in the back where it snaps, and the wood shaft splinters, exploding
Into his lungs. He slumps, spews life's warm streams from his ribcage,
Gasping in agony's long sobs, flailing his sides, body ice-cold.   415
Spinning about, they look all around them. But Nisus grows fiercer:
Look, there's another shaft poised at his ear; and it's balanced for hurling.

While they're in panic, the javelin screams through Tagus's temples,
Both of them, penetrates right through the brain where it warms
    itself, well lodged.
Volcens, brutal with rage, sees no sign of who the assailant   420
Could be or where he could rush in himself and vent all his fury.
'You, though, will pay me in double, for both, in the meantime,'
    he cries out.
'Your warm blood is the penalty fixed.' As he speaks, he is moving
Up on Euryalus, sword unsheathed. Now Nisus is frantic,
Out of his mind, just shrieking in terror. For he can no longer   425
Hide in the safety of shadows, endure such personal anguish.
'Me, look at me, here I am. I'm the killer, Rutulians, attack me!
Leave him alone! The entire scheme was mine. He hadn't the daring,
Even the strength. I call sky's omniscient stars to bear witness:
His crime was too deep a love for a friend who's a curse's
    fulfilment.'   430
As he was speaking, the sword was applied with a thrust of great vigour,
Through the boy's ribs, then across, and it burst his white bosom
    asunder,
Doubling Euryalus over in death. Blood covers his beauteous
Limbs; his neck droops languidly down to recline on his shoulders,
Just as a brightly crimsoned flower shorn down by a
    ploughshare   435
Droops as it dies, or as field poppies lower their heads when their
    slender
Stems grow tired, weighed down by an unpredictable rainstorm.
  Nisus sped into their midst, dashing through all the rest with just
    one goal:
Volcens, and nothing distracts his attack on that one person, Volcens.
Foemen surround him from this side and that, take him on at close
    quarters,   440
Bludgeon him. He presses on, whirling sword like a thunderbolt,
    striking
Randomly till it is plunged down the throat of the screaming Rutulian,
Taking his enemy's life as he dies. He then hurls himself forward,
Utterly mangled, upon the now lifeless corpse of his dear friend.
There he at last, in the stillness of death, finds release from his
    anguish.   445
  Fortune has blessed you both!* If there's magical charm in my verses,
No day will ever delete you from time's recollection, as long as

Sons of Aeneas shall live on the Capitol's* motionless bedrock,
Long as the Father of Rome shall retain his command over peoples.
  Though they've secured both their prey and their plunder, when
    conquering Rutulians   450
Carry the lifeless Volcens back to the camp, they are weeping.
Grief is no less in the camp, where the blood-drained cadaver of
    Rhamnes,
Other chiefs too, have been found: one massacre, numerous victims,
Even Serranus and Numa.* A big rush ensues to the actual
Bodies and half-dead men, to the site still fresh with its
    slaughtered   455
Heaps still dankly warm, to the full-blooded foaming of brooklets.
Passing the spoils hand to hand, they can see it's Messapus's shining
Helmet, and see whose medallions cost so much sweat to recover.

Dawn was already beginning to sprinkle the earth with her new light,
Leaving Tithonus's saffron bed. Sun's rays were already   460
Spreading, already events once concealed were revealed by his
    brightness.
Turnus, himself now fully equipped in his armour, is rousting
Men to take arms. Each chief hones lines that are battle-keen,
    bronze-clad,
Whetting the edge of their wrath with assorted rumours and stories.
Further (and it was a piteous sight) they hoisted on
    spear-points*   465
Heads they'd impaled. When they lined up behind, cheering loudly,
    one's eyesight
Met Nisus, Euryalus.*
Tough as they were, Aeneas's men, who had set their opposing
Lines on the left of the rampart (the right had the river's protection),
And who controlled huge trenches and stood on their towering
    bastions,   470
Now felt depressed. The impaled heads moved them deeply with
    sorrow:
Faces they recognized only too well oozed gory putrescence.
Rumour had now winged swift in her flight through a fluttered and
    panicked
City and swooped with her news on the ears of Euryalus' mother.
All inner warmth fled the poor woman's bones in an instant.
    Her shuttle   475

Shook from her hands and her wool skein unravelled. Her sense of
     fulfilment
Wholly destroyed, she fled out of the house with a ritual, female,
Keening lament, tore her hair in a frenzy, ran up on the ramparts
Straight to the front line, oblivious of male presence, danger, or
     weapons.
That's where she stood and filled heaven with cries of lament and
     of outrage: 480
'Can this be you that I'm seeing, Euryalus? You there, my life's last
Solace in age, could you really have left me so cruelly abandoned?
Didn't they give you a chance for a final word with your poor dear
Mother before you were sent on your way for this dangerous mission?
Now, dear lord, here you lie in an unknown land, feeding
     Latium's   485
Carrion birds and its dogs, while I, your own mother, can't give you
Due rites of burial, close up your eyes, clean your gashes with water,
Drape you in that special robe that I worked day and night in my
     weaving.
Pulling the sley was my solace for all my old-womanly fretting.
Where shall I follow you now? What land has your limbs, your
     dismembered   490
Parts and your mangled cadaver? Is *this* all of you you can bring me,
Son? Is it *this* I've been following over the land and the high seas?
O you Rutulians, if there's the least bit of righteousness in you,
Pierce me, hurl all of your weapons at me, make *me* today's first
     death!
Or, mighty father of gods, you could pity me, blast this accursed   495
Head down to Tartarus' bottommost depths with your own special
     weapon.
I cannot otherwise break off the bonds of my cruel existence.'
Spirits are stunned at this outburst. A ripple of sorrowful moaning
Sweeps through the ranks; battle energy breaks and begins to grow
     sluggish.
She is, in fact, fanning grief into fire. So Idaeus and Actor,   500
On Ilioneus's orders and those of the sobbing Iulus,
Seize her between them, remove her, and put her where no one
     can see her.

Far off, the resonant bronze of a bugle has crackled staccato
Terror. There follows a thunderous cheer bellowed back by the heavens.

Quickly the Volscians* approach in an interlocked tortoise
　　formation,　　　　　　　　　　　　　　　　　　　505
Ready to fill in the trenches, to ram through and rip apart ramparts.
Some look for ways to get in and to scale outer walls upon ladders:
Points undermanned, where the crown of defence admits flickers of
　　daylight
Through less dense crenellations of troops. In response, though, the
　　Teucrians
Blast them with all kinds of weapon, prise ladders away with strong
　　levers.　　　　　　　　　　　　　　　　　　　510
Holding a wall under siege was a skill they'd acquired in prolonged war.
Further, they tried hurling boulders of murderous heaviness, hoping
Somehow to break through this covered attack. But whatever they
　　threw down,
Troops underneath that dense-packed tortoise easily handled.
　　This time they can't manage, though. For the Teucrians are
　　　trundling a massive　　　　　　　　　　　　515
Monster of stone to where sizeable forces are clustered in menace,
Tipping it over. It rolls a long distance, and crushes Rutulians,
Smashes their armoured roof. Though they're bold, these Rutulians
　　find such
Blind attacks now unappealing. The new goal's clearing the ramparts,
Missiles the means.　　　　　　　　　　　　　　520
Elsewhere Mezentius, fearsome to see, whirls round an Etruscan
Pitch-pine brand, fanning smoke-thick flames which he brings for
　　the onslaught.
Neptune's offspring, Messapus,* the tamer of horses, has by now
Torn through the ramparts. He's calling for ladders to tackle the
　　main walls.

Muses, Calliope* too, I now beg you, inspire me as I sing　　525
Carnage wrought there then by the sword, all the slaughter that
　　Turnus
Dealt: who it was that each person dispatched as an offering to Orcus,
Spread out with me war's huge scrolled chart with its landscapes and
　　peoples.
*Goddesses, you can remember it all and can cite it from memory.**
　　Daunting the eye looking up, and equipped with high gangways,
　　　a tower,　　　　　　　　　　　　　　　　　530
Beautifully sited, was under assault. The Italians were trying

First, with all forces, to capture it, then, with all force they could
    muster,
Topple it over. The Trojans, for their part, used rocks to defend it,
Volleyed off arrows and spears through the set-back slits which they
    crowded.
Turnus was taking the lead, and he hurled off a pitch-coated,
    blazing   535
Spear which implanted a flame in its side. The fire, bellowed by
    wind gusts,
Ripped through the planking, ate into the uprights and lodged there
    unsated.
Terrified soldiers inside, wanting vainly to flee the disaster,
Panicked. While huddling together and backing away into corners
Free of the ruinous flames, they provoked an abrupt shift in
    balance.   540
That's when the tower slumped over; its crash crackled thunder
    through heaven.
Men were now falling to earth half-dead with the huge mass behind
    them,
Cruelly impaled on their own arms, chests routed out by the hardwood
Lumber. Helenor was almost alone in surviving; and Lycus*
Also escaped. As for details: Helenor was only a youngster,   545
Born to Maeonia's king by a slave named Licymnia. She raised him
Secretly, sent him to Troy with the weapons denied by his status,
Light arms: sword but no sheath, shield blank,* no marks of distinction.
He, when he saw himself right in the middle of Turnus's thousands,
Latin troops here, there, rank upon rank of them standing
    around him,   550
Much as a wild beast, trapped by a tight-packed circle of hunters,
Snarls at the menacing weapons and hurls herself,* knowing what's
    waiting,
Forward to death in a leap that impales her on spear-points of
    hunters,
So the youth rushes, intent upon death, straight into the foemen's
Midst, heading there where he saw that the weapons were
    thickest.   555
  Lycus is nimbler by far on his feet; and he weaves and he dodges
In between weapons and in between foes, flees as far as the ramparts,
Struggles to claw his way close to the top and to reach for his
    friends' hands.

Turnus, however, whose feet and whose spear have kept track of
    their quarry,
Taunts him in victory: 'Hoped you could somehow escape from
    my clutches,   560
Did you, you fool?' As he speaks, he tears Lycus from where he is
    dangling
Pinioned, and rips away with him a sizeable section of rampart,
Much as when Jupiter's bearer of arms* flies back to the hilltops
Clutching a rabbit or white-bodied swan in the tight grip of talons,
Or when a lamb is the prey, still sought by his mother's
    incessant   565
Bleating, but dragged from its sheep-pen by Mars' beloved wolf.
    There is cheering
Everywhere. Into the trenches they go, fill them up till they're hillocks.
Others pitch torch after blazing torch on the high tops of buildings.
Now Ilioneus,* hefting a rock, a big chunk of a mountain,
Flattens Lucetius who's nearing the gate and who's
    carrying fire.   570
Liger accounts for Emathion, Asilas destroys Corynaeus.
Liger's success is his spear, and Asilas' a sneaked arrow, long range.
Caeneus slaughters Ortygius; Turnus the conquering Caeneus.
Turnus kills Itys and Clonius, Promolus and Dioxippus,
Sagaris too, also Idas, who's holding his post atop turrets.   575
Capys brings death to Privernus,* just recently grazed by Themillas'
Spear and who'd thrown down his shield to attend to the wound it
    inflicted,
Mad as he was. Capys' arrow thus slipped up upon him in winged
    flight
From far away* and it lodged in his left side and there, hidden deeply,
Ruptured his lungs with a gash that brought death as it halted his
    breathing.   580
    There stood Arcens' son* in his most distinctive equipment,
Artwork himself in his needleworked tunic, aglow in Iberian
Rust-red—handsome as well. He'd been sent here by Arcens, his
    father,
After his childhood in Mars' holy grove by the river Symaethus
Where there is also a well-endowed altar to kindly Palicus.   585
Bullets,* not spears, which he set to one side, were Mezentius' selection.
Whirling a taut sling thrice round his head, he fired off a screaming
Shot, struck his foe with its molten lead in between his two temples,

Splitting his forehead and stretching him out full length on the
    deep sand.
   Now's when Ascanius, they say, shot his first swift arrow in battle   590
(Earlier he'd been a terror to only the timider wildlife),
Killing, with his own hand, Numanus, a brave man, and surnamed
Remulus.* He'd just recently made a good marriage alliance,
Taking a younger sister of Turnus as wife; and his new-found
Royalty puffed out his chest. He was out there in front of the
    army's   595
First ranks, pacing, declaiming a mixture of words worth reporting,
Words worth nothing at all,* making loudness a factor of greatness.
'Aren't you ashamed you're besieged yet again and contained by a
    rampart,
Using your walls to protect you from death, you twice-captured
    Phrygians?
Look at these men who demand our brides for themselves,
    or they'll fight us!   600
Which god drove you to Italy, you folk? What utter madness!
Atreus' sons aren't here, nor's Ulysses, inventor of fiction.
We are a species tough from the roots. We carry our new-borns
Straight to the rivers to toughen them up in the cold and the water.
Boyhood means staying awake to go hunting, exhausting the
    forests.   605
Playtime is breaking in horses and firing off shafts with a horn bow.
Youth means dealing with work, getting used to a bare-bones
    existence,
Taming the earth with a rake or shaking up towns in a battle.
Steel grinds our life's every stage; our prod for the ox's
Back when it's tired is our spear-shaft reversed. Old age, as it
    slows us,   610
Can't either lessen our strength or diminish our vigour of spirit.
We hide our grey hairs with our helmets, delight in importing,
Even then, fresh fruits of our hunts, and in living on plunder.
You, with your needleworked saffron and gleamingly purpled apparel,
You take delight in inertia, indulging yourselves in your
    dances.   615
Tunics for you come with sleeves, and your bonnets have nice little
    ribbons.
Phrygian women, not Phrygian men, go to Dindyma's highlands,
Skip to where your double woodwinds* please local ears. Up on Ida,

Mother is calling you now with her soft Berecyntian boxwood
Pipes and her timbrels. Stop playing with steel. Leave arms to the
    real men.'   620
This man's boasting, and chanting of terrible insults,* Ascanius
Couldn't endure. So he faced him directly and notched in an arrow,
Pulled on the bowstring of horse-gut till both arms were parted, and
    then stopped.
First he begged Jupiter's mercy, made vows reinforcing his prayer:
'Almighty Jupiter, favour the boldness of my undertaking!   625
I will myself bring you yearly gifts in a rite at your temple,
Personally set at your altars a bullock with gold on his forehead,
White and unblemished, who carries his head just as high as his
    mother's,
Ready to butt with his horns and to scatter the sand in arenas.'
Jupiter heard him and, out of a clear patch of sky, rattled
    thunder,   630
Off to the left. As he did, the bow loaded with death thumped loudly,
Off sped the torqued-back arrow, released now and hideously
    screeching,
Whipping through Remulus' head as its steel penetrated his hollow
Temples: 'Go on! Mock bravery now with your arrogant speeches!
Here's the retort twice-captured Phrygians send in dispatches!'   635
That's all Ascanius said. And the Teucrians support him by cheering,
Roaring their joy, raising spirits as high as stars in the heavens.

Up in that brilliant zone, as it chanced, sat the long-haired Apollo
Right then observing the lines of Ausonian troops and their city
From his post high on a cloud. And he said to victorious Iulus: 640
'Blessings on your new manhood, my boy. That's the pathway to
    heaven,
You, who are born of a god, and will some day beget gods! For all wars
Fated to come will subside when Assaracus' people is ruling
Justly. And Troy doesn't set its restrictions on you.' When he'd
    said this
Down from the high bright heavens he leaped and he parted the
    breathing   645
Winds on his way to Ascanius, assuming the form of the ancient
Butes, at one time Dardanian Anchises' squire and his trusted
Gatekeeper; later Aeneas had added him on to Ascanius'
Staff as an escort. Apollo, as he moved in, now resembled

This old man, and in every detail; the shade of complexion,   650
Sound of the voice, white hair, and the armour ferociously clanging.*
These are the words he addresses to Iulus, who's fired up for battle.
'Son of Aeneas, you've shot down Numanus and suffered no vengeance:
That should suffice. Great Apollo concedes you first honours. He
   doesn't
Envy your matching his weapons and prowess. But you're still a
   young boy.   655
No further fighting. Give warfare a break . . .' But before he had
   finished
All he had risen to say, or heard any response, he just vanished
Into thin air beyond reach of men's eyesight. He fled human vision.
   Dardan commanders knew *this* was a god and that these were god's
     weapons;
For, as he left, they felt sure they'd heard noise from a rattling
   quiver.   660
Prompted by Phoebus' words and divine presence, they keep Ascanius
Back from the fight, though he hungers for combat, and come to the
   rescue,
Flinging their own lives back into battle and chasms of danger.
   Up goes a cheer that leaps barbicans, runs the full length of the
     rampart.
Bold bows bend, leather thongs torque tight, they are ready for
   action.   665
Soil is a litter of spears, while shields and the hollows of helmets
Clang in collision. The battle is swelling to furious roughness,
Huge as a storm-front's approach from the west at the rise of the rainy
Goat Stars,* when downpours thrash upon earth or when hail-thickened
   cloudbanks
Pelt upon shallows as Jupiter, windblown with southerlies, lashes   670
Spiralling tempests of water and ruptures the sky's hollow cisterns.

Pandarus, Bitias,* sons borne to Alcanor living on Ida,
Youths reared in Jupiter's grove by Iaera, a nymph of the forest,
Tall as their homeland's silver firs, yes, tall as their mountains,
Open the camp-gates wide.* They're in charge by their
   commandant's order,   675
Sure of their prowess and acting alone, they invite the foe's entry
Into the camp. They're positioned inside, in front of the towers,
Right side, left side, armoured in steel, plumes dancing on tall heads,

Just as, up in the air, with the river Livenza* about them—
Or on the banks of the Po or round Adige's dazzling beauty—   680
Twin oak trees [*genus: quercus*]* raise untrimmable tresses
Sky high, capping their rising heads, crowns nodding sublimely.
  Once the Rutulians see it is open, they burst through the entrance.
Instantly Quercens, Aquiculus too (he looks good in his armour),
Tmarus, precipitous spirit, and Haemon the war-god's
  descendant,   685
All their accompanying forces as well, either turn tail, defeated,
Or leave their lives, while attempting to cross, on the gate's very
  threshold.
Anger now grows even stronger in hearts so divided by conflict.
Trojan troops massed deep swarm into this very same sector,
Venture a hand-to-hand fight, risk sallying out ever farther.   690
  Turnus, the leader, who's off elsewhere in his full battle fury,
Wreaking his havoc, receives a report that the enemy's boiling
Forth in a new deadly wave, flinging open its gates as a challenge.
Monstrously angered, abandoning plans now in progress, he rushes
Straight to the gate of the Dardan camp and the towering
  brothers,   695
Killing Antiphates first, since he was the first to oppose him,
Bastard son, by a mother from Thebe, of mighty Sarpedon.
Laying him low with a javelin. The shaft, of Italian cornel,
Flew through the softness of air, struck him full in the stomach,
  shot upwards
Into his chest which it carved to a cavern that foamed out the dark
  wound's   700
Eddies of liquid. The spear-point, lodged in his lungs, begins
  warming.
Next he kills Meropes, Erymas too; brings death to Aphidnus,
Bitias next, with his blazing eyes and his snarling bravado,
Not by a spear-cast—no spear made could ever have taken
This man's life—it's a pike with a yard-long blade and the
  massive   705
Torque of a thunderbolt, catapult launched, that comes screaming
  towards him.
Even a jerkin of two whole oxhides, a corslet of trusty,
Double-laid, gilded, plate-mail cannot withstand it. His mighty
Limbs give way and collapse, earth groans, and his shield clangs
  upon him.

That's how a pre-built stone pier* falls, the type workmen
    assemble   710
Now and then, down at Euboean Baiae's seafront, in giant
Segments and drop in the sea. As it sinks to the bottom and settles,
Under the shallows, it causes precisely this kind of turmoil.
Bubbling seas seethe upswirled sand, churned darkly volcanic,
Prochyta's cliffs shudder echoing roars and Inarime's* bedrock   715
Heavily laid on Typhoeus, at Jupiter's orders, is shivered.

    Mars, raw power in arms, added courage and strength to the
    Latins,
Twisted the sharpened prongs of his goads in their breasts ever deeper,
While he bedevils the Teucrians with Cowardice, Darkness of Terror.
Waves of them roll in from everywhere now there's a chance for a
    real fight.   720
War's god strikes at the soul.

    Pandarus, seeing his brother's corpse laid flat, recognizing
How war's fortunes stand, what circumstance governs its status,
Levers the gate back shut, applies massive force to its hinges
Muscled by ample shoulders, and thus leaves a lot of his own
    troops   725
Locked outside their own walls in a battle intensely contested.
Others, of course, he locks in with himself. They are fleeing;
    he saves them.
He was an idiot not to have seen, in their midst, the Rutulian
King break in, and for causing that king to be locked, like a giant
Tiger let loose among helpless barnyard beasts, in their city.   730

    Instantly, light of a different kind flares Turnus's eyes bright,
Hideous thunder rings from his arms, shivers run down his helmet's
Blood-red plumes. From the orb of his shield he now radiates
    lightning.
Panic sweeps over Aeneas' men. When they see that detested
Face and immense limbs, they know them. Huge Pandarus too has
    his radiance,   735
Boiling with wrath as he is at the death of his brother and shouting:
'This is no honeymoon palace Amata has given as dowry,
Nor central Ardea sheltering Turnus inside daddy's castle.
What you see here is the enemy camp; and you're powerless to leave it.'
Turnus, his heart unruffled and calm, just smiled and responded: 740
'Take the first shot, if your soul's man enough for it. Try me in
    combat.

You'll tell Priam yourself that you've found an Achilles right here too.'
That's all he said. His opponent, with all of the strength he could
    muster,
Whirled off a shaft full of knots, raw, bark-covered, unfinished timber.
Breezes got hold of it right as it came in to strike, and Saturnian   745
Juno wrenched it aside, so the spear hit, and stuck in, a gatepost.
'*You* won't escape this weapon that *my* right hand is employing.
Here's a man who doesn't miss in selecting a weapon and striking.'
Turnus had spoken. He leaped up high, sword held even higher,
Clove the youth's forehead in two at a point in between his
    two temples,   750
Cut right down with a monstrous wound all the way to his beardless
Jaws. There's a crash as the earth shudders, slammed by the huge
    body's impact.
Limbs buckle under, he sprawls on the ground. As he's dying his
    armour
Bloodies with brain, and his head, split in two halves, perfectly equal,
Hangs, splayed this way and that, to the left and the right of his
    shoulders.   755
   Spooked by this figure of terror, the Trojans retreated and scattered.
Had it occurred to the victor, in fact, to break open the barriers
Instantly, using his hand to let allies in through the gateway,
This would have marked Troy's last day* of war, last day of existence.
Fury for battle, however, mad lust for the kill, drove this ardent   760
Warrior's hand straight ahead at the foe.
First catch is Phaleris, followed by Gyges, whose tendons he slashes,
Both on the run. Then he hurls spears plundered from them at the
    fleeing
Backs of the others—for Juno keeps fuelling his strength and his
    courage.
Halys is next; then, clean through his shield, Turnus javelins
    Phegeus,   765
Takes by surprise some troops on the walls who are stirring a rally:
Prytanis, Halius too, and Alcander along with Noëmon.
Lynceus advances upon him and calls on his comrades' assistance.
Turnus's right is exposed to the rampart, yet he, with a glittering
Slash of his sword, lunges in for the kill. Shorn off by a single   770
Close-range stroke, in their sheer, far peace, lie a man's head and helmet.
Amycus, plague among wildlife, was next; no one found more fulfilment
Smearing a spear-shaft or arming the steel tip with poison than he did;

Aeolid Clytius fell, as did Cretheus,* friend to the Muses:

Cretheus, the Muses' companion; for poetry's song and its lyre,   775

Fitting his numbers to strings, always touched a core deep in his being.

His songs were always of horses, of arms, and of men and their battles.

  Finally news of their massacred troops reached the Teucrian
    leaders,*

Mnestheus and fearsome Serestus, who came there and saw that their
    forces

Were in a shambles, that someone had actually let the foe enter.   780

'Where do you think you can run to from here?' said Mnestheus.
    'To what place?

What other walls, what additional cities are in your possession?

Citizens, will it be said that a single human, completely

Trapped in our ramparts, has wrought such incredible city-wide
    slaughter,

And gone unpunished, while sending to Orcus a host of our
    finest   785

Youths? Does betraying your ancient gods and your homeland's
    fulfilment

And great Aeneas not shock, shame, or trouble your pitiful cowardice?'

  Fired by these words, their resolve comes back and they form up
    in close ranks.

Gradually Turnus starts backing away from the fight, and the river

Now is his goal and the section of wall that is moated by water.   790

Teucrians pressure him all the more keenly and raise a loud war-cry,

Ring him around like a big mob of hunters who've circled a savage

Lion, with murderous javelins poised. Terrified, but ferocious,

Savagery flaring his eyes, he retreats. Yet his anger and courage

Won't let him show them his back, though the counter-attack he so
    dearly   795

Wishes to launch cannot be. There are too many weapons and people.

  That's how reluctantly Turnus pulls back in his tracks: an
    unhurried

Path of retreat, though his mind's at a furious boil with resentment.

Twice, even then, he rushed into the thick of his cordoning foemen,

Twice sent them reeling all over walls in disorder and panic.   800

But reinforcements speed from the camp and the front coalesces;

Juno, the daughter of Saturn, no longer dares give him extra

Strength to resist, because Jupiter's now sent Iris from heaven,

Bringing his sister commands that allow her no subtle amendments

If Turnus fails to withdraw from the Teucrians' towered defences. 805
So, the youth hasn't the power in his shield and the force in his
     right hand
Even to stand his own ground. Spears hurled in from so many quarters
Now overwhelm him. The concave helmet encasing his temples
Constantly clangs, the bombardment of stones leaves its solid bronze
     gaping,
Stripped of its plumes,* and its boss can't shelter his head from
     relentless 810
Pounding. The Trojans and Mnestheus himself, now lightning
     in action,
Double their spear-volleys. Sweat oozes out over Turnus's body,
Forms into soot-blackened rivers (he'd had no chance for a breather).
Laboured gasping for air shudders all of his joints. He, at long last,
Leaps, fully armed, from the walls, thus entrusting himself to the
     Tiber's 815
Streaming flow. As he touched it, the river-god caught him and
     raised him
Up in his tawny swirls and he swept him away upon gentle
Currents: returned to his allies content, fully cleansed of his slaughter.

BOOK TEN

Meanwhile Olympus, seat of all power in the universe, opens
Wide for a meeting* the Father of Gods and Ruler of Mortals
Calls to his residence high in the stars. He can monitor from there
All earth, including the Dardan camp and the people of Latium.
Gods take seats in a hall facing sunrise and sunset. He speaks first: 5
'Why have you now reversed your judgement, lords of the heavens?
Why have your passions become so unfair, and your quarrels
  so violent?
I'd disapproved of a war that set Italy fighting the Teucrians:
Why this internal discord contesting what I had forbidden?*
What fear prompted this clique or that to provoke an armed
  conflict?   10
There'll come a time when it's *just* that you fight. Don't rush to
  confront it.
Then fierce Carthage will open the Alps, unleashing a massive
Tide of destruction* on Rome and its citadels. You'll have your licence
Then to compete in your hate, to despoil both cities and substance.
Now let it ride, be content to sustain this ratified treaty.'   15
Jupiter's statement was brief; golden Venus did not respond briefly:
'Father, whose power over men and events is complete and eternal—
What other force can exist that we *could* now make our appeal to?—
Surely you see the Rutulians' arrogance: Turnus careering   20
High on his horses, straight through the ranks, bellied out in his
  onrush
By the success Mars blows his way. No longer are Teucrians
Shielded by well-sealed walls. Instead, they are fighting the battle
Inside the gates, on the ramparts. They're filling the ditches with
  bloodshed.
Not knowing this, Aeneas is gone. Will you never give Trojans   25
Respite from siege and blockade? Once more there's an enemy
  threatening
Reborn Troy's new walls. And there's now an additional army:
Tydeus' son, Diomedes,* sets out from Aetolian Arpi,
Rushes the Teucrians again. More wounds, I suppose, yet await me—
I, your own child, now delay, by my absence, those spear-thrusts
  from mortals.   30

If these Trojans, of course, all sailed for Italy, lacking
Your divine will and consent, let them pay for their sins. Don't assist
    them.
If, though, they followed responses to prayers which voices from heaven,
Voices from ghost worlds, too, kept giving them, why is it *someone*
Can now reverse your commands and set destiny on a new
        basis?   35
Need I remind you of fleets burned up near Sicilian Eryx?*
Or of the ruler of storms, and his winds from Aeolia, bellowed
Into a seething rage, or of Iris dispatched through the cloudbanks?
She's now arousing death's still world, the sole province of nature
Still untried. So Allecto's suddenly launched on the upper   40
World for a Bacchic romp through the heart of Italy's cities.
Visions of empire arouse me no more; I cherished them only
While there was still such a thing as albeit changeable Fortune.
Now let whoever you choose to win, win. If there's no land your
        hard-nosed
Wife will allot to the Teucrians, Father, I beg by the smouldering   45
Ashes and ruins of Troy, grant licence to rescue Ascanius*
Safe and sound from the conflict, grant me my grandson's survival.
As for Aeneas: well, let him indeed be tossed amid unknown
Waters and follow such random course as Fortune devises.
Give me the right to remove this boy from the horrors of warfare.   50
Amathus, Paphos up high, Cythera, Idalia's temples:
These are my lands. Let him set aside weapons and live out his
        life there,
No need for glory! Give orders that Carthage have absolute, crushing
Power on Ausonia's soil. Nothing they've got there* will give any
Tyrian city a problem.

                                    'So, what did they gain by surviving   55
War's scourge, and by escaping the heart of the fires set by Argives,
And by enduring the countless perils of sea and of vast lands—
All in a Teucrian quest for a new-born Troy and for Latium?
Surely the sensible thing would have been to resettle their homeland's
Ashes, the soil where Troy once stood. I beg of you, father,   60
Give the poor Teucrians their Xanthus and Simoïs back! Let them
        relive
Ilium's sorrows and fall.'

                            Then, profoundly enraged, royal Juno
Lashed back: 'Why do you force me to break my self-imposed silence,

Make me degrade hidden pain into words for public consumption?
Did any man, any god, *compel* Aeneas to choose war   65
Or to approach King Latinus* as would some hostile invader?
Granted, he headed for Italy under Fate's authorization,
Prompted by raving Cassandra's words. But did *we* suggest leaving
Camp and then casting his life to the winds? Did *we* suggest trusting
Total command of the war, and defence of his walls, to a
      young boy,   70
Or drive Etruscans to treason, or madden a peace-loving people?
Which god herded him into this trap? Where's my pitiless power-play
Here? Where is Juno in this, or Iris "dispatched through the cloud
      banks"?
What a disgrace that Italians should throw up a circle of fire
Round new Troy as it's born, and that Turnus, Pilumnus's
      grandson,   75
Child of the goddess Venilia, should take a firm stand on his native
Soil! Yet it's right when the Trojans, with torches of fire, attack Latins,
Crush under *their* yoke fields they don't own, take the produce as
      plunder,
Pick out their in-laws and pluck pledged brides from their family's
      bosoms!
They, while their hands offer peace, clear decks and equip them for
      battle.   80
You are empowered to snatch your Aeneas away from attacking
Greeks and replace him with phantoms of cloud, mere air without
      substance;
And you're empowered to transfigure his fleet into so many
      sea-nymphs.*
We, when we counter with aid for Rutulians, are guilty of high crimes.
"Not knowing this, Aeneas is gone." Let him not know and stay
      gone!   85
Paphos is yours, so's Idalium, so are the heights of Cythera.
Why challenge tough hearts, then? and a city pregnant with warriors?
Think! Is it we who are set on capsizing this impotent Phrygian
State in flux?
                     'Who tossed poor Troy to the Greeks in the first place?
What caused *all* this war, what made *all* Europe and Asia   90
Rise up in arms, cast treaties adrift through treacherous thievery?
When the adulterous Dardan prince* took Sparta, was *Juno*
Leading the way? Did I arm him, did *I* use Cupid as war's nurse?
Fairer for you if you'd feared what I'd do to your boys then. It's too late

Now to jump up with your unjust complaints, lodging laughable
    protests.'   95
    Such was the case Juno argued. The sky-dwellers, all in an uproar,
Favoured one side or the other. Like first growled gusts of a tempest
Trapped in a forest, they rumble. The gale's not seen, but the rolling
Roar alerts sailors to storm winds wending their way towards water.
    Then the omnipotent Father, who wields prime power over
    nature,   100
Starts to respond. As he speaks, the high palace of gods becomes silent.
Earth shudders deep through its soil. Silence falls on the summit of
    heaven,
Zephyrs subside, Ocean flattens its waves into lake-still calmness.
'Carry on into your minds* my words, then. Grasp them securely.
Since, evidently, Ausonians will not be allowed to join Teucrians,   105
Linked by a treaty—your own civil wars defy any conclusion—
I'll be impartial. Whatever today's ambitions or fortune
Bring each individual man, Rutulian or Trojan,
Whether the camp is besieged because Italy's fate so demanded
Or because Troy's bad errors and ruinous prophecies* caused it.   110
Nor do I hold the Rutulians exempt. Individual effort
Makes or breaks fortune today. King Jupiter's wholly impartial;
Fates will discover a way.'* Then he swore a great oath by his brother's
Molten, pitch-scorched banks of the Styx, by its dark-eddied torrents,
Marking his oath with a nod that rocked all Olympus with tremors.   115
Thus ended talk about fate.* Rising up from his throne bright and
    golden,
Jupiter, flanked by an escort of sky-dwellers, moved to the doorway.
    Meanwhile, besieging Rutulians pressed their attacks upon all
    gates,
Bent on butchering men and on ringing the ramparts with blazing
Fires. But inside the stockade, penned in, Aeneas's legion   120
Lacks any hope of escape. Troops stand upon high towers, glumly
Hopeless—the circling walls manned here and there by a soldier.
Asius, Imbrasus's son, Hicetaon's child, named Thymoetes,
Two named Assaracus, Thymbris, an old man, along with him Castor:
These are the front lines. And fighting alongside are two of
    Sarpedon's   125
Brothers from mountainous Lycia: Clarus and Thaemon.* Then
    hoisting,
Sinews strained to the full, a gigantic rock, not a trifling
Chunk of a mountain, is Clytius' son, Lyrnesian Acmon,

Proving no lesser a man than his father or brother, Menestheus.*
Javelins, boulders, barrels of fire, arrows notched to the
      bowstring: 130
These are the varied defensive munitions the soldiers compete with.
Look, and you'll see in their midst the Dardan boy,* very justly
Venus's prime concern. With his helmet discarded, his handsome
Head shimmers as does a gem set in tawny gold for a necklace
Or for a crown, or as ivory gleams when inlaid by an artist   135
Into a setting of boxwood or terebinth wood from Dalmatia.
Streaming hair on his milk-white neck has been gathered and ribboned
Into a circlet of soft, supple gold. And, Ismarus, your people,
Proud as they are, saw *you* there too, aiming shots that would draw blood,
Arming your arrows with poison, you noble child of Maeonian   140
Lydia. There men plough rich croplands; the Pactolus* waters
Fields of its farmlands with gold. At his side, Mnestheus* took his
      station,
Hero whose glory soared only yesterday, when he averted
Turnus' assault on the walls, driving Turnus himself from the ramparts;
And Capys*—Capua's named after him, the Campanian city.   145
Hard men fought one another all day in the contest of battle.

    Now in the darkness of midnight, Aeneas is cleaving the water.
Leaving Evander, he'd entered next the Etruscan encampment,
Meeting their king. There he'd briefed that king on his name and his
      background,
Said what he wants and can offer, explained what forces Mezentius 150
Gathers about him, informed him of Turnus's passionate anger,
Offered advice about how much trust may be put in things human,
Mingled a few humble pleas. Not a moment slipped by before Tarchon*
Joined forces, hammered out terms of a treaty. The Lydian people,
Free now of fate's constraints, have entrusted themselves to a foreign
Leader and board their fleet, in accord with divine will. Aeneas   156
Heads the command in his vessel with figures of Phrygian lions
Bearing the prow's beak; looming above them is Ida. How grateful
Exiled Teucrians had been for her shelter and wood!* Great Aeneas
Sits here, re-scrolling the varied events of the war. At his left side   160
Pallas sticks close, asking now about stars guiding night navigation,
Now about all he has suffered and seen upon land, upon high seas.

Goddesses, open up Helicon now, set your music in motion!
Tell of the forces that sailed with Aeneas from Tuscany's coastline.

Who was it armed and equipped these ships, who sailed on the
    salt sea?   165
  Massicus* leads, as he cuts through the waves on the bronze-sided
    Tigress.
Under his banner a thousand youths left Clusium's ramparts,
Left their home city of Cosa: their weapons are arrows and deadly
Bows, quivers light on their shoulders. Fierce Abas is sailing alongside,
His unit all fitted out with elaborate armour, his vessel   170
Glistening in light with its figurehead wrought as a gilded Apollo.
His Populonian motherland gave him a squad of six hundred
Seasoned warriors. And Elba, whose inexhaustible mineworks
Make it an island of iron and forges, has added three hundred.
Third comes Asilas, interpretive link between men and
    immortal   175
Gods, who elicits responses from cattle's innards and heavens'
Stars, from the tongues of the birds, from fire-flashing, ominous
    lightning.
He rushes his dense, spear-spiked force of a thousand to battle.
Pisa, a city in origins Greek, in location Etruscan,
Gave him command of its troops. After him, follows Astyr,*
    supremely   180
Handsome—Astyr, proud of his horse and his colourful weapons.
Three hundred men, all united by one single purpose in coming,
Make up his squad: men of Caere and men from the Minio's
    ploughlands,
Others from Pyrgi, an ancient town, and unhealthy Graviscae.
  Cinyrus,* you I would never omit: of Liguria's captains,   185
You are the bravest; nor you, though your squadron is tiny, Cupavo.
Swan plumes rise from your helmet's crest, signifying your father's
Feathery form. Love, *you* bear the blame for the change that
    transformed him!
Cygnus, wan with grief, people say, for his darling Phaëthon,
Lets the Muse solace his sad love lost, and he sings amid leafy   190
Shadows of poplars, his sisters once. Then, while he is singing,
Sinks wan-white as an old man's hair under plumage of soft down.
Rising from earth, he chases the stars, voice soaring to heaven.
Now with a group of his age-mates aboard, this swan's son, Cupavo,
Powers the oars of the giant *Centaur*, whose figurehead monster   195
Menaces waters ahead, poised high with a great rock to threaten
Surging waves at the prow, as his long keel furrows the salt deep.

There you see Ocnus* as well, son of Manto, the seer, and of Tuscan
Tiber, the river. He's levied a force from the banks of his homeland.
Mantua: Ocnus endowed you with walls, named you after his
    mother;   200
Mantua, heir to an ancestry rich, but not all of one bloodline.
Three distinct peoples are there, each people with four distinct cities.
Mantua heads up their league. Her strength is her blood that's Etruscan.
Hate of Mezentius arms five hundred from here to oppose him.
Mantua's river-god, crowned with his father Benacus's grey
    reeds,   205
Sails as their flagship, the *Mincius*, hate hewn into his pine planks.
Then comes Aulestes. His heavy-built *Triton*,* powered by a hundred
Tree-length wave-lashing oars churns marbled surface to salt spume.
Triton's immense, figured, bristling prow and the conch that he carries
Frighten the dark deep. Down to the flanks, as he swims, he has
    human   210
Form and appearance, but then, from the belly on, he's a monstrous
Sea-beast. Under his hybrid breast brine foams with a dull roar.
Such were the captains elect who sailed to help Troy in their thirty
Vessels,* and cut with their plate-bronze prows through the flatness
    of salt sea.

Day had withdrawn from the heavens, and now, in her wandering
    night drive,   215
Blessèd Phoebe was pounding her course through the heart of Olympus.
Guiding his vessel himself and trimming its canvas, Aeneas
Sat at the steering. Anxiety gave no rest to his body.
    Look, as he's halfway back, he's met by a group of his comrades
Dancing about on the waves: they are nymphs that the blessèd
    Cybele   220
Ordered transfigured from vessels to nymphs, to be gods in the salt sea.
Swimming alongside, they cut through the waves; their number exactly
Matches the number of bronze-figured prows once beached on the
    seashore.
Knowing their ruler at first far glance, they dance in his honour.
Cymodocea, most doctored of these in the fine art of speaking,   225
Follows his wake, grips the stern with her right hand, and arches
    her back up
Out of the sea, while her left hand noiselessly paddles the water.
All unaware though he is, she speaks to him: 'Child of divine blood,

Are you awake?
        'Come, Aeneas, wake up!*
                   'Loose the ropes, give us full sail!
We are what once was your fleet, we're the pines cut from
    sacrosanct Ida's   230
Summit, and now we are nymphs of the sea. When perfidious Turnus
Drove us in panic before him, pursued us with sword and with fire,
We, though not lively about it, did sever your tie-ropes. And since
    then
We've searched seas to find *you*. The Great Mother took pity and
    changed us
Into this shape, made us gods who live on while submerged
    in the water.   235
Your boy, Iulus, however, is penned in by walls and by ditches,
Trapped in a crossfire by Latins alive with the fury of battle.
True, the Arcadian cavalry,* joined by some valiant Etruscans,
Holds the positions assigned. But Turnus, fully determined
Not to permit them to link up camps, sent troops to confront them.   240
   'Up on your feet!
          'Strike first!
                 'Call allies to battle as day dawns!
Seize your invincible shield, with its wrought gold rim, which the
    Fire God
Gave you himself. For tomorrow's first light, if you don't think my
    forecast
Laughable, surely will see massive heaps of Rutulian corpses.'
Though she had no more to say, this nymph did have more to
    contribute.   245
Not unaware of the needed technique, she, using her right hand,
Pushed the high stern. And the ship shot forward over the waters,
Faster than even a javelin flies, or an arrow swift as the breezes.
Prompted by this, other ships quicken pace. Yet Trojan Anchises'
Son stays still as a log. Though prodigiously cheered by the omen,   250
He doesn't grasp what it means. And he prays, glancing up at the
    sky's vault:
'Goddess of Ida, Mother of Gods, and Dindyma's great friend,
Lover of great-towered cities and chariots powered by lions,
You be my battle commander, and you, make this prophecy duly
Prosper. Divine goddess, stand by your Phrygians, a stalwart
    defender.'   255

That's what he said. In the meantime, the day, with its ripening
    sunlight,
Rushed to complete its full circle; the night was now totally routed.
  As a beginning, he orders his allies to follow his signals,
Fire up their spirits for war, ready gear (and themselves)
    for a battle.
Since he's already in sight of the Teucrians and his
    encampment,   260
He, standing high on the aft-deck, hoists, in his left hand, his blazing
Shield from the sky. In response, from the ramparts, the Dardans
Raise up a cheer to the stars, much as cranes coming home to the
    Strymon,
Hidden by dark storm clouds as they wing their way across heaven,
Signal with clangorous cries their flight from the south winds of
    summer.   265
Hands are now volleying spears; hopes raised high kindle their anger.
  But the Rutulian king and the other Ausonian leaders
Find this reaction bizarre—until, looking behind them, they notice
Ships backing onto the beach, the whole sea rolling in with a navy.
There is Aeneas, helmet ablaze, crest vomiting fire,   270
Golden shield-boss erupting with searing flames of destruction.
So comets boding disaster will flare blood-red in the clear night
Skies, on occasion, so Sirius' new-born star, as he rises
Blazes his heat, his diseases, and drought upon sickly and
    death-doomed
Humans. His evil brightness of eye gleams grimly in heaven.   275
  Turnus, as daring as ever, is sure he can still take the seashore
First, and can stop them himself—even drive them away as they're
    landing.
Seizing the chance to raise spirits with words, he now issues this
    challenge:*
'Here's what you've prayed for: a chance for your own hands to
    shatter their forces.
Mars is the power in a hero's hands. Each man must remember   280
Wife, home, deeds that our fathers have done, and recall all their
    glorious
Honours. So let's not wait. Let's confront them down at the water
While they are still disembarking and scared, while their footing
    betrays them.
Fortune favours the bold.'

He, as he speaks, is debating which men he should lead on this
    mission,   285
Which he could trust to sustain his siege of the enemy's fortress.

Meanwhile, Aeneas is landing the allied troops along gangplanks
Lowered from high aft-decks. Many simply wait for the breakers'
Crash, when the sea's spent strength sucks back, then leap in the water;
Some just slide down oars. But Tarchon, surveying the
    coastline,   290
Notes where the shallows are breathlessly calm,* where there's no
    roar of breaking
Waves, where the sea-swell sweeps smooth surf to the shore
    unobstructed.
Suddenly, shifting his course for this point, he appeals to his comrades:
'Men, you're the pick of the best. Now pull full stroke on your stout
    oars,
Make your ships leap, drive them on, cleave enemy earth with
    your armoured   295
Prows. Let your keels plough furrows and plant themselves there on
    the beaches.
Make it to land, that's all. If our ships break up as we beach them,
I'll pay the price.' Once Tarchon has issued these orders, his crewmen
Stand to the oars, press down with their whole body-weight, drive
    the vessels
Onto the Latin shores in a flurry of foam until armoured   300
Prows surge clear of the sea, bite deep in the dry sand, and each one
Settles with undamaged keel. Well, with one exception.* For, Tarchon,
Your vessel ploughed on into the shoals, ran aground on a slanting
Reef where, for some time, it pitched, uneasily balanced, resisting
Wave upon wave. Then its back broke. Men spilled out among
    rollers,   305
Trapped amid broken oars, amid floating benches and planking,
Swept from their feet by the suctioning force of the backflowing
    breakers.
  Turnus reacts decisively, instantly: rushing all units
Straight into action against these Teucrians down on the seashore.
Trumpets sound. First blood in resisting this army of peasants,*   310
Goes—what an omen of war!—to Aeneas, who, starting with giant
Theron (himself intent upon killing Aeneas), now slaughters
Latins. Theron's blood he drained from the flank, as his sword-stroke

Cut through his corslet of bronze and his tunic stiffened with gold
    thread;
Next he struck Lichas, devoted, from childhood, to Phoebus the
    Healer   315
Since he'd been cut from his dead mother's womb and survived
    iron's early
Thrusts; then Aeneas brought death upon those who stood nearby:
    a tough man,
Cisseus, and Gyas, a giant, who were, at that moment, destroying
Rank upon rank with their clubs. Little help were their own Herculean
Weapons or well-muscled arms, or the fact that their father,
    Melampus,   320
Had, for as long as the earth made Hercules suffer through monstrous
Labours, stood at his side.
                     Look! He now aims a javelin at Pharus,
Hitting him full in the mouth as he volleys a barrage of insults.
Cydon, you too could have died while chasing Clytius, your latest
Passion unfulfilled, cheeks showing the first trace of blond fuzz.   325
You'd have been hacked by Aeneas's sword, and released from
    your constant
Preoccupation with youthful amours. You'd be just a pathetic
Corpse if your brothers had not intervened, a platoon of them,
    Phorcus'
Sons—there were seven in all—discharging a volley of seven
Javelins. Some ricocheted off Aeneas's shield and his helmet,   330
Harmlessly, some even grazed him, but slightly, deflected by kindly
Venus. Aeneas now spoke to his faithful companion, Achates:
'Keep me supplied with those spears that once, on the Ilian flatlands,
Lodged in the bodies of Greeks. Not one will be any less lethal
Now, when its target's Rutulian.' He picked up, and fired off,
    a massive   335
Shaft. And it flew through the breezes and whipped through the
    bronze-plate that covered
Maeon's shield, then shattered his chest as it shattered his corslet.
Rushing to help him, his brother Alcanor supports his collapsing
Brother, disarming his own hand; the hurled spear speeds on its
    bloody
Unstopped course, rips on through Alcanor's arm. So his
    sword-hand   340
Hangs from his shoulder, lifeless, and limply attached by its tendons.

Tearing the spear from his brother's corpse, with Aeneas the target,
Numitor* aims. But he isn't allowed to strike home in his vengeance.
All he achieves is a scratch on the thigh of the mighty Achates.

　Clausus* from Cures has his turn now, his confidence based on　345
Youthful physique. His stiff spear-shot strikes Dryops at long
　　range
Under the chin. Its powerful force cuts clean through his windpipe,
Just as he's speaking, and robs him of life as it robs him of
　　language.
All he can strike is the earth, with his head; and his mouth vomits
　　thick blood.
Clausus goes on to destroy six Thracians by various tactics.　　　350
Three were of Boreas' noblest bloodline; three more their father,
Idas, had sent from their fatherland, Ismarus. Then, with Auruncan
Units, Halaesus arrived, followed soon by the Tamer of Horses,
Neptune's offspring, Messapus. And group after group joins the
　　struggle,
Trying to drive the invaders away. Ausonia's gateway,　　　　　355
Italy's shore, is the site of the struggle. Like weather-fronts fiercely
Warring in vast shared skies, with their wind gusts equal in power,
Neither they and their clouds, nor their strong seas, yield in the
　　contest,
Stalled in prolonged deadlock, all nature frozen in conflict,
Just so the Trojan front and the Latin front, as they battled,　　360
Fought, foot jammed against foot, dense packed, man pitted
　　against man.

Elsewhere, though, in a dry river-bed where a torrent had scattered
Huge rocks end over end, ripping trees from the banks, Pallas
　　noticed
How his Arcadian horsemen were running away under Latin
Pressure. The rough terrain had suggested dismounting. They'd
　　done so.　　　　　　　　　　　　　　　　　　　　　　　365
Infantry warfare, however, had not been part of their training.
Such was the crisis that Pallas had only one option: to kindle
Manly pride with a mixture of bitter words and entreaties.
'Comrades, you're running away. Where to? I beg you, by your own
Selves, by your valiant deeds, by the name of your leader,
　　Evander,　　　　　　　　　　　　　　　　　　　　　　370
By all the wars you've won, by my hopes of attaining a glory

Matching my father's, it's not your feet you must trust, but your
     weapons.
That's how to break through the enemy ranks. Where the fighting is
     thickest,
That's where the fatherland now summons you, summons Pallas,
     your leader.
No supernatural forces are crushing us. *Our* foes are human: 375
Men, who like us, can be killed. They have no extra hands, extra
     lifelines.
Look now, the sea locks us in with a wall of salt water. There's no
     land
Left we can run to. So shall we then head for the high seas and Old
     Troy?'*
This said, he charged straight into the fray where the foemen were
     thickest.

     Lagus,* led by an unjust fate, was the first to encounter   380
Pallas, who speared him while he was attempting to rip up a huge rock.
Right through his midriff the javelin spun, where his spine
     separated
Ribs of his ribcage. And Pallas recovered his shaft from the body,
Lodged though it was in the bone, before Hispo,* enraged by the cruel
Death of his friend, could move in, as he hoped, and so gain the
     advantage.   385
Rage made Hispo rash. Pallas caught him instead as he charged in,
Buried his sword in the angrily panting lungs of his foeman.
Sthenius fell to him next, then Anchemolus, scion of Rhoetus'
Ancient house. He had raped his stepmother once in her bedroom.

     Daucus' sons, identical twins, Larides and Thymber—   390
Even their parents—and this confusion delighted them—could not
Tell them apart—you too died then in Rutulia's ploughlands.
Pallas supplies a grim way of distinguishing one from the other:
Thymber, he cuts off your head with Evander's sword, and Larides,
Your right hand, lopped off, now misses its master; its fingers   395
Still have a shadow of life: they twitch and they claw at the
     sword-hilt.

     Pain intermingled with shame sent Arcadians back to the battle,
Courage rekindled by Pallas's words, and by seeing his valour.
Pallas, in fact, speared Rhoeteus* then as he passed in his chariot,
Fleeing the fight. And that's how a reprieve was then granted
     to Ilus.   400

Ilus, you see, was the target of Pallas's powerful spear-shot.

Rhoeteus got in the way while fleeing from you, noble Teuthras,

Both you and Tyres, your brother. He tumbled head first from his
    chariot

Barely alive, and his heels gouged stripes in Rutulian ploughland.

Fires that a shepherd has set at strategic points round a forest   405

(When, as he's hoped, summer winds have arisen) will suck flames

High in an updraft into the centre, creating a single

Frontage of Vulcan's jagged blaze stretched wide on the broad plains,

Meanwhile, gazing down at the fires, rambunctious in triumph,   409

There sits the conquering shepherd. Just so, Pallas, all of the courage

Your men showed coalesced. It delighted (and helped) you.

                                          Halaesus

Moved to oppose them—a tough man who used all his armour's
    protection

Cannily. He killed Ladon and Pheres, Demodocus also,

Cut off Strymonius' hand with a lightning sword-stroke when this man

Threatened his throat, smashed Thoas' face with a boulder and
    showered   415

Fragments of skull far and wide, pulped crimson with brain-spattered
    blood clots.

Fate, through Halaesus' father,* had sung of his doom. So the
    father

Hid him away in the woods. But the fates, when death sank the old
    man's

Eyes into blindness, got hold of him, marked him down for Evander's

Spear. And now Pallas had found him. Before he attacked, Pallas
    prayed thus: 420

'Grant, Father Tiber, good luck to this iron-tipped spear that I balance,

Poised for the cast. May it pierce through the chest of that tough
    man, Halaesus.

You'll have a trophy: his spoils and his armour will honour your oak
    tree.'

And Tiber listened; Halaesus exposed his own chest to Evander's

Spear as the youth tried, unfulfilled, to cover Imaon.   425

Lausus,* a major force in the war, did not allow carnage

Pallas inflicted to panic his troops. He started by killing

Abas, a knot to frustrate any blade, who rose up to oppose him.

Next, he laid waste the Arcadian troops, laid waste the Etruscans,

And you Teucrians too—whose bodies the Greeks had not
    shattered.   430
Column met column, matched both in physical strength and in leaders.
Those in the rear crowd those in the front; sheer masses of soldiers
Stop any movement of weapons or arms. On this side there's Pallas
Straining and pressing, and Lausus on that, both youths of
    outstanding
Beauty, both roughly the same age. But neither, says Fortune,
    will ever   435
Make his way home from the war. Yet the ruler of mighty Olympus
Tolerates no thought of letting them meet one another in combat.
Fate awaits each, very soon, at the hands of a mightier foeman.
   Meanwhile, his sister divine* is admonishing Turnus to rescue
Lausus. He cuts through the ranks in between in his swift-moving
    chariot,   440
Then, upon seeing his comrades, he cries: 'It is time to stop fighting;
Pallas is mine, only mine. Only I have the right to this duel.
Oh, how I'd love this show if his father could be here in person!'
This said, his comrades withdrew from the area, as he'd instructed.
Pallas, amazed at these boastful commands, was, as the
    Rutulians   445
Pulled back, shocked stock-still by his first sight of Turnus. His
    eyes moved,
Scanning the giant body, assessing its strengths at a distance,
Glaring defiance. He fired back words in response to the tyrant's
Own volleyed words: 'Either way, I'll have glory: the Spoils of
    Distinction*
Or a heroic death. My father accepts either outcome.   450
Cut out the threats.' So saying, he entered the clearing established.
Blood rushed cold to Arcadian hearts, gelled thick in their terror.
Turnus leaped from his chariot, setting the style for a close-range
Duel on foot. And the image evoked is that of a lion,
Watching, from high in the hills, as a bull in the grasslands
    below him   455
Thinks about fighting, but makes no move. So he races towards him.
Pallas, as soon as he thinks his opponent has come within spear-shot,
Aims the first blow in the hopes that, although he is no match in
    sheer strength,
Chance may reward him for boldness. He cries these words to the
    heavens:

'Hercules, stand with me now in this challenge supreme, I beseech
    you,   460
Just as my father was there when you came needing food, needing
    shelter.
Grant that my dying foeman may see me stripping his bloodstained
Armour. Let Turnus's very last sight be me in my triumph.'
Hercules heard what the young man said, though he choked back
    a heavy
Groan deep down in his heart. He was weeping tears of
    frustration.   465
Jupiter spoke to him, father to son, with a friend's understanding:
'Each man has his day marked. Life's short years can't be recovered.
That's why a man's real task is to reach beyond life in achievement,
Pass beyond fate, beyond rumour to fame. Troy's towering ramparts
Saw many sons of the gods fall beneath them. One was
    Sarpedon,*   470
Child of my loins. And his fate, even now, is summoning Turnus.
He too has entered the final stretch of the course he's allotted.'
This said, he tears his eyes far away from Rutulian ploughlands.
  Meanwhile Pallas, his spear discharged full force, is already
Gripping his sword, flashing menace, withdrawn from its hollow,
    enclosing   475
Sheath. And the spear, as it flies, penetrates his opponent's
Shield at the rim, pierces armoured plates protecting his shoulders,
Finally grazes the flesh of the mighty Turnus's body.
Turnus, unhurriedly testing his razor-sharp javelin's balance,
Launches its iron-clad tip against Pallas, and cries out a message: 480
'Look, and see whether the weapon I wield cannot penetrate deeper.'*
While he was speaking, his whiplashing javelin's point had already
Drilled through the generous plating of bronze and of iron, through
    oxhide,
Layer upon layer, that covered the shield, struck straight through the
    centre,
Pierced the resistant breastplate and dug through the muscular
    ribcage.   485
Pallas gained nothing by pulling the burning shaft from his wounded
Body. His blood and his life followed fast through the channel created.
Doubling over his wound, he collapsed, as his arms clanged around him,
Biting the enemy dust with jaws gushing blood in his death-throes.
Turnus was now standing over him: 490

'Listen, Arcadians! Echo', he said, 'my words to Evander.
Say he deserves to receive Pallas home in the state that I send him.
Still, I'll bestow such honour as comes with a tomb, and what solace
Burial brings. But the cost of his entertaining Aeneas
Won't come cheaply for him.' As he spoke, he was stamping his
       left foot   495
Firm on the corpse as he stripped off its sword-belt, a work of quite
       monstrous
Weight, stamped heavy with crime. For engraved in gold there by
       Clonus,
Eurytus' son, was a wedding of blood, where, in one night, so many
Bridegrooms* were foully murdered by brides in an orgy of slaughter.
It's now Turnus's spoils. He's happy to have it, triumphant.   500

Witness the human mind, knowing nothing of fate or the future,
Nothing about moderation when puffed with success and good
       fortune!
Turnus will find there's a time when he'll wish he could purchase an
       unscathed
Pallas, a time when he'll hate these spoils and the day that he won them.

Comrades are crowding around Pallas now as he's laid on his
       curving   505
Shield, as they carry him back to their ranks amid weeping and deep
       groans.
Oh, what a sorrow and glory you'll be when you come home to father!
This same day introduced you to war, then withdrew you for ever.
Nonetheless, you leave mounds of Rutulian corpses behind you.
   News of this deadly blow now flies to Aeneas from solid   510
Sources, not rumour. It's clear that the tiniest tip of the balance
Dooms his men, that they're running: it's time that he rescue the
       Teucrians.
Cutting a swath, edge to distant edge of the battlefield, scythes
Anything anywhere close, in a rage, as he seeks you out, Turnus,
Proud of your latest slaughter. It's all there: Pallas, Evander   515
Clear in his mind's eye; the first bread they broke when he came as a
       stranger;
Handshakes of treaty and friendship.
                                       So four youths, seedlings of Sulmo,
And the four Ufens raised, he harvests to be living tribute

Sprinkled with grain for the ghosts of the dead; with the flood of
  their gushing
Prisoners' blood he would dampen the flames* upon Pallas's pyre.   520
  This done, he fired off a spear, long range. And its target was Magus
Who, thinking quickly, ducked. And the quivering spear flew
  above him.
Clasping Aeneas's knees as a suppliant, Magus sought mercy:
'Please, by your father's ghost, by your dreams for your growing
  Iulus,
Save this life, I beg, for another son and his father.   525
I've an impressive house; in its vaults there are masses of well-wrought
Silver, gold by the pound, some in crafted form, some in ingots.
I'm not the pivotal point of a Teucrian victory. One life
Won't make much of a difference, this way or that, in the battle.'
That's what he said. And Aeneas' reply ran somewhat as follows: 530
'Spare these multiple masses of silver and gold that you've mentioned,
Save them for your own sons. This commercial aspect of warfare
Turnus was first to suspend just now by his killing of Pallas.
That's what Anchises' ghost has declared—and so has Iulus.'
This said, his left hand grasps Magus' helmet, and, though he's
  still begging,   535
Bends back his neck. Then he plunges the blade-hilt deep in his
  suppliant.

  Haemon's son, priest of Phoebus and Hecate, gleaming in long white
Robes and insignia, was not far away, his temples for all time
Bound with a chaplet that symbolized life consecrated. Aeneas
Clashed with him, chased him all over the field till he slipped, then
  astride him,   540
Casting a huge shadow, slaughtered him. Stripping his armour,
  Serestus
Shouldered it up as a trophy for you, Mars, Lord of the Soldier.*
  Caeculus, Vulcan's descendant, and Umbro who hails from the
  Marsian
Hills, put *some* new life in their front. But Dardanus' offspring
Rages against it. His sword has just pruned off, along with its
  rounded   545
Shield, the entire left forearm of Anxur.* This man had been spouting
Big talk, believing that words beget force, and perhaps his ambition
Buoyed him to heaven with hope. He had promised himself a long
  lifespan,

Stretched over many more years, that he'd live long enough to have
    white hair.

  Tarquitus next set himself in the path of Aeneas's fury.   550
Born to a nymph, Dryope, and fathered by Faunus, the woodlands'
God, he was prancing, proud in his blazing armour. Aeneas,
Hefting a spear, pinned the massive weight of his shield to his
    breastplate.
As the man begged in vain and prepared to keep pleading, Aeneas
Slashed off his head. When it fell to the ground, he rolled over the
    headless,   555
Still warm trunk with his feet and said this, with a heart full of
    hatred:
'Figure of terror, now lie where you are. Your wonderful mother
Won't ever bury your limbs* in the family tomb. You'll be either
Left here as food for the carrion birds or flung to the surging
Seas where your wounds will be nibbled by starving fish as your
    corpse drifts.'   560
  Off he goes, hot in pursuit of Turnus's best men: Antaeus,
Lucas, and Numa* the Brave, and Camers the Tawny—the richest
Lord of estates in Ausonia, king of Amyclae's Laconic
Peoples,* sparse with their words; he was son of Volcens the
    Great Heart.
Once there was blood on his sword, like the monstrous Aegaeon,
    Aeneas   565
Savaged the whole field of battle. Aegaeon, they say, had a hundred
Arms and a hundred hands, all either clashing their matching
Shields or unsheathing swords. He had fifty chests from which fifty
Mouths flared fire that day when he fought against Jupiter's
    lightning.
Look at him now, in a head-on charge at the oncoming
    four-horse   570
Rig of Niphaeus!* And: it's not *he* but the horses that veer off,
Shying in fright, tearing off from the sight of him, toppling their master
Out, dragging chariot straight for the sea as Aeneas approaches,
Long in his galloping stride, most fierce in his snorting and roaring.
  Lucagus, meanwhile, and Liger, his brother, have charged to the
    forefront,   575
Driving a chariot drawn by a pair of white horses. His brother
Handles the reins as Lucagus whirls drawn sword all around him
Fiercely. Aeneas, unable to stand their madness and fury,

Runs up, appears right in front of them, huge with his menacing
    spear poised.
Liger addresses him: 580
'No, it is not Diomedes' steeds* that you see, or Achilles'
Chariot. These aren't Phrygian plains, they're the land where your
    battles
End now, along with your life.' Such words fly in public from Liger,
Mad beyond help. Yet it's not a reply in words that the Trojan
Hero plans; his response is a javelin torqued at his foeman. 585
Lucagus, stretching forward, as if he were handling a horsewhip,
Goading the pair with the flat of his sword, is advancing his left foot,
Poised for the fight, when that javelin rises, clear through his shining
Shield's lower rim, then drills through his groin. He is hurled by its
    impact
Out of the chariot, down to the ploughlands, tumbling and dying. 590
Righteous Aeneas's words to his foe are ironic and bitter:
'Lucagus, well, we can't blame panicked horses for failing your
    chariot,
Shadowy phantoms did not divert *your* team from the foeman;
You left the rig, jumped clear of the wheels.' He grasps both the
    horses'
Bridles while speaking. The brother slips down from the chariot,
    extending 595
Unarmed hands in an unfulfilled last hope to win pity.
'Think, I beg, of yourself, of the parents who bore you and formed you.
Please, man of Troy, let this life go on. I beg you for mercy.'
'That's not the way you were talking just now,' says Aeneas, who
    cuts off
Further appeals. 'Die now. Don't abandon your brother, good
    brother.' 600
Then he reveals life's lair in the chest with a skilful incision.
  Such were the deaths that the Dardan commander dispensed on
    the flatlands,
Out of control, like a torrent in flood, like a raging tornado
Black in the sky.
              Now Ascanius, the boy, with the other young warriors,
Finally bursts from the camp. For the futile siege has been ended. 605

Jupiter, meanwhile, took action, addressing these comments to Juno:
'Sister and darling wife that you are to me, all in one person,

Oh, how right you have been. Venus, just as you thought, is
    supporting
Trojan successes. It's not their own skill, their own brilliance in battle,
Not their own fierceness and courage, or stubborn endurance of
    peril.'   610
Juno's response was subdued: 'Why disturb me, dear wonderful
    husband,
Now when I'm heartsick and living in fear of your grim resolutions?
If there were still any force, as there once was and, properly, should be
Now, in your love for me, you, with control of the universe, surely
Wouldn't persist in denying me power to steal Turnus from battle, 615
And, in this way, keep him safe and unharmed for his father, for
    Daunus.
Well, let him die, let his righteous blood pay its price to the Teucrians,
This, nonetheless, is a man who derives his name from Pilumnus,
Our stock, four generations ago, a man who has often
Loaded your temple steps with his many, and lavish, donations.'   620
  Briefly the king of Olympus, high in the heavens, responded:
'If what is asked is delay of his death, some time for a young man
Destined to die; if you've grasped that it *is* my resolve that he *must* die,
Get Turnus out, let him run, grab him now! Fate is already pouncing.
There's slack enough to indulge you in this. If your prayers have
    as subtext   625
Any more radical pardon than this, if you're thinking the whole war's
Course can be shifted or changed, then the hopes that you feed on
    are empty.'
  Juno laments: 'Putting fate into words may mean shifting and
    deadening
Meanings the mind would convey. The thought: "life still remains
    for this Turnus"
Yields, if I'm not wrong, the words: "still remains": no more than
    the ghastly   630
Death of an innocent. Please, prove me wrong, overpowered by delusive
Fears. So rephrase what you've started to say for the better.
    For *you can*.'*

This said, she instantly hurled herself from the apex of heaven,
Mantled in dark cloud, storming the air with an onrush of winter,
Straight to the Ilian front and the fort in the Laurentines'
    country.   635

Out of her cloud's hollow veil, Juno tailored a wispy and strengthless
Shadow resembling Aeneas* (the likeness was really astounding),
Armed it with Dardan equipment and copied the godlike Aeneas'
Shield and his plumes. She endowed it with power of speech, but
    not reason:
Sound unsupported by mind. Her art caught his movements
    exactly.   640
  When people die, rumour has it, their shapes simply flutter at
    random;
And, when we sleep, dreams mock and delude our unconscious
    perceptions.
So this mirage now behaves. It happily leaps to the front lines,
Brandishes arms to provoke, yells words that will irritate Turnus.
Turnus attacks it and, though at a distance, discharges a
    screaming   645
Spear. The mirage simply spins in its tracks, shows its back, begins
    running.
Turnus, believing Aeneas has baulked and is fleeing from combat,
Gulps a great draught of illusory hope in emotional tumult:
'Where are you running, Aeneas? You're promised a bride. Don't
    desert her!
My hand will pledge you that portion of earth you sailed oceans in
    quest of!'   650
Such are the boasts he lets fly as he hunts the mirage with his flashing
Sword. He can't see that his joy's just a creature that flies on a
    wind gust.
Moored to a high cliff-ledge, as it chanced, lay a vessel at anchor,
Rope ladders draped from its sides, lowered gangplank ready for
    boarding.
This was the ship King Osinius sailed in from Clusium's
    coastlands;   655
Now it's the hideout the trembling mirage of the fleeing Aeneas
Hurls itself into. Yet Turnus lets nothing obstruct him, but bounding
Hot on its heels, leaps straight up the steep-sloped rise of the gangplank.
Just as he's mounted the deck, Saturn's daughter ruptures the hawsers,
Turns back the tide, tears the ship clear of land, spins it over the
    waters.   660
  So: while Aeneas is challenging Turnus, now absent, to battle,
Slashing the numerous others he meets into so many corpses;
So: while the fleeting mirage, giving up on its search for a hideout,

Soars to the skies, then mingles itself with the mantling dark cloud;*
Turnus is far out to sea, set adrift, spun around by a whirlwind.   665
He, unaware of what's happening, displeased too by his rescue,
Looks back and raises his hands and his voice to the heavens, protesting:
'Father Almighty, did you think *me* so bad as to merit
This much criminal shame? Did you want me punished in this way?
Where am I brought? Where and why did I leave? How can *I* ever
          get back?   670
Will I be able to look at our camp and the Laurentine ramparts
Ever again? My troops, all following me and my banner,
Men (god forbid!) I have left amid indescribable slaughter,
Straggling, yes, I can see them now, I can pick out their dying
Groans. And now I'm doing—what? Could the earth yawn open
          a chasm   675
Deep enough now for my needs? More effective to beg you for pity,
Winds. I, Turnus, implore you, it's my wish: bellow this vessel
Onto a reef or a cliff, sink it deep into merciless quicksands,
Well beyond reach of Rutulians and of omniscient Rumour.'
Now, as his thoughts found words, his mood wavered this way and
          that way.   680
Should he, since overwhelming shame was crippling reason,
Cover up guilt with a sword, run his pitiless blade through his own
          ribs?
Or throw himself in the pitching waves and swim for the curving
Shore, thus restoring himself once more to the fight with the
          Teucrians?
Two choices: each one he tried three times; each time mighty
          Juno   685
Stopped the young man and suppressed the attempt. For she pitied
          him deeply.
Drifting, but favoured by currents and waves, he made way and
          was carried
Landward to Ardea, ancient city of Daunus, his father.

Meanwhile, acting on Jupiter's orders, Mezentius, blazing,
Takes up the fight and attacks the now over-confident Teucrians.   690
Instantly, this one man is the target of every Etruscan
Blade, each volley of spears: the one focus for all of their hatred.
He's like a crag that protrudes in the vast expanses of ocean,
Set in the path of the furious gales and exposed to the breakers,

Bearing the brunt of the threatening onslaught of sky and of
    sea-swell.   695
Standing unshaken and firm, he grinds Dolichaon's son, Hebrus,
Into the ground, kills Latagus next, then swift-running Palmus.
Latagus' face and advancing form he destroys with a massive
Mountain chunk, pure rock. As for Palmus, he severs his tendons,
Leaving him powerless and squirming. He gives the man's armour to
    Lausus: 700
Plumes for his helmet's crest and a breastplate to strap to his shoulders.
   Then, he slew Phrygian Evanthes, and Mimas, Paris' companion,
Even the same age. For Amycus fathered a son that Theano
Brought into life's light the same night Hecuba, pregnant with fire,
Bore Paris. Yet Paris died in his father's city, his homeland.   705
Mimas lies on the Laurentine coast in a land he does not know.
  Still Mezentius fights, like a boar that the snapping of hounds'
    teeth
Flushes from hilltops where he has been sheltered for years by the
    pine-dense
Summits of Vesulus, fed by the forested Laurentine lakelands'
Acres of marsh reeds. He now stands firm as the nets drop
    about him,   710
Snarls, snorts, tenses his shoulders, and arches his back into bristling
Fury. And nobody's quite man enough to go wild and get closer.
Safer to press him with shouts, and to shoot off spears from a distance.
He's not afraid. He takes time, circles this way and that, and he
    lunges,   717
Gnashing his teeth at them all; and he shrugs off spears from his
    tough hide.*   718
So, though they had just reason to hate Mezentius wildly,
All of them lacked raw nerve to unsheathe steel blades and
    attack him.   715
Spears, arrows, thunderous shouts were their weapons, all volleyed
    at long range.
  Then he saw Acron,* who'd come down from Corythus' ancient
    dominions,
Greek-born (but he'd left his wedding for exile, his wife still a
    virgin),   720
Saw him far off in the fierce throes of combat, his plume and his mantle
(Gift of his pledged bride) purpled with dye pounded out from the
    sea-snail.

Often, when starving, a lion who roams all over the high lands
(Hunger's a desperate persuader) will thrill if he glimpses a
     scampering
She-goat or maybe a stag, growing proudly into its antlers;   725
Maw gapes wide, mane bristles erect, ineluctable jaws bite.
Now he is sprawling on guts ripped out, face bloodied and streaming
Horror and gore.
That's how Mezentius leaps at the thick of the foe, how he pounces.
Acron goes down, unfulfilled; and his heels, in his death-throes,   730
Pound earth. *His* blood dyes the now broken spear that has killed him.

  Next was Orodes.* Disdaining the thought of destroying another
Foe on the run and inflicting anonymous wounds with a spear-cast,
Face to opposing face, Mezentius met him in combat,
Man against man. Skill at arms won the day, not tactical cunning.   735
Foot upon fallen foeman's chest, arms tugging the spearshaft,
'Men,' he cried, 'Here lies Orodes, no trivial factor in this war!'
Joining the shout, allies cheered and re-echoed this paean of triumph.
Dying, Orodes responded: 'Whoever you are that has killed me,
Joy won't be yours very long. An identical fate watches over   740
You too. You'll soon gain just the same kind of plot in these
     ploughlands.'
Smiling at this, and yet also enraged, Mezentius answered:
'Die now. In my case, the Father of Gods and the Ruler of Mortals
Handles the details, I think.' Then he tugged the spear out of the body.
Rigid rest and an ironclad sleep slammed eyes into blindness: 745
Light and perception were damned to a night of darkness eternal.

  Caedicus butchered Alcathoüs; and Sacrator, Hydaspes;
Rapo, Parthenius, also the tough and resilient Orses;
Clonius fell to Messapus—Lycaon's son too, Ericetes.
Clonius' horse had no bridle; he'd fallen and sprawled on the
     hard earth.   750
But Ericetes was fighting on foot. When another foot-soldier,
Lycian Agis, advanced, Valerus, whose family were fighters,
Killed him. Then Salius killed Thronius. Salius fell to the hidden
Marksman, Nealces, so lethal with arrows and spears at a distance.

Mars, even-handed and deadly, was dealing out grief and
     destruction   755
On both sides, both equally slaughtering, equally slaughtered,
Victors and victims—no running from battle by one or the other.

Gods within Jupiter's halls pitied each for this furious, wasted
Anger, regretted that creatures who die have to suffer such hardships.
Venus is watching from here; watching there is Saturnian Juno;   760
Pallid Tisiphone's rage rules thousands caught in the middle.
Waving his monstrous spear, Mezentius, whirling destruction,
Strides forth over the battlefield, massive as mighty Orion
Ripping a path midway through the depths of Nereus' ocean,
Marching along on foot, head and shoulders clear of the water,   765
Or, when he carries an ancient ash from the heights of a mountain,
Treading the ground, but plunging his head deep into the cloud-caps.
No less vastly armed than these is Mezentius in action.

Noticing him in the long line of fighters, Aeneas advances,
Ready to fight. And, standing his ground unafraid, his opponent   770
Waits for his great-hearted foeman's attack, his immensity stock-still,
Eyes now gauging the distance between them, the range for a
    spear-cast.
'Right hand, you are my god, and you, javelin that I'm poising,
Ready to throw, give your best! I vow to you, Lausus, that you'll be
Dressed like a trophy* with spoils stripped away from Aeneas,
    this pirate's,   775
Corpse.' This said, he dispatches his spear. Screaming off at its distant
Target, it does hit the shield. But, deflected, it picks out, at random,
Faraway Antores, lodges between the man's flank and his thigh bone.
Antores, one of the best, friend of Hercules, sent out by Argos,
Joined with Evander, and settled within an Italian city.   780
Laid low, unfulfilled, by a wound that was meant for another,
Dying, he stares at the sky, and remembers his dearly loved Argos.

Righteous Aeneas now hurls his spear. And it tears through the triple
Bronze sheets, then through the linen lining, then through the threefold
Stitched oxhides of the hollow shield and it strikes in the lower   785
Part of the groin, but without full force. So, swiftly, Aeneas
Tugs out the sword at his thigh, delighted to see the Etruscan's
Blood, and now hot for the kill, moves in on his quivering foeman.
Lausus, on seeing this sight, groans deeply for love of his
    cherished   790
Father. The tears in waves stream all down his face in his sorrow.

Here I will not pass over in silence the cause of your harsh death,
Or your noble deeds, young man—if tales of the long-gone
Past win belief in such glory. You're worthy of being remembered.

Weighed down, dragging his enemy's spear in his shield now,
    Mezentius   795
Gave ground, defenceless, and tried to pull back. Rushing forward,
    the young man
Hurled himself into the fight in between them the instant Aeneas
Reared up, arm raised, poised for the kill. He himself intercepted,
Parried the stroke and himself took the blow. With a loud shout, his
    comrades
Followed him. Safe beneath his son's shield now, the father
    retreated;   800
They, with a long-range volley of arrows and spears, kept the foeman
Busy. Aeneas was forced to control his own rage and seek cover.
There are those times when the hail pelts down out of menacing
    storm clouds,
Times when all ploughmen, all tillers of land, will scatter from open
Fields, and when travellers huddle away in a spot that's protected,   805
Under the sheltering banks of a stream, or in high, hollow cliff-caves,
While rain pours to the ground and until, with the sun's
    reappearance,
Day and its work can resume.
                          Pinned down by a deluge of weapons
Hurled all around him, Aeneas endures this cloudburst of warfare,
Waits for the thunder to end, cursing Lausus, threatening
    Lausus: 810
'Why all this hurry to die—as you will? You're not up to this challenge,
Your sense of righteous devotion has lured you to rashness!' The other
Still prances madly. Ferocious wrath flares yet more intensely
Now in the Dardan chief. As the Fates pluck the last threads of Lausus'
Lifespan, Aeneas thrusts, full force, with his powerful sword's
    blade   815
Clear through the young man's belly and buries it hilt-deep inside him.
Through the light shield, no match for his challenge, the point,
    penetrating,
Pierces the tunic of soft supple gold that his mother had woven.
Blood gushes over his lap as he sinks; life flees from his body,
Sad on the breath of the winds to its place among lingering
    shadows.   820
    Yet, when he sees the expression that spreads on the face of the dying
Youth, on that face growing stunningly pallid, the son of Anchises
Pities him, utters a groan from his heart, reaches out with his right hand.

Here, mirrored sharp in his thoughts, is his own righteous love for
    his father.
'Poor young lad! What act of respect can Aeneas the Righteous   825
Now do for you to acknowledge and praise such supreme dedication?
Keep your armour, your pride and your joy. And, in case you were
    worried,
Yes, I will send you back to the ashes and ghosts of your parents.
Though you went unfulfilled to your pitiful death, you'll have solace
Knowing you fell by the hand of Aeneas the Great.' Mocking
    Lausus'   830
Comrades, who hold back, he picks up the youth whose blood was
    befouling
Hair once neatly styled, lifts him up from the ground on his shoulders.

Meanwhile his father is stanching and cleansing his wounds at the
    flowing
Waters of Tiber. He's taken the weight off his feet, with his body
Propped for support by the trunk of a tree.* High above, in its
    branching   835
Arms, hangs his helmet of bronze; on the meadow, all peaceful,
    his heavy
Armour lies. Select youths stand round. He, nauseous and gasping,
Favours his neck; and his flowing beard spills over his broad chest.
Constantly asking how Lausus fares, he constantly sends out
Men to recall him and carry commands from his grief-stricken
    father.   840
Weeping companions, however, are already carrying Lausus
Dead, on his armour, a huge man felled by a huge wound inflicted.
He, in his mind, fears the worst. He knows, from afar, why they're
    groaning.
He now filthies his white hair with dust by the fistful; he stretches
Hands to the heavens. Embracing the corpse, he cries out in
    sorrow: 845
'Son, was the pleasure of staying alive so great that it kept me
Back, and that I allowed you, my own child, to replace me in battle,
Facing our enemy's sword? Am I saved, I your father, by your
    wounds?
Living because you died? My exile is now void of any
Sense of fulfilment in misery. This is the wound driven deeply!   850
Son, I'm the very same man whose criminal actions have ruined

Your good name: I was loathed, overthrown, I was stripped of
    my fathers'
Sceptre. I should myself have exacted the judgement my soul's guilt
Owed my land and my people's hate: some death in a thousand
Forms. And I've not yet left these regions of humans and
    daylight.   855
I'm still alive. But I'll leave.' He raises himself on his injured
Thigh as he speaks. Though the depth of his wound does limit his
    movement,
Undeterred, he calls for his stallion, his symbol of glory—
And his companion in grief, upon whom he had ridden victorious
Out of all battles. He speaks these words to his sorrowful partner: 860
'Rhaebus, we've lived long years, if anything's long for us death-doomed
Creatures. Today you will either bring back, in your triumph, Aeneas'
Bloodstained spoils and his head and, together with me, avenge Lausus'
Suffering and pain, or you'll die with me here if our foray just cannot
Force a path open. I do not believe you, bravest of stallions, 865
Will tolerate someone else's control and a Teucrian master.'
This said, he mounts up and settles himself in his usual manner,
Loads up both of his hands with sharp-tipped javelins. Bright bronze
Gleams on his head, and his horsehair plumes stream wildly about him.
Straight to the centre of battle he charges, and here in this single 870
Heart whirls a maelstrom of shame and of grief intermingled with
    madness,
Love lashed to mindless rage, yet courage, controlled and self-conscious.
Three times now he calls a loud call on the name of Aeneas
And, recognizing the voice, Aeneas prays in contentment:
'Father of gods, make it so! Make it so, majestic Apollo! 875
Make your start to the duel!'
That's all he says. Then he comes to confront him, spear at the ready.
'Savage!' the other replies. 'How can *you* scare *me* now you've taken
My son's life? There was no other way that you could have
    destroyed me.
We neither tremble at death nor respect any god whatsoever. 880
Stop all the talk. I have come here to die, and I'm bringing you presents
First. Here they are!' And his javelin spins full force at his foeman.
Then comes another, another again, and they strike as he circles
Widely and swiftly around; but the shield's gold boss takes the
    impact.
Three times he loops to the left round his standing foe at a gallop, 885

Showering spears from his hand. Three times, also turning, the
    Trojan
Hero hefts up a forest of shafts stuck fast in his bronze shield.
Then, when he tires of extended delays and of pulling out countless
Javelins, feeling the pressure of fighting on terms so unequal,
After much thinking, he breaks from defence and he hurls his own
    weapon,   890
Piercing his foe's warhorse clean through at the curve of its temples.
Instantly rearing up, lashing air with his forelegs, the stallion
Bucks off his rider, and then crashes down on top of him, tangling
Harness and man as he plunges and falls, dislocating his shoulder.
Trojans and Latins alike set the heavens ablaze with their
    shouting.   895
Yanking his sword from its sheath, Aeneas flies at him in triumph:
'Where is the fierce Mezentius now?' he enquires. 'Where's the
    famous
Violent power of his soul?' In response, looking up, the Etruscan
Gulps air into his lungs, regaining his senses and day's light:
'Why, bitter foe, do you gloat, making death no more than
    a menace?   900
Butchering me's not a sin. I didn't fight hoping for quarter!
Lausus, my son, settled no such terms with you for our duel.
One thing I beg—if there's this much forgiveness for enemies
    conquered:
Grant that my body be buried. I know that my countrymen's bitter
Hatred has me at its mercy. I beg you to ward off their fury.   905
My son shared my life, my death. Let us share the same tombstone.'
With no illusions, he offers his throat to the sword as he's speaking.
Then, in a torrent of blood, he pours out his life* on his armour.

BOOK ELEVEN

Dawn, as time passed, duly rose and left Ocean. Aeneas,
Up before her with the Morning Star,* thanks gods for his
    conquest.
Even though anguish impels him to take time needed to bury
Comrades lost, though his mind is in turmoil because of the slaughter,
He has set high on a mound an immense oak* whose limbs he has
    pruned back   5
All the way round and arrayed with the gleaming arms and
    equipment
Stripped from the ruler Mezentius. He's turning it into a trophy
Honouring you, War's Lord, great Mars, and attaches the fighter's
Blood-drenched plumes, snapped spears, and the corslet, scored
    by a dozen
Holes* gouged through. To what serves as the left hand, he fastens
    the brass-bound   10
Shield, from its 'neck', he's suspending the sword in its ivory scabbard.
  Seizing his chance—for his captains are all pressing in on him,
    wildly
Cheering—he rallies his troops as they give him a rousing ovation:
'Men, this achievement is huge. All fear must be banished from now on.
These spoils,* my first fruits of the war, have been reaped from a
    proud king!   15
Here is the artwork my hands have created! Behold him, Mezentius!
Now we must march upon one more king and the walls of the Latins.
Ready your weapons! Put war in your souls! Make war what you
    hope for!
Let's not be caught unawares by delays, and impeded the instant
Heaven nods signs to up standards and march the lads out of
    encampment.   20
No dissent must arise out of fear-fraught inertia and slow us.
  'Let us commit to the earth,* as we wait, these friends, these
    unburied
Bodies. In Acheron's depths, that's the only meaningful tribute.
Go!' he said. 'Honour these spirits, the pick of the flock, who with
    their blood
Mothered this new home to life for us all. Give them offerings
    and final   25

Rites. Now our first step should be to have Pallas returned to Evander's
Grief-stricken city. This day, marked black,* has removed him and
    plunged him
Deep in the sourness of death. Yet it found him not lacking in
    courage.'
  Tears fill his eyes as he speaks. He retraces his steps to the dead
    youth's
Quarters. An old man was guarding the laid-out corpse of the lifeless   30
Pallas. Acoetes had earlier served as Arcadian Evander's
Arms-bearer, then was assigned as companion to his beloved Pallas:
This move he made under auspices boding less happy fulfilment.
Gathered around him were all Pallas' slaves, a good number of Trojan
Men, and, with hair flowing free in the fashion of grief, Trojan
    women.   35
Once, though, Aeneas presented himself, after passing the high
    doors,*
Beating of breasts started, moaning notes shrilled up to the starry
Skies and the royal marquee re-intoned lamentations of sorrow.
Now's when his eyes get their first glimpse of Pallas: the snow-cold
    whiteness,
Pillowed head, then the face, the slight chest with the wound an
    Italian   40
Spear left gaping wide. Tears gush from his eyes as he's speaking:
'Poor lad! Was it upon you that Fortune, who came to us smiling,
Cast evil eye to spite *me*, so that your eyes would never see our realm,
And so you'd never ride home to your father's kingdom in triumph?
This isn't what my departing words to your father Evander   45
Promised for you, when he hugged me as I went away, as he sent me
Off to pursue great power. He feared for us. These were, he
    cautioned,
Fierce opponents; we'd battle a tough and resilient people.
He, I suspect, is a prisoner, even now, of delusive
Hope. Chances are that he's still making vows, piling gifts
    upon altars   50
While we are gathered in grief to pay hollow respects to a lifeless
Youth who has no further debt he must pay any god in the heavens.
  'You'll see how cruelly your son died, how you lost what fulfilled you.
Such is our great triumphal return that you've waited and watched for!
Here's how much *my* word is worth! Still, you won't see him come
    back defeated,   55
Scarred by disgraceful wounds. No, Evander, you won't be a father

Wishing death as a curse on a son who's survived.* What a mighty
Guardian, Ausonia, you've lost! What a great loss for you too, Iulus.'
   Ending his tearful lament, he commands them to lift up this
      piteous
Corpse and dispatches the pick of his whole force, as escort and
      final   60
Honour guard—men who would join with his father in weeping.
      A thousand
Troops* were but minimal solace indeed for a grief so immensely
Huge, and yet surely the due that was owed to his father, in pity.
   Others, no less fired up, plait switches of oak and arbutus
Withes into wickerwork, weaving a casket and cushioning bier,   65
Raising a couch wattled over with taut-stretched, shadowing
      branches.
Here, on a farmhand's bedding, they set out their noble young hero
Languid as drooping hyacinth falls,* or limp as a violet
Clipped in its flower by a virgin's thumb, but whose shimmering
      lustre
Lingers, whose perfect form hasn't shrivelled, as yet, though
      its earthen   70
Mother no longer sustains life's vital strength with her nurture.
Then, bearing matching mantles stiffened with gold and with purple
Dye, comes Aeneas. Sidonian Dido herself, with her once live
Hands had produced them for him, as a pair: her labour of rapture,
Threaded with highlights of fine-spun gold worked into the
      cross-weave.*   75
One of the capes, in his grief, he drapes over the youth, a last tribute
Bridling the hair, now damned to the flames, in a veil of
      enshroudment.*
Many more prizes won in the Laurentine battle he also
Stacks up, and orders the plunder conveyed in a lengthy procession,
Adding some horses, and weapons he's stripped from the enemy's
      bodies.   80
Then, hands chained behind backs, come the men he is sending
      for human
Sacrifice,* planning to sprinkle the flames with the blood of their
      slaughter,
Honouring Pallas's ghost. He bids captains convey, with their persons,
Stumps clad in enemy arms, names nailed upon placards as insults.
Wretched Acoetes, enfeebled and robbed of fulfilment in old age,   85

Bruises his chest with his fists, and his nails rip his cheeks as they
    march him,
Pitching down, hurled prone* to the ground the full length of his body.
Then they add chariots, drenched in Rutulian blood, to the march-past.
Aethon, his war-horse, trots past riderless,* stripped of its trappings,
Weeping and dampening its cheeks with a flow of magnificent
    teardrops.   90
Some bear his spear and his helmet—just these, for his conqueror,
    Turnus,
Now has the rest. Then the Teucrians follow, and then the Etruscans,
Full force.* Arcadians, weapons reversed, pass in funeral formation.
After the whole of the escort has passed in review and is moving
Onwards, Aeneas remains where he stands and observes, with
    a deep groan: 95
'Fate, with identical horrors of war, calls *us*, from our tears here,
Elsewhere to others. Goodbye for eternity,* wonderful Pallas,
Through all eternity, here's my farewell!' That was all. He now headed
Back to the high walls, directing his stride straight into the fortress.

Diplomats sent from the Latins' city were now in attendance,   100
Olive-boughs wreathing their brows. They were asking a special
    concession:
Would he turn over the war-dead strewn all over the landscape,
Would he allow them to pass beneath earthen mounds to entombment?
Since no dispute involves those now vanquished and lost to the
    sunlight,
Could he take pity on those once called his in-laws and good
    hosts?   105
Being a good man, Aeneas concedes their request—their petition
Can't very well be denied—and appends these additional
    comments:
'What shabby decoy of fortune has snarled you in such a colossal
War, men of Latium, that *you* flee from *us* who approached you in
    friendship?
Peace for the dead, for the losers in Mars' game of chance, that's
    the only   110
Favour you beg? I'd be willing to grant the same terms to the living!
I wouldn't *be* here, if fate hadn't granted me this place to settle.
I'm not at war with your people. *Your* king walked out* on the
    welcome

We offered, choosing to hazard his fortunes on Turnus's weapons.
Turnus, not they, should have faced this death. That would have
    been fairer.   115
If he's prepared to end war with his hand, and get rid of the Teucrians,
These are the weapons, and I am the man honour called him to
    challenge.
Life would have been the survivor's reward from a god or his own
    strength.
Go now, and kindle the flames beneath your poor citizens' bodies!'
That's what Aeneas said. They were stunned into absolute
    silence,*   120
Kept on exchanging glances without any change of expression.
    Drances,* an older man, quick to show hatred and hurl accusations,
Ever a personal foe of the youthful Turnus, exploited
This opportunity: 'Hero from Troy, rumour said you were mighty,
Arms prove you mightier! How can I praise you as high as the
    heavens?   125
Should I be awed by your justice first, or your prowess in warfare?
We will, with gratitude, bring this report back home to our city
And reunite you, if Fortune discloses a path, with Latinus.
He is our ruler. What Turnus contracts is his personal business.
Raising the predetermined might of your walls, even hauling   130
Stones for your Troy on our shoulders will be, not a task, but a
    pleasure.'
Total assent to his words rang clear, as if one voice had shouted.
Terms for a twelve-day truce were agreed. So with peace as their
    bondsman,
Teucrians mingled with Latins and wandered at will, and securely,
Over the hilltops. The tall ashes ring with the iron of axes,   135
Conifers high as the stars topple downwards. They split with
    their wedges
Fragrant cedar and oak after oak, while, in endless procession,
Wagons groan on their way, transporting their burdens of rowan.

Rumour, just recently telling of Pallas' triumphs in Latium,   141
Now outflew the official reports of this grievous misfortune,   139
Giving Evander himself and Evander's whole city the details.   140
Following ancient practice, Arcadians rushed to the gateways,
Funeral firebrands clutched in their hands. And the flames trace a
    blazing

Pathway of light far over the fields as they march out in order.
Coming the opposite way is the Phrygian multitude,* joining   145
Ranks with the column of mourners. Then mothers, once they have
     seen them
Nearing the walls, set the whole city blazing with shrill lamentation.
No force at all has the power to prevent Evander emerging
Publicly. And when the catafalque carrying Pallas is set down,
He falls upon it and clings to him tightly, weeping and moaning.   150
Once pain's choking has eased, voice finds just enough force to
     break forth:
'Oh Pallas! *This* isn't what you had promised your parent!* How extra
Cautious you'd willingly be when entrusting yourself to the cruel
War-god! I knew how seductive one's newly found glory in combat
Could prove to be: that peculiar sweetness of first battle-honours.   155
These are the piteous marks of your passage to manhood, your basic
Training in local warfare! And here lie my vows and my prayers
Which not one god heard! You died fulfilled, at the right time,
Dearly belovèd wife. You were not kept alive for this anguish!
I, by surviving you, have achieved no more than surpassing   160
My due of life. I'm a father who's outlived his own son. If only
I'd joined my allies from Troy and been raked by Rutulian volleys!
I would have given my life. They'd be bringing home me, and
     not Pallas.
Teucrians, I don't take issue with you, with our treaties or pledges
Sealed with a welcoming handshake. For this was the price that
     my old age   165
Owed as a payment. Indeed, if a premature death was awaiting
This my son, I'll be glad, at some point, that he fell after felling
Thousands of Volsci while leading you Teucrians forward to Latium.
I, in fact, cannot imagine for you any nobler funeral,
Pallas, than this one provided by righteous Aeneas, the mighty   170
Phrygians,* Etruscan lords, and the whole armed force of Etruscans.
They're bringing those that your right hand killed, remounted as
     large-scale
Trophies. And *you'd* stand among them now, a huge tree-trunk in
     armour,*
Turnus, if *you'd* been his age, and you'd both, for your years, had the
     same strength!
Why, though, do my ruined dreams of fulfilment keep Teucrians
     from battle?   175

Go!* And report these directives to your king: be sure you remember!
"I delay death, in a life I hate seeing now Pallas is taken,
Just to put your hand on trial.* You're aware that it owes son
    and father
Turnus as recompense due. And for proving its worth and good
    fortune
There's only one venue open. I am not suing you to bring my life   180
Pleasure, that wouldn't be right, but to please my son in the dead
    world."'

Dawn, meanwhile, who had brought forth her blessing of daylight
    for piteous
Death-doomed humans, commenced bringing back both their
    labour and troubles.
Father Aeneas now built, as did Tarchon, his funeral pyres
Down on the curving beach, where each unit, with its traditional   185
Rites, transported its dead. As the smoke-black brands kindle blazes,
Hot, fiery billows of darkness entomb far reaches of heaven.
Three times, arrayed in their bright-flashing armour, they run round
    the burning
Pyres; three times they ritually circle the funeral's mourning
Flames upon horseback, and howling mouths halloo loud
    lamentation.   190
Earth is bedewed with the same damp tears that bedew all their
    armour.
Shouting of men assaults sky in a roar with the shrilling of trumpets.
One group is now tossing onto the flames spoils ripped from the
    slaughtered
Latins: their helmets, their splendid swords, horse-bridles and trappings,
Red-hot wheels; others offer their own dead's all too familiar   195
Armour: the shields and the spears that fell short of achieving
    fulfilment.
Bodies of oxen killed all round honour Death in abundance;
Coarse-haired boars, flocks stolen from every pasture, have throats slit
Over the flames. Men cover the sea-front and watch as their comrades
Blaze, and maintain their watch as the members subside into
    darkening   200
Embers. Nothing can tear them away until Night's chilly dampness
Takes her turn with the blaze of her stars' lights studding the dark
    skies.

Elsewhere, and no less intently and piteously, Latins constructed
Countless pyres of their own, though they do commit some of the
    many
Human bodies to graves dug into the ground, carry others   205
Home, if their lands are adjacent, or send them back to their cities.
All of the rest, a gigantic heap of unsortable slaughter,
Not honoured, not even counted, they burn. Then everywhere vast
    fields
Rival each other with close-set clusters of blossoming fires.
   Daylight had pushed the cold shadows aside for a third time; the
    mourners   210
Started to break down high-heaped ash and unsortably tangled
Bones from the pyres and compress them beneath a warm earthen
    embankment.
Now's when the real crest, the mightiest wave, of prolonged
    lamentation
Crashed in the homes, in the city of mightily wealthy Latinus.
Mothers and piteously sad widowed brides, loving-hearted and
    grieving   215
Sisters, and children, now fatherless orphans, here, there, began
    screaming
Curses on monstrous war and on Turnus' plans for a wedding.
He's the one, he is the *one*, they demand, whose sword must
    determine
This fight, since he claims Italy's throne for himself, and top honours.
Drances adds weight to these cries in a vicious and sworn
    deposition: 220
One man alone must be called on, yes, *ordered* to fight, and that's
    Turnus.
Many a statement, variously phrased, at the same time supported
Turnus against him. The queen's great name cast an ominous shadow.*
Rumour, enhanced by the trophies he'd earned, further strengthened
    his backing.
   Now, amid all the unrest, as the core of the tumult is blazing,   225
Back come dejected delegates sent to the big city, bringing
Further fuel for the fire: Diomedes' response. Their enormous
Efforts and costly disbursements had all come to nothing. Their
    offerings,
Gold and the power of their prayers, had been worthless. He'd said
    that the Latins

Had to look elsewhere for arms, or beg peace from the king of the
    Trojans.   230
  King Latinus himself gives up* at this national disaster.
Angered gods, fresh tombs they can see, show the verdict of iron
Will and resolve; and they warn that what destiny brings is Aeneas.
He, therefore, summons the council-at-large and his own chief
    advisers,
Since he's empowered to issue a call, to convene behind
    closed doors   235
Inside the palace. They fill up the streets in their rush to assemble.
Both his supreme seniority and the prime power of his sceptre
Grant to the visibly joyless Latinus the seat at the centre.
Here he commands that the mission rebuffed by Aetolia's city
Make its report, and requests that responses received should be
    detailed   240
Fully and point by point. Other tongues are then ordered to silence.
Venulus does as he's told and begins his narration in this wise:
'Citizens, yes, we have seen Diomedes and Argive encampments,
We've run our journey's course, we've passed all its perils triumphant,
We've all shaken the hand that brought Ilium's land to its
    downfall.   245
He, fresh from conquering Garganus' farms in Iapygia, was founding,
Right there, a city called Argyripa,* after his homeland.
  'Once we had entered, and leave had been granted to speak in his
    presence,
We made our offerings, explained who we were and our homeland's
    location,
Who had attacked us, and what motivation had lured us to Arpi.   250
He heard us out; then he made this reply in a voice free of passion.
"Fortune's children, peoples who live under lordship of Saturn,
Ancient Ausonian folk! What changes in fortune are ruffling
Your serene life, prompting *you* to provoke what you don't
    understand: war?
All of us whose swords' blades bloodied Ilian fields in our violence,   255
Have (not to count bitter times we endured as we fought beneath
    Troy's high
Walls, and not counting those swamped by the Simoïs) suffered
    reprisals,
Penalties words can't describe, world-wide, for our criminal actions.
Priam himself might pity our troops. The grim star of Minerva's

Storm, ships wrecked off Euboea, the false shore-lights Caphareus 260
Flared out of vengeance. From warfare to far scattered coasts
    we were driven,
Atreus' son, Menelaus, as far as the pillars of Proteus,*
Exiled. Ulysses has gazed upon Cyclopes' homelands on Etna.
Or Neoptolemus' realm: shall I talk of this? Idomeneus'
Overthrow, maybe? Or Locrians living on Libya's coastline? 265
Even the Mycenaean commander of all the great Argives
Died, as he entered his home, at the hand of a wife I'll leave nameless.
Watching, embedded, for Asia's defeat, his cuckolder* waited.
Gods, one might add, have begrudged me the sight of the marriage
    I longed for
On my return to my homeland's shrines and to Calydon's beauty.* 270
Right now portents that frighten the eye still pursue me. My
    comrades,
Lost to me, soared to the sky* upon wings or are river-birds drifting
Aimlessly. Oh, what a ghastly affliction has punished my people!
Now they are filling the rocks by the coasts with their sorrowful
    screeching.
This was the penalty I should have seen was impending, the
    moment 275
I went mad and assaulted divine bodies too with my iron
Blade, and did actual violence to Venus by wounding her right hand.
Don't ask *me*, don't urge me again into this kind of battle!
Pergamum has been destroyed. There's no war between me and the
    Teucrians
Now. And they give me no joy, I don't even remember, these
    grudges of old days. 280
Those presents you offer me from your homeland's shores you
    should rather
Give to Aeneas. For we have confronted his savaging weapons,
We've fought him, hand to hand. So believe me. I know how immensely
He looms over his shield, how he torques his spear like a whirlwind.
If Ida's land had produced two more such men in addition, 285
Fates would have been reversed. A Dardanian would have
    assaulted
Inachus' cities and Greece would itself be the country in mourning.
Credit for any delay, before tough Troy's walls, that impeded
Greeks and their conquest, repulsing their progress for nine years,
Must be assigned to the hand of Hector, the hand of Aeneas.* 290

Both men were noted for courage, and both for remarkable prowess.
Righteousness was more Aeneas' domain. Let your hands join in
     treaties,
Given a chance. But beware, if your arms join battle with their arms!"
So, most excellent king, you have heard not just the responses
This king gave to our prayers, but the judgement he passed on the
     great war.'   295
   Hardly had delegates ceased, when the varied hum of conflicting
Views rumbled out of Ausonian mouths, the way rocks blocking river
Rapids raise thunder of swirling waters trapped, the way nearby
Banksides rumble the crackling surge of the onrushing torrent.
Once spirits calmed, once the nervous chatter had dwindled to
     silence,   300
High on his throne, the king prayed to the gods, then began his own
     comments:
'Better to have one's policies set in a crisis, Latini,*
Prior to action. This isn't the moment for planning. I'd rather
Not make our council convene when the foe has our city encircled.
Citizens, we are engaged in a war we can't win with a people   305
Born of the gods, men no battles can tire, men who can't be defeated
Since a defeat simply strips off their power to resist further fighting.
Dreams,* if you really *had* any dreams, of Aetolian assistance,
Give them up now. Yes, we each had our dreams. But you see how
     they've shrivelled.
Life has been crushed out of everything round us in general ruin.   310
All of you see it all with your eyes. You can touch it and feel it.
No, I am *not* blaming anyone. Men have done everything manhood
Could have done. This fight was fought by the realm, as a body, united.
So, let me frame, for the record, my hesitant mind's resolution
Which I'll explain very briefly. Now give me your fullest attention.   315
I own* an ancient estate very close to Etruria's river
Stretching far to the west, on into Sicanian holdings:
Hard, hilly land that Auruncans, along with Rutulian farmers,
Seed, and with great effort, plough, though the roughest of tracts are
     for pasture.
All this region, including the high mountain forests of pine-wood,   320
We, I propose, as a good-will gesture, cede to the Teucrians,
Set balanced terms for a treaty, invite them to enter as allies
Into our realm. If they're so much enamoured of us, let them settle,
Build cities. But, if their impetus carries them on to seize someone

Else's domains, other peoples, if *leaving* our soil is their problem,   325
Let's use the strength of Italian oak to construct twenty vessels,
More if they've forces to fill them. We *have* all the lumber that's
     needed
Close to the sea. So let *them* decide numbers and classes of keels laid.
We'd be supplying the brasses, the labour, the tackle and dockyards.
Therefore, I move that we send out a hundred blue-blooded
     Latins*   330
Gifted in language, to state our decision and settle a treaty.
Have them bear olive-boughs, symbols of peace, in their hands on
     the journey,
And bring as gifts large loads both of ivory and of gold bullion,
Also the kingdom's throne and my own ceremonial toga.
Now give us your ideas. Our state is exhausted. Revive it!'   335
     Drances arose. He was hostile as ever. For Turnus's glory
Raked him with jealousy's bitterness, evilled his never directly
Confrontational glance. He was free with his wealth, had a gifted
Tongue, and a hand ice-slow in a war. Though, in planning, considered
Not without value, his strength was subversion. His aristocratic   340
Mother conferred proud blood; he was vague when discussing his
     father.
Now he adds weight to the forces of anger, expands their dimensions.
'No one is blind to this crisis you seek our advice on. It doesn't
Need my voice to explain it, my lord. They admit that they all grasp
History's plan for our people, but limit their comments to
     mumbling.   345
Let this man allow freedom of speech, and suppress his own windy
Bluster. I'll speak, though he threatens to bring me death with a
     sword-thrust.
Thanks to his ill-starred guidance and pestilent conduct, we're seeing
So many leading lights snuffed out, and the whole of our city
Settle like ashes, beleaguered by grief,* while *he* puts the Trojan   350
Camp to the test with a boldness that comes when retreat is an option,
Scaring the air with his spears.
                              'So add one more gift* to the bounty
You order sent, or assigned, to the Dardans, just one further present,
Finest of kings, and let no man's violence deter you: your daughter.
Grant her—as father, you should—to a son-in-law not of the
     common   355
Flock, to a groom who has class. Seal peace in a treaty for ever.

But, if our minds and our hearts are so mightily cramped by our terror,
Let us appeal to the man himself,* beg him for permission,
Ask him to yield and sign over his rights to our king and our country.
Why do you, time and again, cast your poor fellow citizens into　　360
Obvious dangers? You don't just start problems. *You* are the problem!
There's no salvation in war. It's peace we all ask of you, Turnus,
Peace guaranteed by the only pledge that defies violation.
I who, you claim, am your foe (it's a lie but contesting it wastes time),
Look! I'm the first to come begging your mercy. Take pity on
　　　　your own　　365
People. Disarm your aggression. Begone! You are beaten. We're routed,
We've seen enough death, we've turned huge fields into desolate
　　　　wastelands.
If, though, it's rumour that stirs you, if, deep in your breast, you're
　　　　conceiving
Oaken strength, if your heart's set on having a palace as dowry,
Dare to display that spirited heart in confronting your foeman.　　370
We common souls, as it is, must be carpets of unburied, unwept
Nobodies strewn on the plains to ensure that a wife with a palace
Benefits Turnus. So, if there's one speck of might in your own will,
One drop of martial blood in your veins, even you must confront him:
He's challenged you!'*　　375
Turnus's violence flared at the tone of this speech, and emerging
First as a groan, it exploded in words full of heartfelt emotion:
'Drances, you're always so free with your wealth of rhetorical figures
Just when our wars demand action. If meetings of elders are summoned,
You arrive first. But you shouldn't be filling the senate with
　　　　verbal　　380
Blasts that escape you when you're not at risk, when the walls with
　　　　their ramparts
Keep the foe out and the ditches have not become moats from the
　　　　bloodshed.
Go on, maintain your tradition of eloquent thundering, Drances,
Charge me with cowardice, you, since your hand has stacked so many
　　　　slaughtered
Trojans in heaps and built notable trophies all over the
　　　　farmlands.　　385
Now you've a chance for assessing the potent man in your manhood's
Vital force. You see, *we* don't need to go far to find foemen.
They're here, standing around these walls, we're completely encircled.

We're off to face them. You're not. Why so? Will the war-god
    within you
Always reside in your windy tongue and your feet when you're
    speeding   390
Out of a battle?
Me "beaten"? No one will justly claim I am beaten, you filthy
Wretch, when he sees Tiber swelling to flood stage with Ilian
Blood, and the whole of Evander's house uprooted and sprawling
Dead like his offshoot—and all the Arcadians stripped of their
    armour.   395
That's not how Bitias and massive Pandarus found me in battle,
Or how the thousand I vanquished and sent down to Tartarus
    that day
Found me when trapped within enemy walls, fenced in by their
    rampart.
"There's no salvation in war"? Sing that as your dirge to the Dardan's
Head, or your own future prospects, you madman. Persist in
    creating   400
Total chaos with tactics of fear, in extolling the strength of a nation
Conquered twice, while, in contrast, demeaning Latinus's forces.
   'Myrmidon leaders (in his script) are starting to tremble at
    Phrygian
Forces! Both Tydeus' son and Larissan Achilles are panicked!
Aufidus' torrents retreat from the waves of the rough Adriatic!   405
His feigned fear at confronting my menacing insults is only
Criminal artistry sculpting a scowl on his figure of terror.
   'Don't worry, you'll never lose your kind of a soul to my good hand.
Keep it yourself, lodged with you inside your contemptible bosom!
   'Now, father, I am returning to you and your major proposals.   410
If you put no further hope *at all* in our military prowess,
If we are so far gone that a single reversal in battle
Means we are dead at the roots and that Fortune has nowhere to
    come back,
Let's sue for peace, let's extend them our hands which are obviously
    useless.
Yet how I wish we could muster a trace of traditional manhood!   415
Blessed in his labours beyond other men, as I see it, transcending
Ordinary souls is the man who meets death to avoid seeing conduct
Just like this, who bites dirt with his teeth only once and for ever.
But, if we have the resources and youths still able of body,

If there are cities to help us in Italy, peoples surviving,   420
And if the glory the Trojans won cost a great deal of bloodshed—
They had their own losses too, for the storm struck all sides with
        equal
Power—then why do we yield in disgrace on the very first threshold?
Why do our limbs start shaking before any bugle has sounded?
Much does improve in a day. Man's labours vary as seasons   425
Change. And since Fortune must visit so many in turn, she will
        sometimes
Make us look stupid and then set us back in a solid position.
We'll get no help from Aetolian Arpi and her Diomedes.
But there's Messapus, Tolumnius too—he fulfils his objective—
Plus captains so many peoples have sent. There'll be no meagre
        glory   430
Following Latium's recruits and those from the Laurentine farmlands.
Then, from the excellent Volscian people, there's also Camilla,
Leading a cavalry column.* Her squads bloom bright in their
        bronze-plate.
    'Still, if the Teucrians demand that I come out alone for a duel,
And we accept, and if *I'm* such an obstacle blocking the
        common   435
Good, I won't then proceed* to think Victory hates and avoids me
So much that I would refuse any act that might bring my dream closer.
I'll face him bravely, though he may be playing the great role,
        Achilles,
Armed with equipment that's equally fine, handcrafted by Vulcan.
I, Turnus, vow* both to you and my father by marriage, Latinus,   440
My life's blood. I stand second to none, in my manhood, to bygone
Heroes.
        'Aeneas "calls *me* out alone?"* I pray that he *will* call!
Drances must not be the one to atone with *his* death, if the angry
Gods have their way, or win honour, if manhood and fame prove
        decisive.'

While they continued contentious internal debates on disputed   445
Issues, Aeneas was moving his camp and his battle formations.
Look! For the news is now spreading all over the palace and causing
Mighty commotion, it's flooding the city with terror in huge waves:
Teucrian troops, battle-ready, along with the Tuscan contingent,
Are, report says, moving down from the Tiber all over the flatlands. 450

Instantly spirits are roused and the hearts of the ordinary people
Bludgeoned. Their wrath is aroused by no trivially light provocation.
Trembling with rage, they want weapons, yes, 'Weapons!' the young
    men are shouting.
Fathers are saddened. They're weeping and grumbling. Disputes,
    disagreements
Everywhere blend into one huge roar that soars to the heavens,   455
Much as when great flocks of birds just happen to settle on highland
Forests, or when, on Padusa's fish-filled waters, the raucous
Swans trumpet calls all across those ever-talkative marshes.
  'Well now,' Turnus observes, seizing opportunity's offer,
'Summon your council, citizens, praise peace, stay where you're
    seated.   460
They're overrunning your realm with their forces.' He said nothing
    further,
Rushed from the meeting, departed the tall palace building in
    seconds.
'You!' he commands. 'Volusus! Tell Volscian units to arm up!
Lead the Rutulians yourself. Get the cavalry ready, Messapus,
Fan them out over the plains. Coras, help him, along with your
    brother.   465
This group must strengthen the city's gates and take charge of the
    towers.
All other units must join me and march out wherever I order.'
  Father Latinus himself now abandons his meeting and big
    plans,   469
Deeply upset by the grim situation, and seeks an adjournment,   470
Constantly blaming himself for not acting alone and inviting
Dardan Aeneas as son-in-law and as his heir to the city.
  Everyone's swarming up to the walls from all over the city.*   468
Some dig out trenches in front of the gates, bring up boulders and
    sharpened
Posts. As the trumpet's raucous blast gives the signal for warfare's
Bloodshed, housewives and children encircle the wall like a
    floral   475
Wreath. All hands are required for the ultimate task of survival.
Further, the queen is conveyed to the heights of the citadel, Pallas'
Temple, escorted by mothers massed in a huge group, and bringing
Gifts for the goddess.* And there at her side is the virgin Lavinia,
Cause of this great disaster, her eyes so becomingly downcast.   480

In go the mothers and fill up the temple with smoke from their incense,
Pouring their voices of sadness forth from within the high sanctum.
'Mistress of weaponry, spirit of warfare, Virgin of Triton,
Break this Phrygian pirate's sword with your own hand and
    sprawl him
Face down onto the soil. Lay him low at the base of our tall gates.'   485

Turnus is now busy arming himself and impatient for battle.
He has already put on his fire-red corslet. Its bronze scales
Bristle around him. He's strapped gold greaves to his calves, though
    his temples
Still lack a helmet. He's buckled his sword to his side and is blazing
Gold as he speeds from the citadel heights. For his spirits are
    prancing;   490
There in his mind's eye, his hopes, he has already conjured his
    foeman.
He's like a stallion, breaking his tethers, escaping his stable,
Finally free. The whole prairie becomes his domain without fences.
Now he can choose between heading for clusters of mares in the
    pastures
And flashing down to the river he knows for a plunge in familiar   495
Waters. He stretches his neck up high and he whinnies with wanton
Pleasure. His mane streams free on his neck, streams over his
    shoulders.
  But, heading Turnus off, Camilla charged up with her Volscian
Troopers. The queen then leaped from her horse right in front of the
    main gate,
All her battalion followed her lead and dismounted with easy   500
Grace, slipping down in one smooth wave from their horses. She
    spoke thus:
'Turnus, a certain self-confidence is, perhaps, earned by one's valour.
I make so bold as to promise I'll charge at Aeneas's mounted
Forces, head off and engage his Etruscan cavalry units
All by myself. Permit *me* to confront the first dangers of battle,   505
You be the infantryman, stand at the walls, mount guard on the city.'
Turnus, his eyes fixed fast on this virgin, a figure of terror,
Answered: 'What adequate thanks can I offer you, Italy's virgin
Glory? How can I repay you? But now, since your wonderful spirit
Soars above everything, share the great labour with me, as a
    partner.   510

Rumour, and scouts we've deployed, are reporting that ruthless Aeneas
Has, and I trust what they say, just dispatched an advance force of
    light-armed
Cavalry. Purpose? To kick up a noise* on the plains while he marches
Over the ridge, through unguarded mountainous heights, on the city.
I plan a bit of war's banditry there. The trail drops through a
    wooded   515
Gorge. I'll be able to seal both exits with infantry units.
Muster your squads, intercept these Etruscan cavalry forces.
With you the fierce Messapus will ride, Latin companies also,
Tibur's squads too. You will gain a conception of leadership's
    challenge.'
This said, he fires up Messapus and allied leaders for battle,   520
Using almost identical words. Then he moves on his foeman.

There is a valley with tortuous twists, ideal for deceptive
Military ruses. Its flanks press in on the defile, encroaching
On both sides, shedding dense, leaf-canopied darkness,* begrudging
Access to those who would pass the constrictive jaws of its
    entrance.   525
High on the crest of the mountain above it—a good place for
    look-outs—
Lurks a plateau, not known to outsiders, affording good cover
Whether you'd want to engage your foes on the right flank, the left
    flank,
Or just stand on the ridge-top and overwhelm them with boulders.
That's where the young man goes; he, knowing the course of the
    pathways,   530
Takes the terrain and the unfair advantage of woods to set ambush.
  Settled, meanwhile, far above, Latona's daughter* was speaking
Grimly to one of her sacred group of virgin attendants,
Opis, swift on her feet. And Diana was uttering these words:
'Off, my dear virgin, to cruel war goes Camilla, who's bearing   535
Weapons about her, which, though they are ours, won't save her.
    No other
Woman is dearer to me; her love for Diana* is no new
Force that's come over her soul in a sudden upsurge of sweetness.
  'Thrown out because he was proud* in his power—and his rule
    was detested—
Metabus, as he was leaving his ancient city, Privernum,   540

Took, as he fled from the midst of the war and its battles, his infant
Daughter to be his companion in exile. He named her Camilla,
After her mother Casmilla, with just a slight shift in the spelling.
Carrying her for himself in a fold of his robe, he was heading
Up the long ridges of lonely woods. Deadly weapons were
    raining   545
All round, swift-darting Volscian troops were now tightening
    their circle.
Then, blocking off his escape, was the Amasenus in full flood,
Foaming and topping its banks after drenching, torrential
    cloudbursts.
He was preparing to swim, but held back, through love of the infant,
Fearful for his dear burden. And then, as he stirred every option   550
Round in his thoughts, this one swirled up, then, unsteadily, settled.
He was a man at war and, by chance, his masterful right hand
Wielded a javelin, massively oaken, knotted and smoke-cured.
To it he bound his offspring, enclosed in a pastoral, cork-bark*
Cover, then strapped her in place at the shaft's exact centre of
    balance.   555
Gauging the arc of her flight in his great hand, he cried to the
    heavens:
"O blessed virgin, Latona's daughter, O Guardian of Woodlands,
I, who am this child's father, now dedicate her to your service.
Yours are her first weapons grasped as she flies from the foe. She's
    your suppliant!
Goddess, accept her, I beg, as she's cast to the treacherous
    breezes!"   560
This said, he draws back his arm, puts torque on his javelin, hurls it
Off on its way. Waters bellow. Camilla flees over the river's
Rage on a screeching spear: an ill omen for future fulfilment.*
Metabus, though, as the troop of his trackers starts pressing more
    closely,
Leaps in the torrent, defeats it, then plucks out his shaft, with the
    virgin   565
Vowed to the Goddess at Crossroads attached, from the turf of the
    meadow.
  'No city took him within its defences, much less into households.
Nor would this wild human creature have made any gesture to ask
    them.
He led a shepherd's life in the lonely world of the mountains,

Raising his daughter here, in the bush, amid overgrown ranges,   570
Suckling her at the dugs of a mare from a wild herd on untamed
Beast's milk, inserting the teat at her tender lips, squeezing gently.
Once this infant could stand on her feet, take her first steps, her
      father
Armed her hands with a sharpened javelin, then from the tiny
Young child's shoulders, suspended a bow and a quiver of arrows.   575
No gold brooch for her hair, no long cape draping her body:
All down her back, from the top of her head, hung the skin of a
      tigress.
Her tender hands whirled spears, like a boy, not the sley of a girl's
      loom.*
Circling her head was a smooth strap hurling bullets of slingshot,
Shooting a white swan down or perhaps some crane from the
      Strymon.   580
Mothers in every Etruscan town so hopelessly wanted
Her as a bride for their sons. But, contented with only Diana,
She remained virgin and fostered eternal love for her weapons
And for her chastity. Oh, how I wish she had not been seduced by
This kind of military action, attempting to harass the Teucrians.   585
She would be dear to me now and be one of my corps of companions.

      'Go then, my nymph, since *her* bitter fate now closes in quickly,
Slip from the dome of the skies and visit the land of the Latins,
Where there's a grim fight in progress. The omens portend a disaster.
Take these weapons and draw from the quiver an arrow of
      vengeance   590
Which will exact for me, from whatever Italian or Trojan
Violates her sacred body with wounds, like payment in bloodshed.
Afterwards, I'll bear the piteous maiden's corpse and her armour
Undespoiled in a hollow cloud to her homeland for burial.'
Now she had spoken. The nymph spiralled down through the sky's
      subtle breezes   595
Thunderously, swathing her body in black like a swirling tornado.

Meanwhile the Trojan force nears the walls in conjunction with
      captains
Leading Etruscan recruits* now trained and turned into equestrian
Units of uniform size. So the open plains are a whinnying
Tumult of stallions prancing and rearing, of heads tugging
      taut reins   600

This way and that. Now the farms have become vast croplands of iron,
Bristling spear-shafts; plains are a blaze of armaments brandished.
Out to oppose them Messapus rides, and the swift-moving Latins.
Coras, too, with his brother, the squad, too, of virgin Camilla;
All are in view on the plain's far side. Right arms are now either   605
Angled back as they couch the extended reach of their lances
Or making javelins quiver. Advancing men and the horses'
Whinnying heighten the heat. Then they halt. Each side has
    moved into
Javelin range. Of a sudden, a shout. Out they burst in a fury,
Yelling their horses to fury, discharging their spears the way
    blizzards   610
Swirl snow round, weaving sky into one dense shrouding of darkness.
   Levelling lances, Tyrrhenus, and, keen as his spearhead, Aconteus*
Instantly target each other and meet in the battle's first combat,
Crashing together with thunderous noise and complete devastation:
Four-footed horses smash shattered chest against chest at a
    gallop.   615
Pitched from his horse and hurled like a lightning bolt or a huge ball
Powered by torqued ropes, Aconteus spatters his life on the breezes.
   Instantly orderly lines become chaos. The Latins, now routed,
Wheel about, shipping their shields to their backs, gallop straight
    for the city.
Trojans pursue; and Asilas takes charge at the head of their
    squadrons.   620
Once near the gates, though, the Latins again raise a rallying war-cry,
Veer away, rein about supple-necked horses to face them. Pursuers
Now are pursued, swept far to the rear, reins free, through their
    own ranks.
Think of the sea with its alternate swirls of advance and withdrawal:
Charging the land, surging over the rocks with the froth of its
    seething   625
Swell, arched high into breakers that wash through the last spit of
    dry sand,
Then rattle rapidly back, spinning stones in a suctioning backwash,
Leaving the coastal sands as a slithering shallow of liquid.
   Twice Tuscans routed Rutulians, driving them back to their
    ramparts;
Twice, hurled back by spears, they glanced round and covered their
    own backs.   630

After they'd charged one another a third time, however, their forces
Totally tangled and intertwined. Each man picked a man out.
That's when the dying screamed, when the weapons and bodies
    went rolling
Deep in the pooling blood, and when, mingled with carnage of
    humans,
Half-dead horses writhed; for the fight grew ever more brutal.   635
Since Orsilochus* feared to face Remulus' prowess in person,
He flung a spear at his horse, striking under the ear where the iron
Tip stuck. Crazed by the wound and the pain beyond bearing, the
    charger
Reared up, chest raised high, thrashing legs, and then bucking
    its rider,
Spinning him over the ground. And Catillus brought down Iollas,   640
Huge in his courage, along with Herminius, huge in his body
And in the strength of his arms. He wore nothing to cover his golden
Unscissored hair, nothing over his shoulders. For wounds didn't
    scare him.
So much man so exposed to a foeman's arms! Driven through him,
Right between his broad arms, there's a quivering spear. And the
    raw pain   645
Doubles him up. Dark blood gushes everywhere, death clad in iron,
Beautiful death* men yearn to attain through wounds in a battle!

Yet, where the slaughter is thickest, the Amazon prances, exposing
One of her flanks for the fight and equipped with a quiver: Camilla.
Sometimes her hand scatters volley on volley of light, pliant
    javelins,   650
Sometimes she grabs for a strong double axe, for her hand never tires.
Arms from Diana, her golden bow, ring out on her shoulders.
If she's repelled and retreats, she draws out her bow, faces backwards,
Firing her flying shafts from behind her. Her favoured companions
Gather about her: the virgins Larina and Tulla, and also,   655
Wielding an axe made of bronze, Tarpeia. Each girl is Italian,
Chosen by godlike Camilla herself to enhance her own image,
First-rate servants in peacetime and war. They're so like the Thracian
Amazons splashing their way across Thermodon's streams in their
    gaudy
Armour, off to the wars, like Hippolyta's troops. Or perhaps we'd
    imagine   660

Penthesilea the daughter of Mars like this while returning
Home in her chariot, her armies of women tumultuously howling
Mighty halloos as they prance with the crescent-moon shields that
    they brandish.
  Who was the first man you killed with your weapons, you fierce
    young woman?
Who was the last? Bodies spilled to the ground and left dying:
    how many?   665
Clytius' son, Euneus, was first. And she hurled a long pine-shaft
Clear through the chest he exposed when he turned round to face
    her. Collapsing,
Vomiting rivers of blood, he kept biting the ground he'd made gory,
Writhing in spasms of death round the very wound that
    destroyed him.
Then add Liris and Pagasus. Liris, bucked when his stallion   670
Stumbled,* was gathering his reins. And while *he* was slipping,
    the other
Came running up, hands stretched to assist, and thus holding no
    weapons.
Both she sent crashing down to their deaths. Then she adds on Amaster,
Hippotas' son, then pursues and shoots, long-range, with her javelins
Tereus,* also Harpalycus, also Demophoön, Chromis: 675
Each shaft torqued and dispatched by this woman's hand brought a
    Phrygian
Man to his death.
               Far off, wearing unfamiliar equipment,
Mounted upon a horse from Apulia, a hunter is riding.
Ornytus cloaked the whole breadth of his ample shoulders with
    rawhide
Stripped from a bullock (he liked a good fight).* For his head,
    the enormous   680
Gaping mouth and the jaws of a white-toothed wolf give protection.
Arming his hands is a peasant's staff with a hooked point. In *his* troop
He is the central figure and stands a whole head above others.
She intercepts him—it's not very hard, for his column's
    retreating—
Runs him through and then adds these words from a heart full of
    hatred: 685
'Did you think you were out hunting game in the woods, you
    Etruscan?*

Your day of doom has arrived. It refutes, with the weapons of women,
Everything you men say. But still, you will carry no trifling
Name to your fathers' ghosts: you died by the spear of Camilla.'
    Next fell Orsilochus, Butes as well, the two largest of Teucrian   690
Fighters. But Butes *did* have his back turned when she drove her
        javelin
In at that slim gleam of neck between corslet and helmet, his shield was
Merely dangling down from his left arm. He was, in fact, seated.
She, in Orsilochus' case, ran away. Though he chased her in
        great big
Circles, she fooled him by making a tighter loop on the inside.   695
Now the pursued was pursuer. He pleaded and begged as she rose up
Higher and hacked through the arms of the man, through his bones,
        with her mighty
Axe-blade, again and again. Gashes flooded his whole face with
        hot brains.
    Terror immobilized Aunus' son when he saw her and met her
Quite unexpectedly. This man, an Apenniniculan warrior,   700
Lied with Liguria's best while fate let him practise deception.
Once he perceived he could not make an exit in any direction
Quickly enough to get out of a fight or avert the queen's onslaught,
He made a shrewd approach with a well-planned ruse, and
        began thus:
'What so distinguishes you from the herd if you, being female,   705
Need a stud racehorse for courage? Away with escape! Trust resources
You have, and fight me on level turf, on foot, and at close-range.
Hitch yourself up! You will soon know who flatulent glory has
        hoodwinked.'
She was enraged at his words and inflamed by the sharp pain they
        brought her.
Handing her horse to a comrade, she faced him on foot with
        equipment   710
Much like his: bare steel, plain shield, though this didn't scare her.
Thinking his ruse had her beaten, the youth didn't falter. He simply
Lifted the reins, wheeled about, and took off at a runaway gallop,
Spurring his horse to full four-legged speed with a raking of iron.
'You're the one fooled, you Ligurian! Runaway pride gets you
        nowhere!   715
Your slick attempts at your folk's traditional arts have been wasted!
Trickery won't bring *you* home safely to Aunus the Cheater!'

These are the young girl's words. Like fire with the feet of a sprinter,
She outraces his horse, grabs the reins, turns to face him,
    attacks him,
Then penalizes her foeman in blood, casually, like a sacred   720
Predator soaring on wings from a cliff-top, extending his pinions,
Stalking a pretty dove,* over her limits, unbridled, in veiling
Cloud; and he catches her, grasps her, and guts her with curving
Talons. Her blood sputters; plumes wrenched out flutter down
    from the heavens.

This was not something the Sower of Life for the gods and for
    humans   725
Failed to observe from his post on the pinnacled heights* of Olympus.
He, life's begetter, aroused the Etruscan Tarchon for battle's
Savagery, pricked up his wrath with no trivially soft provocation.
Tarchon, then, rode round amidst slaughter and columns
    withdrawing,
Spurring his fleeing wings with his varied words, into action,   730
Calling each trooper by name and reviving the battered for battle:
'What fear has touched you, Etruscans, what monstrous failure of
    courage,
You, so determined you'll never feel pain and who'll always be useless?
Some woman drives you around in a daze, beats back your advances!
What are swords *for*? Why do your right hands wield weapons that
    don't work?   735
You are not lacking in fire for night's bellicose tussles and Venus,
Or when the sound of the curving pipes declares dances for Bacchus!
Keep a sharp eye out for fêtes, and for tables loaded with goblets!
That's what you love, that's your cause, when the seer declares
    omens propitious,
When the host's* challenge to you in the woods is well-marbled
    and juicy.'   740
This said, and ready to die, he's now spurring his horse into combat,
Targeting Venulus, rushing at him like a whirlwind. He grabs him
Up off his horse, pulls him over his lap, and with notable violence
Holds his foe tight with his right hand and carries him off at a gallop.
Shouts ring out to the heavens above them, and all of the
    Latins   745
Turn their eyes his way. For Tarchon is fire racing over the flatlands,
Arms and their man* in his grasp. Then he snaps off Venulus' iron

Spearhead and probes for a gap in his armour, a spot where the
    death-wound
Can be delivered. But Venulus fights back against him. He pushes
Tarchon's hand from his throat, escapes force with the strength of
    his own force.   750
Think of an eagle, high in her flight, all tawny, and holding
Intertwined with her feet and clenched in her talons a captured
Serpent. He's wounded but writhing his rippling coils, and he spirals
Upwards, scales prickled out and erect, stretching higher and higher,
Spitting out hisses. But she doesn't stop her attacks on her
    struggling   755
Prey with her curving beak as her wings thrash flight through the
    heavens.
That is how Tarchon carries away from the forces of Tibur, in
    triumph,
His own burden of prey.* Emulating their captain's achievements,
Lydia's sons, the Etruscans, attack.

                         Fate's dues are awaiting
Arruns, who, javelin poised, is stalking* the speedy Camilla   760
Craftily. That's where he has the edge. He's in quest of the easiest
Chance; so wherever the raging girl plunges into the columns,
Arruns moves stealthily in. And he follows her tracks, never speaking.
Where she returns from a victory won, disengaging from battle,
There the young man goes too, like a thief, with a flick of his
    quick reins.   765
This approach, that approach, each angle offered, and circling, circling
Everywhere, constantly, ruthlessly flexing his unerring javelin.
   Chloreus,* devoted to Cybele's mountain (at one time her priest too),
Was, it chanced, spurring his horse to a froth. He stood out at a
    distance,
Gleaming in Phrygian armour. And so did his horse, with its
    bronze mail   770
Threaded with gold on a backing of leather and looking like plumage.
He was resplendent himself in Iberian rust-red and purple,
Fired arrows made in Crete from a horn bow crafted in Lycia.
Gold-plate covered that bow on his shoulders. The seer wore a
    golden
Helmet as well, and he'd gathered the crackling folds of his
    cotton   775
Cloak, crocus-yellow in hue, with the tawny gold of a fastener.

Ornate needlework patterned his tunic and wild Anatolian leggings.
He was the one that the virgin Camilla, in all the fight's struggles,
Had to pursue. Did she want to display, at the gates of a temple,
Some Trojan armour? Or wear it herself, perhaps, when she went
          hunting?   780
She pursued blindly, recklessly all through the columns,
Hot, but with feminine tastes,* in her passion for booty and plunder.
     Arruns had finally captured his moment. Lurking in ambush,
He, at last, brought his javelin to life and he uttered this prayer:
'Greatest of gods and guardian of holy Soracte, Apollo,*   785
We are your chief devotees and heap up, for rites in your honour,
Bonfires of pine-wood. We walk, for we trust in our righteous devotion,
Straight through the blaze, press the soles of our feet on the
          deep-layered embers.
Father Almighty, permit this disgrace to be purged by my weapons.
I wouldn't strip off her gear, make a trophy out of a beaten   790
Virgin.* I don't want spoils. For my further achievements will
          bring me
Praise. So as long as this pestilent demon may fall when she's beaten,
Wounded by me, I'll go back without fame to my ancestors' city.'
     Phoebus heard all of the prayer and his will allowed one part
          accomplished.
As for the other, he tossed it away on the fluttering breezes.   795
That he lay low with a sudden death the distracted Camilla:
Yes, prayer granted. That hills of his homeland should see him returning:
Not granted. Storms swirled these words away to the whims of the south
          *winds.**
Now, as the javelin hurled by his hand screeched noise through the
          breezes,
Volscians all shifted passions to thoughts of the queen and they
          focused   800
Their keen eyes upon her. She herself noticed neither the moving
Air nor the sound, had no sense of the weapon's descent from the
          heavens,
Nothing, until that javelin passed through the nipple she kept bare,
Stuck where aimed; there it drank deep draughts of her virginal
          lifeblood.
Frantically, comrades converge at a run and support their collapsing 805
Mistress. But running away is the most frightened person around
          them:

Arruns. Elation has mingled with fear and he now doesn't even
Dare put his trust in a spear or face up to a virgin in combat.
He's like the one who conceals himself instantly up in the mountain
Heights, to which no path leads, before hostile weapons pursue him: 810
He is the wolf who has just killed the herdsman or champion bullock,
Fully aware of the rash deed done, tail limp now and quivering,
Tucked away under its womb-like paunch,* heading into the forests.
That is how Arruns, in panic, took off to where eyes couldn't
    see him.
Happy just to escape, he hides himself deep in the fighting. 815
    She, though, is dying. She tugs at the weapon. The spear's tip of iron
Close to her ribs, in between her bones, won't budge. The wound's
    too deep.
She's slipping now, as her life's blood seeps; and her eyes are now
    slipping
Coldly to deadness, the colour once bright in her face has all faded.
Breathing her last breath, she speaks a few phrases to one of her
    girlfriends, 820
Acca, the one she most trusted, the only person Camilla
Shared her concerns with at all. She addressed her much in this
    manner:
'Up to this point, I had strength. Now, Acca my sister,* this vicious
Wound makes me weak. The world round me grows blacker with
    shadows.
Hurry away and convey my final instructions to Turnus. 825
He must take *my* place in battle and keep Trojans out of the city.
Now, farewell.' As she spoke she was loosening her grip on her
    horse's
Reins and was slipping down to the ground, unwittingly this time.
Cold now, and slowly detaching self from her whole body, bowing
Slumped neck and head to her captor, Death, she surrendered her
    weapons. 830
Life flutters off on a groan, under protest, down among shadows.*
    That's when an indescribable roar surged up and assaulted
Golden stars. Now Camilla had fallen, the fighting grew meaner.
Massed for attack they charge all at once: the whole Teucrian
    task force,
Tuscan commanders too, and Evander's Arcadian squadrons. 835

Opis, the Crossroad Goddess's guard, up high atop mountains,

Had, for a long time now, been sitting and watching the battle
Unperturbed. When she saw from afar, in the midst of the raging
Warriors' uproar, the grisly death that had punished Camilla,
She gave a groan and she uttered these words full of heartfelt
    emotion: 840
'You've paid a price too high, too cruel a penalty, poor girl,
Just for attempting to harass the Teucrians during a conflict.
It hasn't helped you that you lived a solitary life for Diana
Out in the wilds, that you've worn our arrows strapped to your
    shoulders.
Still, though, your queen hasn't left you with no honours now in
    this final   845
Hour of your death. For your fate won't be nameless, forgotten by
    nations.
Nor will you suffer from rumours that claim nobody avenged you.
He who has given you wounds did violence to your sacred body.*
He'll meet the death he deserves.'
                        There was once a huge burial-chamber,
Built at the foot of a mountain, and mounded with earth, for the
    long-dead   850
King of the Laurentine people, Dercennus. A shrouding of dark-leaved
Holm-oak covered the mound. In a speedy movement this loveliest
Goddess landed here first. From the top of the rise Opis watches
Arruns. She sees him gleaming in arms, swollen vanity rising.
'Why are you turning away to go off?' she enquired. 'Come
    towards me!   855
Come to your death over here, so you'll get the reward for Camilla
You so deserve! And will you perish, too, on the shafts of Diana?'
This said, the hostile Thracian nymph drew a swift, feathered arrow
Out from her gilded quiver. She first stretched the horn bow* to
    straightness,   859
Then drew it far, far back till the two curved heads came together,
Coupled. Then she could touch, hands levelled, her left to the iron
Tip of her shaft while touching her right to her bowstring and nipple.
Suddenly Arruns heard both the screech of the shaft and the whirring
Air at precisely the instant the iron stuck fast in his body.
Comrades who'd been at his side left him gasping his life out
    and groaning   865
Final groans in anonymous flatland dust, then forgot him.
  Opis soars on her wings to the brightness of heaven's Olympus.

First to break ranks is Camilla's light cavalry, after their leader's
Death. In the rout, the Rutulians break, and Atinas is running,
Officers split from their troops, and platoons left without their
        commanders   870
Seek safe ground, wheel horses about, race back to the city.
No one has strength to contain, in a fight, this murderous Teucrian
Onslaught and no one can stand his ground in its path. So they slacken
Bowstrings, reshoulder their bows upon shoulders slumping and
        sagging.
Cloven-hoofed quadruped clatter kicks clumps, quivers plains at a
        gallop.   875
Whirling dust swirls up to the walls with the blackness of smoking
Fires, mothers drum out grief on their breasts and they howl from
        the watchtowers
Wails only women can wail, high as stars in the heavens above them.
    Gates have been opened. The first wave of fugitives bursts within,
        sprinting,
Pressed by a raging mob of the foe, mixed in with their own lines.   880
Failing to flee a pathetic death on their very own thresholds:
On their homeland's walls or in safe rooms within their own houses.
Skewered by spear-thrusts, they gasp out their souls. Some rash
        individuals
Slam the gates shut. They don't dare keep escape within city
        defences
Open to comrades who plead for admittance. A hideous slaughter   885
Follows. The swords that the fugitives rush on are swords of defenders
Blocking their access. While parents watch, eyes streaming with tears,
Some of the men shut out, as the wild stampede presses onwards,
Spin into trench-pits; some, while careering blindly with free-rein,
Smash, like battering-rams, into gates, into reinforced gateposts.   890
Down from the walls, from the heights of the fray (and in rivalry),
        mothers
Hurl spears shakily handled. They *have* seen Camilla, and real
Patriotism inspires them. They hastily improvise oak-hard
Fencing and fire-toughened poles into copies of iron-tipped
        weapons,
Ardent with passion to be the first women to die for their city.   895

Meanwhile the savaging news reaches Turnus, up in the forest,
Flooding his youthful soul. Acca tells of the ruinous rampage:*

Volscian forces entirely destroyed and Camilla now fallen;
Enemy forces advancing aggressively; Mars going their way;
Foe now in total control; panic already spread to the city.   900
He's in a fury now—that's what Jupiter's brute will requires—
So he abandons his hilltop ambush* and leaves the rough forest.
Scarcely had he disappeared beyond view and set foot on the
    flatlands,
When, marching into the now clear pass, up over the ridge-top,
Father Aeneas emerged on the plain from the forested darkness.   905
Both armies now, full force, make a rapid advance on the city.
Distance between them is measured in strides—indeed, not very
    long ones.
Just as Aeneas observed dust rising like smoke from the meadows,
And got a long-range view of the Laurentine columns, so Turnus
Recognized, at the same moment, the savage Aeneas's armour,   910
Heard too the thumping of feet on the march and the snorting
    of horses.
Trojans* would right then have launched an attack and engaged
    in a battle
If Phoebus hadn't been reddening darkly, and bathing exhausted
Stallions in Spanish tides, bringing night back as daylight was ebbing.
So, they establish a camp and build ramparts in front of the city.   915

BOOK TWELVE

T URNUS, observing that setbacks in battle have broken the Latins,
Sees their morale's given out. Eyes show they expect him
    to honour
Now what he promised before. And he burns with unquenchable
    ardour.*
Raising his courage high, like a lion who, though he has serious
Chest wounds dealt him by hunters in Punic ploughlands of
    Carthage,*   5
Finally puts life back in his limbs, exults as he ruffles
Layers of mane on his neck, and fearlessly snaps off the bandit's
Deep-fixed shaft. Blood pours from his mouth, but he's roaring.
Such is the violence now welling up within Turnus. He's blazing.
That's when he speaks to the king in an outburst of seething
    emotions: 10
'Turnus won't cause a delay. He won't offer Aeneas's cowards
Pretexts for changing their words or reneging on terms they've
    regretted.
I'm on my way out to fight. Start the rites, old sire, draft the treaty.
Either I'll send, with my hand, this deserter of Asia, this Dardan,
Down to the Pit of the Damned*—and the Latins can sit down and
    watch while   15
My lone sword is refuting the charge of dishonour we all share;
Or you must share my defeat. And Lavinia must go as this man's wife.'*
   These words elicit a measured response from Latinus's calm soul:*
'You're an outstandingly brave young man. And the higher your valour's
Wildness ascends, the more scruples I need as I keep the scales
    level,   20
Fearing what *you* won't fear, weighing all that might throw off the
    balance.
You rule the realms of your father, Daunus, and numerous townships
Captured by your own hand. You have gold, and goodwill, from
    Latinus.
Other potential brides, quite respectable stock, live in Latium
And in Laurentian lands. Let me speak, free of any evasion,   25
Frankly. This can't be said gently. Attend to my words and
    digest them.

My proper course was *not* to ally my daughter with *any*
Previous suitor. All gods, all men so sang in their omens.
Love for you vanquished me, though. Common bloodlines
        vanquished my judgement.
So did my sad wife's tears. I broke all bonds of agreement,   30
Took back my son-in-law's promised bride, took up arms in
        unrighteous
Conflict. You see what disasters, what wars, have been dogging me,
        Turnus,
Since then, what terrible suffering you, above all, have to shoulder.
Vanquished in great battles twice, we now barely preserve, in one city,
Italy's hopes. And the Tiber is still running warm with our
        lifeblood,   35
Mighty expanses of plain gleam white with the bones of our people.
Why do I keep going back? What madness is warping my reason?*
If, with no Turnus around, I'm prepared to adopt them as allies,
Why don't I, rather, just end all the strife while he's living and healthy?
What will Rutulians, blood of our blood, what will all the Italians   40
Say if I somehow betray you to death (may no ominous outcome
Follow these words!), while you're seeking to veil my daughter as
        your bride?
Think of the risks and the losses of war. Do pity your father,
Well on in years, grief-stricken, and far off now in his native
Ardea.' These words give no relief to the violence of Turnus'   45
Passion. Attempts at a cure just heighten and worsen the fever.
This is what comes from his lips, when his power of speech is
        recovered:
'Sire, for my sake, lay down, I beseech, any care which, for my sake,
You've been deploying. Permit me to wager my death against glory.
We too, father, can fire off a volley; steel isn't, in our hands,   50
Impotent. Blood does flow out of wounds we inflict. When he's
        fleeing
This time, Mother Divine will be too far off to encloud him
Like a veiled woman, so he can hide* in the blankness of shadows.'
  Now though, the queen* who was weeping, distraught by the new
        terms of combat,
Clung, herself ready to die, to her ardent son-in-law, pleading: 55
'Turnus: by tears that I shed, by whatever regard for Amata
Touches your spirit, I beg you. You're my one hope now, this wretched
Old woman's haven. Latinus has status, has power just so long as

You keep it up. Our whole house, as she sways, seeks repose on your
　　bosom.
My one plea: don't hazard your hand in a fight with the Teucrians.　　60
Any disaster that's waiting for you in this duel, awaits me
Also. For, Turnus, when you leave the envious eye of the day's light,
I go. I won't watch, chained, if my son-in-law must be Aeneas.'
　Tears flowed over Lavinia's fevered cheeks as she listened,
Noting her mother's appeal. An intense blush crimsoned her
　　features,　　65
Spreading its radiant warmth through her face with suffusions
　　of fire.
As when the blood of the sea-mollusc violates Indian ivory's
Pureness, as lilies when set among roses* erupt with a rubied
Tinge to their whiteness, so the girl's face gleamed changes of colour.
Love disturbs Turnus' heart. He stares at the girl, full of longing.　　70
Even more ardent for war, he adds a brief word to Amata:
'Don't, please don't, send me off with your tears or such ominous
　　comments,
Mother. I leave for the brutal war-god's contests of battle.
Turnus, besides, isn't free to delay death's hour or defer it.
Idmon, I want you to take this news to the Phrygian tyrant.　　75
These are my words. He won't like them. "At first light tomorrow
When, as she rides on her crimson wheels, Dawn rubies the heavens,
Don't lead Teucrians out to attack the Rutulians. Both sides
Must have a respite. Let's settle this war, you and I, with our own
　　blood.
In this arena Lavinia's hand must be sought and contested." '　　80
　Once he's declared this, he rushes outside, hurries back to his
　　palace,
Asks for his horses, delights as he watches them whinny before him.
These Orithyia had given Pilumnus, a personal honour,
Brighter than snow in their whiteness, and swifter in pace than the
　　breezes.
Charioteers, all attention, surround and fuss over them: cupped
　　hands　　85
Pat upon echoing chests, combs neatly untangle the flowing
Manes. He proceeds now to buckle his corslet of gold and of paler
Brass plates over his shoulders, and then, all in one burst of action,
Tightens the shield-straps, mounts the red plumes on the horns of
　　his helmet,

Readies his sword, which the god of the flames* once forged for
    his father,   90
Daunus. He'd tempered its white-hot steel in the waters of death-cold
Styx. Turnus seizes his sturdy spear—spoil stripped from Auruncan
Actor and propped, until now, up against a huge, centrally sited
Column. He whirls it around with a violence that sets it vibrating:
'Now,' he exclaims, 'now's your moment, good javelin! You've never
    failed me   95
Yet when I've called on your help. It was once mighty Actor who
    wielded
You in his hand, now it's Turnus. Empower me to shatter his body,
And let my strong right hand tear off this Phrygian eunuch's*
Corslet, rip it to shreds, then drag those curls he's been crimping
Hot on an iron, and slicking with myrrh, through the filth and the
    dry dust.'   100
Such is the madness that drives him. All over his ardent and blazing
Face sparks fly, fire flickers in eyes so intense and ferocious.
He's like a bull* who is trumpeting blood-chilling bellows to herald
Battle's commencement, who's trying to concentrate all of his anger
Into his horn-tips, who'll charge at a tree-trunk and lunge at the
    breezes,   105
Paw at and scatter the sand as he works himself up for the conflict.

Meanwhile Aeneas, who's no less a savage in armour his mother
Gave him, is honing his own martial edge, self-lashed in his anger,
Thrilled that the war's being settled on terms that this treaty has
    offered.
He, then, calms both his troops and the fears of his anxious Iulus,   110
Telling them what fate involves. And he bids men provide King
    Latinus
Definite answers and thus give peace legal basis and wording.

Next day's dawn has just now arisen and started to sparkle
Mountain peaks with its rays—it's the moment when horses of Sunlight
Rise from the sea's depths, nostrils breaking the surface and
    breathing   115
Brightness. Rutulians, Teucrians, marking the plain for the conflict
Under the great city's walls, spread outwards, preparing the grassy
Altars and hearths for the gods, who are dear to both sides, in the centre.
Some carry pure water, some fire; all wear ritual garments,

Foreheads are circled with wreaths of medicinal plants that bring
     healing.   120
Italy's sons march forth as a legion; from densely packed gateways
Close-ranked, spear-armed columns deploy. The Etruscan and Trojan
Forces all rush from their camps in a varied array of equipment,
Armed as if marshalled for war, as if Mars* blared summons to vicious
Battle. Their leaders are present, resplendent in gold and in
     purple,   125
Dashing about in the midst of the thousands of troops. Here is
     Mnestheus,
Born of Assaracus' blood, here's Asilas the Brave, there's Messapus,
Tamer of horses, descendant of Neptune. The moment the signal
Sounds, each captain retires to his own designated position;
All plant spears in the ground, prop shields up against them, at
     angles.   130
Then those who don't bear arms: mothers, ordinary people, the feeble
Older men, pour forth in support, take seats upon towers,
Roofs, even stand atop tall city gates. The besieged are besieging.
     Juno is watching too, high up on what's now called the Alban
Mount (though it wasn't named then, wasn't famed and
     prestigious),   135
Gazing down on the plains, upon both the Laurentian and Trojan
Armies in battle formation, and down on Latinus's city.
Out of the blue, she addresses (as one goddess speaks to another)
Turnus' sister,* whose personal realm is the lakes and the babbling
Streams. It's a sacred distinction the king of the bright skies,
     exalted   140
Jupiter, gave her to recompense rape and virginity ravished.
'Nymph, you're the glory of waters and joy supreme to my own soul,
You, as you know, I've preferred to all women of Latium who've ever
Climbed into great-souled Jupiter's joyless bed. Of them only
You would I gladly place somewhere up in the regions of
     heaven.   145
Learn what your pain is to be so you won't think it *my* fault, Juturna.
When it seemed Fortune permitted, when Destiny's Sisters let Latium
Prosper, I granted your city and Turnus my total protection.
Now I observe the youth off to encounter a fate he's no match for.
Destiny's Sisters and violent hatred are nearing their due date.   150
Here is a fight and a treaty whose terms my eyes cannot witness.
You, if you're daring enough to bring critical help to your brother,

Go on. You should. Something better, perhaps, will ensue from your
    anguish.'
  Tears well up in a flood from Juturna's eyes as she listens.
Three times, four times* she lashes blows on her nobly
    handsome   155
Breast. 'This is not', said Saturnian Juno, 'the moment for weeping.
Hurry, and now, if you can, carry off your brother from death's grip—
Or start war on your own. Let the pact they've conceived be aborted!
I'll show you how to be daring!' Exhorting her thus, she departed,
Left her uncertain, her mind grimly wounded, bewildered, and
    frantic.   160

Back to the kings: in the midst of a host of attendants, Latinus
Drives out his four-horse team; and a gold crown circles his temples
Gleaming with two rows of six bright radiant spikes, symbolizing
Ancestry traced to the Sun.* In a tall chariot drawn by a yoked pair
Turnus drives, and he waves in his hand two spears, tipped with
    broad steel   165
Points.
       Then, on this side, Aeneas, the father, the root-stock of Roman
Growth, sets forth from the camp with his star-bright shield and
    celestial
Armour: a vision of fire. At his side is Ascanius, the second
Hope for the greatness of Rome. And a priest, clad in garments of
    sacred
White, has now brought out the young of a bristling boar, and an
    unshorn   170
Hogget, and already set them in place by the fires of the blazing
Altar. The group turns; everyone's gaze now faces the rising
Sun. Then hands sprinkle salted grain, steel blades sever livestock's
Tufts from their foreheads, and chalices pour out ritual libations.
Righteous Aeneas, sword unsheathed, offers this as his prayer: 175
'Now let the Sun be my witness, and you too, Earth of this country,
You, for whose sake I've been able to bear the extent of my labours;
Also the Father Almighty and you, Saturn's daughter, his consort,
Goddess who now, I pray, are better disposed; also famous
Mars, you're the father, at whose divine will all war is conducted.   180
Fountains and rivers, I call upon you, and I call on whatever
Force keeps Sky in its place, powers ruling the blueness of Ocean.
It is agreed that, if victory happens to go to Ausonian

Turnus, the vanquished will leave for Evander's city.* Iulus
Shall quit this land. And, hereafter, Aeneas's people shall never   185
Mount any further attack on this realm, any act of aggression.
If, though, Victory nods her approval to *our* martial efforts,
As, I suspect, she'd prefer, and I pray the gods make it their
     preference
Too, I will not force Italians to live in subjection to Teucrians,*
I'm not in quest of a realm for myself. Both peoples, unconquered,   190
Under identical laws, must submit to a treaty for all time.
I'll donate gods and their rites.* As my father-in-law,* let Latinus
Keep both his forces and solemn command. For it's Teucrians
     who'll build
My city walls; and Lavinia will give this community her name.'
Thus spoke Aeneas. He'd started. Latinus, who followed him,
     spoke thus,   195
Eyes looking skyward and right hand stretched to the stars of the
     heavens:
'By these same powers, Earth, Sea, Stars, I now swear, Aeneas,
And by Latona's twins, by the two-headed nature of Janus,*
By the infernal power of the gods, by the relics that ruthless
Dis enshrines! Let the Father whose thunderbolts sanctify
     treaties   200
Hear this! I'm touching the altars whose flames and whose powers
     shall be witness:
No dark day shall cause the Italians to shatter this treaty's
Peace-terms, regardless of what may befall, no force ever alter
My resolution,* not even a force that could send forth a deluge
Flooding the earth and make heaven collapse into Tartarus'
     dark pit.   205
My will is much like this sceptre's (it chanced, he was holding a sceptre)
'Never again will it generate shoots or give shade with its green leaves
Now it's been hewn from the trunk of its native plant in the forest,
Torn from its mother, its arms and its tresses sundered by iron.
Tree though it once was, a craftsman's hand has encased it in
     handsome   210
Bronze, as a symbol borne by the governing fathers of Latium.'
     Such were their verbal exchanges confirming the treaty, enacted
Under the eyes of the delegates round them. They next take the duly
Consecrate cattle and sever their throats over fire, ripping innards
Out while the beasts are alive, pile loaded plates upon altars.   215

Still, though, for quite some time, this fight had appeared an
   unequal
Match, in Rutulian eyes; they'd been racked by conflicting emotions,
Deepened now, as they saw, up closer, the physical contrast.
Turnus's silence, his quiet and reverent approach to the altar,
Pleading demeanour and downcast eyes, cheeks drained of their
   colour,   220
Body so young and so pale—all this reinforced their impression.
Once she's observed him becoming more widely the topic of comment,
Seen that morale in the ranks is declining, Juturna, his sister,
Moves to the central formation and feigns the appearance of Camers.*
He, born of old family blood, with a father distinguished for
   valour.   225
Was, when at arms, quite a warrior himself: both fierce and aggressive.
That's why her shrewd sense of tactics sends *her* to the central
   formation.
Scattering gossip around her like mixtures of seed, she harangues
   them:
'Aren't you ashamed, you Rutulian men, to be hurling a single
Soul out to fight for an army like ours? Don't we match them in
   numbers,   230
Match them in strength? Look around! All the Trojans and all the
   Arcadians,
All of Etruria's "agents of fate" full of hatred for Turnus,
Here they are! Fight one on one, and we've hardly enough foes to duel!
He'll soar up, on the rumours of fame, to the gods at whose altars
He's now pledging his life; he'll live on our lips, in our legends.   235
We, now lounging about in the fields, will have lost our own fathers'
Land. We'll be forced to obey the commands of our arrogant masters.'
   Words like these fire young men's minds to a new resolution.
Murmuring writhes through the army's ranks in a constant crescendo.
Even Laurentians are changing their minds, yes, even the Latins.   240
Those who'd been hoping to gain, for themselves, some respite
   from battle,
And, for the state, some security, now want a fight, pray the treaty
Won't work out; and Turnus's lot stirs pity; it's unjust.
   One further, and more persuasive, touch was applied, when Juturna
Staged a display up high in the heavens. No omen has ever   245
Been more effective in baffling and cheating the minds of Italians.*
In flies Jupiter's eagle of gold through sun-reddened clear skies,

Scattering shorebirds away and disrupting the ranks of the raucous
Flying columns. He suddenly swoops straight down to the water,
Wickedly snatching a gorgeous swan in the grip of his talons.   250
That pricked Italian minds to attention. And then all the shorebirds,
Screeching and wheeling about in their flight (seeing it was amazing),
Darkened the bright sky with plumes, formed up like a black veil of
      storm clouds,
Chased their assailant through breezes until, foreclosed by their sheer
      force,
Wilting too from sustaining his load, the bird loosened his talons,   255
Dropping his prey to the stream and withdrawing deep in a fogbank.
Shouting Rutulians, hands outstretched, greet this as an omen
Auguring well for a fight; and Tolumnius first—he's an augur—
Cries: 'This is it! This is just what I've prayed for so often! I witness
Gods' presence and I acknowledge their portents. I'll lead you, I'll
      lead you!   260
Take up arms, poor folk, though this ruthless intruder's aggression
Scares you as if you were strengthless birds, and the power of his
      violence
Devastates you and your coasts. He's the one who'll be fleeing and
      sailing
Deep into far-off seas. Close ranks in defence of your chosen
King, the one *he* has deposed! Fight on, single-hearted, in battle!'   265
      Once he had spoken, he ran to the front and he span off a javelin
Straight at the foe and the horn-tough wood, pitched perfectly,
      sang shrill,
Piercing the air. At the same, very same time, a huge roar erupted.
Orderly ranks became rioting mobs, hearts seething with fury.
On flies the javelin. Right in its path, as it chanced, there were
      standing   270
Nine very beautiful forms, brothers all, who were born of a single
Faithful Etruscan bride to Gylippus, a man from Arcadia.
Close to the waist, where the harness's stitched hem chafes on the
      stomach,
Just where the pin of the belt-buckle bites both side-straps together,
That's where it struck one of these, an outstandingly handsome
      and brightly   275
Armoured youth, through the ribs, spilling him and his life on the
      gold sand.
Oh, what an army his brothers become in the grief that sets courage

Blazing within them, as some draw swords, others grab up their hurling
Spears in a wild, blind onslaught. Responding, Laurentian forces
Counterattack. Then it's Agyllines, Trojans, and gaudily
　　armoured　　　　　　　　　　　　　　　　　　　　　　　　　　280
Squads of Arcadians, wave after wave, thick and fast into battle.
One single passion held all in its grip: to let swords make decisions.
Altars, they just tear down as a whirling tempest of weapons
Fans out over the skies, and the rain lashing down is of iron;
Chalices, hearths become plunder; Latinus himself is removing　　285
Figures of gods roughed up in defeat as the treaties are mangled.
Others hitch horses to chariots, or settle themselves, in a single
Leap, upon horseback and, swords unsheathed, plunge into the action.
　　Eager to tear up the treaty, Messapus is mounted, and charging
Tuscan Aulestes, a king—and, to show it, he wears his regalia.　　290
Scared by the horse, his opponent retreats; the poor wretch
　　tumbles over
Altars behind him, his shoulders and head hit the ground. But
　　Messapus,
Hot in pursuit, looms over him and, as he's desperately pleading,
Deals him, from high up on horseback, a mortal thrust with his
　　long lance
Thick as a rafter. He then, like the fighters in public arenas,　　295
Cries out: 'He's bought it! The gods have been granted a nobler
　　victim!'
Up run Italians; they're starting to strip off his armour from still warm
Limbs. Corynaeus* confronts them and grabs, from an altar, a
　　smouldering
Branch which he thrusts in the face of Ebusus, who's dashing
　　towards him,
Poised to deliver a blow, and his bush-thick beard is ignited,　　300
Flares up, exuding a smouldering stench. Corynaeus advances,
Seizing his frantic foe's hair, with his left knee jamming his body,
Flexing him, bending him down to the ground. Then he gives him
　　the death-blow:
Rigid steel through the flank.
　　　　　　　　　　　　　Here's Podalirius,* chasing
Alsus, a shepherd, who's racing about through the thick of the
　　battle's　　　　　　　　　　　　　　　　　　　　　　　　　305
Front ranks. Sword unsheathed, he's poised for a strike, when the other
Swings back his axe, splits open his lax foe's forehead and jawbone,

Irrigates flanges of armour with spattered blood. And upon him
Rigid repose steals, binding his eyes in a prison of iron
Slumber, their brightness jailed in eternity's night-time of
    blindness.   310
   Righteous Aeneas, his helmet torn from his head, and his right hand
Held up high, but unarmed, keeps shouting appeals to his forces:
'What are you rushing to do?* Why this sudden explosion of discord?
Stifle your anger. A treaty's already been forged, every legal
Detail fixed. So permit me to honour its terms, which endow me,   315
Only *me*, with the right to engage. Don't panic. My hand will
Forge guarantees for this treaty whose terms swear Turnus is *my* due!'
While he is speaking—in fact, well before has finished these
    statements—
See! In screeches an arrow on fletched wings, aimed at the hero.
Whose hand propelled it, what spiral of energy drove it, or
    whether   320
Chance or a god brought such great acclaim to Rutulians isn't
Clear. All credit for this famous deed's been suppressed by tradition;*
No one has boasted that he was the hero who wounded Aeneas.
   Turnus, on seeing Aeneas withdraw from the battle and Trojan
Leaders in panic, felt buoyed by an upsurge of hope, renewed
    ardour.   325
Calling for horses and weapons, he leaped, in a flash, to his chariot,
Grasping the reins in a fever of pride and dispatched, at a gallop,
Many a brave man's body to death, ran down and left dying
Many another while crushing their ranks with his wheels and his horses'
Hoofs, or with spear after spear that he hurls as they scatter
    before him.   330
Now, like Mars unleashing wars in the land of the ice-cold
Hebrus, a vision of blood, his shield vibrating like thunder,
Setting his frenzied stallions loose at a wild gallop over
Sprawling flatlands, faster than southerlies, faster than zephyrs,
Wringing groans from the distant borders of Thrace with their
    hoofbeats,   335
Circled by faces of Dark Terror, Anger, and Ambush, the god's own
Retinue, so too Turnus ferociously lashes his horses,
Steaming with sweat, to the hub of the battle and crushes his grimly
Butchered foe. For the tearing hoofs spurt blood like a morning
Dew on the ground, as the heel-hammered gore turns sand into
    marshland.   340

Sthenelus,* Thamyrus, Pholus: they all are consigned to the slaughter.

Hand-to-hand combat accounts for the last two; the first's hit at
　　long-range.

Long-range shots kill Imbrasus's sons, both Glaucus* and Lades.

Imbrasus armed them himself back in Lycia with matching
　　equipment,

Trained them in combat, in riding a horse even faster than winds
　　blow.   345

　　Now, from another direction, Eumedes, distinguished in warfare,

Drifts to the heart of the battle. He's son of the legendary Dolon*

And, though he's named for his grandfather, seems, both in spirit
　　and prowess,

More like his father who, once in the past, dared ask for Achilles'

Chariot as payment for entering into the Greek camp and spying.   350

Tydeus' son, Diomedes, rewarded his daring with different

Payment, however. He no longer dreams of Achilles' fine horses.

　　Turnus, who's spotted Eumedes now, on the plain, in the distance,

Aims a light javelin off in pursuit through the lengthy and empty

Space in between, and then reins in his pair, leaps down from his
　　chariot,   355

Towering above his supine and half-dead foe. With his foot set

Firm on the man's neck, he wrestles the sword from the grip of his
　　right hand,

Plunges its glittering blade down deep in his throat till it's blood-soaked.

'Here's how you'll lie,' he exclaims, 'to survey and to measure
　　Hesperia's

Lands you attempted to conquer! And here's my repayment for
　　people   360

Daring to test me with steel. Here's the boundary wall they
　　establish.'

Then, with a spear-cast, he sends him Asbytes to be his companion,

Chloreus, Sybaris too, and Dares,* Thersilochus also,

Also Thymoetes who's tossed from the neck of his horse as it's
　　bucking.

　　Just as the blast of the Thracian northerlies roars on Aegean   365

Depths, bringing wave upon wave in their wake, crashing onto the
　　beaches,

And, with the sweep of their winds, sends clouds scudding over the
　　heavens,

So, along Turnus' murderous path, there are columns collapsing,

Battle-lines routed and running. His energy's impetus drives him;
Breezes aroused by his chariot's speed ripple waves through his
    streaming   370
Plumes.
       Then Phegeus,* who couldn't be passive before this persistent
Raging attack, threw himself at the chariot, twisted the racing
Horses' mouths, set frothing by bits, to the side. While he hangs there,
Dragged by the pair, he's exposed at the flank; and a lance with its
    broad shaft
Chases him, pierces the double plates of his corslet and strikes
    home,   375
Merely gaining a taste of his blood, though. The wound's superficial.
He's even tugging his shield to the front and confronting his foeman,
Starting to mount an attack and relying on help from his unsheathed
Sword when the wheel, speeding onwards, the force of the axle in
    motion,
Hurls him aside, pitched down to the ground. Now Turnus is
    on him,   380
Lashes his sword through the gap between helmet and rim of the
    breastplate,
Lops off his head, leaving him on the sand a truncated cadaver.

Now, while the conquering Turnus is dealing out death on the
    flatlands,
Mnestheus and faithful Achates are helping the blood-soaked Aeneas
Back to the camp, with Ascanius right at their sides. He is
    crutching   385
Each second, laboured, step on the lengthy shaft of his war-spear.
Once there, he rages and tugs at the snapped-off head of the arrow,
Telling his men to go straight for the shortest path to recovery:
Slash through the wound with a broad steel blade, tear open the hidden
Site where the arrowhead's deeply lodged, get him back to the
    battle.   390
Now on the scene is Iapyx.* He's Iasus' son and, of all men,
Dearest to Phoebus Apollo, who once, in love's shackles of frenzy,
Happily gave him the choice of his arts as gifts to select from:
Augury, skill with the lyre or with archery's swift-flying arrows.
He, to put off the impending death of his invalid father,   395
Chose, rather, knowledge of herbs and their powers: the practice
    of medicine;

Chose a career without public acclaim in the arts that are silent.
Still on his feet, propped up on his massive spear, stood Aeneas,
Bitterly cursing, encircled by numerous troops, with Iulus
Weeping. His tears left Aeneas unmoved. Now the ageing Iapyx,   400
Robes pinned back and sleeves rolled up in the medical manner,
Fusses about with a doctorly hand and applies, in abundance,
Phoebus' powerful herbs. But it's futile. Extracting the iron,
Either by hand or by using forceps, is equally futile.
No touch of Fortune is guiding his probes, and his teacher,
     Apollo,   405
Gives no assistance. All over the plain, in ferocious crescendo,
Terror is spreading, catastrophe's nearing. They watch while the
     heavens
Thicken with dust as the cavalry charges, as spears and as arrows
Rain on the midst of the camp. Grim cries from the youths ring to
     heaven
While they are fighting, and while, under Mars' harsh rules, they
     are dying.   410
   Much shaken now by her son's undeserved pain, Venus the Mother,*
Harvests some dittany shoots with their fuzzy leaves and their pinkish
Flowers from atop Mount Ida in Crete; it's a curative herbal
Plant that the wild goats know very well to consume when a hunter's
Swift-flying arrow is lodged in their backs. This herb is what
     Venus,   415
Shrouded from sight in the darkness of cloud, now brings for his
     treatment,
Mixing her formula secretly into the clear river water
Already poured* in a clean, bright bowl—with a dash of ambrosial
Extract and curative powers of pure panacea's aroma.
This is the lotion with which, unknowingly, agèd Iapyx   420
Washes the wound. All pain, in an instant, is gone from the body,
Bleeding is stanched deep down in the wound, and, without any
     pressure,
Out comes the arrow, which follows the hand of the surgeon, and
     back comes
All of Aeneas's strength, now restored to its earlier level.
'Hurry, bring arms for the man!' cries Iapyx. 'Don't stand
     around idle!'   425
He, thus, is first to set courage ablaze for a fight with the foemen.
'Human resources and technical skill didn't come to the rescue

Here, and it's not my hand that restores you, Aeneas. Some greater
Power, some god, is at work, and returns you for greater achievements.'
Greedy for battle, he's already buckled his legs into golden   430
Greaves. How he hates the delays! And he's flashing his javelin.
After his shield's set in place at his flank and his corslet's backstraps
Fastened, he gives his Ascanius an armoured embrace and perfunctory
Kisses squeezed through his helmet's visor, then offers these
    comments:
'Learn from me, lad, what courage involves and the meaning of
    effort.   435
Others can teach you of Fortune. My sword-hand will, in this conflict,
Keep you safe and will usher you into a world of great prizes.
You, who will soon reach adulthood, mature, must be sure to
    remember
This moment, and as your mind reflects upon models your family
Set, let your father Aeneas and Hector your uncle inspire you!'   440
    This said, the mighty man went out, without help, through the
        gateway,
Waving a monstrous spear in his hand. And, along with him, Antheus,
Mnestheus too, the entire massed force in a compact formation
Poured from the camp, now deserted. The whole plain billows with
    blinding
Dust and the pounding of feet drums earth to a shudder of terror.   445

Turnus, from high on a facing mound had observed them approaching;
So had Ausonian forces. And deep through their bones ran an icy
Shudder. Juturna was first to detect and to recognize this sound,
Well before all other Latins. It frightened her. So she retreated.
Over the open country Aeneas now hurried his dim, dark   450
Columns. For he swept on like a storm in the hurricane season
Out from the sea onto land. The poor farmers, who've sensed its arrival
Well in advance, are in panic. Its torrents will flatten the grain-crops,
Uproot trees, overwhelming their world with complete devastation.
Winds are the swift-moving heralds that roar its advance to the
    coastline.   455
That's how the leader from coastal Rhoeteum drives forward his frontal
Strike at the foe, each unit densely massed in converging
Wedges.
        A blow of Thymbraeus' sword kills weighty Osiris,*
Mnestheus slaughters Arcetius, Epulo falls to Achates,

Ufens to Gyas. The augur Tolumnius*—*he'd* hurled the first
    spear, 460
Straight at the foe—is himself now a victim of war. And an uproar
Surges to heaven. It's now the Rutulians' turn to be routed,
Showing their backs amid billows of dust as they flee across
    farmlands.
Slaughtering fugitives, though, doesn't seem worthwhile to Aeneas.
He doesn't even pursue those who'd fight him, on foot or on
    horseback, 465
Or those with javelins poised. His eyes, bright lights in the
    dense dark,
Track only one quarry, Turnus, the one man he's seeking to challenge.
  Fear that he'll do so is plaguing Juturna, who thinks like a warrior.
Therefore she flings out Metiscus* who's holding the reins, since
    he's Turnus'
Charioteer. Once he's slipped from the pole, she abandons him
    far back, 470
Flickers the rippling reins in her hands. She becomes his replacement,
Takes all his features, the body, the voice, and the arms of Metiscus.
Think of a black shape flitting through vast estates of a wealthy
Master: a swallow,* who sweeps through his towering halls on her
    feathers
Gleaning the crumbs and the fragments of food for her garrulous
    nestlings, 475
Noisily threading the porticoes' emptiness, circling the still pools'
Waters. Juturna, like her, now careers through the thick of the
    foemen,
Flying about the whole scene on her horses, her chariot swooping,
Giving a glimpse, here and there, of her brother in triumph, permitting
No battle-contact, but winging away, swallowed up in the
    distance. 480
  Undeterred, though, Aeneas unravels the intertwined circles,
Tracking the man to confront him, and calling him loudly through
    columns
Here, columns there. Yet each time his eyes shoot a glance at his
    foeman,
Each time he tries to outrace the retreat of those wing-footed horses,
Off, with a twist of the chariot reins, and away goes Juturna. 485
What can he do? His mind helplessly drifts upon tides that keep
    changing.

And there are different concerns which arise to distract his attention.
Slyly advancing upon him, Messapus selects one of two tough
Spears, iron-tipped, that he happens to have in his left hand, and taking
Deadly aim, spins a lethal shot at Aeneas. The latter   490
Stops still, draws himself fully within the enclosing, protective
Wall of his shield, sinks down upon one knee. The javelin, flung hard,
Still clips the crest of his helmet and shears off the top of his plumage.
That's when his anger explodes. He grasps that the horses have
      veered off:
Turnus' chariot has vanished while he's been the victim of
      ambush.   495
After invoking as witness both Jupiter and the mistreated
Pact many times, he now finally enters the thick of the fighting,
Fearsome, with Mars on his side, wreaking indiscriminate, savage
Slaughter. He throws off all further restraint and unleashes his anger.

Could any god now craft me in verse this suffering's full toll,   500
Detail the carnage, the deaths among princes whom one moment
      Turnus,
Then, at the next, Troy's hero pursues all over the landscape?
Jupiter, was it your will that these peoples who'd one day be living
Bonded for ever in peace should collide in such terrible conflict?
Now it's Aeneas who kills the Rutulian Sucro,* who hardly   505
Halted his stride, though this duel did cause the first break in the
      Teucrian
Onslaught. He thrusts raw steel into Sucro's side, through the ribcage
Shielding the heart, striking home at a point where death is immediate.
Turnus, advancing on foot, strikes Amycus, thrown by his stallion,
Also his brother, Diores:* the one who attacks gets a long spear's   510
Point, and the other a sword's. He decapitates both, and attaches
Both men's heads, still gushing with blood, to his chariot-siding.
Talos and Tanaïs, and, making three in a single encounter,
Valiant Cethegus,* are killed by Aeneas; add gloomy Onites—
Echion's Thebes resonates in the name of this son of Peridia.   515
      Turnus slew brothers who hailed from the Lycian land that Apollo
Loves, and Menoetes,* a young man whose loathing of war didn't
      help him.
He, an Arcadian, practised his art round the waters of Lerna,
Teeming with fish. He was poor, far removed from the halls of the
      mighty,

Child of a father who scattered his seed upon soil he had rented.   520
   Just like burn-off fires that are launched from opposing directions
Into a tinder-dry forest and crackling thickets of laurel,
Or, like foaming torrents that thunder from high in the mountains
Down on their rapid, precipitous course to the sea's level surface,
Each overwhelming all life in its path, so Aeneas and Turnus   525
Wreak devastation together through battle. And, deep in their spirits,
Anger's rip-tides seethe, hearts, void of all concept of yielding,
Burst. All energy drives into massive explosions of slaughter.
Seizing a crag, a huge rock that he spins like a whirlwind, Aeneas
Topples Murranus and empties him onto the ground while he's
      boasting   530
Loudly of ancestors, ancient family names, and unbroken
Lineage traced through Latium's kings. Now he's under the rein-straps,
Under the yoke, rolled over by wheels, thrashed down by the frantic
Hoofbeat of horses who do not remember that he is their master.
Turnus now clashes with Hyllus, who's charging and snarling with
      monstrous   535
Fury, and powers a spear at the gold that encases his temples.
On through his helmet it passes, to lodge in his brain. Nor were you
      saved,
Cretheus, bravest of Greeks, by your prowess in weapons, from Turnus.
Nor did his gods save Cupencus, their priest, from his doom when
      Aeneas
Came at him. For, though he met the attack face on, the poor
      fellow   540
Found that his bronze-clad shield couldn't dampen the impact of iron.
Aeolus, your death too is observed by the Laurentine flatlands,
Watched as you sprawl on your back, spreadeagled. You're dying,
You, the man Argive troops couldn't vanquish in battle formation,
Even Achilles himself—though he toppled the kingdom of
      Priam.   545
Here your race ends. You die. You'd once lived high beneath Ida,
High in Lyrnesus you'd lived; but your tomb's in Laurentian farmland.
   All battle units are now involved in the fight, all the Latins,
All the Dardanians. Mnestheus, along with ferocious Serestus,
Also the tamer of horses, Messapus, and valiant Asilas,   550
Troops of Etruscans, Arcadian squadrons dispatched by Evander.
Each man strives for himself to exert all the force he can manage:
Tense, not a pause, not a break in the vast devastation of conflict.

Now's when his mother, supreme in her beauty, inspired in Aeneas
Thoughts of approaching the walls, of making the city his army's   555
Target, surprising the Latins with threats of immediate disaster.
While hot on Turnus' tracks through the different contingents, Aeneas
Kept realigning his view of the fight. He observed how the city
Rested securely, unarmed and unharmed, in the havoc of warfare.
Instantly, visions of fighting a larger-scale battle are kindled.   560
So, he calls Mnestheus, Sergestus, and valiant Serestus, his captains,
Then he positions himself on a hill. All around, other Teucrian
Legions assemble in mass without grounding their weapons or downing
Shields. And he speaks in their midst from atop the high mound
        where he's standing:
'These are my orders. I want no delays. Here Jupiter stands firm.   565
No one must slacken his pace because plans have been shifted abruptly.
That city, cause of the war, very heart of Latinus's kingdom,
This day, unless they concede to defeat, to our yoke, to obedience,
I will destroy, and I'll level its heights to the ground and to ashes.
Am I supposed just to wait till it takes Turnus' fancy to bother   570
Battling me, till he wants a rematch, though defeated the first time?
Citizens, here is the nub, here's the heart of this criminal warfare.
Rush out the torches. Use flames to demand that this treaty be
        honoured.'
   Once he has finished, they all, in a keen and competitive spirit,
Close ranks, form in a wedge, charge straight at the walls of the
        city.   575
Ladders appear, as from nowhere; there's suddenly fire, there are
        torches.
Some, fanning out, charge gates, overwhelming the front-line defenders,
Others fire javelin volleys so dense that they block out the sunlight.
There, in the first wave, and pointing his sword at the ramparts, Aeneas
Shouts out loud, that Latinus has broken agreements, and
        summons   580
Gods to bear witness that he, yet again, has been forced into battle:
'Twice now Italians have fought us, this treaty's the second they've
        broken.'
Discord erupts among various terrified citizen factions:
Some want the city unbarred, want to open the gates to the Dardans,
Even try dragging their monarch himself out onto the ramparts.   585
Others are seizing their weapons and rushing to man the defences,
So, when a shepherd has tracked down bees in the porous, volcanic

Rock where they hide and has filled its chambers with billows of acrid
Smoke, those insects, afraid for the hive, zoom round through
      their waxen
Fortress and sharpen the sting of their wrath with a furious
      buzzing.   590
Over the rooftops the dark stench rolls, from inside the surrounding
Stones muffled rumbles resound, smoke spills upon air's hollow breezes.
That's how misfortune's befalling the Latins, already exhausted,
Shaking the whole city, down to its very foundations, with anguish.

When, looking out from the palace, the queen* sees the enemy
      coming,   595
Walls being scaled, flames leaping from rooftop to rooftop, but nowhere
Any Rutulian troops to oppose them, nor any of Turnus's units,
She, hopes unfulfilled, believes Turnus has perished in combat,
And, her mind shattered by grief's sudden upsurge of horror,
Screams out that hers is the blame, she's the cause, she's the source
      of disaster,   600
Mindlessly raving out torrents of words in the madness of sorrow,
Rending her purple regalia with hands that will now end her life's span:
She's slung a noose for a hideous death from a beam in the ceiling.
    Once this catastrophe's known to the poor, sad women of Latium
First to react is Lavinia, whose hand rips her own golden tresses,   605
Tears at her rose-coloured cheeks. Then, around her, the rest of the
      household
Riots in grief, the broad palace resounds with their throbbed
      lamentations.
Rumour, fulfilment's foe, makes her death common news through
      the city.
Minds are depressed and Latinus, his garments in shreds, simply
      wanders,
Stunned into shock by the death of his wife and collapse of his city,   610
Fouling his whiteness of hair with the filth of the dust that he sprinkles.
Constantly blaming himself because, earlier, he'd not accepted
*Dardan Aeneas as son-in-law while he could still choose alliance.**
    Meanwhile, warring away at the farthest rim of the flatlands,
Turnus is chasing a handful of stragglers, with no special
      interest   615
Now; he delights less and less in successes his horsemanship garners.
Winds waft out to him here sounds heard from a city in chaos,

Drumming, alerting his ears to the shouts energized by a terror
Eyes can't see, to an uproar that offers no cause for rejoicing.
'Oh, dear god, what's causing such riots of grief on the
            ramparts?   620
Why is the sound of the shouting so clear when the city's so far off?'
That's what he says as he hauls on the reins, stopping short in a panic.
'Keep going this way,' his sister disputes. It is she who's been guiding
Chariot, horses, and reins in the form of his driver, Metiscus,
'Turnus, let's follow these people from Troy in the very
            direction   625
Victory opened a path for us first. There are others', she added,
'Able enough with their hands to conduct a defence of the buildings.
Just as Aeneas attacks the Italians and wrecks them in battle,
So we too should dispense brute death with our hands among
            Teucrians.
You'll kill as many as he, and you'll match him in honours from
            battle.'   630
Turnus replied:
'Sister, I've long known *just* who you are, from the time of the artful
Shambles you made of the treaty, since you first entered the battle.
You don't fool me now, goddess, either. But who has dispatched you
Down from Olympus? Who wished you to suffer such terrible
            hardships?   635
Was it so you'd have to witness your poor brother's cruel extinction?
What can I do? Does some twist in my fortunes now promise me safety?
No man alive's any dearer to me than Murranus. I saw him
Die right in front of my eyes as he called upon me: a prodigious
Man overwhelmed in defeat by a wound that was no less
            prodigious.   640
Ufens died so he'd not lose his sense of fulfilment by watching
My disgrace. Both his armour and corpse have been seized by the
            Teucrians.
Must I now watch as their homes are destroyed? That's my single
            dishonour
Still unachieved. Must my hand not refute the words spoken by
            Drances?
Well, shall I run? Will this land see Turnus's back as he's fleeing?   645
Is dying really so bad? Oh, souls of the dead, I implore you,
Show me some kindness since powers above now *will* my destruction.
Let my soul, unacquainted with charges of cowardice, go down

Pure to your world. Let me never disgrace my ancestral distinction.'
   Just as he finishes, look, here's Saces, struck by an arrow   650
Full in the face, flying up through the thick of the foe on a
    foam-flecked
Steed, calling Turnus's name and beseeching him, still at a gallop:
'Turnus, you're our last hope of salvation. So pity your people.
Thunderbolts blaze from Aeneas's arms, and he brazenly threatens
Total destruction and ruin for Italy's highest defences.   655
Firebrands are leaping to roofs as I speak. It's to you all the Latins
Look with their faces, their eyes. Our ruler, Latinus, just mumbles:
"Possible sons-in-law, which way to lean in the matter of treaties."
She, though, the queen who showed *you* real loyalty, treated you fairly,
Perished by her own hand, fled the brightness of life in her
    terror.   660
Only Messapus in front of the gates and the wily Atinas
Still whet the blades of our troops. And around them on each side,
    a phalanx
Stands massed close. While they're trapped in a cropfield of steel
    with its spiky
Blades unsheathed, you're galloping pastures unplanted and fallow.'
   Shocked stock-still and confused* by the mixture of images
    conjured,   665
Turnus just stood there in silence and stared. In this one heart,
    a maelstrom
Seethed: huge eddies of shame, cross-currents of grief and of
    madness,
Love and courageous awareness of self set boiling by fury.
Then his mind shook off the shadows, its daylight restored.
    He refocused
Eyesight's blazing orbs on the walls, and disturbed by his anguish,   670
Gazed, past the spin of his wheels, at the great city back there,
    behind him.
Look, though: a rolling billow of flames is spiralling skywards,
Up and up, storey by storey, consuming a tower, the tower
He had constructed himself of well-joinered timber, and mounted
Over a platform on wheels and equipped with some high-level
    gangplanks.   675
'Fate has now taken decisive command, sister. Stop your delaying.
Where god, where cruel Fortune is calling us, there let us follow.
I fight Aeneas! It's settled. It's settled: I suffer whatever
Anguish accompanies death! You will never again see me, sister,

So disgraced. Let me rage out my rage while there's still time,
    I beg you.'   680
Out of his chariot onto the fields he leaped when he'd spoken.
On through the foe, through the weapons he crashed. He abandoned
    his grieving
Sister and raced till he burst his way to the heart of the battle.
That's how a mountaintop boulder comes crashing unstoppably
    downwards,
Wrenched by the wind from its bedrock, or washed far away by
    torrential   685
Floods, or perhaps just sapped by the passage of years beyond number.
Down through a chasm its energy drives it, this murderous mountain
Mass, as it bounces in joy on the ground, as it rolls away woodlands,
Cattle, and men. So Turnus too crashes on through the scattering
Ranks, to the city's walls, where the blood pools deepest on
    dampened   690
Earth, to where Air screams loud with the whirring of javelins
    volleyed.
    Once there, he raises his hand and he issues this loud proclamation:
'Spare yourselves now, my Rutulians! Hold back your javelins, Latins!
Anything Fortune may have in her plans is for *me*. It is fairer
I should atone for the treaty alone and decide it in combat.'   695
Everyone then pulls back, leaving him now exposed in the open.
    Father Aeneas, on hearing the mention of Turnus, abandons
Siege of the ramparts, abandons assaults on the citadel's fortress,
Hurries all obstacles out of the way, ends all operations.
Fearsome thunder rings from his arms as he leaps up, exultant,   700
Massive as Athos or massive as Eryx or massive as Father
Apenninus himself when he rattles his shimmering oak trees,
Raising his snow-capped head to the heavens in utter elation.
Now the Rutulians struggle for views, as do Trojans, Italians—
All who'd been holding the battlement's heights, all those who'd
    been pounding   705
Battering-rams at the base of the walls, shifting gaze and attention,
Stripping their shoulders of armour. Latinus himself is astonished,
Speechless that two huge men, born in different parts of the circling
Globe should be coming together and settling issues with iron.
    Now that the field has been cleared, now the flat plain's open
    and empty,   710
Out dash the two, at a spirited run. They put torque on their
    long-range

Javelin-shots, then tear into War with their shields and their clanging
Armour. Earth gives a groan, and they duel away with cascading
Strokes of the sword. What's luck, what's skill, all merges to oneness.
As, in the vastness of Sila, or up in the heights of Taburnus,*   715
Two bulls rush at each other and tangle in hostile encounter,
Head against head, and their herdsmen, scared at the sight, run
            for cover.
Unmoved, cowering mutely, the whole drove stands; heifers lowly
Moot as to who'll hold the woodland's hollows, or who'll lead the
            whole herd.
Mutual wounds are exchanged as the bulls, in an orgy of
            violence,   720
Butt, gore, tangle with horns. Necks, forequarters, dampen with
            streaming
Blood. Moaned moos, low notes reintoned, set the whole hollow
            booming.*
Such is the fight as the Trojan Aeneas and Daunian hero
Clash, at a run, with their shields. Huge crashes resound to the heavens.
Jupiter holds two scales in his hands, balanced evenly, places   725
In them the two men's differing fates so that he can determine
Which one the struggle condemns, under whose weight the scales
            begin sinking.*
    Turnus now glitters and sparks, for he thinks himself safe. So he rises
High as his body will go as he lifts up his sword for a downstroke.
Trojans begin to shout loudly—and so do the worrying Latins;   730
Both forces rise to their feet. The perfidious sword-blade, however,
Shivers to pieces on impact, betraying its fiery owner.
Only his feet come to help. He runs faster than gusts of the east wind
Once he has glanced at the unknown hilt* and his weaponless
            right hand.
Rumour reports he was rushed as he harnessed and mounted
            his horses   735
When battle started, and that he forgot to bring out his ancestral
Sword in his nervous excitement, grabbed that of his driver, Metiscus.
This sword, as long as the Teucrians scattered, retreated, and
            turned tail,
Served well enough. But against weapons forged by a deity, Vulcan,
Mortal steel was as brittle as ice and it shattered on impact: 740
Strewn on the tan-coloured sand, lying scattered as glistening
            fragments.

That's why Turnus is panicked, and runs about this way and that way
Over the different parts of the plain, interweaving erratic
Circles. A dense ring of Teucrians entraps him on all sides; extensive
Marshes contain him on one flank, and high city walls on the
　　　other.　　　　745
Hot in pursuit comes Aeneas who matches the terrified Turnus
Footstep for footstep, though every so often his knees, which the arrow's
Wound slows down, fail to work with his feet and refuse to keep
　　　running.
　　He's like a hunting dog with a stag he's got trapped at a river
Or fenced in by the huntsman's scarecrows* feathered in Punic　　750
Crimson. He races in yelping pursuit. And his panicky quarry,
Hedged in by fear of the treacherous nets and the river-bank's steepness,
Bounds and rebounds on a thousand escape routes. The panting
　　　and lively
Umbrian hound isn't shaken. He's got him, he's got him, he's snapping
Jaws just as if he had got him. He's fooled. For his fangs come up
　　　empty.　　　　755
　　Now's when the shouting intensifies; all around, river-banks, lakelands
Echo the sound, the whole heaven's a riot of thunderous uproar.
He, while he flees for his life, snaps at all the Rutulians, calling
Each by his name; he implores them to bring him the sword he has
　　　trusted.
Instant death is Aeneas' response: he will kill, so he threatens,　　760
Anyone who gets near. They're afraid, and he scares them with constant
Threats to destroy the whole city as well. On he presses, though
　　　wounded.
Five full circles they spin as they run; they unravel as many,
This way and that. They're competing for no insignificant, sporting
Prizes at games. The awards* are the life and the lifeblood of
　　　Turnus.　　　　765
　　Here, so it chanced, a wild olive had stood, consecrated to Faunus.
Sailors had honoured it once (though its bitter leaves marked it for
　　　firewood).
They made a practice, when saved from the seas, of fixing upon it
Gifts for the Laurentine god, and of hanging up garments as offerings.
Teucrians, wanting to fight on a plain free of any obstruction　　770
Made no exceptions and hacked this sacred plant to a low stump.
In it, Aeneas's javelin stood, driven there by the forceful
Power of his cast, deep lodged, fixed firm in the grip of its stubborn

Roots. The Dardanian loomed up, eager to tear the embedded
Steel tip out with his hand and pursue with his spear what he
    couldn't   775
Catch in a foot race. This frightening sight drove Turnus to panic:
'Pity me, Faunus, I beg you!' he prayed. 'Dear earth of my homeland,
Hold that spear! I have always respected your cults and traditions
Which, in contrast, Aeneas's men have defiled in their warfare.'
Faunus was not at all deaf to his prayer and the help he
    requested.   780
Long though Aeneas delays his pursuit as he wrestles the stubborn
Stump, no force he can muster avails to prise open its oaken
Bite. While he struggles, intense and persistent, Juturna the Daunian
Goddess, again takes the form of the chariot-driver, Metiscus,
Runs out to Turnus her brother and brings him the sword he'd
    forgotten.   785
  Venus, enraged that such freedom's allowed to a bold minor spirit,
Strides in, however, and rips out the spear from the roots where it's
    planted.
Both men now stand tall, refitted with weapons and valour.
One puts trust in his sword, one's straightened and honed by his
    spearshaft.
Facing a fight to the death, and each other, they're poised and
    they're breathless.   790

Meanwhile Almighty Olympus's ruler is speaking to Juno
Who, from the golden veil of a cloud, is watching the combat.
'Wife, tell me: how will it come to an end? What remains at this juncture?
You yourself well know, and admit that you know, that Aeneas
Must be the Native Spirit,* who's fated to rise to the sky's stars.   795
What do you hope you can build* in the cold clouds' veiled isolation?
Was it good form that a god suffer wounds from a mortal?* That Turnus'
Sword, stripped away, should then be restored? For without you Juturna
Couldn't have done it. Should violent force be increased in the
    vanquished?
Stop it all now! That's enough! Be moved by my pleas; and,
    so monstrous   800
Pain doesn't gnaw you in silence or anguish stream from your sweet
    mouth
Sourly, time and again, over *me*, be tractable, I beg.
Now comes the moment of truth. You've been able to harry the Trojans

Over the lands and the seas, kindle flames of a war that's atrocious,
Ravage a household, mix wedding anthems with dirges of
     mourning.   805
Don't attempt anything more. I forbid it.'* So Jupiter opened.
   So Saturn's daughter divine replied, with a look of submission:
'Jupiter, I, though reluctant, abandoned both Turnus and solid
Earth, since I know it's your will, great lord: what you wanted.
Otherwise you wouldn't see me alone in this aerial setting   810
Now, taking good with the bad. I'd be circled with flames, I'd be
     standing
Right at the front, dragging Teucrians off to their deaths in a battle.
This I admit: I persuaded Juturna to save her pathetic
Brother, approved of a bolder approach to protect his existence,
Not that she take up arms, though, and draw back the bowstring
     in combat.   815
This I swear by the head of the Styx, whose unpitying waters
Make them the single object of terror to gods in the heavens.
Now I'm conceding defeat. I am leaving the battle. I loathe it.
But, I entreat you, on Latium's behalf, on behalf of your own kin's
Grandeur, for something encompassed by none of fate's legal
     provisions.   820
When, and so be it, they settle their peace in fulfilment of marriage,
When they shape treaties and laws in their confederation together,
Don't require those who were born here, the Latins, to alter their
     ancient
Name, become "Trojans", be known as "The Teucrians", or alter
     their language.
Don't make them change their traditional dress. Let Latium
     continue,   825
Let there be Alban kings who will span all the centuries. And let
Roman stock get its strength from Italian concepts of courage.
Troy is destroyed. Now permit Troy's name to share her destruction.'
   Smiling at her, the deviser of matter, of matters, and humans
Said: 'There's no doubt you're the sister of Jove, second offshoot
     of Saturn's   830
Stock, for your heart churns anger to waves with a hurricane's fury.
Come, though, it's time you gave up on your useless rage.
     For I grant you
All that you wish. I concede. I'm prepared to admit myself beaten.
Italy's people will keep both native language and culture.

Further, their name will remain as it is. Intermarriage will
    thin out   835
What's left of Teucrians: namely, their blood. I'll add rituals and
    customs,
And I'll ensure that they'll all be collectively known as "the Latins".
Out of this blend with Ausonian blood you will see a new nation
Rise, and surpass all men and the gods in its righteous devotion.
No other people will match them in honouring you in their
    worship.'   840
Juno agrees. In delight, she relaxes her stiff, mental tension,
And, as she does so, departs from the sky and the cloud where
    she'd settled.
  This gained, the father took counsel with his own thoughts for
    the next phase:
Getting Juturna detached from her role as her brother's protector.
  Forces exist, people say, twin pestilent powers called the Dirae,* 845
Born with Megaera, their triplet in hell, to the never discerning
Night in the one same moment of birth. Night endowed them with
    matching
Ringlets of snakes and equipped them with wings like the winds they
    would glide through.
This pair appears flanking Jupiter's throne at the savage king's
    threshold,
Honing the fears he inspires among humans, sickly and
    death-doomed,   850
Each time the king of the gods masses hideous death and diseases
Over their heads, or brings terrors of war upon cities that earn them.
  Jupiter sends one of these on her swift way down from the heavens'
Heights, with instructions to come as an omen confronting Juturna.
So, she flies off, dropping swiftly to earth on a whirling tornado, 855
Much like an arrow, propelled through a cloud by the torque of a
    bowstring,
Armed with a savagely virulent poison and fired by a Parthian—
Parthian, or, if you will, a Cydonian*—screaming and swiftly
Carrying unforeseen, incurable wounds through the shadows.
That's how this creature of Night made her way to the earth
    and her target.   860
Sighting the Trojan positions and Turnus's ranks, she compresses
Her full self, in a flash, to the size and the shape of a smallish
Bird* such as settles at night on a funeral site or abandoned

Rooftop to sing a foreboding, late-watch dirge through the ghostly
Shadows. The demon, her face thus changed, swoops down
    into Turnus'   865
Face, swoops, screaming, again and again, bats his shield with
    her beating
Wings. For the first time, shock at a sight disables his body,
Loosens his limbs. Horror bristles his hair, chokes sound behind
    locked jaws.
   But, by the screech of the demon's wings, Juturna, his sister,
Knew from afar who it was. Her hopes of fulfilment were finished.   870
Loosening and tearing her hair, scoring cheeks with her nails, she,
    with clenched fists
Pounded her breast. 'Oh, what help can your sister be now to you,
    Turnus?
Tough as I am, what more can I do? Have I skills to stop daylight
Dead in its rush from your eyes? Can I fight against that kind of
    monster?
Carrion birds, I'm already leaving the battle! I'm frightened,   875
Don't terrorize me! I know that there's death in the sound of your
    wingbeats!
Great-hearted Jupiter sends his proud orders: that doesn't
    escape me.
This is his compensation to me for virginity ravished!
What did he grant me eternal life *for*, stripping me of life's basic
Terms, that we die, and of power to end, as I certainly
    would now,   880
All my pain, and to walk at my poor brother's side through
    the shadows?
I cannot die!* What joy will I have in anything round me,
Brother, without you? Has earth no abyss deep enough to devour,
De-deify me, dispatch me to death's abysmal remoteness?'
Such were her words. Then, shrouding her head with the grey
    of her mantle,   885
Groaning profoundly, the goddess entombs herself deep in her waters.

On and on comes Aeneas, pursuing and raising his spearshaft
Huge as a tree. From his savage heart he taunts him with these words:
'Why dally now at the climax, Turnus, and draw back at *this* point?
We must engage up close and with brute force, not in a foot race!   890
Take any shape, any form that you will, pull in such resources,

Courage or skill, as you have, then pray you can soar to the starry
Heights upon pinions or seal yourself off within earth's hollow chasm.'
He shook his head: 'It's not words you say in a rage that alarm me,
Raging brute! Gods alarm me, and Jupiter. He is my real foe.'   895
Saying no more, he surveys his surroundings and sees a huge boulder
Lying, by chance, on the plain: a huge boulder positioned in old
     times
Marking the property lines—to prevent a dispute over borders!
Even a dozen hand-picked men* of the build earth produces
Now would have trouble just hoisting its great mass up on their
     shoulders.   900
This hero picks up the rock in his trembling hand, races top speed,
Stretches as high as he can to add torque to its flight at the foeman.
Yet he has no sense he's running, no knowledge he's moving or
     hoisting
Up in his hand and hurling a boulder of massive proportions.
Knees buckle, blood sets hard in his veins with the cold ice
     of terror.   905
As for the stone the man threw: it just tumbled through void and
     through empty
Air, fell short of its length, inflicted a blow upon nothing.
   As in a dream,* when languid sleep seals eyes in our night-time
Rest, we're aware, in ourselves, of desperately wanting to reach out
Into some purpose or course; but strength, in the midst of our
     efforts,   910
Fails us. We feebly slump. Our tongues will not function, our usual
Bodily powers don't support us. No sound, no words find expression.
Such was Turnus's plight. Whatever attempt at heroic
Action he made, the grim goddess frustrated. Conflicting emotions
Whirl through his heart as he stares at Rutulians, stares at the city,   915
Hesitates, frightened, and shakes at the sight of the menacing javelin,
Sees no place to pull back to, no force to deploy on his foeman,
No sign at all of his chariot or of its driver, his sister.
And, as he hesitates still, Aeneas with javelin brandished,
Figures the odds of success with his eyes and, mustering his full
     strength,   920
Spins off a long-range shot. No boulder propelled from a taut-torqued
Catapult high on a parapet makes such a crack, and no lightning
Leaps with such crackling, thunderous peal. Like a whirling tornado,
Bearing the fury of death, that shaft rips open his corslet's

Rim* and the outer edge of his shield's seven layers of protection,   925
Screams through the thick of his thigh. And Turnus, felled by the
    impact,
Drops to the ground on his knee; and his knee buckles under his
    hugeness.
Up leaped Rutulians moaning in notes reintoned* in the whole hill's
Rippled response, as their voices are echoed around by the high
    woods.
Low on the ground and on bended knee, he appeals with extended   930
Hand, with an earnest look in his eyes, and declares: 'I've deserved
    this,
Nor am I begging for life. Opportunity's yours; and so use it.
But, if the love of a parent can touch you at all (for you once had
Just such a father, Anchises), I beg you to pity the agèd
Daunus, and give me, or if you prefer, my sightless cadaver,   935
Back to my kin. You've won; the Ausonians have witnessed the
    vanquished
Reaching his hands out to make his appeal. Now Lavinia's
    your wife.
Don't press your hate any further.' Aeneas, relentless in combat,
Stops; and though rolling his eyes, he holds back his hand from the
    death-stroke.
Slowly but surely, the words take effect. He's begun hesitating,   940
But when a harness catches his gaze, high on Turnus's shoulder,
Gleaming with amulet studs, those pleas have no chance of
    fulfilment:
Pallas's oh so familiar belt, which Turnus had shouldered
After defeating and killing the boy. It's the mark of a hated
Personal foe. As his eyes drink in these mementoes of savage   945
Pain, these so bitter spoils, Aeneas grows fearsome in anger,
Burning with fire of the Furies. 'You, dressed in the spoils of my
    dearest,
Think that you could escape *me*? Pallas gives you this death-stroke,
    yes Pallas
Makes you the sacrifice, spills your criminal blood in atonement!'
And, as he speaks, he buries the steel in the heart that
    confronts him,   950
Boiling with rage. Cold shivers send Turnus' limbs into spasm.
Life flutters off on a groan, under protest, down among shadows.*

ANCESTRAL CHART

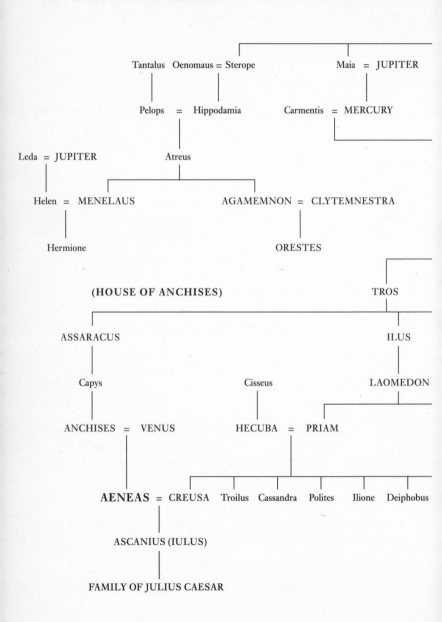

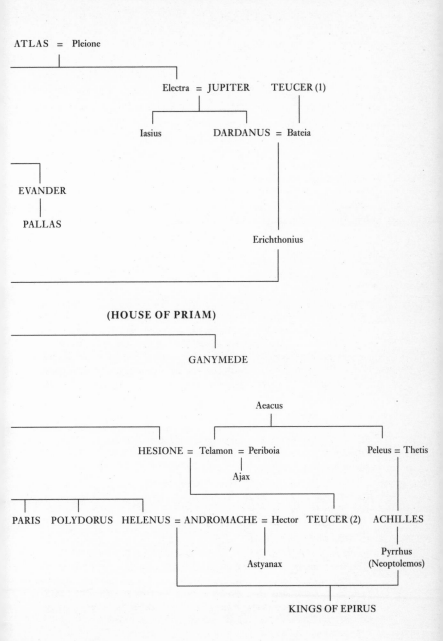

ATLAS = Pleione

Electra = JUPITER   TEUCER (1)

Iasius   DARDANUS = Bateia

EVANDER

PALLAS

Erichthonius

(HOUSE OF PRIAM)

GANYMEDE

Aeacus

HESIONE = Telamon = Periboia   Peleus = Thetis

Ajax

PARIS   POLYDORUS   HELENUS = ANDROMACHE = Hector   TEUCER (2)   ACHILLES

Pyrrhus
(Neoptolemos)

Astyanax

KINGS OF EPIRUS

EXPLANATORY NOTES

BOOK ONE

1a–d *I'm the same man*: the italicized lines were removed by Virgil's editors.

1 *of Troy*: I delete the traditional comma after 'I sing'. Troy refers back to 'arms and the man' as well as forward to 'seashores'.

13 *Carthage*: 'New Town' in the Phoenician/Carthaginian language. It was settled by colonists from Phoenicia (modern Lebanon), whose chief cities were Tyre (hence 'Tyrians') and Sidon, five hundred years *after* Troy fell. Carthage itself was annihilated by the Romans in 146 BC. A Roman colony (named in honour of Juno) was soon proposed for the site; but colonization did not start until 44 BC, under Julius Caesar.

27 *Judgement of Paris*: Juno's causes of anger are given in reverse order. Paris, son of Priam, king of Troy, was asked by Eris (strife as a divine force) to judge which of three goddesses was most beautiful. Each offered him a bribe symbolic of her godhood: Minerva (Gk. Pallas Athena: 'Wisdom'), Juno (Gk. Hera: 'Power'), or Venus (Gk. Aphrodite: 'Love'). He accepted Venus': the most beautiful of women, Helen, who was already married to Menelaus of Sparta. When Paris, accompanied by Aeneas in some traditions, abducted her to Troy, Menelaus called upon all those who had been her suitors (almost all major Greek heroes of the day) to honour their pledge to defend his rights to her. So began the Trojan War (and the linking of Aeneas with Paris). The *Aeneid* is, at the divine level, a continuation of the rivalry between Juno and Venus, 'Power' and 'Love'. Left on the sidelines is Minerva, 'Wisdom'—also overlooked in the art and cult of Augustan Rome.

28 *Ganymede*: usually placed at least one generation before Paris and also (but not always) linked with Mount Ida. He was abducted by Jupiter (Gk. Zeus), made immortal, and required to be (among other things) Jupiter's cup-bearer. His abduction is depicted on a cloak given to the winner of the boat race (5.250–8).

97 *Bravest Danaän of all*: Diomedes, who lurks in the background throughout the *Aeneid*, was Aeneas' greatest Greek adversary. Aeneas is saved from him in *Iliad* 5 (see Introduction). Aeneas' words of despair here are based on Odysseus' similar lament in *Odyssey* 5.

148 *Much the same happens*: the first simile of the *Aeneid* is political and compares divine to human behaviour, not vice versa. Epic similes often highlight differences among things compared. The winds do not act spontaneously as Virgil's rioters do, but because Juno has subverted the hierarchy of command. Some think Octavian is the righteous man to whom Neptune is compared, and are, probably, at least partly right. But there is a risky undertow. Romans knew Octavian had restored order with weapons, not words,

and that Neptune was not his favourite god, but patron deity of his powerful foe during the civil wars: Sextus Pompey, the younger son of Caesar's rival Pompey. Sextus took for himself the same epithet Virgil applies to Aeneas: *Pius*, 'righteous'. He also minted coins bearing the slogan *pietas* along with images of himself and Neptune, and even styled himself 'Son of Neptune'. Octavian suffered heavy losses to Sextus in naval campaigns in Sicilian and Italian waters, and declared, famously, that he would win whether Neptune wished it or not. He even had Neptune's statue removed from a procession on one occasion (see also notes on 5.813; 6.6, 42, 70, 109, 366, 863–4).

161   *It's a natural port*: Servius (on 1.159) says this is an imaginary scene based on the Punic colony New Carthage (Cartagena) in Spain. Virgil appropriately gives it the feel of a stage 'set', since it marks Aeneas' entry into a world and time not his own: Carthage had not yet been founded.

178   *Ceres*: both the goddess who is the energy of crops and the Latin word meaning 'grain'.

226   *light of his glance*: many ancients thought the eyes *emit* the light we see by. This is important in the case of Jupiter and Venus (in conjunction here). For they are not just anthropomorphic beings, but bright planets (or erratic 'stars' as the ancients believed) whose celestial positions vary. But Juno was never a planet. She is associated with air (Gk. Hera was explained as an anagram of *aer*, 'air') and with the clouds veiling the skies (blocking visual contact between earth and heaven). Iris (the Rainbow) is her messenger. Neptune, the Sea, was not a planet either; our Neptune, invisible to the naked eye, was undetected in antiquity. Other solar system gods are Apollo (Sun), Diana (Moon), Mercury, Mars, and Saturn.

237   *whose is the mind*: Venus insinuates that someone else (i.e. Juno) has changed his thinking. For more on this, see 10.628–32 and note.

257   *Cytherea*: a reminder to Venus, born in the sea and washed ashore at the island of Cythera, that what has happened to Aeneas at sea is not necessarily bad.

274   *twin boys*: Romulus and Remus. Romulus founded Rome as a Latin city and, in most traditions, killed his brother Remus, though this is not obvious from Jupiter's words. Jupiter assumes that Venus knows Romulus is raised by a she-wolf, the Latin for which, *lupa*, has a range of meaning like that of 'vixen'. Livy says some took the story as a reference to the wife of the shepherd Faustulus (he found the lads), who lived as 'a she-wolf [i.e. vixen] among shepherds'. Jupiter's comment that Romulus showed appreciation for his wolf-nurse by skinning her and wearing the pelt diverts attention from the double sense of *lupa* here. Romulus, after death, was identified as a god, Quirinus.

279   *Empire that has no end*: Jupiter's resolve to give Rome eternal power follows oddly on his failure to deal with Juno's storm (which might have killed Aeneas). Latin *fatum* means, literally, 'that which is spoken'. So Jupiter's

description of his words as 'destiny' is not quite 'fate' as Christian theologians understand it. He speaks with less certainty at the council of gods in Book 10. Male gods in the *Aeneid* pay attention to human affairs only intermittently.

294 *Portals of War*: the doors of Rome's Temple of Janus, the double-faced god symbolizing entrances (and exits), were closed when Rome was at peace—only three times up to Virgil's day, most recently by Octavian. In 7.607–20 the doors of a similar Temple of Janus in Latinus' city are opened, despite Latinus' objections.

299 *Dido*: founder and ruler of Carthage. Virgil follows the practice of most Greek and Roman poets in placing female characters at the heart of his work. Not only is Carthage ruled by a woman, but the chief gods of the *Aeneid* are female, as is one of the main Italian warriors. The most memorable seer and the demons of the underworld are also female.

346 *Pygmalion*: his name is Phoenician, first found on a Carthaginian pendant made between 673 and 663 BC, the preferred date for the foundation of Carthage (the traditional date is 814 BC). He is represented with Astarte, a Phoenician goddess sharing characteristics of both Venus (with links to Cyprus) and Juno (with links to Carthage). In Punic tradition, Phoenicians established the city of Citium in Cyprus, under Elissa, daughter of Pygmalion before Carthage was founded by Dido and Beles (called Belus by Virgil). In Virgil, Elissa is another name for Dido. Pygmalion's name is usually linked with his skill in making lifelike images. In Ovid he is a Cypriot artist who crafts an image out of ivory (see note to 6.893 on the significance of ivory). He falls in love with his creation, and Venus brings it to life for him (*Metamorphoses* 10.247–93). His descendant, Cinyras, fulfilled a promise to send fifty ships against Troy by sending one real and forty-nine *models*. He was himself deceived by his daughter Myrrha (= myrrh) into making love to her. Their child is Adonis (Phoenician/Hebrew *Adonai*, 'Lord'), born after her metamorphosis into a myrrh tree.

368 *Byrsa, "The Hide"*: the Carthaginians negotiated with local residents for as much land as they could enclose with the hide of one ox (they sliced it into tiny slivers to make a lengthy thread). Aeneas has not yet seen a trace of human habitation. He is still distant from Carthage in time and space.

374 *Venus, the Evening Star*: Venus is also the planet Venus, the evening star.

393 *twelve swans*: the omen implies that Jupiter (rather than Juno) is responsible for the plight of Aeneas' fleet. The swans represent the twelve other surviving ships. Swans are less often associated with Venus than with Apollo in Graeco-Roman myth. Though Jupiter disguises himself as a swan to attack Leda, mother of Helen, his usual bird is the eagle. Battles between swans and eagles, unheard of in nature but common in poetry, usually result in success for the swans, probably because the Swan constellation rises ahead of the Eagle, is pursued by the Eagle across the heavens, but (since it is more northerly) sets later than the Eagle and thus 'survives' the attack. Venus may have 'staged' this omen as Juturna stages a similar omen in 12.244–64 (see note on 12.246).

415–17 *Paphos . . . Sheba*: Venus goes back to her Cypriot cult centre in Paphos (linked with the Pygmalion story). Virgil's emphasis on the Sheban (Arabian) origins of incense (grown, as was the myrrh tree, almost exclusively in Arabia) recalls the Phoenician/Middle Eastern connections of Venus' cult and the story of Cinyras, Myrrha, and Adonis.

429 *stage in the future*: Dido's Carthaginians are building a theatre to stage plays hundreds of years before there were plays to stage. Columns for sets are a feature of Roman, not Greek, theatres. The first permanent stone theatre at Rome was erected in 55 BC. Another was being built as Virgil wrote. So too was Caesar's Roman colony in Carthage, which had a theatre (the old Punic site did not). Trojan War motifs (part of the Caesars' artistic programme) make sense in the new *Roman* Carthage, but not in the Punic city. Since Carthage had been levelled, salted, and cursed in 146 BC, some thought its reconstruction impious.

440 *in their midst unseen*: emphasis on Aeneas' invisibility is apt, not only because this is how Aeneas was protected from his foes at Troy in *Iliad* 5 and 20, but because Aeneas is now doubly displaced, in time as well as in space. He is looking at a city founded five hundred years after Troy's fall which has features of Roman Carthage from yet another five hundred years further on.

463 *this fame*: Latin *fama* carries more shades of meaning than any one English equivalent can bear. It derives from the same root as *fatum*, 'that which is spoken', and means 'rumour', 'gossip', and 'tradition', not just *positive* 'fame' (see also Translator's Note).

469–70 *Rhesus' / Tents*: if Rhesus' horses drank from Troy's rivers, legend reported, the city would not fall. See *Iliad* 10, and Euripides' *Rhesus*— the only surviving Greek tragedy in which Aeneas appears. Troilus' sorrows, the death of Priam, and the exploits of Penthesilea, described in the following lines, are found only in authors after Homer. What the Trojan War means to the Carthaginians (and where their sympathies lie) is a mystery. They boasted no connection to either side until this fictional moment invented by Roman poets.

488 *with Achaean commanders*: Aeneas sees himself mixed in (*permixtum*) with the Greek commanders, either fighting or fraternizing. Virgil situates his only authorial (and non-committal) reference to the negative Aeneas tradition on a building dedicated to an enemy god in an enemy land.

527 *We did not come to annihilate*: the irony is that Aeneas' descendants did come to do so in 146 BC.

592 *Much as a sculptor's hands*: Venus recreates Aeneas (who is from a different time period) so he can meet Dido. Comparison of Venus to a sculptor embellishing a marble statue recalls the illusions wrought by Pygmalion to deceive Dido. And Astarte, on the Phoenician pendant and divine counterpart of Venus, is the consort of Pygmalion who, tradition says, ruled Carthage after Dido's death (see note to 1.346).

619 *Teucer*: Dido is referring, not to Teucer, a founding father of the *Trojan* (Teucrian) people, but to Teucer from Salamis (the island close to Athens), a *Greek* warrior at Troy. His mother was Hesione, sister of Priam, king of Troy, so he is a blood relation of Aeneas. Exiled by his father when he returned from Troy, he went on to found another Salamis in Cyprus. But, as Dido points out, he does so under the patronage of her father, Belus. He is a client king with an overlord (a warning of what Aeneas' relationship to Dido will be, should their peoples join). Virgil's source here may be Sophocles' and Pacuvius' now lost *Teucer* tragedies. See also note to 8.157. 'Teucer' is one of the many famous names in the *Aeneid* applied to two (or more) people. In this case, both Teucers were famous. Often a minor person is given the name of a famous character to elicit 'echoes' of the namesake.

639 *long, skilled toil and the proud purple mollusc*: a disturbing line, which focuses not so much on the beauty of the finished product, but on what went into making it: the hours of toil at the loom, the extraction of the famous Phoenician purple dye from the crushed sea-snails of the Mediterranean (it took some 23,000 sea-snails to produce enough dye for a Roman senator's robe, according to Pliny the Elder). Thus the 'royal' purple is a symbol of both princely pride and princely oppression, as is most brilliantly expressed in Aeschylus' *Agamemnon*, where Clytemnestra cajoles her husband into walking upon purple-dyed tapestries as a symbolic re-enactment of his destruction of beauty (before she kills him). The idea that the sea-snail is proud of its contribution is surely ironic.

650 *Finery . . . Helen had brought*: these (and Ilione's sceptre and crown) are the only items of women's attire mentioned among Aeneas' treasures from Troy. We never learn how he acquired them, why he gives them to Dido, or whether he identifies their previous owners to her. A queen in love might see them as tokens of affection, even a covert hint at marriage. Virgil accords them influence equal to that of Love in shaping Dido's emotions.

658 *Cupid, her own child*: Virgil follows the later Greek tradition of making Cupid (Gk. Eros) the child of Venus rather than a primeval god, predating Venus. Venus' actions recall Apollonius 3, where Eros is recruited by Aphrodite (Venus) to make Medea fall in love with Jason.

667 *Aeneas, your brother*: Cupid, also called Amor ('Love'), is Aeneas' half-brother. And *Amor* is *Roma* (Rome) written backwards (especially apt in Carthage, since Punic, like Hebrew and Arabic, is written right to left). Roman poets often link Rome and Love.

683 *feigning his features*: Dido is again deceived by 'crafted illusions'. Virgil never mentions the restoration of Ascanius, though scholars assume that he is restored after Aeneas leaves Carthage. Some later passages take on added interest if we don't so assume. Ascanius is also known as Iulus.

712 *descendant of Phoenix*: the Latin *Phoenissa* evokes both Dido's Phoenician identity and the phoenix, a mythical bird that lived for five hundred years, then cremated itself. From its ashes arose a new phoenix. Dido vows in Book 4 that an avenger will arise from her bones: a reference critics agree

is 'prophetic' of Hannibal, who inflicted terrible catastrophes on Rome two cycles of the life of the phoenix after the fall of Troy.

713 *Unfulfilled*: see Translator's Note, pp. xlix–l, on this translation of *infelix*. The Roman dictator Sulla translated 'Felix', his nickname, into Greek as 'Epaphroditos', 'Blessed by Aphrodite'. So Dido, in a way, is *infelix* because she is *not* so blessed.

720 *Acidalian*: that is, of Acidalius, a fountain in Boeotia (Central Greece) sacred to the Graces, Venus' daughters. Venus has taken Ascanius to Idalia in Cyprus (1.681, 693); Amor adds two letters and repositions his mother's identity.

752 *Could he describe Diomedes' steeds?*: Dido probably already knows the answers, as she knows much else about the fall of Troy. It is Dido, not Aeneas, who tells us how long Aeneas has been travelling! Since Diomedes won the chariot race in *Iliad* 23 with the horses he captured from Aeneas in *Iliad* 5, Aeneas ought to be able to assess them. See 10.581–601 and note to 10.581. Aeneas does not answer these questions.

BOOK TWO

2 *Aeneas . . . began thus*: Virgil builds on various traditions about Aeneas at Troy, ranging from an heroic withdrawal to an escape negotiated with the Greeks. Octavian would not have sponsored an obviously treacherous Aeneas; but the many influential Romans who accepted Octavian's rule reluctantly would have had no use for an *Aeneid* that parroted imperial propaganda. Virgil's Aeneas makes his 'own' case, in his 'own' voice. He neither confronts nor contradicts negative traditions, but assimilates them with remarkable finesse. He needs finesse on other fronts, too. Like Homer's Odysseus in Phaeacia, he is addressing an inner audience whose goodwill and support are crucial. But both heroes must avoid absorption into their hosts' worlds if they are to fulfil their own goals or obligations. Aeneas' narrative, like Odysseus' in *Odyssey* 9–12, is not just a travelogue, but a shrewd rhetorical design to secure passage out of the host's domain. In Homer, the king wants Odysseus gone; but the king's daughter, backed by the queen, wants to marry him. Odysseus manipulates their differing interests to his own advantage. Aeneas has to deal with Dido who is king, queen, and princess all in one, and thus more dangerous. He must clear his name (but not appear too threatening or desirable to her), and insist, with polite obliquity, that his destiny lies in Italy, not in North Africa.

12 *recoils from the anguish*: Aeneas shows a formidable capacity for analysing how the mind works. He characterizes himself by his tendency to avoid unhappy memories and will later show that this avoidance extends to reactions in his unconscious mind.

66 *You'll learn them all*: Aeneas sets up Sinon as a model of Greek unreliability, as a reason for scepticism about any stories of Troy a Greek (including Homer) might tell. Sinon's voice lets him answer Dido's question

about the horse ('the trap' 1.753) without knowing too much 'himself'. Virgil's model may again have been Sophocles (a master of oblique speech), who wrote tragedies (now lost) named *Laocoön* and *Sinon*.

79 *See, none*: Sinon's name creates wordplay on the Latin *si non* ('if not', 'unless').

82 *Belus' descendant*: to distinguish this Belus too finely from the Phoenician Belus (see note to 1.346) is to miss Aeneas' shrewd rhetoric. Palamedes was credited with inventing a way of writing Greek in letters adapted from the Phoenician alphabet. His death is also linked to his skill in writing. When Ulysses feigned insanity to avoid conscription for the war, it was Palamedes who proved his madness false. Ulysses, in revenge, had his scribes forge a letter indicating Palamedes' intent to betray the Greeks (the subject of Euripides' lost tragedy *Palamedes*). Ulysses had gold 'planted' below Palamedes' bed and left the letter for Agamemnon to find. Palamedes was condemned and stoned to death.

100 *Calchas'*: a Greek seer who helps Ulysses manipulate the ranks through their superstitions.

112 *interlocked maple*: a wood harder than the pine used for the frame.

114 *Eurypylus*: famous for going to Patras after the Trojan War and for *ending* that city's annual sacrifice of its handsomest boy and girl.

118 *the sacrifice human*: Aeneas has Sinon modify the traditional oracle demanding a human sacrifice before the Greeks' return voyage by adding 'Argive, again'. The usual victim is Priam's daughter Polyxena, killed on the grave of Achilles. Human sacrifice is treated as criminal here as in the tragic poets. Cicero calls it 'a monstrous and barbarous custom' (*Pro Fonteio* 31); Julius Caesar says much the same (*Gallic Wars* 6.16). But Octavian sacrificed humans on the anniversary of Julius Caesar's death (Suetonius, *Divus Augustus* 15), and Aeneas later takes prisoners for sacrifice (see notes to 10.520, 558). The practice was not as uncommon at Rome as is sometimes suggested (the closeness of the words for enemy and sacrificial victim, *hostis* and *hostia* respectively, build the idea into the language). Gladiatorial contests were first given at Rome as a sacrifice honouring the dead.

164 *Tydeus' unrighteous son*: Diomedes, unrighteous because he fought the gods.

176 *templed sky*: Latin *extemplo*, 'suddenly', derives from *templum*, 'temple', not just a building but a region of the sky for taking auspices (that is, omens from the flight of birds).

263 *first was Machaon*: Aeneas' list suggests an eyewitness account, especially in its adjustment of the order of their appearance.

286 *wounded*: Aeneas contends (*a*) that he was asleep when the Greeks left the horse; (*b*) that his unconscious mind had not accepted Hector's death; (*c*) that his unconscious had rationalized Hector's death as a long, inexplicable absence and could not account for Hector's lacerated condition, which he obviously knew about consciously but had rejected subconsciously.

This is the most complex ancient account I know of suppression by the unconscious of fact known to the conscious mind.

318 *Panthus*: a Greek from Delphi abducted to Troy, father of one of Troy's wisest and best warriors, Polydamas. Priam made him priest of Apollo in compensation for his abduction. The grandson with him is, possibly, Polydamas' child Leocritus. Polydamas himself is not named in the *Aeneid*.

339–41 *Rhipeus . . . Coroebus*: only Coroebus figures in other traditions (in Euripides' *Rhesus*). Virgil assigns him the role Homer gives to Othryoneus (*Iliad* 13.363 ff.).

395 *each one arming himself*: Aeneas shows Coroebus taking the lead, and does not describe his own donning of Greek armour (the verbs are in the third person). But it becomes clear that he too was in Greek armour, as the verbs revert to first person plural. It would thus be easy to confuse him with the Greeks.

396 *we mixed with Danaäns*: Aeneas has now explained why he could be represented as 'mixed in with' Danaän leaders, even as fighting on the Greek side, on the temple reliefs in Book 1.

437 *wound from Ulysses*: Ulysses' wounding of Pelias draws attention to Aeneas' failure to name any Greek warrior he fought personally.

441 *tortoise formation*: a Roman rather than Greek siege tactic: the infantry's shields were linked to form a 'roof' over their heads as the legions assaulted enemy defences.

457 *Dragging*: the tower Aeneas ascends is the one to whose pinnacle Astyanax, son of Hector and Andromache, was dragged in theatrical versions of the fall of Troy (e.g. Seneca's *Trojan Women*) and thrown to his death. Aeneas undermines this tradition by claiming he was on and destroyed that tower *before the siege ended*. Perhaps the negative tradition suggested that he witnessed Astyanax' death.

470 *Pyrrhus dances*: the *pyrrhicha*, a dance performed in armour, was allegedly named after Pyrrhus.

482 *Opening up a great window*: Aeneas now places himself at ground level *outside* the palace, as if he were with the Greeks, looking over Pyrrhus' shoulder.

506 *Priam's fate*: Aeneas re-frames Priam's death from the Trojan side, as if he were on a rooftop *inside* the palace compound. For once, the two opposing Aeneases of tradition are juxtaposed, not assimilated. But the 'Trojan' version is the one from which his narrative continues.

518 *the arms of his young days*: Priam, unlike the snake to which Pyrrhus is compared, cannot regain his youth by donning the warrior 'skin' of his youth.

543 *Hector's . . . corpse*: in *Iliad* 24, Achilles pities Priam and returns Hector's body for burial.

555 *spectator at Troy's Fires*: Aeneas, a non-intervening observer, presents Priam as himself reduced by old age to the role of spectator at Troy's fall,

then butchered when he tries to intervene. But when he adds that Priam's headless corpse lies on the seashore, he is adducing yet another tradition in which Priam was executed on the beach. Some see Virgil intruding upon Aeneas' narrative here with a reference to the death of Julius Caesar's adversary, Pompey, in his own way 'Ruler of Asia'. Pompey was killed by a Macedonian (named Achillas!) on the coast of Egypt, where he fled after his defeat in 48 BC.

567 *I was the last one alive*: lines 567–88 are not in the major manuscripts. Servius says this passage was removed by Virgil's editors. Many think these lines are not genuine; but omitting them creates as many problems as it solves since it leaves a gap in the narrative: what scholars call a *lacuna*. The only similarly large *lacuna* postulated in Latin epic is in Silius 8.29–192 (which also shows Aeneas in what some would consider a 'bad light').

568 *on guard . . . at Vesta's / Shrine*: the idea of killing Helen as she hides in Vesta's shrine is a clever touch, whether one accepts this passage as genuine or not. Girls selected to guard Vesta's temple at Rome had to remain virgins through thirty years of service. If they did not they were buried alive.

569 *Tyndareus' daughter*: Helen is sometimes daughter of Zeus, sometimes (especially when belittled) daughter of Tyndareus, king of Sparta.

577 *her uncle's*: reading *patruas*, not Servius' reading *patrias*: 'her father's'.

587 *Vengeance we burned for*: reading *flammae* ('flames'), not *famam* ('rumour', 'reputation') with the manuscripts.

602 *gods' inclemency*: clemency was deemed the most godlike of virtues. The description, by Venus' son and attributed to Venus, of Troy's destruction by the gods' inclemency is dubious in Stoic terms; in Epicurean terms, impious. His point is that no human is to blame for Troy's fall: not Helen, not Paris, not himself.

615–16 *Pallas . . . aegis and gorgon*: Pallas is Virgil's preferred name for Minerva. She is traditionally represented with her shield, the aegis, whose central motif is Medusa's head, which turns to stone those who gaze upon it.

632–3 *the goddess / Guiding me*: Aeneas stays in the foreground of his narrative after Venus' intervention, and emphasizes the divine influences that prompt him to escape Troy.

642–3 *Troy / Fall once*: Hercules had conquered Troy earlier; see note to 8.157.

649 *Blasted me down*: Jupiter punished Anchises for his affair with Venus by maiming and disfiguring him.

671 *Buckling a sword on again*: Aeneas implies that he laid down his arms on reaching home, although he wants everyone to leave with him immediately, perhaps to establish that he is no longer wearing Greek armour. Presumably he now dons a second set of Trojan armour. Epic warriors, regardless of rank, normally own only one. He puts armour on yet again at 2.749 to return to Troy.

676 *Taking up arms*: one cannot take up arms without 'laying down' (that is, placing) hope in their success.

691 *augural sign*: following Servius' reading *augurium*; the manuscripts have *auxilium*, 'help'.

711 *and my wife follow on*: Pausanias (10.26.1) reports a tradition dating back to the *Cypria* (an early Greek epic) that Aeneas' wife was named Eurydice. So Aeneas is probably building on the myth of Eurydice, wife of Orpheus, here and linking it with his own 'experience'. The dead Eurydice was to follow Orpheus back out of the underworld, if he did not look back, and be restored to life. Aeneas' wife will be lost because he *fails* to look back.

714 *Temple of Ceres*: in the negative tradition, this was the site arranged with the Greeks as a rendezvous for those Trojans allowed to leave.

740 *never restored to my eyesight*: but in 2.772 he tells of seeing her ghost, which, though not the same as seeing *her*, suggests her (temporary) restoration to his vision. See also next note.

746 *crueller sight*: the sight, presumably, of the whole group with Creusa alone missing.

760 *I revisit the . . . palace of Priam*: since Aeneas went to the palace *before* going home for Creusa and Anchises, there was no particular reason to suspect Creusa would be there. But his frenzied search for her affords a chance to dispose of accounts that place him in Troy among the Greeks after the fall.

772–84 *the ghost of Creusa*: the conjuring of Creusa's ghost would (*a*) remind Dido of her husband's ghost urging her to leave Phoenicia; (*b*) absolve Aeneas of responsibility for Creusa's death; (*c*) authorize his leaving the city; and (*d*) tell him where he must go: to the Lydian Tiber, namely Italy (not Carthage). Aeneas indicates no recollection of Creusa's injunction to look for the Lydian Tiber as his travels begin in Book 3. If we feel like prompting him by echoing Creusa's words we are responding exactly as Aeneas' formidable rhetoric expects Dido to respond: 'You must settle and marry a new wife in Italy, not Thrace, not Crete, not . . . Carthage.'

775 *to allay my concerns*: see note to 3.153.

797 *Influx of newcomers*: at the Temple of Ceres.

801 *Venus, star of the morning*: Venus is both the morning and the evening star, depending on whether she precedes sunrise or follows sunset.

BOOK THREE

1 *After the powers on high had approved*: Aeneas represents the gods as more organized than Virgil 'himself' does, and notes his ritual attempts to gain insight into what he sees as the collective divine will. He also portrays himself as deferential to his father Anchises and conveys his righteousness, *pietas*.

5–7 *we constructed . . . Ships*: Homer's Troy had no navy. Aeneas does not explain how he could build and launch a fleet near Troy so soon after Troy fell.

18 *Aeneadae*: Aineia (in Thrace) proclaimed its foundation by Aeneas on coins and held a festival in his honour. It may also have claimed his tomb, which Virgil had to eliminate. Cities seized on myths to link themselves with travellers such as Odysseus and Aeneas. It was not enough to say: 'Aeneas slept here.' He had to sleep *with* someone and have a child or, failing that, die and have a cult tomb. The *Odyssey*, among the first works written down in Greek, could brush aside unwanted prior traditions. But Virgil had to set Aeneas in an established path. See A. Erskine, *Troy between Greece and Rome: Local Tradition and Imperial Power* (Oxford, 2001), 93–8. Aeneas places himself at a tomb rather than in one: that of Polydorus. It is a regally Trojan, yet problematic, substitution, for it makes Aeneas' first landfall just where Agamemnon's Greek fleet stopped on its return voyage: the realm of Polymestor of Thrace (see Euripides' *Hecuba*).

19 *Dione's / Child*: Dione is more often the mother, by Tantalus, of Pelops, the ancestor of the house of Atreus, than the mother of Venus. In using this pedigree for his mother, Aeneas establishes a genealogical link between himself and Agamemnon, son of Atreus. Virgil calls Caesar 'son of Dione' (*Eclogue* 9.47).

45 *Polydorus*: Euripides' *Hecuba* opens with the ghost of Polydorus, son of Priam, telling of his murder by Polymestor. In Pacuvius' lost *Iliona*, it is not Polydorus but Polymestor's own son Deipylus who is killed. Polymestor's wife Ilione (Iliona in Pacuvius) switched the two children when babies, without her husband's knowledge. When Iliona discovered Polymestor's murder of their son she blinded and killed him. In Pacuvius, then, Polydorus survives: if Aeneas arrived after Agamemnon, Polydorus would have been alive and Ilione a widow.

46 *sharp-pointed spear-shafts*: covering the mound are myrtle and dogwood (cornel), both used to make spears and arrows. Aeneas is tugging at weapons that have grown back as the plants from which they were made. In a picture, it might be hard to tell whether he was inserting or extracting the spears. Aeneas has Polydorus' ghost clear him of blame, and gives Euripides', not Pacuvius' account of the Thracian murder. Since Aeneas founds Aeneadae close to the time of Polydorus' murder, some accounts might have shown him disposing of Polydorus as a rival. Among Aeneas' gifts to Dido are the sceptre and crown of Ilione (1.653), which Aeneas presumably obtained here. How and why they were available to him is a mystery, since Aeneas does not mention meeting Ilione.

78–9 *calmest / Welcome*: Delos, subject to stormy weather, is notoriously difficult to land on or leave.

80 *Anius*: Dionysius (1.59.3) says one of Anius' daughters was given to Aeneas, and that her name was Launa (that is, Lavinia), and that Lavinium was named after her (Erskine, *Troy between Greece and Rome*, 185–8). Virgil does not dispose of this tradition until Book 7 (note to 7.71).

Meanwhile Aeneas distracts our attention. He has his father misinterpret an oracle and thus send the Trojans to Crete (not on any prior itinerary for Aeneas). When disaster ensues, Anchises redirects them to Delos. But the return voyage is pre-empted by the household gods who direct Aeneas, finally, to Italy.

94 *Dardanus' rugged sons*: Aeneas shows that Apollo is directing them to Italy, where Dardanus was born. He again emphasizes that he had as yet no clear sense of his family's origins.

107 *Teucer*: Anchises takes the Trojans to be sons of Teucer (that is, Teucrians) and thus of Cretan origin rather than sons of Dardanus (that is, Dardanians) and of Italian origin.

111 *Great Mother*: Cybele. Her cult, linked with Phrygia in Asia Minor, was brought to Rome towards the end of the Second Punic War (Silius 16.1–45). A prophecy claimed that an invading foreign army could be expelled only if Cybele's cult were transferred to Rome. Her festival, the *Megalensia*, became one of Rome's most important. The Corybants were Cybele's followers. Wild dances and music were part of her cult. She had a male consort, Attis, who got into a frenzy or was unfaithful to Cybele (or both), castrated himself, and eventually died—though his body was preserved, at Cybele's request. Cybele's priests, called *galli*, practised self-castration (*Gallus* is a multiple pun in Latin, meaning 'Gaul' and 'rooster' as well as '(castrated) priest'). Roman citizens were not allowed to serve as her priests, and official art, including coins, is silent about Attis. Poets are not. Catullus 63 tells of Attis' self-castration and prays the frenzy won't strike him. But Attis is never mentioned in the *Aeneid*, though there are comments on 'Phrygian' lack of masculinity. To Iarbas, Aeneas is 'helped by his eunuch entourage, this latter-day Paris' (4.215).

121 *Idomeneus*: king of Crete and a major Greek warrior at Troy. He alone reached home with his squad intact, but was exiled for sacrificing his son (having vowed, rashly, to sacrifice the first thing he saw on returning home). Aeneas does not mention until later that Idomeneus was exiled to *Italy*.

147–8 *conscious / Creatures*: Latin *animalia*. That which is *animal*, says Cicero, 'is driven by its own personal and internal motion', as distinct from the inanimate, 'which is acted upon by external force' (*Tusculan Disputations* 1. 23. 54). See also 4.522 ff., 8.26–7, and 9.224.

153 *allay my concerns*: this line is identical with 2.775 and 8.35. I could not make them completely identical in English because of needed changes in gender, verb person, and number.

164 *'Twilight Land'*: Latin *Hesperia* (Gk. *Hesperios*, 'evening'); used of the western Mediterranean generally, but in Virgil usually of Italy.

171 *Ausonia . . . Dicte*: Ausonia is a Greek name for Italy (see note to 7.206). *Dicte*, a mountain in Crete famous for its curative herb, dittany, is often used to designate Crete as a whole. Here it also establishes a pun. Jupiter's *dicta* ('decrees') bar Aeneas from *Dicte*'s land. Since no prior tradition

sends Aeneas to Crete, it is worth noting that the Cretans were proverbially liars. Odysseus, famous as a liar, assumes a Cretan identity when spinning his false identities in *Odyssey* 13–21.

211 *Harpies*: Aeneas' sequel to a famous episode in Apollonius is his only full encounter with the fantastical creatures of the *Odyssey* and *Argonautica*, though he at least sees Polyphemus the Cyclops later in the book. Homer had situated them beyond the known world, but Apollonius moved them within it. The Harpy episode centres on attempts made by the Trojans to set out tables to dine. And Aeneas is telling the story immediately after the lavish banquet Dido has set for them.

222 *In we rush*: Aeneas describes his arrival as a savage onslaught on an idyllic scene, but never suggests he tried to stop it. In Apollonius, Jason's crew drives the Harpies away from their homeland to save a starving, blind man whom the Harpies attack when he tries to eat. In the *Aeneid*, the Harpies keep possession of their depleted herds and relatively new land (though Celaeno's reference to it as the 'land of our fathers' gives the impression that they have always been there (249)). The episode recalls the attack of Odysseus' last surviving companions on the cattle of the Sun in the *Odyssey*.

241 *foul . . . seabirds*: Latin *ob-scenae*, 'kept from display, obscene', acquires a secondary sense in this context of dining (*cena*): *obs-cena*, 'kept from dining'.

247 *Sons of Laomedon*: Laomedon was Priam's father and proverbial for perfidy; see note to 8.157. This is a curious (and ominous) reminder that Trojans cannot always be relied on to keep their word. If Aeneas wants to be able to leave Carthage, he must not make the Trojans (or himself) too appealing to Dido.

250 *Carry on into your minds*: see 10.104, where Jupiter says the same line. In Latin, *accipite ergo* is apt for Celaeno. She is a 'bird of prey' and *accipiter* = 'hawk'. It is apt for Jupiter, too, whose bird is the eagle.

252 *direst of Demons*: Harpies are demons (Latin *Dirae*) associated with famine rather than Furies, the avengers of bloodshed (see note to 6.555). Celaeno's Greek name means 'the Dark One'.

256 *Till dire famine*: this prophecy makes it clear that Dido's ample tables, the setting of Aeneas' narration, cannot mark the end of his travels. Perhaps that is why Aeneas attributes the prophecy of eating tables in desperation to the one mythical monster he claims to have met personally. When one adds the later account (3.622–38) of Polyphemus cracking Ulysses' crewmen like eggs and eating them alive, one can see that Aeneas is deploying themes not ideal for a state banquet, even when tables are removed. See note to 7.122.

270–4 *Zacynthus . . . Leucas's cloudy peaks*: tradition had Aeneas visit Zacynthus and Leucas and found temples. Aeneas 'relocates' these traditions to Actium, some distance away. Virgil is intruding his authorial presence here.

Octavian defeated Antony and Cleopatra off Actium in 31 BC, in a naval victory that won him control of the Roman world and the opportunity to construct his own New Troy (see note to 8.675). Since Aeneas cannot know about this victory, Virgil is not obliged to digress into panegyric.

288 *Arms from Danaän victors*: a rare reference in epic to writing. The defeated Aeneas celebrates a personal triumph at Actium, memorializing in bronze his victory over a *Danaän* (Greek) warrior whose name is identical with that of Abas, the father of *Danaë*. See note to 7.410. The name 'Aeneas' resembles in spelling the Latin word *aëneus*, 'made of bronze'.

291 *we tuck out of sight*: Latin *abscondimus*. Aeneas bypasses not only Zacynthus and Leucas but the arguably fictional Phaeacia where Odysseus narrates his travels (*Odyssey* 6–12).

295 *Helenus, Priam's son*: Helenus, twin brother of Cassandra, whose prophecies no one believed, supported Troy until Paris' death, then left Troy, offended that Priam had given the widowed Helen to Deiphobus (see 6.494 ff. and notes), not to him. Since only he knew how the Greeks could take Troy, the Greeks captured him. He told them that success required the help of Pyrrhus and of Philoctetes, heir to the bow of Hercules (Sophocles, *Philoctetes* 603–21). He also saved Pyrrhus' life by advising him to return to Greece by land when the war ended (most of those who returned by sea died in shipwrecks). The grateful Pyrrhus made Helenus heir to his possessions, which included Andromache, Hector's widow, awarded as a war-prize (Euripides, *Andromache* and *Trojan Women*). Helenus and Andromache moved to Buthrotum in Epirus. Later Macedonian and Epirote kings claimed links with all three. Alexander the Great's mother was said to be the descendant of both Helenus and Pyrrhus. King Pyrrhus (who invaded Italy in 280 BC) named his son Helenus. See Erskine, *Troy between Greece and Rome*, 122–3.

309 *she could speak*: Aeneas, on poor terms with Hector's family in the *Iliad*, foregrounds his brusque treatment of Andromache, but also shows that neither Andromache nor Helenus holds any ill-will for him. The scene resonates with echoes of tragedy; uncannily so, since Aeneas' voice predates the works it echoes.

317 *what befell to uplift you*: Aeneas' emphasis on 'picking up' the 'fallen' Andromache highlights the sense of 'falling'—in Latin, *casus*, 'event, chance'—an apposite metaphor for Andromache's sorrows: her son had been 'allowed to fall', as Seneca's Calchas says, 'from the top of a high tower' (see note to 2.457).

319 *spousal relations*: this phrase doesn't say: 'Are you still enslaved to a marriage with Pyrrhus?' Latin has *servare*, 'maintain', not *servire*, 'be a slave to'. Aeneas' question is cruel; for he has already heard of Pyrrhus' death and of Andromache's marriage to Helenus.

322 *Single daughter left virgin*: Polyxena, daughter of Priam, was sacrificed on Achilles' grave by Pyrrhus.

330 *now enter Orestes*: the most frequently occurring character in surviving
Greek tragedy. Andromache is aware of herself as a character in drama
and draws on Euripides' play about her, *Andromache*. In it, her life is
threatened by Hermione, Pyrrhus' jealous Greek wife, until Orestes
arrives with Pyrrhus' body and ready to marry Hermione himself. Her
Orestes, 'maddened by ghosts of his crimes', is echoed, with slight
modification, in 4.471 where Orestes is 'driven mad in a drama'. Among
his crimes was the killing of his mother, Clytemnestra, to avenge her
killing of his father, Agamemnon.

341 *his lost mother*: Aeneas has Andromache affirm his account of Creusa's
death (though how she knows about it isn't clear). Ascanius remembers
her, as we see in 9.298; Aeneas never refers to her again after this.

348 *sob through the flood*: Aeneas, aptly, uses *singula* for the 'individual' words
interrupted by Helenus' weeping, since it suggests *singultus*, 'sobbing'.

382 *Ignorant man*: Aeneas has Helenus reaffirm what he himself insists on in
Books 2 and 3: his own ignorance. Why Juno has the power to censor
Apollo's seer is unclear. So too is the line between Helenus' ignorance and
what censorship forbids him to say.

390–2 *Under the bankside's . . . in a cluster*: repeated at 8.43–6, see note there
and on 8.85. I make the sow albino, not simply white (as in Latin), to keep
the pun on Alba (*alba* = 'white'). Some think there is a pun on Troia
(Troy) and *troia*, a word for 'sow' not found until over five hundred years
after Virgil. Romans loved puns too much to miss one so obvious for so
long if it had been available.

395 *Fates will discover a way*: Jupiter uses the same words in 10.113.

405 *mantle of purple*: Romans veiled their heads for sacrifice; Greeks did not.

443 *mad seer*: the Sibyl of Cumae; see note to 6.10 for details.

464–5 *sawn elephantine / Ivory*: the epithet 'sawn' makes the phrase echo
Odyssey 19.562–7 (see note to 6.893). Latin *elephantus,*'elephant', rarely
means 'ivory'. The usual word is *ebur*. Virgil probably has Aeneas use this
expression because Romans got their first glimpse of elephants when
Pyrrhus of Epirus (Helenus' distant successor) invaded Italy in 280 BC
and brought war-elephants. He defeated the Romans but lost so many
troops that he had to withdraw: hence the phrase, 'a Pyrrhic victory'.
Statues were sometimes decorated with a *combination* of gold and ivory,
most famously that of Athena in the Parthenon at Athens.

466 *Brought from Dodona*: site of a shrine of Jupiter, reputedly the oldest
oracle in Greece, plundered and destroyed first in the third century BC
and again by the Romans in 168–167 BC. The Latin indicates the origin
of these cauldrons, not whether they reached Helenus as 'imports' or
'plunder'. 'Neoptolemus' armour' takes the ambiguous imagery further.
Neoptolemus (another name for Pyrrhus) had been denied possession of
his father's armour. So his own armour marks a new start. When Helenus
inherits it he is marked as Pyrrhus' heir. In passing it on to Aeneas,

Helenus makes Aeneas his heir and betrays his Epirote New Troy as he reportedly betrayed Old Troy. Aeneas' descendants will destroy Buthrotum and refound it as a Roman colony. All Aeneas can see is the armour of the youth over whose shoulder he saw into the palace of Old Troy as it fell to the Greeks.

484 *a Phrygian cloak*: Andromache honours Ascanius as the image of her dead Astyanax, who is himself the image of his father Hector. In Seneca's *Trojan Women*, based on Greek originals, she keeps Astyanax's cloak as he is taken to be killed because it has been touched by Hector's ashes. She defines herself here by her past, speaking of herself not as Helenus' wife, but as Hector's.

499 *hindrance to Greeks*: Aeneas' self-narrated prophesy is grim with irony, as he holds Pyrrhus' armour.

507 *shortest of crossings*: Aeneas does not cross from Onchesmus (the traditional point), probably because it claimed Anchises' grave, which Aeneas places in Sicily.

515 *progression of stars*: these constellations are not all visible at the same moment, so Palinurus' observations take time. Line 516 repeats 1.744, which refers to the skies as presented by the Carthaginian poet Iopas. But when Aeneas adds Orion in the next line, the picture changes. Orion was proverbially menacing to sailors, particularly in winter, when it rises close to dawn. Hesiod warns sailors to secure their ships to land then; Polybius says a Roman fleet was lost because it sailed just after the rising of Orion. In summer, Orion rises around midnight. So Palinurus times his own rising to observe Orion's appearance in the skies.

526 *unmixed wine*: Romans, like Greeks, diluted wine with water.

541 *trained for the chariot*: the notion of the chariot as symbolic of peace is puzzling. Chariots were vehicles of war in many ancient societies. But Romans normally used chariots for races. Chariots are a sensitive topic for Aeneas, who lost his to Diomedes in *Iliad* 5. He always fights on foot in the *Aeneid*.

553 *the sailor's / Graveyard*: not simply an allusion to a remote myth of singing mermaids luring sailors to death upon the rocks. In 42 BC Octavian had seen the wreckage when Sextus Pompey defeated his navy off that same Scyllaean promontory; Scylla and Charybdis were not just poetic images for him.

578 *Enceladus' body*: see Glossary; most writers say it is Typhoeus (Typhon) under Etna.

610 *Anchises . . . took his hand*: Anchises plays the welcoming role Priam played to Sinon in Book 2. But Achaemenides is not part of a Greek plot to destroy the Trojans. This incident is probably Aeneas' fiction. It has no known precursor and Achaemenides is not mentioned elsewhere in the *Aeneid*. Aeneas positions himself in Odysseus' wake, claims moral superiority over Odysseus, and subverts the tradition that Odysseus was the

lone survivor of his voyage. Yet there's a flaw. Odysseus visits the Cyclopes in the first year or so of his travels. Aeneas, starting at about the same time, meets Achaemenides in his sixth year. Since Achaemenides claims he has been stranded just three months, the chronology doesn't fit. What the narrative does achieve, however, is to move Aeneas close enough to Ulysses (that is, Odysseus) in his travels that their paths almost cross in Sicily: at a safe distance from Rome. For one troublesome strand of the tradition makes Aeneas joint founder of Rome with Odysseus. The emphasis on Ulysses as *infelix*, 'who found no fulfilment', is therefore important.

684–5 *that I hold not . . . Charybdis or Scylla*: most manuscripts have *teneant*, 'that they hold'. But the sense requires either *teneamus*, 'that we hold' (which won't scan) or *teneam*, 'that I hold', which scans and is supported by several editors. The shortest crossing between Sicily and Italy is at the Straits of Messina (now bridged), notorious for difficult currents and linked mythically with Scylla (which tears ships apart) and Charybdis (which swallows ships beneath its surface).

705 *Selinus*: named for the wild celery, the emblem on its coins and used to make the victor's garland at the Isthmian games. Selinus was destroyed in 409 BC, rebuilt, destroyed again during the Second Punic War, then abandoned. So there is pathos underlying Aeneas' jesting remark. 'Palms', as in English, are both palm trees and the generic term for top honours awarded at games, as well as the palms of the hand.

707 *Drepanum's harbour*: the westernmost port on his circumnavigation of Sicily, the turning point before the home stretch to Italy. But Juno's storm sends Aeneas off the course altogether, to Carthage. Much of western Sicily, including Drepanum, was controlled by or allied with Carthage until the end of the Second Punic War. Drepanum is a fair distance from Segesta, where Aeneas celebrates games in honour of Anchises (Book 5), but the tradition that Segesta was founded by Trojans dates back at least as far as Thucydides (6.2) in the fifth century BC.

715 *a god drove me clear off the course*: Aeneas' last words show Carthage is not his destination but an unwanted digression. This land belongs to 'your' (*vestris*) people, not to us. Again, he publicly, though diplomatically, rejects Dido's offer to share Carthage. These are his last words in direct speech until 4.333, where he reaffirms the point directly in private conversation with Dido.

716 *gods' story of Fate*: Aeneas has indeed reframed 'the tale of destiny' in his own terms.

BOOK FOUR

9 *Anna my sister*: Anna is only the third Carthaginian so far named in the *Aeneid*, after Dido and Iopas in Book 1 (or the fourth, if we assume Bitias in 1.738 is Carthaginian not Trojan). Servius (on 4.682) says Varro claimed it was Anna who loved Aeneas. If so, there are two traditions current.

Virgil 'reconciles' them by making Anna Dido's sister and spiritual double. Anna was at some point identified with a Roman goddess, Anna Perenna. Ovid (*Fasti* 3.523–654) and Silius (*Punica* 8.29–192) say Anna sought refuge with Aeneas in Italy, only to flee when warned by Dido's ghost that Aeneas' Italian wife was jealous. She drowned in the river Numicus (also the site of Aeneas' death). Julius Caesar, who revised the Roman calendar, was killed on Anna Perenna's feast day: the Ides of March.

29 *unlovely confinement*: wordplay on *sepulchrum* and *pulchrum*, sepulchre and beauty, occurs even on a tombstone: as if 'se-' in 'sepulchre' were the separative prefix 'se-' as in 'secession'.

33 *and those sweet sons?*: not only Aeneas, but the child introduced to Dido as Ascanius, are sons of Venus. Minor adjustment is needed to keep Anna's unconscious irony. 'Venus' is in the centre of the Latin line where it can be taken either with 'sons' or 'delights' (depending on where one makes the metrical break).

38 *Africa, goldfield for triumphs*: Anna thinks of victorious African chieftains, but Virgil's contemporaries would think of Romans in triumph over Africa. This is probably why 'Africa' rather than the more usual 'Libya' is used. Publius Cornelius Scipio was named 'Africanus' for defeating Hannibal in 202 BC. His descendant won the same honour for destroying Carthage in 146 BC. North Africa was a rich prize for its Roman conquerors, most recently for Octavian, who had annexed Egypt.

46 *Juno's approval*: as divine patron not only of Carthage, but also of marriage.

67 *won't offer responses*: Latin *tacitus*. Dido is asking the 'hearts' of cattle to speak when she herself refuses to speak.

72 *Dicte's*: this Cretan mountain is home, ironically, to dittany, a medicinal herb used to heal wounds. Venus uses it on Aeneas' wound in 12.411–19.

85 *Love's*: Dido may still be taking Love (Cupid) not Ascanius onto her lap.

113 *rights to implore him*: Venus uses the same approach to Juno that Aeolus uses in 1.76–80.

120 *wings flurry their flanks*: flanking 'wings' (*alae*) of cavalry frighten the quarry into the centre where hunters are poised. The image also suggests a (game-)bird frantically flapping its wings against its own flanks. Juno plans to make the hunters the quarry of her own expedition.

126 *I'll designate her . . . marriage*: repeats 1.73, where Juno promises Aeolus the nymph Deiopea.

167 *the shrewd sky's brilliance*: Virgil makes use of the philosophers' notion that the skies are suffused with reason—the same idea that occurs at the beginning of St John's Gospel: 'In the beginning was rational power (*logos*).'

169 *That first day*: Dido's troubles have already started. What begins is hatred between Rome and Carthage, which, mythically at least, would not have arisen had Dido and Aeneas kept their distance.

195 *gossip the foul goddess*: 'foul' could, in Latin, refer to the goddess, her talk, or both. I link it to the goddess since, despite the seventeen-line preamble,

the four-line summary is concise and, essentially, true. In lines 220–1, Aeneas and Dido don't grasp the need for positive rumour (that is, a good public image). Since Virgil reports Rumour in *indirect speech*, we can't know what elements he, as reporter of rumour, is 'editing out'. In Books 2 and 3, internal narrators 'mask' Virgil's opinions. In Book 4, indirect speech 'masks' Aeneas' thoughts.

198 *Ammon*: Jupiter's Egyptian counterpart, whose oracle at Siwah was visited by Alexander the Great and, in Virgil's day, by Julius Caesar's opponent, Cato (see first note to 6.841 and note to 8.670).

203–4 *Rumour dissolves . . . their altars*: the Latin is full of wordplay based on *amor*: *amens*, '(the *amans* (lover) turned) mindless'; *amor*, 'love': *amarus*, '(love turned) bitter'; its burning bitterness, in turn, leads Iarbas to pray at the fires of the altars: *aras*.

215 *his eunuch entourage*: for this slur on Phrygian masculinity, see note to 3.111.

218 *faith in . . . Rumour*: the rumour Virgil reports about Iarbas' reaction to the rumour he hears about Dido leads Iarbas, Jupiter's son, to conclude that Jupiter himself is just a rumour. Iarbas is the only person in the *Aeneid* who speaks of himself entirely in the royal first person plural—and while addressing Jupiter! But his insult finally gets Jupiter's attention and prompts his intervention.

228 *God knows*: Latin *ideo*. Roman writers often make wordplays on forms of *deus*, 'god', particularly on the dative/ablative *deo*, even in the most 'serious' contexts. Cicero has a speaker return from a digression to the divine subject with the remark: 'Now I go back (*reDEO*) to the gods (*ad DEOS*)' (*De natura deorum* 1.80).

234 *Rome to Ascanius*: both Aeneas and Ascanius will be long dead before Rome is founded. So Jupiter is either exaggerating or alluding to the Greek tradition in which Aeneas did found Rome. Each time Jupiter speaks, his view of what destiny holds is different.

235 *he can build*: 'Build' is crucial. Jupiter sees something we don't yet see. He also views Carthage as an enemy nation—which it will be a thousand years after Aeneas' death—but Aeneas surely does not. Jupiter seems not to grasp that Aeneas' departure will *cause* that enmity.

238–9 *these parental / Orders*: Virgil echoes Homer's description of the dispatch of Hermes to Calypso in *Odyssey* 5.43 ff. Since Odysseus is held in Calypso's power against his will in a mythic land, unable to leave, Zeus sends Hermes to Calypso with orders that she must release him. Here Mercury is sent to Aeneas, who *does* have the power to leave and is not held against his will. Though Aeneas is not in his own time and space, he is, unlike Odysseus, in a city that does, for some centuries, exist in time and space.

242 *Orcus*: Death as an Italian god who devours all things. See the note to 6.273.

248 *Atlas, whose pine-covered head*: Atlas (a mountain and range in North Africa) is envisaged as both a geographical mass and a sensate divine being

who supports the heavens on his shoulders. Mercury, born on Mount Cyllene in the Peloponnesus and a descendant of Atlas on his mother's side, descends the living face of his maternal grandfather before plunging towards the sea like a gull. Atlas is not on the direct route between Olympus and Carthage. Mercury goes out of his way to retrace his genealogical 'descent'.

259 *outskirts*: Latin *magalia*, the Romanized form of a Punic word meaning 'huts', 'tents', but also the general name for the outskirts of Carthage.

260 *refurbishing houses*: Aeneas, dressed as Dido's consort, is overseeing the building of Carthage. Jupiter meant 'build' quite literally in line 235. Latin *novare* means 'to build something anew' rather than simply 'to build something new'. Scholars opt for the latter, seeing Carthage as a city newly built, rather than rebuilt. But the architecture of Virgil's Carthage is Roman, and Virgil's Rome was following Caesar's lead and rebuilding the city.

264 *Threaded with highlights . . . cross-weave*: this line is repeated at 11.75 in a surprising context.

271 *you deserter*: Mercury substitutes a wordplay on *terra*, 'land', and *teris*, 'wear down', for Jupiter's words about Carthage as enemy, which would make no sense to Aeneas.

278 *Vanished away*: gods often leave before finishing speeches in the *Aeneid*: Iris in Book 5 and Apollo in Book 9, for example. They say only what is needed to precipitate the action required.

283–84 *get round the besotted / Ruler*: the exact phrasing of Aeneas' thoughts is beyond reach in indirect speech, since the reporter can superimpose or substitute his own attitudes, as Mercury has just demonstrated. Aeneas could have been thinking: 'How can I broach this matter with my darling Dido?' or 'How can I broach the matter with this besotted ruler?'

292 *great love affair*: singular *amor* = 'love', plural *amores* = 'love affair(s)'.

295 *They all were delighted*: the Trojans were not easy with Aeneas' affair with Dido, as Odysseus represents his crew as critical of his dalliance with Circe in the *Odyssey*.

296 *Who could fool a lover?*: an odd question. Lovers are proverbially gullible. The issue is why Aeneas cannot deceive Dido. Refitting a storm-damaged navy in Carthaginian harbours could not go undetected for long, and Aeneas waits too long. When Dido challenges his planned departure, she echoes his 'confidential' instructions to Mnestheus precisely. Rumour, even if unrighteous, supplies information the righteous Aeneas does not.

301 *resembling a Thyiad*: The rites of Bacchus (Dionysus), though banned in Rome, were celebrated by the women of Thebes (in Greece) on Mount Cithaeron. They dressed in animal skins and carried a staff called a thyrsus. In their divine intoxication they were allegedly capable of tearing cattle (and humans) to pieces. Poets called them 'Maenads' ('Mad women') or 'Thyiads' ('Women who offer living sacrifices'). Their most famous description is in Euripides' *Bacchae*. See also 7.394–404.

305 *perfidious:* in calling Aeneas perfidious, Dido is reversing the Roman convention that the Carthaginians are 'perfidious': breakers of agreements and other pledges of honour (and she does so again at 4.367 and 4.421). The Latin queen Amata also accuses him of perfidy in 7.362. The only other person so characterized is Turnus, in 12.31; the only object so described is Turnus' sword in 12.731.

308 *doomed to a cruel death*: the first of Dido's hints that she will kill herself if Aeneas leaves.

324 *partner in marriage*: Dido's complaint recalls Creusa's protest, as reported by Aeneas, when he prepares to leave his family behind in the house and go forth to die (2.675–8). But this time there is no child over whose head a divine flame can flicker to change Aeneas' resolve.

328 *a baby Aeneas*: Julius Caesar's affair with Cleopatra, in contrast, did produce a child, Caesarion, who was killed on Octavian's orders after the defeat of Antony and Cleopatra.

333 *That I owe you, my ruler*: these are the first direct words Virgil has given Aeneas since the end of Book 3. We are allowed no insight into his feelings about Dido; their affair is presented in terms of her feelings towards him and the way their relationship looks to others.

335 *missing Elissa*: the 'distance' Aeneas creates by referring to Dido in the third person and as, for the first time in the epic, 'Elissa' (see note to 1.346), is profound. It is further intensified by the soundplay between *Elissa* and *meminisse* ('remembering'), which evokes the Latin *elisae* = 'of the woman erased' (as in the English 'elision') and thus adds a touch of ambiguity. Dido does not miss the undertone: she calls herself Elissa in line 610, where I add 'forgotten' to compensate for what I could not convey here. Compare Seneca, *Medea* 556–61, where Medea sees that her request for the anger between herself and Jason to be 'obliterated' (*irae . . . oblitterentur*) results in his being utterly 'oblivious' (*oblitus*) of her. He erases everything with the anagram: *omnia ex animo expuli*, (roughly) 'I've wiped my (mental) *slate* of all our *tales* . . .'

337 *a few words in defence*: Aeneas answers as if charged in court with breach of contract (*foedus*). The Latin phrase *pro re*, which I render 'in defence', is the legal formula in Roman courts for addressing the charges brought. But Dido's charge is breach of faith (*fides*); she concedes that no contract exists. Aeneas deals similarly with her charge that he intended to slip away silently. He is reported to have avowed to others *an intent* to talk to her before leaving, even though he has ordered the preparations to be made in silence. His rhetorical skill enables him to inflect language to his purposes without actually lying.

352–3 *Anchises' / Angry face*: Virgil mentions no dream visions of Anchises in this context.

361 *Going to Italy's not my choice*: nor is staying with Dido, as she suspects and as he affirms. There is no reason to think that he had ever told her he would stay indefinitely.

395 *force of love's power*: Virgil does not specify whose love: her love for him, his love for her, or love's power in general. But there is no reason to suppose that Aeneas (before this ambiguous moment) shares Dido's obsession. That suggestion was made to accommodate him first to Christian, then to Victorian sensibilities. Rejecting Dido's approaches would have made bad politics. And readers have long recognized the influence of Apollonius' Jason and Medea on Virgil's shaping of the relationship between Aeneas and Dido. Ancient poetry abounds with instances of one-sided love relationships from Homer onwards.

402 *Ants getting ready for winter*: in 1.430–6 the Carthaginians are like bees in summer, building hives, harvesting pollen; here, the Trojans are ants preparing for winter, plundering what others have harvested (as humans plunder beehives). Neither insect affords a happy model for a society that allows individuals freedom of action or choice. Virgil reworks Ennius' description of Punic *elephants* lumbering along. The tiny can be as destructive as the huge. See also note to 6.898.

422 *Trusts with his innermost secrets*: that Aeneas has a relationship with Anna, which continues after he breaks contact with Dido, is a surprise. And the notion that he has inner secrets to which we have even less access than Dido is maddening. Given the tradition that makes Anna his lover, possibilities abound. But Virgil makes the relationship a wholly private domain, denying even Rumour a few words. He never hints that Dido is jealous of Anna. Rather, Dido authorizes contact between them by using Anna as a go-between.

436 *when my time expires*: Dido cannot possibly be stating outright that she intends to kill herself at the end of this extension of time, as some translations imply. It is important that Anna does not grasp that Dido intends to kill herself. Dido is using a financial metaphor for which Aeneas has set the tone by describing their relationship in legal, contractual terms. Dido employs the terminology of a mortgage (in which property offered as security for a loan is 'dead'—hence the 'mort-' element in 'mortgage'—to the owner until the amount of the loan, plus interest, is repaid). In Dido's case, what is borrowed is time, and the security offered is her life.

444–5 *the old oak tree / Sticks to the crags*: a paradoxical simile when used of someone resolved to go away. This is a variation on *Iliad* 8.16, where Homer suggests that Tartarus is as far below us as heaven is above us. Virgil does another 'take' of this Homeric line in 6.577–9, where he tells us that Tartarus extends down twice as far as heaven extends upwards.

468 *desolate landscapes*: in her dreams, Dido herself now seems displaced in time, a lost ghost hunting her lost people after Rome annihilates Punic Carthage. The illusory reality she has inhabited since Aeneas' arrival, which collapses historical time into a single mythic frame, makes her an allegory of Carthage itself. Her death will be the death of her whole culture.

470 *Seeing the sole sun*: from Euripides, *Bacchae* 918–19, with only a change in the person of the verb.

469–73 *She was like Pentheus . . . sit waiting*: Pentheus and Orestes are not in Dido's dreams. They tell us how Virgil sees her, not how she saw herself. The simile inverts sexual roles and juxtaposes two Euripidean heroes. One, Pentheus, is killed by his mother; the other is his mother's killer. Virgil makes Pentheus more like Orestes by changing Euripides' Maenads into Furies. Each experiences pluralized visions of reality: madness is inflicted on Pentheus by Bacchus, and on Orestes by the Furies (and his conscience). But neither is in love or intent on suicide.

486 *sleep-bringing opium poppy*: a preamble to what follows, not an addition to what precedes it. There is no point in having a guardian if part of its attendant's duties are to drug it to sleep. In Apollonius 4.156–7, Medea drugs the dragon guarding the Golden Fleece in violation of her duties so she can help Jason steal it.

508 *his person, in effigy*: Dido, like Pygmalion and Venus, is crafting illusions. Dido's plans for her death recall two unmentioned tragic heroes: Hercules, victim of his wife's love and suspicions, who cremates himself on a pyre in Sophocles' *Women of Trachis*; and Ajax, the only character in Greek tragedy arguably killed on stage. In Sophocles' *Ajax* he dies on his own sword. Ajax is brother of the first Greek Dido mentions: Teucer (1.619–22). Dido chooses a heroic male model for suicide, not the traditional noose of the lovelorn woman. Since she uses both fire *and* sword, she is committing a symbolically civic suicide: one destroys a city rather than a person by fire and the sword. The 'female' qualities for which she had hoped to be remembered, her loyalty and chastity, have been lost because of her affair with Aeneas. Yet she deludes Anna by playing the role of Medea, a woman attempting to destroy her unfaithful lover by witchcraft. If Virgil is attempting to insinuate his Dido into the firmament of great tragic heroes, he has to give her death both the resolution of an Ajax and the flamboyance of a Hercules, but leave us to make the connections he omits.

511–12 *Hecate . . . Avernus*: see notes to 6.13 and 126.

529 *descendant of Phoenix*: see note to 1.712.

556 *some shape of a god*: Latin has no definite or indefinite articles. *Forma dei* can indicate everything from '(a) shape of (a) god' to '(the) shape of (the) god'. If this *is* Mercury, Virgil's emphasis on how *similar* it is to Mercury is odd. The vision is self-presented and self-erasing: Virgil uses reflexive verbs and describes it in terms of 'phantoms, ghosts, shadows', which come up (from below) suddenly (line 571). So Aeneas' declaration that the vision is a god *sent* to him from heaven differs from Virgil's authorial view. Aeneas extrapolates his notion that heaven is *again* sending him a divine messenger from the accuracy with which the vision reproduces the image of Mercury; he displaces the dream's element of uncertainty into a vagueness as to which god he has seen. The nearest parallel is the appearance of Apollo (in disguise) to Ascanius in 9.638–51 (9.650–1 are similar in many details to 4.558–9). See also the fake Aeneas Juno devises

in 10.636–44. It dispels itself back into the clouds (10.664) from which she had formed it in a phrase identical to the ending of line 4.570 except that it has 'clouds' instead of 'night'.

569 *Hang the delays!*: Latin *mora*, 'delay', has undertones of death because its sound is close to that of *mors*, 'death'. Much that the vision says is misleading; and the idea that the woman is the changeable factor in this relationship is absurd. Further, it is winter (Greeks and Romans did not sail the open seas in winter); when the Trojans are at sea in Book 5, they encounter a storm. Dido is planning suicide not murder. Though she thinks of attacking Aeneas' fleet, she dismisses the idea.

580 *Lightning flash*: the flash of his sword blinds us to the absence of lightning from heaven confirming the dream as ominous. The image also symbolizes the end of sexual involvement, as in Ovid's story of Cinyras and Myrrha (*Metamorphoses* 10.298–502). See F. Ahl, *Metaformations: Soundplay and Wordplay in Ovid and Other Classical Poets* (Ithaca, NY, and London, 1985), 213–29. There is also a possible wordplay on Punic *barcas*, 'lightning'. See note to 4.632.

586 *noticed the fleet under full sail*: the description recalls Catullus 64.126–7, where Ariadne looks for Theseus, the lover who has left her. This echo has further resonances, since Aeneas has a close relationship with his lover's sister, as Theseus later has with Phaedra, Ariadne's sister (whom he marries); Theseus too founds a state, Athens: he is the Greek parallel for Romulus in Plutarch's *Lives*.

596 *your unrighteous acts come to haunt you*: I read this sentence as an exclamation, not as a question.

597 *the appropriate course*: some take this line to mean: 'That was the time for restraint: when you were giving him your power.' But Dido is saying she should have acted against him (instead of becoming his lover) when he was at her mercy. It is too late to act against him now her honour is lost.

602 *a treat for his banqueting father*: as Procne serves Itys (Itylos in Homer) to her husband Tereus (Zethos in Homer), to punish his rape and mutilation of her sister Philomela (some poets reverse the sisters' names). This mythic precedent is closer than the male Atreus who serves his brother Thyestes' children to him.

603 *could not have been*: Dido's correction of verb tense and mood reveals her first thoughts about what to do when the Trojans arrived: she had calculated the risks of military action, but decided they were too high.

610 *forgotten Elissa*: see note to line 335 for the addition of 'forgotten'.

615 *Let him be hammered in war*: some of Dido's prayers are partially fulfilled in Books 7–12. Aeneas' death, referred to (but not narrated), occurs at the river Numicus in Italy.

623 *ritual gifts to my ashes*: Rome's wars against the Carthaginian Hannibal (Dido's future 'avenger') and the Numidian prince, Jugurtha, and Rome's own civil wars fought in Africa are often represented in Latin poetry as an

offering of blood to the ashes of Carthage (and thus of Dido). The idea is reinforced with wordplay between *Poeni*, 'Carthaginians', and *poena*, 'punishment'. Hannibal himself is never named in the *Aeneid*.

632 *Barce*: Virgil's use of *Sychaeus*' nurse for this mission not only brings Anna to witness Dido's last moments, but ensures that Barce, Dido's last connection with her dead husband, witnesses it too. Barce's name derives from *Barcas*, a Punic heroic epithet: 'Gleaming Sword'. Anna has so far been playing the role of the Nurse in a tragedy. Now Virgil accommodates a tradition in which Dido (or Anna) dies with Sychaeus' nurse in attendance. Barce's name also recalls (*a*) the Barcaeans, who are among Dido's North African foes (4.42–3), and (*b*) the Carthaginian Barcas family, the most famous of whom was Hannibal (Silius 10.355).

638 *Stygian Jupiter's rites*: of Dis (Pluto), Death as the divine force ruling the underworld.

662 *our death*: Dido's shift to the first person plural emphasizes that Aeneas will share in the death prompted by his abandonment of her love. She will die on his sword, next to his effigy, on a pyre whose fire his eyes will have to drink in and keep as a memory to haunt him for ever.

670 *Carthage . . . faced final collapse*: the simile makes explicit the equation between Dido's death and the annihilation of Carthage by Rome in 146 BC. Her three efforts to raise herself up may also symbolize the three Punic Wars between Rome and Carthage.

672 *soul now lost to her body*: Anna is Dido's 'other self' (4.8), the sharer of her soul, and has, in a way, lost her soul (Latin *anima*). She is thus *exanimis*, 'without soul, dead'. Anna, not Dido, gives the last speech from the pyre (as she would in a scene based on Varro's 'other' version).

BOOK FIVE

1 *Meanwhile*: Aeneas returns to his own times. Book 5 is set in Sicily, amid traditions of Trojan and Greek colonies there, and of the island's absorption into the Roman world. The west of Sicily was dominated by Carthage, the east by Greeks until Rome took over during the Punic Wars. But in Virgil's day Sicily had been fiercely contested during the civil wars. From 43 to 36 BC it was controlled by Sextus Pompey. Wresting Sicily and the seas from him was Octavian's hardest task, and there are numerous 'echoes' of it in Books 5 and 6, not least because Sextus and Aeneas shared the epithet *Pius*, Righteous. See note to 1.148.

8–11 *Now . . . darkness*: almost the same as 3.192–5, where Aeneas sails from a fictional visit to (real) Crete to the (fantastical) Harpies. He now returns from a fictional visit to (real) Carthage to his traditional travels. The visit to Carthage is set between two storms, as Odysseus' visit to Phaeacia is set between periods of sleep (*Odyssey* 6–13). No gods start this storm: it is just the wrong season to be at sea.

24 *Eryx's coasts*: Eryx was the son of Venus, by Neptune (or Butes, an Argonaut). Traditionally, he built a city, a temple to Venus, gave his name to a mountain, challenged Hercules to box, and was killed. The actual temple at Eryx was first built by Carthaginians and dedicated to Astarte (Venus). The city kept ties with Carthage until captured by Rome in the First Punic War. It is an apt landfall for Aeneas on his way back from Carthage.

35 *Acestes*: founder of Segesta (Gk. Aegesta), son of Aegesta, who fled Troy during Hercules' attack, and of the river Crimisus (the manuscripts' Crinisus is an error) who mated with her in the form of a dog or bear (Acestes wears a she-bear's skin). Segesta had a turbulent history (Acestes is happy to see an *allied* fleet) and co-operated with Carthage until the First Punic War, when it joined the Romans and was rewarded with increased territory, probably including nearby Eryx.

49 *if I've not made a slip*: Aeneas' abrupt departure from Africa and the ensuing weather (rather than planning) allow a chance for rites not performed when Anchises died.

60 *my city is founded*: presumably Lavinium, his settlement in Latium (Italy).

66 *a boat race*: the precursor of Virgil's funeral games is *Iliad* 23 (the games for Patroclus), but Virgil substitutes a boat race for Homer's chariot race. Perhaps chariots are too sensitive a subject for Aeneas, who lost his rig to Diomedes in *Iliad* 5 (see Introduction). A boat race also recalls the contemporary struggle for control of the seas around Sicily, since Virgil pointedly specifies the Roman connections of some contestants. He makes Homer's Greek boxing match a lethal Romano–Sicilian style contest between the Trojan Dares and the ancient son of Sicilian soil, Entellus. Finally, he modifies and repositions in Sicily elements of the tradition that Rome was founded after the burning of the Trojan fleet.

73 *Helymus*: a son of Anchises and half-brother to Aeneas (though Virgil is silent about this). His name evokes the Elymi, who, with the Carthaginians, occupied most of western Sicily before the Punic Wars and who, Thucydides says (6.2), also came from Troy.

83 *Ausonian Tiber*: Aeneas' ignorance of the Tiber is coupled oddly with his 'learned' use of 'Ausonian' to describe it. Ausonia (named for Auson, son of Odysseus by Circe or Calypso) was an ancient name for Italy.

91 *bowls*: Latin *pateras*, apt for vessels used for offerings to one's father, *pater*. The wordplay (which has no manageable English equivalent) underscores Aeneas' suspicion that the snake might be his father's 'familiar' (as a black cat is a witch's 'familiar' spirit). The same wordplay recurs in line 98.

95 *local god*: usually the soul of a dead local hero whose identity is unknown to the foreign visitor, but who must be treated with respect. See note to 7.136.

104 *Phaëthon*: = 'shining one', epithet of the Sun; also the name of the Sun's child, Phaëthon, who drove the solar chariot for one disastrous day (see 10.185–8 and note to 10.85). Reference to him forebodes catastrophe.

115 *Pristis*: a name for huge (but sometimes 'real') sea-creatures. The other
ships are named after monsters that Epicureans claimed never existed.
Mnestheus, captain of the *Pristis*, is ancestor of the Memmius clan, whose
only notable members both made their names as tribunes of the people (see
note to 6.842) in 111 and 66 BC respectively. The elder Memmius accused
the Roman nobility of corruption when an African prince named Jugurtha
bribed many senators. He tried to have Jugurtha interrogated, but failed.
He ran for the consulship in 99 BC but was killed by his rival for office. The
younger Memmius (a member of the Epicurean school of philosophy!)
attacked the wealthy Lucullus and his family and, at first, opposed Julius
Caesar. He even married Fausta, the daughter of the dictator Sulla, but
then divorced her, and joined Caesar. Fausta promptly married a supporter
of Pompey, and between them they ruined Memmius' political career.
He went into exile in Athens and probably died there. He was a wealthy
man, an orator, philosopher, poet, and patron of Lucretius, who dedicated
his epic to him. He also sought out the company of Catullus (but Catullus
disliked him); and Cicero prevented him from buying Epicurus' house in
Athens.

118 *Gyas . . . the Chimaera*: no Roman link is given for the captain of the
largest ship. Servius proposes the Geganius family; but it had vanished
from records long before Virgil. 'Gyas' suggests strength of limb, like the
Latin warrior Gyas in 10.318, or Gyes, a monster with a hundred arms
(M. Paschalis, *Virgil's Aeneid: Semantic Relations and Proper Names* (Oxford,
1997), 187)—apt for the captain of an oared galley. The mythic Chimaera,
also used as a symbol by Turnus (in 7.785), was a predatory, fire-breathing monster that roved Asia Minor and was killed there by the hero
Bellerophon. Plutarch thought it symbolic of a pirate; and *Chimaera* is a
war galley: a trireme. If there is a Roman link, it may be too controversial
to be stated.

121 *Centaur . . . Sergestus*: centaurs, half-human, half-horse, were thought
clever, crafty, and treacherous. The only important Sergius is Lucius
Sergius Catilina, who planned a revolution at Rome in 63 BC but was
stopped by Cicero. He is depicted on Aeneas' shield in 8.668. Sergestus
is one of Aeneas' chief officers.

122–3 *Cloanthus . . . Cluentius*: since the Cluentius family is of Oscan rather
than Latin roots, the epithet 'Roman' is rather odd. Oscan was a language
related to Latin, widely spoken in the areas south of Latium and especially among the Samnites, the most durable of Rome's rivals in Italy
until their annihilation by Sulla in 82 BC. Lucius Cluentius was defeated
and killed by Sulla in 89 BC during Rome's wars with her Italian allies
(Appian, *Civil Wars* 1.50.221). He was a *meddix*, an Oscan magistrate
whose rank corresponds with that of a consul at Rome (although the
title is conventionally rendered in Latin as *praetor*, the next most senior
magistracy at Rome after consul). Another Cluentius, Aulus Cluentius
Habitus, from Larinum (on the border between Apulia and the territory

of the Frentani) died the following year (Cicero, *Pro Cluentio* 11). Cicero defended his son, charged with homicide, in a case of family vendettas and poisonings involving his murderous mother, Sassia (the name of Cloanthus' ship, *Scylla*, means 'bitch', as well as the sea-monster Scylla of 3.424–8). The three identified captains, then, have descendants who challenged Rome's ruling elite in the days of Virgil's father and grand-father. They look suspiciously like the kind of reformers, intellectuals, revolutionaries, and gangsters that critics said were the basis of Sextus Pompey's forces in Sicily during the civil wars. Since Virgil's competitors in the boat race are as fictional as the race itself, he could have selected any Roman families he wished. So one has to wonder why he chose these.

175 *Tosses him . . . into the sea*: if Gyas has an unnamed Roman descendant, Menoetes may give the clue. Octavian's rival in Sicily, Sextus, had a second in command, Menodorus (also called Menas). Menodorus left Sextus' navy after Sextus refused to have all three enemy leaders (Octavian, Mark Antony, and Lepidus) murdered when they were on board his flagship negotiating terms. They were, he argued, his guests. Menodorus concluded that Sextus was not ruthless enough to win and changed sides. But Sextus had a loyal admiral, Menecrates, who, when critically wounded, threw himself into the sea rather than surrender. At that time Sextus, with his crews of Romans, Greeks, slaves, and pirates (many from Asia Minor), controlled Sicily. He surrendered to (and was executed by) Octavian's forces in Miletus (in Asia Minor) in 36 BC.

182 *Teucrians still laugh*: no one goes back to pick him up. Similarly, when Aeneas' helmsman goes overboard (5.858–9), no one tries to find and bury his body.

213 *frighten a dove*: at this very moment someone is out catching a dove for use as a target in the archery contest.

243 *Faster . . . than an arrow*: Cloanthus' arrow outpaces Mnestheus' dove. But Virgil later (5.493) describes Mnestheus as the winner, as if such were his original intent. Having an Epicurean's ancestor win a race of ships named for mythical monsters he claimed could not exist would have been a nice touch. But having him come second because the gods help his rival isn't bad either.

248 *talent*: a measure of weight; see note to 9.265.

260 *Demoleos*: an odd combination of two Greek words meaning 'people'.

270 *How they jeered him!*: yet Virgil applauds him, not the winners, for sea-manship. That Catiline's ancestor wins plaudits (echoed by Aeneas) is baffling unless it is displaced praise for Catiline's conqueror, Cicero (never named), or unless Virgil's politics are more radical than anyone suspects. Virgil is free to refer to Catiline's and Cluentius' ancestors, but not to Cicero's. Yet mention of Catiline or Cluentius (even Memmius) stirs memories of Cicero. Octavian must have been emphatic that Cicero's name (like Sextus Pompey's) was 'out'. Cicero, who supported Caesar's

opponents, was executed on Mark Antony's orders in 43 BC. Since this boat race is Virgil's fiction, there is probably a reason why 'Cluentius' wins (Cicero's Cluentius did), why 'Memmius' runs him a close second, and why 'Catiline' comes last. But this is not the place for such speculation. Since Aeneas' fleet is now his 'Troy', a state without a city, the metaphor of the ship of state has great power in *Aeneid* 5: this is, perhaps, Rome *after* the Punic Wars, brought close to ruin by factions in the first century BC.

273–4 *on a raised road's / Flagstones*: the snake's error is wandering onto a roadway instead of remaining concealed. This may be a continuation of the allusion to Catiline who 'breaks cover' prematurely in his conspiracy. If so it is also evocative of Cicero's arrest on the road when trying to escape Antony's troops.

285 *Pholoë*: her name echoes that of the centaur, Pholus, killed accidentally by Hercules (and mentioned by Virgil, 8.294 and *Georgics* 2.456), an ironically apt prize for the captain of the *Centaur*.

292 *They come thronging*: though the foot race is more democratic than the boat race, where the oarsmen are anonymous, Virgil names just seven sprinters: three Trojans, two Greeks, and two Sicilians. No Roman pedigrees are suggested. The prizes offered are less lavish than those for the boat race.

316 *is heard*: I keep what I can of Virgil's order; one sees a race start before hearing the starting signal.

333 *unclean sludge*: in *Iliad* 23.773 ff., Ajax slips in the dung of sacrificial animals during the foot race, leaving victory to Odysseus. Here, an idealized contest becomes a dishonest scramble for honours in a field sodden with sacrificial waste. Virgil briefly deludes us into thinking he approves of Nisus' cheating, since he intrudes no negative moralizing. His most biting irony is saved, as in the boat race, for the spectators.

334–5 *Euryalus . . . Salius*: each name contains 'leaping' in Greek and in Latin. Paschalis (*Virgil's Aeneid*, 190) nicely points out that the *eury-*, 'wide', in 'Euryalus' gives him the added ability to do a 'broad' jump over his fallen rivals. But the *hal-* element in Euryalus' name also suggests the 'salt' sea, as in Homer's *póntos halós*: 'the sea of salt' (*Iliad* 21.59). And Virgil activates that sense in 9.433. For possible allusions to historical figures in Nisus and Euryalus, see note to 9.465.

360 *Stolen by Greeks*: Nisus, who cheats, is given a prize stolen by Greeks from a holy place. No obligation is felt to return the stolen item to the god.

364 *palms wreathed . . . in leather*: the winners of other contests receive palm wreaths; for the boxing they bring the 'wreathed' palms of their own hands. The prize is a bull, marked for sacrifice by gilded horns and garlands (and the boxing gloves are made of bulls' hides). The first contestant, Dares, has a name thought to derive from the skinning of a sacrificial animal (Paschalis, *Virgil's Aeneid*, 192): 'Flayer'.

367 *the vanquished*: losers usually survived Greek boxing matches. But reference to Amycus of Bebrycia (on the Black Sea), who forced visitors to box with him and killed them, raises doubts. Amycus is killed by Pollux in Apollonius; in Theocritus, Pollux thrashes him and makes him promise to be kind to future visitors.

372 *Bebrycian Butes*: Virgil's invention. In Apollonius, Butes is an Argonaut not a Bebrycian. A boxer named Butes is linked with the foundation of Lilybaeum in Sicily and is father of Eryx (5.24 and note).

379 *Nobody dares*: avoiding this wordplay (not in the Latin) was impossible.

387 *Entellus*: Virgil's invention; linked with the earth of his land, Latin *tellus* (Paschalis, *Virgil's Aeneid*, 193) and a protégé of Eryx (see note to 5.24). He recalls Hercules' African rival Antaeus, whose strength comes from the earth.

405 *rigid with iron and lead*: they are Roman boxing gloves, *caestus*, designed to kill (*caedere*) the opponent, not to protect the fighter's hands.

416 *both of my temples*: *tempus* means (1) 'time' and (2) 'temple' (of the head), a doubleness underscored by *geminis*, 'twin'. Old age has the (twin) advantages of time and his (two) whitening temples. The boxing match recalls in many details the fight between Odysseus and Iros the beggar in the *Odyssey*.

481 *lies the great ox*: the first actual killing in Book 5; the second is also of an animal, a dove. The single human 'killing' in this book is Palinurus'. In Book 6 no human 'killings' occur, and there are no animal killings in Book 2 (the bull Laocoön tries to sacrifice escapes; and the wooden horse actually 'gives birth').

489 *shoot . . . arrows*: the contest follows and expands *Iliad* 23.850 ff. The dove, seen earlier as a simile, is now a live target attached to a mast. Hippocoön and Eurytion are not in earlier writers.

493 *his boat race victory*: Virgil implies that Mnestheus won; but he came second (5.243). His shot, aptly, liberates the dove, for he is the person compared to the liberated dove in 5.209–17. But the liberated dove is caught by the arrow, just as his boat was caught by the arrow-like speed of Cloanthus' vessel.

496 *by breaking . . . a solemn agreement*: Pandarus broke the truce between Greeks and Trojans in *Iliad* 4.72 ff., by shooting an arrow that wounded Menelaus.

521 *Technical art arched tense*: in reproducing Virgil's anagrams and sound-plays, I have made the bowstring more musical than in the original.

524 *loudly, but too late*: an ambiguous omen. Some scholars think it refers to Caesar's murder a millennium later. But comets tend to forecast impending rather than (or as well as) distant events. The archery contest takes place near the ships, and the target dove is tied to a mast. So the prodigy warns that the ships are under threat or that they will pass on to an immortality of their own (or both, since both are accomplished).

536 *Cisseus*: the father of Hecuba (wife of Priam). Thus the bowl is one of Aeneas' family heirlooms—a special gift indeed at the funeral games of his father Anchises, but unwittingly ominous, for Hecuba dreamed she was pregnant with fire. See lines 636–7 below and note on 7.319.

564 *Polites*: Aeneas had watched his father and grandfather being killed at Troy. A town of the Latin League (see note to 6.773–5), Politorium, reputedly founded by Polites, is listed by Pliny, *Natural History* 3.68–9, as among those that had vanished without trace. Turnus also rides a Thracian piebald in 9.49–50.

568 *Latins of Atius' clan*: Octavian's mother Atia was the daughter of Gaius Atius Balbus.

570 *his mount a Sidonian*: as Dido retains Aeneas' gifts, so Aeneas and Iulus keep hers—though it is surprising that they had time to embark a horse in their haste to leave Carthage.

588 *There was a labyrinth*: in Knossos, Crete, a large complex, now known as the Palace of Minos, was built into a hillside on many interconnected levels. Coins from Knossos often show a labyrinth motif (see note on 6.27). Pliny (*Natural History* 36. 91–3) notes that 'the labyrinth' is also a marked walk on complex patterns of tiles, and the name of a ceremonial game performed by young Roman riders in the Campus Martius (see note to 6.127). Comparison of cavalry manoeuvres to a labyrinth may derive from Etruscan usage. An Etruscan vase depicting a maze and cavalry bears the inscription *Truia*, taken to mean 'complex movement' or 'maze dance' in Etruscan. Romans probably connected *truia* and *Troia*, creating the notion that the exercise was Trojan. They celebrated this display as the 'Game of Troy'. Comparison of choreographed motion to a static architectural labyrinth as designs baffling the eye prepares us for the labyrinthine imagery in Book 6.

606 *sent Iris down*: Juno uses Iris (as in 4.693–705), this time in an assault on the ships (compare 9.2, which is identical with this line, and also heralds an attack on Trojan ships). Book 5, dominated by men's games, is capped by actions taken by women, who are excluded from watching or participating in official events. Virgil is absorbing the tradition, recorded in Dionysius, that Rome was founded by a woman, Rhome, after the Trojan ships were burned; but he localizes the incident in Sicily and robs Rhome of her glory.

620 *Beroë*: Iris' choice of identity looks solidly bourgeois until one examines the name. In *Georgics* 4. 341 she is a nymph, the daughter of Ocean. See Paschalis, *Virgil's Aeneid*, 207, for (*a*) the connection with Juno–Beroë who causes Bacchus' mother Semele to be blasted with fire, and (*b*) the presence of *mare*, 'sea', in the name of Tmarian Doryclus (whose own name means 'famous for his spear' in Greek).

693–4 *unprecedented / Storm*: the rainstorm follows immediately after Aeneas' prayer, but Virgil makes no causal connection such as scholars tend to infer.

He leaves open the possibility of coincidence; and Aeneas seems to regard the storm as coincidence, not as a divine response to his prayer. His reaction is not gratitude, but disheartenment. Extinguishing fires is easier than rekindling Aeneas' resolution.

709 *follow where fate drags*: a variant of a Stoic saying, whose classic form is that fate *leads* the willing and *drags* the unwilling. Nautes ('sailor' in Greek) must be the only known mythic 'Nautes', who received Pallas' shrine, the Palladium (see 2.166–83), when Diomedes restored it to the Trojans. But Nautes' philosophical and practical advice doesn't cheer Aeneas any more than the storm does.

722 *Down from the skies*: the vision comes *down* from the skies (not *up* from the world of ghosts), looks like (rather than 'is') Anchises, and, though it appears at night, is not linked with a dream. Contrast the vision resembling Mercury in 4.556 (and note). It is the vision, not Virgil as author, who claims Jupiter has sent it. Virgil again 'distances' his account through other voices.

742 *Who are you running away from?*: Aeneas' words echo Dido's question to him when he plans to leave Carthage (4.314); and he uses exactly these words to her ghost at 6.466. Similarly, Odysseus begs his mother's ghost not to go from him in *Odyssey* 11.210.

747 *Jupiter's mandates*: Aeneas divides the vision's words into three distinct authorizations: (1) Jupiter's mandate, (2) Anchises' instructions, (3) his own orders. He allows no debate, and gives Acestes no choice. Note the official change of citizenship for the *matres*, the married women who have had children. The Latin is *transcribunt*, 'transfer', not *adscribunt*, 'add'. Families are being separated by this action. See 9.284–91.

781 *defies saturation*: Virgil uses a rare adjective, *exsaturabile*, to describe Juno's heart. Juno's insatiable anger is very un-Saturn-like behaviour for the daughter of Saturn (thought of as a banished god who had presided over a Golden Age of peace and prosperity), as Neptune, himself a child of Saturn, would know.

798 *Destiny's thread-spinning Sisters*: Latin *Parcae*. They represent a different way of viewing causality. The three sisters (Clotho, Lachesis, and Atropos) spin, measure, and cut the thread for each individual life. Fate, by contrast, is destiny as *spoken* by the gods.

809 *I snatched him away*: Neptune rescued Aeneas from Achilles in *Iliad* 20.158 ff. Add the storm in Book 1, and this makes the third time Neptune has saved Aeneas' life.

813 *port of Avernus*: Lake Avernus, near Cumae in Italy, did not become a naval port until the wars with Sextus Pompey, whose patron deity was Neptune (43–36 BC). Octavian's admiral Agrippa built new fleets there to replace Octavian's losses in storms and battles.

814 *You will search for him*: Palinurus, Aeneas' helmsman, occupies in the *Aeneid* the place Elpenor occupies in the *Odyssey*. Surprised by Odysseus'

sudden departure, Elpenor ('Hope of Man') forgets he is on a rooftop in his rush to join his comrades in book 10 and falls to his death. Odysseus tells of meeting his ghost in book 11, and of burying his body in book 12. Aeneas, however, does not search for and bury Palinurus' body (see note to 6.366). Palinurus is not always *Aeneas*' helmsman. In some writers, he is Odysseus' helmsman, even Hannibal's.

819 *skims sea's surface*: words recalling 1.187 where Neptune calms the storm. One ship was lost then; one man will be lost to the seas now. Virgil brings us back to motifs with which the *Aeneid* opens.

822 *Comrades of varied appearance*: the picture Virgil presents recalls the numerous Roman mosaics depicting Neptune surrounded by sea-creatures. But some of these assorted nymphs assume a life of their own in epic. Thetis, after all, is the mother of Achilles; and Cymodoce's virtual namesake, Cymodocea, will have things to do and say later in the *Aeneid* (10.25–48). For some of Aeneas' vessels will be transformed into sea-nymphs after being attacked with fire again in 9.109–22.

838 *Sleep*: until now sleep has been represented as the unconscious state in which the mind is open to manipulation by gods or other forces, not a deity acting in its own right with its own agenda, as it is here.

842 *Phorbas' features*: Phorbas, 'He who leads to pasture', is best known as the shepherd in Seneca's *Oedipus*, whose testimony, under torture, convinces Oedipus he has killed his father and married his mother. The etymology of Palinurus' name suggests he should *come back* to Italy (Gk. *palin*, 'back'), and the name of his ancestral father Iasus is identical with that of the brother of the very Dardanus who left Italy for Asia Minor. Palinurus is linked with the tradition that Aeneas arrived in Italy at Velia, but Virgil jettisons Velia (and Palinurus) and redirects the fleet to Cumae.

846 *I will spell you*: literally: 'I will undertake (initiate) your duties (rites) for you', that is to say: 'I'll do your duties for you' *or* 'I'll start your funeral rites'.

864 *Sirens*: the sea-nymphs whose song lures sailors to death on the rocks; Odysseus has his crewmen seal their ears with wax and tie him to the mast so he can hear their song and not leap into the sea (*Odyssey* 12.39 ff.). Virgil relegates this myth to the remote past, and nudges Aeneas out of the Homeric world (contrast the end of Book 3 where Aeneas visits the land of the Cyclopes three months after Odysseus). The Sirens are for Virgil the Sirenusae islands off the Italian coast and their song the sound of surf. Aeneas passes without noticing either them or the loss of his helmsman until he is near the Italian coast. The calm seas are noted by Virgil, authorially, and by Aeneas. Octavian would have had different memories. Cassius Dio (49.1) narrates that when Octavian was on his way to Sicily, passing Cape Palinurus, a storm fell upon him. It destroyed many ships, and Menodorus (Sextus Pompey's admiral) attacked the surviving vessels and burned or towed many away. Velleius 2.79.3 notes the same disaster: 'a violent African wind wrecked by far the greater part of

his fleet near Velia and the promontory of Palinurus.' See notes to 5.175 and 6.70, 109, and 366).

BOOK SIX

2 *Cumae*: the first Greek colony in Italy (and where, traditionally, the Latin alphabet was adapted from the Greek), settled from Chalcis in Euboea around 750 BC.

5 *patterned / Fringe*: like that of a Roman toga. This is possibly a reference to the resorts of the area in Virgil's day. Ovid talks of 'patterned beaches' at the nearby resort of Baiae.

6 *Twilight's Land*: Hesperia, Italy (see note to 3.164); also = 'land of the dead'. The 'Twilight god' in Sophocles is Death. Virgil's contemporary, Strabo (5.4.5), says Cumae and Avernus were thought to be the site of Homer's book of the dead (*Odyssey* 11), but had been demystified when Agrippa cut down its forests to rebuild Octavian's fleet and militarized the area after Sextus Pompey defeated Octavian off Cumae in 39 BC.

8 *find streams*: there are none. The *only* waterway was Agrippa's military conduit between Lake Avernus and the Lucrine Lake (*Georgics* 2.159–62 f.: 'Julian waters gush into Avernus').

10 *Sibyl*: there had been two Sibylline shrines nearby, one by Avernus, one at Cumae. Virgil treats them as the same. They were not established in Aeneas' time and closed after Rome conquered Cumae in 338 BC. Virgil's shrine is 'his invention and not based directly on any recent procedure of consultation at Cumae' (H. W. Parke, *Sibyls and Sibylline Prophecy in Classical Antiquity*, ed. B. C. McGing (London, 1988), 80–1; 96 and n. 20).

13 *Goddess at Crossroads*: Hecate, often identified with Diana. Her shrine is at Avernus, Apollo's in Cumae, Virgil merges two priestly roles into one Sibyl.

14 *Daedalus*: an Athenian artist, employed by King Minos of Crete, designed a 'cow-suit' for Minos' wife Pasiphaë so she could seduce a bull; also the labyrinth in which her hybrid child, unjustly named *Mino*taur, was contained. He gave Minos' daughter Ariadne a thread to help Theseus escape the labyrinth after killing the Minotaur. Finally, Minos imprisoned Daedalus in his own labyrinth, along with his son Icarus. Daedalus escaped by devising wings. But Icarus perished because he flew too close to the sun. Daedalus epitomizes the uneasy relationship between artist and powerful patrons: imprisoned in his own creation, harmed by his own skills. Virgil is actually first to set Daedalus' initial landfall in Cumae.

15 *ominous swift wings*: a bird was of good omen if it flew directly toward its goal or sought a special place to settle. Daedalus became his own 'bird of omen' when he flew.

16 *Bear Stars*: ancient poets claimed that sailors navigated by either the Greater or Lesser Bear constellations. Daedalus is unique because he steers *towards* them, not *by* them.

19 *Wings . . . as oars*: also used of Mercury's flight in 1.300–1; in Lucretius (6.740–6), birds fall from the sky, 'forgetful of their oarage of wings', into Lake Avernus.

20 *Androgeos' murder . . . Cecrops's children*: Androgeos, son of Minos, was killed in Athens by rivals he defeated at the games. Cecrops, mythical first king of Athens, was, like the Minotaur, of hybrid form: half-human, half-snake.

22 *Seven live bodies of sons*: most traditions have seven men *and* seven women (corresponding to the seven Pleiades and seven Hyades, the main stars in the constellation Taurus (the Bull)).

    lots drawn: Athenians decided many public duties and offices by lottery.

27 *intricate puzzle*: a mental and physical wandering, continued in the notion of ruses and mazes (see note to 5.588). Virgil draws on Herodotus' account (2.148) of the great Egyptian labyrinth, most of which one crossed in darkness (Pliny, *Natural History*, 36.85–6; 88). Its lower areas, like cathedral crypts, housed royal tombs.

28 *pitied a ruler*: this statement looks 'back' to Pasiphaë and 'forward' to Pasiphaë's daughter Ariadne, who loved Theseus, one of the Athenians destined for sacrifice.

33 *what fell were your father's hands*: grief leaves Daedalus unable to complete the story. The fall of Icarus is missing; the viewer's eye must generate the image and explain its absence or fail to understand the picture. Here (unusually) Virgil supplies what is missing with his authorial voice.

35 *Deiphobe*: Virgil is first to give the Sibyl a name and parentage. Glaucus, a fisherman turned into a sea-monster, is used in Plato's *Republic* to exemplify how the soul keeps its nature despite changes in appearance.

36 *sightseeing*: Latin *spectacula*. When Statius (*Silvae* 3.5.95–7) invites his wife to join him at Naples, he mentions the oracle at Cumae as a local *tourist attraction*.

42 *Mined*: huge excavations for military works occurred here in 37 BC in connection with Octavian's plans to use Avernus as a naval base (Strabo 5.4.5).

70 *Marble temple*: there is no tradition that Aeneas built such a temple. His words recall Octavian's vow, made in 36 BC (after defeating Sextus Pompey), and fulfilled in 28 BC when he dedicated a solid marble temple to Apollo in Rome to celebrate victory at Actium. He did not build a temple to Diana (Hecate), but set her statue next to Apollo's. The festivals are the 'Apollonian Games', established in 212 BC; perhaps also the 'Centennial Games', celebrated two years after Virgil's death, but planned during his lifetime.

72 *store your responses*: Octavian transferred the Sibylline Books (a collection of Sibylline prophecies) and the priests who looked after them to Apollo's temple in 28 BC.

80 *shapes her with pressure*: controlling the Sibyl's mind and body in a kind of spiritual rape. Apollo's priestesses resist mental as well as physical possession by him.

84–5 *the Dardanians . . . Lavinium*: that is, the Dardanians will return to their 'ancestral' home. Lavinium will be the first and only city Aeneas actually founds in Italy.

88 *Simoïs, Xanthus, the Dorian camp*: the Simois and Xanthus are rivers near Troy; Tiber and Numicus are their Italian counterparts (7.150–1, 242, 797). What awaits is a new Trojan War. The counterpart of the Dorian (i.e. Greek) camp is less clear (the Trojans are the invaders this time). The only Greeks fighting as a group in Books 7–12 are on Aeneas' side; but his rival Turnus traces his origins to Greece (7.371).

89 *another Achilles*: *Latio* is ambiguous: the new Achilles is born either 'for Latium' or 'in Latium': he could be Aeneas or his opponent, Turnus. All are sons of goddesses: Aeneas of sea-born Venus; Achilles of Thetis, a sea-deity; Turnus of Venilia (identical with Salacia, goddess of Salt Water).

96 *any way*: reading Latin *qua*, 'by which way, where' (as cited in Seneca, *Epistles* 82.18), rather than *quam*, 'than'—as in the older manuscripts and Servius.

97 *Greek city's*: Evander's Pallanteum, on the site of Rome, which Aeneas visits in Book 8.

99 *obscurity's riddles*: oracles usually allow more than one interpretation.

104 *as news*: much was forecast by Creusa, Helenus, and Anchises. Helenus said the Sibyl would say how to cope with each impending trial (3.458–60). She does not; but Anchises' ghost does in 6.890–2. Virgil, however, doesn't tell *us* what Anchises says.

107 *Acheron*: a river linked with death and 'Twilight Lands'. Virgil has it spill into Avernus or the Acherusian lake between Cumae and Misenum.

109 *teach me the route*: Aeneas wants to enter the underworld, not bring the dead to him as Odysseus does. His journey recalls Socrates' 'Myth of Er' in Plato, *Republic* 10: Er, left for dead, comes back to life and reports what he has seen in the underworld. An incident in the Roman civil wars gave Socrates' story new vigour. According to Pliny, one of Octavian's soldiers, Gabienus, came back to life mysteriously after being found dead on a beach in Sicily, and prophesied to Sextus Pompey victory for the 'righteous' side, which Sextus took to mean his own, since he was *Pius*, 'Righteous'. Virgil's *Pius Aeneas* may be following in the steps of one of Octavian's rivals here.

119–23 *Orpheus . . . Hercules*: each goes to bring something *out* of the under-world (and either fails or pays a penalty): Orpheus to reclaim his wife Eurydice; Pollux, to get his brother Castor; Theseus, to help Pirithoüs carry off Proserpina; Hercules to kidnap Cerberus. Orpheus loses Eurydice on the way back; Pollux helps his brother share life only by shar-ing his brother's death; Theseus is kept among the damned in Tartarus (6.606–7); Hercules goes mad and destroys his family on his return.

126 *Avernus*: used by the Sibyl for the whole underworld, not just its local point of access. Lucretius (6.748) talks generically of 'Avernian places and lakes'.

127 *Dis's*: *Dis pater* = 'Rich Father', Roman god of the dead (Gk. Pluto). A king, it is said, was told his sick children could be cured if they drank water from the Tiber boiled on the altar of Dis and Proserpina at Tarentum. He thought the city Tarentum was meant, but found a place named Tarentum in the Campus Martius at Rome (see Map 2) and an altar dedicated to the two gods. Notable Romans were buried on the Campus Martius, including Octavian's heir-apparent Marcellus (who died after a failed 'water-cure') (see note to 6.863–4). The Sibyl says Dis's portals are always open; but the Campus Martius shrine was opened only when sacrifices were offered to *both* gods. Aeneas takes an offering to Proserpina only.

132 *Cocytus'*: a tributary of Acheron. Its (Greek) name suggests lament.

134–5 *twice gaze upon . . . Tartarus*: see second note to line 561.

138 *Sacred . . . to the underworld's Juno*: i.e. Proserpina. Scholars since antiquity have suspected that Virgil invented the golden bough. The description recalls mistletoe and its harvesting. See Pliny, *Natural History* 24.12.

149 *a friend of yours*: Aeneas, who knows Palinurus is dead, has no idea what body the Sibyl is referring to. See note to 6.366 and Lucretius (6.703–11). If there is more than one corpse, why was Neptune so insistent at 5.814–15 that only one would die, and why has no one noticed the other's absence?

160 *scatter . . . chatter*: *sermo*, 'conversation', was thought to derive from *serere*, 'to sow'.

163 *Misenus*: At 3.239–40 he sounds the attack against the Harpies. Aeolus, god of winds, is a good father for a bugler. In the accusative case his name is identical with Misenum (a city farther along the coast). Ovid (*Metamorphoses* 14.103) says he was a companion of Odysseus.

179 *an ancient forest*: Octavian cut down this forest to build a fleet and new base at Misenum (Strabo 5.4.5). It became the permanent headquarters for the Roman fleet. Destroying ancient forests was often condemned as sacrilege (note to 7.47; and see 9.80–122); Virgil masks this risky reference with echoes of Ennius' description of woodcutting (*Annales* 187–97).

185 *As he surveys*: Aeneas often goes through the formalities of a required action while thinking of something else. Compare lines 37 and 703.

190 *twin doves*: doves or (carrier) pigeons, sacred to Venus, are natural messengers. Suetonius (*Divus Augustus* 94) says pigeons nesting in a palm tree presaged Caesar's victory over Pompey's sons at Munda in 45 BC.

210 *though it struggles*: compare the Sybil's words at 6.415–8.

237 *high cavern*: the 'Grotto of the Sibyl' on the south shore of Avernus.

242 *Birdless*: the etymology Aornos > Avernus is made by Lucretius 6.740–3. This line was generally considered an interpolation by ancient scholars.

243 *black-skinned*: animals sacrificed to underworld gods were usually black.

249 *Furies'*: the original has the Greek term *Eumenides*, 'the Well-Meaning Ones', a euphemism for their 'real' name, *Erinyes*, 'the spirits of strife', who punish murder, perjury, and failure to respect the old (or suppliants).

They are similar to Roman demons called *Dirae*, whose mother is Night (7.331; 12.845–8, 860) and whose sister is Earth.

258 *the deity's advent*: Apollonius 3.1212–24 gives more details about Hecate.

260 *blade from its sheath*: Aeneas may need to frighten ghosts as does Odysseus in *Odyssey* 10.535–6; 11.48. But see 6.290–4 and note to 6.93. Some see a sexual undertone. Latin *vagina* means 'sheath', and was used metaphorically of the vagina. See D. Gillis, *Eros and Death in the Aeneid* (Rome, 1983), 15–36.

265 *Chaos*: the origin of everything (Hesiod, *Theogony* 123) is a primal oneness, like a black hole—but infinite void, not infinite density. Varro says *caelum*, 'sky', derives from *chaos*.

273 *Orcus*: a Roman underworld god, related to 'ogre': apt here, given the monsters that follow. Orcus' 'gullet' suggests the passage, like a throat, leading into the *vestibulum* of a Roman house, hence *orca*, 'funeral urn' (with a narrow neck).

274 *Sorrows*: the 'real' horrors at the entrance contrast with the imaginary horrors listed next, much as the 'true ghosts' contrast with 'false dreams' at the underworld's exit.

282–9 *a dark elm . . . shadow*: Romans used the elm, as the English once used the birch, as a tree of punishment. Centaurs, half-horse, half-human, and Scyllas are not previously monsters of hell, though the horse is linked with cults of the dead. The Chimaera (see note to 5.118) is often in the underworld. Harpies (notes to 3.211 and 3.222) carry people off to death in *Odyssey* 1.241. Gorgons are sea-creatures whose faces turn those who look at them to stone. Fear of Gorgons ends Odysseus' consultation of the dead (*Odyssey* 11.633–5). Hydra, a many-headed water-snake killed by Hercules, is an underworld monster in *Theogony* 305 ff. The 'three-bodied shadow' is Geryon, whose cattle Hercules stole (*Aeneid* 8.201–4; *Theogony* 305 ff.). Briareus is a hundred-armed giant dungeoned in the underworld (*Theogony* 617).

293–4 *bodiless . . . shaped form*: Ghosts, as memories of the 'real', have an irrational fear of weapons. Chimaeras and Scyllas are fantasies against which weapons are useless (unless, like Bellerophon, who kills the Chimaera, you have another fantasy creature (Pegasus) to fight them).

297 *thick silt*: perhaps a reference to the problems which made Octavian abandon Avernus in favour of Misenum because the harbour silted up (Strabo 5.4.5).

298 *Charon*: usually a character in comedy or satire (Aristophanes' *Frogs* and Lucian's underworld dialogues). The dying Alcestis has a vision of him in Euripides' *Alcestis* (a substitute for a satyr play).

306–8 *mothers . . . watching*: Servius says Virgil rewrote the end of *Georgics* 4 after his friend Gallus fell from favour and committed suicide in 26 BC and incorporated in it echoes of *Aeneid* 6. These lines are similar to *Georgics* 4.474–6 and, like 6.438–9 (common to both *Aeneid* 6 and *Georgics* 4), recall his sorrow for Gallus which, Servius says, he dared refer to only obliquely for fear of offending Octavian.

309 *leaves*: leaves fall and die, but migratory birds return to nest as seasons change. The similes evoke *Georgics* 4.472 ff., where they merge into one: ghosts are like birds hiding among leaves. Note also that Glaucus (*Iliad* 6.146–9) compares human lives to leaves and is the descendant of Bellerophon who killed the Chimaera. The Sibyl, who prophesies with leaves, is daughter of (a) Glaucus.

333 *Leucaspis*: not mentioned elsewhere in the *Aeneid*. In *Iliad* 22.294 the word (meaning 'white shield'—the blank shield without motto carried by a novice warrior) is used of Deiphobus (6.494 ff. and notes). *Orontes* drowns in the storm in 1.113–17.

338 *from Carthage*: Virgil says he drowned on the voyage from *Sicily* in 5.827 ff.

341 *Which one of the gods*: Aeneas said Palinurus died through negligent overconfidence (5.870–1) and did not mention a prophecy by Apollo about him. He now discreetly prompts Palinurus to explain what occurred.

347 *cauldron of Phoebus*: a vessel within a sacred tripod at Apollo's shrines.

348 *no god plunged me*: he did not know a god was throwing him overboard; but the seas weren't heavy. He makes the seas rough and attributes his death to tribesmen on the shore. Aeneas does not correct him.

366 *Velia's harbour*: Dionysius (1.53.2) says Velia was Aeneas' first landfall in Italy. Virgil's Aeneas never goes there. Servius, on 6.378, says Palinurus' lack of burial caused a plague in that area, which lasted until his ghost was placated. But this is hundreds of years later. Palinurus will have a long wait. Velia had bad memories for Octavian (see note to 5.864). After his fleet was destroyed off Cape Palinurus, Octavian took refuge in Velia, to rescue crews and repair his fleet. Aeneas' neglect may cause his 'descendant' to pay a price.

398 *the god who . . . defied death*: the text has *Amphrysia*, 'of Amphrysus', a river in Thessaly, where Apollo served as a slave to Admetus after breaking an oath by the Styx. In return for Admetus' kindness, Apollo granted Admetus extended life if someone agreed to die in his place. Admetus' wife Alcestis did so, but was rescued by Hercules. See note to 9.105.

426 *children*: Virgil's focus on those who died before speaking (Latin *infans*) contrasts with Socrates' indifference in *Republic* 615c: 'they are not worth mentioning'.

432 *Minos presides*: his cruelty does not disqualify him. Crete was famous for its laws; the earliest Greek law code is inscribed on stone at Gortyn, in Crete. Minos judges those falsely condemned by human courts and listens to the false charges again. But no real *hearing* can be given to those *silent* or *unable to speak*.

436 *How they'd long*: a poignant variant of the remark by Achilles' ghost in *Odyssey* 11: that he would rather be the slave of the poorest man on earth

than king of the dead. Virgil applies it to souls who have the eternal despair of knowing they did the wrong thing.

438–9 *grim . . . constriction*: identical with *Georgics* 4.478–9.

445–8 *Phaedra . . . Caeneus*: female victims of passion, recalling the heroines in *Odyssey* 11.321 ff. For individual details, see the Indexed Glossary.

450 *among women of Greece*: I add the phrase to underscore Virgil's introduction of a woman from outside Greek tradition, now marked among the famous women of epic. Notice that no such accommodation is made for Creusa, Aeneas' wife, whom he neither sees nor asks about in the underworld.

460 *withdraw from your country*: adapted from Catullus 66.39, itself translating a lost poem of Callimachus, where the speaker is a lock of hair apologizing to Queen Berenice for leaving her head. Aeneas tries to be courtly: he, like the lock, had no choice about leaving (see 4.361). More grimly, the echo recalls Iris cutting a lock from Dido's head to allow her to die (4.702–5).

463 *I couldn't believe*: i.e. he *refused* to believe her vows to die if he left (4.308, 323, 385–6). He doesn't say how he heard the news or whether he knew she'd used *his* sword.

466 *Who are you running from?*: an ironic echo of Dido (4.314) when she realizes Aeneas is going to leave: 'Could you be running from me?'

471 *the crags of Marpessus in Paros*: Parian marble, recalling Venus' enhancement of Aeneas' first appearance to Dido (1.593) and his hardness denounced by Dido in 4.366–7. Virgil compared him to an oak with roots reaching down to Tartarus in 4.441–9. Now Dido is paradoxically immovable in her determination to pull away from him.

479–80 *Tydeus . . . Adrastus*: three of the 'Seven against Thebes'. Tydeus is named first probably because he was father of Aeneas' adversary Diomedes. See entry in the Indexed Glossary for the 'Seven'. They are the *only* really famous warriors Aeneas meets in the underworld.

483 *Glaucus . . . Medon . . . Thersilochus*: three minor Trojan warriors in a verbatim translation of *Iliad* 17.216. Virgil foregrounds warriors that Homer's Hector calls on as among 'countless hordes' of allies at the edge of Troy's realm. Thersilochus is one of seven men Achilles kills in two lines (*Iliad* 21.209–10). See also 12.363 and note. Glaucus is not the famous Glaucus of *Iliad* 6.119–236, second in command of the Lycians. Medon is unknown; the Medon of *Iliad* 15.332–6 is a Greek, half-brother of Ajax son of Oileus.

484–5 *Three sons of Antenor . . . Idaeus*: again, verbatim from the *Iliad* (11.59). In *Iliad* 11.56–66, Antenor's sons gather around the famous trio of Hector, Polydamas (one of Troy's best warriors), and Aeneas. *Polyboetes* is unknown elsewhere. *Idaeus* is Priam's driver and herald, noted for bringing the ransom for Hector's body (*Iliad* 24.324–5) and for negotiating a truce (*Iliad* 7.365–420). The omission of top Trojans readies us for the omission of top Greeks and famous Romans.

489 *Agamemnon*: his name merely designates who commanded the Greek army, and thus highlights the total absence of important warriors from the Trojan War.

494 *Priam's son*: not Hector, but Deiphobus, Helen's second Trojan husband, the only (somewhat) important Trojan warrior (*Iliad* 13.402–539) Aeneas meets in the underworld.

500 *Master of weapons*: it would be hard to find a *less* apt epithet for Deiphobus, as we shall see.

507 *your name and your arms*: Aeneas' claim does not wholly conflict with Deiphobus' account which follows, but it raises questions. How did Aeneas acquire Deiphobus' armour without his body? And why is he at the port of Rhoeteum after Troy's fall? He told Dido he had headed directly to Mount Ida, and later built his fleet under Antandros in the southern Troad, far from Rhoeteum (3.5–7 and note). See also Map 1. Servius suggests the arms were represented pictorially on the tomb; the text clearly says they were real.

517 *in a circle around it*: Deiphobus' story echoes and modifies its archetype in *Odyssey* 4, where Menelaus tells of Helen circling the horse with Deiphobus, and imitating the voices of the wives of the warriors in it to induce them to betray themselves. With the noise described here, no one would have heard a cry from inside the horse. Odysseus would not have had to silence Anticlus and save the day.

524 *Strips . . . all arms*: if Deiphobus is right, Aeneas must have obtained Deiphobus' armour directly or indirectly from Helen. Aeneas has also somehow obtained Helen's regalia from her marriage with Paris (1.647–52).

529 *Aeolus' spawn*: Ulysses, a great talker, is as aptly linked to the wind god, as is Misenus (6.164). Sophocles and Ovid make Ulysses grandson of Aeolus and bastard son of the notorious liar Sisyphus. In the *Odyssey*, he massacres his wife's suitors in a room from which he, like Helen here, has had all weapons removed.

535 *Dawn*: the contrast between the dark underworld and rosy Dawn is striking. Deiphobus is made as conscious of darkness as his female namesake Deiphobe, priestess to Apollo, is conscious of light, as if in allusion to the Sun (Phoebus) and Moon (Phoebe) in inverted roles.

542 *Elysium*: Homer's abode for the blessed after death (*Odyssey* 4.561 ff.). The most detailed description is in Plato, *Republic* 10. The road to the Blessed usually runs 'to the right' and that of the damned 'to the left', the ill-omened side (Plato, *Republic* 10.614c).

555 *Tisiphone*: one of the *Dirae* (demons of ill-omen, fulfillers of curses), like Allecto and Megaera (7.324–53 and 12.845–55). The Harpy Celaeno is also a *Dira* (see note to 3.252). Except in Dido's dream and the similes following it, where imagery is nightmarishly confused (4.465–73 and notes), the *Dirae* are not identical with the Furies (spirits of blood vengeance).

Despite her Greek name, suggesting punishment (*tisis*), Tisiphone has roles only in *Roman* poetry.

561 *I'm hearing*: following manuscript P, which reads *aures*, 'ears' (hence 'hearing'). Manuscripts M and R have *auras*, 'breezes'. Aeneas is interested in hearing what the punishments are like.

565 *took me through*: the Sibyl has just said the innocent are not allowed to enter. We assume, then, that 'took me through' means simply 'explained'. But her use of *vidi*, 'I saw', later dismisses that illusion. Perhaps she isn't innocent; perhaps exceptions are made for administrators, or for women. All those punished in Tartarus are male. And how *Aeneas* is going to see Tartarus at all, let alone twice, as the Sibyl has said in 6.133–5, is less clear. In the earlier lines she perhaps uses 'Tartarus' for the underworld in general.

578 *twice as far*: Homer and Hesiod say Tartarus extends down the *same* distance as sky extends upwards. Virgil's damned need twice as much room. See also 4.445–6 and note.

580 *Titans*: gods of an earlier generation who rebelled against Jupiter. The most famous were Ocean and Saturn (Gk. Kronos) whom Virgil can't name without undermining the myth of the Saturnian Age (see Book 7). Those he names are not Titans, but *are* listed (with one exception) in *Odyssey* 11. Virgil omits Prometheus, man's benefactor, from Odysseus' list and transfers his punishment to *Tityos* (line 595). He includes only those who assault Olympus in some way, and his punishments differ from the 'canonical'.

582 *Aloeus's twins*, his stepchildren Otus and Ephialtes piled Mount Pelion on Mount Ossa (in some versions, earthly Olympus too) to attack heavenly Olympus.

585 *Salmoneus*: a mortal among monsters, rarely mentioned elsewhere. This version is the longest in ancient literature and the longest account of punishment in the Sibyl's Tartarus. He is singled out because he demands worship as a god and builds his city at Olympia in Elis, the cult centre of Jupiter. The Sibyl daringly places him between the adopted children of Aloeus and the adopted child of Earth, Tityos. Octavian, who honoured his adoptive father Caesar as a god and called himself son of the Divine Julius, 'lightnings' his way to the Euphrates and makes his way to Olympus in *Georgics* 4.559–61.

595 *Tityos*: a giant killed by Apollo and Diana for attempting to rape their mother Latona. His flesh is constantly reborn in an eternity of torment: a ghastly and constant reincarnation, contrasting with the *psychological* terror inflicted on Pirithous and Ixion, listed next.

601 *Pirithoüs, Ixion*: Zetzel observes ('*Romane Memento:* Justice and Judgment in *Aeneid* 6', *TAPA* 119 (1989), 269): 'the names and the punishments are familiar, but the combination is extremely odd. Ixion is normally found on his wheel, Pirithoüs on his throne, paired with Theseus;

while the punishment described is normally attached to Tantalus (cf. *Odyssey* 11.582–92).' See note to 6.119–23. Virgil refers to Ixion's wheel in *Georgics* 4.483. Most Greek writers set Tantalus' punishment beneath an overhanging rock.

605 *that direst of Demons*: Aeneas says the Harpy Celaeno boasts that she is the 'direst of Demons' and calls her the greatest plague ever to emerge from Stygian waters (3.252, 214–15). This Demon (whoever she is), like Celaeno, prevents people from eating.

614 *don't ask me*: Romans were doubtless curious about which Romans had spots reserved in Tartarus: Marius, Cinna, and Sulla, for instance, who between them had slaughtered thousands. Their legacy was too politically sensitive for Virgil to risk naming them. Caesar, for one, was linked with Marius. Knowing about them might also curb Aeneas' enthusiasm. But omitting them is like omitting Stalin from a history of Russia. For a possible reference to Marius and Sulla see note to 9.334.

618 *Phlegyas*: Ixion's father, also linked with Theseus in Valerius Flaccus 2.192 ff. Both are doomed to sit at a banquet like the one described in 6.603–5. Virgil is the first to place Theseus, unifier of the Athenian state (and Romulus' parallel Life in Plutarch), in Tartarus.

621 *sold his country*: the historian Sallust says an African prince, Jugurtha, once described Rome as a city for sale. Servius thought Virgil's lines (said to be adapted from a work by Virgil's friend and editor Varius) referred to Scribonius Curio, a tribune who supported Julius Caesar when he was poised to invade Italy. Lucan says this man sold Rome to Julius Caesar: there were many potential buyers (Marius, Sulla, Cinna, and the whole line of Caesars) but Curio was unique: he brokered the sale.

625 *hundred mouths*: Virgil says (6.43–4) she *does* have a hundred mouths.

641 *shining only for them*: Elysium is, like Tartarus, exclusively male. It is a very upper-class preserve, based on Plato's myth of Er: no women, children, or ordinary people. Status in the afterlife is determined by status in life. The poet supreme here is a mythic disciple of the mythic Orpheus, Musaeus, whose works, if they ever existed, did not survive in Virgil's day. No other Greek or Roman poet or philosopher is named as a resident of Elysium.

650 *Ilus . . . Dardanus*: Dardanus was father of Erichthonius and grandfather of Ilus, Assaracus, and Ganymede. Ilus was father of Laomedon, the father of Priam (see note to 8.157). These are the founders of Troy. Virgil says nothing about them. Aeneas can have no idea who they are, and shows no interest in meeting them. No Trojan from the two generations before Aeneas (except Anchises) is named as present in Elysium, and no one else but Musaeus.

658 *Eridanus*: a river name, linked with various rivers real and imaginary. See Virgil's description of it (as the Rhône) in *Georgics* 4.317 ff. and the note on *Aeneid* 9.35. It is often used of rivers in the remote west and north where amber, famous for its preservative properties, was found: hence its

associations with death and immortality. Apollonius says Eridanus rises at the world's end, at the gates of night; Aratus identifies it with the celestial River constellation. It is the *philosophers'* otherworldly river.

670 *what district*: Rome was divided into *regiones* like our 'quarters' or 'districts', and Octavian systematized them. The Sibyl is asking for Anchises' address, which she thinks he has been assigned to, not chosen. She is as ignorant about the philosophers' Elysium as she is knowledgeable about traditional mythic Tartarus and has clearly never been there before. She too needs a guide and doesn't speak again after asking this question.

681 *holding a census*: Anchises is depicted as a Roman censor, an official elected, periodically, to review the citizenship and Senate rolls and remove all those not qualified, financially or morally. Anchises counts only those he deems worthy of recognition as Romans and thus 'censors' the account of Rome's 'future'. The closer he gets to Virgil's own day, the more extensive his censorship becomes. The office of censor would have been on Roman minds as Virgil wrote, because the last censors ever appointed at Rome (except for an attempt by the emperor Claudius to revive the office in AD 47) were for 22 BC. They were unable to complete their work, for reasons not entirely clear. But one religious reason for invalidating a census arose if the censor looked upon a dead person (Cassius Dio 54.28). Octavian abolished the office (which would place its holder above him in certain judicial areas) and assigned the duties to a lower magistrate, an aedile, and appointed Agrippa, who had held the highest offices of state (see note to 6.767). So Anchises, like Octavian, is editing the rolls himself. That is why I have provided more detailed information about persons named or alluded to here than elsewhere in these notes. Anchises' census yields only one further clearly named person whose role in public life belongs to the hundred years before Virgil's day (call it 20 BC): Octavian's recently deceased heir apparent, Marcellus. Two names mentioned could have resonance for that century, but could also be referring to more remote ancestors: Brutus and Cato. Two other persons from the period are obviously referred to but not named: Julius Caesar and Pompey. The majority named belong either to undatable prehistory or to the period between about 700 and 120 BC. Anchises' future Romans are all dead as Virgil writes, except for Octavian.

697 *Etruscan waters*: Aeneas identifies Cumae in terms of the *Etruscan* settlement in that part of Campania (perhaps to avoid alarming Anchises by suggesting he is among Greeks). But how does he know about the Etruscan settlement? Nobody else has mentioned it.

703 *Through this*: the ghost eludes Aeneas, as Aeneas claims Creusa's ghost eluded him in Troy. Aeneas' attention also drifts, as in a dream (6.37, 185).

705 *river Lethe*: Virgil's version of Plato's 'River of Indifference' yields a pun on Latin *letum*, 'death'. In Greek *lēthē* means 'forgetfulness'. In the Myth of Er, souls about to enter bodies drink of the River of Indifference, whose waters induce forgetfulness (*lēthē*). Er does not drink, so he is not subject

to *lēthē*. In Greek, the prefix 'a-' forms a negative, as it can in English: *a*moral, *a*sexual. *Alēthēs*, the adjective translated into English as 'true', was taken by Plato to mean 'non-forgetful', and its noun, *alētheia* ('truth'), to mean 'non-forgetfulness'. *Alēthēs* also makes a pun with *alētheis*, 'having wandered', in the *Odyssey*. And Socrates, in Plato's *Cratylus*, describes truth as a 'divine wandering', a *theia alē* (the anagram of *alētheia*).

707 *bees*: some thought them part of the divine mind (*Georgics* 4.219–21), which may account for their presence here. Their structured societies create a collective identity with little room for individual choice, and humans harness their productivity for human use. See 1.430–6.

712 *crowded the banks*: like those crossing the Styx into the underworld in 6.317–20.

720 *reincarnation*: Anchises offers no answer to this question. Souls have no choice about being reincarnated. In Plato they can at least select their new lives.

726 *Feed on internal Energy*: Anchises takes elements from several ancient philosophical schools here (scholars have found traces of Heraclitus, the Stoics, even Aristotle, in addition to Plato and the Pythagoreans) and presents them in a style that evokes Virgil's epic predecessor, the Epicurean Lucretius. Anchises is presenting a generic 'philosophers' view' of life and death rather than the dogma of any particular school, in contrast to the Homeric 'poets' view', in terms of which the rest of the underworld is framed. The Christian reading of the *Aeneid*, sanctified in Dante's *Divine Comedy* and still dominating scholarship, tends to assume that Anchises is voicing Virgil's own beliefs. But Virgil's Epicurean background (see Introduction) should warn us that attributing to him any personal belief in an afterlife is problematic, much less one advanced by Anchises (who proves to be a very unreliable source of information in this book, as elsewhere in the *Aeneid*).

743 *Each of us suffers his ghostly pain*: torture in the philosophers' Elysium is called purification. Obsession with purity turns Elysium into a sunlit Tartarus. Anchises does not explain why he himself has been so quickly purified, why exceptions are made, why purified souls are put back in bodies, or what powers lie behind the processes. In juxtaposing traditional myths and philosophical theories about death and knowledge, Virgil shows us how little they really differ and how easily the eye can be deceived. It is also possible that he is punning on 'Elysium' and *elisum*, 'erased' (6.542, 744), as he puns on 'Elissa' and *elisa* (see note to 4.335), given the context of censorship and recollection.

748–9 *a thousand / Years*: as in the myth of Er (*Republic* 615a) and in Aeschylus' *Prometheus Bound*. Plato's Socrates follows the Pythagorean philosophers in maintaining that the 'soul' continues to exist after death, is purged of its flaws for a thousand years, then put back in some other human or animal body; and that what we regard as knowledge is recollection of what our souls knew before they were put into bodies.

756 *glory that follows*: Anchises omits almost all Romans who brought suffering on Rome. He 'censors' carefully. Since Troy falls a thousand years before Virgil's day, the souls will be queuing for a long time.

763 *your posthumous offspring*: the Latin *postuma* would usually mean 'posthumous', though it was argued that the original meaning was simply 'last'. Servius, commenting here and on 1.270, says Aeneas' future wife was pregnant when he died. Afraid of Iulus' reaction, she fled to the woods and reared Silvius there. Livy (1.3.6) makes Silvius the son of Iulus rather than Aeneas. In Roman law, *postumus* is used both of children born after the father's death, and of those born after the father has made his last will (Gaius, *Institutes* 1.147; Ulpian, *Digest* 26.2.5). Their late arrival leaves them with no formal status as heirs and thus 'posthumous' as far as claims to their father's estate are concerned.

764 *advanced old age*: Jupiter (1.265 ff.) implies that Aeneas will live just three years after arriving in Latium. Servius' suggestion that 'advanced old age' means 'immortality' is nonsense.

766 *masters of Alba*: the Alban kings, therefore, are descended from Silvius, not from Iulus, which goes against what we (and Aeneas) have been told previously. The connection between Iulus and the Julian clan, then, becomes tenuous. This is where Silvius' posthumous status becomes important. For Octavian too was a 'posthumous' son, adopted by Caesar in his will. This adoption gave him precedence in Roman law over Caesarion, Caesar's biological son by Cleopatra, who would not have been recognized as a Roman citizen.

767 *Procas*: Servius says Procas was the twelfth not the second king. So Anchises' 'next' is misleading. Almost nothing is known about him. If Procas was the 'glory of Troy', no one knows why. There were fourteen Alban kings; all founded cities. Virgil mentions five. Notable omissions are Alba himself, Latinus (already alive in *Aeneid* 7–12), and Agrippa. 'Agrippa' is also the name of Octavian's admiral, designated his successor after Marcellus' death (see note to 6.865). Maecenas (a friend of Virgil and Octavian) said Octavian made Agrippa so great that he had to make him his son-in-law or kill him (Dio 54.6.5). It would have been politically risky for Virgil to set Agrippa's namesake among the kings.

768–9 *Capys, Numitor . . . Silvius Aeneas*: Capys founded Capua. Servius says he was the sixth Alban king. Numitor, grandfather of Romulus and Remus, was deposed by his brother Amulius. Livy (1.3.10–11) says Amulius killed Numitor's sons and made his daughter, Rhea Silvia, a Vestal virgin. She was raped by Mars and bore Romulus and Remus. Anchises mentions neither Numitor's relationship to Romulus nor the existence (and treachery) of Amulius. Nor does he mention Remus. He hurries on to Silvius Aeneas who, Servius says, was kept from power for fifty-three years. Hence Anchises' doubts about his ever becoming king.

773–5 *Nomentum . . . Cora*: Anchises lists eight cities founded by Alba Longa. Others list up to twenty-nine. All were members of the Latin League,

Latinum nomen (*nomen* means both 'name' and 'league'). These cities (and Alba) had been destroyed by Rome, abandoned, or absorbed into other towns by Virgil's day. Once substance without name, they are now names without substance: 'ghost towns'. See note to 5.564.

778 *Romulus*: Anchises does not make it clear that Romulus is the founder of Rome, and attaches him to the Alban rather than the Roman kings (see note to 1.274). Scholars dispute whether 'father' in 6.780 means Mars or the (supreme) father, Jupiter. I leave the text ambiguous.

781 *Here's the man*: Octavian, placed immediately after Romulus, but not named until after a discussion of Cybele (who rates almost as many words as Romulus). Octavian is thus flanked by two gods. The arrangement mirrors Octavian's positioning of his palace on the Palatine Hill, opposite Cybele's temple and right by the 'Hut of Romulus'. Anchises places Octavian in the centre of his 'Parade of Kings'.

784 *Cybele*: see 3.111–14 and note to 3.111. Construction of her temple on the Palatine was no accident. It officially reaffirmed a Trojan identity for Rome and juxtaposed it to the Romulan traditions of Rome's origins.

789 *Caesar is here*: Octavian, not Julius Caesar. 'Born of a god' would mislead Aeneas (who would assume divine birth such as his own). Octavian's father by posthumous adoption also became a god posthumously, by a vote of the Roman Senate.

794–8 *Garamantes . . . Caspian kingdoms*: Anchises diminishes Bacchus and Hercules, the only heroes whose exploits earned them universal acceptance as gods (contrast the hymn of praise to Hercules in 8.285–302). He also exaggerates the achievements of Octavian, who neither made nor aspired to such conquests in the East; he strove to secure, not expand, Rome's eastern frontiers. It was Alexander the Great who conquered these areas and Julius Caesar who dreamed of rivalling Alexander. Alexander represented himself as successor to Hercules and Bacchus, and identified places he reached in his advance towards India as sites they had visited. Alexander, whose empire was larger than Rome's, is never mentioned in the *Aeneid*. But Virgil's audience knew of him—none better than Octavian, who had overthrown his last successor in Egypt.

810 *Roman king*: Rome's second king, Numa (around 700 BC), is credited with establishing Rome's religious and legal practices and bringing peace. His home town, Cures, was in Sabine territory. The omission of his name would baffle Aeneas (and Roman readers) but let Octavian see an allusion to himself as a follower of Numa's precedent.

812 *Tullus*: Tullus Hostilius, Rome's third king (early seventh century), noted for his thirty-two-year reign, his sack of Alba Longa (not mentioned by Anchises), and his execution of Mettius Fufetius (8.642–5 and note to 8.643).

815 *Ancus*: the fourth king, Ancus Marcius (mid-seventh century), founded Rome's port, Ostia, and refined procedures for declaring war. No one else

mentions his boastfulness, which may be an allusion to those who claimed descent from him: the Marcius Rex family, which justified its last name (= 'king') by alleged links with Ancus. Julius Caesar claimed such descent on his mother's side (Suetonius, *Divus Iulius* 6).

817 *Tarquin kings*: Priscus and Superbus (i.e. Tarquin 'the Proud') are the fifth and seventh kings of Rome, and Etruscan, not Latin. Anchises omits the sixth king, Servius Tullius, perhaps because he has the same clan name as Marcus Tullius Cicero. The *fasces* (axes enclosed by rods) symbolized authority to kill or flog. Anchises gives Aeneas no clue that the Tarquins mark a turning point in Roman history: in 510 BC. Tarquin the Proud was expelled and a Republic founded by Lucius Junius Brutus and Lucius Tarquinius Collatinus, who became Rome's first consuls. Rather, Anchises takes Tarquin's epithet, 'Proud', and attaches it to Brutus. Lucius Brutus was claimed as ancestor (and precedent for restoring the Republic) by Caesar's killer, Marcus Brutus, who used the slogan *libertas*, 'freedom', on his coinage ('freedom' occurs only three times in the *Aeneid*). Anchises blurs the line between monarchy and Republic because (*a*) it is arguably not clear: Brutus' fellow first consul is himself a Tarquin; and (*b*) a clear line would draw attention to his placement of Octavian at the centre of the age of kings. Lucius Brutus' first use of the *fasces* was to execute his own sons for plotting to bring back the Tarquins. Anchises' last remark about posterity must refer to Marcus Brutus' killing of Caesar. See also note to 11.747.

824–5 *Decii . . . Camillus*: Romans of the Republican era. Publius Decius Mus, father (340 BC) and son (295 BC), gave their lives for Rome in a ritual *devotio*, 'offering oneself up for death'; the best-known Drusi are Octavian's wife Livia and his stepson, the future emperor Tiberius. Others include the Drusus who defeated the Carthaginian Hasdrubal, and Marcus Livius Drusus, who followed in the tradition of the Gracchi (see note to 6.842). Titus Manlius Imperiosus Torquatus, consul in 397, executed his son for disobedience in battle. Marcus Furius Camillus, censor in 401 BC, remained loyal to Rome even when mistreated, prosecuted on trivial charges, and exiled to Ardea (home town of Turnus, Aeneas' antagonist in Books 7–12). He was recalled after the Gauls captured Rome in 390 and were bought off at huge expense. Tradition held that Camillus attacked the Gauls and recovered the ransom. Anchises totally omits the Gallic disaster and substitutes military 'standards' for ransom, as if a battle, not a war, had been lost (see notes to 7.717, 8.652, 657, and 659). Octavian might see this modification as a reference to his own negotiations for the standards lost to the Parthians in 53 BC.

826 *souls . . . in identical armour*: unnamed Romans of the Republican era. Julius Caesar, the 'father-in-law', Gnaeus Pompeius Magnus (Pompey), the 'son-in-law', are not named here by Anchises or elsewhere by Virgil. In 49 BC Caesar, fresh from conquering Gaul, invaded Italy by the coastal route from Monaco and Nice, halted at the Rubicon (the boundary between

Gaul and Italy), and demanded to be allowed to keep his army and run for the consulship *in absentia*. The Senate refused him, and ordered Pompey (previously married to Caesar's daughter Julia and thus Caesar's son-in-law) to defend the state. Pompey had no reliable troops in Italy and withdrew to Greece. There he mustered an army from the eastern Mediterranean. Caesar crossed into Greece the next year and defeated Pompey, who fled to Egypt where he was murdered on orders from King Ptolemy.

836–8 *That man . . . That man*: unnamed Romans of the Republican era. Lucius Mummius destroyed Corinth in 146 BC; Lucius Aemilius Paulus defeated Perseus, king of Macedonia, in 168 BC and destroyed most of Epirus.

841 *Great Cato*: ambiguously named Romans of the Republican era. There were two famous Catos: Cato Major (Greater or Elder), consul in 195 BC, once thought to be the father of Latin history; and Cato Minor (Lesser or Younger), his descendant. 'Great' (*Magnus*) sits noncommittally between them. The Elder advocated the destruction of Carthage (and got his way in 146 BC); the Younger killed himself in North Africa in 46 BC to avoid being 'pardoned' by Caesar for fighting for the Republic. Both opposed what they saw as the ambitious militarism of their rivals: the Elder Cato was an ideological foe of Scipio Africanus (see note to 6.842), as his descendant was of Julius Caesar. As censor (184), the Elder Cato secured Scipio's trial and exile. Anchises' words exclude neither. See also note to 8.670.

Cossus: another named Roman of the Republican era. Aulus Cornelius Cossus killed Tolumnius, king of Veii, in either 437 or 426 BC in single combat and was the second to dedicate the *spolia opima* ('Spoils of Distinction'), the weapons taken from an enemy leader killed in a duel with the Roman commander. The first was Romulus, who killed Acron, king of Caenina, and carried his armour to the Capitoline Hill, later consecrated to Jupiter Feretrius. The final winner of the spoils was Marcellus in 222 BC (see note to 6.855). Marcus Licinius Crassus, grandson of Julius Caesar's partner (and rival) in power, wanted to dedicate them in 29 BC, but was denied on the grounds that he did not hold full 'power of command' at the time. The date of Cossus' dedication was critical. If it was 437, when Cossus was a lowly military tribune, Crassus had a precedent: if 426, when he was consul, Crassus did not. Octavian said he had found an inscription on a linen corslet dedicated by Cossus to Jupiter Feretrius which proved he was consul when he won his Spoils: so Crassus had no precedent. How the corslet lasted four centuries in the Temple of Jupiter (which had no roof) is unclear. Octavian probably worried that the prestige might make Crassus a rival. See R. M. Ogilvie, *A Commentary on Livy, Books 1–5* (Oxford, 1970), 71–3 and 563–67.

842 *Gracchus's stock*: ambiguously named Romans of the Republican era. The Gracchi were a powerful and influential family in the third and second

centuries BC; best known are the brothers Tiberius (tribune of the people in 133) and Gaius (tribune of the people in 122 and 121), who tried to introduce reforms at Rome. Both were killed in mob violence orchestrated by the conservative elite. Caius allied himself with Fulvius Flaccus (consul in 125 BC, tribune in 121), who wanted to extend citizenship to all free Italians. As tribunes they could (and did) block Senate proceedings with their veto (see note to 12.806) and introduce legislation. Many saw in their failure the seeds of later civil wars.

843 *Scipiadae*: 'Sons of Scipio'. Ambiguously named Romans of the Republican era. I retain the calculatedly Greek form since it is probably a comment on the family's famous love of Greek culture. It also echoes Lucretius (3.1034): 'Scipiadas, the lightning bolt, the terror of Carthage', and goes one better than Lucretius by doubling the singular son. Anchises is also making a cross-language pun: Latin Scipio = 'staff' = Gk. *skeptron*, 'staff'; and Gk. *skeptós* = 'thunderbolt'. For a moment we imagine the Gracchi are the thunderbolts of war (as they were, in a way) before the Latin points us to the Scipios. But which Scipios? I leave the issue ambiguous. The Latin *cladem Libyae* can yield 'a disaster' inflicted either '*by* Africa' or '*on* Africa'. Servius assumes the first: his Scipios are two brothers, killed fighting Hannibal in Spain in 211 BC. If so, there may also be an allusion to the battle of Thapsus (46 BC) in the civil wars in which both opposing armies were, technically, commanded by a Scipio. Modern scholars assume the second sense: the Scipios are: (*a*) Publius Cornelius Scipio Africanus, son and nephew of the Scipio brothers who died in 211; (*b*) Africanus' grandson by adoption, Scipio Aemilianus (son of Aemilius Paullus (6.836–8 and note)). Africanus defeated Hannibal in 202 and Aemilianus destroyed Carthage in 146. And Africanus' daughter was mother of the Gracchi.

Fabricius: a named Roman of the Republican era. Caius Fabricius Luscinus (censor in 275 BC) fought Pyrrhus of Epirus when Pyrrhus won his Pyrrhic victory (see note to 3.464–5).

844 *Serranus*: nickname of a Roman of the Republican era, Caius Atilius Regulus (consul in 257 BC), a general in the First Punic War, proverbial for being true to his word and for being called to the consulship while sowing in his fields (Latin *serere* = 'to sow', hence the pun on Serranus). Modern scholars prefer an etymology from Saranum in Umbria. It could as easily derive from *Sarranus*, 'Phoenician', 'Semitic', as in *Georgics* 2.506 and Silius 8.46, and refer to his exploits and sufferings in Carthage.

845 *Fabii*: named and ambiguously named Romans of the Republican era. The Fabii rewrote history (as Anchises does) to emphasize their selfsacrifices in national crises. In 479 BC three hundred and six Fabii were allegedly killed in an enemy ambush; the only survivor was also a Fabius. The family was probably trying to match the three hundred Spartans who had died fighting the Persians at Thermopylae the year before (Herodotus 7.221). The greatest Fabius was Quintus Fabius Maximus Cunctator

(the 'Delayer') whose guerrilla strategy prevented Hannibal from consolidating victory after Cannae in 216 BC. Line 846 is taken from Ennius, with just a change of person: Ennius has 'one man', Virgil 'you'. Octavian, whose motto was *festina lente*, 'make haste slowly', claimed that he had restored the Republic (as Fabius did). By having Anchises cite Ennius, Virgil evades responsibility for words that could mean Fabius *alone* had the right to claim he had restored the Republic. These words conclude Anchises' list of Republican heroes.

847 *Others*: a curious assertion of non-Roman superiority in arts and sciences, given Octavian's boast of building a city of marble and Julius Caesar's recent reform of the calendar, which survives, with fine tuning, to the present day. This may be Virgil's response to Octavian's neglect of Minerva, Pallas Athena, goddess of the arts and of Athens, who was overlooked in the Augustan religious revival. Anchises does not suggest other peoples will produce better poets.

853 *Mercy*: Anchises re-echoes his plea from line 835 to (the unnamed) Julius Caesar, that he be first to show clemency. Caesar usually did, and was killed. Octavian usually did not. He died of old age.

855 *Marcellus*: a named Roman of the Republican era. Marcus Claudius Marcellus conquered Syracuse (Sicily) in 212–211 BC. He is often represented as a horseman (see line 859); and was on horseback when killed in 208 BC (Silius 15.370–80). Anchises places first (and thus emphasizes) Marcellus' stabilizing of the Roman state (lines 857–8) as Fabius *restores* the state (line 846). The Marcelli fought *against* Caesar during Rome's civil wars.

859 *spoils*: Marcellus killed Viridomarus (a Gallic chief) in 222 BC. Anchises' statement that Marcellus dedicated spoils to Quirinus (a lesser class of spoils) is interesting in light of the controversy over Crassus. Other sources, including coinage issued by a family member in 45 BC, show Marcellus making the dedication to Jupiter Feretrius, not Quirinus (Plutarch, *Marcellus* 7; Propertius 4.10.39–40). Anchises lessens Marcellus' honours as Octavian lessens Crassus' honours. See also note to 11.15.

862 *expression*: Latin *vultus*, 'face', was thought to betray what one wishes (*vult*).

863–4 *Who's . . . noble descendant?*: Latin *nepos* indicates 'grandson', 'descendant', and 'nephew'. Marcus Claudius Marcellus (born in 42 BC was both a *descendant* of the famous Marcellus (above) and a *nephew* of Octavian (the son of his sister, Octavia). Octavian chose to marry his daughter Julia in 25 BC to Marcellus in an effort at partisan reconciliation. Marcellus, originally betrothed to Sextus Pompey's daughter, was now to be heir apparent to Caesar, not Pompey.

873 *Massed lamentations*: Marcellus died in 23 BC at Baiae, near the Sibyl's Cumae and Avernus, where Aeneas enters the underworld (Propertius 3.18 has details). The cause of his death was the same 'water cure' that

was earlier credited with saving Octavian's life, and it was prescribed by Octavian's doctor. Marcellus was buried in the Campus Martius where the shrine to Dis and Proserpina was situated (see note to 6.127) in the building Octavian had created to be his own tomb. Mars was linked with the cult of the dead and the earth, and with an Italian horse-god, Mares. Note Marcellus as horseman (line 883) and his nourishment by the earth (see also next note).

879 *Never defeated*: Marcellus accompanied Octavian on one campaign when he was 16.

885 *an offering*: Marcellus presented *munera*, 'offerings' (that is, games), during his only known (and junior) public office. Now, in the underworld, a *munus* (usually the tribute of the living for the dead) is offered to the unborn Marcellus by the dead Anchises. The net effect is to leave Octavian alone: the one person still alive in Rome's 'future', but without an heir. The parade of the future ends with the funeral of Octavian's future.

893 *Sleep opens twin double portals*: in *Odyssey* 19.562–7, Penelope claims to the disguised Odysseus that she has had a dream: an eagle kills her pet geese then says it is Odysseus and the geese her suitors. When she asks Odysseus what the dream means, he says it means just what she has said. But Penelope warns him not to be so sure: 'There are double gates of dreams that do not stay: the first are built of horn [*keraon*], the second of ivory [*elephanti*]. Those dreams that come through those of *sawn ivory* [*pristou elephantos*] deceive [*elephairontai*], for they bring things that cannot be made real [*akraanta*]. But those that come out through the gates of polished horn [*keraon*] bring real things [*etyma*] to reality [*krainousi*], whenever some mortal sees them' (*Odyssey* 19. 562–7). The gates are of 'sawn ivory' *because* they 'deceive', and of 'horn', *because* they 'are fulfilled'. The dreams are decided by the material, not vice versa. 'Ivory' is *ebur* in Latin. *Elephantus* means 'elephant'. To say 'ivory' with *elephantus* one says: 'horn (or tooth) of the elephant'. Virgil has already used Homer's phrase 'sawn (or cut) ivory' at 3.464–5 (see note there). Here the only sign of tooth is inside the word *candenti*, 'gleaming white'. Virgil is straining Latin to keep Homer's elephant (see next note).

898 *through the ivory portal*: here Virgil uses the normal Latin for ivory, *ebur*. I suspect he wanted the elephant earlier because it provides the archetype for two etymologies of Caesar's name. Servius, on *Aeneid* 1.286, says Caesar was so named either because his mother's womb was cut into (*caesus*, by 'Caesarian' section), or because his grandfather killed an elephant, *caesar* in Punic. Caesar proclaimed this latter Punic etymology on his first and most common coinage issued when he had captured Rome and taken the title of perpetual dictator (49–48 BC). On its reverse is an elephant trampling a snake, with CAESAR inscribed below. When victorious, Caesar rode to the Capitol accompanied by forty elephants carrying torches. The elephant was, Juvenal says, 'Caesar's beast of burden'. Artemidorus of Daldi in his *Oneirocrita* says that in Italy an elephant in a dream

symbolizes 'a master, a king'. Will the dream be fulfilled with Julius Caesar dead? As Penelope notes, elephantine dreams may be fantasy. See also note to 12.68.

900 *Caieta's port*: a port north of the Gulf of Naples, named for Aeneas' nurse, who died there.

901 *Anchors . . . seashore* a repetition of *Aeneid* 3.277, but apt here too.

BOOK SEVEN

11 *child of the Sun*: Circe is the sister of Aeëtes, king of Colchis (on the Black Sea coast of what is now Georgia) and of Pasiphaë, mother of the Minotaur. In some traditions her mother is Hecate. Like Aeëtes' daughter Medea, Circe is a witch. Her special power is that of changing men into beasts, though she spends most of her time weaving and singing. Among her victims is the Latin king Picus, whom she turns into a woodpecker. The notion of human souls inside animal bodies (the darker side of doctrines of reincarnation) is not part of Virgil's underworld in Book 6 as it is of Plato's Myth of Er. Odysseus says he visited Circe's land before his consultation of the dead and that he returned there afterwards (*Odyssey* 10 and 12). Virgil keeps Circe out until after his 'book of the dead', and then has Aeneas bypass her. But there is much shape-changing in Books 7–12, so Circe is often present vicariously. By Virgil's day her land, Aeaea, was identified with what is now called Monte Circeo, roughly halfway between Cumae and the Tiber estuary.

37 *Erato*: the Muse of love as well as love poetry. Roman poets assume that sexual desire is a form of aggression whose goal is the possession of the beloved. Thus war is sexual not just in the mythic sense that disputes over women lead nations to war, but because Virgil saw physical aggression as rooted in sexuality, a theme he explores fully in Book 11. He dwells on the close relationship between *Roma* and *Amor*, mirror images even as words, and knows that in Greek *romē* means 'strength'. Love for a person is never as detached from sexuality in pre-Christian Rome as it can be in our usage. And Aeneas is the child of Venus, goddess of sexual love, and halfbrother of Amor (Love). *Venus* is both a common noun for the sexual urge and a name for the goddess. As with Ceres (grain) and Bacchus (wine), the god and the natural energy (s)he represents are one and the same. By invoking Erato, Virgil is defying historians such as Sallust and Livy, who rationalized the confused legends of Rome's beginnings into prose history with a very pro-Roman bias (as opposed to his own more even-handedly *Italian* perspective) and who sometimes dismissed the accounts of bardic poets (Latin *vates*) with scorn. Virgil also reclaims the title *vates* for himself (7.41), and *vates* is the word he uses to describe the Sibyl and Helenus. What follows echoes Sallust (*Jugurtha* 5; *Catiline* 6.20).

40–1 *explain . . . prompt your seer*: Virgil will narrate (*expediam* is a favourite verb of historians), Erato will advise. The Sibyl, in 6.86–93, foresees 'hideous warfare'. Virgil will spell it out, and 'speak', not 'sing', as in Book 1. Books 7–12 are largely the product of Virgil's vatic conception: they are his originals, not variants on the creations of others. He asks Erato to midwife his vision to birth, a metaphor echoed in Propertius: 'A little something is being born that is greater than the *Iliad*' (2.34.66).

47 *Faunus's*: a forest deity, understandably dedicated to trees. The transformation of his father Picus into a woodpecker, then, has a specially vindictive aptness. Virgil routinely emphasizes the sacredness of trees and forests. See 9.79–122 and note to 9.79; 12.766–71; and the note to 6.179. Nothing much is known about Marica outside Virgil and his commentators. She appears to be a kind of double for Circe.

56 *queen of the Latins*: Amata, not actually named until 7.343, though it should not be surprising, after this characterization, that her name has 'love' in it.

59 *laurel*: a bay rather than a laurel; but to translate it as 'bay' means losing the critical pun with 'Laurentine', and the implied etymology for the name of Lavinia, Latinus' daughter. See note to 7.71.

64 *bees in a dense swarm*: whether this omen is good or bad depends on whether the observer is Greek or Roman: to the Greeks a swarm of bees is usually a good omen, to the Romans a bad omen.

71 *Lavinia*: Virgil now disposes of a tradition he evaded earlier (see note to 3.80). Dionysius (1.59.3) says Lavinia was Launa, daughter of King Anius of Delos. Delos, birthplace of Apollo, made a cult of the palm tree under which the god was born. But Apollo's (and Octavian's) favourite tree was the laurel (see note to 7.59), not the palm. Virgil connects Launa/Lavinia, through the laurel, with the Laurentines, blots out Anius' unmentioned daughter, and allows Latinus' city, also never named, to blend quietly into the city Aeneas will found: Lavinium.

73 *Seemed*: some think the fire 'real' rather than a prophetic illusion. But a 'real' fire that melts the crown on Lavinia's head would, at best, leave her scarred. There's no reason to think her beauty damaged.

83 *Albunea's heights*: near Lavinium, and noted for their whitish, sulphurous waters.

86 *priestess*: Virgil does not specify the gender. I follow Fairclough and others in making the priest female. The rites are typical of an 'incubation oracle' in which the consultant or priest slept on the hides of sacrificed animals, often in total darkness, waiting for prophetic dreams.

98 *from a foreign world*: Rome's ruling class in Virgil's day almost never married outside its own inner elite, much less with non-Romans, which is why the major figures in Rome's civil wars are related by marriage to their worst enemies. Alexander the Great's model of unifying a world empire by encouraging marriage outside one's ethnic group may well have

motivated Julius Caesar's and Antony's relations with Cleopatra. But it was anathema to many traditionalists because it was linked with a monarchical form of government. Indeed, much of Octavian's appeal lay in his opposition to this 'Alexandrian' model. So the Aeneas myth was more problematic for him than for Julius Caesar. The efforts made in Book 7 to prove Turnus is 'Greek' so he can qualify for marriage with Lavinia would have seemed bizarre to traditionalists; and marrying Lavinia to a Phrygian, such as Aeneas, would have been 'unthinkable' in their contemporary environment.

105 *Laomedon's youth*: that is, the Trojans, identified as descendants of Laomedon, father of Priam, who broke his word to the gods. See notes to 8.18 and 8.157. It is perhaps an ominous designation here, since we are about to see the 'fulfilment' of a prophecy attributed to the Harpy Celaeno by Aeneas in his narration to Dido. Celaeno had begun by addressing the Trojans as 'Sons of Laomedon' (3.247).

119 *corralled these words*: to validate an omen one had to be alert to the opportunity (and ritually qualified) to declare it fulfilled. See 5.530–2.

122 *my father*: Aeneas narrated a similar (but more threatening) famine prophecy to an audience of Trojans and Carthaginians in 3.246 ff. and attributed it to the Harpy Celaeno. Now, when his audience is exclusively Trojan, he attributes a more encouraging famine prophecy to a private communication from Anchises, and his changes go unchallenged. Scholars usually argue that Virgil is either showing he knows more than one tradition of the prophecy or unwittingly creating an inconsistency to be ironed out during final revision. Neither takes account of the different circumstances on the two occasions. The 'Harpy prophecy' is made after a lavish banquet at Carthage, as part of a rhetorical strategy that insists on Italy as the Trojans' destination. Thus the Harpy's terrifying predictions of a dire famine before the Trojans can settle makes the lavishness of Dido's tables 'proof' that Carthage cannot be the end of their journey. Aeneas was declining Dido's invitation to stay, and reassuring Trojans of eventual departure from Carthage and reversing his procedure in the dream of Hector (2.268–97). Gods create visual omens to manipulate human perceptions; poets and rhetoricians use words. Here Aeneas discloses to his crew what subtended his Harpy narrative and tells them they have arrived and can now settle. See notes to 2.2, 286; 3.256.

129 *exile*: I follow R. D. Williams here in reading *exiliis* (exile) for the manuscripts' *exitiis* (catastrophes). The latter would yield the meaning: 'Sure to set bounds for disasters.'

136 *local spirit*: the most important such divinity was called the *Indiges*, the Native Spirit or Hero, not necessarily born in the land that honours him, even though the term sometimes has this literal sense. In Sallust's *Epistle of Pompey* 5, Pompey sarcastically calls Sertorius, a Spanish-born Roman who led a rebellion against Rome, Spain's *indiges*, its native-son 'hero'. Aeneas is described by Livy (1.2.6) as the Indigenous Jupiter honoured at

the river Numicus, not far from where Aeneas is now encamped and which his scouts discover the next day. Virgil's Jupiter prefers to call him 'the Indigenous' in 12.795, where I render it as 'the Native Spirit'. The inhabitants of the Numicus area are all allied against Aeneas by the end of Book 7. See also 5.95 and note.

140 *in Erebus' darkness*: an odd location for Anchises, whom he has just visited in the brightness of Elysium.

152 *gifted in language*: the Latin has *oratores* (trained public speakers). Virgil's world is not, like Homer's, united under one language. The poet alludes to the use of Greek, Sabine, Oscan, and Etruscan and even glosses some 'foreign' names with Latin equivalents. He depicts Aeneas as aware of other languages. In Troy, differences in speech betray Aeneas' men to the Greeks even when they are clad in Greek armour. Virgil also has Jupiter specify that the Latins won't have to give up their language when accepting Trojan rule. Aeneas' huge delegation is probably in response to his scouts' reports. Virgil's reference to the 'august royal palace' in line 153 warns us that Latinus' city is larger than we would have expected—hence his selection of a cross-section of his forces to communicate with Latin counterparts at all social levels, but also to indicate his own strength.

157–8 *his city's / Bounds*: one usually consulted local peoples *before* setting up a colony—as the Phoenician settlers at Carthage had done. Aeneas seizes territory as an enemy invader would and forces the Latins either to accept him or fight him. No name is given to either Aeneas' camp or Latinus' city.

164 *Dart arched bows' taut strings*: Virgil's language is dense with alliterative anagrams here, suggesting the conversion of energy into bodily strength to take full advantage of each weapon. The fortified Laurentine city and militarized youth come as a surprise, since Virgil led us to expect a peaceful 'Saturnian' people. The setting resembles Rome, displaced in time and space, a city that has not yet taken root. More specifically, it resembles Rome's Capitoline Hill. Latium has a double reality: a militarized and powerful urban upper class and a generally peaceful rural peasantry.

170–1 *a hundred / Columns*: Virgil expands on 7.153. The palace is a religious and political centre, like the Temple of Capitoline Jupiter. The hundred columns make it larger than the Parthenon: an amazing edifice for Picus (a forest king transformed into a woodpecker).

173 *fasces*: the first of many *Roman* features of custom and costume in Latinus' city, closely followed by *curia*, 'senate (house)' (see note to 6.817). The Roman Senate often met in the Temple of Capitoline Jupiter. Romans also celebrated the 'Feast of Jupiter' on the Capitol, and feasted there after military triumphs.

178 *Italus, father Sabinus*: Italus was the hero Italy was named for (1.533 and 3.166). Virgil usually elides a final vowel when the next word begins with a vowel but does not do so before *Italusque* here. He may be using the

hiatus to suggest the presence of a consonant or semi-consonant, as in the Samnite coin inscription where Italia is *Viteliu* (= Gk. *hitalos*, 'bullock'). This sets up a play on *vitisator*, 'sower of vines' (viticulturalist), the epithet of Sabinus, ancestor of the Sabines, whose name some thought derived from *sator* + *vinum* (wine). Then Virgil endows Sabinus with the sickle (usually linked with Saturn) before introducing the original *sator*, Saturn. Central and southern Italy were called, generically, *Oenotria*, the land of *oinos* ('wine', in Greek), named, Varro tells us, for Oenotrus, king of the Sabines. Virgil's ordering principle here is etymological rather than genealogical, as is Plato's in the *Cratylus*.

180 *Janus*: see note to 1.294, and 7.607–20 with note to 7.607. Janus marks transitions: the end of the old year to the beginning of the new; peace to war; and in this instance, order to chaos.

186 *And spears and shields and rams*: not only minor gods and heroes crowd in, but the (surely thousands of) *wounded* in battle and the prizes and debris of conquest. The palace begins to resemble an overstuffed attic. The contrast with the elegant Carthage in Book 1 is striking.

187–8 *small, striped / Toga*: the *trabea*, worn by kings, augurs, and consuls on solemn occasions. Here, uniquely, it is small. The *lituus*, 'staff', was a symbol of augural office, as the 'crook' is of a bishop's authority. It was called Quirinus' staff in honour either of the deified Romulus under whose auspices Rome was founded, or of Cures, home of Numa (credited with establishing Rome's religious laws (6.810 and note)). Add the *ancile*, Numa's sacral shield (see note to 8.663), and Picus might resemble Numa in all but one detail.

191 *striping his plumage*: some species of woodpecker, an augural bird, have black-and-white stripes on the undersides of their wing plumage. That is Libanus' point when he sees a woodpecker pecking an elm (the tree of punishment: see note to 6.282–9) in Plautus, *Asinaria* 262–4, it is an omen of 'stripes' (*virgae*), i.e. a whipping for the speaker. Since the salient feature of Picus' striped toga is its small size, Virgil implies that Picus is represented heraldically with the features of a woodpecker.

202 *Don't avoid being our guests*: Latinus pretends that he thinks Aeneas' arrival is accidental and his camp a temporary fort (and thus not the violation of protocol it appears to be).

206 *Auruncan*: Auruncans are people the Greeks called Ausonians. Virgil uses both terms; Ausonia and Ausonian are often generic for Italy and its early peoples. Auruncan is usually more specific: the Oscan-speaking peoples between the Liris and Volturnus rivers, south of Volscian territory.

208 *Samothrace*: an island in the north-east Aegean, famous for its still elusive mysteries. It was, in some accounts, originally called Dardania. It then became the Samos of the Thracians; but when exiles from Samos took over it became the Thrace of the Samians. Dardanus belongs to the remote past.

209 *Corythus' home*: Corythus seems to be a person, not a place. But Latinus is emphatic that he belongs in Etruria (not in Latium). If so, the Trojans are on the wrong side of the Tiber.

210–11 *sits on a throne in . . . Heaven*: no one but Latinus sets Dardanus in heaven.

212 *Ilioneus*: the Trojan spokesman, as in 1.52 ff., but now without a concealed Aeneas to step from a cloud to the rescue. In addressing the son of Faunus (Rome's equivalent of the goat-god Pan) a diplomat should not use a word-play on *rex* and *grex* (the king (*rex*) outstanding within the flock (*grex*)). And his claim of descent from Jupiter (much superior to Faunus) with grand epic words lifted from Aratus would win him no plaudits in a school of rhetoric. Finally, his flat contradiction of Latinus' hypothesis of their accidental arrival serves only to confirm that, at best, he and Aeneas are ignorant of protocol or, at worst, arrogantly flouting it.

219 *In our beginnings was Jove*: Ilioneus is (anachronistically) citing the opening of Aratus' *Phaenomena*, a Greek epic about the heavens. The phrase is also used by Theocritus, *Idylls* 17.1, in a pastoral context (as in Virgil's own *Eclogues* 3.60). Lines 222 ff. show that Ilioneus has Aratus in mind.

220 *Grandfather*: the Latin, *avo*, is a dilemma for translators. Dardanus was six generations back from Aeneas; but if 'ancestor' is substituted (which would be fine if the context were generalizing, e.g. 'in our grandfathers' days'), this would suppress readers' awareness that Ilioneus is making Dardanus seem closer than he is to his own day, as Aeneas does when talking of Dardanus to Evander (8.134 ff. and note to 8.134).

242 *Numicus*: sacred as the site of Aeneas' death (see note to 7.136).

246 *regalia Priam would wear*: as when Aeneas gives royal gifts to Dido in 1.650–5, we should ask how and where he acquired them (see notes to 3.46 and 6.524). They are, after all, Troy's Crown Jewels.

253 *holding him back*: Aeneas' and Ilioneus' poor diplomacy must be a factor. Aeneas has already staked a claim on his lands and confronted him with a fait accompli: is this the kind of person he wants his daughter to marry, sight unseen? But there is the prophecy; and Aeneas' gifts imply a concession of sovereignty to him and a kind of payment. Besides, the alternative is clearly war. For the Trojans will not leave if he says 'no'. Mustering a show of joy, then, takes time.

262 *Troy's great endowments*: presumably Priam's regalia, now in his hands, and which he will not regard as exclusively his. It doesn't make much sense as a reference to Aeneas' camp (which some claim is named 'Troy' despite Virgil's silence). It would take an army to expel the Trojans at this point.

266 *the hand of the tyrant*: 'tyrant' is the routine word in Latin and Greek for someone who takes power by unconstitutional or illegal means. Substituting an innocuous word such as 'chief' or 'leader', as some translators do, weakens the force of Latinus' comment unjustifiably. Neither god nor fate confers upon Aeneas legal title to the land he has seized. Latinus is careful to

phrase his comment obliquely, as if he were quoting some treaty formula used by an earlier poet and to follow it instantly by calling Aeneas 'your king'.

280 *a chariot*: a gift not put to use: Aeneas fights on foot in the *Aeneid*. He seems to have given up on chariots since he lost one to Diomedes in *Iliad* 5. Compare Latinus' own chariot in 12.161–6.

283 *Daedalan cunning*: see note to 6.14.

293 *Damn these creatures*: Juno, gone since the end of Book 5, finds the Trojans in Italy and prepares to unleash not a storm, as in Book 1, but a war. There is no Neptune to halt the uproar: the Trojans are ashore.

305 *Lapiths*: their only crime was their failure to honour Mars at Pirithous' wedding.

306 *Calydon*: Oeneus, king of Calydon, failed to sacrifice to Diana. In punishment she sent the Calydonian boar to ravage his kingdom.

318 *Rutulian*: a term used of the Latin peoples of Ardea, the city of Turnus.

319 *Bellona*: an Italian war-goddess. See 8.702–3. In the Latin text, Hecuba (line 320) is Cisseis, the daughter of the Thracian Cisseus (see 5.536 and note), as in Euripides' *Hecuba* 3 (set in Thrace), not daughter of Dymas, a Phrygian king (as in *Iliad* 16.718). Her dream of impregnation by a firebrand is in Euripides' *Trojan Women* 922.

325 *Allecto*: her name comes from Gk. *allektos*, 'unstoppable', 'insatiable' (Latin *insaturabilis*). She is the essence of Juno's determination, capable (unlike the gods) of sustained focus on a project and of interconnected strategies of action. Though she may be Virgil's invention, she has characteristics of a traditional Greek Erinys (Fury), and operates mostly by insinuating herself into people's *minds*.

363 *Phrygian sheep-boy*: Paris. Lavinia, unlike Helen, will be a virgin when abducted.

371 *Turnus' roots . . . ancestry*: Amata's argument that the designation 'foreign' includes any state not directly under Latinus' control would allow Latinus to think of Ardea as foreign (see note to 7.98). But Faunus' oracle has further prohibited Lavinia's marriage to anyone within the Latin alliance, which would include Ardea. So she argues a Greek genealogy for Turnus and assigns Inachus (father of Io) and Acrisius (father of Danaë) to Mycenae, a city more ancient than their traditional Argos. See also 7.409–12. Turnus, as we shall see, also subscribes to this notion and has Io as the motto on his shield (7.788–92 and note to 7.789). Neither Amata nor Latinus considers offering Lavinia's hand to real Greeks resident in Italy: Diomedes, say, or Idomeneus (Evander is presumably too old and Pallas too young).

390 *the gentling thyrsus*: Latin *mollis* indicates (*a*) the civilizing (or effeminizing) power of the thyrsus (the Bacchic wand), or (*b*) the thyrsus' (possibly) flexible wood.

410 *Acrisionian settlers*: Danaë, called Acrisione by Homer (*Iliad* 14.319), was put in a chest and set adrift at sea by her father Acrisius, who feared that her son would, as prophesied, kill him. Virgil (uniquely) represents her as an exile coming ashore with fellow settlers at Ardea. Acrisius was the son of Abas. And Aeneas has already dedicated a shield won from a person named Abas (3.288 and note).

412 *Ardea*: compare the way Carthage is described (1.12–13) and other cities of the Latin League (6.773–5 and note).

419 *Calybe*: her name, meaning 'hut' or perhaps 'hideaway', derives from the Greek root *kalyp-*, 'conceal', found also in Calypso. The only other known Calybe is a nymph in *Iliad* 6.21–6 (see Paschalis, *Virgil's Aeneid*, 256). There she is mother of Boukolion ('Cowherd') by Laomedon. Virgil's Allecto is herself quite a country girl: at home in the woods and on the hunt, so her choice of a masking identity is not accidental. Yet, ironically for a demon, she grasps what Juno never does: that there is a *logical* strategy available to Turnus that will yield the results both he and Juno want, and that she can convey it to him best by *disguising* her nature as a spirit of madness. Unfortunately, her choice of *persona* and her 'old hag' make-up are totally wrong. They generate a character from rustic comedy, and produce, until discarded, comic results. Her best advice (to burn the Trojan navy now) is lost until too late.

440 *decades in this spot*: the Latin is curiously ambiguous: *victa* means 'conquered' and (less commonly) 'lived'; *situ* both 'place' and 'decay'. At the two extremes it yields: 'lived in place' and 'conquered by decay'. Which, then, does the sleeping Turnus mean? If the former, he is being patronizing; if the latter, he is delivering arguably the rudest insult in the *Aeneid*. His use of *mater*, 'mother', seems courteous; so I have gone with the former. But the rustic Allecto clearly understands it the other way. The expression *victa situ* is attached to old age when Turnus uses it, but to 'I' when Allecto uses it. In reproducing the effect I have had to alter the pun so that it will work in English. (And 'decades' should be pronounced with the accent on the last syllable, not on the first.)

447 *Raw Strife*: *Erinys* in the original (from Gk. *eris*, 'strife'). This is the 'true' name for one of the spirits called (to avoid offence) *Eumenides*, 'the well-disposed ones'.

457 *torches of death*: Latin *taedae*, 'torches', is often a poetic shorthand for marriage; but the word is also used for funeral torches. Both senses are apt here.

479 *girl from the Cocytus*: Cocytus is of course the underworld river. But Virgil quickly shows us that Allecto knows not only how to hunt, but how to pick out an animal whose killing will start a war.

483 *antlers*: wherever this word appears in the translation, the Latin is *cornu*, 'horn'. Modern English isn't happy about calling a stag's antlers 'horns'.

491   *sylvan*: I have added this word to enable the reader in English to connect the forests (*silvae*) with Silvia's name, as they are connected in Latin.

498   *His hand strayed*: Ascanius both hits and misses his mark. He strikes the stag, but fails to kill it immediately, and the stag gets away. No hunter wins praise for this least desirable of shots. The consequences are worse than they would have been if he had missed altogether. It is not clear which god's presence is marked by the masculine *deus*.

526   *unsheathed swords*: Virgil leaves us to notice that the battle is between fully armed Trojan soldiers and Italian peasants with improvised clubs and stakes. No Trojan casualties are listed.

540   *Mars favouring neither*: despite the inequalities of weaponry, the Latins are holding their own.

558   *what the Great Father would wish*: but when Juno later agrees to stop interfering in the war, Virgil draws attention to the twin powers of hell that flank Jupiter's throne. See 12.845–52 and note to 12.845.

565   *Ampsanctus Valley*: known as the 'umbilical' of Italy (as Delphi was the 'umbilical' of Greece), where there was a sanctuary of Mephitis (the 'Sulphurous' deity). The volcanic exhalations were thought lethal in antiquity, so it is an apt point of departure for Allecto. Lines 565–6 are almost identical with 11.523–4 (the pass where Turnus plans to ambush Aeneas—itself similar to the site of the battle of the Caudine Forks (Livy 9.2.7), where the Romans were disastrously defeated by the (rustic) Samnites in 321 BC).

586–7   *like a crag . . . like a crag*: part of line 586 is repeated in line 587 with an important modification. In line 586 the crag is a landmass resisting the sea; in line 587 it is part of the sea: a boundary belongs to both worlds it divides.

601–4   *Men had a custom . . . to the Getae*: the first letters of these four lines spell out 'Mars'. Acrostics occur in several places in the *Aeneid*, but this is the only one I have reproduced. 'Mars' is the same in English as in Latin and is the subject of the lines marked by the acrostic. It is clearly deliberate, as I am sure the others are. But they are hard to reproduce without altering the 'literal' meaning.

604–6   *Say, for example . . . from the Parthians*: the only real wars and victories lurking here are those of Marcus Licinius Crassus, who won major victories in Thrace over the neighbours of the Getae, for which he was awarded a triumph in 29 BC, when Octavian denied him the 'Spoils of Distinction' (see note to 6.841); and the exploits of Aelius Gallus in what is now Yemen in 25 BC. Aelius Gallus was the successor to Virgil's friend Caius Cornelius Gallus (see note to 6.306–8) who had led an expeditionary force into southern Egypt. The Hyrcanians (in northern Iran) and Indians were never on Rome's military horizons (though Octavian received trade delegations from India in 26 and 20 BC). The only Roman who had achieved any military success against the Parthians was Mark Antony, and even he lost over 22,000 men (and yet more Roman standards) in his ill-fated attack on Phraaspa, the capital of Media. Octavian finally negotiated with the Parthians for the return of both Antony's and the elder Crassus' standards. Compare Anchises' similarly false claims at 6.794–807 (and note to 6.794–8).

607 *War has twin matched portals*: the gates of the Temple of Janus (see 1.294 and note). What is most striking here is the 'reading back' onto early Latium of specific details about officials and garments (and styles of wearing them) introduced after Rome's foundation. The royal toga of Quirinus was worn by consuls only at this ceremony. But there are no 'consuls' in Latinus' city, and the Gabine style of wearing the toga refers to the manner in which it was secured in a battle between Rome and Gabii hundreds of years later.

630 *Amitina*: the manuscripts have Atina, which is too far away to be likely. Hülsen's emendation, Amitina, followed by Horsfall, brings the city within plausible range. If Atina is retained the beginning of the line should be changed to read: 'There is Atina . . .' None of the cities listed was ever very big.

637 *token symbolic of war*: not necessarily a tablet inscribed with a password but some prearranged object.

641 *Goddesses*: the Muses of Helicon (in central Greece), as in Hesiod, *Theogony* 1 ff., not the Muses of Olympus as in Homer, *Iliad* 2.484, or of Pieria, as in Hesiod, *Works and Days*, or Statius, *Thebaid*, perhaps because what matters most is who the *descendants* of these kings are. Since most combatants listed are not found in other versions of the Aeneas legend, the poet needs all the divine help he can get, as line 646 makes clear. Giving notes on all names in the catalogue that follows would require an extra volume. I single out those I find particularly intriguing or puzzling. Roman readers would have known most of them: this is their home territory. The catalogue lines up almost all Italy's peoples against Aeneas, except the Greeks and some Etruscan allies. Virgil is looking back on early Italy as we might look back upon Britain when William the Conqueror invaded. Virgil's Italy had been, and still was, a patchwork of different cultures and languages. There was nothing quite corresponding to Ireland on his map, and ours would have no equivalent for Italy's Greek colonies except perhaps the Latin-speaking religious communities. If one ignores classifications of languages and takes the Welsh as equivalents for the Etruscans, the Gaelic-speaking Scots for some of the various Oscan-speakers (notably the Samnites and the Marsi), the Gauls as the Danes and other Vikings, the Angles and Saxons as Sabines and Latins, and the Trojans as Normans, one can get some sense of the variety of conflicting interests and sympathies. Then imagine the poet as someone of Scottish and Welsh ancestry generating a tale of the Norman invasion in English, but charging it with strange resonances of later British history; where you catch a glimpse of Owen Glendower fighting the English, of the massacre of Scots at Culloden, of Cromwell and the Civil War.

648 *Mezentius*: writers before Virgil or contemporary with him (*a*) do not separate Mezentius from the rest of the Etruscans, (*b*) have him outlive
Aeneas, and (*c*) have him either fall by or make peace with Ascanius. The
epithet 'god-despising' links him to Capaneus, one of the 'Seven against
Thebes' in Aeschylus, *Seven* 441, and in Statius, *Thebaid* (but it does not
prevent him from acting on Jupiter's orders at 10.689). We are not told
here why he was so unworthy a father to Lausus, and when details
are supplied (8.481 ff.) they come from Evander rather than from the
authorial Virgil.

652 *Agylla*: another name for the Etruscan city Caere (Cerveteri), or its port,
Pyrgi. Perhaps Virgil uses this name to avoid overstressing the fact that
Aeneas' fleet later sets out from Caere with a contingent from Caere led
by Astyr. See 10.183; and note to 10.169–84.

655 *Aventinus*: Virgil's invention, named for the Aventine Hill where Remus
later took unsuccessful omens in competition with his twin Romulus to
decide who would name the new city. Romulus took omens from the
Palatine Hill. Aventinus' mother's name is identical with that of
Romulus' and Remus' mother, but his father is Hercules, not Mars, and
his conception occurred during Hercules' visit to the site of Rome (narrated in Book 8). When Aeneas visits the site of Rome in Book 8, he goes
to the Palatine. For in 8.190–267 the Aventine is home to the monster
Cacus. In the myth-history of Rome, the Aventine is associated not only
with the vanquished Remus, but with the secessions of the plebeians, who
established themselves there in their struggles against the dominant patri-
cian families. It is a kind of counter-Rome with a counter-mythology to
which Virgil adds. See also next note.

665 *Samnian rapier*: if the lion-skin marks Aventinus' links with Hercules, the
Samnian (Samnite) rapier connects him with early Rome's most formidable foes in Italy. The Samnites (along with the Marsi) were among the
leading peoples in the 'Social War' in 90–89 BC during which the non-
Latin allies of Rome seceded and established a capital at Corfinium which
they renamed Italia. Among the cities that joined the confederacy was
Alba Longa. See also note to 12.103.

671 *Tiburtus*: *Tiburti*, in Latin, can be both a nominative plural ('the Tiburti',
the people of Tibur) and a genitive singular ('of Tiburtus', the brother).
In this context it is, grammatically, the latter— though Virgil plays on its
identity with the former. It's hard to catch this little witticism in English.

674 *birthed from the clouds*: the centaurs are the descendants of Ixion, who
attempted to rape Juno. Jupiter substituted a cloud made to resemble
Juno (= Gk. Hera, etymologized as *aer*, 'air'). The child born of this rape
was called Centaurus—hence the association of centaurs with clouds.
Such ancestry is appropriate for Catillus and Coras who are from Tibur,
modern Tivoli, famous for its precipitous watercourses with their clouds
of spray, and who gallop about amid *hailstorms* of spears.

678 *Praeneste's founder*: Praeneste (Palestrina), on an outcrop of the Apennines on the north-west border of Latium about 22 miles from Rome, was probably founded by Illyrians, but was by historical times a mixture of Latins, Samnites, and Etruscans. It was at war with Rome throughout much of the fourth century BC and was later one of the main urban casualties during the struggle for power at Rome between Marius and Sulla, when it was sacked after Sulla's brutal victory in 82 BC and many of its inhabitants massacred. Perhaps that is what underlies the slightly ominous way the city and its founder are introduced. Some scholars see a connection between Caeculus and the famous Roman clan Caecilius, the Caecilii Metelli in particular, one of the most important families at Rome over many generations. If so, the echo is ironic, since the Metelli were, by and large, staunch supporters of Sulla. See note to 8.561.

691 *Messapus*: usually the hero of the Messapian peoples of southern Italy (Calabria). The poet Ennius is said to have claimed descent from him (Cicero, *Brutus* 18.72). So Messapus' singing, swan-stepping contingent would be an oblique compliment to Ennius, were it not assembled from communities *north* of the Tiber and thus far distant from Ennius' birthplace. And Fescennium is associated with ribald songs and farces of the sort Julius Caesar's soldiers sang in (playful) mockery of him in his Gallic triumph (Suetonius, *Divus Julius* 49), not epic.

702 *Loops in its pools*: the Latin anagram, *pulsa palus*, makes up the only two words in the line. Several Virgilian half-lines seem to contain anagrams. See 9.466–7. See Translator's Note, p. xlviii.

706 *Clausus*: this Sabine from King Numa's town, Cures, is ancestor of the many branches of the Claudius clan, including the elder and younger Marcellus whose souls Anchises presents to Aeneas (see 6.855–85 and notes) and the Appius Claudius family, distinguished for many generations, but omitted from Anchises' parade perhaps because their most recent members had opposed Julius Caesar and were not yet, like the Marcelli, on Octavian's agenda for reconciliation. The most important Claudius of Virgil's day had to be treated carefully. This was Tiberius Claudius Nero, Octavian's eventual successor, but already bypassed in favour of Claudius Marcellus, and about to be bypassed again in favour of Agrippa. The rambunctiously complimentary wordplay suggests that Virgil has a contemporary in mind for his audience's amusement and that rules out the Marcelli. If so, Tiberius, already launched on his military career, is a contender. See note to 10.345.

717 *Allia*: on 18 July 390 BC Gallic invaders defeated the Romans at the river Allia and went on to capture Rome. The day was marked black on the Roman calendar, as was the day of Hannibal's victory at Cannae. There are no allusions to the sites of Hannibal's victories in Italy in this catalogue or that of Book 10.

723 *Agamemnon's lad*: if 10.417 ff. represent Virgil's view of how Halaesus' *aged father* protected him from the fates until *blindness* stopped his vigilance,

Halaesus is not Agamemnon's son. Virgil uses *Agamemnonius* in 6.489–90 to indicate 'under Agamemnon's command'; it does not have to indicate fatherhood. Halaesus could have served under Agamemnon or simply idolized him. I translate 'lad' to allow all variant interpretations. But Halaesus, like Messapus, seems to be attached to the wrong forces. He is the 'name hero' of the Falisci, Falaesus (initial Gk. 'h' = 'f' before 'a' or 'o' in Italic). But Virgil's Falisci are commanded by Messapus.

725 *Massicus' soil*: the Massicus range produced some of Italy's most prized wines: 'Massic wine'.

733 *our writs of epic*: early Roman laws were often formulated in verse and called *carmina*, a word which indicates laws and judicial formulas as well as incantations or poems. Oebalus is a Teleboean (a people noted for breaking the law, as pirates) and his name evokes Oebalus king of Sparta and father of Tyndareus, the mortal 'father' of Helen and Clytemnestra. Tyndareus has his moment on stage in Euripides' *Orestes* where his pre-occupation is 'the Law', as is traditional among early Spartan kings (such as Lycurgus). Demaratus, exiled king of Sparta, talks of the Law in Herodotus' *Histories*.

740 *city of orchards*: ancient Abellae in Campania was famous for its hazelnuts (*abellana* is the Latin for 'hazelnut'). In calling Abellae *maliferae* (uniquely in Latin literature) Virgil reminds us that Abellae produces other fruits too. But *malum* is open to punning. With a short 'a' it means 'misfortune', and with a long 'a' is the proverbial fruit of discord, the apple. The poet Naevius was so arrogant that the noble Metelli threatened to give him *malum*, that is, 'misfortune' rather than 'an apple'. Since Naevius was from Campania, this may be an oblique reference to him.

741 *Oscan style*: the unchallenged manuscript reading, *Teutonico*, 'in the manner of the Teutones', is baffling. The Teutones were Celtic-Germanic peoples from central Denmark who attacked Roman territory in the late second century BC and were finally defeated by Gaius Marius. They never got as far south as Rome, much less Campania. There's nothing in Caesar, Tacitus, or Pliny to suggest that Celts or Germans used boomerangs (as in this line, traditionally read), much less helmets made of cork-oak, a tree that does not grow in northerly climates. Abellae's Oscan neighbours, however, referred to themselves as *touto*, 'people', a word cognate with Celtic *tuath*, and the common Celtic-Germanic root *teut-* in 'Teutones'. I suspect Virgil wrote *tutico* or *toutonico* rather than *teutonico*, and that the manuscripts assimilated it to the (more familiar) *teutonico*. The Oscan adjective *tovtiks* normally yields Latin *tuticus*. If *Teutonico* is read, 'Celtic' or 'Teuton' must be substituted for 'Oscan'. *Cateia* is clearly a boomerang. Isidore of Seville notes (*Etymologiae* 18.7.7): 'it comes back to the person who sent it', much as Naevius' criticism of the Metelli did.

743 *bronze glitters light*: Virgil uses long syllables to suggest that the usually lightweight shields (*peltae* in Latin) are made weighty by the unusual

addition of bronze-plating. Bronze swords (lighter than iron swords) have a traditional (and lighter) glint.

746 *Aequiculi . . . can't be equalled*: the Aequicoli, 'cultivators of "equal" [i.e. just and flat] land', work on a land that is 'unequal' and harsh, and practise the unjust art of banditry.

753 *Umbro's*: after assorted farmers and bandits we get a medicine man/poet who, in life, uses nature's power to calm snakes and heal snake-bites; in death, he squeezes tears from snake-nurturing water. He precedes a person brought back to life by Asclepius (god of medicine and curative snakes).

761 *Hippolytus' stem*: Euripides' *Hippolytus* tells of a virginal youth dedicated to Artemis, who rejects sexuality and the worship of Aphrodite and is destroyed by her. Hippolytus dies before the eyes of his father Theseus, who cursed him in the mistaken belief that the youth had assaulted Phaedra, his wife and Hippolytus' stepmother. Phaedra, made to fall in love with Hippolytus by Aphrodite, killed herself when he rejected her indirect overtures, but left a note falsely accusing him of rape. In response to Theseus' curse, a bull rose from the sea and frightened Hippolytus' horses. They threw him from his chariot and dragged him to his death. Callimachus, Servius tells us, connected this myth with an Italian deity, Virbius, whose cult prohibited the use of horses. Virgil takes the story from there at line 765.

772 *Phoebus's own son*: (i.e. Asclepius), reading *Phoebigenam*. I could not get the alternative reading, *Poenigenam*, 'Penalty's child', to work without a gnarled and lengthy note. I use the more familiar 'Asclepius' rather than the Latin 'Aesculapius' for Phoebus' son, the god of medicine.

777 *by erasing its meaning*: the phrase says, literally, 'the name [*or* meaning] being turned around'. Virbius is an anagram of *viribus*, 'strength', lost in reassembling the elements of the mutilated Hippolytus. The 'horse' (Gk. *hippo*-) becomes 'man' (Latin *vir*); the 'destruction' in Gk. *lytos* becomes 'life', Gk. *bios* (but with Latin spelling, '*bius*'). Hippolytus lives, but his strength and identity are gone. Servius proposed that Virbius = *vir bis* = 'a man twice'—which adds a letter but does not rearrange the name and identity.

781 *his son*: for Hippolytus to have a son at all is a denial of the relentless chastity that led to his terrible death. That death is his name and his identity: Hippolytus = Destroyed by Horses. Perhaps that is why the last glimpse we get of Virbius junior is in line 782, as he races his horses across the sea-flat plains as his father did in the last instants of his life. Virgil has restored him to his pristine state as Hippolytus, then, the verbal magic complete, for ever abandons him.

785 *Chimaera*: see note to 5.118. The Chimaera, whose home is in Asia Minor but whose fire is that of Sicilian Etna, is, curiously enough, the victim of the most Hippolytus-like of other Greek heroes: Bellerophon. He too was the object of a married woman's unwanted passion. She tried to arrange a

meeting with him. He refused, and she accused him to her husband, Proetus of Tiryns, of trying to seduce her. Proetus wrote a letter to his father-in-law Iobates, demanding that the bearer of the letter (the first letter mentioned in Western literature) be put to death. Iobates refused to kill him because Bellerophon was his guest and sent him instead on a number of Herculean missions designed to cause his death. But with divine help and his magical horse Pegasus, Bellerophon triumphed over all adversaries, including the Chimaera. He died only when he tried to ride Pegasus up to the heavens to the domains of Jupiter. At that point, Jupiter killed him with a thunderbolt.

789 *Io*: unlike the Chimaera, Io is the victim not the predator. She is turned into a beast because she has attracted Jupiter's attention. This Argive daughter of Inachus, the river of Argos, has been transformed into a cow, to conceal her from a suspicious Juno, and she is guarded by an unsleeping sentinel Argus (who is finally killed by Mercury). Io wanders the world in bovine form before her sorrows end. Her travels take her to Egypt, where she is identified with the supreme Egyptian goddess Isis. And Isis is the one god whose temple at Rome Octavian later demolished (in AD 9). Here I think Virgil is raising an interesting issue. If Latium must have a foreign ruler, is Turnus, at the outset, not foreign enough? But, in using Io as his symbol, does he become too foreign as Io moves from Greece to Egypt?

797-8 *Numicus' / Sacred banks*: the third reference to the Numicus in Book 7. The peoples of Latium are fighting the man whose spirit will be their Indigenous god. See note to 7.136.

801 *Ufens*: the second mention of Ufens, who appeared at 7.745 as a swashbuckling bandit, but who is now the river from whom his name derives flowing to constant death in the sea.

803 *Volscian people*: the Volsci moved south-east out of the Umbrian mountains at the time of the Tarquins (sixth century BC) and threatened the coastal areas of central Italy ruled by the Etruscans and Latins. Virgil situates them in those very coastal areas, between the Latins and the Rutulians.

803-4 *Camilla' / Leading a cavalry column*: this line is repeated at 11.433. Camilla is Virgil's invention. But no Roman could have heard her name without thinking of Camillus, the hero who saved Rome's dignity and fortunes after the disastrous capture of Rome by the Gauls in 390 BC (note to 6.824-5). Although Camillus' connection is with Etruscan Veii, not with the Volscians, we should not rule out some link between their names, since evidence suggests that Camillus may be the name of the Etruscan equivalent for Mercury. Camilla's literary career begins when the witch Medea disguises herself as an attendant, *camilla*, of the goddess Diana, in Pacuvius' tragedy *Medus* (fr. 247), set in Colchis. Medea comes close to outfoxing herself in the play. Her son Medus has also arrived in Colchis, and is pretending to be the son of her old enemy, Creon of Corinth.

When she hears that Creon's son is present, Medea tells King Perses that the young man is really Medus, sent by Medea, to assassinate him, and asks permission to kill him. Permission is granted. But Medea recognizes her son at the last moment, and Medus kills Perses, turning her lie into the truth. Pacuvius' speciality was giving plots an extra twist; so too is Virgil's. But Varro notes that *casmilla* indicates an attendant at the mystery cult of Samothrace. So Virgil's new heroine with superhuman abilities may owe something to older links with the divine.

817　*myrtle*: a tree sacred to Venus. Phaedra is said to have fallen in love with Hippolytus while observing him from behind a myrtle.

BOOK EIGHT

9　*Venulus*: his name reads as 'Little Venus': the sort of nickname Romans gave pretty slave-boys. In 11.742–57, in fact, Venulus is carried off by Tarchon, much as Ganymede is abducted by Jupiter (see notes to 11.726, 747, and 758). His name is an odd choice, considering that Venus is Aeneas' mother and was wounded by Diomedes in *Iliad* 5, as she reminds Jupiter in 10.27–30. Virgil does not say who authorizes this legation. If Diomedes joins the Latins, it is unlikely that Aeneas will defeat him.

17　*their king or their king*: the double use of 'king' hints that the state is torn between two kings. A third (Aeneas) claims kingship, and poses a potential threat to Diomedes' domains. The legation is perhaps charged with conveying obliquely that there is an opening for another king with clearer vision.

18　*Laomedon's kinsman*: Laomedon was father of Priam. His perjury led to the first sack of Troy by Hercules. His name occurs more often in Book 8 than in any other book. See note to 8.157.

26　*Night reigned*: an echo of 3.147 where Aeneas says his household gods direct him to Italy; also of 4.522, where sleep comes to all but Dido.

35　*allay his concerns*: see note to 3.153.

42–6　*Now, here's proof . . . troubles*: these lines repeat Helenus' prophecy in 3.390–3. Only the last line is a problem. The Tiber, flowing among, and defining several peoples, has understandably divided loyalties. He says Aeneas' victory will be the reward for his advice; he also saves Turnus' life at the end of Book 9.

51　*Pallas*: this Pallas was the great-grandfather of Evander. Evander's son Pallas (introduced later) is named after him. This is not, then, Pallas Athena (Minerva). But as the presence of Pallas (the goddess) and her Palladium were fundamental to Troy's existence, so the Arcadian Pallas' settlement, on the Palatine, is central to Rome's identity. Virgil's point may be that Pallas (in all applications of the name) is missing from Octavian's new Rome. The goddess whose Palladium symbolized Troy (and Athens) is notably absent from contemporary building programmes.

77 *Hesperidean*: Aeneas' choice of the *Hesperides*, rather than Virgil's more usual *Hesperius*, flatters Tiber: he is not just lord of rivers in Italy, but of rivers in the paradisiacal gardens of the Hesperides. Aeneas' vows to Tiber (not Juno, whom he ignores) go against the instructions Tiber has given him.

82 *Eyes brought to bear on a sow*: the Latin gives us an odd double-take. There are two verbs: the first is active (*praebuit*, 'showed'), the second passive (*conspicitur*, 'is seen'). *Conspicit* without the final unaccented *-ur* is active ('sees'). But the metre throws an accent on *-ur*: it precedes a monosyllable that ends the line: *sus*, 'sow'. The combination sounds like *conspicit ursus*, 'a bear sees', not *conspicitur sus*: 'a sow is seen'.

85 *slaughters*: neither Helenus nor Tiberinus says anything about killing them. Although both declare that pig and piglets represent the thirty years between Aeneas' foundation of Lavinium and the foundation of Alba Longa, others took them to symbolize the thirty cities of the Latin League. Indeed, when the Italic communities seceded from Rome (91 BC) they made the Alban sow a symbol on their coins. In terms of *this* symbolism, the founder of the Roman people is here wiping out the Latin League (as his descendants will do) even before the cities are founded.

91 *amazing the waters*: the Tiber is (and was) too shallow for routine navigation in any but small vessels. If Tiber had not dammed his waters, Aeneas could not have sailed to Rome in a warship, as Romans would know. Virgil allows the landscape to share the astonishment. Readers of Apollonius will recall the Argonauts sailing up (over the Alps!) to Lake Constance from the Adriatic, or portaging *Argo* across the Sahara.

100 *Evander's impoverished holdings*: Aeneas has reached the site of Rome with his elite troops. It has nothing like the formidable palace of Latinus. The entire population is outside the walls celebrating the feast of Hercules. No one has anticipated (for obvious reasons) the arrival of warships. Pallanteum is his for the taking. Indeed, there was a tradition that Aeneas founded Rome (with the help of Odysseus). But prophecies have focused Aeneas' attention on founding Lavinium so his son may in due course found Alba. None point him to Rome itself. There is no reason to think Aeneas ever grasps that this will be Rome. So the city's foundation is postponed for a half-millennium. See note to 9.9; also 12.183–6 and note to 12.184.

103 *Amphitryon's son*: Hercules was the son of Amphitryon's wife Alcmena, but his father is Jupiter (Zeus) disguised as Amphitryon in literary tradition. For the rites, see 8.185 ff. and notes.

105 *penniless senate*: substantial wealth was a *requirement* for admission to the Roman Senate.

118 *We sought asylum*: requests for asylum are not usually accompanied by the demand that the host country cede sovereignty of its lands to the asylum seekers.

119 *Bring him this news, men*: Aeneas abruptly changes from second person singular to second plural, which suggests that Pallas was not alone in his curiosity about the strangers, though Virgil singles him out.

134 *Dardanus*: after the effort spent arguing Dardanus' Italian connections, Aeneas now shows his Greek connections. Aeneas' venture into genealogy gives Dardanus seniority over Evander, since Dardanus is the son of Atlas, whereas Evander is Atlas' grandson. Aeneas overlooks the six mythic generations between Dardanus and himself, and shrewdly uses the plural form 'you' (*vobis*) when noting that Evander's father is Mercury, saying, in effect, 'your family's father'. He does not need ambassadors to make crafty approaches. He hasn't even said who he is.

149 *Upper and Lower*: the Adriatic and Tuscan Seas. Neither Latinus nor Turnus has any such agenda.

155 *Bravest of Teucrians*: after Aeneas' talk of Dardanus, Evander pointedly addresses him as a Teucrian (see also line 161), recognizes his visitor is Aeneas, and says he knew Anchises personally. Aeneas' Hesiodic genealogy looks silly when juxtaposed to personal memories: there were close ties of guest-friendship to build on, ties about which Virgil makes Aeneas (humiliatingly) ignorant.

157 *Hesione's kingdom*: Hesione was daughter of Laomedon and sister of Priam. Evander is referring to Priam, not Anchises, at first, and much more emphatically than can be conveyed in English. Laomedon, famous for perjury, promised to pay Apollo and Neptune for building Troy's walls, then refused when they were complete. The gods sent a monster, to which his daughter Hesione was about to be sacrificed when Hercules arrived and said he would kill the beast for a reward. Laomedon agreed, but when the monster was dead and Hesione safe, he failed to honour his word. Hercules brought an army and sacked Troy. Hesione was given as a war-prize to Telamon and taken to his home on the island of Salamis. She was allowed, for a small price, to bring Priam with her. And some maintained that Priam's name recalled that transaction (deriving Gk. *Priamos* from *epríato*, 'bought'). Hesione's children by Telamon were Ajax and Teucer—the Teucer Dido's father met in Cyprus (1.619–26 and note to 1.619). Evander's tale, like Dido's tale of Teucer, allows the speaker to establish a prior link of friendship with Trojan (that is, Teucrian) guests. This done, Evander invites the Trojans to join him in honouring Hercules who, though he sacked the first Troy, allowed Priam to live and eventually re-found the city.

185 *sacred rites*: celebrated at the *Ara Maxima* (Altar Supreme) in the *Forum Boarium* (Cattle Exchange) in Virgil's day. Livy (1.7.15) says the rites were imported by Romulus.

192 *Cave-dwelling*: on Rome's Aventine Hill.

194–5 *Hiding within it . . . Cacus*: I follow the manuscripts' *tegebat*, 'covered', rather then the popular emendation *tenebat*, 'held, lived in'. The problem with *tegebat* arises from an assumption that Virgil's 'face of Cacus' is equivalent to 'Cacus' alone. It is significant that the tale of Cacus is told by a Greek. In the earliest Latin version, cited by Servius (on 8.203), Cacus is a *god* on the *Palatine* (Romulus' hill) whose cattle are stolen by Geranes. In the Greek tradition, followed by poets from Ennius on and by Livy (1.7.3–15), whose version is similar to Virgil's, Cacus lives on the Aventine (Remus' hill). And he is a cattle-thief, but not, in Livy, a fire-breathing monster. In Virgil, Cacus steals only eight animals out of an entire herd that his victim, Hercules, has himself stolen from Geryon (see next note). 'Cacus' suggests Gk. *kakós* ('bad') and Evander's name suggests 'Good guy'.

202 *all three of Geryon's bodies*: Geryon, a three-bodied monster, was said to have lived on a mythical island, Erythia, usually situated in Spain. Geryon's name makes an easy substitute for the Geranes of old Latin tradition.

210 *by their tails*: as Hermes does in the Homeric *Hymn to Apollo* 314 ff.

228 *stone-built Tiryns's child*: Hercules is linked with two Greek cities: Thebes (home of Amphitryon) his birthplace, and the massive fortress of Tiryns (near Nafplion in the Peloponnesus), his 'base' while performing his labours. I add 'stone-built' to help readers grasp why he is identified with Tiryns here.

230 *Aventine*: for the significance of the Aventine Hill, see note to 7.655.

263 *whose theft he'd denied*: a detail not mentioned by Evander, but found in Dionysius of Halicarnassus 1.39.3. Such allusions to omitted details are common in the *Aeneid*. Indeed, there are dimensions to Evander that Virgil never notes (e.g. his introduction of the Latin alphabet, mentioned by Tacitus, *Annals* 11.14). The text has some further oddities. Evander began as if Hercules' killing of Cacus had occurred in his own lifetime (see 8.363 and Pallas' prayer in 10.460–3). But at line 265 he speaks as if he had not viewed Cacus' corpse, and by 269 ff. sounds like a Roman summarizing ancient tradition. See next note.

268–72 *Since then . . . greatest*: these lines are italicized because they cannot have been spoken by Evander. They are a gloss added either by Virgil or someone else.

281 *Potitius*: the Roman clans of Potitius and Pinarius supervised the Hercules cult at the Ara Maxima until 312 BC (Livy 1.7.12; 9.29.9 ff.). Their names mark them as Italic intruders in Evander's Greek city, though the cults they serve are of great antiquity. Livy states that the Potitii were taught by Evander. During the reign of King Numa a sacred shield allegedly fell from the sky into the king's hands. A smith named Marmurius Veturius was asked to make eleven replicas, and the Salii were founded to guard them, since Rome's prosperity depended on the preservation of the original shield. The Salii ('Leapers') were a College of Dancing Priests (one thinks of the Dervishes). Aeneas' own celestial armour similarly drops from the sky later (8.524–9). Pallanteum is a doublet of Latinus' unnamed

city and its Laurentine inhabitants, but it accommodates Greek (rather than Latin) traditions of Rome's foundation. It is, like the kingdom of Latinus, the mythic past overlaid with events and customs familiar from later Roman tradition (see note to 11.178).

292 *Difficult labours*: Hercules does countless labours in addition to the canonical twelve performed for King Eurystheus. The hymns sung here celebrate, among other things, Hercules' destruction of Troy coupled with his destruction of Oechalia, a much lesser city.

296 *Orcus's guardian*: Cerberus. There is a nice irony here. Aeneas saw Cerberus (and multiple Hydras) in the underworld, but not Hercules himself (whom Odysseus claims to have seen in *Odyssey* 11). This exaltation of Hercules contrasts with Anchises' disparaging comments (6.801–5 and note on 6.794–8).

313 *Evander, the Roman citadel's founder*: in Evander's city we have the topography of Rome, many Roman institutions, and the founder of the Palatine, its citadel (*arx*). Romulus has yet to be born. If Evander founds the Roman citadel (*arx*), Romulus the Roman city (*urbs*), Aeneas the Roman 'race' (*gens*), then the question: 'Who founded Rome?' becomes almost meaningless. The chief figure displaced is Latinus. He becomes part of the genealogy only if his daughter marries Aeneas; and, though his city has many Roman institutions, it is given no clear location on a map.

314 *indigenous Fauns*: the archetypal 'Faun' is Faunus, father of Latinus, who is a kind of tree-spirit. But Evander pluralizes Faunus into Fauni, much as Latinus pluralizes himself as Latini, 'Latins'. The Latins, like the Fauns, are displaced, as was Aeneas at Carthage, in time and space. Perhaps Virgil is referring to the centuries of shoddy treatment the Romans gave their Latin allies and the various Oscan-speaking friends (like the Sabines) and foes (like the Samnites) who lived around them.

323 *made Latium its name*: Virgil's most untranslatable Latin etymology. *Latium* is an exact anagram of *maluit*, 'preferred'. Within Saturn's preference lurked the letters, the elements, of the name he chose for the place where 'he'd . . . lain hidden', *latuisset* (a routine wordplay on 'Latium' and 'latent').

327 *love became greed*: in a context of anagrams, *Amor*, 'Love', is itself an anagram of *Roma*, 'Rome'.

328 *Ausonians . . . and Sicanian peoples*: see note to 7.206; the Sicanians were an ancient people of Sicilian origin.

329 *surrendered its name*: Evander refers to Italy in general rather than to Latium. Saturn's land became known by many different names (Hesperia, Oenotria, and Ausonia) before being named Italy.

331 *we Italians*: as inventor of the Latin alphabet, and widowed husband of a Sabine wife (8.510–11; 11.158–60), Evander has a right to this claim; Greek commentators sometimes use *Italoi* to designate early Greek settlers in Italy as well as indigenous peoples. In the *Aeneid*, peoples we call Italian (or more properly, Italic) usually refer to themselves by specific

sub-identities such as Rutulians, Latins, or Volscians. Ancient Italy, unlike Greece, was not a land with essentially one language and a common culture. Evander, uniquely in the *Aeneid*, adopts a broader identity encompassing all Italians.

332 *Albula*: the ancient name for the Tiber, renamed in honour of a brutal conqueror. Pallanteum will also be renamed 'Rome'.

335 *Carmentis*: also known as Carmenta; some make her Evander's wife not his mother. She had a cult at Rome connected with prophecy and child-birth, and festivals on 11 and 15 January.

342 *passing the great park Romulus*: Virgil fills in for us (but not for Aeneas) what Evander cannot know. The park was later known as the Asylum (from the Gk. *asylon*, 'unplundered'). Romulus made Rome a place of refuge for those exiled or otherwise dispossessed.

343 *Lupercal*: a grotto at the base of the Palatine Hill, dedicated to Faunus Lupercus, the woodland deity, in combination with the cult of the wolf, which had been restored on Octavian's orders. Ovid (*Fasti* 2.271 ff.) says this is where the she-wolf nursed Romulus and Remus. Evander identifies Faunus with Arcadian Pan Lykaios. But Arcadia was a land not only of idyllic rustic life. It had (as does Evander himself) an obverse and more darkly primitive side. The most famous shrine on Arcadian Mount Lykaios was that of Zeus, with traditions of human sacrifice and of metamorphosis into wolves: lycanthropy. At the feast of the Lupercalia young aristocrats ran naked through the Roman forum lashing passers-by with strands of goat-hide. Ovid explains this as a fertility rite. But since the festival was celebrated on 15 February during the three-day *Parentalia* (honouring dead ancestors), the rites may have been to protect the living from the dead (who might reappear as wolves).

345 *Argiletum*: Virgil assumes our familiarity with traditions about Evander, including the charge that he murdered a guest named Argus (as Mercury killed the Argus who guarded Io). Evander is understandably vague on this subject since it might worry his new guest, Aeneas. The mythic murder of a guest by another Arcadian, Lycaon (= 'Wolf-man'), and the cooking of that Dalmatian (!) guest as food for the gods, is presented most famously by Ovid, in *Metamorphoses* 1. Other ancient authors mention further crimes attributed to Evander (including parricide). Virgil may be alluding to a Roman ceremony held on 16–17 March to commemorate Hercules' Argive soldiers, mentioned at 10.779–82 below. If so, Evander has taken us through three major festivals in the first three months of the not yet imagined Julian calendar.

347 *Tarpeia's rock*: the Capitoline was also called the Tarpeian Hill. The rock, on its south-west side, was named after Tarpeia, daughter of one of Romulus' generals. She was thrown from it for betraying Rome, and it became the traditional place for the execution of traitors. The Capitoline Hill was the site of the Temple of Jupiter Optimus Maximus, restored on Octavian's orders in 26 BC, and of the Temple of Jupiter Tonans dedicated

by Octavian in 22 BC. The Capitoline had previously been the site of
Saturnia, founded by Saturn. So the exiled god of the Golden Age had been
doubly displaced by his son Jupiter, who had already expelled him from
Olympus. Ironically, that displacement was engineered by the emperor
who claimed to have brought about a new Saturnian Golden Age.

358 *Janiculum*: possibly on the Janiculum Hill (modern Gianicolo) though
some say this Janiculum was also on the Capitoline. Evander describes
both sites as ruins in his day. The cult of Janus seems to thrive, however,
in Latinus' unnamed city. Janiculum survived as a place name, Saturnia
did not. Evander does not say who destroyed the kingdom of Saturn. But,
as Tiberinus noted, and as Evander will indicate in his account of his
attack on Praeneste, Evander was no friend of Latium's native peoples.

361 *Carinae*: on the Esquiline Hill; one of Rome's fashionable districts in
Virgil's day.

368 *Libyan sow-bear*: exactly what Acestes wears in 5.37 (see note to 5.35),
given further resonance here by the odd glimpse of a bear we get as
Aeneas catches sight of the sow symbolic of Alba at 8.82–3 (and notes to
8.85 and 8.641). There is still a touch of Carthage marking Aeneas. It
recalls Hannibal, who appeared to have Rome in his grasp, but didn't
take it. Aeneas has Rome, but doesn't know he's there.

381 *Rutulian coastlands*: Venus' use of Rutulian is misleading. The Rutulians
are centred in Ardea, Turnus' city, and Aeneas is in Pallanteum, the
future Rome. Nor is Aeneas' camp in Rutulian territory.

383 *Motherhood's goddess*: Venus wisely refers to Vulcan as a revered divine
power (not as husband) and to herself as Venus Genetrix, 'Venus the
Mother', her cult title (not as *mater*, Aeneas' birth-mother, since Aeneas
is her bastard child by Anchises). Caution was needed for two reasons: (*a*)
Vulcan had made a gift, a necklace, for Harmonia, another bastard child
of hers (by Mars), when Harmonia married Cadmus. The necklace
brought nothing but misfortune on its holders (the best description is in
Statius, *Thebaid* 2); (*b*) Octavian had been working on a law which crimin-
alized adultery (the *Lex Iulia de adulteriis coercendis*), a law not actually
ratified until a year after Virgil's death. Octavian's claim of Julian descent
from Venus and Anchises makes his own family descendants of an adulterous liaison. And his father by adoption, Julius Caesar, had had a notorious affair with Cleopatra. Virgil is taking quite a risk in creating this
scene. Writers were aware that readers would see parallels between divine
and human behaviour. Some two centuries after Virgil, Apuleius has
Jupiter complain that Cupid caused him to violate the Julian Law on
adultery (*Golden Ass* 6.22). See note to 8.688.

384 *Nereus' child and Tithonus's wife*: Thetis, mother of Achilles: daughter of the
sea-god Nereus and wife of Peleus. Tithonus' wife was Aurora, mother of
Memnon, an Ethiopian ally of Troy. Both were goddesses of lower status
than Venus and both were married to mortals (Tithonus was granted
immortality but not eternal youth). Anchises, like Pelias and (at the outset)

Tithonus, is mortal, but he is not Venus' husband. Thetis requests armour for Achilles in *Iliad* 18.428 ff. Vulcan's armour did not save Memnon from death at Achilles' hands.

387 *he still hesitated*: Venus' rhetorical manoeuvre does not alter the fact that Aeneas is not *Vulcan's* son.

392 *explosion of thunder*: the Igniter of Fire becomes as hot as his own forges under Venus' caresses and as fierce as one of his own thunderbolts.

394 *Chained*: compare *Odyssey* 8.266–366 where Hephaestus (Vulcan) devises chain-nets to trap his wife in bed with Ares (Mars) and invites the gods to witness the proof of her infidelity. Now Vulcan, ironically called 'the father' here, is trapped by the metaphorical chains of passion Venus has wrought.

399 *Ten years for Troy*: if destiny can be put off for ten years, the notion of fate is subverted, since the causal nexus would be altered. Anchises would be dead (as would Priam too, in all likelihood) and even the reluctant Latinus would not have dared delay Lavinia's marriage so long. Troy's fall, as related in the *Aeneid*, arises from Venus' failure to request arms for Aeneas earlier, if Vulcan is correct. Yet even now Venus is arming Aeneas for a war against Turnus instead of telling him where he is, thereby postponing Rome's foundation for a half-millennium. See notes to 9.759 and 11.902, and 12.183–6 (and note to 12.184).

415 *attend to his tasks*: this image of Vulcan draws on Homer, *Iliad* 12.433 ff., and Apollonius 3.291 ff. and 4.1062 ff., all describing *women* at work. Vulcan, however, has no hope of keeping his marriage bed chaste.

454 *Lemnos*: the Greek island where Vulcan landed after being hurled from Olympus.

462 *retainers*: Evander is the old-fashioned hunter-king (like the young Telemachus in *Odyssey* 2.11) of a bygone era, attended by dogs, not armed guards. His mixed clothing (Etruscan sandals and a Tegean (that is, Arcadian) sword) marks his mixed identity; the pantherskin adds a touch of the exotic.

480 *long ago*: Evander, quietly but firmly, has the Etruscans arrive from Asia Minor long before the Trojans.

502–3 *Italian / Leadership*: though Evander talks of himself as if he were Italian, he is not Italian in the eyes of others (8.331 and note), hence the Etruscan approach to him as a potential foreign leader.

520 *Scarcely had he said this when—no*: Virgil's self-interruption draws attention to the devastating turning point of the *Aeneid*. Aeneas, on the site of Rome itself, recognizes the arrival of his divine armour and sees it flashing to earth. The arms and the man are within reach of one another at Rome for the first and last time in the epic. Aeneas does not know he has reached the city whose foundation is the goal of his labours. One thinks of the city emblazoned on Homer's shield of Achilles—a sad symbol for a warrior who will never again enter a city. By the time Aeneas picks up his weapons, he has left Rome, never to return.

561 *siege of Praeneste*: this siege (and Evander's adversary Erulus—a kind of doublet for Geryon, Hercules' victim) is Virgil's invention. Killing such a leader would have earned him the supreme 'Spoils of Distinction'! But mention of the siege of Praeneste stirs memories of Roman civil wars. In 82 BC Praeneste was the last refuge of Marius' son during the vicious struggle for power between Marius and Sulla, culminating in a battle fought at Rome's Colline Gate. Sulla won, and his troops butchered their Praenestine, Samnite, and Etruscan prisoners, then sacked Praeneste itself. The Elder Marius, like Erulus, proved harder to kill. See note to 7.678. It is also possible that the threefold life of Erulus is a reference to the three wars Rome fought against the Samnites beginning in the fourth century.

601 *Silvanus*: the forest land as god. Silvanus, like Faunus, is identified with Pan. He was a mischievous god, especially threatening to new-born children. Pilumnus (see note to 9.4) was one of the deities who protected the household against him. Silvanus was most noted in Roman history for declaring, after a hard-fought battle between Romans and Etruscans in 509 BC, that the Romans had won because they had lost one fewer soldier (Livy 2.7.2–3). Silvanus' voice was crucial, for the Etruscans were attempting to restore the recently expelled Tarquins to power. Two lines after Silvanus is mentioned, Virgil points out that the forest is on the Latin–Etruscan border. There the forces of the Etruscan Tarchon have camped. They will accompany Aeneas in his assault on Latinus' city. And it is on the banks of the river of (Etruscan) Caere, not in Rome, that Aeneas is given the arms made by Vulcan.

616 *Set the arms under an oak-tree's radiate branches*: an image Virgil develops with increasing pathos later (10.834–7).

629 *set in order*: we must distinguish what is *on* the shield from Virgil's comments *about* it. Though Vulcan's artistry is as much Virgil's invention as is his narrative, it has its own 'voice'. Like Harmonia's necklace (see note to 8.383), it is not a selection of things all good. Rather, it shows a side of Roman history that Anchises suppresses in Book 6: Rome fighting for survival. Curiously, the events and persons depicted are, with two exceptions, either from the very early history of the Roman state, or from the Battle of Actium in 31 BC. The wars with Carthage (and Hannibal) are missing, as are the wars with Pyrrhus, the Samnites, the 'Social' Wars, and the civil wars involving Marius and Sulla, Julius Caesar, Pompey, Sextus Pompey, Brutus and Cassius, and all wars of foreign conquest. The scenes represented run from the foundation by Romulus in 753 BC to the capture of Rome by the Gauls in 390/387 BC; there is nothing after that until Cleopatra's defeat at Actium, apart from the contrasting representations of Catiline (the descendant of Aeneas' Sergestus and conspirator in 63 BC) and Cato the Younger (who opposed Catiline and Julius Caesar, and who committed suicide in 46 BC), who seem to symbolize the unrighteous and the righteous faces of Rome.

631 *and the twin boys she nurtured*: the shield carries no indication that the she-wolf is only their surrogate mother and that one brother (Romulus) will kill the other (Remus).

640 *still armed*: there will be further wars between Romans and Sabines. Titus Tatius and Romulus are father-in-law and son-in-law. The Romans under Romulus were not considered fit sons-in-law by their Sabine neighbours and had to abduct wives, which they did at a public festival.

641 *treaties*: Servius, on 1.62, says that *foedus*, 'treaty', derives from 'the mistreatment [*foede*] by laceration of a female pig [*porca*]—killing it with stones'. *Porca* may be used rather than *sus*, which has the same meaning, because the sacrifice was thought to restrain (*porcere*) people from violating the treaty. The pig killed when treaties were made is usually male. The changed gender links it with Aeneas' slaughter of the sow at the site of Alba. A Roman priest proclaimed to the Alban people, just before they and the Romans agreed to abide by the outcome of a duel between three Roman Horatii and three Alban Curiatii, that Rome would abide by the outcome (Livy 1.24): 'If Rome fails to comply, by public decision and by evil treachery, then may Great Father Day (Jupiter), strike down the Roman people as I now strike down this pig.' He killed the pig with a blow from a flintstone.

643 *Mettius*: called Mettus by Virgil, since Mettius won't work in a Latin hexameter. Servius, with sick humour, says Virgil mutilated his name for the sake of the metre. Rome's wars with Alba and the Latin League are civil wars among kindred peoples. The Alban city, Fidenae, an early foe of Rome (Livy 1.13–14), gave it one of the bloodiest of its battles (Livy 1.27). See note to 6.812. Livy notes the brutal treatment of Mettius Fufetius, the Alban leader, torn between loyalties to Rome and Fidenae: accused by the Roman king, Tullus Hostilius, of failing to maintain 'good faith and treaties' (*foedera*), he was torn apart by two four-horse chariots moving in opposite directions; all eyes turned away from the horror—*foeditate*—of the sight (1.28.7–11). It was 'the first and last execution among the Romans of a kind that has little recollection of human laws' (1.28.11). Virgil's narrative overlay, not Vulcan's artwork, supplies the moral commentary. Mettius is condemned for perfidy, though Virgil wisely does not use this word, linked as it is with Aeneas in 4.305, 366, 421; 7.362.

646 *Lars Porsenna*: Etruscan king of Clusium (Chiusi), who probably captured Rome for himself in 508 BC (Tacitus, *Histories* 3.72.1), but whom Livy and Virgil's over-narrative here represent as trying to restore the Tarquins. The next line contains only the second use of *libertas*, 'freedom', in the epic. These images recall the period of Etruscan domination of Rome.

650 *Cocles . . . Cloelia*: whether they are on the shield or are part of the narrative overlay (to explain Porsenna's angry look) isn't clear. Early tradition (Polybius 6.55.1–4) has Cocles performing a *devotio* (see note to 6.824–5) to consecrate the Sublician Bridge, and drowning rather than

defending the bridge and surviving, as here and in Livy's version, commemorated in English in Macaulay's *Lays of Ancient Rome*. Cloelia saves some fellow hostages by breaking her chains and swimming the Tiber (or riding across it in some versions). Both incidents occur during Porsenna's attack on Rome. Curiously, the Sublician Bridge had just been washed away by floods when Virgil was writing.

652 *Tarpeia's citadel rock*: see note to 8.347. Marcus Manlius saved the Capitoline when the Gauls took Rome in 390 BC. But he was later convicted of treason and thrown from the Tarpeian Rock himself (in 384 BC).

656 *Gallic*: *Gallus* means a Gaul, or a rooster, or a eunuch (especially a castrated priest of Cybele). Since the usual Latin word for 'cockcrow' is *gallicinium*, 'the song of the *gallus*', a goose singing out that the Galli are coming triggers a pun between two of these meanings. The humour is, of course, verbal, not visual: the narrator's, not Vulcan's. The Gallic invasion and capture of Rome is one of the lowest points of Roman history, so the contrast of tone is intense.

659 *unscissored hair*: Latin *caesaries*, which, in this context, can hardly fail to evoke thoughts of Julius Caesar who had conquered the Gauls in his campaigns between 59 and 49 BC and make one ask why Virgil's Vulcan depicts the Gauls capturing Rome rather than Caesar conquering Gaul and why the poet is so silent about one of Rome's greatest (if most controversial) men. There were, of course, a lot of Gallic soldiers in Caesar's army when he crossed the Rubicon in 49 BC.

664 *shields*: see note to 8.281. There was only one 'original'; the other eleven were copies. Latin has more words for 'shield' than English does, and it is hard to show the difference. The Gauls in line 662 carry an infantry shield called the *scutum*, the same kind used by Roman legionaries, framed in wood and covered with leather. The shield Vulcan makes for Aeneas is a *clipeus* (round and usually made of bronze and also used by infantry). The shield that falls from the sky is an *ancile*, a small, oval shield, associated particularly with the 'sky shield' of Numa because of its supposed etymology (from *caelum*, 'sky'). Further, the art of engraving designs on metalwork is, in Latin, *caelatura* and its verb is *caelare*. Romans also saw a link between *caelum* and *celare*, 'conceal'. In Ovid, the Dolphin constellation is *c(a)elatum stellis*, 'engraved in stars', or 'hidden in stars' (depending on your knowledge of astronomy), and 'enskied in stars': all in the same two words. Similarly, Vulcan here is engraving 'sky shields' (both the original and the copies) on Aeneas' mortal shield, *clipeus*, which is itself round like the heavens.

668 *Catiline*: see notes to 5.121 and 10.185.

670 *Cato*: see also 6.841 and note. Vulcan contrasts Cato with Catiline, presumably because of the similarity of their names and the antithetical nature of their politics. Sallust makes the contrast between Caesar and Cato. There may be a deeper level of allusion to Cato's own sacrificial death. Some writers talk of the sacred sword of Cato with which he took

his own life. And his clan name, Porcius, can be linked with the language of treaty-sacrifice.

675 *Actium*: the battle that made Octavian ruler of the Roman world. His fleet, commanded by his admiral, Agrippa, defeated the combined navies of Mark Antony, Julius Caesar's principal aide, and Cleopatra, queen of Egypt and Caesar's former lover, now Antony's wife, in 31 BC.

681 *paternal star*: after Caesar's death a comet appeared which was interpreted by some as marking his soul's ascent among the gods. Octavian (whom Virgil here calls by the title Augustus, which he had not yet assumed in 31 BC) used it as his symbol, along with the twin crests, suggesting Romulus (see 6.779).

684 *Naval Crown*: Marcus Agrippa was awarded this honour for defeating Sextus Pompey at the battle of Naulochus in 36 BC. Vulcan appears to be according a greater military status to Agrippa, mentioned here for the only time in the epic. See notes to 3.270–4; 6.6, 70, 109, and 366.

688 *his wife, who's Egyptian*: Cleopatra. Virgil is not showing ethnic prejudice against Macedonian Egyptians, but condemning Antony's marriage in the only safe terms available. See note to 7.98. Antony had abandoned his wife Octavia (Octavian's sister) to marry Cleopatra under Egyptian or Macedonian, not Roman, law. Therefore the relationship was adulterous. Virgil would hardly want to frame the issue in these terms, given Octavian's pending legislation on adultery (see note to 8.383). Virgil's authorial 'disapproval' of an Egyptian wife masks Vulcan's suggestions (*a*) that Mark Antony actually conquered eastern peoples (he fought off a Parthian invasion and won victories against the Parthians between 36 and 31 BC); (*b*) that his troops included (but were not limited to) non-Italians; (*c*) that Antony, not the unnamed Cleopatra, is in command. The details are important: they define the battle as part of a *civil* war (further reinforced by the central figure of Discord, the Demon of civil war in 701–2). Official propaganda made Cleopatra the leader and Antony her lackey (thereby making it a *foreign* war in which Antony traitorously assists the foe). Romans could not celebrate triumphs in civil wars, so some generals represented their citizen opponents as servants of foreign powers.

691–2 *Cycladic / Islands uprooted*: ancient historians comment on the unusually large size of Antony's warships. Tradition held that Delos (one of the Cyclades) had been a floating island before the births of Diana and Apollo. To reach Actium, all of the Cyclades would have had to drift to the other side of Greece.

696–7 *sistrum . . . twin snakes*: on returning to Egypt, Cleopatra killed herself (with poisonous snakes, asps, in the best-known tradition) when the alternative was surrender. Though unnamed, Cleopatra occupies more narrative space than any other figure on the shield, and is the only human leader described during the fighting. She is thus at the artistic focus of Aeneas' shield. Since she carries the traditional symbol of Isis, the sistrum (a kind of rattle), Cleopatra may be portrayed (as would be common in Ptolemaic art) as the Egyptian goddess Isis. And Isis is routinely identified with the Greek Io whose image is at the centre of *Turnus'* shield (see notes to 7.371, 789). So the two shields may well resemble each other. Octavian destroyed the temple of Isis at Rome at a cost greater than that of constructing Apollo's Temple.

698 *barking Anubis*: a dog-headed god, the only Egyptian god named. The gods in motion or fighting are Mars, Discord (Civil War), and Bellona, an Italian war-goddess. Others named are poised or watching.

714 *Caesar*: that is, Octavian. But he is not, as we might expect, in action during the battle. Virgil (and perhaps Vulcan) breaks off the account of Actium to bring us to Rome for Octavian's triumph.

719 *young bulls slaughtered for Caesar*: the Latin for 'slaughtered' is *caesi*. For the association of this word with Caesar, see note to 6.898.

721 *with pride at its portals*: the wording echoes 8.196 (Cacus' case). Octavian built Rome's first Temple of Apollo in solid (white) Luna marble, set on the Palatine Hill, as he had vowed in darker days. See note to 6.70.

729 *Such is the tale*: many ideas resonate here. Aeneas shoulders the future as he shouldered the past (Anchises) in Book 2. The only figures he would recognize from the underworld on the shield are Octavian and possibly Cato. But it is surprising he does not recognize the Palatine and other sites that he has just visited, despite the new buildings. But one often doesn't see what one isn't looking for.

BOOK NINE

1 *While these actions occurred*: Virgil marks his transition here with one of Julius Caesar's favourite phrases in his *Gallic Wars*. But the military action of the previous book is limited to the future events that have been hammered onto Aeneas' armour in Vulcan's underground caverns.

4 *Pilumnus*: Turnus' grandfather, a god who protected new-born children, named after the pestle (*pilum*) with which grain is ground (and *pilum* also means 'spear'). See note to 8.601.

9 *in pursuit of the sceptre . . . of Evander*: Iris' assumption that Aeneas intends to take over Pallanteum draws attention to Aeneas' failure to see the connection between Rome and Pallanteum. See note to 8.100.

29 *[Passing along . . . the others]*: this line is identical with 7.784, is not in the best manuscripts, and should be omitted.

30 *Ganges*: the holy river of India. This powerful simile compares a fictional army, as it advances upon Aeneas' camp by the Tiber across a dry, dusty plain, with the majestic, constant flow of the Ganges, a river his audience had seen only symbolically, in delegations sent by Indian rajahs to Rome during Octavian's reign (see note to 7.604–6), or in literary descriptions such as his own. Even Alexander the Great had not conquered India, and Indians were coming to Rome, not vice versa. The seven tributaries of the

Ganges, taken with the seven mouths of the Nile, are a reminder of what is within, and what is beyond, Rome's reach. Virgil portrays Egypt's great river in ebb, returning from summer floods to within its 'regular' banks. Romans would have seen captured Egyptians at Octavian's triumph following the annexation of Egypt. But seasons change, the Nile will rise again. In larger perspectives of geography and time, the Tiber, even when flooded by poetic hyperbole to carry fleets, does not bear comparison. And Italy's warring armies have turned her farmland to dust. See also next note.

35 *Caïcus*: the army is first noticed by a Trojan sentinel whose name is that of one of the great rivers of Asia Minor, famous for its springtime floods: Caïcus. Virgil's sense of the civilizing energy of rivers is perhaps best seen in *Georgics* 4.317 ff., where Cyrene is a cavernous underground source for many rivers (the Tiber, Nile and Caïcus—but not the Ganges).

69 *The fleet!*: this second attempt to burn Aeneas' fleet was suggested to Turnus by Allecto (7.430–1). Iris has prompted him to launch an attack, but has not suggested how to carry it out. Contrast 5.618 ff.

78–9 *For belief in the story / Died long ago*: Virgil prepares us for an incredible story and gives us one, to the dismay of those critics who have missed his point. Virgil is stirring more recent (and still sensitive) memories. Cybele's appeal stresses the special circumstances under which she permitted the *sacred* forests on Mount Ida to be logged for ship-building, an action which would otherwise have been *sacrilegious*. In Virgil's day, vast forests had been logged for ship-building during the civil wars. Cumae and Avernus had been deforested to replace Octavian's heavy losses in war-galleys during battles and storms (notes to 6.6, 179; 7.47). And Octavian had been the driving force behind the development of the cults of Mount Ida's Cybele and Cumae's Apollo at Rome. (See 3.111–14; 6.784–7; and notes to 3.111 and 6.784).

84 *Now that you've tamed Mount Olympus*: a discreet reference to the tradition that she (*a*) saved Jupiter from being eaten (as were his brothers and sisters) by Saturn, and (*b*) helped him defeat the Titans.

95 *the right to be deathless*: Jupiter takes a utilitarian (and non-conservationist!) position. He concedes sanctity only to such pines as survive their use as ships to convey the Trojans to Italy. When they are turned into sea-nymphs they are sunk rather than burned. Neptune acquired many new nymphs in Rome's civil wars.

105 *Styx*: the most famous underworld river, by which the gods swore their most binding oaths, and most appropriate in this watery context. Jupiter swears again by the Styx at 10.113–14, and Virgil uses the same sentence to describe it. The brother of Jupiter is Dis, = Hades or Pluto.

112 *Corybant*: see note to 3.111.

116 *my sacred pines*: see note to 9.79.

121 *[Matching the number . . . seashore]*: this line, identical with 10.223, is not in the major manuscripts and is not needed.

127 *issued this challenge*: this whole line is repeated at 10.278. It fits both contexts.

148 *arms made by Vulcan*: probably Achilles' armour (*Iliad* 18.478 ff.) rather than that of Aeneas, which he may not yet know about (he does know about it in 11.438–9); but he is forgetting something we learn later: that he owns a sword made for his father Daunus by Vulcan (12.90–1, 734–41).

151 *Stealing the statue . . . sentries*: some feel that this line, very similar to 2.166, is a gloss, not an integral part of the text and omit it. I think the echo serves well.

161 *Fourteen Rutulians*: twice as many guards as are posted in *Iliad* 9.85 to guard the Greek camp.

164 *Then they're sprawling*: discipline quickly breaks down among the Latins, as command structures do in the *Aeneid*. Messapus, the duty-officer, is himself asleep when we next see him.

171 *Mnestheus*: captain of the *Pristis* in 5.115 ff. Serestus is captain of the ship to whose mast the target, a dove, is attached in the archery contest (5.487) just before the women set fire to the ships.

176 *Nisus*: this episode seems detachable. Its self-contained nature is the key to its importance. It did not *have* to happen. It results from a series of dubious policy decisions: Aeneas' establishment of a colony without consulting local residents, his dispatch of a legation to Latinus rather than visiting him in person, and his sub-delegation of command of the main force to Mnestheus and Serestus so that he can himself visit the Greek king, Evander, at what proves to be the future site of Rome. Notable features of this episode are that it occurs at night and ends, as it begins, at the gates of Aeneas' beleaguered camp (or small city). It thus evokes not only the sack of Troy but also a major historical battle, fought at the Colline Gate of Rome in 82 BC, during the revolt of Rome's Oscan-speaking allies and some Etruscans, and when the struggle for power between Marius and Sulla was at its height. Since Virgil avoids mentioning Marius and Sulla openly in the *Aeneid*, the obliquity of allusion should not be surprising. Unusually in ancient warfare, the battle of the Colline Gate continued into, and was decided during, the night. The several references to decapitation as cutting the *collum*, 'neck', may also constitute a pun on *collis*, 'hill' (and thus Rome's *Colline* Gate, facing the hills). Nisus and Euryalus, the main characters, are familiar from the foot race in 5.294 ff. The incident itself has a literary base in Homer, *Iliad* 10, and Euripides, *Rhesus*, where Odysseus and Diomedes capture a Trojan spy, Dolon, who reveals to them where a late-arriving Trojan ally, Rhesus, is camped. If Rhesus' horses drink of Troy's rivers, the city will never fall. Odysseus and Diomedes kill Dolon, enter Rhesus' camp, kill him and his troops, and take his horses away.

189 *They're asleep . . . drunk*: as were the Trojans the night Troy fell, according to Aeneas.

196 *under that mound*: Latin *tumulus* indicates either a 'rise' or (more ominously) a tomb. Whether Aeneas will be in Pallanteum at this point is problematic. He seems to spend only a night there.

201 *Opheltes*: there is a mythic Opheltes, infant child of Lycurgus king of Nemea, who is killed accidentally when his nurse Hypsipyle leaves him to guide the Argive 'Seven against Thebes' to a source of water. The Nemean games were founded in his honour. The most familiar version is probably that of Statius in *Thebaid* 4. The sense of 'offering due' implied in the name has resonance here for Euryalus, who has himself been a competitor in similar games in Sicily.

224 *conscious creatures*: see note to 3.147–8.

234 *sons of Aeneas*: Virgil uses patronymics (Greek surnames which explain whose son or descendant someone is) extensively throughout this episode. Here, Hyrtacus' son (Nisus) is asked by Iulus to say what he wants. Since Iulus is not in command of the camp, Nisus is not looking for his authorization. But Iulus is Aeneas' son, and Nisus would not want to insult him. Since it is acceptable to refer to the Trojans collectively as 'Aeneas' sons', Nisus shrewdly uses this mode of address to call in the real commanders, without excluding the crown prince. In doing so, however, he makes it embarrassing for them to speak before Iulus, since Iulus is, literally, Aeneas' son. As a result, the child Iulus becomes the prime negotiator, first with Nisus, and then with Euryalus, who is not much older than himself; and childish extravagance and childlike emotions dominate the exchanges (and, later, the conclusion of the episode). Aeneas has, unintentionally, created a situation in which social protocol undermines and paralyses the command structure. He has, in effect, left Iulus in charge of his camp. And Mnestheus and Serestus make no attempt to take command of the camp until the very end of Book 9.

246 *Aletes*: mentioned in 1.121 as a very old man (his name means 'the Wanderer'). The name recalls one of Hercules' descendants, born to an exiled father, who succeeded in taking control of Corinth and who would have taken Athens too if the Athenian king, Codrus, had not committed suicide. There was an oracle that Aletes would capture Athens if he spared its king. So Codrus killed himself so that he could not be spared. The story had resonance in Virgil's day because the Younger Cato had committed suicide to avoid being spared by Julius Caesar.

265 *gold: two talents of bullion*: in the *Iliad*, a talent is a fairly modest amount: about the price of an ox. But the Attic talent is about 57 pounds in crude weight. Precise equivalency is hard to calculate since a talent of gold sometimes means the equivalent, in gold, of a talent weight of silver. Virgil's Latin has 'big' talents, so he does not have Homer in mind. Two talents of gold is a very large sum of money (enough to stir even a congressman's interest).

270 *his armour*: Iulus' promises would, among other things, deprive Aeneas of the opportunity for dedicating Turnus' armaments as his 'Spoils of Distinction' (see notes to 6.841, 859; 10.449–50; 11.15). The catalogue of rewards is a crescendo of extravagance. Bestowal of even part of Latinus'

estates would require their confiscation by Aeneas (which would not make for good relations with his future father-in-law). Virgil's audience might see an allusion to the 'proscriptions' carried out some sixty years earlier by Sulla, after the battle of the Colline Gate (see note to 9.175) and some twenty years earlier the second triumvirate (Octavian, Antony, and Lepidus) or to the so-called 'Donations of Alexandria', in which Mark Antony (who had a son named Iullus) gave away parts of the Roman Empire to Cleopatra and others. People throughout Italy (including Virgil) had their estates confiscated, were driven from their homes, and often outlawed during the proscriptions. Should Nisus demand the fulfilment of Iulus' pledge, Aeneas would have trouble denying him. Neither Mnestheus nor Serestus, the designated commanders, protests Iulus' promised prizes.

283 *more than all gifts*: Euryalus gently reminds Iulus that the only reward *he* has been offered is that of being Iulus' friend and companion, which won't mean much once Iulus has given a lot of his potential patrimony to Nisus (already Euryalus' close friend). Euryalus' reply is impressive. He neither accepts nor rejects Iulus' offer, but vows to continue in a heroic path, in so far as Fortune permits.

292 *Old sons of Dardanus*: *Dardanidae*, the patronymic, shows us how these older men (even the grandfatherly Aletes) are drawn into the frame of reference established by Nisus and Iulus.

294 *Touched by this image . . . for a father*: Iulus' first words recall the price paid for Aeneas' *pietas* towards Anchises: the loss of Creusa, Iulus' mother. Her name was last mentioned in Book 3, when Andromache asked Aeneas if Iulus still remembered his mother (and got no reply). We may recall the tug-of-war between Creusa and Aeneas (in which Iulus is at the centre) when Aeneas prepares to leave his family to chance and set out to die in the fighting because the stubborn Anchises refuses to leave Troy. It is the fire over Iulus' head that decides the day, and makes possible the departure that saves everyone but Creusa. Facing Iulus now is a youth of his own age, about to leave his own mother on a mission to Iulus' father: to have him rescue his son again.

301 *to you if you come back*: all the 'you'\'s here are singular and do not include Nisus—a technicality of great importance, since all Iulus has promised Euryalus is friendship.

304 *Lycaon of Knossos*: both names are ominous, but together they create an otherwise unknown new person. The name of Lycaon conjures *lykos*, 'wolf', Arcadia, human sacrifice, and cannibalism. 'Knossos' conjures Crete, artistry, labyrinths, and hybrid monsters.

313 *meaningless present*: like all the presents he has promised.

325 *Rhamnes*: his name is like that of one of the three original tribes of Rome designated by Romulus: Ramnes, a name Roman writers linked with Romulus himself.

330 *Remus'*: the namesake of Remus, Romulus' brother, which makes it more
likely that Virgil is linking Rhamnes with Romulus. As in the massacre of
the suitors in the *Odyssey*, the scene is a strange mixture of hideous death
and the ludicrous.

334 *Lamyrus now, now it's Lamus*: Lamyrus ('gluttonous' in Greek) is aptly
linked with Lamos ('throat' in Greek), the name of the Laestrygonian cannibal king in *Odyssey* 10.81 (see Paschalis, *Virgil's Aeneid*, 325–8). Appreciation
of this jest may have changed an original spelling from Lamirus to Lamyrus.
The combination *Lamirumque Lamumque* in the nominative, *Lamirusque
Lamusque*, yields the anagram of Marius and Sulla. If we take the whole line
segment in the nominative we get *necnon Lamirusque, Lamusque*, which
yields an anagrammatic question: *nonne C.que Marius L.que Sulla?* 'Aren't
they Marius and Sulla?': two of Rome's bloodiest leaders.

335 *Youthful Serranus*: the namesake of a famous Roman general (see note to
6.844).

344 *Herbesus*: from *herba*, 'grass', + *esus*, 'eaten'; this is among the oddest of
the names. Other names yield possible connections outside this context,
but would take too long to expound here. Rhoetus cannot be the same
Rhoetus as in 10.388 for obvious reasons, unless Virgil is following
Homeric practice: letting a warrior killed in one book fight again in
another. He visits him twice in this passage, as if correcting himself in his
rush to keep track of the slaughter.

356 *We've drunk deep*: Latin *exhaustum*. The metaphor is both apt and grotesque
in this context of butchering people who have drunk themselves to sleep.
Nisus failed to win the foot race in Book 5 because he slipped in the blood
and waste of sacrifice. He doesn't want to slip in blood again.

362 *Remulus*: since Remus is named in the preceding slaughter and Romulus
alluded to in Rhamnes, Remulus seems like a bizarre combination of the
opposed twins.

364 *These he strapped on*: as Euryalus dons his slain enemies' weapons, we
recall the similar actions of Coroebus, Aeneas, and other Trojans in
Aeneas' account of the sack of Troy. Virgil places special emphasis on this
captured weaponry, and particularly on the sword harness (which foreshadows Turnus' fateful donning of Pallas' harness in Book 10). These
pieces have changed owners too frequently to be healthy. And this brings
to three the number of suits of armour Euryalus (like Aeneas at Troy) has
worn within an hour or so. His most fateful exchange is of the helmet just
given to him by the *long-lived* Aletes for the helmet belonging to Messapus,
which he gains by theft not by conquest. Messapus makes a good stopping
point for the killing since, if Virgil is to be consistent, Messapus cannot
be destroyed by iron or fire (7.691–3).

370 *Volcens*: though Virgil calls him a Rutulian (9.442), his name suggests the
Samnite town of Volcei (site of a Temple of Vulcan), and could evoke the
Volcentes of Lucania in southern Italy, or even the Volcae of Gaul, given

the geographical separation implied in the names of his two troopers. See note to 9.412.

374 *moonbeam*: it is not dawn that betrays them, as Nisus had feared, but the moon.

389 *It was useless*: Nisus, after escaping, realizes he has lost Euryalus, as Aeneas on escaping Troy, realizes he has lost Creusa. He must now plunge back into the dangers he has just escaped.

412 *Sulmo*: his name is that of a town in an upland valley in Samnite territory near Corfinium, the rebel capital during the 'Social' Wars. Nisus' next victim has the name of the Tagus river in Spain. After the sack of Praeneste and the confiscations of Sulla, many Samnites migrated to Spain or northern (Gallic) Italy. For just such a departure, see Virgil's own first *Eclogue*. It is possible that Virgil's father and mother Magia (an Oscan name) were displaced to Mantua at that time.

446 *Fortune has blessed you both!*: Virgil's authorial eulogy for Nisus and Euryalus, when one adds the lengthy lament of Euryalus' mother, is the longest tribute to anyone in the epic. (I suspect there were contemporaries subtending Euryalus and Nisus. See note to 9.467.)

448 *the Capitol's*: Virgil encapsulates the essence of Rome in the hill that seems to correspond to Latinus' city, rather than in the Palatine Hill of Evander, Romulus, and Octavian.

454 *Numa*: yet another name with Roman historical resonance is added: Numa was Rome's second king. See notes to 6.810; 7.187–8; 8.664.

465 *hoisted on spear-points*: Sulla had the head of Pontius Telesinus the Samnite leader displayed to the defenders at Praeneste after his victory (and massacre) at the Colline Gate. The son of Marius, one of the leaders defending Praeneste, committed suicide, and Praeneste was sacked. For Virgil's ominous mentions of Praeneste, see notes to 7.678 and 8.561.

467 *Nisus, Euryalus*: the Latin is *Euryali et Nisi*. Virgil's half-lines sometimes contain anagrams (see note to 7.691); and 467 is a half-line. I noted at 5.334–5 that the *hal-* element in Euryalus' name suggests the 'salt' sea, as in Homer's *póntos halós*: 'the sea of salt' (*Iliad* 21.59), and also, that Lamirus and Lamus may yield Marius and Sulla (note to 9.334). A similar approach here to *Euryali et Nisi* (if we use the accusative, *Eurialum et Nisum*) yields *TelesinuMariuum*, from which we can extract both Marius and Telesinus. And the Homeric *póntos halós* might even suggest Telesinus' clan name. Perhaps the tale of Nisus and Euryalus is more than fiction: it is subtended by allusions to the extinction of the main Oscan opponents of Rome in Italy at the battle of the Colline Gate, much as the tale of Dido is subtended by the destruction of Carthage. The Italy Virgil recalls is not limited to its triumphant Latin speakers, even if the names must be carefully encrypted.

505 *Volscians*: see note to 7.802. For the tortoise formation, see note to 2.441.

523 *Neptune's offspring, Messapus*: the line repeats 7.691, and is fittingly formulaic.

525 *Calliope*: Virgil finally invokes the Muse of epic to describe the assault on Aeneas' camp.

529 *Goddesses . . . memory*: this entire line repeats 7.645 and is rightly omitted from most manuscripts here.

544 *Helenor . . . Lycus*: Helenor = 'Man-destroyer' and *Lykos* = 'Wolf' in Greek. They create a composite identity as a pair. The name of Helenor's mother recalls Licymnios the son of Electryon and a Phrygian slave-woman: the only child of Electryon to survive an attack by the Taphians. He became Hercules' uncle by marriage, and later travelled from city to city before settling in Argos, where he was killed by his cousin Tlepolemos. Lycus also has a connection with Hercules: as the tyrant who took over Thebes in Hercules' absence (the theme of Euripides' *Heracles*).

548 *shield blank*: i.e. *leukaspis*, 'white shield', in Greek. See note to 6.333.

552 *hurls herself*: Virgil here shows a formula developed most fully in 11.721, 726, 747 ff.: when he compares someone to a bird or other animal, he follows the grammatical gender of the animal compared throughout the simile. Here Helenor becomes a *fera*, 'a wild beast' (feminine in gender).

563 *bearer of arms*: the eagle. Virgil avoids changing Turnus' gender in the simile at line 563 by using *armiger* for 'eagle' rather than *aquila* (which is feminine), because he is about to exchange the eagle for the masculine *lupus*, 'wolf', and convert Lycus from a wolf into a lamb. Turnus as wolf is sacred to Mars, Rome's Wolf God.

569 *Ilioneus*: familiar as the Trojan spokesman in Books 1 and 7; for Liger (line 571), see 10.575–601 and note to 10.581; Asilas cannot be the Asilas of 10.175–8, 11.620, and 12.127 and 550, who has not yet arrived; and Corynaeus cannot be the Corynaeus of 12.298 unless we have the dead fighting again. Some of the others listed have mythic resonances too long to explore here. Virgil, like most epic poets, does not like to leave even the fictional dead unnamed. Each 'casualty' is an individual human life ended.

576 *Capys . . . Privernus*: Capys is Aeneas' cousin, sometimes identified as founder of Capua, a city in Campania with a history of troubled relations with Rome. During the Second Punic War it sided with Hannibal, and was treated harshly by Rome when victory was won. Privernus is named after Privernum, a Volscian town near the borders of Latium which often aided the Samnites during their fourth-century wars with Rome and also opposed Rome during the Second Punic War.

579 *From far away*: the manuscripts' reading *lateri manus*, implying that the arrow pinned Privernus' hand to his side before killing him, is probably not right. Housman's emendation, *alte lateri*, 'deeply in his side', is widely accepted by English editors. Yet if this is what Virgil wrote, it is hard to imagine how it could have been changed into what the manuscripts have; and the idea of the wound's depth, the essence of Housman's conjecture, is already convered by *intus*, 'inside', in the next line. I follow Gemoll's earlier emendation: *lateri eminus*.

581 *Arcens' son*: the warrior himself is not named, which is unusual, since the form used is not a patronymic but a full phrase. Since these lines resemble 7.761–4 describing Virbius, the son of another Virbius (Hippolytus reborn), perhaps we may infer that Arcens' son also had the same name (*Arcens* = 'the Protector'). The river Symaethus is in eastern Sicily and the Palici (represented here as one singular deity) are Sicilian gods, twin sons of Jupiter and Etna (or Thaleia, a daughter of Vulcan). They were born from the ground where their mother had hidden them for fear of Juno's anger, and are thus called Palici, 'the Returners'. The Sicilians swore their solemn oaths by these gods. Since there is no known grove of Mars by the Symaethus, editors often prefer the anagram *matris*, 'of his mother', to the manuscripts' *Martis*, 'of Mars'.

586 *Bullets*: Mezentius selects an appropriate weapon for this attack on a youth whose outfit is remarkable for its Iberian rust-red colour. Iberians were also famous for their prowess with slings. The placement of the death-wound may be significant; the Palici punished those who invoked them falsely by striking them blind.

592–3 *Numanus . . . Remulus*: his name suggests Romulus, Remus, and Numa all in one diminutive package.

596–7 *words worth reporting, / Words worth nothing at all*: Virgil denounces a speaker most often when disclaiming responsibility for what is being said. Iarbas (4.215–17) and Turnus (12.75, 96–100) both mock the Trojans (and Aeneas) as effeminate Phrygians.

618 *double woodwinds*: the Greek *aulos*, with its two distinct 'pipes'. See note to 10.207. Its Latin counterpart was the Roman *tibiae pares*, which was played in southern Italy (especially in Lucanian Sila), Sardinia, and Sicily until modern times (called either *fischietto a pariglia* or *fiscarol*). The 'Phrygian' was considered the most lascivious and decadent of Greek musical modes by critics. The boxwood aulos, producing a mellow (and to some ears 'effeminate') tone, was less favoured by those preferring the more robust tones of blackwood pipes. I add 'soft' to the translation (line 619) to convey Numanus' mockery of the rites of Cybele.

621 *chanting of terrible insults*: the Latin is *dira canentem*, often taken to mean 'singing ominous warnings'. But Numanus is, rather, mocking 'Phrygians' in accordance with standard Greek and Roman stereotypes.

650–1 *This old man . . . armour ferociously clanging*: the lines resemble 4.558–9. See note to 4.556.

669 *Goat Stars*: we now call them collectively Auriga, 'the Charioteer'.

672 *Pandarus, Bitias*: Pandarus is the namesake of Homer's Pandarus, who breaks the truce in *Iliad* 4.7 ff. and who is mentioned by Virgil at 5.495. And, like the Homeric Pandarus, Virgil's Pandarus changes the course of the epic. He breaks a violently fought stalemate by opening the gates (Latin *pandere*, 'to lay open'). The only word close enough to Bitias is *bitumen*, the pitch used to seal ships' timbers and make poultices for

livestock (*Georgics* 3.448–51, where it is used in combination with other ingredients, including pine-resin from Ida). Both men were reared by a wood-nymph (with the same name as a Homeric sea-nymph in *Iliad* 18.42), in a grove among the conifers of Ida. They are as tall as trees and are positioned at the gateposts of their camp. I suspect Virgil has encrypted a historical name here too, but it would take too long to explain it in this context.

675 *Open the camp-gates wide*: Virgil's points of departure are *Iliad* 12.127 ff. and (possibly) a lost passage of Ennius. The similes and metaphors direct attention to north-east Italy (from the Po's plains to the Alpine heights where Italy merged with the Celtic world in Virgil's day and now with the Germanic.

679 *Livenza*: major manuscripts have *liquentia*, 'liquid'. Servius reads *Liquetia*, the river now named Livenza, and this seems preferable, given Virgil's mention here of two other rivers flowing through the coastal regions south of the Dolomites, the Po and the Adige, home territory to Virgil. The course of the Adige is so beautiful that the flat rendition of *amoenus* as 'pleasant', as in the notion of the *locus amoenus*, the 'pretty spot' of bucolic poetry, seems inadequate. I use modern names here.

681 *[genus: quercus]*: the botanical gloss is intruded to maintain Virgil's word-play. As often, Virgil blurs the line between mythic person and mythic or natural landscape. This is a collision of landscapes, not only of people. Pandarus and Bitias are, in their first tree simile, firs on their native Mount Ida. Now they are oaks in Italy's Alpine and sub-Alpine north-east, Virgil's home territory. The first enemy they encounter at the gates is Quercens, whose name is resonant of *quercus*, the Latin for 'oak'. Aquiculus' name, suggesting 'water-dweller' and perhaps 'watercourse', introduces the rivers; and Tmarus (a mountain in Epirus, but also evocative of the Tamarus river in Italy's Samnite country) and Haemon (resonant of Mount Haemus in Thessaly) the mountains. I translate Tmarus' epithet, *praeceps*, as 'precipitous', to preserve his geological origins, rather than 'impulsive', which loses the mountain while preserving the man.

710 *pre-built stone pier*: Virgil draws attention to a practice that Roman satirists, particularly Juvenal, lambast. The Campanian coast was not only built up with military works at Cumae and Misenum. Parts were converted into a resort area for the outrageously rich by building villas out over the sea. Virgil's naming of Baiae focuses the reference on the resort areas. See notes to 6.5, 36, and 42.

715 *Inarime's*: Inarime is a back-formation from the Greek phrase *ein Arimois* in *Iliad* 2.783. As Malcolm Willcock observes (*A Commentary on Homer's Iliad, Books 1–6* (London, 1970), 83): 'whether this is Arima (a place), Arimoi (mountains) or Arimoi (a people) was uncertain even in ancient times.' If by this name Virgil is, as some think, referring to Ischia, Prochyta's larger neighbour, he is alone in doing so. Greek and Roman writers usually call that island Ischia Aenaria, honouring Aeneas who, in some traditions, made his first landfall in Italy there (Pliny, *Natural*

History 3.6.12). But Virgil has made Cumae Aeneas' landing point, and reference to Ischia Aenaria here would undercut his own narrative. He may be referring, rather, to the more distant Mount Etna, where the mythic Typhoeus is usually said to be buried (Pindar, *Pythian* 1.28).

759 *Troy's last day*: again, as in Venus' failure to request divine armour for Aeneas during the Trojan War, or in Aeneas' lack of awareness that he is in the city that will be Rome, an oversight changes events totally (see 8.396–9 and note to 8.399; compare 11.902 and note).

774 *Cretheus*: his name belongs to no pattern of reference that I can discern from line 762 onwards. There is a Cretheus, a son of Aeolus, grandfather of Jason, who founded Iolcos. So Virgil may be alluding to Apollonius (who wrote the *Argonautica*); but the omission of any mention of ships makes this less likely. Lynceus also brings Apollonius to mind, since one of his mythic namesakes was the Argonaut noted for his keen sight. Other names conjure famous archetypes briefly: Gyges, king of Lydia; Halys, the river dividing Asia Minor, whose crossing caused Croesus to destroy his own empire.

778 *Finally news . . . reached the Teucrian leaders*: this line is a stunning prelude to the debate in heaven in Book 10. Mnestheus and Serestus have deferred to Iulus' pre-distribution of the prizes of victory, and are not described as fighting or even watching the course of the battle until this point.

810 *Stripped of its plumes*: the translation of the last part of the Latin line depends on where it is punctuated. I follow Hirtzel and Mynors in putting a comma after *iubae*, 'plumes'. Others put a comma after the next word, *capiti*, 'head'. The alternative punctuation yields: 'Stripped off the plumes from his head, and the boss can't endure the relentless | Pounding.' This reading shifts attention from the helmet to the head and encourages a further shift of focus: taking 'boss' as the boss on the shield rather than on the helmet (to which the plumes were attached).

BOOK TEN

2 *a meeting*: Virgil's first indication that the gods have a forum like the 'Councils of the gods' in *Iliad* 5, 8, 15, and 20. Servius says he is also using the (now fragmentary) first satire of Lucilius. Virgil's tone is satirical: as if he were showing a meeting of the Roman Senate, with Jupiter presiding. Jupiter claims the gods have voted on a course of action he approved but then done what he forbade. His final decision, however, is a concession to the quarrelling factions. Only three gods speak: Jupiter, Venus, and Juno. Roman readers might see an allusion to the uneasy triumvirates (juntas of three leaders) that led to civil war in the first century BC.

9 *I had forbidden*: the Latin *vetitum* recalls the power to 'veto' senatorial decisions which Octavian asked from the Senate in 27 BC. But Jupiter does not use a veto here. See 12.806 and note.

13 *Tide of destruction*: the Second Punic War (218–202 BC), when Rome almost fell to Hannibal.

28 *Diomedes*: the Latins sent him a delegation in Book 7; he has not answered, much less set out with an army. Venus remembers he wounded her hand (*Iliad* 5.336 ff.) when Apollo rescued Aeneas from him.

36 *Sicilian Eryx*: Venus had a temple there: Venus Erycina (see note to 5.24).

46 *licence to rescue Ascanius*: Venus wants to take him where she has already transported him (1.691–4) after substituting Amor (Cupid). No mention has been made of his return.

54 *Nothing they've got there*: this collective insult to Latins, Greeks, Etruscans, Celtic, and Oscan peoples living in Italy would draw a hiss from almost everyone in Virgil's Roman audience.

66 *approach King Latinus*: Juno is exaggerating rather than lying. Aeneas sent *ambassadors* to Latinus, but visited Evander and the Arcadians *in person*. He left senior officers in charge of his camp, but they deferred to Ascanius and were not vigilant.

83 *transfigure his fleet into so many sea-nymphs*: Juno may not know that Cybele did this, with Jupiter's assent (9.77–122).

92 *adulterous Dardan prince*: Paris, who abducted Helen.

104 *Carry on into your minds*: the same line Aeneas attributes to Celaeno at 3.250 (see note there).

110 *ruinous prophecies*: perhaps Jupiter is aware that the prophecies have kept Aeneas from the site of Rome rather than helped him to recognize it. See notes to 8.100 and 8.399.

113 *Fates will discover a way*: the exact formula Aeneas says Helenus uses in 3.395 when speaking about Celaeno's prediction of famine. When Virgil puts echoes of Celaeno and Helenus in Jupiter's speech and has him allude to 'ruinous prophecies', doubts emerge as to Aeneas' 'destiny', and how 'fixed' it is. What Jupiter says to the assembled gods differs radically from what he says to individual gods. He talks to Venus in 1.257–8 as if his word and fate were the same: he now implies that they are not.

116 *talk about fate*: *fatum*, 'fate', and *fandi*, 'talking', come from the same root as *fama* ('rumour'). Jupiter disavows further involvement in the 'fate-making' process, and binds himself with an oath sworn by the Styx to enforce his current, vague ruling: that each individual's fortune will determine events. Jupiter's is just like his first oath by the Styx in 9.104–6. See also note to 6.398.

123–6 *Asius ... Thaemon*: Asius and Thymoetes are minor Trojans (*Iliad* 3.146–7 and 12.96); the Assaracuses, minor descendants of a major Trojan; Clarus and Thaemon, minor brothers of Sarpedon.

128–9 *Clytius' son ... Menestheus*: neither Clytius nor his father are noted elsewhere. Nor is Menestheus, whose name is similar to that of Aeneas' officer, Mnestheus.

132 *the Dardan boy*: usually Ganymede (abducted by Jupiter); here Iulus (abducted by Venus), described as if he were a work of creative art not a real person (see note to 10.46).

141 *Pactolus*: the river where the mythic Midas of Phrygia was purged of his magical touch that turned everything into gold. Pactolus was itself a source of gold.

142 *Mnestheus*: Virgil's summary of 9.779–812 is misleading. Turnus was assaulting the walls from *inside* the camp; and Mnestheus had not noticed Turnus was there until after he had wrought havoc.

145 *Capys*: Aeneas' cousin is not much discussed by Virgil. Tradition links him with (*a*) the betrayal of Troy to the Greeks, and (*b*) with Capua, which came to terms with Hannibal during the Punic Wars.

153 *Tarchon*: in other traditions, he led the Etruscans from Lydia to Italy and founded the cities of Mantua and Cortona, in addition to Tarquineia. His name obviously evokes the Tarquins, Etruscan kings of Rome—though Virgil never states the connection. To do so might give too overt an impression that Aeneas is installing an Etruscan monarchy (see note to 6.817). Virgil carefully distinguishes Etruscan immigrants from Trojans by incorporating them as allies seeking, not leadership, but a subservient role. Evander says they felt bound by prophecies to choose a foreign leader (8.503). The term for such non-citizen rulers was *tyrannus*, 'tyrant', itself derived from the possibly Etruscan word *turan*, 'lord'.

159 *shelter and wood*: these lines remind us that most of Aeneas' original vessels are sea-nymphs. His fleet is now largely Etruscan. Their port of departure is presumably Pyrgi, the port of Caere. If Aeneas is sailing with them on the *sea* (10.227) his own vessel is Etruscan, since he sent his own ships back down the Tiber from Pallanteum (8.548–50). This is probably Virgil's way of subsuming the tradition that Etruscans founded Rome.

166 *Massicus*: a name derived from Mount Massicus in Campania, famous for its fine wines (as Virgil notes in 7.725). His vessel is called *Tigris* ('Tigress') probably in honour of Bacchus, whose chariot is often represented as drawn by tigers, as Cybele's is by lions. The force he is bringing, however, is from Clusium (Chiusi), later home to one of Rome's greatest foes, Lars Porsenna (see 8.646 ff. and note) who tried to bring the Tarquins back to Rome. The Etruscans sail in an order that starts with those nearest the Tiber and moves north up the coast to Liguria, then across to north-east Italy.

169–80 *Abas . . . Asilas . . . Astyr*: I assume there is a *rationale* for Virgil's assignment of names here, but am not sure I've found it. Abas (see Glossary) is also the name of (*a*) a companion of Aeneas and (*b*) of an Argive warrior he killed, and whose name he inscribes on his victim's shield. The only important mythic Abas is the son of Hypermestra, the only daughter of Danaus who does not kill her husband (see note to 10.499): a mixture of Greek and Egyptian bloodlines. The name Abas tends to appear in contexts specifying weapons and their use or non-use (even in death he is a 'knot to frustrate any blade' (10.428)). It seems right for the leader of an area rich in iron that has a name suggesting 'despoiling' (Latin *populari*, de-people, despoil) as well as *populus* (poplar tree) and evocative of the cult of Juno Populonia, the goddess who protects people from plunder. *Asilas* is linked with priestly activities, so his name is likely to recall some Etruscan priestly office. Many Roman religious practices seem to be of Etruscan origin. With *Astyr*, personal beauty and his horse are the definers. Greek *aster*, 'star', makes a beginning (Paschalis, *Virgil's Aeneid*, 350). And the Asturians in Spain were famous for their horses. Silius says Asturians claimed descent from the Homeric Memnon's charioteer (3.332–4). What needs to be added is that Asturian cavalry were a major element in Hannibal's army when he invaded Italy; some of his major victories were won in Etruscan territory. Astyr's name, then, has ominous associations.

185 *Cinyrus*: there are several textual alternatives for this name (e.g. Cinyras, Cunarus). Cinyrus seems to me the most plausible because, in Greek, it carries the same sense of plaintive musicality as does *ligys*, the word sometimes seen as the root of 'Ligurian'. And in the *Palatine Anthology* (2.72 (414)) Virgil himself is described as a clear-voiced and melancholy (*ligys*) swan. Cinyrus' squadrons come from areas where Etruscans mingled with Gallic and other non-Italian peoples. Each leader and vessel has some associations with music. Prominence is given to his son Cupavo with a massive ship but a small squadron (appropriate for a large bird, rare in Italy). His own odd name has multiple resonances (Cupid + *avis* ('bird') = 'Bird-lover' or Cupid + Juno's special bird *pavo* ('peacock')) and leads into the story of Cygnus (= 'Swan'), metamorphosed into the bird (whose name he already has) through his love for Phaëthon. Phaëthon' sisters are changed into poplars, which give us a punning link back to Abas' Populonian motherland and its undertones of Juno Populonia. The Phaëthon myth also opens more distant links with Gaul and northern Europe (6.658 and note); Apollonius (4.611–17) thought it of Celtic, that is, Gallic, origin. Further, Cupavo's vessel has the same name as Sergestus' vessel in the boat race: *Centaur*. Sergestus' descendant, Catiline, gathered his army to overthrow the Roman state in Etruria, was allied with Gauls, and was defeated, in Etruria. There are menacing undertones here, as with Tarchon, Lars Porsenna's Clusium, and Astyr, echoing the grimmer themes on Vulcan's shield, which Aeneas now possesses, and which flashes destructive fire and flame like the Dog Star of summer when he disembarks.

198 *Ocnus*: the name suggests Gk. *okneo*, 'shrink from', 'avoid'. Mantua is the home town of Virgil, its most famous prophetic bard. In *Eclogues* 9.60 its foundation is linked with Bianor, but here it is derived from Manto (Gk. *mantis* = 'seer, prophetic singer'), best known as the daughter of the seer Teiresias in Seneca's *Oedipus*. Among its three peoples are Etruscans and Gauls. Mantua's river, the Mincius, is the smallest tributary of the Po whose source is Benacus (Lake Garda). In *Georgics* 3, Virgil vows to build a temple

(commemorating Octavian's exploits) on the banks of the *huge* Mincius (huge only in spring when its floodwaters wreak havoc). How Mantua could have sent ships from the Po to the Tiber so speedily is a mystery.

207 *Aulestes. His heavy-built Triton*: 'Aulestes' suggests the Greek *aulos* (a double-stemmed reed instrument) and might evoke the name of Ptolemy Auletes, a Macedonian king of Egypt. See note to 9.618. His ship's figurehead is the musical monster Triton who killed Misenus (6.173).

213–14 *their thirty / Vessels*: larger than Aeneas' own fleet had been; their number is the same as the traditional number of cities in the future Latin League, established around Alba Longa.

229 *Come, Aeneas, wake up!*: Cymodoce, with other sea-creatures, pushed Cloanthus to victory in the boat race (5.826). Here we have Cymodocea, a slightly different name: a sea-nymph, newly created from ship's timbers; Virgil puns on the element *-doce* in her name as if it were from the Latin *doce-*, 'teach, instruct'. Expertise in language came to her more speedily than to the other former pines. She addresses Aeneas, awake (in body at least) a couple of lines earlier, as if she had found him sleeping. Curiously, Suetonius (*Divus Augustus* 16) says that just before Agrippa's decisive sea-battle against Sextus Pompey (36 BC), Octavian was so fast asleep that friends had to wake him to give the battle signal.

238 *Arcadian cavalry*: part of the Arcadian contingent, then, has already arrived while Pallas and Aeneas are at sea. No Trojan other than Iulus is mentioned. The active defence is conducted by allies.

278 *Seizing . . . issues this challenge*: repeats 9.127. Though missing in two major manuscripts, the line fits in perfectly: Turnus is taking the initiative, as usual. Leaving it out muddies the transition.

291 *breathlessly calm*: reading *spirant*, 'breathe' (with manuscript *M*), not *sperat*, 'he expects' (with manuscripts *P*, *R*, and Servius).

302 *with one exception*: why Tarchon? Perhaps because his descendant was Tarquin the Proud, the first foe of Rome to come to grief before Lars Porsenna, Gallic invaders, and Catiline, hints of whom lurk in this Etruscan fleet. Catiline's ancestor ran his vessel aground in the boat race.

310 *peasants*: as in Book 7, Virgil emphasizes the rustic nature and arms of the Latin forces. Yet only one of those listed sounds even faintly Latin, and few sound like farmers. Romans would have noticed this instantly. But Virgil offers even less help than he does with the Etruscan catalogue. Here is what Romans might have noticed. The unknown Theron that Aeneas kills wears expensive armour and has a Greek–Sicilian name. Lichas' (Greek) name recalls Hercules' herald who indirectly causes Hercules' death (and whose birth by posthumous Caesarian section is described in words that studiously *avoid* echoes of Caesar's name). Cisseus has the same name as Hecuba's father and Gyas is the namesake of the mysterious Trojan officer in the boat race (see notes to 5.118 and 175), even if both Latins wield clubs and are sons of Melampus (a Thessalian prophet not

usually closely linked with Hercules). Pharus ('Lighthouse') is a mythic sea-captain in whose boat Helen and Menelaus were travelling when shipwrecked in Egypt. Cydon was the mythic founder of Cydonia in Crete. Phorcus, father of the brothers who rescue Cydon, is a Greek sea-god. Maeon is a Theban prophet. Alcanor (Gk. 'Man's Strength') is unknown, but brother of the first Italian-sounding person in the episode, Numitor.

343 *Numitor*: he fails to kill Aeneas, but Aeneas does not kill him either. He is the namesake of an Alban king, the grandfather of Romulus and brother of Romulus' wicked uncle Amulius. See note to 6.768-9.

345 *Clausus*: this Latin-Sabine name is familiar from the catalogue in 7.706-9 (and see note to 7.706). Virgil has switched to talking about the casualties Latins inflict on the Trojans and their allies. The ancestor of the Claudius clan strikes the first blows in response.

378 *Old Troy*: Pallas' allusion to an imagined voyage (back) to Troy is oddly addressed to Arcadians who did not come from Troy. Virgil is, perhaps, showing him 'echoing' what Aeneas might say.

380 *Lagus*: his name means 'hare' in Greek.

384 *Hispo*: the manuscripts have Hisbo; but since there is a Roman name Hispo, I have changed the spelling.

399 *Rhoeteus*: his name, like that of Ilus (line 401), conjures images of Troy, not of Italy. The famous Ilus was the founder of Troy's citadel, and Rhoeteum was one of the ports in the Troad.

417 *Halaesus' father*: see note to 7.724.

426 *Lausus*: son of Mezentius, the Etruscan who heads the catalogue of Turnus' allies in 7.648-54.

439 *sister divine*: Virgil now tells us that Turnus has a divine sister, but does not name her until 12.146, the most extraordinary postponement of identification in epic.

449 *Spoils of Distinction*: Pallas, already talking of dedicating spoils (10.421-3), is now hoping to win the most distinguished of all spoils. See notes to 6.841, 859; 9.270; 11.15. There is much talk of spoils as symbols of glory in Book 10. In Book 11 the trophies created seem less glamorous.

470 *Sarpedon*: Jupiter's son, killed at Troy. This passage is based in *Iliad* 16.459 ff. Here is a point where 'fate' coincides with individual fortune. Pallas enters a contest he lacks the prowess to win.

481 *penetrate deeper*: this is a contest of masculinity. See notes to 11.721, 747, 760, and 790-1.

499 *Bridegrooms*: in Aeschylus' *Suppliants*, the fifty daughters of Danaus, descendants of the Argive princess Io, come back to Argos from Egypt, looking like foreigners, and beg (and are granted) protection from King Pelasgus. They fled Egypt to avoid a forced marriage with the sons of Aegyptus. In the lost second and third plays of Aeschylus' trilogy, they are forced to marry Aegyptus' sons but, with the exception of

Hypermestra, kill their husbands on their wedding night. Hypermestra is put on trial for breaking the oath to kill (which all the daughters took), but acquitted, thanks to the intervention of Aphrodite. Virgil's exclamation at lines 501–2 has such an Aeschylean flavour that it might be adapted from one of the two lost plays. A curious mythic dialogue is at work here, because Turnus himself claims Argive descent, and bears the image of Io on his shield. With Pallas' sword-belt he has acquired a matching piece. But Virgil, unlike Aeschylus, expresses disapproval of the murders committed by Danaus' daughters.

520 *dampen the flames*: he captures enemy soldiers to use as human sacrifices, as does Achilles in *Iliad* 21.27 ff. See also note to 11.97. Sulmo (9.412) and Ufens (7.745 ff.) are names of both warriors and, respectively, a town and river.

542 *Mars, Lord of the Soldier*: Latin *Gradivus*, a title of Mars who 'treads heavily'. Aeneas rededicates Haemon, priest of Apollo while alive, to Mars in death.

546 *Anxur*: his name is also the Volscian name for Tarracina in Latium; Umbro means 'an Umbrian'.

558 *Won't ever bury your limbs*: His words combine those spoken by Odysseus in *Iliad* 11.452 ff., with their menace of carrion birds, and those of Achilles in *Iliad* 21.122 ff., when each denies an opponent burial. Neither Greek makes any pretence of more civilized behaviour. Aeneas becomes progressively less civilized as he moves from depression and defeat to anger and victory, earning comparison with the giant Aegaeon (10.565–9). See also note to 11.22. There is grim humour in the 'topping' of the son of the forest-god Faunus and a nymph named Dryope ('Oak Face').

561–2 *Antaeus . . . Numa*: Antaeus is also the name of a Libyan giant whose strength was maintained by his native earth. He was killed by Hercules, who lifted him up and strangled him. The Numa here is the second namesake of Rome's second king to be killed in action. The other was killed by Nisus in 9.454.

563–4 *Amyclae's Laconic / Peoples*: Camers' city in Latium has the same name as Sparta's twin city in the Greek province of Laconia, famous for the terse speech of its 'laconic' people. See 12.224–6. His father Volcens was killed by Nisus in 9.442. The tradition that Latin Amyclae vanished after an infestation by snakes probably arises from wordplay between Gk. *Opheis*, 'snakes', and *Opikoi*, 'Oscans', as Servius suggests.

571 *Niphaeus*: the name means 'Snowy'. From what follows, this ought to be Virbius, the doublet of the Greek Hippolytus, who is in the catalogue of troops in Book 7 but is never shown fighting. Aeneas appears like the bull from the sea in Euripides' *Hippolytus* that frightens Hippolytus' horses, which drag him to his death. This is the first of two consecutive encounters by Aeneas, fighting on foot, with charioteers.

581 *Diomedes' steeds*: Dido had asked Aeneas to describe Diomedes' horses and the greatness of Achilles in 1.752. Now the matter of Aeneas'

withdrawal when confronted by Diomedes and Achilles becomes a sarcastic taunt from Liger. See the Introduction for details of the passages in the
Iliad. This scene draws some details from *Iliad* 6, where Diomedes
encounters (but does not kill) Glaucus. Curiously, the anagram of the
Latin *Lucage* in line 592 is *Glauce*.

628–32 *'Putting fate into words . . . For you can'*: these are very hard lines.
I could not get across what Juno is doing without restructuring the phrasing. 'Fate' is in Latin 'that which is spoken', and Juno is talking of how
fate can be changed in the transition between intent and word. She takes
mente ('mind') and sees its elements, represented by letters, as unscram-
bling themselves into *maneret* ('would remain'). One could remove the
doubtful element ('would') and leave *manet* (remains) which itself contains a punning allusion to *manes* ('ghost'). Fate becomes fixed at the point
where the scrambling process stops. But the 'fate' spoken does not necessarily express the full nature of the thought that subtends it. Juno is trying
to give Jupiter another way of interpreting his own thoughts, as Venus
suspects she has done in 1.237. She is the 'mind' behind the throne of
heaven—up to a point, at least.

637 *Shadow resembling Aeneas*: Juno steals a trick from Apollo and Venus and
reuses the phantom Aeneas ploy from *Iliad* 5.449 ff., where Aeneas is
saved from Diomedes, but with a twist. In this version, Turnus is the one
being saved. It is the would-be killer that is doubled, not the victim.

664 *mingles itself . . . cloud*: as the vision of Mercury in 4.570 mingles with
night (and see note to 4.556).

717–18 *He's not afraid . . . tough hide*: almost all editors agree that these two
lines are misplaced in the manuscripts.

719 *Acron*: namesake of the warrior Romulus killed to earn his 'Spoils of
Distinction' (see note to 6.841); and he comes from the home town of
Dardanus, one of Troy's founding fathers.

732 *Orodes*: an allusion to the Parthian king who defeated the Romans at
Carrhae in 53 BC, captured their standards, and executed their commander Crassus, grandfather of the Crassus who claimed the 'Spoils of
Distinction'. The emphasis on certain details (that Mezentius' victory
was won face to face, and by skill at arms, not tactical cunning) suggests
Virgil had the Parthian Orodes in mind. For Parthian tactics involved
feigned cavalry retreats which induced the Roman infantry to break ranks
and pursue, and the Parthians were trained to shoot arrows behind them
as they retreated. Hardly any Roman writer of the age fails to mention
Parthian tactics. Mezentius does what no Roman ever did: defeat (an)
Orodes. Only Mark Antony had any military success against the Parthians.

775 *Dressed like a trophy*: as a despiser of gods, Mezentius would not vow his
spoils to Jupiter if he won them but use them to adorn his beloved son.
The standard Roman 'trophy' was made of a tree, with its limbs trimmed
back, decorated with the armour of the vanquished. See 11.5–11 and 11.84.

835 *by the trunk of a tree*: the second image of arms and a tree (see 8.616 and note); the scene is ominously suggestive of a partially finished 'trophy'.

908 *he pours out his life*: Virgil does not describe how Aeneas kills Mezentius: the Etruscan offers his throat, then blood spills over his armour. This leaves us with a puzzle in the opening lines of Book 11.

BOOK ELEVEN

2 *Morning Star*: Virgil uses the Greek Eos (dawn) for the Morning Star.

5 *an immense oak*: the third image of arms and a tree. See 8.616 and 10.835.

9–10 *a dozen / Holes*: Aeneas either let foes lacerate Mezentius' body or did more than just administer a death-blow. He now memorializes his killing with a 'trophy'. He accepts the *principle* of stripping a dead foe's equipment (as is traditional in epic) even if he can't forgive others for doing so.

15 *These spoils*: not quite Romulus' 'Spoils of Distinction'. Virgil makes Mezentius an exiled tyrant (not an official commander) who takes orders from Turnus, who holds no official command (11.128–9). Killing Turnus might not win the *spolia* either, though Pallas, a junior officer in Aeneas' forces, thought it would (10.449–50). The Trojans give Aeneas an ovation, a lesser triumph than that awarded the younger Crassus (see notes to 6.841 and 859). Poets can inscribe the past as definitively as emperors can.

22 *commit to the earth*: Aeneas, who denied Tarquitus burial (10.557–60) but granted it to Lausus (10.825–8), now authorizes burial for the allied dead and later allows a truce the foe requests to bury its dead. He is silent about Mezentius' burial. Failure to permit burial of the enemy dead (as in Sophocles' *Antigone*) was regarded as impious, if not criminal, by the ancients. An exceptional commander would himself ensure the burial of enemy dead, as Hannibal did after his victory at Cannae.

27 *day, marked black*: Romans marked days of major catastrophes 'black' on the calendar.

36 *passing the high doors*: the large marquee and numerous attendants contrast with Evander's small residence in Pallanteum. The lamenting Trojan women recall tragic choruses and the rituals of women's lament still practised in Greece. Such mourners often reserve their dirges until the bereaved enter.

57 *a curse on a son who's survived*: reading *sospiti* for the manuscripts' *sospite*. The manuscript reading yields: 'Praying to die a cursed death since his son has survived.'

61–2 *A thousand / Troops*: a huge escort. 'Kings spare nothing in their grief' (Seneca, *Trojan Women* 485–6). Perhaps Marcellus' state funeral (6.860–5) is on Virgil's mind. Or perhaps there is method in Aeneas' extravagance. Evander might now want to break off the alliance. He sends enough other troops to discourage such a move.

68 *hyacinth falls*: whatever Virgil's hyacinth was (an iris, whose droopy lower petals are called 'falls', or some early flower that wilts quickly when plucked, like a bluebell), it was not the same as *our* hyacinth. But I can't jettison the reference to Hyacinth, celebrated as the mythic youth who dies prematurely, symbolic of all young men killed in the spring of their lives.

75 *Threaded with highlights . . . cross-weave*: the same line is used to describe the robe Aeneas wears when building Carthage (4.264). Perhaps Dido made a pair. As Aeneas adds this to the bier, and war-booty, trophies, and prisoners for sacrifice to the procession, the scene changes from rustic funeral to state funeral.

77 *veil of enshroudment*: Virgil alludes to two Roman rituals: (*a*) the veiling of a bride in a fiery red veil (*flammeum*); and (*b*) the hooding or veiling of a person condemned to execution.

81–2 *human / Sacrifice*: they were captured by him at 10.517–20. See notes on 2.118; 8.343.

87 *Pitching down, hurled prone*: the Latin *sternitur* can be reflexive: 'pitches oneself down'. But it follows *ducitur*, always passive. Does Acoetes hurl himself down or is he hurled by others, or by the impetus of the procession? I leave the issue ambiguous. He might be held partly accountable (as guardian) for Pallas' death.

89 *riderless*: implied, not stated, by Virgil—a familiar symbol in a state funeral. The weeping horse has been criticized as 'exaggerated', as if the whole passage were not a comment on the excesses of orchestrated official grief for one nobleman's death.

92–3 *the Etruscans, / Full force*: the Etruscans are in full force, not the Arcadians, as we (and Evander) might expect. Evander notes the full Etruscan presence at line 11.171.

97 *Goodbye for eternity*: Achilles says much the same at Patroclus' funeral, which he attends (*Iliad* 23.19). Tomb inscriptions show it was a Roman ritual formula. Compare Catullus' lament for his brother (101.10). Aeneas neither attends Pallas' funeral nor delegates a senior officer as his representative—even when the Latins negotiate a twelve-day truce. His failure to attend does not spare the lives of the youths captured for sacrifice on Pallas' pyre. They are in the procession. Virgil keeps us back to watch what happens to the bodies of the ordinary soldiers. And Aeneas misses a chance to see the site of Rome again and have Evander, perhaps, recognize the topography on his shield.

113 *Your king walked out*: Aeneas either doesn't know what Latinus said in Book 7 (he did not visit him) or is distorting his words. Latinus urged the Trojans not to flee *his* welcome, and offered Lavinia's hand on the single condition that Aeneas meet him in person. When hostilities arose, Latinus refused to declare war.

120 *stunned into . . . silence*: not surprisingly. Latinus did not do what Aeneas says he did; and, in line 112, Aeneas declares that fate awards

him their lands. The delegates are in no position to accept or contest his claims.

122 *Drances*: Virgil's invention. Despite Virgil's preamble, Drances hurls no accusations here, ignores Aeneas' charges, and, from a position of power-lessness, secures the desired truce through courtly flattery without making binding concessions. Can an ambassador do any better?

145 *Phrygian multitude*: these words evoke the rites of the Phrygian goddess Cybele, noted for their frenzy and self-mutilation (see note to 3.111).

152 *promised your parent*: keeping the manuscripts' reading *parenti*, 'parent', which has a secondary sense of 'obeying': i.e. this is not what you prom-ised your parent, who 'obeyed' your request to go to war.

170–1 *mighty / Phrygians*: 'mighty' seems sarcastic when used with 'Phrygians'. Evander's trust in Aeneas is shaken (Aeneas' failure to come to the funeral can't have helped). Hence his challenge to Aeneas to prove his worth.

173 *a huge tree-trunk in armour*: Evander's comment is prompted by the armoured trophies in the procession. That's why *armis* ('arms', 'weapons') not *arvis* ('fields') is the better reading here. If *arvis* is read, the line reads: 'Trophies. And you'd stand among them now in the fields, an enormous . . .'.

176 *Go!*: Evander dismisses the Trojans *before* the funeral starts and uses them collectively as messengers to deliver his call to Aeneas for action. His message, which follows, supplies his last words in the epic.

178 *hand on trial*: Evander uses legal language, as if issuing a court summons for a debt due. Hence 'trial', 'recompense', 'venue', and 'suing'. 'Venue' is legal shorthand for the 'court' in which a trial is to be held. Evander leaves the date to be determined. He frames his agreements with Aeneas as legal obligations. This view may also figure in Aeneas' notion that he is exacting punishment due from Turnus in Book 12.

223 *ominous shadow*: because the queen supports Turnus, some fear opposing her.

231 *King Latinus himself gives up*: Latinus, though opposing war, would rather not accept Aeneas (his speech at lines 243 ff. confirms this). Diomedes' refusal to join the Latins is a lethal blow.

247 *Argyripa*: = Arpi, as in line 250. There is a rich tradition about Diomedes in Italy. See I. Malkin, *The Returns of Odysseus* (Berkeley, 1998). His speech, however, is kept at a distance by Virgil (who reports it through Venulus). Virgil cannot plausibly create a fiction in which Aeneas kills Diomedes. Some local traditions maintained that Diomedes was killed by Daunus, Turnus' father.

259–62 *Minerva's storm . . . Caphareus . . . pillars of Proteus*: three episodes from the disastrous return of the Greeks from Troy. Minerva hurled a thun-derbolt to destroy Ajax, son of Oileus, who had tried to rape her priestess Cassandra (see 1.39–45); Nauplius, father of Palamedes (see 2.82), decoyed the fleet onto the rocks of Caphareus to avenge his son; and Menelaus was shipwrecked in Egypt. The pillars of the Egyptian king Proteus are

Virgil's invention, a counterpart to the pillars of Hercules at Gibraltar, western limit of the Mediterranean.

268 *his cuckolder*: Aegisthus, Agamemnon's cousin, was the lover of Clytemnestra, Agamemnon's wife.

270 *Calydon's beauty*: Diomedes is identified with two Greek cities: (1) Argos and (2) Calydon in Aetolia, more often the latter. Diomedes' juxtaposition of his own wife to Clytemnestra, whom he refuses to name, may hint at the tradition that Diomedes, like Agamemnon, was betrayed by his wife.

271–2 *My comrades . . . soared to the sky*: See Pliny, *Natural History* 10.126, and Ovid, *Metamorphoses* 14.497 ff.

290 *the hand of Hector, the hand of Aeneas*: Diomedes, as reported by Venulus, sets Aeneas on a par with Hector, as neither Homer nor Virgil (in his authorial voice) do. We have no means of knowing whether Venulus is modifying what has been said (Virgil's characters do so routinely) to further some agenda of his legation.

302 *Latini*: the Latins are a pluralization of Latinus himself: Latinus' children.

308 *Dreams*: Latin *spes* is often used as we use 'dream': of a *consciously* imagined future. Latinus coaxes his citizens to accept a future which conflicts with their own and (he implies) his dreams. And he offers a new dream: that the Trojans will ultimately go elsewhere. Since their fleet no longer exists, new ships must be built. In case the Trojans have simply piratical goals (as Amata suggests), he offers them much of the wealth they would gain if they sacked the city. But he does *not* renew the offer of Lavinia's hand.

316 *I own*: Latinus notes that the (rough, hilly) land is his (rather than the state's) and extends into non-Latin territory, and he refers to the Tiber as an Etruscan river. He minimizes any sense that the Latins are giving up *their* land. There is some threat to (Rutulian) Turnus: Latinus' land is worked by Auruncans and Rutulians.

330 *a hundred blue-blooded Latins*: in 7.265, Latinus is dismayed that Aeneas has not come in person, but has sent a delegation of a hundred men ('gifted in language, / Picked from among all ranks', 7.152–3). He now makes a response in kind, but upgrades his delegation to an entirely aristocratic hundred. Given the practice of sending noble youths as hostages, he is also, though not explicitly, offering hostages.

350 *beleaguered by grief*: depending on context, the Latin means either 'sink down' or 'besiege'.

352 *add one more gift*: Drances notes Latinus' omission of Lavinia from his proposal. Under the guise of chastising Turnus, Drances forces Latinus to reinsert it.

358 *the man himself*: Turnus.

375 *He's challenged you!*: Aeneas actually said (11.115) that Turnus ought to challenge *him* and that he would readily respond.

433 *Leading a cavalry column*: repeats 7.804, unusual in that a mortal character is echoing something said by Virgil in his authorial voice. And Camilla is the last person in Turnus' abbreviated 'catalogue' as she is in 'Virgil's' catalogue in Book 7.

436 *I won't . . . proceed*: the Latin *adeo* is an adverb ('to such an extent') not the verb 'I go towards'. But for a moment, the last word of line 435 and the first words of line 436 (*obsto non adeo*) flash before us the sense: 'I'm in the way, I'm not going.' Turnus is not eager to fight Aeneas and he envisages defeat.

440 *I, Turnus, vow*: Turnus publicly dedicates himself to death in a *devotio*, a ritual act of self-sacrifice of which English 'devotion' is a pale shadow. The vow is a self-imposed sentence of sacrificial death for one's country, exemplified by (among others) the Decii, whose souls are shown to Aeneas in 6.824.

442 *Aeneas "calls me out alone?"*: Turnus works Drances' distortion of Aeneas' words to his advantage. He relies on his hearers to recall that Aeneas issued no such challenge (see note to 11.375) rather than reminds them of the facts: that Aeneas was awaiting *his* challenge—which he might then be obliged to issue!

468 *Everyone's swarming . . . city*: I reposition this line to make a smoother transition.

477–9 *Further, the queen . . . for the goddess*: this passage recalls *Iliad* 6.297 ff. (also *Aeneid* 1.479 ff.) where women of Troy bring offerings to the other major Pallas of the *Aeneid*: Minerva (the Virgin of Triton). Women appeal to her in a crisis. She lurks in the background of the *Aeneid*, but is not a character in it. She is also absent from Octavian's religious revival (see note to 8.51), much as Aeneas is absent from his Pallas' funeral.

513 *To kick up a noise*: I take *quaterent* in its commonest sense: 'causing something to shake'. Camilla's hope of leading the attack while Turnus guards the home base (inverting the usual male/female roles) is foiled. Adding Messapus and the Latin and Tiburtine cavalry to Camilla's also lessens her hope of personal glory.

523–4 *encroaching . . . darkness*: these lines repeat, verbatim, the description of the Ampsanctus Valley in 7.565–6 and recall Livy's description of the Caudine Forks (9.2.7), where two Roman legions were ambushed by the Samnites in one of Rome's most humiliating defeats (321 BC). Turnus' choice of a site hints that disaster awaits Aeneas.

532 *Latona's daughter*: Diana, Apollo's sister, often identified with the Goddess at Crossroads, and linked with such Italian warriors as Virbius and Camilla. Apollo supports, intermittently, Aeneas and his allies.

537 *love for Diana*: some translate as 'Diana's love'. But that makes Diana talk about herself in the third person, as does Julius Caesar in his commentaries, and undermines the rationale for an account of how Camilla's attachment to *her* came about.

539 *because he was proud*: like Tarquin and Mezentius. Virgil appears to have invented Camilla, though her name and provenance evoke Camillus (6.824–5 and note).

554 *cork-bark*: suggesting a Roman book-scroll (the Latin for 'bark' also means 'book'). Metabus not only saves his child, but makes her a local legend.

563 *ill omen for future fulfilment*: Camilla, once saved by a spear, will die by a spear.

578 *the sley of a girl's loom*: Roman girls were trained to use a loom not weapons. But Latin *tela*, used for the warp-threads on the loom (often for the whole loom), is identical with the plural of *telum* ('weapon'). The closest parallel I could think of was a technical term from weaving: 'sley', the loom's reed (Latin *pecten*), with its implicit pun on 'slay'. Camilla also circled her head with a sling, not ribbons. I don't know where she found the tigerskin in Italy; Cassius Dio (54.9) says tigers were first seen by the Romans in 20 BC when brought by a delegation from India. If so, Virgil is not only showing her early (and ultimately fatal) taste for exotic fashion, but making what is arguably his latest datable reference to his contemporary world.

598 *Etruscan recruits*: the Etruscan mounted division is of horse-owners and riders, not trained cavalry. They were drilled into a fighting force during their advance. This idea is expressed in syllabic play: *Etrusci* become part of (an) *exercitus*, 'army', quite literally.

612 *Aconteus*: his name derives from a Greek word meaning a pointed spear, so his jousting (and death) are quite appropriate. I expand 'keen' into 'keen as his spearhead' so the point, as it were, isn't lost.

636 *Orsilochus*: the name means 'rising from ambush'.

647 *Beautiful death*: an ironic echo of Horace's famous words: 'it is sweet and comely to die for one's country' (*dulce et decorum est pro patria mori*).

671 *Stumbled*: I read *suffuso*, 'sprawled, tripped', not *suffosso*, 'stabbed from below [that is, hamstrung]'. A horse that has stumbled may be unhurt; no rider would attempt to remount a hamstrung horse.

675 *Tereus*: the name evokes a mythical king of Thrace, who married Procne, but raped her sister Philomela and cut out her tongue. He is juxtaposed with a male version of Thracian Harpalyce ('Rapacious Wolf') who can 'tire out a racehorse' (1.316). They are apt victims for Camilla.

680 *(he liked a good fight)*: the Latin has *pugnatori*, 'fighter', which could refer to either the bullock or Ornytus. A great hunter wearing the hide of a *young* bull is odd, as is much about Ornytus. Virgil positions 'huge' ambiguously in line 680, leaving us to decide whether the wolf's jaws or Ornytus' head (or both) are unusually large. In line 682, the Latin word I translate as 'peasant' could refer to his hands, his spear, or both. Like Herminius (line 641), Ornytus wrongly assumes that rustic prowess trains him for war.

686　*you Etruscan*: Camilla uses a colloquial ethnic slur in which Etruscan =
'lazy idiot'. Compare Tarchon's comment at 11.732–3, and Virgil's slap
at the Ligurians at 11.701.

722　*Stalking a pretty dove*: Camilla is the male, and her victim female in this
simile. And 'sacred' makes the generic winged predator not only, technically,
a 'sacred' falcon rather than a 'common' hawk but suggests Jupiter, who
assumes bird wings to attack women. And the dove is Venus' bird.
'Beautiful' and 'over one's limits' are both present in the Latin *sublimem*.
Doves don't normally fly high. This dove exposes herself to danger by surpassing the 'norm', as does Camilla's victim. Further, Latin *nubes* means
'veil'—hence 'cloud'—and, by extension, 'bride' (*nubere* = 'marry'), since
brides are veiled. The language of sexual attack runs close with that of
killing in Latin.

726　*pinnacled heights*: Jupiter (his bird is the eagle and he is described in his
sexual role as sower of life) is watching from an even higher elevation and
intervenes (through an intermediary), inspiring the male Tarchon to
carry off the male Venulus as a (female) eagle carries off a (male) snake
(lines 751–8). See note to 8.9.

740　*the host's*: Tarchon puns on *hostia*, 'sacrificial victim' (hence the 'host' at
the Eucharist), and *hostis*, 'enemy'. The sacrificed animal was food for a
feast: Etruscans are readier for parties than wars.

747　*Arms and their man*: an echo of 1.1. Tarchon threatens to abduct the epic,
not just Venulus. He is a forerunner of the Etruscan kings of Rome,
the Tarquins (see note to 6.817), and a potential rival for Aeneas. Had
the Tarquins survived, Rome might have been Etruscan, not Latin (and
Trojan). Tarquinius Priscus was marked for power (as was Octavian
(Suetonius, *Divus Augustus* 94.7)) by the appearance of an eagle (Livy
1.34). Since this episode is prompted by Jupiter, the eagle and its prey
further suggest the myth of Jupiter's own abduction (as an eagle) of the
Trojan boy, Ganymede, a cause of Juno's violent anger against Troy and
its descendants. The imagery of war and sexuality acquires a homosexual
undertone here. Perhaps all violence is sexual, as Virgil's invocation of the
Muse Erato in Book 7 implies.

758　*burden of prey*: Virgil's wordplay is on *alis*, 'wings', and *aliter*, 'otherwise',
as in his description of Mercury in 4.238–58.

760　*Arruns . . . is stalking*: Arruns is an Etruscan name; Tarquinius Priscus'
brother and son were both called Arruns. The Tarquins gained power
thanks to Priscus' scheming wife and lost it because of Sextus Tarquinius'
rape of Lucretia. So Virgil's selection of Arruns as the killer of Camilla is
apt. Arruns stalks the virgin Camilla as she threads through enemy
columns, much as the predator falcon stalks the dove.

768　*Chloreus*: a warrior with a flair for feminine fashion. I sharpen Latin *pere-
grina*, 'foreign', to 'Iberian' (red dye was imported from Spain). I reduce
Gortynia (from Gortyn in Crete) to 'Cretan'. I make the leggings

Anatolian (the Latin 'barbarian' means unacceptably 'foreign' rather than 'crude', as in English). Crudely made Gallic and German leggings would not be favoured by Chloreus over the stylish Anatolian versions. The Latin for 'cotton' also means 'linen'. Cotton was not grown in Italy, but flax (for linen) was; I opt for the import. Crocus-yellow is a feminine (and 'priestly') colour in ancient authors. As a former priest of Cybele, Chloreus would have been a eunuch (see note to 3.111): another variant in the sexual interactions of Book 11.

780–2 *when she went hunting . . . but with feminine tastes*: I take *venatrix*, 'huntress', with 'wear' (rather than with 'pursued', in line 781). Camilla *is* a hunter even if her tastes in clothing are like Venus' in Book 1; and hunters pursue carefully. It is not that passion for plunder is peculiarly female, but that Chloreus' outfit appeals to Camilla as a woman. Her tastes give Arruns his chance and cost Camilla her life.

785 *Apollo*: Apollo and his sister Diana are on opposite sides, yet neither conflict nor converse; Diana does not help Camilla or persuade Apollo to stay Arruns' hand. Arruns' prayer marks him as the precursor of the pathological sexual stalker/killer of modern times: a religious fanatic attracted to and disgusted by what he thinks is the improper conduct of a particular woman or group of women: hence the purging of 'this disgrace' by his weapons. Virgil does not enhance the image of Apollo (Octavian's favourite god) by having him grant Arruns' prayer, given Octavian's own concern for moral legislation. And in Arruns' prayer there is an eerie echo of Aeneas' comment about killing Helen in the disputed 'Helen episode' (2.567–88 and note to 2.567).

790–1 *beaten / Virgin*: the use of *pulsa*, 'beaten', twice in Arruns' speech is odd. It isn't the ideal verb to describe killing with a spear and carries, as does this whole segment, sexual undertones.

796–8 *That he lay low . . . south winds*: these lines are generally thought not to be Virgil's.

813 *womb-like paunch*: Latin *utero*, which normally means 'womb'. The Latin wolf is masculine (*lupus* not feminine *lupa*), and *cauda* ('tail') often has the secondary sense of 'penis'. The use of *uterus* for belly feminizes the already shrivelled masculinity implied. Arruns becomes strangely neuter, like Chloreus whose attire caught Camilla's eye. Camilla, whose prowess with the spear makes her a woman acting out a male role, however, is never sexually neutral. Mothers want her as a wife for their sons.

823 *Acca my sister*: these words recall Dido's first words to Anna in 4.9. Echoes of Dido and Anna abound in this scene of Camilla and Acca. Again a woman wants to maintain the fight against the Trojans. Camilla's request, ironically, saves Aeneas from ambush.

831 *Life flutters off . . . among shadows*: see 12.952 and note.

848 *violence to your sacred body*: in Opis' terms, the killing is, in effect, a form of rape.

859 *the horn bow*: there are sexual undertones in the language of the bow in Latin as in Greek. Opis' approach to Arruns is a killing framed almost as a seduction.

897 *Acca tells of . . . rampage*: we never learn if Acca tells Turnus that Camilla wanted him to avenge her death. She tells him only news that makes him abandon his ambush.

902 *abandons his . . . ambush*: without Turnus' temper (and Chloreus' wild tailoring, Camilla's obsession with it, Arruns' desire to kill Camilla, Camilla's request to Acca, and Acca's omission of the core of Camilla's message), Aeneas would have been ambushed, and the story would have ended differently.

911 *Trojans*: the context suggests that Virgil's 'they' are the Trojan forces.

BOOK TWELVE

3 *ardour*: Turnus' home town Ardea is often echoed in words describing his (ardent) passions.

5 *in Punic ploughlands of Carthage*: recalling the hunt in 4.129–68. Here the hunt is in farmlands, the quarry Turnus, the hunters bandits who, like the lion, intrude on civilization.

15 *Pit of the Damned*: Latin *Tartarus*. Turnus accuses Aeneas of criminally abandoning Troy; the sharpness of his words is offset by his awareness that the charge of cowardice can also be raised against himself.

17 *Lavinia must go as this man's wife*: words echoed in his last statement to Aeneas (12.937).

18 *Latinus's calm soul*: Latinus is devious. Though carefully set out, the disguises are obvious to Turnus. Plutarch notes that blunt self-expression is not only more dangerous than figured speech, but usually less *effective*, even with friends (*Moralia* 66 E–74 E); we should beware of 'counterfeit bluntness'—a sign of flattering insincerity (*Moralia* 59 D).

37 *What madness is warping my reason?*: exactly Dido's words at 4.595. But Latinus' emotion is feigned. He took no active part in causing war with the Trojans as he suggests he did.

53 *so he can hide*: I read *ut* rather than *et*, i.e. so that *Aeneas* won't be able to hide behind his mother's veil, rather than 'and his mother won't be able to hide him'.

54 *Now though, the queen*: this formula highlights Dido's increasing anguish in 4.1, 296, and 504. But Virgil does not suggest that Amata's love for Turnus is caused by gods.

68 *lilies when set among roses*: crimson and purple dyes came most famously from the Phoenician (Punic) sea-snail's blood (it took 23,000 to yield enough for a senator's toga). Ivory, *ebur*, 'blushes red' in the anagram *rubet* as it does under the effects of dye. Then the blush 'disturbs' (*turbat*)

Turnus, sending him back to the bloodshed when Dawn's Punic wheels crimson the skies (line 77). He goes to his white horses and mounts red plumes on his helmet. The ivory simile derives from *Iliad* 4.141, where it describes blood staining Menelaus' legs when Pandarus' arrow wounds him, thereby breaking the truce negotiated so that he and Paris can end the war by fighting a duel for Helen. In another sense the ivoried dream of Book 6 is being bloodied over. See notes to 6.893 and 898.

90 *sword, which the god of the flames*: Daunus is not always the pitiful, aged father represented by speakers in the *Aeneid*. Elsewhere he is a formidable warrior, worthy of divine weapons, who first welcomes, then kills Diomedes. Yet Turnus looks to the spear taken from the otherwise unknown Actor, rather than his father's sword. Note that he 'readies' the sword, but does not put it on.

98 *Phrygian eunuch's*: an echo of 4.215–17, recalling Iarbas' insults about Aeneas, and the second time Turnus calls Aeneas 'Phrygian' here (see 12.75). Lavinia, unlike Dido, cannot choose her partner and would probably not choose Aeneas if she could.

103 *like a bull*: there is a lot of 'bull imagery' in Book 12. In many Oscan-speaking communities the word for bull was a pun on the word for Italy: *viteliu* (and other variants). The symbol of resistance to Rome in the Social War was a bull goring a wolf, and the capital of the confederacy was renamed *Italia* (land of the bull). See notes to 7.173 and 665, and to 12.715.

124 *Mars*: though present everywhere as the idea of war and in similes (see 12.331–7), Mars makes no personal appearance in the *Aeneid*.

139 *Turnus' sister*: her existence is first noted at 10.439 and she is not named until 12.154. By then, Roman readers would have concluded that the goddess must be Juturna, since Juno is on the Alban Mount from which a stream flowed into Lake Juturna. Juturna had a festival and a temple at Rome. Virgil is probably the first to identify her as Turnus' sister. Her relationship with Turnus evokes Anna's relationship with Dido.

155 *three times, four times*: words first used by Aeneas, in reaction to Juno's storm in 1.94. And Juno interrupts Juturna as Neptune interrupts himself in 1.135. The whole line is virtually identical with 4.589 (spoken by Dido on finding that Aeneas has left).

164 *Ancestry traced to the Sun*: as either son or grandson of Circe. His horses and equipment evoke the solar chariot (12.113–16). In Book 7, Latinus was presented as Faunus' son, descendant of Picus who refused Circe's overtures. But Latinus, like Turnus or prominent Romans, represents his ancestry in accordance with political needs at a given time.

184 *Evander's city*: if Aeneas is killed, the terms of the treaty will settle Trojans on the site of Rome five hundred years earlier than if he wins, presuming the unconsulted Evander welcomes them. Aeneas' victory is, in a way, a setback to Rome's development. See notes to 8.100, 399, and 729.

189 *Teucrians*: Aeneas wisely chooses the less threatening designation 'Teucrians' for his people in the event he loses, since it implies no special

claims upon Italy. His claim not to be seeking a realm for himself contradicts what he has said on previous occasions.

192 *gods and their rites*: most likely Cybele and the deities whose cult statues
he says were entrusted to him by the vision of Hector (2.293).

As my father-in-law: this term of kinship calls to mind the failed agreements between Caesar and Pompey which preceded the civil wars. See the
Introduction.

198 *Janus*: the quintessentially Roman god whose shrine is opened in wartime
is an equally appropriate god (given his two faces) for negotiating treaties
between warring parties. See notes to 1.294 and 7.180, 607.

203–4 *alter / My resolution*: Latinus' will is irrelevant. He, though technically
in command, is undermined by subordinates at 12.266 (with some divine
help), much as Jupiter's command structure for the winds is undermined by
Juno and Aeolus in 1.52–82. The battle, when it starts, is compared to a
tempest (12.283 ff.). This time there is no Neptune to stop it, as in 1.124–53.

224 *Camers*: see also 10.562 ff. and note to 10.563–4.

246 *cheating the minds of Italians*: Virgil's observation, as writer of an epic full
of omens and their interpretation, is cynical. Juturna's fabricated omen
resembles the one Venus reports to Aeneas near Carthage (1.393 ff. and
note). Here, the eagle symbolizes not Jupiter but Aeneas, and is designed
to provoke not forecast action, or, as in Venus' omen, report covertly what
is happening.

298 *Corynaeus*: perhaps the Corynaeus of 6.228 (who officiates in religious rituals). A different Corynaeus is killed in 9.571. The fact that so many soldiers
on either side have the same names enhances the sense that this is a civil war.

304 *Podalirius*: there was a Greek Podalirius, a physician, brother of Machaon
and child of Asclepius, who cured Philoctetes' wound, and whose life was
once *saved* by a herdsman. He had a shrine in Italy. The Podalirius here
dies just before Aeneas is wounded and needs medical help.

313 *What are you rushing to do?*: Aeneas' words echo Virgil's friend Horace
(*Epodes* 7), who expresses dismay at the Roman civil wars.

322 *suppressed by tradition*: Virgil poses as a historian, and ironically: since
there is no known tradition of the wounding of Aeneas, there is no tradition
of who wounded him. The incident recalls the wounding of Menelaus in
Iliad 4.104 ff. The Homeric parallel casts Aeneas as Menelaus even though,
in Turnus' eyes, Aeneas is the Paris figure.

341 *Sthenelus*: his name is the same as Homer's (Greek) warrior, Diomedes'
close friend and charioteer. But this Sthenelus fights on the Trojan side.
Thamyrus is unknown, but Pholus is also the name of (among others) a
Greek warrior, king of the Dolopians, who fought at Troy.

343 *Glaucus*: one of Virgil's favourite multiply used names. Since this one is
from Lycia he recalls the Glaucus son of Hippolochus in *Iliad* 6 (see note
to 6.483), who exchanges armour with Diomedes; this Glaucus is son of
Imbrasus (usually from Thrace, not Lycia).

347 *Dolon*: this really is the son of a character in the *Iliad*. The incident (*Iliad* 10.314 ff.) was so famous that Virgil did not need to include (for a Roman reader) the details he includes. The details afford another opportunity to bring Diomedes to mind in the context of horses and chariots. The implicit comparison of Turnus to Diomedes is another reminder that the real Diomedes is not in the battle.

363 *Dares*: the defeated Trojan boxer in Book 5. For the colourful Chloreus, see 11.768; for Thymoetes, see 10.123. Thersilochus is a Trojan ghost in 6.483 (and note); and since Virgil includes his name in precisely the same phrase (derived ultimately from *Iliad* 17.216), he knows it. See the Indexed Glossary for the others.

371 *Phegeus*: Turnus has already killed one Phegeus (9.765). There is a mythic character from Arcadia named Phegeus who was the son of Inachus. Inachus was the father of Io, whose image is on Turnus' shield because Turnus claimed descent from Inachus' family. Although this Phegeus cannot be the same, Virgil may have invented him to suggest that connection.

391 *Iapyx*: his name suggests he is from Iapygia in southern Italy, but also evokes the Greek verb 'to heal' (*iasthai* < *iatros* = doctor), as does his father's name, Iasus. There is a tradition that he came from Crete (home to the curative herb dittany) and thus from Mount Dicte rather than Ida. Ambrosia is the honey-like food of the gods and panacea (= all-curing) a mythic curative.

411 *Venus the Mother*: Virgil here uses the word *Genetrix*, which is one of her cult titles rather than simply a designation of her status as Aeneas' mother.

417–18 *water / Already poured*: Virgil uses a passive verb 'poured' here without indicating who did the pouring. Venus is doctoring a basin of water that Iapyx (or others) set out to lave the wound. Venus again rescues Aeneas. But this time she uses the cloud to veil herself, not him.

458 *Thymbraeus' sword kills . . . Osiris*: no Trojan or Italian warrior with either name is mentioned elsewhere. But the first is often used as an epithet of Apollo who had a shrine in Thymbra, and Osiris is an Egyptian god, husband of Isis.

460 *Tolumnius*: namesake of the king of Veii killed by Cossus when he won the 'Spoils of Distinction' (note to 6.841).

469 *flings out Metiscus*: as Gyas (recently mentioned again) flings his helmsman overboard in Book 5. Athena displaces Sthenelus, Diomedes' charioteer, in *Iliad* 5.835.

474 *a swallow*: in the empty, static, lines of columns in a portico, the swallow's only thought as she swoops is of keeping her chicks alive; she, like Juturna, is an intruder in a huge alien structure she can nest in but never own. But Juturna is threading through a moving landscape of armies. The Latin pun echoed in 'swallows' is on *avis*, 'bird', and *avia*, 'trackless'. But another, more sinister bird will soon intrude.

505 *Sucro*: another Rutulian with a name linked with Spain (the river Xucar and the town of Sueca), place of exile for many Italians displaced by Rome's generals during the first century BC.

510 *Diores*: the contestant who comes in third in the foot race in Book 5.

513–14 *Talos . . . Tanaïs . . . Cethegus*: again, minor warriors whose names recall more familiar people and places. Talos is the bronze man in Apollonius 4; Tanaïs is the river Don; and Cethegus has the same name as one of the conspirators in Catiline's planned revolution in 63 BC.

517 *Menoetes*: not the same as Gyas' old helmsman in the boat race, but perhaps recalling the older Menoetes and the imagery linked with him. See note to 5.175.

595 *the queen*: Amata. But the simile of the bees and the already established echoes of Dido recall Carthage, too. So does Turnus' reaction when the sounds waft to him at a distance, as the sight of the fire on the Carthaginian shore causes anguish in Trojan hearts in 5.6–7.

612–13 *Constantly blaming himself . . . alliance*: these lines (not in the major manuscripts) are largely identical with 11.471–2. They are probably not written for this context.

665 *Shocked stock-still and confused*: Turnus' dazed state recalls Aeneas' description of himself during the fall of Troy in Book 2.

715 *Sila . . . Taburnus*: Sila (see note to 9.618) is a massive highland area in Lucania and Taburnus a mountain of south Italy: Samnite territory. These areas were among the last refuges of Rome's greatest Italic rivals for power, the Samnites, who were crushed at the battle of the Colline Gate in 82 BC and in the ensuing sack of Praeneste. See note to 8.561. This contest will decide which of the two Italian bulls will rule Italy, the 'bull' country: the Oscan (Samnite) or the Roman. See notes to 7.178, 9.465, and 12.103.

722 *the whole hollow booming*: Virgil plays on the juxtaposed sounds of *nemus*, 'grove', and *omne*, 'whole' or 'all'. I render *nemus* as '[wooded] hollow' to permit a somewhat similar wordplay with 'whole', even though *nemus*, strictly speaking, means 'woodland' or 'grove'. Wordplay is so abundant in this bull simile that one cannot convey its effect without offering some equivalent in English.

727 *the scales begin sinking*: so Jupiter has been watching all along, as Juno and Juturna violate his instructions. He now weighs the 'fates' of the two heroes, as if he did not know the outcome. Unlike Homer, from whose *Iliad* 22.209 ff. the passage derives, Virgil does not tell us which fate sinks down. Numerous echoes of *Iliad* 22 here underscore parallels between Aeneas and Achilles, Turnus and Hector.

734 *the unknown hilt*: Turnus' distraction, which caused him to leave behind the sword Vulcan had forged (see 12.90–2 and note to 12.90), is a decisive factor now. As in his premature abandonment of the ambush in Book 11, Turnus' errors (and chance) loom large in his doom.

750 *scarecrows*: I know of no precise English word for these Roman hunting devices used to frighten the quarry away from paths other than those the hunters wish them to take. They functioned much as scarecrows do. The wounded lion to which Turnus was compared at the beginning of Book 12 is now a deer (like Dido in 4.69 ff.), and his pursuer, Aeneas, is (ironically) compared to an Italian hound. The simile is based on *Iliad* 22.188 ff. where the hunter is Achilles and the hunted is Hector.

765 *The awards*: the words derive from *Iliad* 22.159 (said of Hector). Unlike the boxing match in Book 5, this duel holds no hope for the survival of the vanquished. Note that the prize is Turnus' (not Aeneas') life.

795 *Native Spirit*: the Latin is *Indiges*, 'Spirit resident in the land' (Livy 1.1.4–5 and Ogilvie, *Commentary on Livy*, 39–43).

796 *build*: a literal translation of Latin *struis*, 'build', as in 4.235, where, using the identical phrase, Jupiter reacts to what he sees Aeneas doing in Carthage. Here Jupiter is talking of things Virgil does not permit us to see at all, and we have no means of assessing his truthfulness. Turnus' sword, he claims, was *torn from his grasp*, as if he had done so himself. Virgil, authorially, has noted a rumour that Turnus *forgot* the sword.

797 *a god suffer wounds from a mortal*: these words evoke Venus' complaint in 10.29–33 about her wound inflicted by Diomedes. Jupiter is referring to the wounding of Aeneas (a future god) by unknown hands. His words might also apply (unintentionally on his part) to the Trojan descration of Faunus' sacred tree.

806 *I forbid it*: Latin *veto*, 'I forbid', is politically charged. In the Roman Republic, tribunes of the people had the right to close Senate proceedings by saying: '*Veto!*' Octavian assumed this right of veto for himself when he took control of Rome, by making the Senate give him the powers of a tribune. From this point, the veto became the right of the self-established executive branch of government to act as if it were the people's representative. It was to be the basis of Octavian's authority. Here Jupiter assumes the right to veto the procedures of other gods and end the war. But since he does so in a private consultation with Juno, not in an open council, it may not be sustainable on all occasions, as we see in 10.6–90.

845 *powers called the Dirae*: once Jupiter claims the right to veto, the Dirae, demonic powers until now associated with Tartarus, are seen flanking Jupiter's heavenly throne. The reference to Megaera suggests that the other two are Tisiphone and Allecto (though the Harpy Celaeno is a candidate too). Which one is sent Virgil does not say. The hitherto inattentive Jupiter now employs powers which Juno told Allecto he would not tolerate in heaven (7.557–8). Opinions vary as to whether this improves the situation for mankind.

858 *or, if you will, a Cydonian*: Virgil pointedly offers a less menacing Cydonian (Cretan) alternative to the Parthian archers (who had wrought havoc with

the Roman army at Carrhae in 53 BC). Since Jupiter has sent the demon, he is the point of comparison with the archer in the simile.

863 *Bird*: like the screech owl whose cry disturbs Dido (4.461–3).

882 *I cannot die!*: Juturna is a double victim of Jupiter's rape. Immortality means her sorrows can never end.

899 *hand-picked men*: in the *Iliad*, men of yore were stronger than men of the poet's day; Virgil echoes *Iliad* 12.445–9, where Hector does the lifting. He links Turnus' greatest feat of strength with his time of utter impotence.

908 *As in a dream*: Virgil builds on a dream simile from the duel between Hector and Achilles in *Iliad* 22.199 ff. but assimilates it to *our* dreams of powerlessness. His reality is like our worst nightmares.

924–5 *rips open his corslet's / Rim*: Aeneas' javelin pierces his corslet, his shield, then his thigh. Turnus is not facing his foe (or does not have his shield in front of him) when the shaft hits, and he is struck from behind.

928 *moaning in notes reintoned*: the phrase itself echoes the simile comparing the impending conflict to a battle between bulls for dominance over the herd in 12.715–27.

952 *Life flutters off . . . among shadows*: The last line is identical with 11.831 describing Camilla's death. 'Native' Italy is dead.

INDEX AND GLOSSARY

All names of persons mentioned in the text are included, and all lines or passages including a character's name are noted, except in the case of Aeneas. Individual mentions of geographical regions and of tribal and other collective names, however, are not generally noted. Since references are to book and line numbers, the glossary will work either with this translation or with the Latin original; line numbers usually refer to the Latin but are either identical to those of the translation or one before or one after. An 'n.' after a reference (e.g. Anchises, 9.294 n.) indicates that the name is discussed in the note on that line, but is not present in the text at that point. Persons named in the notes only are not included in this glossary, unless the text is unquestionably referring to them.

Pronunciation guide. English-speakers pronounce Latin as if it were English, so treating Latin names as English will usually yield the conventional pronunciation with only a few modifications. All words are stressed on the first syllable unless marked with an acute accent (´) to indicate that the stress falls on some other syllable. Final '-e' and '-es' are *always* pronounced, as '-ee' and '-eez' respectively; '-ae' and '-oe' are usually pronounced '-ee', but, when italicized, as '-eye' and '-oy' respectively. Both 'c' and 'ch' are pronounced 'k'. In a few names where 'c' is traditionally pronounced 's', the 'c' is italicized. Greek words are spelled and accented in the Roman/English, not the Greek manner (Andrómache, not Andromákhe), except when thoroughly familiarized to English-speakers in their Greek spelling and pronunciation (e.g. Mýkonos).

Apennines, mountain range in Italy,
12.703; an Apenniniculan is
someone who lives in the
Apennines, 11.700

Aphídnus, a Trojan, 9.702

Apóllo, god of prophecy, music, the
bow, and the sun, also known as
Phoebus, 2.114–21, 319, 429;
3.75–101, 119, 144, 154–63, 189,
251–2, 274–5, 359–60, 372, 395,
434–5, 474, 479, 637; 4.7, 58,
143–9, 345–6, 376; 6.9–13,
17–20, 36, 56, 69–72, 77–80,
100–1, 341 n., 343–7, 398 n.,
535 n., 595; 7.62, 71 n., 241, 771;
8.157 n., 336, 692 n., 698 n., 703,
720–1; 9.79 n., 638–61; 10.28 n.,
171, 315, 537, 542 n., 637 n., 875;
11.532 n., 785–98, 913–14;
12.164 n., 392, 403–5, 458 n., 516

Aquículus, a Rutulian., 9.684

Arab(s), 7.605; 8.706

Ar*ae*, 'Altars', reef-like islands between
Sicily and North Africa, 1.109

Aráxes, a river running through
Armenia which was, more or less,
the eastern boundary of Roman
power, 8.728

Arcádia, a province in the
Peloponnese, Greece, famous both
for its beauty and its barbarity,
5.299; 8.159, 573; 10.425–9; 12.272;
Arcadians, 8.51, 102, 129, 352, 518;
10.239, 364, 397, 452, 491; 11.93,
142, 395, 835; 12.231, 281, 518, 551

Arcens, a Sicilian, 9.581, 583

Arcétius, a Rutulian, 12.459

Archíppus, an Umbrian, 7.752

Arctúrus, a bright star whose rising
and setting bring bad weather,
1.744; 3.516

Ardea, Turnus' home town, capital
of the Rutulians, 7.411, 412, 631;
9.738; 12.44

Arethúsa, a fountain near Syracuse
in Sicily, 3.696

Argilétum, a street in Rome
connecting the Forum with the
Suburra, 8.345; thought to
commemorate the death of
Evander's guest, Argus (2)

Argos, city in the Peloponnese,
successor to the power of Mycenae;
sacred to Juno; symbolic of Greece
and Greek power, 1.24, 285; 2.95,
178, 326; 6.838; 7.286; 10.779, 782;
its inhabitants, the Argives, often =
the Greeks, 1.40, 650; 2.55, 78, 119,
177, 254, 393; 3.283, 547, 637; 5.52,
314, 672; 7.672, 794; 8.374; 9.202;
10.56; 11.243; 12.544

Argus, (1) the hundred-eyed guardian
Juno sent to keep Jupiter away from
Io, daughter of Inachus, king of
Argos, killed by Mercury, 7.791; (2)
guest of Evander, 8.346

Arícia, a town in Latium and the name
of a nymph who lived there, 7.762

Arísba, a town near the Troad, 9.264

Arpi (= Argyripa), a town in Apulia,
founded by Diomedes, 10.28;
11.246–50, 428

Arruns, the Etruscan who kills
Camilla, 11.759, 763, 784, 806, 814,
853, 864

Asbýtes, a Trojan, 12.362

Ascánius, = Iulus, son of Aeneas and
Creusa, 1.267–71, 288, 556, 645–6,
659–94, 709–10; 2.563, 598, 651,
666, 674–86, 710–11, 722–4, 747;
3.339–41, 484; 4.84–5, 140–1,
156–9, 274, 354, 602, 616; 5.374,
546–51, 569–72, 596, 667–74;
6.364, 763 n., 766 n., 789; 7.107–16,
477–8, 493–9, 522; 8.47–8, 550,
628–9; 9.232–3, 255–80, 293–313,
501–2, 590–3, 621–63; 10.45–62,
69–71, 236–7, 524, 534, 604–5;
11.58; 12.168–9, 184–5, 385,
399–400, 433–40

Asílas, an Etruscan, 9.571; 10.175–8;
11.620; 12.127, 550

Drusi, members of the aristocratic Roman Drusus family, 6.824

Dryope, a nymph, 10.551

Dryopes, an early people of Greece, 4.146

Dryops, a Trojan, 10.346

Dulíchium, an island near Ithaca, 3.271

Dymas, a Trojan, 2.340, 394, 428

Earth (personification), 4.166; 7.137

Ebysus, a Trojan, 12.299

Echion, a Greek who helped Cadmus build Thebes, 12.515

Edónians, a people of Thrace, 12.365

Egéria, a nymph of Latium, wife of King Numa, 7.763, 775

Egyptian wife, = Cleopatra (not named by Virgil), last Macedonian ruler of Egypt, 8.687–8, 705

Elba, island off the coast of Etruria, 10.173

Eléctra, daughter of Atlas, 8.135, 136

Elis, site of Olympia (Greece) and the Olympic games, 3.694; 6.588

Elíssa, another name for Dido, 1.346 n.; 4.335, 610; 5.3

Elýsium, underworld home of the blessed and of souls to be reborn, 5.735; 6.744–52

Emáthion, a Rutulian, 9.571

Encéladus, a giant, killed by Jupiter and buried under Mount Etna, 3.578; 4.179

Entéllus, a Sicilian boxer, 5.387–472, 387 n.

Epéus, inventor of the Trojan horse, 2.264

Epirus, a district of north-west Greece on the Adriatic coast, 3.292, 513

Epulo, a Latin, 12.459

Epytídes, guardian of Ascanius, 5.547, 579

Epytus, a Trojan, 2.340

Erato, Muse of love poetry, 7.37; see also Muse

Erebus, Darkness; the underworld, 4.26, 510; 6.247, 404, 671; 7.140

Erétum, a Sabine city on the Tiber, 7.711

Ericétes, a Trojan, 10.749

Erídanus, river situated by Virgil in Elysium, 6.659 and note

Erínys, a Fury, 2.337, 573; 7.447, 570

Eriphýle, wife of Amphiaraus, one of the 'Seven against Thebes', and mother of Alcmaeon, 6.445

Erulus, a king of Praeneste, 8.563

Erymánthus, a mountain in Arcadia (Greece), 5.448; 6.802

Erymas, a Trojan, 9.702

Eryx, (1) a son of Venus and king in Sicily, 1.570; 5.24 and note, 392, 402, 412, 419, 483, 630, 772; (2) Sicilian mountain and town, 5.759; 10.36; 12.701

Etna, volcanic mountain in Sicily, 3.554–79, 674–8; 7.786; 8.419, 440; 11.263

Etrúria, the country of the Etruscans (Tuscans), in Italy (Tuscany), 8.494; 12.232

Etruscans, the people of Etruria, the Etruscans, 8.480, 503; 9.150, 521; 10.148, 180, 238, 429; 11.598

Eubóea, the long island east of Attica and Boeotia, 6.2, 42; 9.710; 11.260

Eumédes, a Trojan, 12.346

Eumelus, a Trojan, 5.665

Euménides, the Furies, 4.469; 6.250, 280, 375

Euneus, a Trojan, 11.666

Euphrátes, a river in the Middle East, 8.726

Europe, the continent, 1.385; 7.224; 10.91

Eurótas, a river in Laconia, where Sparta is situated, 1.498

Eurýalus, a Trojan, friend of Nisus, 5.294, 295–343 and note; 9.179–98, 231, 281, 320, 342, 359, 373, 384–96, 424, 433, 467, 475, 481

Eurýpylus, a Greek, 2.114

Eurýstheus, a king of Tiryns, whom Hercules was forced to serve, 8.292

Eurýtion, a Trojan competitor in the archery contest, 5.495, 514, 541

Eurytus, father of Clonus, 10.499

Evádne, wife of Capaneus, one of the 'Seven against Thebes', who burned herself on her husband's funeral pyre, 6.447

Evánder, king of Pallanteum, 8.52, 100, 119, 185, 313, 360, 455, 545, 558; 9.9; 10.148, 370, 394, 420, 492, 515, 780; 11.26, 31–55, 140, 148, 394, 835; 12.184, 551

Evánthes, a Phrygian in Aeneas' army, 10.702

Evening Star (Venus, Hesperus), 1.374; 5.19; 8.280; see also Hesperia

Fabaris, a tributary of the Tiber, 7.715

Fabii, the Roman Fabius family, especially Quintus Fabius Maximus, the famous general who resisted Hannibal with a strategy of delay and guerrilla warfare, 6.845 and note

Fabrícius, conqueror of Pyrrhus, king of Epirus, 6.844

Fadus, a Rutulian, 9.344

Fates(s), (1) = the pronouncement(s) made by Jupiter (Latin *fatum* = 'that which is spoken'); often used loosely in the sense of 'determining force(s), destiny': 1.2, 32, 39, 205, 229, 258, 262, 382, 546; 2.14, 34, 54, 121, 194, 257, 294, 433, 738; 3.7, 9, 17, 337, 376, 378, 395, 444, 700, 717; 4.110, 225, 340, 440, 519, 614, 651; 5.82, 656, 702, 709, 784, 798; 6.68, 72, 147, 170, 197, 376, 409, 459, 466, 511, 546, 683, 714, 869, 882; 7.50, 79, 81, 114, 120, 123, 223, 234, 239, 255, 273, 314, 584, 594; 8.39, 133, 293, 333, 340, 398, 477, 499, 511, 575, 731; 9.94, 107, 135, 137, 643; 10.35, 67, 109, 113, 117, 155, 380, 417–18, 501, 623, 628–32, 815; 11.97, 112, 233, 286, 701; 12.111, 147–50, 232, 676, 795, 820; (2) = death or

menacing situation: 1.222; 2.506, 562, 654; 3.494; 4.678; 5.725; 6.515; 10.438, 469, 471, 624, 740; 11.587, 759, 847; 12.149; (3) the threads spun, measured, and cut by the sisters Clotho, Lachesis, and Atropos respectively (and called, collectively, *Parcae* in Latin). The length of the thread spun determines an individual's length of life or destiny: 1.22; 5.798; 10.814; 12.147–50; (4) as a system of balances: 12.725–7

Faunus, son of Picus, father of Latinus; identified with the Greek Pan, 7.47–8, 81, 102, 213, 254, 368; 8.314; 10.551; 12.766, 777

Fear (personification), 6.276

Ferónia, an Italian goddess, 7.800; 8.564

Fescénnia, a town of Etruria, 7.695

Fidénae, a town of Latium, five miles north of Rome, 6.773

Flavínia, area of Etruria, 7.696

Fortune, a divine or semi-divine force, more random than fate and not actually controlled by the Olympian gods; often a personification: sometimes like our 'History', sometimes like our 'Chance' or 'Luck': 1.95, 240, 613, 628; 2.79, 350, 385, 387, 656; 3.16, 53, 318, 493, 609, 615; 4.109, 434, 653; 5.22, 210, 356, 604, 625, 710; 6.96, 533, 639, 683; 7.243; 8.16, 127, 333, 578; 9.41, 214, 240, 260, 282, 446, 723; 10.43, 49, 107, 112, 284, 435, 502; 11.42, 108, 114, 128, 139, 179, 252–3, 413, 426, 12.147, 405, 436, 637, 677, 694

Foruli, a Sabine town, 7.714

Fucínus, a lake in Latium, 7.759

Fury, a demon goddess called *Erínys* (plural: *Erínyes*) by the Greeks, who prompts strife and separation, *eris*, unlike *eros*, 'desire', prompter of (sexual) love and of joining. The Latin word *furor*, however, highlights

Maeónia, a name for Lydia and for Etruria (since Etruscans came from Lydia), 4.216; 8.499; 9.546; 10.141; 11.759

Maeótia, area round the Sea of Azov, home to the nomadic Maeotians, 6.799

Magus, a Rutulian, 10.521

Maia, mother of Mercury, daughter of Atlas; one of the Pleiades, 1.297; 8.138, 140

Malea, a promontory in the south-east Peloponnese, 5.193

Manlius, Manlius Capitolinus, who saved the Capitol at Rome from the Gauls, 8.652

Manto, a prophetess, married to Tiberinus, god of the Tiber, 10.199

Marcéllus, a family name in the Claudius 'clan'; especially, Marcus Claudius Marcellus, who fought Hannibal and conquered Syracuse, and his descendant with the same name, nephew and adopted son of Octavian, who died in 23 BC, 6.855, 883

Maríca, a nymph, 7.47

Marpéssus, a mountain on the island of Paros, famous for marble, 6.471

Marrúvium, a city of Latium where the Marsi lived, 7.750

Mars, god of war, war itself, 1.4, 276; 3.13, 35; 6.777, 872; 7.182; 8.630, 700; 9.566, 685; 10.542, 755; 11.389, 661; 12.124 and note, 179, 332

Marsi, a Sabellian tribe in Italy, 7.758; 10.544

Massicus, (1) a mountain on the border between Latium and Campania (Italy), 7.726; (2) an Etruscan warrior, 10.166

Massylians, a people of North Africa, 4.132, 483; 6.60

Media, Asian land of the Caspian, part of the Parthian Empire, 4.211

Medon, a Trojan, 6.483

Megáera, one of the Furies, 12.846

Megara, a town in Sicily, 3.689

Melámpus, a Latin seer, 10.320

Meliboéa, a town in Thessaly known for its purple dyes, 3.401; 5.251

Melite, a sea-nymph, 5.825

Mella, a river of Cisalpine Gaul flowing through modern Brescia, 4.278

Memmius, a Roman 'clan' name, 5.115–17

Memnon, king of Ethiopia, son of Tithonus and Aurora, 1.489

Meneláus, Agamemnon's brother, Helen's husband, 2.264; 6.525; 11.262

Menéstheus, a Trojan, 10.129

Menóetes, (1) a Trojan, Gyas' helmsman in the boat race, 5.161–82 and note to 175; (2) an Arcadian, 12.517

Mercury (Gk. Hermes), messenger of the gods; son of Jupiter and Maia, 1.297–304; 4.222–78, 239 n., 248 n., 358–9, 556 n.; 558; 6.19 n.; 7.803 n.; 8.134 n., 138; 9.650 n; 10.664 n.; 11.758 n.

Merópes, a Trojan, 9.702

Messápus, usually the hero of Messapia or Iapygia (south-east Italy), but leading troops from north of the Tiber in the *Aeneid*, 7.691; 8.6; 9.27, 124, 160, 351, 365, 458, 523; 10.354, 749; 11.429, 464, 518–20, 603; 12.128, 289, 294, 488, 550, 661

Metabus, a Volscian, father of Camilla, 11.540, 564

Metíscus, a Rutulian, charioteer of Turnus, 12.469, 472, 623, 737, 784

Mettius, Mettius Fufetius, dictator of Alba, torn apart by horses, 8.642

Mezéntius, an exiled Etruscan tyrant, 7.648, 654; 8.7, 482, 501, 569; 9.522, 586; 10.150, 204, 689, 714, 729, 742, 762, 768, 897; 11.7, 16

Mimas, a Trojan, 10.702, 706

Mincius, smallest tributary of the river Po (Italy), 10.206

Ocean, the mythic river surrounding Earth, 1.287, 745; 2.250; 4.139, 480; 7.101, 226; 8.589; 11.1

Ocnus, founder of Mantua, 10.198

Oebalus, a king in Campania, 7.734

Oechália, a town in Euboea, 8.291

Oenótria, old name for the southern part of Italy, 7.85; Oenotrians, 1.532; 3.165

Oileus, father of the 'Lesser' Ajax, 1.41

Oléaros, an island of the Cyclades (Antiparos), 3.126

Olýmpus, the heavens, sky; also Mount Olympus in Greece, 1.374; 2.779; 4.268, 694; 5.533; 6.579, 586, 782, 834; 7.218, 558; 8.280, 319, 533; 9.84, 106; 10.1, 115, 216, 437, 621; 11.726, 867; 12.634, 791

Onítes, a Rutulian, 12.514

Ophéltes, a Trojan, 9.201

Opis, a companion of Diana, 11.532, 836, 867

Orcus, a Roman god of the underworld, Death; also, the underworld itself, 2.398; 4.242, 699; 6.273; 8.296; 9.527, 785

Oréstes, son of Agamemnon and Clytemnestra; he killed his mother and was driven mad by the Furies, 3.331; 4.471

Oricum, a town in Epirus, 10.136

Oríon, a mythic hunter; the constellation Orion, 1.535; 3.517; 4.52; 7.719; 10.763

Orithýia, a daughter of Erechtheus, king of Athens, 12.83

Ornytus, an Etruscan, 11.677

Oródes, a warrior with a Parthian (Persian) name, allied with Aenéas, 10.732

Oróntes, a Lycian ally of Aeneas whose ship sinks in a storm, 1.114, 220; 6.334

Orpheus, a bard, whose musical skill would have won his wife Eurydice back from the dead if he had not

disobeyed instructions and looked back, 6.119

Orses, a Trojan, 10.748

Orsílochus, a Trojan, 11.636, 690–4

Orta, a town in Etruria on the Tiber, 7.716

Ortýgia, (1) = Delos, 3.124, 143, 154; (2) an island in Syracuse's harbour, 3.694

Ortýgius, a Rutulian, 9.573

Oscans, a people of Campania (Italy), 9.573

Osínius, a king of Clusium (Etruria), 10.655

Osíris, a Rutulian, 12.458

Othrys, (1) father of Panthus, 2.319, 336; (2) a mountain in Thessaly, 7.675

Pachynus, promontory in south-east Sicily, 3.429, 699; 7.289

Pactolus, a river in Lydia (Asia Minor), 10.142

Padúsa, one of the mouths of the river Po, 11.457

Paeon, a god of medicine, 7.769; 12.401

Pagasus, an Etruscan, 11.670

Paláemon, son of Athamas and Ino, changed to a sea-god, 5.823

Palamédes, a Greek hero, ruined by Ulysses' schemes, 2.82

Palatine, the Palatine Hill, home to the most powerful at Rome, 9.9

Palicus (more usually in plural: Palici), the name of twin sons of Jupiter by Etna or Thalia, worshipped in Sicily, 9.581–5 and note to 581

Palinúrus, Aeneas' helmsman, 3.202, 513, 562; 5.12, 833–71; 6.337–81

Palládium, statue of Pallas stolen from Troy by Ulysses and Diomedes, 2.166–83; 9.151

Pallantéum, a city built on the future site of Rome by Evander, 8.54, 341; 9.196, 241

Pheneus, a town in Arcadia, 8.165

Philoctétes, son of Poeas, king of Meliboea, in Thessaly; from Hercules he inherited the poisoned arrows without which Troy could not be taken, and with which he slew Paris; after the war he founded Petelia in Italy, 3.402

Phineus, son of Agenor and king of Thrace, who was struck blind by the gods and tormented by the Harpies for putting out the eyes of his sons, 3.212

Phlegethon, a river of fire in Tartarus, 6.265, 551

Phlegyas, a son of Mars, and father of Ixion; he was punished in the underworld for the impious act of burning Apollo's temple at Delphi, 6.618

Phoebe, a name of Diana, as moon-goddess, 10.216

Phoebígena, son of Phoebus, i.e. Aesculapius, 7.772 n.

Phoebus, *see* Apollo

Phoenícian, a person from Phoenicia (Lebanon), often in reference to Dido, 1.302, 338–44, 442, 567, 670, 714; 4.49, 134, 348, 529; 6.450, 858; 12.4

Phoenix, (1) son of Amyntor and companion of Achilles, 2.762; (2) mythic father of the Phoenician people, 1.72; (3) the mythic bird, the phoenix, 1.712 n.

Pholoë, a Cretan prisoner given as a prize to Sergestus, 5.285

Pholus, (1) a Centaur, accidentally killed by one of Hercules' arrows, 8.294; (2) a Trojan, 12.341

Phorbas, a Trojan, 5.842

Phorcus, (1) a sea-god, 5.240, 824; (2) a Latin warrior, 10.327

Phrygia, the area of Asia Minor to which Troy belonged; thus 'Phrygian' often = Trojan, though usually with overtones suggesting

effeminacy, one of the most common names for the Trojans, throughout

Phthia, a district of Thessaly, home of Achilles, 1.284

Picus, son of Saturn, father of Faunus; changed by Circe into a woodpecker, 7.48, 171, 189

Pilúmnus, son of Daunus and ancestor of Turnus, 9.4; 10.76, 619; 12.83

Pinárius, member of a family who, with the Potitius family, presided over the rites of Hercules at Pallanteum and Rome, 8.269–70, 281

Piríthoüs, son of Ixion, who tried to abduct Proserpina from the underworld, 6.393, 601

Pisa, a town in Etruria, a colony from Pisa in Elis (Greece), 10.179

Plemýrium, a promontory near Syracuse, Sicily, 3.693

Pluto, brother of Jupiter and king of the underworld, 7.327

Podalírius, a Greek physician, 12.304

Polítes, a son of Priam, killed by Pyrrhus, 2.526; 5.564

Pollux, brother of Castor; as son of Jove, he was immortal, and on the death of Castor he was allowed to share his immortality with his brother on alternate days, 6.121

Polybóetes, a Trojan, priest of Ceres, 6.484

Polydórus, son of Priam, killed in Thrace, 3.41–55, 62–8

Polyphémus, a Cyclops, blinded by Ulysses, 3.641, 657

Pométii, a Volscian town, 6.775

Populónia, a city on the coast of Etruria, 10.172

Porsénna, a king of Etruria, who tried to restore Tarquins as kings of Rome, 8.646

Portúnus, god of harbours, = Greek Palaemon, 5.241

Potítius, *see* Pinarius

Praenéste, an ancient Sabine town on the eastern borders of Latium, 7.678–82; 8.561

Priam, (1) son of Laomedon and king of Troy, 1.458, 487, 654, 750; 2.22, 56, 146–52, 190, 291, 344, 403, 435, 454, 484, 506–58 and notes to 506, 518, 543, and 555, 562, 581, 760; 3.1, 49–52, 295, 321, 346; 4.343; 6.494, 509; 7.252; (2) son of Polites, and grandson of (1), 5.564

Pristis, name of a ship, 5.115–16 and note to 115, 154–6, 187, 218

Privérnum, a town of the Volsci, in Latium, 11.540

Privérnus, a Volscian warrior fighting for Turnus, 9.576

Procas, a king of Alba, 6.767

Prochyta, an island off the coast of Campania, 9.715

Procris, wife of Cephalus, who shot her while he was out hunting, 6.445

Promolus, a Trojan, 9.574

Prosérpina, Ceres' daughter, abducted by Pluto, 4.698; 6.142, 402, 487

Proteus, a sea-god who could changing into all kinds of forms, 11.262

Prytanis, a Trojan, 9.767

Punic, *see* Carthage *and* Phoenician

Pygmálion, Dido's brother and killer of her husband, 1.347, 364; 4.325

Pyrácmon, a Cyclops, 8.425

Pyrgi, the port of Caere in Etruria, 10.184

Pyrgo, the nurse of Priam's children, 5.645

Pyrrhus, the son of Achilles; also called Neoptolemus (*see also that listing*); after the Trojan War he founded a kingdom in Epirus, 2.469, 491, 526–9, 547, 662; 3.296, 319

Quercens, a Rutulian, 9.681

Quirínus, the name given to the deified Romulus, 1.292; 6.859; 7.187, 612

Quirítes, Roman citizens, 7.710

Rapo, a Rutulian, 10.747

Remulus, a Rutulian, 9.360, 593, 633; (2) another Latin warrior, 11.636

Remus, (1) brother of Romulus, 1.292; (2) a Rutulian, 9.330

Rhadamánthus, Minos' brother, and a judge in the underworld, 6.566

Rhaebus, Mezentius' horse, 10.861

Rhamnes, a Rutulian, Turnus' augur (taker of omens), 9.325, 359, 452

Rhea, priestess, mother of Aventinus, 7.659

Rhesus, a king of Thrace, whose horses were captured by Ulysses and Diomedes, 1.469

Rhipeus, a Trojan, 2.339, 394, 426

Rhoeteum, a promontory near Troy; hence 'Rhoetians' = Trojans, 3.108; 5.646; 12.456

Rhoetéus, a Rutulian, 6.505

Rhoetus, (1) a Rutulian, 9.344, 345; (2) a king of the Marsi, 10.388

Rome, 1.7; 5.601; 6.781; 7.603, 709; 8.635; 12.168

Romulus, mythical founder of Rome, 1.276; 6.564, 778, 876; 8.342, 638

Rosea, a district in central Italy, 7.712

Rufrae, a town in Campania (Italy), 7.739

Rutúlians, a people of Latium, whose capital was Ardea, 1.266; 7.318, 409, 472, 475, 795, 798; 8.381, 430, 473, 492; 9.65, 113, 123, 130, 161, 188, 236, 363, 428, 442, 450, 494, 517, 519, 635, 683, 728 10.20, 84, 108, 111, 118, 232, 245, 267, 334, 390, 404, 445, 473, 509, 678; 11.88, 162, 318, 464, 629, 869 12.40, 78–9, 117, 216, 229, 257, 321, 463, 505, 597, 693, 704, 758, 915, 928

Saba, *see* Sheba

Sabínus, mythical ancestor of the Sabines, 7.178. The Sabines were one of the originally Oscan Sabellian peoples of central Italy: those closest to Latium (sometimes in Latium) and most 'Latinized' are Sabines, those more distant and still dominantly Oscan in Virgil's day (those in the mountainous centre and in Italy south of Latium) are called Samnites

Saces, a Rutulian, 12.651

Sacráni, a people of early Latium, 7.796

Sacrátor, a Rutulian, 10.747

Sagaris, a slave of Mnestheus, 5.263; 9.575

Salamis, island off coastal Attica, home of the 'Greater' Ajax and Telamon, 8.158

Salii, the twelve dancing priests of Mars, 8.285, 663

Salius, (1) a competitor in the foot race, 5.298, 321, 335–56 and note to 334–5; (2) an Etruscan, 10.753

Salénto, an area of Calabria (Italy), 3.400

Salmóneus, a son of Aeolus, ruler of Elis, punished for imitating the thunder and lightning of Jupiter, 6.585

Same, an Island in the Ionian Sea (Cephallenia), 3.271

Samnites, see Sabellians

Samos, (1) an island off Asia Minor, 1.16; (2) another name for Samothrace, 7.208

Samothrace, an island off the coast of Thrace, 7.208

Sarnus, a river in Campania (Italy), 7.738

Sarpédon, a son of Jupiter, king of Lycia, killed at Troy, 1.100; 9.697; 10.125, 471

Sarrástes, a people of Campania, 7.738

Satícula, a hill town in Campania, 7.729

Satúra, a lake in Latium, 7.801

Saturn, exiled god, father of Jupiter, Juno, and Neptune, identified with an early king of Latium who presided over a Golden Age of peace and prosperity, 1.23, 569; 3.380; 4.92, 372; 5.606, 799; 6.794; 7.49, 180, 203, 428, 560, 572, 622; 8.319, 329, 358, 357; 9.2, 745, 802; 10.659, 760; 11.252; 12.156, 178, 807, 830

Scaean, name of Troy's west gate, facing the sea, 2.612; 3.351

Scipio, member of a famous family of Rome; Publius Cornelius Scipio defeated Hannibal in 202 BC, and his descendant destroyed Carthage in 146 BC, 6.843

Scylacéum, a town in southern Italy, 3.553

Scylla, (1) a sea-monster dwelling on one side of the straits of Messena, between Italy and Sicily, 1.200; 3.420–4, 432, 684; 6.286; 7.302; (2) the ship captained by Cloanthus, 5.122

Scyros, an island north-east of Euboea, 2.477

Sebethis, a nymph, 7.734

Selínus, a town on the south-west coast of Sicily, 3.705

Seréstus, a Trojan captain, 1.611; 4.288; 5.487; 9.171, 779; 10.541; 12.549, 561

Sergéstus, a Trojan captain, 1.510; 4.288; 5.121 and note, 184–203, 221, 272, 282; 12.561

Sergius, name of a Roman 'clan', the most famous member of which was Catiline, 5.121

Serránus, (1) a nickname of Regulus, who was ploughing when told of his election as consul, 6.844 and note; (2) a Rutulian, 9.335, 454

'Seven against Thebes', the grand tale of civil war between Polynices, son of Oedipus, and his brother Eteocles in the generation before the Trojan War. The *Thebaid*, Statius' Latin version, survives, as does Aeschylus' tragedy, *Seven against Thebes*. Six warriors joined Polynices, son of Oedipus, in his attempt to capture the throne of Thebes: those mentioned or alluded to in the *Aeneid* are: Adrastus, Amphiaraus, Capaneus, Parthenopaeus, Tydeus;